CONTENT-BASED

BASED

CURRICULUM

CONTENT-
BASED
CURRICULUM
for high-ability learners
second edition

edited by

Joyce VanTassel-Baska, Ed.D.,
& Catherine A. Little, Ph.D.

PRUFROCK PRESS INC.
WACO, TEXAS

Library of Congress Cataloging-in-Publication Data

Content-based curriculum for high-ability learners / edited by Joyce VanTassel-Baska & Catherine A. Little. --
2nd ed.
    p. cm.
Includes bibliographical references and index.
ISBN 978-1-59363-399-8 (hardback)
1. Gifted children--Education--United States. 2. Curriculum planning--United States. I. VanTassel-Baska, Joyce.
II. Little, Catherine A.
LC3993.2.C64 2010
371.95'3--dc22
                            2010015402

Copyright ©2011, Prufrock Press Inc.
Edited by Jennifer Robins
Cover and Layout Design by Marjorie Parker

ISBN-13: 978-1-59363-399-8

Printed in the United States of America.

At the time of this book's publication, all facts and figures cited are the most current available. All telephone
numbers, addresses, and website URLs are accurate and active. All publications, organizations, website, and
other resources exist as described in the book, and all have been verified. The authors and Prufrock Press Inc.
make no warranty or guarantee concerning the information and materials given out by organizations or content
found at website, and we are not responsible for any changes that occur after this book's publication. If you find
an error, please contact Prufrock Press Inc.

Prufrock Press Inc.
P.O. Box 8813
Waco, TX 76714-8813
Phone: (800) 998-2208
Fax: (800) 240-0333
http://www.prufrock.com

Table of Contents

LIST OF TABLES

LIST OF FIGURES

Chapter 1

An Introduction
to the Book

Joyce VanTassel-Baska

Any book on curriculum has to begin at the beginning in respect
to the beliefs and values that drive curriculum decisions. It
has to provide a reasonable explanation of how curriculum has
come to be interpreted in schools, the major ideas about what
curriculum should be, and the key figures who have explicated
them. Because this also is a book on curriculum for the gifted,
it has to provide some explanation of existing approaches to
curriculum development for that special population and how
the Integrated Curriculum Model (ICM), used to frame this
book, fits into the larger schema of thought.

PHILOSOPHIES OF CURRICULUM

The world of schooling presents very different orientations to thinking about what matters in curriculum. Although
the standards movement has attempted to answer the question
about which philosophies of schooling matter, in reality the

TABLE 1.1

Curriculum Philosophies

Curriculum paradigm	Ontology	Epistemology	Axiology	Methodology	Influences/ precursors
Traditionalist (academic rationalism)	Reality is manifested in representational modes.	The world is knowable through studying the products of the past.	Quality matters.	Reading and discussion of ideas, issues, and themes.	Adler (1984)
Social reconstructionism	Reality is socially constructed.	The world is knowable through social actions that promote equality or inequality.	Equity matters.	Challenging existing social order.	Banks (1975)
Cognitive constructivism	Reality is individually constructed.	The world is knowable by experiencing and applying key skills and concepts.	Direct experiences, mediated by social interactions, matter.	Cooperative/ collaborative learning that is engaging.	Vygotsky (1978)
Behavioristic positivism	Reality is observation and perception of behaviors with mastery as a goal.	The world is knowable by verification of observations and incrementalism.	Skepticism matters.	Scientific method; emphasis on assessment of learning to reflect mastery.	Skinner (1967)
Postpositivism	Reality is limited to consensual communities.	The world is knowable "through a glass darkly."	Person-context interaction matters.	Depth of understanding; use of schemas and scaffolds to enhance connections and sense making.	Gardner (1983)

standards only serve to confuse the issue as they represent multiple perspectives themselves, suggesting that the philosophies are compatible at some level and helpful in deliberating on curriculum decisions for any special population. Yet none is so distinctive as to hold sway over the entire enterprise for long. Table 1.1 presents five curriculum paradigms with their ontology, epistemology, axiology, methodology, and leading influence. These philosophies have affected how we have defined what curriculum is and how we organize and deliver curriculum to learners, based on our conceptions about reality.

Several philosophies also abound about the purpose of curricula in programs for gifted learners. In a sense, each of these philosophies contributes a

TABLE 1.2

Models of Curriculum Organization in Gifted Education Linked to Paradigms

Models	Paradigms
Renzulli's Schoolwide Enrichment Model	Cognitive constructivism
Ford's multicultural curriculum model	Social reconstructionism
Stanley's diagnostic-prescriptive model of acceleration	Behavioristic positivism
VanTassel-Baska's Integrated Curriculum Model	Academic rationalism
Tomlinson et al. Parallel Curriculum Model	Postpositivism

competing paradigm. Table 1.2 shows the links of gifted education curriculum models to existing paradigms about the overall educational enterprise, each of which exerts some influence over how schooling is carried out.

The cognitive constructivist model is represented in the gifted literature by Renzulli's Schoolwide Enrichment Model (see Renzulli & Reis, 1985) and other similar approaches that place the responsibility for learning at advanced levels primarily on the student, with the teacher serving as a facilitator to the learning enterprise by providing materials and resources, asking probing questions, and introducing students to skill sets that will promote higher level thinking processes and problem-solving approaches.

The social reconstructionist model is best represented in gifted education by the ideas of Ford (see Ford, 1996) in espousing a multicultural curriculum, one that examines multiple perspectives and voices in understanding phenomena and events. It also emphasizes the psychological need of a society to move beyond the stereotypes and barriers that prevent the eradication of racism, classism, and sexism to create a better world, suggesting that students are active agents in creating plans and policies to improve their world.

The behavioral positivist model aligns well with the work of Julian Stanley and his associates (see Swiatek, 2002), who have promoted the talent search model for gifted learners. Based on the assumption that gifted learners can progress more rapidly through traditional curriculum experiences if these experiences are well-organized for advanced learning, this paradigm also acknowledges the systems that drive educational environments, based on the premise of learning progress in a time-linear way. The model also purports to plan, monitor, and assess learning in traditional ways that provide quantitative demonstrations of learning achieved.

The academic rationalist model is most closely aligned with the work of VanTassel-Baska and her associates (see VanTassel-Baska & Wood, 2009), the Integrated Curriculum Model, which presupposes that gifted learners have differentiated needs that may be best satisfied through multiple pathways to learning—accelerative and advanced, higher level thinking and problem solving, and conceptual. The work also suggests that the dynamic interaction of teacher and learner produces optimal learning, which is best stimulated through exposure to challenging ideas and products, from all cultures and ages. This can be emulated as students seek to understand existing knowledge in the disciplines and to construct meaning for themselves.

The postpositivist model may best be explicated using the Parallel Curriculum Model from gifted education as an exemplum (see Tomlinson et al., 2002). The model is grounded in the recognition that gifted students represent multiple selves whose learning states may shift as they mature and grow at irregular rates. Thus, learning pathways must be constructed that invite them to focus on school-based learning at advanced levels, on the work of the professions in using the tools and practices of real-world practitioners, on identity formation that will shape their professional futures, and on big ideas that permeate understanding of the world across disciplines.

Although these paradigms may be viewed as competitive, they also may be seen as complementary when translated into the context of classroom practice. In fact, many gifted programs try to be eclectic in their curricular orientation, never ascribing totally to one view over another. This is especially apparent in gifted program goal structures, which tend to include an emphasis on each of these orientations to learning. What varies is the context for the curriculum focus. For example, the Stanley approach often is an augmentation to the school curriculum, taking place through online and summer opportunities to learn, while the use of project-based learning, as espoused by Renzulli, may more likely occur in schoolwide settings. The ICM may more likely be found in content-based programs for providing gifted instruction as it is aligned with the relevant content standards.

ABOUT THE SECOND EDITION

The intention of this book is to provide a clear and cogent way to approach the development of curriculum for gifted and high-ability learners that is substantive, rigorous, and aligns with the paradigm of academic rationalism via the ICM. Such an approach is still the most viable, given the renewed interest in national content standards and the recognition that accountability must extend to assessing students' authentic learning, not just their short-term achievement in all relevant areas of learning.

In the intervening years since the first edition of this text was published, greater emphasis has been accorded to high-stakes state assessments in schools, and less emphasis has been placed on the curriculum standards directly, with studies showing the use of only a limited number of standards at lower levels of cognition for purposes of assessing learning, a situation which in turn has led to instructional devolution whereby teachers teach only to the content to be covered on these assessments. In respect to gifted learners, this situation has further exacerbated the need for challenging curriculum delivered in a context of dynamic, inquiry-based instruction. Within gifted education, the response to the mandate of No Child Left Behind (NCLB, 2001), the policy engine that has fueled the degradation of standards and the elevation of assessments, has been to adopt the philosophy of differentiation for all, using resource consulting teachers trained in gifted pedagogy to work in inclusion classrooms, in the hopes of reaching the gifted learners in these contexts. To date, little evidence exists to suggest that this strategy is working. In fact, data appear to suggest just the opposite—that the majority of classrooms still do not practice differentiation for the gifted (Westberg & Daoust, 2003) and are not grouping gifted learners in any configuration that would allow for meaningful differentiation to occur. Given this situation, an emphasis on high-quality curriculum and instruction for all learners seems even more imperative.

From its inception 22 years ago, our curriculum work at the Center for Gifted Education has been nested in several assumptions that make it valuable to the broader audience of all school practitioners, not just to the teachers and administrators of gifted programs.

- We assume that all children can learn challenging material, and we have set about to demonstrate the truth of that assumption by using high-powered curriculum, designed for gifted learners, with all learners in some of the poorest schools in our nation.

- We assume that higher level thinking can be taught best through the core domains of learning. We have systematically tested this assumption by assessing critical thinking and problem-solving abilities through language arts, science, mathematics, and social studies curriculum.

- We assume that the use of graphic organizers to scaffold instruction facilitates learning, especially for promising learners from low-income backgrounds and other diverse learners. Our research evidence suggests that such scaffolds are clearly contributory to the learning gains of students using our curriculum materials.

- We assume that multiple pathways to learning, as well as multiple approaches to assessment of that learning, enhance the likelihood that students will benefit from planned instruction. Our work has consistently employed multiple models and assessment tools, including performance-based, portfolio, and standardized, to capture the nature and extent of the authentic learning of students.

- We assume that professional development must augment the development and dissemination of curriculum materials in order for the learning of students to be optimized. Toward that end, we have offered ongoing professional development opportunities to schools, school districts, states, and university groups that wish to implement our curriculum units of study. (VanTassel-Baska & Stambaugh, 2008, p. 3)

These assumptions are best operationalized through showing the importance of the connective tissue among curriculum, instruction, assessment, and professional development in the work of positive educational change. Consequently, in this edition we have added a chapter on professional development to provide specific commentary on its importance in developing learning coherence. The ICM also has relevance to other areas of the curriculum such as the arts, technology, and foreign language. Thus, we have added chapters on these three areas of curriculum, each of which is so important to gifted learners and each of which may be aligned with the differentiation principles of the ICM. Because the template of the standards has always been a backdrop to the work done at The College of William and Mary and continues to be a forceful guide in effecting differentiation, we have added a chapter to focus on how standards may be best differentiated for the gifted in relevant subject areas.

Finally, we hope this second edition of the text provides educators with additional data to support using effective differentiation strategies for the gifted, including the use of research-based curricular materials, delivered in flexible grouping arrangements. Our claims remain similar, however, to those in the first edition—we assert that it is possible to develop high-powered, rich, and complex curricula that treat content, process, and product considerations as equal partners in the task of educating gifted learners. Furthermore, we argue that an overarching concept or theme can bind curriculum study together within and across areas of learning so students can appreciate the world of ideas as a superordinate bridge to understanding their world.

REFERENCES

Adler, M. (1984). *The Paideia program.* New York, NY: MacMillan.

Banks, J. A. (1975) *Teaching strategies for ethnic studies.* Boston, MA: Allyn & Bacon.

Ford, D. Y. (1996). *Reversing underachievement among gifted Black students: Promising practices and programs.* New York, NY: Teachers College Press.

Gardner, H. (1983). *Frames of mind: The theory of multiple intelligences.* New York, NY: Basic Books.

No Child Left Behind Act, 20 U.S.C. §6301 (2001).

Renzulli, J. S., & Reis, S. M. (1985). *The Schoolwide Enrichment Model: A comprehensive plan for educational excellence.* Mansfield Center, CT: Creative Learning Press.

Skinner, B. F. (1967). *Science and human behavior.* New York, NY: Free Press.

Swiatek, M. A. (2002). A decade of longitudinal research on academic acceleration through the Study of Mathematically Precocious Youth. *Roeper Review, 24,* 141–144.

Tomlinson, C. A., Kaplan, S. N., Renzulli, J. S., Purcell, J., Leppien, J., & Burns, D. (2002). *The parallel curriculum: A design to develop high potential and challenge high-ability learners.* Thousand Oaks, CA: Corwin Press.

VanTassel-Baska, J., & Stambaugh, T. (2008). *What works: 20 years of curriculum development and research.* Waco, TX: Prufrock Press.

VanTassel-Baska, J., & Wood, S. (2009). The Integrated Curriculum Model. In J. S. Renzulli, E. J. Gubbins, K. S. McMillen, R. D. Eckert, & C. A. Little (Eds.), *Systems and models for developing programs for the gifted and talented* (2nd ed., pp. 655–691). Mansfield Center, CT: Creative Learning Press.

Vygotsky, L. S. (1978). *Mind in society: The development of higher psychological processes.* Cambridge, MA: Harvard University Press.

Westberg, K. L., & Daoust, M. E. (2003, Fall). The results of the replication of the classroom practices survey replication in two states. *The National Research Center on the Gifted and Talented Newsletter*, 3–8.

Chapter 2

An Introduction to the Integrated Curriculum Model

Joyce VanTassel-Baska

This chapter explores several facets of conceptualizing curriculum, instruction, and assessment for gifted learners. It begins by defining a differentiated curriculum for this population. A rationale is then provided for an integrated approach to the development of curricula. Next, the chapter presents the Integrated Curriculum Model (ICM) with the types of applications made in curriculum units developed by the Center for Gifted Education at The College of William and Mary. Key curriculum reform elements are presented to illustrate how they have been incorporated into the structure of these units. Finally, a discussion of implementation considerations explores the respective roles of the nature of the learner and the context variables of flexibility, grouping, climate, and teacher quality.

WHAT IS A DIFFERENTIATED CURRICULUM?

Differentiated Curriculum

Defining differentiation for the gifted requires recognition of the inter-related importance of curriculum, instruction, and assessment. A differentiated curriculum for the gifted is one that is tailored to the needs of groups of gifted learners and/or individual students, that provides experiences sufficiently different from the norm to justify specialized intervention, and that is delivered by a trained educator of the gifted using appropriate instructional and assessment processes to optimize learning.

Curriculum design is one major component of a differentiated curriculum for the gifted, as it delineates key features that constitute any worthwhile curriculum. What is important for these students to know and be able to do at what stages of development? A nonnegotiable foundation in a curriculum for gifted learners is a sound design that links general curriculum principles to subject matter features and gifted learner characteristics. A well-constructed curriculum for the gifted has to identify appropriate goals and outcomes and related activities that support their achievement. How do planned learning activities focus on meaningful experiences that provide depth and complexity at a pace that honors the gifted learner's rate of advancement through material? The curriculum for the gifted also must be exemplary for the subject matter under study, meaning that it should be standards-based and grounded in the habits of mind of the discipline. Thus, it must be relevant to the thinking and doing of real-world professionals who practice writing, pose and solve mathematical problems, or engage in scientific inquiry for a living. Moreover, it should be designed to honor high-ability students' needs for advanced challenge, in-depth thinking and doing, and abstract conceptualization. Some general questions to ask in judging appropriate differentiation for the gifted are included below:

- Is the curriculum sufficiently advanced for the strongest learners in the group?
- Is the curriculum complex enough for the best learners, requiring multiple levels of thinking, use of resources, and/or variables to manipulate?
- Is the curriculum sufficiently in-depth to allow students to study important issues and problems related to a topic under study?
- Is the curriculum sufficiently encouraging of creativity, stimulating open-ended responses and providing high-level choices?

Typically, a curriculum is organized according to grade levels, with each subsequent grade-level expectation being more demanding than the preceding. In this way, we can calibrate level of difficulty to ensure that students are working in their zone of proximal development (Vygotsky, 1978). When we differentiate curricula for the gifted, we must move to a higher level of expectation in respect to content, process, and concept demands. Thus, one way of accommodating higher expectations effectively is to make *more advanced curricula* available at younger ages, ensuring that all levels of the standards are traversed in the process. In language arts, for example, this should mean reading more challenging books that are above the functional reading level of gifted learners. Differentiating curricula then requires attention to the level of functional learning matched to advanced expectations. Adaptation of advanced learning expectations needs to occur, as well. It may be insufficient merely to move students through the next stage of the curriculum without a concomitant appreciation for depth and complexity of the underlying experiences to be provided. Thus, the curriculum level for gifted learners must be adapted to their needs for advancement, depth, complexity, and creative opportunity. Each of the content chapters in this book demonstrates ways that these differentiation principles are incorporated.

Project work also needs to be carefully differentiated for the gifted, in order to meet the criterion of creativity. As more emphasis is placed on collaborative project work at all levels of schooling, it is critical that educators of the gifted use a set of standards to judge whether or not such work is sufficiently challenging for this group of learners and whether or not the contextual settings in which the work is carried out will promote sufficient growth for them. Differentiation of project work may be judged based on the medium in which the project is done and the variables and skills addressed by the demands of the work. Provision of alternatives for student products also enhances the creativity dimension of the curriculum. For example, students might write a poetry book using their choice of poetry forms. Chapter 6 explores the dimension of project/product development and its concomitant skill sets.

Differentiated Curriculum Resources

Because differentiation of the curriculum is so central to the enterprise of gifted education, it would follow that the choice of differentiated curriculum resources would be critical in curriculum planning and delivery of instruction to ensure that the appropriate level of challenge is provided in each content area. We have a strong evidential base that suggests that materials constitute the curriculum in most classrooms (Apple, 1991) and that most basal materials are inappropriately geared to challenging gifted students (Johnson, Boyce, & VanTassel-Baska, 1995). Taken together, these findings suggest the need for careful selection of materials that meet basic specifications for exemplary curricula in the subject area in question, as well as appropriate curricula for the gifted based on differentiation features. Although the selection of nationally

1. Does the material address the goals and outcomes of the curriculum framework?

2. Is the material differentiated for the gifted in respect to advancement, complexity, and creativity?

3. Is the material well-designed in respect to emphasizing research-based strategies, such as concept mapping, metacognition, and articulation of thinking?

4. Is the material aligned with standards in the relevant subject area or _easy_ to align?

Figure 2.1. Guiding questions for selecting curricular materials for gifted students.

---

available materials meeting these specifications for the gifted may be small, such materials do exist and should be used to guide the differentiation process for curricula. There also are criteria available to guide the development of differentiated materials (Purcell, Burns, Tomlinson, Imbeau, & Martin, 2002); these criteria have been used by the National Association for Gifted Children (NAGC) to recognize exemplary curriculum units that have been developed by various individuals and groups and implemented in classrooms.

Differentiated curricular materials for gifted students should go beyond a single text as resource, provide advanced readings, present interesting and challenging ideas, treat knowledge as tentative and open-ended, and provide a conceptual depth that allows students to make interdisciplinary connections. High-quality technology resources that meet the same criteria should be used as an important part of integrated learning.

It is useful for schools to appoint a materials selection committee that can review materials in each subject area, with an eye to principles of differentiation and exemplary content (VanTassel-Baska, 2004). Figure 2.1 provides a few guiding questions that should influence the process. The materials selection committee then may rate each resource reviewed and make decisions for use based on the data collected. Chapter 14 in this volume contains a more complete checklist of criteria and guidelines for selecting differentiated materials.

Instructional Differentiation

Another aspect of differentiation that needs clarification is in the *choice of instructional strategies*. In many respects, there are no strategies that are differentiated only for the gifted. Rather, strategy use is inextricably tied to the nature and level of the curriculum being addressed. Thus, the reason that the diagnostic-prescriptive approach to instruction is so powerful with the gifted is that it allows for a process by which curricular level can be efficaciously discerned and addressed in an adaptive fashion. Yet we know that some strategies are highly effective with the gifted in combination with an advanced curriculum. For example, questioning can be a powerful tool for evincing high-level discussions in gifted clusters, if the stimulus reading or viewing also is challenging. Use of open-ended activities also can prove effective if they are of requisite difficulty.

Problem-based learning (PBL), because of the sheer demands of working on ill-structured problems, poses a particularly appropriate instructional approach for gifted program use. Thus, strategy differentiation involves a set of techniques that need to be matched to advanced curricula in order to be effective for advancing the learning of gifted students. Instructional approaches that foster differentiated responses among diverse learners include those that are inquiry-based and open-ended and that employ flexible grouping practices (VanTassel-Baska & Brown, 2007). Three such approaches are highlighted here as examples and treated more extensively within later chapters in this book.

Problem-based learning. An example of an effective inquiry-based model is problem-based learning, which has the learner (a) encounter a real-world problem sculpted by the teacher out of key learning to be acquired in a given subject; (b) proceed to inquire about the nature of the problem, as well as effective avenues to research about it; and (c) pursue sources for acquiring relevant data. The instructional techniques needed by the teacher include high-level questioning skills, listening skills, conferencing skills, and tutorial abilities in order to guide the process to successful learning closure in a classroom. PBL also requires the use of flexible team grouping and whole-class discussion. Problem resolution requires student-initiated projects and presentations, guided by the teacher. Thus, effective instruction must include the selection of a few core teaching models that successfully highlight the intended outcomes of the curriculum.

Higher level questioning techniques. The use of high-level questions is another key instructional method for ensuring that gifted students are being challenged. Many questioning models have been employed to promote higher level thinking, including the simple PBL model:

- What do we know?
- What do we need to know?
- How can we find out?

More complex models involve key elements of reasoning:

- What is the issue?
- What perspectives are there on the issue?
- What are the assumptions of each stakeholder group on the issue?
- What would be the consequences of each perspective holding sway?

These models of questioning, among others, promote advanced learning in the gifted as well as other students and are addressed in Chapter 5 of this book in greater detail, as teaching to higher level process skills is examined.

Concept development. Part of what makes constructivism such a powerful approach to learning is that it provides a context for students to create their own understanding of an important concept at several levels: basic, applied to individual subject area; and global, applied to the universe. Basic concepts like time and space may be introduced to students early, yet continue to be learned through ongoing application in related subject matter. Subject-based concepts like magnetism and photosynthesis can be mastered through the study of a particular content area, in this case science. Global concepts, like *systems* and *patterns of change*, become known by continual applications in multiple spheres of knowledge. Thus, the idea of a concept is subject to level and type of application.

Teaching to conceptual understanding is one of the central learning approaches recommended by Bransford and Donovan (2003) in all subject areas. Yet, it requires a heuristic that elevates the learning for students. By asking students in small groups to identify examples of the concept, categorize the examples, come up with counterexamples, and develop generalizations about the concept under study, teachers help students begin to derive definitions that they have constructed but that have their own validity, given the process employed. At all levels, conceptual learning can be attained if it is addressed systematically in the instructional process.

Assessment Differentiation

Just as differentiation involves careful selection of core materials and curriculum that underlies them and the deliberate choice of high-powered instructional approaches, it also requires the choice of differentiated assessment protocols that reflect the high level of learning attained. High-stakes assessments, such as the Scholastic Aptitude Test (SAT), Advanced Placement exams (AP), and even state assessments required by NCLB, are the standardized symbols of how well gifted students are doing in comparison to others of their age. Secondary schools, in order to be considered high quality, must be producing students scoring at the top levels on nationally normed instruments. Yet deep preparation for success on these tests rests in individual classrooms. Even strong learners like the gifted cannot do as well as they could without adequate preparation in relevant content-based curriculum archetypes. The use of assessments as planning tools for direct instruction in each relevant subject area is a key to overall improvement in student performance. Administrators responsible for the review of teacher lesson plans need to know how such assessment models can be converted into work in classrooms. Curriculum directors and departments need to spend planning time on strategies for incorporating such elements. Because such assessments are a reality of NCLB and viewed by our society as crucial indicators of student progress in school, we need to make them work for us rather than against us in the public arena.

In addition to standardized measures being employed to assess student learning, it also is crucial that more performance-based tools be used to assess individual growth and development (VanTassel-Baska, 2008). In tandem with more standardized measures, they provide a more complete picture of individual progress toward specific education goals. For gifted learners, in particular, the quality of performance on such measures may be a better indicator of skills and concepts deeply mastered than paper-and-pencil measures, because performance-based assessments require students to articulate an understanding of the learning process as well as provide responses to multipart and open-ended questions and tasks (VanTassel-Baska, Johnson, & Avery, 2002). More specific examples are provided in Chapter 16 of this volume.

Quality Teaching

Just as the roles of curriculum, instruction, and assessment are central to the differentiation process, so too is the teacher. In the absence of a well-trained teacher, differentiation of materials is insufficient to affect student growth. Access to high-quality, well-trained teachers in specific subject areas who can provide challenge and nurturance for our best learners is clearly a critical issue in appropriate education of the gifted. Without thoughtful teachers, the best curricula will lie dormant in classrooms, unable to be energized and vivified by expert instruction. Teachers with only strong management skills also will fail to excite the gifted if lack of knowledge is apparent.

What are the critical requirements for identifying high-quality teachers of the gifted? First of all, teachers of the gifted need to be lifelong learners themselves, open to new experiences and able to appreciate the value of new learning and how it applies to the classroom. Second, they need to be passionate about at least one area of knowledge that they know well, and be able to communicate that passion and its underlying expertise to students. This would imply deep knowledge in a subject area, coupled with the ability to use the skills associated with that knowledge domain at a high level. Third, they need to be good thinkers, able to manipulate ideas at analysis, synthesis, and evaluation levels with their students within and across areas of knowledge. Such facility would imply that they themselves were strong students in college and scored well on tests of reasoning, like the Scholastic Aptitude Test (SAT) and the Graduate Record Exam (GRE). Fourth, teachers of the gifted must be capable of processing information in a simultaneity mode, meaning that they need to be able to address multiple objectives at the same time, recognize how students might manipulate different higher level skills in the same task demand, and easily align lower level tasks within those that require higher level skills and concepts. In addition, they must be creative engineers, able to structure lessons and learning opportunities shaped by available student data and an intuitive sense of student need in an area of learning.

In addition to these prerequisites for effective teachers of the gifted, there also is an approved set of national standards for preparing teachers in this field. Developed jointly by NAGC and Council for Exceptional Children, The Association for the Gifted (CEC-TAG), the standards delineate 77 indicators of teacher preparedness to work effectively with the gifted, usually requiring at least 12 hours of university coursework to become competent in them (VanTassel-Baska & Johnsen, 2007). Teacher preparation is an essential undergirding to delivering differentiated content, instructional processes, materials, and assessment for gifted learners. A copy of these standards may be found in the Appendix; they also are referenced throughout the book to demonstrate alignment to the ideas expressed about provisions and services for gifted learners.

RATIONALE FOR AN INTEGRATED CURRICULUM MODEL

The ICM is one approach to curriculum development that demonstrates alignment with the curriculum reform paradigm and is responsive to students talented in traditional academic areas (Little, 2009; VanTassel-Baska & Wood, 2009). This approach has relied on the key factors of curricular reform to guide the development process. It also has employed three dimensions to differentiating content, process, product, and concepts.

Although schools have used many approaches in their programs for the gifted, the use of systematic, challenging curricular intervention has been lacking. Moreover, planned curricular experiences have not been sustained over time. What the field has lacked is a comprehensive and cohesive curricular framework that uses good curricular design, considers the features of the disciplines under study, and sufficiently differentiates for talented students. Thus, an integrated model of curriculum for gifted learners, one that is sensitive to all aspects of their learning needs, is essential. Salient characteristics of the gifted learner may be handled simultaneously in such a scheme, attending to precocity, intensity, and complexity as integrated characteristics representing cognitive and affective dimensions.

A second reason for an integrated curriculum relates to current delivery models. As pull-out programs have decreased in number, more gifted students are being served in heterogeneous or self-contained settings, contexts in which integrated curricular approaches can work well if applied diligently and systematically. Because an integrated curriculum represents a total curricular package in an area of learning, rather than an add-on curriculum, it provides the needed differentiation within traditional areas of learning for which schools are accountable. Thus, an integrated curriculum model would work well in cluster-grouped classrooms in which gifted students are congregated for advanced learning, as well as in subject-based classes or in gifted schools where differentiation is needed across all subjects.

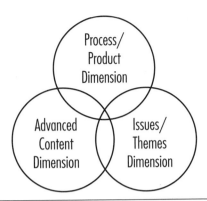

Figure 2.2. Integrated Curriculum Model for Gifted Learners. From "The Development of Talent Through Curriculum," by J. VanTassel-Baska, 1995, *Roeper Review, 18,* p. 99. Copyright © 1995 by The Board of Trustees of the Roeper School. Reprinted with permission.

A third reason for an integrated approach rests with recent research on learning. Studies have documented that better transfer of learning occurs when higher order thinking skills are embedded in subject matter (NRC, 2000), and teaching concepts in a discipline is a better way to produce long-term learning than teaching facts and rules (Bransford & Donovan, 2003). Our understanding of creativity also has shifted toward the need for strong subject matter knowledge as a prerequisite (Simonton, 2000).

A fourth reason for using an integrated model is related to a clear shift of emphasis in the field from the focus on the individual gifted learner to the process of collective talent development for all learners. As this shift has occurred, curricular principles important for the gifted have been seen as the province of all learners developing talents in both traditional and nontraditional domains, accomplished through employing interdisciplinary, concept-based curricula and higher order thinking. This development calls for a close alignment of meaningful subject matter with its higher order manipulation of skills and ideas.

For all of these reasons, an integrated curriculum model provides a strong research-based foundation for design and development work in all subject area disciplines to differentiate effectively for the needs of gifted learners.

THE INTEGRATED CURRICULUM MODEL

The Integrated Curriculum Model, first proposed by VanTassel-Baska in 1986 and further explicated in subsequent publications across the last three decades (Little, 2009; VanTassel-Baska, 1998, 2003; VanTassel-Baska & Stambaugh, 2006a, 2008), comprises three interrelated dimensions that are responsive to very different aspects of the gifted learner (see Figure 2.2). These dimensions may be thought of as described below.

The ICM emphasizes advanced content knowledge that frames disciplines of study. Honoring the talent search concept, this facet of the model ensures that careful, diagnostic-prescriptive approaches are employed to ensure new learning as opposed to remedial instruction. Curricula based on the model represent appropriate advanced learning in that area. For example, teachers routinely determine what students already know about their yearly instructional plan by testing them on end-of-year or end-of-chapter material before it is taught and then adjusting classroom instruction to their level of learning.

The ICM provides higher order thinking and processing. This facet of the model promotes student opportunities for manipulating information at complex levels by employing generic thinking models like Paul's (1992) Elements of Reasoning and more discipline-specific ones like Sher's (1993) Nature of the Scientific Process. This facet of the ICM also implies the utilization of information in some generative way, whether it be a project or a fruitful discussion. For example, students may use the reasoning element "point of view" to discuss and write about a short story by William Faulkner. Students may conduct a science experiment reflecting on whether or not their findings supported their research question, and if not, why?

The ICM focuses learning experiences around major issues, themes, and ideas that define both real-world applications and theoretical modeling within and across areas of study. This facet of the ICM honors the idea of scaffolding curricula for talented learners around the important aspects of a discipline and emphasizing these aspects in a systematic way (Ward, 1981). Thus, themes and ideas are selected based on careful research of the primary area of study to determine the most worthy and important issues and ideas for curriculum development, a theme consistent with curricular specifications that have guided standards development and other major initiatives (American Association for the Advancement of Science, 1990; Perkins, 1992). These ideas become an important framework for curriculum development. The goal of such an approach is to ensure deep understanding of ideas, rather than superficial responding.

This model synthesizes the three best approaches to curriculum development and implementation documented in the literature for talented learners (e.g., Benbow & Stanley, 1983; Lubinski & Benbow, 2006; Maker, 2003; Ward, 1981). Recent reviews of curricular models for the gifted have found the greatest effectiveness prevailing in the accelerative approach, guided by content modification (Johnsen, 2000; VanTassel-Baska & Brown, 2000, 2007). The fusion of these approaches is central to the development of a coherent curriculum that is responsive to diverse needs of talented students while also providing rich challenges to all for optimal learning.

Translation Into Curriculum Units of Study

The ICM has been translated into a curriculum framework and sets of teaching units, as well as supplementary materials, in the areas of science, language arts, mathematics, and social studies. To date, these four curricular areas represent the best examples of a deliberate effort to translate the model into written materials. The translation of the ICM was accomplished by developing a curricular framework addressing each of its dimensions in an integrated way.

In order to satisfy the need for advanced content, the language arts curriculum (Center for Gifted Education, 1999), developed for grades K–12, used advanced literature selections that were 2 years beyond grade reading level, used advanced language, and contained multiple levels of meaning. The writing emphasis was placed on persuasive essays that developed an argument, which is a more advanced form of writing than is typically taught at elementary levels. Use of advanced vocabulary and the mastery of English syntax at the elementary level also was stressed.

The process/product dimension of the curriculum was addressed by embedding the Elements of Reasoning developed by Paul (1992) and by using a research model developed to aid students in generating original work (Boyce, 1997). Products were encouraged through both written and oral work. In the newer curriculum developed through Project Athena, another language arts study funded by the Javits program, the *Jacob's Ladder* program is organized by levels of reading comprehension, linked to Paul's Elements of Reasoning, in order to provide students the scaffolding necessary to handle drawing consequences and implications, using data and evidence to make inferences, and exploring multiple perspectives in order to create original work from selected readings (VanTassel-Baska & Stambaugh, 2006b).

The issues/themes dimension of the curriculum was explicated by focusing on the theme of *change* as it applied to works of literature selected for the unit, the writing process, language study, and learners' reflections on their own learning throughout the unit. Additionally, studying an issue of significance was emphasized as a part of the research strand for each unit. To date, 10 units have been developed, validated, piloted, and revised using this framework (Center for Gifted Education, 1999; VanTassel-Baska, Zuo, Avery, & Little, 2002).

The translation of the ICM to the National Science Curriculum Project for High-Ability Learners was driven by the overarching theme of *systems*, which became the conceptual organizing influence in each of the seven units of study (Center for Gifted Education, 1997). Students learned the elements, boundaries, inputs, and outputs, as well as the interactions, of selected systems. Through a problem-based learning approach, they also learned about how science systems interact with real-world social, political, and economic systems. The process/product dimension of the curricular model was addressed by engaging students in a scientific research process that led them to create their own experiments and design their own solutions to each unit's central problem. The advanced content dimension was addressed by selecting advanced science content for inclusion in each unit and encouraging in-depth study of selected content relevant to understanding the central problem of the unit. These units are being used in classrooms across the country to incorporate the new science emphasis and have been found successful in heterogeneous settings, as well as with more restricted groups (VanTassel-Baska, Bass, Ries, Poland, & Avery, 1998). In later units developed for primary age children, under Project Clarion, the concepts of both *systems* and *change* were used to enhance concept development at basic levels, at science topical levels, and at macro concept levels. Moreover, scientific process attainment also was stressed, along with content mastery linked to standards (VanTassel-Baska, 2008).

The translation of the ICM to social studies was driven by the theme or concept of *systems* for several units, with the concepts of *change* and *cause and effect* explored in additional units. The concept of *systems* was applied to understanding structures in society, such as economic and political systems; other units emphasized connected chains of causes and effects to help students understand multiple causation in history and to recognize that historical events were not inevitable. As in the language arts units, the process/product dimension of the model was addressed through embedded use of Paul's (1992) Elements of Reasoning, as well as through a heavy emphasis on historical analysis. Products included written and oral presentations of research efforts and other activities. The advanced content dimension was addressed through the selection of advanced reading materials, including many primary source documents, as well as secondary sources and historical fiction, and through early introduction of advanced skills and ideas (Little et al., 2007).

The translation of the ICM into mathematics units follows a similar design, with advanced content being a primary concern along with higher level mathematical processes, special math projects, and a concept-based orientation. The concept of models is the one most employed in the units developed to date. Because there are fewer math units developed by the Center for Gifted Education, and because they have not been rigorously tested in classrooms beyond tryouts and piloting, we have not reported on them more extensively here. Chapter 9 contains more commentary on both the design and development aspects of these units of study.

An example of the translation of the ICM to the specific disciplines may be found in Table 2.1, which portrays the ICM as it has been applied to the exemplary curriculum units developed at the Center for Gifted Education at The College of William and Mary. These curriculum units will be discussed further as examples of content-based curricula for high-ability learners throughout this text.

TABLE 2.1

Application of the Integrated Curriculum Model to William and Mary
Science, Language Arts, and Social Studies Curricular Units

Dimension	Science Units	Language Arts Units	Social Studies Units
Advanced Content	• Student-determined mastery of science content through a problem-based approach • Formative and summative assessment of science content learning	• Advanced reading selections • Corresponding advanced vocabulary work • D-P approach used to teach grammar • Expository/personal essay writing	• Advanced in-depth study of key periods in U.S. and world history that were influential, with an emphasis on the use of primary sources
Process/ Product	• Use of scientific process embedded in problem-based learning • Preparation of problem resolution and presentation to class	• Use of writing process model coupled with self, peer, and teacher assessment approaches • Use of Paul's Elements of Reasoning (1992) to explore meaning in literature and to conduct real-world research • Production of research project/oral presentation of findings	• Emphasis on Paul's Elements of Reasoning (1992) as a basis for oral and written argument in the analysis of complex social and historical issues • Emphasis on historical analysis skills applied to primary and secondary sources • Emphasis on research products
Issues/ Themes	• Organized around the concept of systems • Teaching to underlying generalizations about systems	• Organized around the concept of change • Teaching to underlying generalizations about change	• Organized around the concept of social, geographical, political, and economic systems that define the history of ancient and modern civilizations • Subconcepts of structure, function, pattern, and cause and effect are also explored • Emphasis on complexity of causality in human interactions throughout history

Theoretical Underpinnings

The theoretical support for the Integrated Curriculum Model comes primarily from two sources. One source is the work of Vygotsky (1978) in three aspects of his theoretical orientation. One aspect critical to the model is the zone of proximal development, which implies that learners must be exposed to material slightly above their tested level in order to feel challenged by the learning experience. This idea was expanded on by Csikszentmihalyi (1991) in his concept of flow and his studies showing that gifted learners demonstrated a broader and deeper capacity to engage learning than did typical students (Csikszentmihalyi, Rathunde, & Whalen, 1993).

A second aspect of the Vygotsky (1978) theory of learning influential to the model is his view of interactionism, whereby the learner increases learning depth by interacting with others in the environment to enhance understanding of concepts and ideas. Ideas are validated and understood through the articulation of tentative connections made based on a stimulus such as a literary artifact, a film, a piece of music, or a problem. Learning increases as interactions provide the scaffolding necessary to structure thinking about the stimulus.

A third aspect of Vygotsky's (1978) theory applicable to the development of the ICM was his theory of constructivism, whereby learners constructed knowledge for themselves. This theory is central to the tenets of the teaching and learning models found in the ICM curriculum and a central thesis to the model itself, as students must be in charge of their own learning in respect to each dimension of the model, whether it be content acceleration, project-based learning opportunities such as PBL, or discussion-laden experiences in which concepts, issues, and themes are explored.

Another theoretical influence on the model was the work of Mortimer Adler (1984) and his Paideia Proposal, which posited the importance of rich content representing the best products of world civilization coupled with the relevant cognitive skills to study them, appropriately linked to the intellectual ideas that spawned the work of the disciplines and philosophy. His worldview of curriculum was highly influential in thinking about the role of academic rationalism in a curriculum for the gifted, even as cognitive science was the predominant force in the larger environment.

Finally, the theory of multiculturalism espoused by James Banks (1994, 2001) speaks to the aspect of the ICM concerned with students making a better world through deliberate social action, whether through the resolutions brought to policy makers as a result of PBL work or the studies of technology used in researching issues or the concerns for censorship in the history of great literature. Moreover, this theoretical orientation also provided a major emphasis on the works of minority authors from both this country and abroad as an attempt to acknowledge multiple perspectives in student understanding of any content area, especially history.

CURRICULUM REFORM DESIGN ELEMENTS

The ICM-based national curriculum projects for high-ability learners were developed with an understanding of appropriate curricular dimensions for gifted students, but they also demonstrate the use of key design features of curriculum reform strongly advocated by the national standards projects (O'Day & Smith, 1993) and the middle school movement (Erb, 1994). In more recent years, these ideas have been subjected to rigorous testing of their validity and may be found in the "what works" publications of the National Research Council. Thus, the curriculum employs the following emphases:

- Is *meaning-based*, in that the curriculum emphasizes depth over breadth and concepts over facts, and is grounded in real-world issues and problems that students care about or need to know. In science, students study the implications of acid spills on interstate highway systems. In language arts, they relate to how the impact of the treatment of minorities in this country has changed over a 60-year period. In social studies, students examine documents within context and explore the influence of various individuals and groups in order to understand the complexity of historical events and decisions. Moreover, the pedagogy of the curriculum across content areas is constructivist in orientation, helping students to construct their own meaning from the events, artifacts, and problems studied.

- Employs *higher order thinking and reasoning* as integral components to all content areas. The units provide students opportunities to demonstrate their understanding of advanced content and interdisciplinary ideas through strategies such as concept mapping, persuasive writing, and designing experiments.

- Emphasizes *intradisciplinary and interdisciplinary connections* by using overarching concepts, issues, and themes as major organizers. Thus, students study systems of cities, government, economies, and language, as well as chemistry and biology. The concept of *change* in language arts is relevant to literature, writing, and language, as well as to mathematics, art, and music.

- Provides opportunities for *metacognition* (student reflection on learning processes). Students are involved in consciously planning, monitoring, and assessing their own learning for efficient and effective use of time and resources. In social studies, for example, students pursue alternative paths to a real-world problem resolution in their particular area of study through a deliberative group process that engages them in metacognitive skills.

- Develops *habits of mind* through cultivating modes of thinking that resemble those of professionals in various fields with respect to skills, predispositions, and attitudes. In science, curiosity, objectivity, and skepticism are openly nurtured. In language arts, the mode of reflection and revision is consistently encouraged. In social studies, experiences develop awareness of the complexity of causality, the importance of exploring bias, and the need to avoid present-mindedness.

- Promotes *inquiry-based learning and problem solving* by having students take charge of their own learning. In the problem-based science units, students find out what they know, what they need to know, and how to pursue important knowledge in working on a real-world problem in small investigatory teams. In language arts, students work in teams to discover how language functions and is structured. In social studies, students work together to explore different aspects of a culture or historical period and then share their findings.

- Uses various new *technologies as tools* for the learning process, from doing background research via the Internet, to creating digital written and visual products to be shared with authentic audiences locally and at a distance, to communicating with students around the world through a variety of technological means. The units of study in each area incorporate activities that require these applications.

- Focuses on *learner outcomes of significance*, those that advance higher level skills and conceptual understandings. Expectations for learning are identified at targeted grade levels that reflect the priorities of the new curriculum for being broad-based, conceptual, and relevant to real-world application. In each set of units, learner outcomes reflect content, process/product, and concept emphases.

- Employs *authentic assessment* by tapping into what students know as a result of meaningful instruction. Using approaches like portfolios and performance-based activities, the units engage learners in assessment as an active part of the learning process.

- Is sensitive to *multicultural and global concerns*. In the case of language arts and social studies, it ensures a strong representational pattern of multicultural readings and materials, as well as a focus on the important skill of viewing issues from multiple perspectives. History is deliberately taught from the viewpoint of multiple perspectives in minority and majority groups.

- Focuses on an *overarching concept* as a frame for development and implementation. Language arts units employ the concept of *change*, while science and social studies work with the concept of *systems* with the overlap of change over time and cause and effect in the study of history.

- Employs *multiple resources and materials* that allow flexibility, variety, and sophistication in delivery patterns. Students may read different texts, for example, yet respond to a common set of questions about them.

- Focuses on *substantive content*: key ideas, principles, and structures that students need to master in the discipline in order to become proficient. The content is organized to provide an understanding of the structure of language arts, science, and the social sciences.

All of these reform elements formed the basis for initial curriculum development work. A model of the elements taken together may be seen in

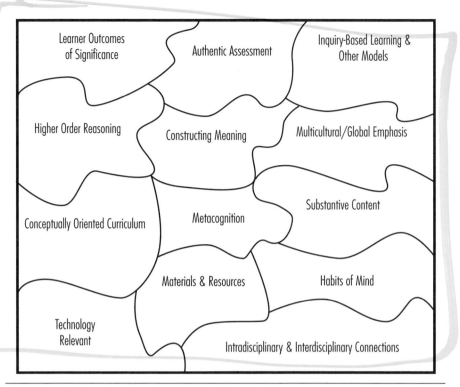

Figure 2.3. A model for curricular reform.

Figure 2.3. The puzzle represents a holistic way to represent the interlocking nature of these elements, yet it reveals the clear boundaries of each that may be used in teacher training.

Systematic tailoring of the curriculum for gifted learners occurred through ensuring the following kinds of additional emphasis:

- provisions for acceleration and compression of content;
- use of interrelated higher order thinking skills (e.g., analysis, synthesis, and evaluation);
- integration of content by key ideas, issues, and themes;
- advanced reading level of materials employed;
- opportunities for students to develop advanced products;
- opportunities for independent learning based on student capacity and interest; and
- consistently focused use of inquiry-based instructional techniques.

Thus, the systematic fusion of integrated curricular considerations with reform principles was effected.

BEST PRACTICE AND IMPLEMENTATION CONSIDERATIONS

In a study of all extant curriculum models in gifted education, VanTassel-Baska and Brown (2007) found that across models, the following best practices could be derived, well-supported by the research from several sources. All of these practices are strongly advocated throughout this book as we examine content-based curriculum more fully in all of its dimensions.

- Best practice is to group gifted students instructionally by subject area for advanced curriculum work that is flexibly organized and implemented, based on the student's documented level of learning within the subject area.
- Best practice suggests embedding multiple higher level thinking models and skills within core subject area teaching to enhance learning.
- Best practice suggests the use of inquiry as a central strategy to promote gifted student learning in multiple modalities.
- Best practice calls for the use of student-centered learning opportunities that are issue- or problem-based and relevant to the student's world.

Yet the implementation of any curriculum model is based on several considerations in the school setting. Most important among them is the nature of the learner. For talented students, regardless of the richness of the core curricular base, there will be a need to address certain powerful characteristics through flexible implementation of a model.

The Learner: Characteristics, Aptitudes, and Predispositions

There are many characteristics of gifted learners on which one might focus for a discussion of creating an optimal match between learner and curriculum. Several lists have been discussed as a basis for curriculum work (e.g., Maker, 2003; VanTassel-Baska, 1998). However, in studies of curriculum, it has become apparent that three such characteristics remain pivotal for purposes of curricular planning and development: precocity, intensity, and complexity.

Precocity. The precocity of the learner is a key characteristic to consider in curriculum development. Gifted learners, almost by definition, evidence advanced development in some school-related curricular area. The most commonly tested areas for such development are in the verbal and mathematical subject domains. Most students identified for gifted programs are at least 2 years advanced in one or both areas. Such evidence of advanced development provides a basis for curricular planning at a more advanced level and the expectation that such students can master new materials in one third to one half of the time of typical learners. For acutely gifted learners, there is a powerful motivation to learn fast and move ahead.

Intensity. In addition to precocity, another key characteristic that deserves attention for curriculum development is the intensity of gifted learners. This intensity may be manifested affectively in the realm of emotional responsiveness, such as when students react strongly to the death of a pet or a classroom injustice committed by a teacher. But, this characteristic also has salience in the cognitive realm. Students exhibit intensity through the capacity to focus and concentrate for long periods of time on a subject that fascinates them or an idea they find intriguing. Such a characteristic can just as quickly become dissipated in uninteresting busywork or lack of depth in the exploration even of a subject of interest. This characteristic, like precocity, needs curricular attention.

Complexity. The third learner characteristic of curricular interest is complexity, the capacity of gifted learners to engage in higher level and abstract thinking even at young ages. It also refers to their preference for hard and challenging work, often at levels beyond current functioning. They enjoy working on multiple levels simultaneously, such as when solving complex real-world problems that have many parts and perspectives to study. Just as with precocity and intensity, the characteristic of complexity in the gifted demands curricular responsiveness because it is openly desired by the learner and often indicated by his or her behavior in the classroom.

These three characteristics each dictate an approach to the curriculum that honors the various facets of the gifted mind and personality. Whereas other curricular models have addressed a particular facet of the gifted learner, the Integrated Curriculum Model represents a fusion of several approaches such that the most powerful characteristics of the gifted are directly reflected in the curricular intervention.

Although this model has salience for all learners, based on a talent development paradigm, the variable of time becomes crucial in implementation. Not all learners will be ready at the same stage of development in each area for the advanced, intensive, and complex study required by the curriculum. For example, reading selections in the language arts curriculum may be appropriate for high-ability fifth graders, but too difficult based on reading level for average fifth graders. Teachers, then, would need to decide whether to substitute more accessible literature and still employ the unit with all students or to differentiate instruction in the classroom, using the unit only with a cluster group of high-ability learners. The judicious application of this curricular model for all learners is thus advised.

The Context Variables

Although the need for a match between the learner and the intervention has already been described, it also is important to highlight contextual considerations that could affect the successful use of this curricular model in school settings. There are at least four variables that must be considered: flexibility in student placement and progress, grouping, teacher training, and climate of excellence.

Flexibility in student placement and progress. Even an enriched and accelerated curriculum developed for high-ability learners that addresses all of the educational reform principles cannot be used without careful consideration of entry skills, rates of learning, and special interests and needs. Thus, ungraded multiage contexts in which high-ability learners access appropriate work groups and curricular stations represent a critical component of the implementation context. Pretesting of students on relevant skills is a central part of the Center for Gifted Education's curricular projects, and diagnosing unusual readiness or developmental spurts that may occur in a curricular sequence also is important. Schools may notice and use such data as a basis for more in-depth work in an area of a particular teaching unit.

Grouping. As a curriculum for high-ability learners is implemented, attention must be paid to the beneficial impact of grouping for instruction. As Kulik's (1993) reanalysis of the grouping data demonstrated, when curricula are modified for gifted students, the positive effects of grouping become more prominent. Moreover, recent classroom studies have verified that little differentiation is occurring in heterogeneous classrooms for gifted students (Westberg & Daoust, 2003), and the majority of teachers in our schools are not trained to teach gifted learners (Johnsen, VanTassel-Baska, & Robinson, 2008). Thus, forming instructional groups of gifted students for implementation of a differentiated curriculum is clearly the most effective and efficient way to deliver it. Whether such grouping occurs in separately designated classes or in regular classrooms is a local consideration.

Teacher training. Based on data confirming the significant role of teacher training in providing differentiated instruction for the gifted (Hansen & Feldhusen, 1994; Tomlinson & Strickland, 2004; VanTassel-Baska & Johnsen, 2007) and the availability of coursework in the education of the gifted (Johnsen et al., 2008), there is good reason to place gifted students with teachers who have received at least 12 university credit hours of professional training. The benefits to gifted learners become greater when a differentiated curriculum is handled by those sensitive to the nature and needs of such students. Some training in the direct implementation of curricular materials to be used is also desirable. For example, in my experience with the Center for Gifted Education materials, about 3 days of training in the various approaches employed in the materials have generally supported initial implementation, depending on the experience of the teachers involved, followed by in situ professional development and classroom monitoring of implementation across at least 2 years.

Earlier in this chapter, I delineated the characteristics and qualities necessary for effective teachers of the gifted. However, there is little substitute for systematic preparation of teachers to ensure that gifted learners are well-served in schools.

Climate of excellence. In order for gifted learners to perform at optimal levels, the educational context must offer challenging opportunities that tap deeply into students' psychological states (Csikszentmihalyi et al., 1993), provide generative situations (VanTassel-Baska, 1998), and also demand high standards of excellence that correspond to expectations for high-level productivity in any field (Ochse, 1990). More than ever, the climate of a school for excellence matters if curriculum standards are to be raised successfully for any student. For gifted students in particular, this type of climate must be in place to ensure optimal development, positive attitudes toward learning, and engagement. Such a climate also is essential for disadvantaged gifted youth who are put more at risk by lowered expectations for performance (VanTassel-Baska, 2009).

CONCLUSION

This opening chapter has established the landscape of what constitutes appropriate curricula for the gifted and why such a multidimensional approach is required. Succeeding chapters will provide concrete applications of the ICM at work with gifted students across subject areas, levels of instruction, and dimensions of learning. Only through careful curriculum development practices can we help promote optimal learning opportunities for minds of promise.

KEY POINTS SUMMARY

- Differentiated curricula for the gifted involve the features of advanced level, choice of instructional strategies that promote thinking, selection of appropriate materials, generative project work, and alternative assessment approaches to measure authentic learning.
- Differentiation of the curriculum may occur through the adaptation of level, depth, complexity, challenge, and creative opportunity.
- The quality of teaching is a central tenet of effective curriculum differentiation, requiring teachers to be trained in the principles of gifted education best practices.
- Best practice principles should be followed in the selection or development of a curriculum for the gifted.
- Curricula for the gifted should align with existing state and national standards to be effective and demonstrate how key features of learning research may be applied.
- Implementation of a curriculum must honor the specific characteristics of

the learners being taught and provide a flexible and supportive environment for learning.

REFERENCES

Adler, M. (1984). *The Paideia program.* New York, NY: MacMillan.

American Association for the Advancement of Science. (1990). *Science for all Americans.* New York, NY: Oxford University Press.

Apple, M. W. (1991). The culture and commerce of the textbook. In M. W. Apple & L. K. Christian-Smith (Eds.), *The politics of the textbook* (pp. 22–40). New York, NY: Routledge.

Banks, J. (1994). *An introduction to multicultural education.* Boston, MA: Allyn & Bacon.

Banks, J. (2001). *Cultural diversity and education: Foundations, curriculum and teaching.* Boston, MA: Allyn & Bacon.

Benbow, C. P., & Stanley, J. C. (Eds.). (1983). *Academic precocity: Aspects of its development.* Baltimore, MD: Johns Hopkins University Press.

Boyce, L. N. (1997). *A guide to teaching research skills and strategies for grades 4–12.* Williamsburg, VA: Center for Gifted Education, The College of William and Mary.

Bransford, J. D., & Donovan, S. (Eds.). (2003). *How students learn: History, mathematics, and science in the classroom.* Washington, DC: National Academy Press.

Center for Gifted Education. (1997). *Guide to teaching a problem-based science curriculum.* Dubuque, IA: Kendall/Hunt.

Center for Gifted Education. (1999). *Guide to teaching a language arts curriculum for high-ability learners.* Dubuque, IA: Kendall/Hunt.

Csikszentmihalyi, M. (1991). *Flow: The psychology of optimal experience.* New York, NY: HarperPerennial.

Csikszentmihalyi, M., Rathunde, K., & Whalen, S. (1993). *Talented teenagers: The roots of success and failure.* New York, NY: Cambridge University Press.

Erb, T. (1994). The middle school: Mimicking the success routes of the information age. *Journal for the Education of the Gifted, 17,* 385–406.

Hansen, J., & Feldhusen, J. (1994). Comparison of trained and untrained teachers of the gifted. *Gifted Child Quarterly, 38,* 115–123.

Johnsen, S. K. (2000, Summer). What the research says about curriculum. *Tempo, 20,* 25–30.

Johnsen, S. K., VanTassel-Baska, J., & Robinson, A. (2008). *Using the national gifted education standards for university teacher preparation programs.* Thousand Oaks, CA: Corwin Press.

Johnson, D. T., Boyce, L. N., & VanTassel-Baska, J. (1995). Science curriculum review: Evaluating materials for high-ability learners. *Gifted Child Quarterly, 39,* 36–43.

Kulik, J. (1993). *An analysis of the research on ability grouping: Historical and contemporary perspectives.* Storrs: University of Connecticut, The National Research Center on the Gifted and Talented.

Little, C. A. (2009). *The Integrated Curriculum Model.* In B. MacFarlane & T. Stambaugh

(Eds.), *Leading in gifted education: The festschrift of Dr. Joyce VanTassel-Baska* (pp. 271–284). Waco, TX: Prufrock Press.

Little, C. A., Feng, A. X., VanTassel-Baska, J., Rogers, K. B., & Avery, L. D. (2007). A study of curriculum effectiveness in social studies. *Gifted Child Quarterly, 51,* 272–284.

Lubinski, D., & Benbow, C. (2006) Study of Mathematically Precocious Youth after 35 years: Uncovering antecedents for the development of math-science expertise. *Perspectives on Psychological Science, 1,* 316–345.

Maker, C. J. (2003). *Curriculum development for the gifted* (2nd ed.). Rockville, MD: Aspen Systems.

Ochse, R. (1990). *Before the gates of excellence: Determinants of creative genius.* Cambridge, England: Cambridge University Press.

National Research Council. (2000). *How people learn: Brain, mind, experience and school.* Washington, DC: National Academy Press.

O'Day, J. A., & Smith, M. S. (1993). Systemic reform and educational opportunity. In S. H. Fuhrman (Ed.), *Designing coherent educational policy* (pp. 250–311). San Francisco, CA: Jossey-Bass.

Paul, R. (1992). *Critical thinking: What every person needs to survive in a rapidly changing world.* Rohnert Park, CA: Foundation for Critical Thinking.

Perkins, D. (1992). Selecting fertile themes for integrated learning. In H. Hayes Jacobs (Ed.), *Interdisciplinary curriculum: Design and implementation* (pp. 67–75). Alexandria, VA: Association for Supervision and Curriculum Development.

Purcell, J. H., Burns, D. E., Tomlinson, C. A., Imbeau, M. B., & Martin, J. L. (2002). Bridging the gap: A tool and technique to analyze and evaluate gifted education curricular units. *Gifted Child Quarterly, 46,* 306–321.

Sher, B. T. (1993). *A guide to key science concepts.* Williamsburg, VA: Center for Gifted Education.

Simonton, D. K. (2000). Cognitive, personal, developmental, and social aspects. *American Psychologist, 55,* 151–158.

Tomlinson, C., & Strickland, C. (2004). *Differentiation in practice: A resource guide for differentiating curriculum.* Alexandria, VA: Association for Supervision and Curriculum Development.

VanTassel-Baska, J. (1986). Effective curriculum and instructional models for the gifted. *Gifted Child Quarterly, 30,* 164–169.

VanTassel-Baska, J. (Ed.). (1998). *Excellence in educating gifted and talented learners* (3rd ed.). Denver, CO: Love.

VanTassel-Baska, J. (2003). *Curriculum planning and instructional design for gifted learners.* Denver, CO: Love.

VanTassel-Baska, J. (2004, Winter). The case for a systems approach to curriculum differentiation. *Tempo, 24,* 5–24.

VanTassel-Baska, J. (Ed.). (2008). *Alternative assessments with gifted and talented students.* Waco, TX: Prufrock Press.

VanTassel-Baska, J. (Ed.). (2009). *Patterns and profiles of promising learners from poverty.* Waco, TX: Prufrock Press.

VanTassel-Baska, J., Bass, G., Ries, R., Poland, D., & Avery, L. D. (1998). A national study of science curriculum effectiveness with high-ability students. *Gifted Child Quarterly, 42*, 200–211.

VanTassel-Baska, J., & Brown, E. (2000). An analysis of gifted curriculum models. In F. A. Karnes & S. M. Bean (Eds.), *Methods and materials for teaching the gifted* (pp. 91–131). Waco, TX: Prufrock Press.

VanTassel-Baska, J., & Brown, E. F. (2007). Toward best practice: An analysis of the efficacy of curriculum models in gifted education. *Gifted Child Quarterly, 51*, 35–40.

VanTassel-Baska, J., & Johnsen, S. K. (2007). Teacher education standards for the field of gifted education: A vision of coherence for personnel preparation in the 21st century. *Gifted Child Quarterly, 51*, 182–205.

VanTassel-Baska, J., Johnson, D., & Avery, L. D. (2002). Using performance tasks in the identification of economically disadvantaged and minority gifted learners: Findings from Project STAR. *Gifted Child Quarterly, 46*, 110–123.

VanTassel-Baska, J., & Stambaugh, T. (2006a). *Comprehensive curriculum for gifted learners* (3rd ed.). Needham Heights, MA: Allyn & Bacon.

VanTassel-Baska, J., & Stambaugh, T. (2006b). Project Athena: A pathway to advanced literacy development for children of poverty. *Gifted Child Today, 29*, 58–63.

VanTassel-Baska, J., & Stambaugh, T. (2008). *What works: 20 years of curriculum development and research*. Waco, TX: Prufrock Press.

VanTassel-Baska, J., & Wood, S. (2009). The Integrated Curriculum Model. In J. S. Renzulli, E. J. Gubbins, K. S. McMillen, R. D. Eckert, & C. A. Little (Eds.), *Systems and models for developing programs for the gifted and talented* (2nd ed., pp. 655–691). Mansfield Center, CT: Creative Learning Press.

VanTassel-Baska, J., Zuo, L., Avery, L. D., & Little, C. A. (2002). A curriculum study of gifted student learning in the language arts. *Gifted Child Quarterly, 46*, 30–44.

Vygotsky, L. S. (1978). *Mind in society: The development of higher psychological processes*. Cambridge, MA: Harvard University Press.

Ward, V. (1981). *Differential education for the gifted*. Ventura County, CA: Office of the Superintendent of Schools.

Westberg, K. L., & Daoust, M. E. (2003, Fall). The results of the replication of the Classroom Practices Survey replication in two states. *The National Research Center on the Gifted and Talented Newsletter*, 3–8.

Chapter 3

Who Is the Target Population for Gifted Curriculum?

Elissa F. Brown

OVERVIEW OF HISTORICAL CONCEPTIONS OF INTELLIGENCE

For more than a century, researchers have posited different conceptions of intelligence and ways in which intelligence is a useful construct for understanding behaviors and learning propensities. Some researchers have focused on the central ability known as "g" for general intelligence (Hollingworth, 1926; Spearman, 1904; Terman, 1925). Others have chosen to approach intelligence from primary mental abilities such as verbal comprehension, memory, and perceptual speed, based on the work of Thurstone (1938) and factor analysis. The term giftedness was synonymous with "intellectual giftedness," and the pioneering researchers investigated the nature and characteristics of gifted individuals only *after* setting minimal IQ standards for identification. Conceptions of giftedness are central to gifted education because, depending upon the theory or conception adopted by a school district, all aspects of the resulting program are driven by the understanding of the adopted conception of giftedness.

More recent modeling of human intelligence has focused on information processing structures (Sternberg, 1991, 2008) that serve as macro abilities of metacomponents, performance components, and knowledge acquisition components with an emphasis that intelligence is context-bound versus earlier constructs that held that intelligence is genetically endowed and fixed. Conceptions and definitions of intelligence vary within the broader field of education according to disparate theories of talent development, student demographic characteristics (e.g., language and cultural backgrounds), nonintellective factors considered important in the definition of exceptionality, different autonomous intelligences (Benbow & Stanley, 1996; Bracken & McCallum, 1998; Carroll, 1993; Csikszentmihalyi, 2000; Gardner, 1993), and the degree to which one's abilities and the context in which the individual operates interact (Gagné, 2007). These differing conceptions of intelligence have shaped our understanding and use of the construct of giftedness. Depending upon how a state or school district defines giftedness, there are implications for identification processes and policy, as well as the ways in which educators and schools group, instruct, and assess gifted students. Bloom (1985) noted:

> no matter what the initial characteristics (or gifts) of the individuals, unless there is a long and intensive process of encouragement, nurturance, education, and training, the individuals will not attain extreme levels of capability. (p. 11)

TARGET POPULATION

In order to focus on a talent development model of giftedness that supports the notion of students' abilities changing as they progress through school, moving from a more general ability in the early years to a specialized ability in a field of study as they grow older, this chapter will focus on giftedness as it relates to a specific demonstrated ability nested within a domain area, such as mathematics. Because most school districts identify children for programs that are related to a specific content area (e.g., mathematics), focusing on a school-based conception of giftedness encourages clearer communication and has implications for the roles and responsibilities of our schools in developing talent.

According to Coleman and Cross (2005), the rationale for considering this type of definition is as follows:
- A school-based conception of giftedness recognizes the relative stability of interests that are evident by age 12 in many people (Albert, 1980; Hildreth, 1966).

- It recognizes the cumulative effects of development (Simonton, 1997), demonstrating that involvement in a domain becomes more evident as one begins to master the field (Bloom & Sosniak, 1981; Feldman, 1997; Sosniak, 1997), and speaks to a talent development model that occurs over time. It also pays attention to the fact that many gifted children do not perform well on standardized tests, but show promise in a field of study.
- It recognizes that the peak performance in most gifted people's careers comes in early adulthood, and signs of this performance are evident in their adolescence. The assumption is that people may be born with the potential to be gifted and precocious in a domain area, but many do not realize this potential because a specific domain is needed to transmit the ability. The view of giftedness as developing expertise is defined as the ongoing process of the acquisition and consolidation of a set of skills needed for a high level of mastery in one or more domains of life performance.

One of the limitations of using a school-based conception of giftedness is that most schools and school districts use intelligence tests within their overall system of identification and often do not retest students. Therefore, a score on an intelligence measure denotes one point in time. Using a developing expertise within a domain model limits the use of intelligence tests as measuring this aspect. There are several assumptions when employing a school-based conception of giftedness. Some of those assumptions are as follows:

- Giftedness in one domain is just as important as giftedness expressed in another.
- Giftedness in any domain can be the impetus for the presence of potential giftedness in another area.
- All populations have gifted children who exhibit sophisticated behaviors that underscore developing expertise in a domain.
- Strategic and carefully planned assessment techniques can be used effectively to indicate needed services.

One might assume with a school-based, domain-specific definition of giftedness that everyone is gifted. This is a false assumption because although everyone has strengths, these strengths may not rise to the level of giftedness. Gifted and talented students possess learning characteristics and needs that differ from those of their chronological age peers: They typically learn faster, have the capacity to understand concepts at a greater depth, and concentrate on tasks longer (VanTassel-Baska, 1998). They are more curious and prefer solving more complex problems than their chronological age peers. Gifted children at some point in time must be able to display or show performance in their high-ability domain. This becomes more important as they grow and mature because the indication of potential is no longer sufficient in an adult world. A person must demonstrate his or her abilities in a field or endeavor.

These differences in conceptualizing giftedness call for challenging educational opportunities in which gifted and talented students can learn with and from intellectual peers. Special programming and services are essential in order for gifted and talented students to maximize their potential. Gross (1998) stated that gifted learners will not thrive socially or emotionally if their giftedness goes unrecognized.

Great diversity exists within the population of gifted and talented learners with respect to areas of academic and artistic giftedness, degree of giftedness within those areas, qualities such as motivation and persistence, and level of performance in school subjects. A recent task force through the National Association for Gifted Children (NAGC, 2010) has been developing a new working definition and defines giftedness as the following:

> Gifted individuals are those who demonstrate outstanding levels of aptitude (defined as an exceptional ability to reason and learn) or competence (documented performance or achievement in the top 10% or rarer) in one or more domains. Domains include any structured area of activity with its own symbol system (e.g., mathematics, music, language) and/or set of sensorimotor skills (e.g., painting, dance, sports).
>
> The development of ability or talent is a lifelong process. It can be evident in young children as exceptional performance on tests and/ or other measures of ability or as a rapid rate of learning, compared to other students of the same age, or in actual achievement in a domain. As individuals mature through childhood to adolescence, however, achievement and high levels of motivation in the domain become the primary characteristics of their giftedness. Various factors can either enhance or inhibit the development and expression of abilities.
>
> *Implications for Educators.* Exceptionally capable learners are children who progress in learning at a significantly faster pace than do other children of the same age, often resulting in high levels of achievement. Such children are found in all segments of society. Beginning in early childhood, their optimal development requires differentiated educational experiences, both of a general nature and, increasingly over time, targeting those domains in which they demonstrate the capacity for high levels of performance. Such differentiated educational experiences consist of adjustments in the level, depth, and pacing of curriculum and outside-of-school programs to match their current levels of achievement and learning rates. Marked differences among gifted learners sometimes require additional and unusual interventions. Additional support services include more comprehensive assessment,

counseling, parent education, and specially designed programs, including those typically afforded older students.

Barriers to attainment. Some gifted individuals with exceptional aptitude may not demonstrate outstanding levels of achievement due to environmental circumstances such as limited opportunities to learn as a result of poverty, discrimination, or cultural barriers; due to physical or learning disabilities; or due to motivational or emotional problems. Identification of these students will need to emphasize aptitude rather than relying only on demonstrated achievement. Such students will need challenging programs and additional support services if they are to develop their ability and realize optimal levels of performance.

Adulthood. As individuals transition to appropriate higher education and specialized training, and eventually to independence, they will profit from targeted guidance and support. Continuing high levels of exceptional adult performance will require, in addition to advanced knowledge and skills, high levels of motivation, perseverance, and creative problem-solving. Exceptionally capable adults are among those most likely to contribute to the advancement of society and its scientific, humanistic, and social goals.

Implications for Policy Makers. Policy Makers should be aware that the gifted persons described here will comprise a large proportion of the leadership of the next generation in the arts, sciences, letters, politics, etc. If we provide this group with a mediocre education we doom ourselves to a mediocre society a generation forward. Educators know how to provide an excellent education for these students, but it will not happen by accident or benign neglect. Policy Makers control the allocation of resources, and trained educators of exceptionally capable students know how to use these resources constructively. These resources and expertise should be brought into alignment for the benefit of all. Does this mean that we tear these scarce resources away from other students, including those with disabilities or those who are living in troubled circumstances? No, quite the contrary. A moral society must care for and enhance the development of all of its citizens. Specific investment in the gifted is one way to build a society that can help solve the society's need with creative innovations and organizations. (n.p.)

This working definition developed by experts and practitioners across the country supports the notion of a school-based concept of giftedness and recognizes the range and diversity of gifted learners from all populations and economic strata. Additionally, it recognizes that giftedness is a lifelong process, and continuing high levels of performance may result in a synergistic effect between gifted individuals and society's needs.

Students of Poverty

According to demographer Harold Hodgkinson (2007), poverty is the biggest risk factor for young children, and 22% of children in the United States live in poverty. Researchers have documented for years that the first years of life are the most important in terms of cognitive and social/emotional development. The number of high-achieving lower income students nationally is larger than the individual populations of 21 states (Wyner, Bridgeland, & DiIulio, 2007), yet these learners receive limited support from schools for their advanced abilities. Children living in higher socioeconomic status (SES) environments have qualitatively and quantitatively more opportunities to develop their gifts and talents than students of poverty (Ford, 2007; Rothstein 2004; Wilson, 2000). Therefore, beginning as early as prekindergarten, achievement gaps occur in educational attainment between students of poverty and their counterparts from low-middle to upper-middle-class income families. This gap in academic achievement is widely recognized as one of the most significant challenges facing educators and families. Children from lower income backgrounds may have the most difficulty in being identified for gifted programs (VanTassel-Baska, 2009) because they may not have a family background that is rich in language or may not have family members who have had positive school experiences or who have attained a higher education degree.

A word of caution is warranted in that there is great variation among families of poverty and, thus, there are no "typical" low-income gifted learners. Therefore, students of poverty are underrepresented in gifted programs due to their unique experiences and varied environments. Typical assessment procedures for identifying such gifted learners for services and programming may not be a good match for this group of learners because they often have neither been acculturated to middle-class values, nor do they have the robust language or environmental experiences of their more affluent peers. Ensuring early and ongoing identification processes that are more dynamic and authentic in nature is critical in finding more gifted students of poverty.

Culturally Diverse Learners

The limited number of gifted learners from culturally diverse backgrounds identified and served in programs for the gifted has been a major concern in the field over the past five decades. Refereed articles have underscored the many variables and constraints precluding these children from being appropriately identified and served in order to maximize their potential and demonstrate high performance in domain-specific areas. Barriers include everything from screening and identification processes and policies, to teachers' conceptions of giftedness and student self- and peer perception.

Ogbu (1995) discovered that many minority students may feel pressured to reject any attempts to develop their intellectual skills because of "psychological pressures against 'acting white' that are just as effective in discouraging involuntary minority students from striving for academic success. The dilemma of involuntary minority students is that they may have to choose between 'acting white' and 'acting black'" (p. 588). Hébert (2000) showed in his study that urban males who participated in activities and developed friendships outside of their ethnic group had a stronger sense of self and were able to resist pressure to reject attempts to develop their intellectual ability. Frasier and Passow (1994) suggested that regardless of cultural background, gifted students demonstrate the following abilities:

- a strong desire to learn;
- an intense, sometimes unusual interest;
- an unusual ability to communicate in words, numbers, or symbols;
- effective, often inventive strategies for recognizing and solving problems;
- a large storehouse of information;
- a quick grasp of new concepts;
- logical approaches to solutions;
- many highly original ideas; and
- an unusual sense of humor.

In spite of many internal or external obstacles for culturally diverse gifted students, these students often display the ability to rise above their circumstances and showcase their giftedness.

Twice-Exceptional Learners

Gifted students with disabilities are a heterogeneous group of individuals with a variety of handicapping conditions. The most typical definition for twice-exceptional gifted learners is one that describes evidence of high performance in an area combined with a disability that suppresses the student's ability to achieve according to his or her potential (Brody & Mills, 1997) and speaks to gifted children with learning disabilities. Gifted students with a disability must handle two roles—being gifted in a domain and having some sort of disability. Conducting research on twice-exceptional children is difficult because there are dissimilarities among their disabilities. Another complication is that exceptional children's programming may focus on remediating the deficit rather than enriching the area of giftedness. For a twice-exceptional gifted learner, getting identified in both areas and receiving appropriate programming is critically important.

SYSTEMS FOR SUPPORTING GIFTED LEARNERS

It is not enough to have a conceptual definition of gifted learners that is inclusive, equitable, and comprehensive. Gifted learners require supportive systems that support their identification and undergird the context in order for learners to be able to demonstrate ability in a field or endeavor. There are many support structures that need to be in place for identifying and serving gifted learners, but there are three overarching support structures that must be in place in order to customize and maximize educational opportunities. They are as follows:

- *Policies*: Identification and supplemental policies at state and local levels.
- *Teacher standards*: Standards for teacher preparation and professional development.
- *High-powered curriculum*: Differentiated curriculum designed for gifted learners that is responsive to their intellectual and emotional needs.

Identification Policies for Gifted Learners

Uncertain definitions of giftedness and the varied procedures for identifying gifted and talented students have long plagued the field and have created a complex and challenging conundrum for teachers, counselors, and administrators. Definitions of giftedness and appropriate identification measures are consistently the most frequently cited barriers to identifying, placing, and providing appropriate services to gifted learners (Clasen, Middleton, & Connell, 1994; Maker, 1996; Pfeiffer, 2003; Sarouphim, 1999).

Concerns about assessment and identification are exacerbated for nontraditional learners who come from culturally diverse or different backgrounds, from low-SES households, or who have limited English language proficiency (Bracken & McCallum, 1998; Ford & Harmon, 2001; McCallum, Bracken, & Wasserman, 2001). The establishment of appropriate gifted identification practices is critical if equity in placement is deemed important. Equitable and accurate identification helps ensure fair access to services, programs, and resources to all students. If identification of gifted students is to be comprehensive, accessible, and fair, then efforts to identify students should be undergirded by local and state policies that ensure that attention, subsequent programming, and funding are provided for this target population. Once definitional issues are resolved, identification policy that is comprehensive, equitable, and inclusive must be mandated.

The attention that has been focused on identification since the release of the Marland report (1972) and the *National Excellence* report (U.S. Department of Education, 1993) has clearly helped the field to clarify definitions of gifted and is inclusive of underrepresentation of key groups. Although there are few studies in the area of gifted education policy, there are two consistent findings that are noted. First, mandates matter. States that do not mandate gifted education have experienced significant cuts in programming or the elimination of programs (Brown, 2001; Landrum, Katsiyannis, & DeWaard, 1998; Purcell, 1995). Although mandates do not guarantee meaningful education (U.S. Department of Education, 1993) or cohesive implementation, states with accountability systems enjoy higher academic results (Carnoy & Loeb, 2002). Second, perceptions matter. State policies can legitimize the perception of the need for gifted services and set the stage for dispelling misconceptions associated with giftedness. Mandated state policies guarantee movement on the issue of gifted education as stakeholders come to value the need for provisions for this targeted population.

In the spring of 2003, the Center for Gifted Education at The College of William and Mary contracted with the Ohio Department of Education (ODOE) to conduct a policy review study across five states to determine the nature, extent, and relative success of policies governing programs for the gifted. Attention to identification issues received the greatest emphasis in all state regulations as seen through the number of rules and regulations governing this process (Brown, Avery, VanTassel-Baska, Worley, & Stambaugh, 2006). Components of a high-quality state identification policy (Clinkenbeard, Kolloff, & Lord, 2007) include the following:

- contains an operational definition of gifted and talented;
- uses multiple criteria;
- uses assessment tools that are sensitive to inclusion of underrepresented groups;
- ensures identification processes that match the operational definition;
- calls for coherence between identification, curriculum, and service; and
- outlines a process for decision-making and appeals concerning screening, identification, and service.

If states delegate the responsibility for developing identification policy to local school districts, then there needs to be a repository of information on what local decisions have been made as these choices significantly impact program development within the field. Other specific policies regarding acceleration, weighted grades, Advanced Placement, testing out of standards, and dual enrollment are all areas highly relevant to gifted learners. State policies are needed in each of these areas to maximize benefits to gifted learners.

Teacher Standards

Another necessary support structure for gifted learners is teacher preparation to ensure that gifted learners are appropriately identified and nurtured by qualified personnel. Teachers and school leaders need to be educated in relevant theory, research, instructional approaches, program development, and evaluation that develop and sustain best practices in the classroom. One way to provide personnel preparation is through a standards-based approach. The National Council for Accreditation of Teacher Education (NCATE) provides a set of teacher preparation standards for institutions of higher education. These standards serve as markers for coursework and assessment employed in different colleges and universities in a variety of teacher education programs. The standards are designed on a model of professional competencies and represent a broad consensus of the values, skills, and knowledge that teachers need to acquire to be effective in teaching. Since 1985, the field of gifted education had worked on a set of standards through the Council for Exceptional Children, The Association for Gifted division (CEC-TAG). Since that time, a new set of standards, based on the early work of CEC-TAG, has been formulated through a collaborative process between the National Association for Gifted Children (NAGC) and CEC-TAG. After many years and revisions, the final set of standards was approved by the respective association governing boards in 2006 and lastly by NCATE's Specialty Areas Studies Board. Universities that house a program for educator preparation in gifted education had to begin using the new standards in spring 2008 (VanTassel-Baska & Johnsen, 2007).

There are 10 standards, each with a set of knowledge and/or skills for educators of gifted learners to know and be able to demonstrate competency (see the Appendix). The implications of having these standards in place for gifted learners help to ensure a consensus on what teachers of the gifted must understand and be able to demonstrate. However, not all states have universities that offer gifted education coursework or policies on teacher preparation to work with gifted learners. Kitano, Montgomery, VanTassel-Baska, and Johnsen (2008) suggested best practices for translating the teacher standards for higher education into enhancing professional development at K–12 levels in order to ensure measures of quality that are consistent nationally for school districts and universities. A school district or school could use these standards as benchmarks for determining the level of expertise that teachers need and then provide the subsequent training or target professional development on a particular standard. Just as important as who is the target population for gifted curriculum is the question of who is qualified to teach that population.

High-Powered Curriculum for Gifted Learners

The third overarching support system for gifted learners is high-powered curriculum. Curriculum is one of the strongest support structures for ensuring that gifted learners, at all stages of development, are provided with educational experiences that match their rate and level of learning. Whitehurst (2009), as part of his work with the Brookings Institution, conducted a cursory exploration of topic reports from the What Works Clearinghouse and revealed that curricular interventions had moderate to large effect sizes on student outcomes. He argued that effective curricula, compared with other policy levers such as reconstituting the teacher workforce, are not only cost-effective but produce larger effects on student achievement than other approaches. In other words, curriculum matters.

If curriculum matters, then providing a differentiated curriculum to gifted learners is nonnegotiable. Central to the argument for providing differentiated curriculum for gifted learners is the recognition of the learner in terms of his or her capacity for increasing levels of complexity, depth, and pace. Gifted learners not only can handle increased complexity and abstract connections, but require a differentiated curriculum to maximize their potential and respond to their readiness levels and interests. There may not be a single best curriculum earmarked for gifted learners, but there is sufficient evidence to suggest that there are well-designed curricula available for use or modeling in classrooms nationwide.

Two overarching approaches have been used historically when developing or implementing curriculum for gifted learners. They are acceleration and enrichment. Beyond these two approaches, several other curriculum models have shown evidence of effectiveness when working with gifted learners in a variety of settings and in different domains. VanTassel-Baska and Brown (2007) reviewed existing program/curriculum models in the field for their use with gifted learners, based on criteria cited as effective and comprehensive. They found that the use of advanced curricula in core areas of learning at an accelerated rate had the strongest body of research evidence. Data on curriculum models favored a discipline or domain-specific approach, although the delivery methods varied.

The Integrated Curriculum Model (ICM) is one such model. It is a curriculum framework developed for general intellectual and specific aptitude learners that integrates a strong content emphasis with conceptual and critical thinking skills components. The Center for Gifted Education at The College of William and Mary developed a series of curricular units in relevant content areas based on the ICM, drawing on the traditions of acceleration and enrichment. Evidence from studies of classroom implementation supports the applicability and flexibility of the ICM in a variety of settings with gifted learners at multiple stages of development (see Chapter 19 for specific details).

Moreover, using the ICM in core areas of learning, such as language arts, was found effective on measures of critical thinking and reading comprehension with more typical and diverse learners in Title I settings (VanTassel-Baska, Bracken, Feng, & Brown, 2009), suggesting that other groups of learners benefit from high-powered curriculum designed for gifted learners.

If one considers our earlier definition of giftedness presented in this chapter (NAGC, 2010), which focuses on a school-based or content-specific definition, then providing an accelerated and complex curriculum that is content-specific matches the target gifted population seen to be most in need of services.

Curriculum combines with teacher preparation, professional development, resource allocation, and targeted policies to represent a comprehensive and coordinated set of structures that foster the identification and development of gifted learners.

CONCLUSION

This chapter has focused on a school-based concept of giftedness wherein an individual demonstrates outstanding levels of achievement or competence in one or more domains. The conception of giftedness employed by a school district is the foundation for all subsequent decisions such as identification, programming, curricula, teacher preparation, and program evaluation. Additionally, given the diverse needs of gifted and talented students, policies must be in place and programming must be flexible and responsive to the needs of particular learners at a given stage of development in order for a student's ability in a domain to be realized and demonstrated. Teachers who work with these learners must be carefully selected and trained in gifted education. Finally, gifted learners require high-powered curriculum to ensure a depth and sophistication of content, commensurate with their unique needs.

KEY POINTS SUMMARY

- Theories and conceptions of giftedness are the catalyst to subsequent school district processes for identification, service delivery, and program evaluation.
- A school-based conception of giftedness, focusing on domain-specific giftedness, proves useful when considering concomitant identification and programming.
- Poverty may be the single most prohibitive barrier for both identification and service for gifted learners.
- Culturally diverse gifted learners demonstrate similar abilities regardless of their background and have been chronically underidentified and underserved.
- Twice-exceptional learners should be identified and served for both abilities and disabilities where warranted.
- Gifted learners are found in all segments of society, and require different kinds of educational experiences for their development in the domains in which they demonstrate the capacity for high levels of achievement.

- The ICM is a flexible curriculum framework that can accommodate all types of gifted learners as evidenced by the effectiveness research.
- Characteristics and needs for all types of gifted learners, identification protocols, and programming approaches are delineated in the teacher education standards, which should be used as a basis for professional development and university training.
- Support structures such as policies, teacher preparation, and high-powered curriculum must be in place to ensure that programs for the gifted are institutionalized.

REFERENCES

Albert, R. S. (1980). Exceptional gifted boys and their parents. *Gifted Child Quarterly, 24*, 174–179.

Benbow, C. P., & Stanley, J. C. (1996). Inequity in equity. *Psychology, Public Policy, and Law, 2*, 249–292.

Bloom, B. (1985). *Developing talent in young people*. New York, NY: Ballantine Books.

Bloom, B. S., & Sosniak, L. A. (1981). Talent development vs. schooling. *Educational Leadership, 39*, 86–94.

Bracken, B. A., & McCallum, S. R. (1998). *Universal nonverbal intelligence test*. Itasca, IL: Riverside.

Brody, L. E., & Mills, C. J. (1997), Gifted children with learning disabilities: A review of the issues. *Journal of Learning Disabilities, 30*, 282–297.

Brown, E., Avery, L., VanTassel-Baska, J., Worley, B., & Stambaugh, T. (2006). A five-state analysis of gifted education policy. *Roeper Review, 29, 11–16*.

Brown, E. F. (2001). *Systemic reform: The impact of North Carolina's state-initiated policies on local gifted programs* (Unpublished doctoral dissertation). The College of William and Mary, Williamsburg, VA.

Carnoy, M., & Loeb, S. (2002). Does external accountability affect student outcomes? A cross-state analysis. *Educational Evaluation and Policy Analysis, 24*, 305–331.

Carroll, I. E. (1993). Four systems for emotion activation: Cognitive and noncognitive processes. *Psychological Review, 100*, 68–90.

Clasen, D., Middleton, J., & Connell, T. (1994). Assessing artistic and problem-solving performance in minority and nonminority students using a nontraditional multidimensional approach. *Gifted Child Quarterly, 38*, 27–37.

Clinkenbeard, P. R., Kolloff, P. B, & Lord, E. W. (2007). *A guide to state policies in gifted education*. Washington, DC: National Association for Gifted Children.

Coleman, L. J., & Cross, T. L. (2005) *Being gifted in school* (2nd ed.). Waco, TX: Prufrock Press.

Csikszentmihalyi, M. (2000). Positive psychology: The emerging paradigm. *NAMTA Journal, 25*, 5–25.

Feldman, D. H. (1997, August). *Developmental theory and the expression of talent*. Paper presented at the conference of the World Council for Gifted and Talented, Seattle, WA.

Ford, D. Y. (2007). Diamonds in the rough: Recognizing and meeting the needs of gifted children from low SES backgrounds. In J. VanTassel-Baska & T. Stambaugh (Eds.), *Overlooked gems: A national perspective on low-income promising learners* (pp. 37–41). Washington DC: National Association for Gifted Children.

Ford, D. Y., & Harmon, D. (2001). Providing access to gifted education for culturally diverse students. *Journal of Secondary Gifted Education, 3,* 141–143.

Frasier, M., & Passow, A. H. (1994). *Toward a new paradigm for identifying talent potential* (Research Monograph 94112). Storrs: University of Connecticut, The National Research Center on the Gifted and Talented.

Gagné, F. (2007). Ten commandments for academic talent development. *Gifted Child Quarterly, 51,* 93–118.

Gardner, H. E. (1993). *Frames of mind: The theory of multiple intelligences.* New York, NY: Basic Books.

Gross, M. U. M. (1998). The "me" behind the mask: Intellectually gifted students and the search for identify. *Roeper Review, 20,* 167–174.

Hébert, T. P. (2000). Defining belief in self: Intelligent young men in an urban high school. *Gifted Child Quarterly, 44,* 85–103.

Hildreth, G. H. (1966). *Introduction to the gifted.* New York, NY: McGraw-Hill.

Hodgkinson, H. (2007). Leaving too many children behind: A demographer's view on the neglect of America's youngest children. In J. VanTassel-Baska & T. Stambaugh (Eds.), *Overlooked gems: A national perspective on low-income promising learners* (pp. 7–22). Washington, DC: National Association for Gifted Children.

Hollingworth, L. S. (1926). *Gifted children: Their nature and nurture.* New York, NY: Macmillan.

Kitano, M., Montgomery, D., VanTassel-Baska, J., & Johnsen, S. K. (2008). *Using the national gifted education standards for pre-K professional development.* Thousand Oaks, CA: Corwin Press.

Landrum, M. S., Katsiyannis, A., & DeWaard, J. (1998). A national survey of current legislative and policy trends in gifted education: Life after the National Excellence report. *Journal for the Education of the Gifted, 21,* 352–371.

Maker, J. (1996). Identification of gifted minority students: A national problem, needed changes, and a promising solution. *Gifted Child Quarterly, 40,* 41–50.

Marland, S. P., Jr. (1972). *Education of the gifted and talented: Report to the Congress of the United States by the U.S. Commissioner of Education and background papers submitted to the U.S. Office of Education,* 2 vols. Washington, DC: U.S. Government Printing Office.

McCallum, R. S., Bracken, B. A., & Wasserman, J. (2001). *Essentials of nonverbal assessment.* New York, NY: Wiley.

National Association for Gifted Children. (2010). *Task force statement on defining giftedness.* Unpublished manuscript.

Ogbu, J. U. (1995). Understanding culturally diversity and learning. In J. A. Banks & C. A. Banks (Eds.), *Handbook of research on multicultural education* (pp. 582–593). New York, NY: Macmillan.

Pfeiffer, S. I. (2003). Challenges and opportunities for students who are gifted: What the experts say. *Gifted Child Quarterly, 47,* 161–169.

Purcell, J. (1995). Gifted education at a crossroads: The program status study. *Gifted Child Quarterly, 35,* 26–35.

Rothstein, R. (2004). A wider lens on the Black-White achievement gap. *Phi Delta Kappan, 86,* 105–110.

Sarouphim, K. M. (1999). Discovering multiple intelligences through a performance-based assessment: Consistency with independent ratings. *Exceptional Children, 65,* 151–161.

Simonton, D. (1997). When giftedness becomes genius: How does talent achieve eminence? In N. Colangelo & G. A. Davis (Eds.), *Handbook of gifted education* (2nd ed., pp. 335–349). Boston, MA: Allyn & Bacon.

Sosniak, L. (1997). The tortoise, the hare, and the development of talent. In N. Colangelo & G. A. Davis (Eds.), *Handbook of gifted education* (2nd ed., pp. 207–217). Boston, MA: Allyn & Bacon.

Spearman, C. (1904). General intelligence, objectively determined and measured. *American Journal of Psychology, 15,* 201–293.

Sternberg, R. (1991). Giftedness according to the triarchic theory of human intelligence. In N. Colangelo & G. A. Davis (Eds.), *Handbook of gifted education* (pp. 45–54). Boston, MA: Allyn & Bacon.

Sternberg, R. J. (2008). Increasing academic excellence and enhancing diversity are compatible goals. *Education Policy, 22,* 487–514.

Terman, L. M. (1925). *Mental and physical traits of a thousand gifted children: Genetic studies of genius, Vol. 1.* Stanford, CA: Stanford University Press.

Thurstone, L. (1938). *Primary mental abilities.* Chicago, IL: University of Chicago Press.

U.S. Department of Education, Office of Educational Research and Improvement. (1993). *National excellence: A case for developing America's talent.* Washington, DC: U.S. Government Printing Office.

VanTassel-Baska, J. (1998). *Excellence in educating gifted and talented learners* (3rd ed.). Denver, CO: Love.

VanTassel-Baska, J. (Ed.). (2009) *Patterns and profiles of promising learners from poverty.* Waco, TX: Prufrock Press.

VanTassel-Baska, J., Bracken, B., Feng, A., & Brown, E. (2009). A longitudinal study of enhancing critical thinking and reading comprehension in Title 1 classrooms. *Journal for the Education of the Gifted, 33,* 7–37.

VanTassel-Baska, J., & Brown, E. (2007). Toward best practice: An analysis of the efficacy of curriculum models in gifted education. *Gifted Child Quarterly, 51,* 342–358.

VanTassel-Baska, J., & Johnsen, S. K. (2007). Teacher education standards for the field of gifted education. *Gifted Child Quarterly, 51,* 182–205.

Whitehurst, G. J. (2009). *Don't forget curriculum.* Washington, DC: The Brookings Institution.

Wilson, C. A. (2000). Race, poverty, and test scores. *Negro Educational Review, 51,* 23–26.

Wyner, J. S., Bridgeland, J. M., & DiIulio, J. J. (2007). *Achievement trap: How American is failing millions of high-achieving students from lower-income families.* Lansdowne, VA: Jack Kent Cooke Foundation.

Chapter 4

Accelerating Learning Experiences in Core Content Areas

Joyce VanTassel-Baska and Beverly T. Sher

You are a primary teacher of the gifted and have just begun your third year of teaching. Because you are now off probation, you feel you can begin to experiment a bit with the curriculum, as you have noticed that some of your students seem bored and distracted by what constitutes grade-level curriculum. In fact, the mother of one of your students has already scheduled an appointment with you to discuss how you plan to differentiate for her child in the regular classroom. Yet you have 22 other students whose needs also must be considered. How do you satisfy the needs of advanced learners and their families while also attending to the full range of student needs?

Acceleration of gifted students is the first consideration in planning an appropriate curriculum for them. Each of these learners is typically identified based on advanced development in one or more areas of the curriculum. This higher level of functioning demands that the level of curricular challenge be raised to ensure a good match to the child's readiness pattern for learning. Thus, acceleration has to precede enrichment within core areas of learning.

There are several myths associated with the advancement of children beyond grade-level expectations. The following list is typical in that it explores various misconceptions about acceleration that both educators and parents hold.

Myth #1: Gifted children will become social and emotional misfits if they are accelerated. No studies suggest that acceleration causes such problems in the gifted (Gross, 1994, 2004; Neihart, 2007). Ironically, just the opposite may be true. When forced to socialize with age-mates in a lower level curriculum, gifted children may become socially withdrawn and alienated over time.

Myth #2: Gifted children benefit more when their learning is controlled, even when advancement is a part of the plan. For example, students may go ahead a half-year in math, but no more. This myth is dangerous in that it implies a one-size-fits-all mentality when working with the gifted. Individual differences prevail in ways that make artificial boundaries for learning a subject inhibitory. Each student should be encouraged to learn as much as possible in subject areas for which he or she must demonstrate proficiency (Schiever & Maker, 1997).

Myth #3: Gifted children benefit from enrichment more than acceleration. Studies over the past century have continued to demonstrate that acceleration is twice as powerful as enrichment when dealing with gifted students (e.g., Kulik & Kulik, 1992). Moreover, gifted students enjoy moving at a fast pace through subject material, gobbling up new information as they go. For many gifted students, their major interest area is also the area of learning in which they are most precocious, thus adding to their desire for advanced work in that area.

Myth #4: Gifted children will run out of curriculum or have to repeat it in later years because of early exposure to advanced-level work. The new standards have clearly demonstrated the scope of material that needs to be mastered in each subject area, an amount requiring more instructional time than is currently available in schools (Marzano, 1999). Consequently, there will always be more to learn, even for the gifted, at every stage of development. Schools need to be sensitive, however, to K–12 curricular planning for the gifted that would allow for effective use of school time in a subject area augmented with outside opportunities.

Myth #5: Gifted children will be more normalized by staying with age-mates. The reality of giftedness is its unique trajectory for learning that does not conform to age-grade expectations. Consequently, staying with age-mates and being discouraged from learning at one's own comfortable rate invites under-achievement patterns of behavior, including acting up and out, refusing to do assigned work, and loss of motivation for learning (Colangelo, Assouline & Gross, 2004; Gallagher & Gallagher, 1994).

These are but a few of the common ideas we hold about the dangers of acceleration of gifted learners. Yet these myths are strongly dispelled by the actual research literature on acceleration. In truth, our gifted programs are far less effective than they might be if strong acceleration policies were enacted.

REVIEW OF RESEARCH

Perhaps more has been written about the efficacy of accelerative practices with the gifted than about any other single educational intervention with any population. Reviews of the literature on acceleration have appeared with some regularity over the last 30 years (Benbow, 1991; Daurio, 1979; Gross & van Vliet, 2003; Kulik & Kulik, 1984; Reynolds, Birch, & Tuseth, 1962). Each review has carefully noted the overall positive impact of acceleration on gifted individuals at various stages in the lifespan. Successful programs of acceleration, most notably offshoots of the basic talent search model developed by Julian Stanley and others in the 1970s, have demonstrated and continue to demonstrate the significant positive impact on the learning of students from using accelerative practices (Benbow & Stanley, 1983; Gross, 2004; Kulik & Kulik, 1992; Lubinski, & Benbow, 2006; Swiatek, 2007; Swiatek & Benbow, 1991a, 1991b).

Moreover, a broad-based research agenda has emerged in the field of gifted education, dedicated to understanding the long-term effects of educational acceleration of the gifted (Brody, Assouline, & Stanley, 1990; Brody & Benbow, 1987; Brody & Stanley, 1991; Robinson & Janos, 1986; Swiatek & Benbow, 1991a, 1991b). These studies continue to show positive results in cognitive development from acceleration. It also has been found that accelerated students generally earned more overall honors and attended more prestigious colleges (Hany & Grosch, 2007). Brody et al. (1990) found that among accelerated students, the best predictor of college achievement was early and continued Advanced Placement (AP) course-taking, suggesting that advanced challenging work on an ongoing basis is a powerful inducement to later achievement.

Often, there is concern about the social and emotional development of young accelerants. Yet studies and reviews of the literature on this issue continue to suggest the absence of adverse effects (Neihart, 2007). Even at young ages, Proctor, Black, and Feldhusen (1986) found generally positive results from early admission to school and other forms of acceleration. Richardson and Benbow (1990) and Swiatek and Benbow (1991b) reported no harmful effects of acceleration on social and emotional development or academic achievement after college graduation. Janos, Robinson, and Lunneborg (1989) reported no detrimental effects of acceleration on young entrants to college, and Noble et al. (2007) found only positive benefits of early entrance to university for precocious learners. In another study, Robinson and Janos (1986) found similar adjustment patterns for early entrants in comparison to three equally able nonaccelerated comparison groups, noting only unconventionality as a distinguishing characteristic of the early entrants. In another study of female-only early college entrants, positive personality growth during the accelerated first year of the program was found (Cornell, Callahan, & Loyd, 1991).

Using the existing research base on acceleration effectively to improve practices in classrooms is clearly a priority of high-quality education and the mark of educators who are visionary in their work. Key approaches to using acceleration, the differing patterns of students who can benefit from it, and the teacher competencies necessary to do it well are central aspects of implementation.

CLASSROOM-BASED ACCELERATION

For the clear majority of gifted and high-ability learners in school, the use of classroom-based acceleration practices is an essential part of making learning meaningful for them. A system for diagnosing and prescribing the appropriate level of instruction for these learners was developed in the 1970s by Julian Stanley and has been used worldwide in programs for the gifted ever since (Benbow & Stanley, 1983; Swiatek, 2007). For a teacher with gifted and high-ability children in the class, what approaches are essential to employ? The core of the approach may be summarized in three steps: diagnostic assessment, cluster grouping, and follow-up curricular intervention.

Step 1: Diagnostic Assessment

Perhaps the central strategy that is called for is effective diagnostic assessment of those learners whom a teacher suspects of having advanced abilities in the core areas of learning: reading and math. This diagnostic assessment should be buttressed by the previous year's achievement data and other records. Utilizing multiple sources of data for making decisions is important. Possible sources of diagnostic data include the following:

- *End-of-year assessments to be employed at the grade level.* In September, teachers can give their students the end-of-year reading comprehension test, the spelling test, and the English usage test in language arts; in math, they can give them the end-of-year computation, measurement, and number theory assessment. In each of these areas, the high-ability learners are likely to score 75% or higher, necessitating the need for compressed instruction and advanced work on other aspects of the language arts and math curricula.
- *Formal diagnostic instruments.* Teachers can give students the Gates-MacGinitie diagnostic reading test and the Orleans-Hanna math test to

assess functional level in these skill areas. Teachers also may administer an individual achievement test in these key areas of learning.

- *Chapter tests that cluster items across topics in math.* Because of the incremental nature of math study, teachers may want to assess students on more discrete aspects of the curriculum as the year progresses. Although this approach inhibits accelerative practices, it does allow students to avoid being remediated.

Such diagnostic assessment is a crucial first step in finding students who need advanced instruction in basic areas of the curriculum.

Step 2: Cluster Grouping

Follow-up instructional intervention must then be based on the diagnostic results. These results should be analyzed for patterns within and across student profiles. Students who are reasonably close in scores (i.e., within 10 percentage points) should be cluster-grouped for advanced instruction. These groups may range from two to five students in number. If a teacher has only one student who is very advanced, that student should be cluster-grouped with other students at a comparable level either at the same grade level or at the next grade level for instruction in reading, math, or both. It is not appropriate to have gifted students working independently throughout the year in a core area of the curriculum when they could be working with intellectual peers and learning more.

Step 3: Intervention With Curricular Materials

Beyond the instructional grouping decision lies the issue of a differentiated instructional plan for these students in reading and mathematics. Figure 4.1 suggests packaged curricular materials that could be employed with these cluster groups to address a differentiated plan for learning. Such interventions should make the delivery of the differentiated instructional plan feasible, as materials that are already differentiated can be put in student hands, relieving the teacher of the necessity of creating activities and projects from scratch.

The combinatory power of diagnostic testing, cluster grouping based on results, and follow-up intervention with proven materials would be a major improvement in all classrooms and ease the concerns of parents of the gifted whose children feel trapped by grade-level work. By the same token, the use of prepared materials eases the teacher's burden of creating differentiated lessons on the fly. Moreover, prepared materials typically provide enough curricula for a year's worth of work.

Mathematics

Target group:
  Advanced students whose results suggest 1–2 years beyond grade-level expectations.

Curricular interventions:
  • Fast-paced use of math text in gap areas, working out of the current and next 2 years text materials in the district
  • Compression of the math standards for the group, consistent with diagnostic results
  • Use of leveled materials as supplementary resources (e.g., Techniques of Problem Solving [TOPS] materials)
  • Use of math manipulatives
  • Use of games and puzzles in a structured math center

Reading

Target group:
  Advanced students who score 1–3 years beyond grade level expectations in reading skills and comprehension.

Curricular interventions:
  • The Center for Gifted Education Language Arts units
  • Junior Great Books as supplementary reading material
  • Compression of the state language arts standards that relate to reading skills, including analysis and evaluation of text
  • Independent reading program, based on tailored bibliographies

Figure 4.1. Mathematics and reading packaged curricula for high-ability learners.

ISSUES IN IMPLEMENTING A DIAGNOSTIC-PRESCRIPTIVE APPROACH

Many teachers find that they can only accommodate limited numbers of classroom groups successfully. If a teacher can maintain three such groups, it is sufficient to the tasks outlined above. Teachers should provide direct instruction to such groups on a rotating model so that instructional time is shared equally across the classroom. Gifted and high-ability students need direct instruction, too—just at their level of learning.

Teachers often complain that they have no support for these techniques from other teachers or the principal. These approaches require the support of whole schools in order to make them work. Individual teachers cannot effectively implement these strategies in the absence of cross-grade collaboration and principal approval and support. Consequently, careful up-front planning is necessary across staff to make the model work effectively.

Across multiple years, schools must articulate their work with high-ability learners to the next level of learning in the school district, typically middle and high schools. Curriculum coordinators in each of the disciplines must be made cognizant of the implications for accelerated learning and become supportive of such efforts.

Sometimes, the cluster-grouping model used initially in each area is insufficient in terms of containing students ready to do the advanced work. Adding and removing students from the cluster should be ongoing as new students surface who can handle the challenge, and current students fail to perform.

Teachers frequently feel they lack the skill to work with an advanced group in their classroom. This problem may be alleviated by differentiating the staffing within a school such that the most skilled teacher in a particular area like math can be assigned to work with the math high-ability clusters at least one day a week or obtain the use of expert volunteers in a similar capacity. Resource teachers of the gifted also may be employed in this fashion.

ACCELERATED LEARNING ACROSS GRADE LEVELS

A basic principle of instruction for gifted students is that many of them need content acceleration continuously and at a number of specific stages in their development (VanTassel-Baska, 1986, 1998). Although a district's programs may include classroom-based adaptations of basic materials and activities that enrich, expand, and enhance learning opportunities such as have just been described, it must be recognized that a student's need for accelerated learning will extend beyond what a given teacher can provide. It may be difficult to obtain a program that is consistently fast-paced, enriching, and well organized. Yet such goals must be targeted if the students' needs are to be met. As an example, in a comprehensive language arts program for elementary students reading at advanced levels, the following program attributes would be appropriate:

- use of advanced reading materials such as those suggested in Figure 4.1;
- participation in an inquiry-based study of appropriate children's literature (e.g., Junior Great Books);
- inclusion of a writing program that encourages elaboration and incorporation of ideas from literature into stories;
- use of supplementary materials for the development of vocabulary skills;
- reading of selected biographies and books in the content areas (including subjects dealing with multicultural issues);
- inclusion of experiences in foreign language;
- emphasis on the development and use of logic and critical thinking;
- spelling work derived from both basal and literary reading selections;
- telling stories and reading personal works; and
- encouragement and provision of time to pursue free reading based on children's interests.

Although the overall emphasis of the program is an integrated language experience with a strong emphasis on enrichment of the basic curriculum, the underlying issue of appropriate level of instruction is stressed through careful assessment of reading skill levels at various stages each year, access to advanced reading materials, and a vocabulary and spelling program that corresponds with the level of reading instruction. This list of interventions for gifted learners at the elementary level shows the scope of activities that acceleration should provide in setting the curricular pattern in a given content area.

Subject matter acceleration in other content areas also has importance for students in the elementary grades. In mathematics, for example, there also is the need to consider the following instructional emphases across years:

- a focus on developing spatial skills and concepts through geometry and other forms of spatial problem solving;
- a focus on problem-solving skills with appropriately challenging problems;
- an emphasis on the use of calculators and computers as tools in the problem-solving process;
- more emphasis on mathematical concepts and less on computational skills;
- a focus on logic problems that require deductive thinking skills and inference;
- an emphasis on applications of mathematics in the real world through creation of projects that provide experience;
- an emphasis on algebraic manipulations; and
- work with statistics and probability.

For many gifted students, accelerative options are necessary outside the regular classroom and over the developmental course of their K–12 years. Table 4.1 contains options that educators and parents need to consider as a core part of curricular planning for high-ability and gifted learners. Again, the accelerated curriculum is balanced with a strong enrichment element; but, at the same time, it allows for skills, concepts, and requisite materials to be at a challenging level for the child, rather than being geared to grade-level considerations.

APPLICATIONS OF ACCELERATED PATTERNS: CASE STUDIES

The following two case studies have been drawn from the authors' direct experience with gifted children and their developmental trajectories of learning. Each case reflects very different student profiles and predispositions for schoolwork. Each profile also accentuates the need for different accelerative opportunities based on aptitude areas and levels. Finally, the case studies illustrate the uniqueness of gifted students' development and, to some extent, the lack of predictability in it.

TABLE 4.1

Archetypal Features of Candidates for Acceleration Matched With Intervention

Early Admission	Content Acceleration	Grade Advancement	Early Exit From High School
Developmentally advanced in all academic areas by at least 2 years; identified by parents and confirmed by a psychologist.	Precocity in verbal areas; above average in other academic endeavors; identified by teachers during the primary years of schooling.	Developmentally advanced in all academic areas with above-average (not outstanding) grades; is bored by the school's regular and gifted program; identified by parents/self through talent search participation at junior high level.	Highly motivated student who is excelling in all areas at the high school level; identified by teachers and awards.
Suggested Intervention: Early entrance to kindergarten with an appropriately advanced curriculum, careful monitoring of progress throughout early elementary years. Additional acceleration will probably be warranted by junior high school. Early graduation from high school may also be considered (Proctor, Black, & Feldhusen, 1986).	*Suggested Intervention:* Content acceleration to appropriately challenging levels in reading; early application of verbal abilities to writing, dramatics, and debate; formation of literary discussion group that provides a peer-group context (Davis & Rimm, 1988).	*Suggested Intervention:* Grade acceleration to high school; course selection and program guided by academic strengths and interests; careful monitoring of performance in advanced classes to ensure both challenge and success (Stanley, 1979).	*Suggested Intervention:* Early graduation from high school with emphasis on career counseling and college selection of liberal arts study (Stanley, 1979).

Acceleration Case Study #1

Lewis was an intellectually precocious infant. He was fascinated by books at the age of 6 months, and he would listen to his parents read for hours at a time by 12 months. He knew all of the uppercase and lowercase letters and their sounds by 18 months, and he was reading before age 2. He also showed signs of mathematical talent, as he was doing double-digit addition and subtraction in his head at 26 months. He could count past 1,000 at age 2 ½.

He entered Montessori preschool 4 months before his fourth birthday. Montessori was an excellent fit for him: He loved working at his own pace on reading, math, and geography. By kindergarten, Woodcock-Johnson testing revealed that he was working at the late elementary level in all subject areas, and his Montessori teacher had created an individualized, advanced curriculum for him.

At 6, he entered a Montessori elementary program as a first-year student. His teachers brought advanced math work down from the upper elementary classroom for him; he loved extracting square roots using the Montessori materials. He also enjoyed working with the school's periodic table materials, usually used by upper elementary students to "build" atoms of different elements by adding the proper number of protons and neutrons to the nucleus and the proper number of electrons to the electron shells surrounding the nucleus.

By second grade, he had exhausted the Montessori elementary math materials, which included algebra and geometry work. Fortunately, the Education Program for Gifted Youth (EPGY) became available as a distance-learning program from Stanford that year. He started the EPGY K–8 math sequence at the second-grade level in October and had finished the eighth-grade level by Christmas. He took the EPGY Logic of Algebra and Spatial Visualization courses to finish off his second-grade year.

In third grade, he was promoted to the upper elementary classroom, normally reserved for fourth through sixth graders. He took the EPGY Algebra I and Algebra II courses, earning A's. In fourth grade, he did essentially no math. He spent the year finishing the Montessori grammar boxes and polishing his essay skills; he became a competent chess player, an adept Civilization II strategist, and a Civil War buff. He enjoyed Bruce Catton's Civil War books and Winston Churchill's multivolume history of World War II. The Montessori school agreed to skip him a grade so he could participate in the Johns Hopkins' Center for Talented Youth's (CTY) drama course for young students in the summer, where he read Ibsen, Chekhov, and Shakespeare.

In sixth grade, Lewis took EPGY's precalculus course, earning an A, and worked through Harold Jacobs' geometry textbook on his own in his Montessori classroom. He qualified for the Johns Hopkins' Study of Exceptional Talent (SET) program with a 790 on the SAT-M just after his 11th birthday; he earned a 600 on the SAT-V. He took CTY's Bay Ecology course over the summer.

His parents felt that his intellectual and social needs could not have been met in a traditional elementary school program. In Montessori school, he was able to work at his own rapid pace in all subject areas, but was also able to socialize with other elementary students in a multiage classroom. The noncompetitive Montessori environment kept his intellectual accomplishments from making other students (and their parents) feel threatened; this smoothed his social path through elementary school.

After graduating from his Montessori elementary program, Lewis moved on to public middle school at age 11. Because he was working so far ahead of grade level, the middle school agreed to skip him a second grade, and he entered middle school as an eighth grader. The middle school allowed him to take an exceptionally flexible schedule, hoping to meet both his social and his intellectual needs. He split his school day between the local university, eighth-grade classes, and sixth-grade classes.

At the university, he took the first two semesters of college calculus, earning A's. At the middle school, he took the eighth-grade Spanish I course and the eighth-grade world history course. He used Bay Ecology to place out of middle school science and used CTY's Level III distance writing tutorial in place of middle school English. He took physical education, beginning band (he started French horn that fall), and other "specials" with his sixth-grade age peers. He moved to the eighth-grade band at the end of the first semester and was first chair French horn in the top middle school band by the end of the school year. He participated in MATHCOUNTS, a middle school mathematics team competition offered in selected school districts nationally (Northrop Grumman Foundation, n.d.). His team won the regional competition and placed fourth in the state; he was second in the regional individual competition and seventh in the state individual competition.

Middle school was a less happy experience for Lewis than Montessori elementary school had been. He found his middle school classes slow and boring, and he was bullied by some of the other students. Fortunately, he had allies in the building: The gifted resource teacher was always available to help him, and he found social acceptance in the band and on the MATHCOUNTS team. Now, he sees his year in middle school as being the equivalent of military boot camp: It was tough, but it taught him the public school social skills needed for survival in high school. At the end of eighth grade, though, he was convinced that he wanted to skip high school and go straight to college. His parents convinced him to give high school a try for a year, and they promised that he could go on to the local university at the end of ninth grade if he wanted to; the admissions office at the university supported this plan.

In ninth grade, Lewis took the multivariable calculus and differential equations courses at the university, earning A's. He took CTY's Level IV writing tutorial in place of ninth-grade English. He used CTY's Fast-Paced High School Biology course, taken the previous summer, to place out of high school biology. Other classes included Art Foundations (a mistake, for social reasons), chemistry, AP economics, Spanish II and III, and band. He was the second chair French horn in the All-District Symphonic Band and placed 40th out of 57 in All-State Band/Orchestra auditions. He also played in the local youth orchestra. He participated in Math League competitions and took CTY's Number Theory course in the summer.

Compared with middle school, high school seemed like "paradise" to Lewis. He had a social niche in band and had a supportive gifted resource teacher. He found his schedule adequately challenging, thanks to his college math courses and his AP course. He decided that he wanted to stay in high school for the full 4 years and graduate with his class.

In 10th grade, Lewis took the university's introductory computer science course for majors and Foundations of Mathematics, the last course required for math majors, earning A's. He finished EPGY's linear algebra course, which he had started the previous spring, earning an A. His high school courses included English 10, AP biology, Spanish IV, Advanced Spanish Conversation, and band. He started the high school world geography course, which was required for graduation, but found it much too easy, so he compacted out. He took two high school world history courses through the University of Missouri's distance-learning program to meet high school graduation requirements. He continued to participate in Math League competitions and others. He was first chair French horn in the top band at school, as well as in All-District Symphonic Band and All-State Symphonic Band, also continuing to play French horn in the local youth orchestra. He placed third in All-State Band/Orchestra auditions.

Lewis split his time between the university and the high school for another 2 years. He took almost every AP class offered by the high school and continued taking the math and computer science courses required for an applied math major at the university. He was ranked first in his high school class, with straight A's and a large number of weighted courses on his transcript. He looked forward to another 2 years in the high school music program, and thought about adding the university's orchestra to his list of outside activities. High school was a happy experience for him, both socially and intellectually, and he saw no reason to leave before graduation.

In the years since the first edition of this book was published, Lewis graduated as valedictorian of his high school class and matriculated, at age 16, into one of the most selective private universities in the United States. There, he majored in mathematics and minored in physics; in his free time, he continued his involvement in music, playing French horn and mellophone in five different musical ensembles during his undergraduate years. He spent two summers doing undergraduate research in mathematics and physics through National Science Foundation (NSF) funded Research Experiences for Undergraduates (REU) programs, and returned to his mathematics REU institution for a second summer of research that resulted in publishable work. He did exceptionally well academically, earning straight A's as an undergraduate, and was elected to Phi Beta Kappa at the end of his junior year. He graduated college at age 20 with both a bachelor's and a master's degree in mathematics and a music performance certificate and enrolled the following fall in a doctoral program in mathematics at an institution that is ranked in the top five in the United States in his field. He has chosen a thesis advisor and embarked on the research that will lead to his Ph.D. thesis. He is still passionately involved in classical music. He also has discovered a passion for teaching, and has become an effective, caring teaching assistant. He hopes to eventually become a mathematics professor with a career that combines research and teaching.

Acceleration Case Study #2

A second, less radical acceleration case study involves Samantha, a young girl who evinced early signs of verbal giftedness by learning the alphabet at age 2, memorizing whole books for recitation as early as age 3, and reading by age 5. Early testing (age 5) on the Peabody Individual Achievement Test revealed high verbal and general information scores (99%) with lower levels in math problem solving and concepts (85%). The Ravens Matrices showed her to be at 99% for her age group on both the Colored and Standard forms. An individual Stanford-Binet administered at age 10 revealed a 155+ score, with clear superiority in verbal areas. Although standardized achievement and aptitude measures revealed potential and capacity for high performance, she struggled in school, typically receiving B's instead of A's at most stages of development. Habits of procrastination, not completing assignments, and experiencing difficulty with math also were chronic problems. SAT results in seventh grade revealed strong aptitude in both math and verbal areas, qualifying her to participate in summer programs sponsored by Northwestern University. High school assessment results continued to show high-level performance, with PSAT scores at 1370 and SAT scores of 1360, each favoring high verbal performance (720 on the PSAT and 750 on the SAT).

Attendance at a Montessori school from ages 2–5 characterized early development. Participation in Saturday and summer programs at two local universities also characterized extra school enrichment opportunities from age 5 on. Courses taken in the two university programs were broad-based, including two courses in mathematics, one in science, an art course, a geography course, journalism, and literature and writing options.

The public school accommodations for gifted children in elementary and early middle school years were minimal, with participation in a 45-minute once-a-week pullout experience of limited educational value. The Saturday and summer experiences were necessary augmentations to keep interest in learning high. Family travel also spurred interest at these ages. Private school placement at middle school levels was important in receiving a more personalized education, albeit not a stronger one academically. Acceleration in foreign language coursework and participation in a nongraded drama group that included students from grades 7–12 promoted both interest and accelerated skill development during these years. The need for a math tutorial became apparent when Samantha began taking Algebra I as an eighth grader.

She attended a small, private parochial school from eighth grade through her sophomore year in high school. Advantages of this particular setting for her included the opportunity to work with a superb Latin teacher and a strong math teacher, the drama opportunities mentioned earlier, the establishment of social interaction with other gifted young people, and the smaller, more struc-

TABLE 4.2

Acceleration Pattern

Grade	Accelerated Options
7	Homeschooling/tutorial (Latin I) Northwestern University — Literary Analysis (summer)
8	Latin II Northwestern University — Creative Writing (summer)
9	Latin III Northwestern University — AP English (summer)
10	AP Latin IV (Vergil) College French I & II (summer)
11	AP Latin V Catullus & Horace (independent study) French III & IV (block schedule at high school) AP American History
12	AP Government Dual enrollment (French) Early graduation (January)

tured environment. Disadvantages for Samantha at this school included a lack of school flexibility regarding course taking beyond the institution, a narrow view of education, and a disdain for students with atypical problems and learning needs. The last year and a half of high school were spent in a large, public institution that offered greater flexibility, but lacked necessary structure and attention to individual needs.

Block scheduling proved overwhelming in respect to keeping up with homework expectations as Samantha was diagnosed as having both a learning disability and Attention Deficit Disorder (ADD) in her junior year. Advanced Placement courses, while a joy during her summer experience at Northwestern University and during her sophomore year at the private school, became drudgery on the block model. Because of summer course credits and dual enrollment, she was able to graduate in January of her senior year and begin college work, much to her relief. Despite her problems, awards and honors typified Samantha's experiences in school. She usually was on the honor roll, had won fourth place in the regional spelling bee in fourth grade, and had received both music and drama awards. She also was a Commended Scholar in the National Merit Program and an AP scholar by junior year. She received Latin awards for the National Latin Exam for 5 consecutive years, recording a perfect score her freshman year on the Latin III exam. She was one of 43 students selected statewide to participate in the Governor's School Latin Academy at the end of her junior year.

Table 4.2 characterizes the path of acceleration employed in Samantha's case, starting in seventh grade. For Samantha, the benefits of accelerated study included early college entrance, earning 17 college credits, earning 15 high school credits during 3 weeks in the summer, and having courses waived at the university, including a freshman writing seminar.

Samantha hoped to obtain her doctorate some day and planned to become an English major and classics minor at a selective public university where she currently resides. Her goals, however, have been hampered by the persistence of learning problems, coupled with ancillary health difficulties.

In the update on Samantha for this edition, she did indeed attend the local selective university (top 35 in the country), graduating from high school one semester early. She graduated from college with a degree in the classics, taking 5 years to do so, including a one year medical leave precipitated by treatment of a brain tumor during her freshman year. She recovered enough to continue with college by living at home but switched majors from English to the classics, which required fewer papers. Problems with memory and cognition plagued her, as well as chronic pain, which had been diagnosed at the health center as fibromyalgia during her freshman year. Her interest in drama continued during college, and she appeared in several student-produced plays and one mainstage event. Her real talent for theatre also emerged during this period in the form of editing and directing ancient plays for the classics department. She single-handedly obtained funding and put on Aristophanes' *The Birds*, Plautus' comedy *Pseudolus*, and Euripides' *Hippolatus* across her final 3 years of college. Her graduation in August was marked by an immediate opportunity to move to a large metropolitan area and begin teaching without an education endorsement. She is now a teacher of Latin, Introduction to Foreign Language, and Theatre. For the last 5 years, she has attended a local university to obtain certification as a teacher and to begin a master's program in gifted education. Her dream of a doctorate is still alive, and her remarkable progress, despite physical disabilities and learning problems, is inspiring.

Both Lewis and Samantha represent atypical gifted learners in respect to aptitudes, interests, and developed skills. Lewis is clearly functioning at a highly gifted level, such that schooling had to be arranged around him. Samantha, while also highly gifted verbally, had an uneven profile of abilities and learning problems that lowered her level of functioning. Yet, over the years, both were buoyed by accelerated experiences that impacted them positively at the right time in growth and development in all spheres of learning—the cognitive, affective, social, and aesthetic. For Lewis, that accelerated cycle has continued to spiral well into his doctoral program. For Samantha, acceleration served her well at key stages of development, allowing her to amass credits needed later for both high school and college graduation when health problems intervened dramatically.

WHO CAN WORK WITH ACCELERATED LEARNERS?

Good teachers can accommodate the placement of a precocious child in their classes. If, however, an instructional option is seriously intended to provide an opportunity to accelerate a capable child's learning, it will take a teacher who is trained in gifted education and sensitive to some central issues. For many educators of the gifted, even acceleration is not a program option of choice (Southern & Jones, 1991). Therefore, there are several important qualities that should be sought in teachers of accelerated students:

- *Eager backing of acceleration options for able learners.* The attitude of the teacher toward acceleration will have a critical influence on the adaptation and progress of accelerated students. Whereas accelerants are likely to have difficulties in classes in which teachers attribute most problems to their young age, it should also not be expected that they will fare well in classrooms where their advanced placements are merely tolerated. A teacher should be able to rise to the challenge of accelerating the learning of capable students. Such a teacher will furnish educational activities, plan and follow strategies, and set expectations that will promote and maintain accelerated achievement. Teachers need to carry out frequent assessments of the accelerant's achievement and adjustment. If difficulties appear, they should be analyzed and dealt with promptly and rationally.

- *Capability to adapt and modify a curriculum to provide accelerative experiences.* Teachers chosen to work with these students need to understand how to compress material, select key concepts for emphasis, and share knowledge systems with their students. They should not double the homework amount or "cover" more material in class (VanTassel-Baska & Olszewski-Kubilius, 1988).

- *Adequate training and competence for teaching in the content area of the program.* Capable learners should have teachers who are eminently prepared to teach subject matter. This is especially true of accelerated learners. Their exceptional aptitudes will allow them to acquire new skills and knowledge rapidly and also to explore issues that students in the regular class programs will not have time to address. Teachers need to prepare for incorporating appropriate content expertise (Gallagher & Gallagher, 1994), arranging mentorships, and arranging alternate learning placements, such as laboratories, clinics, and internships (VanTassel-Baska & Olszewski-Kubilius, 1988).

- *Preparation in organizing and managing classroom activities.* A teacher of an accelerated program of study must be particularly conscious of the differences within an accelerated group of learners. Some will be capable of moving quite rapidly; others may wish to explore an area of interest in depth. Classroom environments should be flexible enough to accommodate for such individual differences. Skill in the use of cluster grouping and regrouping within an accelerated program is highly desirable for such teachers. Teachers of accelerated students can use student contracts, academic centers in the room, independent reading time, and library-based study to assure integration of the range of student needs.

MAKING ACCELERATION A USEFUL OPTION

School districts will need to plan and prepare carefully to assure that accelerative experiences will have beneficial effects for students. Networks of content-area experts, artists, and educators from all levels and sectors of the community should be developed to discuss acceleration issues, produce cooperative plans, and identify mentors and resource persons. Preschool educators and university experts in early childhood should be involved from the beginning because early referral is an important aspect of any acceleration plan. Such a task force should, for example, address the need to devise appropriate curricula and to examine logistical issues regarding early entrance and early exit options. Provisions need to be considered for at least the following opportunities:

1. continuous progress based on ability and performance, not age or grade, in individual curricular areas;
2. early entrance to school;
3. appropriate credit, placement, or both for advanced coursework taken off campus, given validation of proficiency; and
4. early involvement in college work through the College Board Advanced Placement program, International Baccalaureate program, and/or dual-enrollment options with institutions of higher education.

Several recent guides have been developed to assist educators and parents in making choices and applying them appropriately to acceleration decisions (Assouline et al, 2008; VanTassel-Baska, 2004).

ACCELERATION POLICIES FOR THE GIFTED LEARNER

In order to maximize curricular and program flexibility, it may be appropriate to develop written policy statements regarding acceleration. Indefensible restrictions should be removed to assure that capable students have maximum opportunities in the educational system, rather than being merely confined in it.

Each learner is entitled to experience learning at a level of challenge, defined as the task difficulty level being slightly above the skill mastery needed to complete the task. For gifted learners, this implies the opportunity for continuous progress through the basic curriculum based on demonstrated mastery of prior material. In all planned curriculum experiences for the gifted, care must be taken to ensure that students are placed at their instructional level. This level may be determined by diagnostic testing, observation of mastery, or performance-based assessments.

Gifted learners should be afforded the opportunity to begin school-based experiences based on readiness and to exit them based on proficiency. Thus, both early entrance and early exit options should be provided. The gifted learner requires a school system to be flexible about when and where learning takes place. Optimally, some students can be best served by a prereading program at age 4; other students may be well served by college opportunities at age 16. Individual variables must be honored in an overall flexible system of implementation.

Some gifted learners may profit from telescoping 2 years of education into one or by bypassing a particular grade level. Provision for such advanced placement should be made based on individual student demonstration of capacity, readiness, and motivation. Placement in actual grade levels should be determined by many factors beyond age. Tailoring learning levels, as well as bypassing them, is another important way to ensure implementation of this policy.

CONCLUSION

Although educators have every reason to show concern about the practice of acceleration, there is little basis in either research or effective practice not to utilize it with selected individuals or groups of gifted and high-ability learners in the area of proven competency. Candidates for acceleration vary among themselves, and the nature of the acceleration practice should be responsive to those individual variations. Schools, however, need to ensure that support structures for accelerative practices are in place and that competent teachers are available to carry out such programs. Only then will the high-ability learner be well served in our schools.

KEY POINTS SUMMARY

- Accelerating gifted and high-ability learners requires teachers to set aside harmful myths about the process and employ research-based practices.
- Accelerating students in the classroom involves a three-step process of diagnostic assessment, cluster grouping based on results, and follow-up curricular intervention.

- Acceleration beyond the classroom involves programmatic emphasis in each curricular area that would be available to gifted learners over the K–12 years of schooling.
- Use of accelerative practices such as early admission, content acceleration, grade advancement, and early exit from high school depends on the individual and group profile of learners.
- Students with different profiles can benefit from varied forms of acceleration at key stages of development for different purposes.
- Teachers who work with accelerative practices must understand the nature of the learner, as well as the content area(s) involved.
- Crafting an acceleration policy for use in schools highlights common approaches to employ and reduces the amount of time needed to address each case.

REFERENCES

Assouline, S. G., Colangelo, N., Lupkowski-Shoplik, A., Lipscomb, J. B., & Forstadt, L. (2008). *Iowa acceleration scale manual: A guide for whole grade acceleration K–8* (2nd ed.). Scottsdale, AR: Great Potential Press.

Benbow, C. P. (1991). Meeting the needs of gifted students through use of acceleration. In M. C. Wang, M. C. Reynolds, & H. J. Walberg (Eds.), *Handbook of special education* (Vol. 4, pp. 23–36). Elmsford, NY: Pergamon.

Benbow, C. P., & Stanley, J. C. (Eds.). (1983). *Academic precocity: Aspects of its development.* Baltimore, MD: Johns Hopkins University Press.

Brody, L., Assouline, S., & Stanley, J. (1990). Five years of early entrants: Predicting successful achievement in college. *Gifted Child Quarterly, 34,* 138–142.

Brody, L. E., & Benbow, C. P. (1987). Accelerative strategies: How effective are they for the gifted? *Gifted Child Quarterly, 31,* 105–110.

Brody, L. E., & Stanley, J. C. (1991). Young college students: Assessing factors that contribute to success. In W. T. Southern & E. D. Jones (Eds.), *Academic acceleration of gifted children* (pp. 102–132). New York, NY: Teachers College Press.

Cornell, D., Callahan, C., & Loyd, B. (1991). Personality growth of female early college entrants: A controlled prospective study. *Gifted Child Quarterly, 35,* 135–143.

Colangelo, N., Assouline, S. G., & Gross, M. U. M. (2004). *A nation deceived: How schools hold back America's brightest students* (Vol. 1). Iowa City: The University of Iowa, The Connie Belin & Jacqueline N. Blank International Center for Gifted Education and Talent Development.

Daurio, S. P. (1979). Educational enrichment versus acceleration: A review of the literature. In W. C. George, S. J. Cohn, & J. C. Stanley (Eds.), *Educating the gifted: Acceleration and enrichment* (pp. 13–53). Baltimore, MD: Johns Hopkins University Press.

Gallagher, J. J., & Gallagher, S. A. (1994). *Teaching the gifted child* (4th ed.). Boston, MA: Allyn & Bacon.

Gross, M. U. M. (1994). Radical acceleration: Responding to academic and social needs of extremely gifted adolescents. *Journal of Secondary Gifted Education, 5,* 27–34.

Gross, M. U. M. (2004). *Exceptionally gifted children.* London, England: Routledge.

Gross, M. U. M., & van Vliet, H. E. (2003). *Radical acceleration of highly gifted children: An annotated bibliography of international research on highly gifted children who graduate from high school three or more years early.* Sydney, Australia: University of New South Wales.

Hany, E. & Grosch, C. (2007). Long term effects of enrichment summer courses on the academic performance of gifted adolescents. *Educational Research and Evaluation, 13,* 521–537.

Janos, P. M., Robinson, N., & Lunneborg, C. E. (1989). Markedly early entrance to college: A multi-year comparative study of academic performance and psychological adjustment. *Journal of Higher Education, 60,* 496–518.

Kulik, J. A., & Kulik, C. C. (1984). Synthesis of research on effects of accelerated instruction. *Educational Leadership, 42,* 84–89.

Kulik, J. A., & Kulik, C. C. (1992). Meta-analytic findings on grouping programs. *Gifted Child Quarterly, 36,* 73–77.

Lubinski, D., & Benbow, C. (2006) Study of Mathematically Precocious Youth after 35 years: Uncovering antecedents for the development of math-science expertise. *Perspectives on Psychological Science, 1,* 316–345.

Marzano, R. (1999). *An analysis of national standards in relationship to instructional time.* Aurora, CO: McRel.

Northrop Grumman Foundation. (n.d.). *About MATHCOUNTS.* Retrieved from http://mathcounts.org/Page.aspx?pid=202

Neihart, M. (2007). The socioaffective impact of acceleration and ability grouping: Recommendations for best practice. *Gifted Child Quarterly, 51,* 330–341.

Noble, K. D., Vaughan, R. C., Chan, C., Childers, S., Chow, B., Federow, A., & Hughes, S. (2007). Love and work: The legacy of early university entrance. *Gifted Child Quarterly, 51,* 152–166.

Proctor, T. B., Black, K. N., & Feldhusen, J. F. (1986). Early admission of selected children to elementary school: A review of the literature. *Journal of Educational Research, 80,* 70–76.

Reynolds, M., Birch, J., & Tuseth, A. (1962). Review of research on early admission. In M. Reynolds (Ed.), *Early school admission for mentally advanced children* (pp. 7–18). Reston, VA: Council for Exceptional Children.

Richardson, T. M., & Benbow, C. P. (1990). Long-term effects of acceleration on the social-emotional adjustment of mathematically precocious youth. *Journal of Educational Psychology, 82,* 464–470.

Robinson, N., & Janos, P. (1986). Psychological adjustment in a college-level program of marked academic acceleration. *Journal of Youth and Adolescence, 15,* 51–60.

Schiever, S. W., & Maker, C. J. (1997). Enrichment and acceleration: An overview and new directions. In N. Colangelo & G. A. Davis (Eds.), *Handbook of gifted education* (2nd ed., pp. 113–125). Boston, MA: Allyn & Bacon.

Southern, W. T., & Jones, E. D. (Eds.). (1991). *Academic acceleration of gifted children.* New York, NY: Teachers College Press.

Swiatek, M. A., & Benbow, C. P. (1991a). Effects of fast-paced mathematics courses on the development of mathematically precocious students. *Journal of Research in Mathematics Education, 22,* 139–150.

Swiatek, M. A., & Benbow, C. P. (1991b). Ten-year longitudinal follow-up of ability-matched accelerated and unaccelerated gifted students. *Journal of Educational Psychology, 83,* 528–538.

Swiatek, M. (2007). The talent search model: Past, present and future. *Gifted Child Quarterly, 51,* 320–329.

VanTassel-Baska, J. (1986). Effective curriculum and instructional models for talented students. *Gifted Child Quarterly, 30,* 164-169.

VanTassel-Baska, J. (1998). *Excellence in educating gifted and talented learners* (3rd ed.). Denver, CO: Love.

VanTassel-Baska, J. (2004). *The acceleration of gifted students' programs and curricula.* Waco, TX: Prufrock Press.

VanTassel-Baska, J., & Olszewski-Kubilius, P. (Eds.). (1988). *Patterns of influence on gifted learners.* New York, NY: Teachers College Press.

Chapter 5

Integrating Higher Order Process Skills and Content

Jeanne M. Struck and Catherine A. Little

Y

You are concerned that the emphasis areas in your state tests are not presenting your students with tasks that truly challenge their thinking and encourage them to integrate multiple processes at higher levels. You also notice that your students do not seem to be engaging in class discussions, and you are reexamining your questioning strategies to respond to that issue. You wonder whether your students are able to transfer their developing skills in thinking and problem solving across multiple content areas. You are looking for ways to use questioning in the classroom and higher level activities across content areas to strengthen your students' reasoning skills.

Throughout many schools and classrooms across the United States, the accountability movement has led to tensions between the need to ensure minimum levels of competence for all students and an emphasis on developing more advanced skills in critical and conceptual thinking within and across content areas. In addition, although an emphasis on higher level skills is evident or at least applicable in many content standards, many assessment systems incorporate a greater percentage of tasks that require lower levels of thinking, in part because of the increased cost of developing and scoring more complex, higher level items (Toch, 2006). The focus on ensuring that no child is left behind in developing basic skills, combined with an emphasis on preparing for tests that activate lower levels of thinking, has led to serious concern about whether high-ability learners are being provided with opportunities to make progress in their learning across those areas in which they are already functioning beyond "proficient" levels (Loveless, Farkas, & Duffett, 2008; Wyner, Bridgeland, & DiIulio, 2007), as well as whether students are being prepared for the demands of higher education (Brown & Conley, 2007; Eckert, 2008).

Eisner (1988) observed that humans construct meaning, rather than discovering it. Meanings are represented through an array of forms, and part of the educational experience should be focused on learning strategies for interpreting and using these different forms and reflecting on one's own process of making meaning. To challenge advanced learners, in particular, teachers need to provide learning experiences that require these students to apply higher order processes to advanced content, and to engage in analysis and reflection about the processes they are using and how they may transfer their learning to other contexts.

This chapter explores ways of providing high-ability learners with meaningful, challenging experiences by integrating higher order process skills such as critical thinking and problem solving into any given content area under study. This chapter includes examples of higher order process models and strategies that can be applied within and across subject areas, encouraging transfer of learning and metacognition. The chapter also works hand in hand with the following chapter on student products to provide an overview of ways of approaching the process/product dimension of the Integrated Curriculum Model in constructing and implementing curriculum for high-ability learners.

A key emphasis throughout this chapter will be learning outcomes and experiences that require students to engage in higher levels of thinking and processing, with facilitation and modeling from their teachers. A second key emphasis is the importance within the curriculum of student awareness and reflection on their own processes, as a component of building a repertoire of strategies they may use to approach new problems and questions. Therefore, the overall focus is on providing curriculum and learning experiences that engage students in higher order thinking within content areas and simultaneously increase their awareness of specific thinking strategies that are applicable across multiple contexts. Such experiences are facilitated through focused teacher questioning and through instruction in particular models of higher order process skills.

WHY TEACH HIGHER ORDER PROCESS SKILLS?

What distinguishes humans from other animals is our capacity for higher order mental activity. Reasoning and problem solving are part of every individual's daily activities. The abilities to reason, make decisions, solve problems, analyze, interpret, and think creatively are necessary to survive in the world of work and to deal with complex family, community, and societal issues. Thus, supporting students in thinking critically benefits both individual and societal needs. Seiger-Ehrenberg (1985), who developed several thinking skills programs, stated:

> By the time students graduate from high school, they should be able to consistently and effectively take intelligent ethical action to accomplish the tasks society legitimately expects of all its members and to establish and pursue worthwhile goals of their own choosing. (p. 7)

By "intelligent ethical action," Seiger-Ehrenberg (1985) meant an individual's ability to arrive at a decision using rational thought processes, while taking into account the well being of others who will be affected. She proposed that these outcomes could best be accomplished through increased emphasis on the teaching of higher order process skills within curricula.

Concerns over limited attention to such higher order skills in schools, however, have emerged on a regular basis over the last several decades. *A Nation at Risk* (National Commission on Excellence in Education, 1983) cited higher order process skills as a major weakness in U.S. education: "American students lack rigorous thought and perhaps even thinking is not valued in our schools" (p. 2). The main message in most U.S. schools is to provide "the right answer." Data from the *National Excellence* report (U.S. Department of Education, 1993) confirmed the prevailing viewpoint that schools offer unchallenging curricula and have low academic expectations for students. Top U.S. students had unimpressive results on assessments requiring higher level thinking. The report noted that "Students going on to a university education in other countries are expected to know more than American students and to be able to think and write analytically about that knowledge on challenging exams" (p. 12). In response to these reports, educational reformers have advocated repeatedly for intellectually challenging instruction in U.S. schools that is deeply rooted in the academic disciplines (Cohen & Spillane, 1993). However, despite strong disciplinary emphasis within content standards (e.g., National Council of Teachers of Mathematics, 2000), many state assessments continue to reflect a greater emphasis on lower level skills, and classroom practice continues to focus on the types of skills measured on the assessments (Toch, 2006).

Nevertheless, many educators and researchers continue to advocate for strengthening attention to higher order process skill instruction in schools, and for the necessity of guiding students more effectively in their ability to access and use information at their fingertips rather than to memorize it (e.g., Partnership for 21st Century Skills, 2009). Such skills represent aspects of "successful intelligence," a term coined by the psychologist Robert J. Sternberg (1997). He has explained it as a three-point foundation of analytical, practical, and creative skills in today's economy. It is not what one knows—it is how one uses what he or she knows to create new ways to get work done, solve problems, or construct new knowledge (Fadel, Honey, & Pasnik, 2007). The teaching of higher order reasoning provides a link between learner outcomes of significance and a curricular base so that students engage in "successful intelligence" as they encounter substantive content and construct meaning.

DEFINING HIGHER ORDER PROCESS SKILLS: CLASSIFYING SKILLS AND OUTCOMES

In order to incorporate higher order process skills effectively into curriculum, curriculum developers and teachers must first have a clear sense of what defines higher order versus lower order processes, as well as how these levels are integrated with one another and with specific content. Most educators are familiar with Bloom's taxonomy of cognitive objectives (Bloom, 1956), which has long been used as a guideline for defining lower and higher order thinking. Bloom's six levels—knowledge, comprehension, application, analysis, synthesis, and evaluation—were originally designed to classify instructional objectives and test items in a hierarchical fashion, with knowledge at the lowest level of difficulty and evaluation at the highest. Their application has been broad-based and has included use as a model for "conceptualizing higher-level thinking skills in gifted learners" (Feldhusen, 1994a) and as a basis for differentiation. However, the taxonomy has also been criticized—even, to a certain degree, by its authors—for oversimplifying thinking processes and for the underlying assumption that *difficulty* was the primary distinction separating levels, which has not consistently been supported by research (Marzano, 2001).

In recent years, there have been several efforts to redefine a taxonomy of thinking skills or processes, expanding on and revising Bloom's work. Anderson and Krathwohl and their colleagues (2000) constructed a revised taxonomy that uses verbs for each level to reflect the active process of thinking and also begins to incorporate metacognition as part of the level of "evaluating." These authors specified individual cognitive processes within each level, identifying a total of 19 processes, and reversed the fifth and sixth levels of the original taxonomy (synthesis and evaluation). They also brought to the forefront an emphasis on the different types of knowledge—factual, conceptual, procedural, and metacognitive—which may serve as the basis for a thinker's engagement with each of the cognitive processes; types of knowledge also were included in the original work, but often not emphasized in the version teachers learned. Table 5.1 provides examples of the types of activities in which students may engage at each level of the original and revised taxonomies.

Marzano (2000; Marzano & Kendall, 2007) revised the taxonomy still further, arguing that thinking involves three systems—the self system, the metacognitive system, and the cognitive system—all working on a person's knowledge as he or she engages with a new task. This "New Taxonomy" also uses six levels:

1. Retrieval
2. Comprehension
3. Analysis   } Cognitive System
4. Knowledge Utilization
5. Metacognitive System
6. Self-System

Marzano's taxonomy emphasizes that first an individual must make choices to engage with a new task (self-system) and then engage the metacognitive system in setting goals, making plans, and monitoring progress; the metacognitive and self-systems then interact with the cognitive system as the individual works to process information. The taxonomy specifies processes at each level, ranging from processes such as recall at the retrieval level, to classification and error analysis at the analysis level, to goal specification at the level of the metacognitive system and examining importance and efficacy at the self-system level. This taxonomy integrates an emphasis on the thinker's motivation and goal-setting with a task, as well as the specific cognitive processes of the task itself, thereby refining understanding of the varied systems involved in a thinking task (Marzano, 2000; see also Kendall et al., 2008).

As teachers and curriculum developers prepare outcomes and activities for learners, a taxonomy of objectives can be a useful tool for planning and evaluating the level of integration of higher order process skills with the content under study. For example, the following description of a learning experience identifies the levels of cognitive process of each segment of the activity, referring to both the Anderson and Marzano taxonomies:

> While reading *The Phantom Tollbooth* by Norton Juster (1961), direct the students in learning definitions and examples of different types of figurative language, including simile, metaphor, hyperbole, personification, alliteration, and onomatopoeia (remembering/retrieval). As

TABLE 5.1

Taxonomy Levels and Sample Activities

Level in revised taxonomy (original taxonomy level in parentheses)	Examples of cognitive processes by level	Examples of classroom activities
Remembering (Knowledge)	retrieving, recalling, recognizing	• List the branches of the government and the duties of persons elected or assigned to each branch. • Describe the phases of the water cycle. • Outline the stages of the scientific method.
Understanding (Comprehension)	explaining, interpreting, summarizing, paraphrasing, classifying	• Explain the events that led to the Revolutionary War. • Convert a mathematical problem using manipulatives into a numerical or algebraic equation. • Distinguish between historical fiction and a nonfiction book pertaining to an historical event.
Applying (Application)	executing, transferring, implementing procedures	• Demonstrate how to solve an algebraic equation using manipulatives. • Use the principles of bridge design to construct your own stable span. • Use a word processing program to rewrite a handwritten report. Edit the paper using computer tools.
Analyzing (Analysis)	differentiating, organizing, exploring relationships, distinguishing between components or parts	• Diagram a compound sentence. • Read about the battles of the French and Indian War and infer why each battle was won or lost. • Estimate how many linked tabs from soda cans would stretch around the walls of the school building.
Evaluating (Evaluation*)	judging, critiquing, making recommendations	• Compare the writing styles of Gary Paulsen and Judy Blume. • Pick a way of solving a mathematical equation and justify why you chose the method you did. • Criticize and debate the President's tax plan.
Creating (Synthesis*)	reorganizing, generating new ideas, planning, producing	• Paint a picture using the techniques of Monet and Renoir. • Design a brochure to inform the public about an infectious disease or chronic ailment. • Write a story about schools in America today from the perspective of a teacher or student from colonial times.

* *Note* that in the original taxonomy (Bloom, 1956), Synthesis was Level 5 and Evaluation was Level 6. Anderson and Krathwohl and their colleagues (2000) reversed the two levels.

the students are reading, ask them to identify various uses of figurative language and explain each use and its meaning in the sentence (understanding/comprehension). After reading the novel, read aloud some stories that include figurative language and guide the students to identify the type (applying/analysis). At this point, ask each student to pick a particular type of figurative language to focus on, and tell the students to compare and contrast different authors' uses of the same figurative language devices to express an idea (analyzing/analysis).

Ask the students next to evaluate their authors' uses of the figurative language device—how effective it is and what changes they would recommend (evaluating/knowledge utilization). Next, tell the students they are to write a story or poem using the type of figurative language they researched; however, they can incorporate other types of figurative language as well (creating/knowledge utilization). Guide the students to develop a plan for writing and to complete a self-evaluation of their final piece and their process (evaluating/metacognitive system).

Marzano (2001) emphasized that the thinker's level of knowledge relevant to the particular task is significant in determining the challenge the task presents and the likelihood of success in the task. Therefore, reflecting the criticisms noted above about the original taxonomy, this later version emphasizes that it is not necessarily the taxonomic level of the task that makes it difficult, but instead may be the level of the task *combined with* the complexity of the knowledge required to undertake it. This is a critical consideration in using any version of the taxonomy of cognitive objectives to provide differentiation for learners of varying readiness and ability levels. All students should have opportunities to engage in all of the levels of cognitive process and to engage their metacognitive systems and self-systems; however, highly able students should be challenged to think at higher levels more frequently and with more advanced content knowledge. For example, the figurative language lesson described above might be differentiated across a range of student readiness levels by changing the number of figurative language devices introduced, assigning particular devices to particular students based on different levels of complexity and abstraction, and varying the literature selections used in the activity. Such modifications would continue to engage all students across multiple levels of the taxonomy while still providing advanced stimuli for high-ability learners.

THINKING CRITICALLY AND CREATIVELY

Many of the processes identified at higher levels of the taxonomies described above may be classified under the overarching headings of critical and creative thinking. Critical and creative thinking skills are part of everyone's daily repertoire. Broadly speaking, critical thinking is reasonable, reflective, and focuses on deciding what to believe or do in response to a question or problem at issue (Ennis, 1985), whereas creative thinking is "the ability to generate novel and interesting ideas" (Sternberg & Grigorenko, 2007, p. 59). When individuals are thinking critically, they also may be thinking creatively. According to Paul and Elder (2001), critical thinking incorporates three key abilities: the ability to analyze thinking, the ability to assess thinking, and the ability to improve thinking. Therefore, when an individual thinks critically, he or she is analyzing, evaluating, and being creative. For example, when planning a vacation, most people gather material pertaining to the places they would like to visit. When in the process of deciding where to stay, what route to travel, and what places to tour (analysis thinking), the people traveling make decisions based on how much money they have to spend, their personal preferences, and how much time they will have for vacation (evaluative thinking). Many travelers become very creative in their thinking when they are deciding what route to follow; they map out routes that will "beat the traffic" and get them to their destination sooner, or they find new ways to combine sites during a single day's travel (creative thinking).

When individuals are thinking critically or creatively, they are using similar cognitive operations, such as observing, comparing, and inferring (Marzano et al., 1988), and most higher order processes involve some combination of critical and creative thinking. Again, it is not the level of the process that necessarily makes a task challenging or difficult, but rather the integration of the process with challenging content and the expectation for focused awareness and evaluation of the thinking processes being employed. For example, making choices about what to cook for dinner or what to wear to a party requires critical and creative thinking, but may perhaps be less challenging than the thinking and content knowledge involved in deciding to start a new business or respond to a significant change in organizational policy.

Paul (1992) argued that critical thinking is an awareness, an attention to the thought processes that we undergo. He suggested that all thought and behavior are based on assumptions we make and the conceptual creations we use to organize our world, and that "critical thinkers . . . attempt to heighten their awareness of the conditions under which their self-created conceptualizations—and inferences from them—are rationally justified" (Paul, 1992, p. 25). Therefore, part of the challenge for teachers and curriculum developers is not just to engage students in thinking processes, but to help increase students' awareness of these processes and their developing capacities for applying the processes in new contexts to build strong conceptualizations and inferences. For example, within several of the Center for Gifted Education's curricular series, careful attention is given to teaching Paul's Elements of Reasoning as a specific model of reasoning and then employing the model in multiple contexts throughout a unit of study. To illustrate this combination of teaching the model directly and applying it to specific content across multiple areas, we describe the model and several of its uses in the following section.

Reasoning: Elements and Standards of Thinking

Paul's (1992) eight Elements of Reasoning represent a model of key building blocks of productive thinking. They are implicit in the process when we gather, conceptualize, apply, analyze, synthesize, or evaluate information (Foundation for Critical Thinking, 1996; Paul, 1992). Taken together, these building blocks provide a general logic to reasoning. In document interpretation and listening, awareness of the elements may assist in making sense of an author's or speaker's reasoning. Through attention to the reasoning elements evident in what they write and say, authors and speakers are able to strengthen their arguments.

Purpose, goal, or end in view. Individuals reason to achieve some objective, satisfy a desire, or fulfill some need. For example, if my computer is not working when I arrive at work, the purpose of my reasoning is to determine how to get it fixed and how to complete the day's work. Reasoning is often poor due to a defect at the level of goal, purpose, or end. If the goal is unrealistic, contradictory to an individual's other goals, or muddled in some way, then the reasoning used to achieve it may be problematic. If we are clear on the purpose of a document or speech, it will help to focus the message in a coherent direction.

Question at issue (or problem to be solved). When individuals attempt to reason something out, there is at least one question at issue or problem to be solved (if not, there is no reasoning required). If a person is not clear about what the question or problem is, it is unlikely that he or she will find a reasonable answer or one that will serve his or her purpose. As part of the reasoning process, a person should be able to formulate the question to be answered or the issue to be addressed. For example, why won't my computer work? Or, should libraries censor materials that contain objectionable language? Throughout the reasoning process, the skilled and aware thinker revisits the question regularly to determine whether the same question is still in focus or if it has changed in some way.

Points of view or frame of reference. As people take on an issue they care about, they bring their own point of view to the reasoning process. For example, parents of young children may have a different point of view pertaining to censorship of books than librarians do. The price of a car may seem low to one person and high to another due to different frames of reference. A person always brings a point of view or frame of reference to a problem, but should be aware that it is a possible source of problems in his or her reasoning. An individual's point of view may be too narrow, not precise enough, unfairly biased, and so forth. By considering multiple points of view, individuals may sharpen or broaden their thinking. Arguments for or against an issue can be strengthened when others' points of view are considered and acknowledged. In listening and reading, thinkers need to identify the perspective of the speaker or author and understand how it affects the message being delivered. In writing and speaking, a person's careful exploration of his or her own point of view and acknowledgement of the points of view of other stakeholders are important in presenting a reasoned argument.

Point of view can be influenced by many factors, including personal and experiential factors such as age/generation group, cultural background, family background, and education. In addition, how much actual experience the person has had with a specific issue, problem, or event affects his or her thinking. An individual's emotional involvement based on his or her values can also influence perspectives.

Experience, data, evidence. When people reason, they must be able to support their point of view and inferences with reasons or evidence. Evidence is important in distinguishing opinions from reasons and creating a reasoned judgment. Thinkers can evaluate the strength of an argument or the validity of a statement by examining the supporting data or evidence. Personal experiences, as well as more formal "data," also can contribute to the evidence base to support a person's reasoning.

Concepts and ideas. Reasoning requires the understanding and use of concepts and ideas (including definitional terms, principles, rules, or theories). When people are learning content, they should ask themselves, "What are the key ideas presented?" Thoughts should be examined and organized around the substance of concepts and ideas. Some examples of concepts are *freedom*, *systems*, and *survival*.

Assumptions. People need to take some things for granted when they reason, but they need to be aware of the assumptions they have made and the assumptions of others, because assumptions are at the base of reasoning and of different points of view. Assumptions represent what people believe, value, or take for granted around the issue or problem and its central concepts. Reasoning involves recognizing whether differences in point of view represent different assumptions at a fundamental level, as well as examining one's own assumptions and beliefs about the issue and about one's audience. As a reader or listener, an effective critical thinker also works to identify the assumptions of the writer or speaker.

People formulate assumptions based on beliefs and presuppositions. When reasoning, a thinker must clarify in his or her own mind the points of view and assumptions of different stakeholders affected by the issue, and trace inferences carefully back to supporting evidence rather than only assumptions.

Inferences. Reasoning involves inference-making, or drawing conclusions and giving meaning to data. An inference is a small step of the mind in which a person makes a conclusion based on available evidence. For example, if we know that a train departs for our destination at 7, that it takes 30 minutes to get from our current location to the train station, and that it is now 6:45, we can infer that we will miss the train. The conclusions are interpretations of raw data; thus, they depend on the skill of the individual making sense of his or her situation and also on the reliability of the data available. Many inferences are justified and reasonable, but some are not. People need to distinguish between the raw data of their experiences and their interpretations of those experiences. They also must come to understand the degree to which a person's point of view and assumptions heavily influence inferences.

Implications and consequences. The ability to reason well is measured in part by an ability to understand and articulate the implications and consequences of the reasoning. When individuals argue and support their perspectives on issues and questions, solid reasoning requires that they consider the implications of following that path and what the consequences are of taking the course they support. When people read or listen to an argument, they need to ask themselves what follows from that way of thinking. For example, if a student does not do the assigned homework, then he or she may have to stay after school; if someone puts gas in the car when it has a quarter of a tank left, then the car will take longer to run out of gas.

According to Paul (1992), all eight of these elements are components of our thinking about any issue or problem, although we may not always be aware of the degree to which the elements are coming into play as we make decisions and work to resolve issues. In addition to the elements, another component of the total model is consideration of standards of reasoning, or the criteria against which we may judge the quality of our own or others' reasoning. Among Paul's standards of reasoning are clarity, accuracy, precision, relevance, depth, breadth, logic, and fairness. These standards, like the elements of thought, may be taught directly and modeled for students, as well as infused into various activities, to help provide students with tools they may use to strengthen their own reasoning.

Applications of the Model

The elements and standards of reasoning (Paul, 1992) may be translated into specific kinds of learning activities that engage students in examining the elements within the context of specific content, thereby also reinforcing the flexible application of the elements across multiple experiences and questions.

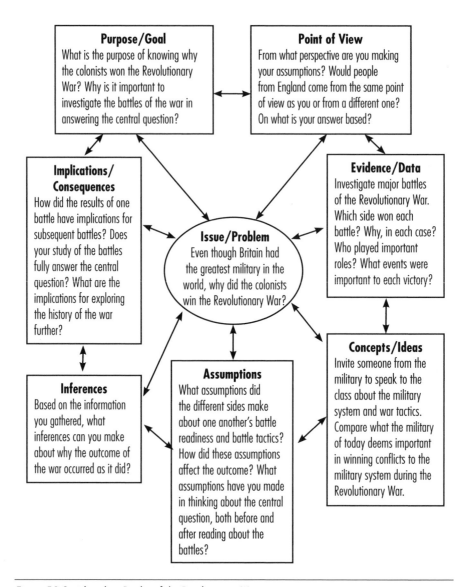

Figure 5.1. Social studies: Battles of the Revolutionary War.

The initial introduction of the elements may be done through application to a particular problem situation relevant to the students' own lives. For example, the sample discussion that follows, Elements of Reasoning, demonstrates questions about each element as it relates to the scenario given.

Paul's (1992) Wheel of Reasoning, representing the elements in a visible format, can be used as a framework for developing lessons in various subject areas that link the elements directly to the content through questioning. Figures 5.1, 5.2, and 5.3 are examples of applications of the model in social studies, science, and language arts. The elements of thought do not have to be analyzed in any particular order; however, one should identify the assump-

SAMPLE DISCUSSION:
ELEMENTS OF REASONING

Instructional Purpose:
- To introduce the elements of reasoning.
- To apply elements of reasoning to a problem situation.

Scenario:

It's the end of the summer, and you need to get a new pair of athletic shoes for school. Your dad wants you to buy good shoes that he can afford, but you want the most expensive brand that you know "everyone" at school will be wearing.

Questions and Sample Responses:

What is the problem or issue?
- You and your dad are not agreeing on the brand of shoes to buy.

Why are we reasoning about it?
- You and your dad would like to try to reach an agreement that is acceptable to both of you.

What are the different points of view?
- Dad has a budget and does not feel he can afford the expensive shoes; he also feels that advertising and peer pressure are having too much of an effect on you.
- You have an image you want to keep up among your peers. You also believe that the more expensive shoes will let you be more successful in sports.

What are the key concepts underlying the issue?
- Popularity, trends, and peer pressure
- Value, quality, and cost
- Making economic choices

What are some of the assumptions that affect the points of view and inferences?
- You are assuming that aspects of your status and popularity are affected by the brand of shoes you wear.
- Your dad is assuming that the amount of money he will spend is a more important consideration than the image the shoes might give you.
- You may be assuming that image and status are more important considerations than quality.

What evidence might support each point of view?

- You want some data to present to your dad to support your point of view. You start asking other kids you see in the community what kinds of shoes they are going to have for school, and you keep a tally of different types. You also ask kids who play sports locally about the types of shoes they wear.
- Your dad collects some information about the different brands of shoes from consumer magazines that give ratings on the quality of the shoes.
- You collect advertisements on different shoes and information on the athletes who appear in the ads.

What inferences can be made from the evidence?

- Your survey of other kids' chosen brands may allow you to draw some conclusions about what the most popular brands will be at school this year.
- You and your dad can draw inferences from the consumer magazines about various qualities of the shoes relative to their cost; you may have different points of view on the relative value or importance of these different qualities, though!
- You may infer from advertisements that the shoes are the most important factor in the athletes' success; this may be a faulty inference, however, and information on the athletes' background and training regimen may provide better evidence for more accurate inferences.

What are the implications and consequences of your thinking?

- You may decide from your research that it is OK to buy a less-expensive shoe, or that you would rather go without something else or get a job in order to purchase the more expensive shoe.
- If you get the more expensive shoes, you may have to wear them longer than if you get less expensive shoes.

tions that guided thinking in connection with key concepts, the evidence that supports particular inferences, and the connections between assumptions as a starting place and inferences as conclusions. This process will assist the thinker in gaining command over thinking. When coming to a conclusion, the thinker should consider supporting evidence, identify the underlying assumptions, and ask, "Are the inferences I made justifiable?"

Assessment of student thinking is essential for monitoring student progress in a subject area, and self-assessment of thinking helps to strengthen reasoning processes overall. The standards of reasoning noted above can be used as a basis for self-assessment of reasoning, as well as for peer and teacher assessment.

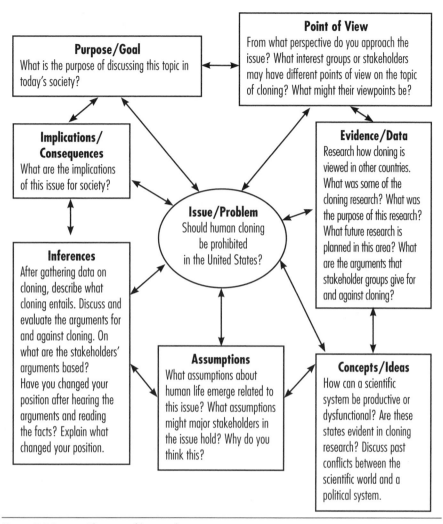

Figure 5.2. Science: The issue of human cloning.

Figure 5.4 is an authentic assessment tool, adapted from the standards, that can be implemented when students write persuasive essays about a given issue.

The reasoning model described here also serves as a starting place and guide for more extended consideration of an issue, the perspectives on it, and the evidence and reasoning to support different points of view; this type of extended application may be translated into a research project that guides students through varied forms of information-gathering and decision-making about an issue. The applications of the reasoning model to research activities and products are discussed in more detail in Chapter 6.

By teaching students the specific elements of reasoning and then reinforcing them through a variety of activities and applications, teachers provide a common language for discussing critical thinking, as well as heightening students' awareness of their own thinking as it progresses. Teachers and cur-

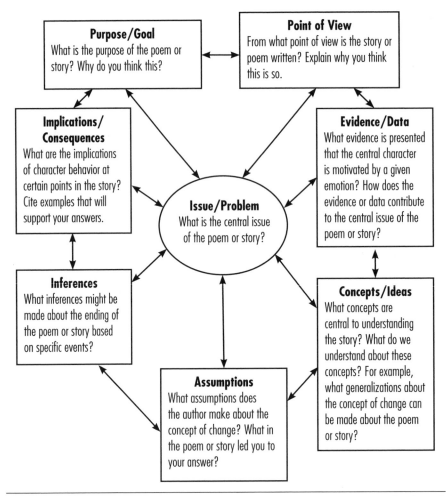

Figure 5.3. Language arts: Literature study. From *A Guide to Teaching a Language Arts Curriculum for High-Ability Learners* (p. 59), by the Center for Gifted Education, 1999, Dubuque, IA: Kendall/Hunt. Copyright © 1999 by the Center for Gifted Education. Reprinted with permission.

riculum developers help to provide practice and experience with the model through questioning and specific activities. In the following sections, we will address questioning to promote higher order processing more broadly, and we will delineate several additional models and learning activities that engage students in practicing and strengthening their understanding of key thinking processes. Questioning and instruction in specific models are closely interrelated, because questioning is used to prompt students to activate different processes, and the process models provide structures and question frameworks for teachers as well as students.

Directions: Rate each standard according to the following:

        3 = Strong   2 = Adequate   1 = Needs Improvement

1. Are there *enough reasons* to make a convincing argument? One or two reasons might not be enough to show your point of view so as to be understood fully.

2. Is the evidence *correct or right*?

3. Are the reasons *clear*? Is the meaning understandable by anyone who reads or hears the argument? Are they explained well, or is more information needed?

4. Are *specific* reasons or examples included, rather than vague generalizations?

5. Are the arguments and reasons *strong and important*? Or do they seem to be included just to have something to say?

6. Is the thinking *logical*? Does the paragraph follow an understandable path, or is it just a disconnected group of statements? Do the sentences seem to go together and to be in the right order?

Figure 5.4. Teacher assessment of student thinking. From *Literary Reflections* (p. 111), by the Center for Gifted Education, 1998, Dubuque, IA: Kendall/Hunt. Copyright © 1998 by the Center for Gifted Education. Reprinted with permission.

QUESTIONING AND FACILITATING DISCUSSION

Questions are perhaps a teacher's strongest tool for engaging students in any kind of cognitive processes, as well as for promoting metacognition and personal connections with the learning experience. Questioning provides the prompt to initiate processing of information, and it can inspire dialogue, discussion, and further questioning, both in an oral discussion and internally. Within a context that emphasizes supporting students in constructing meaning and engaging in metacognition, a teacher's questioning also serves as a model for students as they build skills for asking questions about the new information and tasks they encounter; such skills promote deeper learning by guiding students to interact with greater purpose and engagement with new content and concepts.

There are, of course, multiple types and levels of questions that promote engagement to varying degrees. Costa (2001) classified classroom interactions as generally representing either *recitation* or *dialogue*; recitation involves a teacher-centered succession of teacher questions and student answers, while dialogue is characterized by a broader interaction in which ideas and questions are shared, with the teacher as facilitator instead of the center of the interaction. Unfortunately, the prevalent mode of questioning in classrooms often reflects the recitation format, also known as the initiate-respond-evaluate model, which is highly teacher-centered instead of student-centered and is unlikely to promote deeper understanding (Allen, 2008).

Teachers ask dozens or even hundreds of questions a day, yet evidence suggests that the majority of those questions in most classrooms tend to be lower level questions. Tienken, Goldberg, and DiRocco (2009) documented more than 2,300 questions sampled from 98 teachers across grades 3–12. They classified the questions into two categories: *reproductive* questions, which included mostly lower level questions requiring students to retrieve and reproduce an expected response, and *productive* questions, which tended to be more open-ended and divergent, focusing on creating, analyzing, and evaluating. The study found that around 75% of the documented questions were the lower level reproductive questions, and this distribution varied only slightly across novice and experienced teachers.

Costa (2001) and Gallagher (2007), among others, have emphasized that teachers should monitor their own questioning to examine the types and levels of questions being asked, and that teachers should take time to formulate questions carefully in advance of classroom interactions to ensure purposeful questioning at higher levels. Planning and analysis of questions may use one of the taxonomies described above to classify the types of cognitive processes expected within questions; teachers also may consider how they might answer their own questions, or criteria they would use to evaluate responses, in order to evaluate the strength of the questions themselves.

Appropriate planning of questions guides students to initiate cognitive processes at multiple levels (e.g., retrieving information in order to solve a problem or analyze errors, rather than just to retrieve the information for its own sake). Such planning and monitoring on the teacher's part helps to ensure maintenance of questioning at higher levels and also helps to model complex questioning for students.

Costa (2001) suggested that powerful questions are those that (a) are invitational, (b) engage specific cognitive operations at various levels of complexity, and (c) address internal or external content that is relevant to the learner (see pp. 360–361). Conversely, some questioning patterns that should be avoided include those that really only invite agreement with a stated opinion or fact, without encouraging reasoning about points of view; those that may be answered only with "yes" or "no"; and those in which the answer is given within the question (Costa, 2001; Gallagher, 2007).

The questions themselves are, of course, the central component of effective questioning in the classroom. However, they are not the only component; teachers promote interaction around questioning through behaviors beyond just asking the questions. Wait time has long been recognized as a key factor in engaging students with the learning process (Rowe, 1974), and both the wait time after a question and the wait time after a student gives a response are important in promoting dialogue and engagement. Teachers' responses following student responses also are important in the questioning interaction; responses and follow-up questions that help students clarify or extend their thinking are useful in promoting learning and ongoing discussion. Responses that are intended to praise or reinforce student responses should provide specific praise that demonstrates the criteria upon which the praise is given (Costa, 2001).

As with the questions themselves, teacher responses to student responses also provide modeling and scaffolding for students to engage in their own thinking and follow-up to one another's comments. Several frameworks have been developed to guide classroom discussion in ways that encourage students to continue to engage with questions and with one another's thoughts and responses. Chapin, O'Connor, and Anderson (2003) identified several key "talk moves" that teachers should use and encourage in promoting classroom discourse, specifically focusing on mathematics. These moves include revoicing a student's comment, asking another student to restate someone else's reasoning or idea, asking students to indicate their agreement or disagreement with something that has been stated and explain why, and prompting for further participation or "adding on" to what has been said, as well as wait time. Similarly, the framework for "accountable talk," developed by Resnick and colleagues, guides teachers in encouraging students to interpret and use one another's statements, press one another for clarification and explanation, recognize and challenge misconceptions, and ask for evidence for claims and justification of proposals (Fisher & Frey, 2007; Michaels, O'Connor, & Resnick, 2008). In each of these frameworks, the focus is on building students' capacity to engage in productive dialogue with one another; the goal would be for teachers to be able to decrease their demonstration of the talk moves over time as students become more comfortable with using them.

Socratic Questioning

The points noted above reflect an approach to teaching that is organized around purposeful questioning and follow-up questioning; such an approach is grounded in a very old form of teaching, the Socratic discussion. Socratic teaching is one of the oldest and most effective teaching strategies for cultivating higher order process skills. By using Socratic discussion and questioning techniques, instructors can continually probe students' thoughts on a subject and encourage students in habits of questioning and reflecting upon their own thinking. A response to a question elicits another question and another response, followed by yet another question and response, "which forces the students to think more deeply about the heart of an issue and explore its many sides" (VanTassel-Baska, 1992, p. 113).

According to Adler (1982, 1983), Socratic questioning brings students' ideas to birth, while the awakening of creative and inquisitive powers stimulates imagination and intellect. Socratic discussion enhances clarity of thought, as well as critical and reflective thinking. While engaging in discourse, learners continually analyze their own and others' values and ideas. Paul and Elder (2007; Elder & Paul, 2007) noted that Socratic questioning probes both the *parts* of thinking and the *quality* of reasoning, encouraging students to dig deeper into their thoughts and ideas in a disciplined manner to clarify and strengthen reasoning. In their explanations of Socratic questioning, students are encouraged to examine the elements of thought and standards for reasoning described earlier in the chapter through questioning that targets student attention to these features.

Adler (1982) emphasized that before engaging in discourse on a topic, students should have read various types of literature on it. These might include historical, scientific, and philosophical books; poems; short stories; essays; plays; and authentic documents. The literature should be "products of human artistry" (Adler, 1982, p. 29) and not textbooks. According to Adler (1982), in-depth reading of a topic will assist the students in coming to the discussion with a common vocabulary of ideas. Similarly, by teaching students a structured model that identifies the elements of thought, teachers also provide students with a common vocabulary regarding thinking and reasoning that can be used in discussion (Paul & Elder, 2007). For example, Paul's (1992) elements and standards may provide a shared language for a Socratic discussion.

One way of engaging in Socratic teaching is to have Socratic seminars (Horn, 2001). A Socratic seminar is an opportunity for thoughtful and collaborative dialogue to take place within an open-ended discussion. It is a time when multiple viewpoints are respected and a shared understanding is established.

Based on successful implementation of Socratic seminars, the Fairfax County Public School District in Virginia outlined some key suggestions on how to conduct this type of seminar (Horn, 2001). Before a Socratic seminar, teachers should work with students to establish guidelines. Let the students know it is OK to refer to the text when needed; to "pass" if asked to contribute; and, if confused, to ask for clarification. Every person involved in the seminar should have read or examined the stimulus material (e.g., short story, poem, historical document, play, or art print) at least once in class and, preferably, a second time at home. The piece of writing or art should address complex issues and ideas, connect to the curriculum, and be ambiguous, challenging, and lead to enduring understandings.

Effective Socratic questioners (a) allow students to have wait time to consider the question and frame an answer before requesting a response, (b) maintain an intellectual discussion, (c) ask probing questions that stimulate in-depth thinking, (d) occasionally summarize what has and has not been discussed, and (e) encourage as many students as possible to participate in the discussion.

Three types of questions may be asked during a Socratic seminar. The lowest level of questioning asks the students to gather or recall information.

This type of questioning is useful in gaining clarity, sequencing, and asking for details. For example, a teacher might use Paul Revere's etching of the Boston Massacre (see Archiving Early America, 1996) and related primary source accounts and secondary source retellings in a social studies lesson. In such a lesson, this lowest level of questioning might include the following: "What is the definition of a massacre?" and "What facts from the written accounts of the incident are not portrayed in the etching?"

Another type of questioning asks the students to make sense of the information they gathered, assists them in processing it, and is helpful for analyzing. Continuing the specific example lesson from above, sample questions at this level might include: "How did Paul Revere use color to make the portrayal more powerful?" and "Is the etching an example of propaganda? Why or why not?"

The first question posed at the Socratic seminar should be at the highest level. It should be open-ended and result in students' applying and evaluating information. This type of question should lead the students to cite rich and significant details and to have insight on the issue at hand. Examples of this type of questioning for the sample social studies lesson are as follows: "How do you think the patriots or the loyalists would interpret Paul Revere's etching?" and "Why do you think that the etching was such an effective piece of propaganda?"

Each of these levels of questioning represents an important component of an effective Socratic seminar, but not all questions for such a seminar can be prepared in advance. A key element of Socratic questioning is the teacher's skill at probing student responses to the questions with further questions, moving among the questioning levels to elicit deeper, more carefully reasoned and complex thoughts from students.

The Socratic seminar is a powerful teaching and learning strategy for all children, but it can be particularly effective when used with gifted children. Teachers guide, as well as challenge, their students to use critical and creative thinking skills to understand important ideas and concepts.

Paul and Elder (2008) identified three types of Socratic approaches that might be employed, in a seminar format or otherwise: focused, exploratory, and spontaneous or unplanned. Their description of a focused Socratic discussion is much like the seminar format described above, with specific questions planned in advance to guide the discussion around a particular issue, topic, or text. Exploratory Socratic discussions are useful for both introducing topics and reviewing or assessing what students know about topics; these discussions ask students to demonstrate the depth of their understanding through explanations of key ideas and comparisons of concepts. Finally, spontaneous or unplanned Socratic questioning emerges in response to a particular point or question raised by a student or the teacher. Questions may include many of the "moves" discussed in the previous section, such as asking for evidence or reasons to support a position, asking students whether they agree or disagree with a point and why, asking for examples and counterexamples, and asking for rephrasing or restating of points that have been made (Paul & Elder, 2008, p. 34).

OTHER MODELS AND ACTIVITIES TO SCAFFOLD LEARNING AND UNDERSTANDING

As noted above, teacher questioning also can serve as a model for student questioning as students learn to engage actively with new information through questions they ask themselves and one another. Another approach that may be combined with the guidelines above is to teach students specific questioning structures that they may use to guide their understanding of something that they read, hear, or see. For example, Beck and McKeown (2001) developed the "Questioning the Author" (QtA) approach to encourage students to engage more deeply with text ideas. In this approach, students are guided to focus on text as the product of an author's ideas and process; therefore, they learn to consider issues such as bias; choices made in the structure, presentation, and content of text; and the fallibility of authors. They also learn to link their own writing process with the process that led to what they read.

In the QtA framework, teachers provide initial queries that encourage students to explain what they understand about what they read in terms of what an author intended to convey. For example, the teacher might initiate discussion with a question such as, "What is the author trying to say?" or "What does the author want us to know?" The teacher then asks follow-up questions based on student responses, asking them to dig deeper into their understanding and the evidence to support their inferences. The questioning happens during the process of reading, with students encouraged to ask questions as they read and not just at the end of reading, therefore actively constructing meaning as they read.

Research on the QtA framework has demonstrated that when students were asked to describe what goes on in their reading or social studies classes that used QtA, they overwhelmingly focused on describing their thinking process rather than the specific format or activity; for example, they noted "coming to conclusions" or "talking about what it means" rather than statements such as "talking about the story" or "getting in pairs" (McKeown & Beck, 1998). Such evidence provides support for an approach that focuses students on engaging actively with constructing meaning and understanding the components of the process.

In the Center for Gifted Education's curriculum units across various content areas, students are provided with models for analyzing text that build from a foundational set of questions relevant to the particular content area and key reasoning processes. Students are guided to practice these models with multiple stimuli over the course of the unit so that they become very comfortable with the specific models and questions and are able to apply them to new texts that they encounter. For example, students use a Literature Web to help them identify components such as key ideas, images, and structural elements in a literature selection, and they use a model for analyzing primary sources to guide their historical analysis process in social studies. See Chapters 8 through 11 for further discussion of these and other models for guiding student thinking within particular content areas.

Problem Solving: Modeling the Process

Problem solving is a major higher order process that is used across disciplines, although it is perhaps primarily viewed as an area of focus in mathematics. The National Council of Teachers of Mathematics (2000) has defined problem solving as "engaging in a task for which the solution is not known in advance" (p. 52). It also appears as one of the "Knowledge Utilization" cognitive processes in the taxonomy proposed by Marzano (2000) and discussed above.

Polya (1957) identified four key phases involved in approaching and solving problems. Although he was a mathematician and viewed the process from a mathematical perspective, these phases are themselves applicable across many disciplines and contexts. His argument was that teachers find themselves asking students the same questions or types of questions repeatedly in problem-solving contexts, so these questions and steps should be taught directly to students to encourage them to pursue the problem-solving process with greater self-direction. Polya's phases are as follows:

1. Understand the problem.
2. Devise a plan.
3. Carry out the plan.
4. Look back.

Across these phases, students are encouraged to ask themselves additional questions and to make connections to prior knowledge. For example, in the phase of devising a plan, students should be asking themselves if they know of other problems similar to the one they are attempting to solve, in order to determine whether similar solution methods may be used. At the fourth phase of looking back, students are reflecting on their solution and process to determine the effectiveness of the plan, the degree to which the original problem has been answered, and whether the solution makes practical sense in the context of the situation.

Each of Polya's (1957) phases is an important aspect of thinking across all domains and disciplines. Considering the first two phases of *understand the problem* and *devise a plan,* teachers should guide students in each content area to analyze problems and questions, seek connections to similar problems and questions they have encountered before, and create representations of the problem that may help them to see directions for their solution. Such guidance for students may occur within the general structure of Polya's phases or within a more detailed process that applies more specifically to a content-based task. For example, Raphael's Question-Answer Relationships strategy encourages students to analyze questions about text to determine whether the answer is to be found directly in the text ("Right There" questions), in the text but requiring inferential thinking ("Think and Search" Questions), in a combination of text ideas and readers' ideas and applications ("Author and Me" Questions), or in students' own experiences and point of view ("On My Own" Questions; see Raphael & Au, 2005; Raphael, Highfield, & Au, 2006). Like the Polya phase of understanding the problem, this framework reminds students to focus on what they are being asked first in order to devise an approach to finding an answer.

Within the ICM, the process/product dimension represents both the higher order processes in which students engage and the culminating products that result from their work. Thus, the discussion of such processes in this chapter integrates with the discussion of product development in the next chapter. For example, while the focus here has been on the key pieces of understanding problems and questions and devising plans, the process of creative problem solving and the problem-based learning approach are discussed in the next chapter in light of their product development goals.

Metacognition

A crucial aspect of higher order thinking processes, as highlighted in Marzano's (2000) taxonomy, is metacognition. Both cognition and metacognition are mental processes of knowing. Cognition includes learning knowledge, comprehending, perceiving, reasoning, and judging, whereas metacognition is the "process of developing awareness of one's own thinking and techniques for controlling and improving thinking activities" (Feldhusen, 1994b, p. 320). Metacognition requires cognitive processes; however, cognition does not necessarily mean someone is thinking metacognitively. Conscious, careful planning, monitoring, and evaluating of the thinking processes surrounding a problem or question are the key components of metacognition; bringing awareness of thinking and assessment of thinking to students' attention helps them to hone their skills at addressing new tasks and problems effectively.

There are three main areas of metacognitive activity and questions to ask oneself (Beyer, 1987, as cited in Feldhusen, 1994a) when planning, monitoring progress, and assessing performance:

1. Task analysis and planning
   - What is the goal?
   - What do I need to do to reach the goal?

- What should I do first? Second? Third?
- What do I already know that can help me?
- What more do I need to know?
- What obstacles must be overcome?
- How can I fix potential errors?
- What will the solution look like?

2. Monitoring progress
  - Am I progressing toward my goal?
  - What is my next step?
  - Have I reached all necessary subgoals?
  - Am I ready for the next steps?
  - Does this strategy seem to be working?
  - Are there any other strategies I could use?
  - Have I made any mistakes?
  - How can I fix any of my mistakes?

3. Assessing performance
  - Did I reach my goal?
  - Does my solution fit my prediction?
  - Did I do what I planned to do?
  - Did I fix all of my mistakes?
  - Did I use my time well?
  - How could I do better next time?

One of the most important components of encouraging higher order processes is engaging students in thinking about their thinking. They should be encouraged to monitor the clarity, accuracy, logic, and fairness of their thinking throughout any problem-solving or related process. Metacognition also assists students in checking the quality of their work, and it infuses an inner voice that is a guide to better planning and reasoning.

CONCLUSION

Engaging gifted learners in higher order process skills is an important element in the ICM and in implementing effective curricula for gifted and high-ability learners. Gifted students need to become proficient in thinking and problem-solving strategies that help them to examine concepts central to specific disciplines, but also are common to different fields of study. Moreover, they need opportunities to practice these processes in connection with advanced content and concepts, as well as to increase their awareness of and reflection upon their own thinking. Central to all of this is an acknowledgement that the emphasis is not on "right" answers, but rather on the processes students use to engage with content and the justifications they can provide to explain the answers they reach. As teachers and curriculum developers work to infuse a greater emphasis on higher order processes and metacognition throughout all content areas, they may use specific models both to guide planning and as part of the content of instruction, thereby equipping students with process tools and giving them opportunities to practice with them in multiple contexts to promote transfer and reflection.

KEY POINTS SUMMARY

- Higher order processes are part of everyone's daily repertoire, but applications of them to challenging content may sometimes be lacking in students' classroom experiences.
- Higher order processes may be supported through direct teaching of process models, integration of process models across multiple contexts, and modeling of thinking behaviors and metacognition.
- Several taxonomies of cognitive processes provide the basis for considering the levels of complexity and specific thinking skills required by different tasks. Levels in these taxonomies are not separated solely by difficulty; rather, they reflect different types of processes that offer increasing levels of difficulty when combined with increasingly challenging content applications.
- Developing effective thinking skills requires not only a focus on practicing the skills themselves but on developing awareness and self-assessment around thinking. Therefore, metacognition should be a major focus in connection with teaching thinking skills.
- Paul's (1992) Elements of Reasoning represent a model designed for individuals to draw justifiable conclusions based on evidence or data about an issue, question, or problem. This model is an example of a framework for thinking that can be directly taught and applied across multiple content areas to strengthen student thinking.
- Effective questioning promotes student thinking through inviting engagement at higher levels of thought and facilitating ongoing interactions and meaning construction. Such questioning, including Socratic questioning, requires planning and appropriate implementation, including thoughtful response behaviors from the teacher.
- Higher order processes are integrated in the curriculum with student product development and applied to specific, advanced content and concepts.

REFERENCES

Adler, M. J. (1982). *The Paideia proposal: An educational manifesto*. New York, NY: Macmillan.

Adler, M. J. (1983). *Paideia problems and possibilities: A consideration of questions raised by the Paideia proposal*. New York, NY: Macmillan.

Allen, R. (2008). Analyzing classroom discourse to advance teaching and learning. *Education Update, 50*(2), 1, 3, 7.

Anderson, L. W., & Krathwohl, D. R. (Eds.). (2000). *A taxonomy for learning, teaching, and assessing: A revision of Bloom's taxonomy of educational objectives*. Boston, MA: Allyn & Bacon.

Archiving Early America. (1996). The Boston massacre: A behind-the-scenes look at Paul Revere's most famous engraving. *The Early America Review, 1*. Retrieved from http://earlyamerica.com/review/winter96/massacre.html

Beck, I. L., & McKeown, M. G. (2001). Inviting students into the pursuit of meaning. *Educational Psychology Review, 13*, 225–241.

Bloom, B. S. (Ed.). (1956*). Taxonomy of educational objectives: The classification of educational goals. Handbook 1: Cognitive domain*. New York, NY: McKay.

Brown, R. S., & Conley, D. T. (2007). Comparing state high school assessments to standards for success in entry-level university courses. *Educational Assessment, 12*, 137–160.

Chapin, S. H., O'Connor, C., & Anderson, N. C. (2003). *Classroom discussions: Using math talk to help students learn, grades 1–6*. Sausalito, CA: Math Solutions.

Cohen, D. K., & Spillane, J. P. (1993). Policy and practice: The relations between governance and instruction. In S. H. Fuhrman (Ed.), *Designing coherent education policy: Improving the system* (pp. 35–95). San Francisco, CA: Jossey-Bass.

Costa, A. L. (2001). Teacher behaviors that enable student thinking. In A. L. Costa (Ed.), *Developing minds: A resource book for teaching thinking* (3rd ed., pp. 359–369). Alexandria, VA: Association for Supervision and Curriculum Development.

Eckert, L. S. (2008). Bridging the pedagogical gap: Intersections between literary and reading theories in secondary and postsecondary literacy instruction. *Journal of Adolescent and Adult Literacy, 52*, 110–118.

Eisner, E. (1988). The celebration of thinking. *National Forum: Phi Kappa Phi Journal, 68*, 30–33.

Elder, L., & Paul, R. (2007). Critical thinking: The art of Socratic questioning, part II. *Journal of Developmental Education, 31*(2), 32–33.

Ennis, R. H. (1985). Goals for a critical thinking curriculum. In A. Costa (Ed.), *Developing minds: A resource book for teaching thinking* (pp. 54–57). Alexandria, VA: Association for Supervision and Curriculum Development.

Fadel, C., Honey, M., & Pasnik, S. (2007, May 23). Assessment in the age of innovation. *Education Week, 26*, 34, 40.

Feldhusen, J. F. (1994a). Strategies for teaching the gifted. In J. VanTassel-Baska (Ed.), *Comprehensive curriculum for gifted learners* (2nd ed., pp. 366–378). Boston, MA: Allyn & Bacon.

Feldhusen, J. F. (1994b). Thinking skills and curriculum development. In J. VanTassel-

Baska (Ed.), *Comprehensive curriculum for gifted learners* (2nd ed., pp. 301–324). Boston, MA: Allyn & Bacon.

Fisher, D., & Frey, N. (2007). *Checking for understanding: Formative assessment techniques for your classroom.* Alexandria, VA: Association for Supervision and Curriculum Development.

Foundation for Critical Thinking. (1996). *Critical thinking workshop handbook.* Rohnert Park, CA: Center for Critical Thinking.

Gallagher, S. (2007, November). *What is an effective question, anyway?* Presentation at the annual convention of the National Association for Gifted Children, Minneapolis, MN.

Horn, C. (2001, March). *Socratic seminar: A dynamic search for understanding.* Presentation at the National Curriculum Network Conference, Center for Gifted Education, College of William and Mary, Williamsburg, VA.

Juster, N. (1961). *The phantom tollbooth.* New York, NY: Random House.

Kendall, J. S., Ryan, S., Weeks, S., Alpert, A., Schwols, A., & Moore, L. (2008). *Thinking & learning skills: What do we expect of students?* Denver, CO: Mid-Continent Research for Education and Learning. Retrieved from http://www.mcrel.org.

Loveless, T., Farkas, S., & Duffett, A. (2008). *High-achieving students in the era of No Child Left Behind.* Washington, DC: Thomas B. Fordham Institute.

Marzano, R. J. (2000). *Designing a new taxonomy of educational objectives.* Thousand Oaks, CA: Corwin Press.

Marzano, R. J. (2001). A new taxonomy of educational objectives. In A. L. Costa (Ed.), *Developing minds: A resource book for teaching thinking* (3rd ed., pp. 181–188). Alexandria, VA: Association for Supervision and Curriculum Development.

Marzano, R. J., & Kendall, J. S. (2007). *The new taxonomy of educational objectives* (2nd ed.). Thousand Oaks, CA: Corwin Press.

Marzano, R. J., Brandt, R. S., Hughes, C. S., Jones, B. F., Presseisen, B. Z., Rankin, S. C., & Suhor, C. (1988). *Dimensions of thinking: A framework for curriculum and instruction.* Alexandria, VA: Association for Supervision and Curriculum Development.

McKeown, M. G., & Beck, I. L. (1998). Talking to an author: Readers taking charge of the reading process. In R. Calfee & N. Nelson (Eds.), *The reading-writing connection: Ninety-seventh yearbook for the National Society for the Study of Education* (pp. 112–130). Chicago, IL: National Society for the Study of Education.

Michaels, S., O'Connor, C., & Resnick, L. B. (2008). Deliberative discourse idealized and realized: Accountable talk in the classroom and in civic life. *Studies in Philosophy and Education, 27,* 283–297.

National Commission on Excellence in Education. (1983). *A nation at risk: The imperative for educational reform.* Washington, DC: U.S. Government Printing Office.

National Council of Teachers of Mathematics. (2000). *Principles and standards for school mathematics.* Reston, VA: Author.

Partnership for 21st Century Skills. (2009). *Framework for 21st century learning.* Tucson, AZ: Author. Retrieved from http://www.21stcenturyskills.org

Paul, R. (1992). *Critical thinking: What every person needs to survive in a rapidly changing world.* Rohnert Park, CA: Foundation for Critical Thinking.

Paul, R., & Elder, L. (2001). *Critical thinking: Tools for taking charge of your learning and your life.* Upper Saddle River, NJ: Prentice Hall.

Paul, R., & Elder, L. (2007). Critical thinking: The art of Socratic questioning. *Journal of Developmental Education, 31,* 36–37.

Paul, R., & Elder, L. (2008). Critical thinking: The art of Socratic questioning, part III. *Journal of Developmental Education, 31,* 34–35.

Polya, G. (1957). *How to solve it: A new aspect of mathematical method* (2nd ed.). Princeton, NJ: Princeton University Press.

Raphael, T. E., & Au, K. H. (2005). QAR: Enhancing comprehension and test taking across grades and content areas. *The Reading Teacher, 59,* 206–221. doi:10.1598/RT.59.3.1

Raphael, T. E., Highfield, K., & Au, K. H. (2006). *QAR now: A powerful and practical framework that develops comprehension and higher-level thinking in all students.* New York, NY: Scholastic.

Rowe, M. B. (1974). Wait-time and rewards as instructional variables, their influence on language, logic, and fate control: Part one—wait time. *Journal of Research in Science Teaching, 11,* 81–94.

Seiger-Ehrenberg, S. (1985). Educational outcomes for a K–12 curriculum. In A. Costa (Ed.), *Developing minds: A resource book for teaching thinking* (pp. 7–10). Alexandria, VA: Association for Supervision and Curriculum Development.

Sternberg, R. J. (1997). *Successful intelligence.* New York, NY: Plume.

Sternberg, R. J., & Grigorenko, E. L. (2007). *Teaching for successful intelligence* (2nd ed.). Thousand Oaks, CA: Corwin Press.

Tienken, C. H., Goldberg, S., & DiRocco, D. (2009, October). Questioning the questions. *Kappa Delta Pi Record,* 39–43.

Toch, T. (2006). Turmoil in the testing industry. *Educational Leadership, 64,* 53–57.

U.S. Department of Education, Office of Educational Research and Improvement. (1993). *National excellence: A case for developing America's talent.* Washington, DC: U.S. Government Printing Office.

VanTassel-Baska, J. (1992). *Planning effective curriculum for gifted learners.* Denver, CO: Love.

Wyner, J. S., Bridgeland, J. M., & DiIulio, J. J. (2007). *Achievement trap: How America is failing millions of high-achieving students from lower-income families.* Lansdowne, VA: Jack Kent Cooke Foundation.

Chapter 6

Product Development: Using Higher Order Skills and Processes to Create

Joyce VanTassel-Baska

You are an elementary teacher at the fourth-grade level who is familiar with national and state standards that require students to understand key concepts, develop requisite skills, and acquire habits of mind in each core area of learning. These same standards demand a learner-centered curriculum that will prepare students for various roles within the community and the world. You often worry about finding sufficient time to help your students achieve required learning goals and objectives in each area. Therefore, you urgently seek ways of maximizing instructional time by creating challenging project-based opportunities that cut across subject area skills and concepts that require students to construct their own meaning through independent and group research activities.

The role of product development in the Integrated Curriculum Model (ICM) has been explicated in Chapter 2 of this text. However, it is important to articulate the role of project-based learning in the education of the gifted. This term encompasses several models used in this chapter and others that engage learners directly in constructing meaning for themselves that result in a quality product, achieved in a group or independently. The product may be linked to one subject area or several and preferably demonstrates cross-disciplinary skills and concept learning. The term *product development* then is inextricably linked to using higher level process skills including critical thinking, creative thinking, problem solving, and research. Yet it also involves the use of metacognitive skills, those skills that allow students to plan and organize their work and reflect on progress made at key stages of the task. This chapter will focus on some of the myths associated with project work for the gifted, delineate useful heuristics and models to use in facilitating student work with projects, provide sample ideas for projects, and conclude with guidelines for independent project work.

The field of gifted education has long been enamored of the role of product development in promoting learning, often suggesting that it is the real sign of giftedness in children to be able to produce original work at the level of practicing professionals. Yet, to some extent, this claim of students' producing work at the level of a practicing professional is mythology, as our studies of expertise suggest that even prodigies do not perform at the highest level of adult production at young ages, even though they have mastered the skills of some professions early such as mathematics and music (Ericsson, 2007). It may be useful to clarify some of the myths associated with product development and the gifted.

MYTH #1: PRODUCTS ARE A GOOD TOOL FOR IDENTIFYING GIFTEDNESS

Although the arts community has used portfolios of products done over time as authentic examples of artistic ability for entry to arts schools, awarding of scholarships, and other meritorious purposes, the translation of this concept is challenging to the world of gifted education identification. As a field, we do not possess the expertise to guide the development of worthwhile products in specific domains and lack the mechanisms to do so over time. Thus, when we use this approach to identification, it is done without the knowledge of the process or context under which products were developed, the criteria used and their relationship to appropriate criteria within a field, and the implications for programs and services required as a result of the identification.

MYTH #2: QUALITY PRODUCTS ARE CREATED OUTSIDE THE DOMAINS OF SCHOOL-BASED SUBJECTS, THUS THEY ARE CONTENT-FREE

Recent work in creativity (see Amabile, Barsade, Mueller, & Staw, 2005; Simonton, 2006) has suggested that the construct is domain-specific. Consequently, quality products should be judged by the rules and standards of disciplines to which they belong and by those whose judgment is expert within each domain (Csikszentmihalyi, 2000). If we want gifted learners to develop creative abilities, then they must be cultivated within academic and artistic arenas, not outside them. Elementary projects, conceived as student-directed in the absence of knowledge in relevant subject areas, are doomed not to meet the test of quality.

MYTH #3: GIFTED LEARNERS CAN INDEPENDENTLY DEVELOP HIGH-LEVEL PRODUCTS IF THEY ARE GIVEN TIME AND SPACE

There is no evidence that gifted learners as a group or even individually have the capacity to develop worthwhile products in the absence of direct instruction in the skills necessary to create such products—thinking, problem solving, and research. Teachers are needed to work with such learners in the development of these skills as well as to help them build the knowledge base within the disciplines relevant to the product under consideration. Metacognitive skills also require time to impart and develop.

MYTH #4: HIGH-QUALITY PRODUCTS ARE DEVELOPED IN THE ABSENCE OF RULES AND ALGORITHMS; RATHER, THEY ARE OPEN-ENDED OPPORTUNITIES

Perhaps this myth is the most insidious as it pits a worthwhile creative strategy of "open-endedness" against the parameters needed to create any product of worth in any area of human endeavor. It ignores the requisite need to create within a form, whether it be scientific investigation or poetry or historical commentary. It ignores the need for specificity in what makes a product desirable in any form—that is, what makes a good experiment, a good poem, or a good historical analysis. In the absence of deep knowledge and critical judgment in an area of learning, creative products are not likely to result.

MYTH #5: WORTHWHILE PRODUCTS OF THE GIFTED MUST BE INDIVIDUALLY DETERMINED AND WORKED ON FOR LONG PERIODS OF TIME

Many products that gifted students conceive and carry out can be done collaboratively and in a reasonably short period of time. Part of the purpose of product development is having students create meaning and practice their developing skills at the same time, providing hands-on and minds-on opportunities for learning. Thus, research projects that take only 3–10 days to complete, with half the time occurring in class, may be a propitious way to maximize the learning potential of project work.

THE LEARNING STATE FOR INDEPENDENT WORK

Bishop (2000) found that the process of developing and assigning independent research projects must be one that is done with a consideration of developmental issues and an emphasis on authentic learning experiences. Teachers must design research projects so that the research process is fully understood by the students, with the steps of the process well articulated for incorporation into a project.

One idea that is highly important to product development for gifted learners is the state of mind of the developer. Heightened affect and motivation typically accompany the creative process, enabling an individual to rise above the mediocre in an area of development. Csikszentmihalyi (2000) studied creativity from the vantage point of adult creators who had made significant contributions to a field of study. He found these individuals to possess a high degree of intrinsic motivation, characterized by a mental state of "flow," which had the following characteristics:

- challenging but doable tasks,
- time and space to concentrate on those tasks,
- goal-oriented tasks with a feedback mechanism,
- high level of task involvement to the exclusion of everyday concerns (e.g., eating, sleeping),
- loss of self consciousness replaced by task orientation, and
- time passing unnoticed.

Such characteristics speak to the level and type of connection creative people have to their work, a model to be emulated in work with the gifted by providing the parameters of tasks to be accomplished, assessing the degree of challenge they possess, and providing a supportive context for carrying out the tasks that includes formative assessment approaches to the incipient product under development.

Ideas about authentic learning also are critical to consider in designing independent study options for the gifted learner. Newmann, Secada, and Wehlage (1995) found that the following key criteria must be satisfied if authentic learning is to occur:

- *Construction of knowledge*: the expression of knowledge in written or oral discourse.
- *Disciplined inquiry*: emphasizes cognitive processes (consists of: use of prior knowledge base, striving for in-depth understanding, and expressing conclusions through complex communication).
- *Value beyond school*: student accomplishment that has a value beyond being an indicator for success in school.

Educators of the gifted need to ensure that these features are satisfied in product development work in order to have students exhibit deep generative learning (Renzulli & Callahan, 2008).

Bishop (2000) also suggested the following practical approaches be taken to ensure the authenticity of the learning:

- Plan and work with school media specialists throughout the project.
- Discuss both the cognitive and affective aspects of the research project, using a research model.
- Use the phrase "exploring a problem" rather than "selecting a topic."
- Allow students to select their problem and product, but include some type of writing in the problem-formulation stage and/or the final product.
- Interact frequently with each student during the process.
- Include the students in the evaluation of the product and process.
- Remember that each student is unique. Learn and utilize as much information as you can about each student, including his or her interests, abilities, and learning styles.

TEACHING TO HIGHER LEVEL SKILLS AS PRELUDE TO PRODUCT DEVELOPMENT

To teach the higher order process skills of critical thinking and creativity to gifted learners is to engage them in lifelong learning skills that provide the scaffolding for all worthwhile generative product development in the future.

It is "teaching them to fish," not providing fish to be eaten for only a day. This constructivist approach to learning, however, requires similar approaches to be employed by the teacher, requiring long-term investment in learning new ways to think as well as teach. Because higher order thought and creativity are not formulaic, they require being open to the moment, asking the probing question at the right time, engaging the students in the right activity based on when they most need it, and assessing levels of functioning with regularity. Constructive teaching also requires teachers to provide students with useful models in order to have schema on which to hang their ideas. However, even useful models cannot be taught mechanistically; they must be thoughtfully applied and used idiosyncratically by gifted learners so that the greatest benefits accrue. Finally, teachers must help students understand that real thinking is hard work, that it takes effort over time to improve, and that the outcome is frequently uncertain. These skills also are best taught through project-based approaches that require students to generate a product, either individually or collectively. The models described next are those best done in small groups, with a group product being the end point of the learning.

Creative Problem Solving

Problem recognition and delineation as a critical element of the creative problem-solving process was first identified by Getzels and Csikszentmihalyi (1976) in their pioneering study of artists' approaches to the problem of depicting some aspects of human experiences. They found that creative artists who were able to sustain careers in art were more effective at problem-finding—not problem solving—than less successful fellow students. These findings spawned many models that provided a more balanced perspective between the two types of skills.

Problem solving formally may be described as a series of steps. Beyer (2000) set forth such a model in his broader taxonomy of thinking skills:

- Recognize a problem.
- Represent the problem.
- Deliver/choose a solution plan.
- Execute the plan.
- Evaluate the solution.

The formal steps may or may not characterize students' cognitive activity in a real problem situation. In a sense, they represent an ideal. The steps also define a convergent conception in that a single solution is envisioned, although the language of the model is open to alternative solutions from different problem solvers.

Another complex form of problem solving that involves both critical and creative thinking, widely applied in gifted programs and special extracurricular programs like Odyssey of the Mind and Future Problem Solving, is creative problem solving (CPS; Isaksen, Dorval, & Treffinger, 2000). Six steps or processes characterize the model:

1. mess finding,
2. data finding,
3. problem finding,
4. idea finding,
5. solution finding, and
6. acceptance finding.

The main characteristic of "mess finding" is to sort through a problem situation and find direction toward a broad goal or solution. In "data finding," participants sort through all available information about the mess and clarify the steps or direction to a solution. In "problem finding," a specific problem statement is formulated. "Idea finding" is a processing of many ideas for solution to the problem or parts of the problem. "Solution finding" is an evaluation or judgmental process of sorting among the ideas produced in the last step and selecting those most likely to produce solutions. Finally, in "acceptance finding," a plan is devised for implementing the best solution. An adaptation of the CPS model is called Future Problem Solving. It involves the application of the CPS model to studies of the future and to problems that are now emerging as major concerns (Volk, 2004).

Treffinger, Isaksen, and Dorval (2000) extended the creative problem solving model by suggesting that Stage One should include opportunities for participants to identify their own problem within a specific domain of interest or study. They also suggested that the solution finding stage should involve more than selecting best ideas; it should often involve synthesizing the best ideas into a more complex and creative solution.

Problem-Based Learning

Another model that promotes higher level problem solving in the service of product development in the form of problem resolution is problem-based learning (PBL), a curriculum and instructional model that is highly constructivist in design and execution. First used in the medical profession to better socialize doctors to patient real-world concerns, it is now selectively employed in educational settings at elementary and secondary levels with gifted learners (Boyce, VanTassel-Baska, Burruss, Sher, & Johnson, 1997; Gallagher, 2000; Gallagher, Stepien, Sher, & Workman, 1995). The technique involves several important features:

1. Students are in charge of their own learning. By working in small investigatory teams, they grapple with a real-world unstructured problem that they have a stake in and must solve within a short period of time.

Students become motivated to learn because they are in charge at every stage of the process.

2. The problem statement is ambiguous, incomplete, and yet appealing to students because of its real-world quality and the stakeholder role that they assume in it. For example, students may be given roles as scientists, engineers, politicians, or important project-based administrators whose job it is to deal with the problem expeditiously.

3. The role of the teacher is facilitative, not directive, aiding students primarily through asking questions and providing additional scaffolding of the problem with new information or resources needed. The teacher becomes a metacognitive coach, urging students through probing questions to deepen their inquiry.

4. The students complete a Need to Know Board early in their investigation that allows them to plan out how they will attack the problem, first by identifying what they already know from the problem statement, what they need to know, and how they will find it out. They then can prioritize what they need to know, make assignments, and set up timelines for the next phase of work. Such an emphasis on constructed metacognitive behavior is central to the learning benefits of the approach.

These features work together then in engaging the learner in important problems that matter in their world. Many times, problems are constructed around specific situations involving pollution of water or air, dangerous chemicals, spread of infectious disease, or energy source problems. Students learn that the real world is interdisciplinary in orientation, requiring the use of many different thinking skills and many different kinds of expertise in order to solve problems.

In order to work through a PBL episode, students must be able to analyze, synthesize, evaluate, and create—all higher level thinking tasks according to Anderson and Krathwohl (2000). The following problem and its levels of complex thinking is illustrative of a problem-based learning episode.

Problem: There is a lack of mass transit into and out of a central city. You are an urban planner, given one month to come up with a viable plan. However, your resources have been used on another project, that of city beautification. A new airport is about to be built 20 miles out from the city, but negotiations are stalled. What do you do?

Higher level skills needed to address the problem include:
- Analysis of what the real problem is—mass transit, airport construction, beautification?
- Synthesis of the aspects of the problem—is there a creative synthesis of each facet of the problems noted?

- Evaluation of alternative strategies to be employed—can I shift funds, can I employ a transportation expert, can I deal with the airport negotiations?
- Creation of the plan of action that will need to be sold to the city council.

The plan of action in this case becomes the product of the student work in small groups to address this real-world problem. The next step is for them to plan and execute a presentation to the city council. Problem-based learning then illustrates a model for group problem solving that interprets products as being both written and oral in nature, with group results fostered by individual contributions.

Combining Higher Level Thinking and Problem Solving

Teaching a combination of critical and creative thinking skills through relevant models (see Chapter 5 for Paul's [1992] Elements of Reasoning model) also can do double duty in respect to learning. It can promote strong content-based understanding at a deeper level as well as teach the skills of creativity and problem solving. Consider the following outcomes of learning as a result of students dealing with the options that President Truman faced in ending the war against Japan (see Figure 6.1). All of these outcomes are simultaneously achievable within a learning episode in which students engage directly with a real-world problem and take charge of the learning pace, style, and organization. Autonomy in learning takes center stage in this model that also fosters collaboration and shared responsibility.

Metacognition

Students also need to learn how to regulate specific learning behaviors and deliberately use executive processes in order for deeper learning to be achieved (Schunk, 2000). These behaviors are critical for long-term project work and research, thus serving as an important bridge to that section of the chapter. Metacognition refers to two types of knowledge: self-knowledge in respect to declarative, procedural, and conditional situations (Bereiter, 2002) and self-knowledge in respect to controlling how knowledge is used—the planning, monitoring, and assessing of the process in oneself (Beyer, 2000). Each aspect is a necessary way of conceptualizing the skills needed for gifted learners to become effective in their thinking and problem-solving activities.

Research suggests that metacognition is developmental, beginning early but continuing well into adulthood. It also appears to be more advanced in adults than children, and in gifted students than in typical students, especially in transferring the skills to new domains of activity. Metacognition is easier to teach to gifted learners as well and they appear to benefit more from being

After resolving the problem of "Ending the War Against Japan," the student will:

History
- Understand the range of choices facing President Truman and the Interim Committee related to a strategy for ending the war with Japan.
- Develop a recommendation for ending the war with Japan that is defensible given the war goals of the U.S. in 1945, the military and diplomatic events between 1941 and 1945, and the evolution of the relationship between the U.S. and Soviet Union up to 1945.
- Explain why President Truman decided to use the atomic bomb in preference to other options open to him in concluding the war with Japan.

Ethics
- Make an ethically defensible recommendation regarding the use of the atomic bomb to help end the war with Japan that recognizes the conflicting ethical appeals present in the possible options to end the war.

Critical Thinking
- Select a point of view to argue regarding the use of the atomic bomb.
- Write an essay that outlines the implications and consequences for the U.S. based on the outcomes of the war with Japan.
- Explain different stakeholders' assumptions about war.

Problem Solving
- Use the concept of "problem space" as a tool in defining a problem.
- Recognize the gap between the "real" and "ideal" as the area in which problem resolution takes place.
- Enlarge his database in preparation for forming decision options.
- Generate a resolution for the problem of ending the war in the Pacific that is defensible within the context provided by the events of 1945 and ethically acceptable.
- Refine his personal problem-solving strategy to make his skills more effective, efficient, and humane through self-evaluation.

Creativity
- Apply fluency, flexibility, and elaboration skills to his problem-solving behaviors.
- Generate original solutions to the problem.
- Display positive attitudes for a creative climate.

Figure 6.1. Outcomes for "Ending the War Against Japan."

taught the strategies than other learners. Gifted learners work harder at learning the strategies and appear to be more motivated than nongifted students. Perhaps this is due to a larger information base that they have that supports metacognitive regulation strategies, because we know that metacognition improves with more knowledge in a domain (Sternberg, 2001).

The findings from the research literature on metacognition strongly suggest the value of direct instruction, collaborative learning across age levels, and reflection techniques such as journaling, discussion, and introspection (Schraw & Graham, 1997). Several models of teaching also are useful in promoting these skills in project-based contexts. Two of them are cited here as examples of group approaches to problem solving that require both cognitive and meta-cognitive skills.

One approach is synectics, originally developed by Gordon (1961) and used in gifted programs with even young children (Meador, 1994) to exploit putting two dissimilar ideas together to force-fit a new solution to a problem. Students must work together to solve a common problem in their environment by using metaphor and analogy as a central part of the process. In groups of three to five, they discuss and collaborate on answering questions about their problem, as in the following example:

Problem: Reduce noise in the school cafeteria
- Direct: How is noise muffled in nature?
- Personal: How would you like to be captured if you were noise?
- Symbol: How could noise be represented in the problem?
- Fantasy: How could you create an ideal eating place?

Another model that has been used frequently to foster creative thinking for purposes of product development is the Six Hats (De Bono, 1985). In this model, students take on various perspectives about a problem or issue and then move toward a solution. Each student in a group of six wears a different hat to reflect the role to be undertaken. The following colors reflect the particular orientation to be taken to a problem:
- White: Research orientation
- Green: Creative ideas to address the project
- Yellow: Feasible approaches
- Black: Downside considerations
- Red: Gut reactions/hunches
- Blue: Recap/status/synopsis

This technique can be applied to problems as diverse as the economic stimulus package, to the need to expand energy sources, to conservation strategies. It also can be applied to issues like controlling technology, cloning, and abortion rights.

DESIGNING TASK DEMANDS
FOR MEETING STANDARDS

Beyond the use of models for designing projects, teachers also can generate good domain-specific projects by using the content standards they are teaching to anyway. Two examples follow, based on high school standards in English and physics, respectively. Each product demand has been carefully delineated in respect to expectations and linked to relevant rubric dimensions.

Subject: Language Arts

Curricular outcomes: Use language and visual images for persuasion.

Product task demand: Design an advertisement for a company product that will target a given audience through a given publication outlet. Select the product, audience, and publication outlet from the following choices or create your own. Explain the process of design and the choices you made in creating the ad.

Company products: a new hand lotion, a new car, a redesigned cereal, or one of your choice

Audience profiles: teenagers, young professionals, or people over 50

Publication types: popular magazine, news magazine, *The Strait Times*, or one of your choice.

Rubric dimensions to be placed on a 1–3 scale, with 3 being high:
- Product emphases for persuasion
- Creativity and innovativeness
- Effectiveness of the product based on audience and publication outlet
- Soundness of design processes employed

Subject: Physics

Curricular outcomes: Solve new problems using principles of motion.

Product task demand: You are approaching an intersection where the light has turned amber. You need to decide whether to stop or go through the light. What should you do? Analyze the duration of the yellow light at a given location, minimum speed necessary to go through the light safely, and distance to be traversed. Explain the assumptions you made to solve the problem; outline the steps taken, including measurements; and present your solution using graphical representations.

Rubric dimensions to be placed on a 1–5 scale, 5 being high:
- Validity of the assumptions
- Processes used to solve the problem
- Clarity of the representation to solve the problem
- Explanation of the solution

USING EMBEDDED RESEARCH PROJECTS

Many research-based curriculum materials for the gifted will have designed into the materials a research project that relates to the study of a particular book, period of time, or other cultural idea. The *Navigator* series, developed by William and Mary staff and graduate students, also provide specific research projects as a part of the differentiated task demands. Two examples follow that illustrate the embedded nature of the projects and the short-term product development period.

Snow Treasure: Research the German invasion of Norway during World War II. Find out how different Norwegians reacted to the situation—some worked to resist the Germans, while others worked with the Germans instead. Think about the decision that Norwegians had to make and write a persuasive essay that takes one point of view or the other.

Tuck Everlasting: Recently in the news there has been a lot of coverage of ways in which science might be able to alter the life cycle through cryogenics, genetic re-mapping, cloning, or other methods. Develop a researchable question related to this issue.

The following examples of research projects come from the William and Mary language arts units. Each project is fully described in the unit, with a project rubric for judging the quality of the resulting product.

- *Beyond Words*: changes in language (Center for Gifted Education, 2010b)
- *Journeys and Destinations*: point of view on the best way to preserve memories (Center for Gifted Education, 2010c)
- *Autobiographies*: writing one's own autobiography as a talent development model (Center for Gifted Education, 2010a)
- *Utopia*: impact of the quest for utopia throughout history (Center for Gifted Education, 2010d)

AUTHENTIC AREAS OF INTEREST TO STUDENTS

Many times, students cast around for research ideas when their interests for areas to study may be found in their lives in school, making them highly relevant to enhanced learning and convertible to issues that can be debated. Ideas for such projects that may be relevant to students at elementary and middle school levels follow. Each of these could be done individually or in a small group, self-selected or negotiated with the teacher, and developed in order to provide the structure necessary for product completion and assessment.

- School uniforms for students
- Use of instructional time
- Provision of fine arts classes in school program
- Recess time and its use

- Fitness and fighting obesity issues for students
- School lunches and nutrition issues
- How days missed due to inclement weather should be made up
- Provision of seatbelts on school buses
- Marketing of products to children through commercials

The William and Mary Research Model that follows provides opportunities for students to explore any of the projects listed or research issues presented in individual units of study in the William and Mary series. It differs from traditional research models in several respects. One, it is organized by questions to deliberately engage learners in the inquiry process from the beginning of their independent study. Two, it focuses equal attention on all aspects of the research process, including the synthesizing of data from multiple sources and the manipulation of that data into charts and graphs, two areas of the research process often overlooked in models. Three, it requires that learners communicate findings to multiple audiences in both oral and written formats, a facet of real-world research. Finally, the model challenges the learner within each stage of the process to think about what she is doing, a metacognitive tool to enhance the overall work.

This research model is used throughout the William and Mary units to encourage the use of inquiry as a tool for learning in the form of questions to guide student thinking about the nature of the research they are to undertake; as a heuristic to guide research study in any area of learning, with the questions at Step 3 to be reorganized, given the type of study to be undertaken (e.g., observational, descriptive, experimental, or qualitative); and as a tool for focusing more sharply on one aspect of the research process that students need more support for accomplishing.

INDEPENDENT PROJECT ISSUES AND CONCERNS

There are many good reasons we want to expose gifted learners early to independent study work. The process has several strengths that deserve commentary. First, if it is done well, with consideration for student challenge and capability, it offers a comfortable and flexible form of learning for many gifted students, especially those who are creative and are easily stifled under more rigidly imposed forms of learning. Second, there is little argument that it builds self-reliance and individual resourcefulness in the learning process, making gifted learners responsible for both what they learn and how they learn it with multiple pathways to the learning act. Third, independent study thrusts teachers into a supportive role as resources to students in their learning rather

THE WILLIAM AND MARY
RESEARCH MODEL

Step 1: Identify your issue or problem.
- What is the issue or problem?
- Who are the stakeholders and what are their positions?
- What is my position on this issue?

Step 2: Read about your issue and identify points of view or arguments through information sources.
- What are my print sources?
- What are my media sources?
- What are my people sources?
- What primary and secondary source documents might I use?
- What are my preliminary findings based on a review of existing sources?

Step 3: Form a set of questions that can be answered by a specific set of data.
- What would be the results of _____?
- Who would benefit and by how much?
- Who would be harmed and by how much?
- My research questions:

Step 4: Gather evidence through research techniques such as surveys, interviews, or analysis of primary and secondary source documents.
- What survey questions should I ask?
- What interview questions should I ask?
- What generalizations do secondary sources give?
- What data and evidence can I find in primary sources to support different sides of the issue?

Step 5: Manipulate and transform data so that they can be interpreted.
- How can I summarize what I found out?
- Should I develop charts, diagrams, or graphs to represent my data?

Step 6: Draw conclusions and make inferences.
- What do the data mean? How can I interpret what I found out?
- How do the data support my original point of view?
- How do they support other points of view?
- What conclusions can I make about the issue?

Step 7: Determine implications and consequences.
- What are the consequences of following the point of view that I support?
- Do I know enough or are there now new questions to be answered?

Step 8: Communicate your findings. (Prepare an oral presentation for classmates based on note cards and a written report.)
- What are my purpose, issue, and point of view, and how will I explain them?
- What data will I use to support my point of view?
- How will I conclude my presentation?

than direct purveyors of that learning. They assume the role of consultant and sometimes manager of the learning process to assure that necessary skills are mastered and content explored. It also puts them in a position of monitoring individual skill needs as they occur, rather than assuming that students have or do not have the necessary understandings for application.

However, there are some limitations to the process as well. Any instructional process that is overused is likely to decrease motivation, interest, and ultimately performance—even among the gifted. Thus, using independent project work judiciously in respect to frequency and the nature of the project required is wise. At the middle school level, for example, to have one major project each quarter across subject areas would seem prudent, rather than multiple ones in each subject area that take both instructional and homework time. A second problem may arise with how open-ended the projects undertaken are. If too much divergence is allowed in respect to expectations, students may not be learning what the standards call for or may be off track on outcomes entirely, merely going through the motions without sufficient substance to the resulting product. Sharing criteria for what makes a type of product worthwhile can help but still may not solve the problem entirely if students are not focused on the audience and the profession within which their product is to be developed. Lastly, gifted students often suffer from procrastination and other self-discipline problems associated with long-term individual work assignments. Consequently, even though they have the ability to complete such project work, they often do not or turn in an inferior product. This problem has been well-documented in the Texas Product Development Project, conducted in the early part of this decade to establish assessment protocols for products developed in gifted programs. Many teachers consistently reported lower level products than what was expected, given the students' level of ability. Although some of the blame may be on the initial project specification design, student reaction to the process also is at work.

So what may be a remedy to these and other concerns with project-based work with the gifted? One approach may be to provide more direct instruction on the processes necessary to conduct meaningful individual project work (i.e., independent study). Areas in which students often require some degree of direct instruction to be successful with independent study (Boyce, 1997) include using information strategies to research an issue or problem, researching an issue of significance, using reasoning skills during the research process, and using metacognition for independent and interdependent learning. These skills can be taught to individual and small groups of learners, as well as to whole classes, in order to raise the competency level in conducting research independently.

Another approach is to have teachers evaluate common problems that others have encountered with assigning independent projects. Our work at William and Mary with school districts nationally has suggested several that teachers may want to weigh carefully in organizing such work. The following issues should be considered in order to maximize the benefits to students in undertaking the processes and products of independent project work.

Independent Versus Group Work

If students are experiencing difficulties with independent study, one might try a small-group project as an interim measure that is well-monitored by the teacher to assess areas of difficulty and how weaknesses may be addressed by a partner. Dyads may work well for this approach, as would shorter term projects. Each approach offers greater support for individual students and abbreviates the process so that learning can occur and be assessed expeditiously.

Self-Selected or Mutually Negotiated Projects

Sometimes gifted students overestimate or underestimate their own abilities, especially when it comes to independent work. Thus, it may be prudent to guide the student in deciding the nature of the project to be undertaken and the degree to which it constitutes something sufficiently challenging but not beyond her grasp. Conferencing with students on these issues is one way to ensure that communication about projects is ongoing and open.

Targeted to a Given Subject Area or Interdisciplinary

Most projects by their very nature are interdisciplinary, especially if they are conducted on a real-world problem or issue. However, sometimes it is useful to bound the nature of the project in such a way that the learning accrued is more tightly focused. For example, in a science investigation where the teacher is concerned about students' learning to interpret data correctly, the project may highlight this aspect of the investigation process over others and keep the connections to other aspects of learning diminished.

Topical or Issue/Problem-Oriented

Teachers also have choices in respect to the subject matter that students may study in an independent learning model. Topics are endless but also more flat in respect to what students may learn about them; they are especially susceptible to Internet source learning where secondary sources become the basis for understanding. Issue-based and problem-based research, on the other hand, involve students in actively seeking information from multiple sources and collecting their own. For the promotion of greater motivation in learning, using real-world issues, themes, and problems may be a superior organizational tool. However, teachers will need to provide examples for students of how to convert topics of interest to issues. A few examples follow:

Topic: Animal habitats
Issue: How do animal habitats contribute to or impede extinction?

Topic: The Iraq War
Issue: What were the aspects of the Iraq situation that may have justified our involvement? How has the situation changed to support our decision to withdraw?

Topic: Literature of the 1980s
Issue: How did selected writers of the 1980s capture the spirit of the decade and its major events?

Completed During School Time or Worked on as Homework

Project work has a way of taking on a life of its own unless it is carefully bounded by deadlines and design specifications that students can handle. It is dubious that more than half of the time to complete a project should be done during school instructional time, as much of the work can best be conducted alone without classroom distractions and requires construction time that cannot be completed within a limited time frame. Project work should be done outside of class time predominantly, as serious study requires a different context. Class time should be used to learn a set of skills needed to complete the project, to get questions answered, to seek help in finding resources, and to receive feedback on progress to date.

CONCLUSION

Project work for gifted learners is a necessary staple of their differentiated curriculum design. In fact, it is an essential element of all learning that is meaningful to students over time. We remember what we do and experience, not what we are told. We apply concepts that matter in the real world over and over, not those that are bounded by exercises in books. We learn information that is important for solving problems, not information that is random. We are motivated to learn by our curiosity about how the world works, not by being given the blueprint for figuring it out. Generative product development elevates learning to an adult level in the sense that it requires students to "figure it out" for themselves, in groups or individually. No better learning environment could be devised than one in which gifted learners are consistently challenged to reach new levels of understanding about their world.

KEY POINTS SUMMARY

- The application of authentic learning principles is of paramount consideration in designing product demands for gifted learners.
- Worthwhile product development for the gifted requires a recognition that students cannot be left on their own to produce; rather, they require support in skill development and content knowledge within relevant domains.
- Assignment of worthwhile projects that maximize student learning is key to the continued development of students' critical and creative higher level thinking abilities.
- Fostering the development of quality student products is an iterative process that requires careful structuring of the task demand and supportive feedback regarding students' progress toward standards of excellence.
- Models that can scaffold collaborative work on real-world problems provide a pathway for group product development that can transfer to individual work.
- Products designed for gifted students involve specific task demands linked to rubric dimensions for consideration in assessment at the front end of the process. Exemplars of sample products in the domain also are useful in helping students understand expectations.

REFERENCES

Amabile, T. M., Barsade, S. G., Mueller, J. S., & Staw, B. M. (2005). Affect and creativity at work. *Administrative Science Quarterly, 50,* 367–403.

Anderson, L. W., & Krathwohl, D. R. (Eds.). (2000). *A taxonomy for learning, teaching, and assessing: A revision of Bloom's taxonomy of educational objectives.* Boston, MA: Allyn & Bacon.

Bereiter, C. (2002). *Education and mind in the knowledge age.* New York, NY: Lawrence Erlbaum.

Beyer, B. K. (2000). *Improving student thinking: A comprehensive approach.* Boston, MA: Allyn & Bacon.

Bishop, K. (2000). The research process of gifted students: A case study. *Gifted Child Quarterly, 44,* 54–64.

Boyce, L. N. (1997). *A guide to teaching research skills and strategies for grades 4–12.* Williamsburg, VA: The College of William and Mary, Center for Gifted Education.

Boyce, L. N., VanTassel-Baska, J., Burruss, J., Sher, B. T., & Johnson, D. T. (1997). A problem-based curriculum: Parallel learning opportunities for students and teachers. *Journal for the Education of the Gifted, 20,* 363–379.

Center for Gifted Education. (2010a). *Autobiographies* (2nd ed.). Dubuque, IA: Kendall/Hunt.

Center for Gifted Education. (2010b). *Beyond words* (2nd ed.). Dubuque, IA: Kendall/Hunt.

Center for Gifted Education. (2010c). *Journeys and destinations* (2nd ed.). Dubuque, IA: Kendall/Hunt.

Center for Gifted Education. (2010d). *Utopia* (2nd ed.). Dubuque, IA: Kendall/Hunt.

Csikszentmihalyi, M. (2000). *Beyond boredom and anxiety: Experiencing flow in work and play.* San Francisco, CA: Jossey-Bass.

De Bono, E. (1985). *Six thinking hats.* Boston, MA: Little, Brown.

Ericsson, K. A. (2007). Deliberate practice and the modifiability of body and mind: Toward a science of the structure and acquisition of expert and elite performance. *International Journal of Sport Psychology, 38,* 4–34.

Gallagher, J. J. (2000). Teaching for understanding and application of science knowledge. *School Science and Mathematics, 100,* 310–318.

Gallagher, S., Stepien, W., Sher, B., & Workman, D. (1995). Implementing problem-based learning in science classrooms. *School Science and Mathematics, 95,* 136–146.

Getzels, J., & Csikszentmihalyi, M. (1976). *The creative vision: A longitudinal study of problem finding in art.* New York, NY: Wiley.

Gordon, W. J. J. (1961). *Synectics: The development of creative capacity.* New York, NY: Harper and Row.

Isaksen, S. G., Dorval, K. B., & Treffinger, D. J. (2000). *Creative approaches to problem solving: A framework for change* (2nd ed.). Dubuque, IA: Kendall/Hunt.

Meador, K. S. (1994). The effect of synectics training on gifted and nongifted kindergarten students. *Journal for the Education of the Gifted, 18,* 55–73.

Newmann, F. N., Secada, W. G., & Wehlage, G. G. (1995). *A guide to authentic instruction and assessment: Vision, standards, and scoring.* Madison, WI: Wisconsin Center for Education Research.

Paul, R. (1992). *Critical thinking: What every person needs to survive in a rapidly changing world.* Rohnert Park, CA: Foundation for Critical Thinking.

Renzulli, J. S., & Callahan, C. M. (2008). Product assessment. In J. VanTassel-Baska (Ed.), *Alternative assessment with gifted learners* (pp. 259–283). Waco, TX: Prufrock Press.

Schraw, G., & Graham, T. (1997). Helping gifted students develop metacognitive awareness. *Roeper Review, 20,* 4–8.

Schunk, D. H. (2000). Motivation for achievement: Past, present, and future. *Issues in Education: Contributions From Educational Psychology, 6*, 161–165.

Simonton, D. K. (2006). Scientific status of disciplines, individuals, and ideas: Empirical analyses of the potential impact of theory. *Review of General Psychology, 10*, 98–112.

Sternberg, R. J. (2001). *Complex cognition: The psychology of human thought.* Oxford, England: Oxford University Press.

Treffinger, D. J., Isaksen, S. G., & Dorval, K. B. (2000). *Creative problem solving: An introduction.* Waco, TX: Prufrock Press.

Volk, V. (2004). *Confidence building and problem solving skills: An investigation into the impact of the Future Problem Solving Program on secondary school students' sense of self-efficacy in problem solving, in research, in teamwork, and in coping with the future.* Sydney, Australia: University of New South Wales.

Chapter 7

Concept Development and Learning

Linda D. Avery and Catherine A. Little

*The Constitutional Convention. Converting fractions to deci-
mals. The solar system.* Maniac Magee, Bridge to Terabithia,
A Wrinkle in Time. *The discrete stimuli and content elements
that fill your plan book have begun to seem alarmingly disconnected, and you recognize from their behavior that your students
are learning information for tests and promptly forgetting it. You
are searching for ways to provide a curriculum that connects—not
only across subject areas or segments of the school year, but also to
students' lives and experiences in ways that will help them more
readily retain what they learn in school. Plus, you are searching for
ways to deepen your curriculum so that it becomes more engaging
and more challenging for your gifted students. What can you do?*

In the middle of the last century, scholars gathered
together the texts that made up the Western world's traditional literary canon into a collection they titled *The Great
Ideas: A Syntopicon of Great Books of the Western World* (Adler,
1952). Within this collection, the editor presented a list of

central concepts fundamental to the literature and, indeed, to the history of the Western world. A review of these concepts today, even in a more global and diversity-conscious society, demonstrates that many or most of the ideas can be generalized beyond *The Great Ideas* to fit the human condition, although their definitions and specific structures may vary from culture to culture and time to time. Among these common concepts are *family, authority, faith, love, change, causality, truth,* and *wisdom.*

The concepts fundamental to the human condition also are fundamental to human learning—to our understanding of the world around us and within us. Consequently, such ideas can and should be fundamental to the educational process. The Integrated Curriculum Model (ICM; VanTassel-Baska, 1986, 1995; VanTassel-Baska & Wood, 2009), outlined in Chapter 2 and discussed throughout this book, places concept learning as one of its three primary dimensions, with the recognition that concept learning is crucial to the understanding of any discipline and the relationships among disciplines.

This chapter will focus on the use of concepts in curriculum development and in instruction. After discussing further the rationale for concept-based curriculum and instruction, the chapter introduces a specific model for concept development that provides a point of entry to concept study in any discipline. The chapter then explores various ways of embedding concept study within the curriculum. As with other chapters throughout the book, the emphasis here is on how to use concepts as a basis for differentiating curricula for gifted students, even as they are used as a foundation for strong curricula in general.

THE IMPORTANCE OF CONCEPT LEARNING

Many architects of curricula for the gifted have recognized the importance of concepts as central to the organization and content of units of instruction. In one of his principles of differential education, Ward (1961) advocated that "the content of the curriculum should be organized in a manner which reduces to generic areas the concepts undertaken for instruction" (p. 148). Feldhusen (1988) described an ideal program for the gifted as one that "involves them in ideational challenges and activity as a vehicle to learn subject matter and as stimulus for their cognitive development" (p. 119). Perkins (1993) recommended an education organized around "generative knowledge," which is "a powerful conceptual system that yields insight and implications in many circumstances" (p. 91). VanTassel-Baska (1995), as noted previously, identified concept learning as one of the three key dimensions of her ICM. Moreover, she emphasized that learning fewer concepts in greater depth is advisable over trying to address too many concepts at a surface level. This reflects the position of the American Association for the Advancement of Science (AAAS, 1990), which identified six central concepts for science learning across K–12 education (see Chapter 10 for further discussion).

Concepts are, by definition, abstractions, and they require higher levels of thought to absorb, understand, and extend. Concept learning is fundamental to knowledge acquisition in every discipline and in everyday living, and our comprehension of abstract ideas affects our behavior from kindergarten to the corporation, in the classroom and in the community. We cannot function effectively in society without understanding concepts such as *justice, authority, responsibility,* and *honor.* Concepts such as *change, systems,* and *patterns* may first be introduced in the elementary curriculum, but students will continue to study them in various disciplines through advanced graduate work. Fullan (e.g., 1991, 1993, 2010) has made his reputation in the field of education by synthesizing the research on change in relation to school systems, while graduate programs in educational leadership have incorporated a systems perspective in conceptualizing the function of administration. The investigation of patterns of behavior and occurrence is a central direction for research across many of the social and physical sciences.

Our knowledge of concepts of such breadth is always evolving and paradigmatic, requiring that we revisit ideas over and over to understand them fully. Concept learning also is instrumental in facilitating reasoning processes. We use concept learning to negotiate the application of deductive and inductive thinking. Inferring from the specific to the general or deducing from the general to the specific involves understanding the nature of generalities, and generalities are conceptual understandings. Analogical reasoning and problem-solving tasks also relate closely to concept learning. For example, several studies demonstrated the power of analogical reasoning in building from a familiar to an unfamiliar example of a concept through a popular analogy problem linking the destruction of a tumor surrounded by healthy tissue to the destruction of a fortified city (Gick & Holyoak, 1980, 1983, as cited in Goswami, 1991). Bryce and MacMillan (2005) found that using bridging analogies in teaching physics to teens improved conceptual understanding.

VanTassel-Baska (1998) noted that concepts and themes provide "important pathways between the disciplines so that separate aspects of knowledge are understood as being integrated" (p. 347). Schack (1994) recognized the power of concepts to draw students and teachers alike more deeply into material, provoking curiosity and inquiry. Wiggins and McTighe (1998) recommended that curriculum focus around ideas, topics, or processes that (a) represent a "big idea" with enduring value beyond the classroom, (b) reside at the heart of the discipline, (c) require uncoverage, and (d) offer potential for engaging students. Because concepts are truly relevant to our lives, our ability to identify and connect with them infuses them with vitality and dynamism. Thus, concepts not only link disciplines together, they also link the learner to the content.

Research on how people learn has emphasized the connection between concept learning and metacognition (National Research Council, 2000). We know that learners construct new understandings based on their current knowledge, and in order for teachers to assess fault-lines or misconceptions in this preconceived base, they must "make students' thinking visible and find ways to help them reconceptualize" erroneous understandings (National Research Council, 2000, p. 71). Coll, France, and Taylor (2005) reported on the role of models and analogies in science education and suggested that in order for students to develop conceptual understandings accurately and comprehensively, they need to be able to reflect on and discuss these understandings as they are in the process of developing them. Barton and Levstik (2004) emphasized the importance of encouraging students to express their understanding of key ideas in history, highlighting several types of misconceptions likely to develop unnoticed by teachers unless students were given opportunities to share their understanding in their own words.

Erickson (2007) stated that "there will not be a significant improvement in education until teachers understand the importance of concepts and conceptual understanding to intellectual development, deeper understanding, and motivation for learning" (p. 78). She further noted that teachers who fail to structure the curriculum around concepts and essential understandings tend to differentiate by varying the quantity and not the quality of expectations for student work. This chapter can help teachers learn to avoid this pitfall as they design and implement educationally relevant and challenging curricula.

WHAT IS A CONCEPT?

Concepts are mental representations of objects, events, or other entities (Jonassen, 2006). One of the difficulties inherent in defining *concept* is that the term itself names a concept. Language (also a concept) relies on common understandings of concept labels and of the defining characteristics that group objects or ideas under these labels. Ehrenberg (1981) described some of the key features of concepts. First, all concepts are abstract, because a concept "constitutes a generalized mental image of the characteristics that make items examples" (p. 37). Concept labels are terms that are used to describe any and all examples of a concept. For instance, the label *fruit* refers to the characteristic part of a plant that contains the seeds. In fact, the concepts (or sets of attributes or characteristics) are used interchangeably with the labels.

Although concepts themselves are abstract, the individual characteristics that define an item as belonging to the concept may be concrete, abstract, or a combination of both. For example, the characteristics that designate an apple as a fruit are more concrete than the characteristics that define an action as just or moral. When we speak of concept learning in curriculum development, especially with regard to interdisciplinary concepts that can serve as central organizers for curriculum, we are generally referring to those concepts with characteristics that are more abstract in nature—the "big ideas" discussed earlier in this chapter.

A second feature of concepts is that they cannot be verified, like facts, as being "right" or "wrong." Their meaning is socially constructed. This means that our understanding of concepts must be dynamic. Ehrenberg (1981) used the concept of family to illustrate this point, exploring changing definitions of the term across time and place to encompass nuclear, extended, blended, and other forms of the family.

Beyond this recognition of the dynamic social construction of concepts, it also is important to recognize that individual understanding of concepts is a constructive process. Learning involves the establishment of conceptual understandings based on experiences of the world. A child's initial conception of *dog* may be related to the characteristics of his or her own pet until experiences with other dogs, in person or through books and pictures, help to broaden and solidify the concept in the child's mind. Similarly, experiences with literature, history, and real-world interactions can broaden a child's conceptions of truth, change, patterns, and wisdom. Moreover, discussions of the varying individual and social constructions of specific concepts over time, as expressed through behaviors and writings of individuals and groups across time periods and cultures, can bring to consciousness the reasoning processes that underlie concept construction.

Ehrenberg's (1981) third key point about concepts is the idea that concepts are hierarchical: "some classes include other classes" (p. 39). The example of fruit as a concept was given above; apple is a concept within the larger concept of fruit, but fruit also is a component of the larger concept of plant, which falls under the class of living things. When teachers encourage students to recognize classes of concepts, they support students in reasoning about connections within and between classes, as well as the features that distinguish one class from another. Careful consideration of conceptual hierarchies also ensures that central concepts selected for curricula are sufficiently broad to encourage such deep reasoning and opportunities for comparison and contrast. Several broad concepts useful in curriculum development are illustrated in Table 7.1. These concepts, because of their universality and relevance to specific disciplines, can form the centerpiece of a curriculum that encourages students to explore and deepen their understanding by analyzing instances of the concept in discipline-relevant materials and questions.

In addition to the hierarchical nature of concepts, two distinct types of core concepts are identified in the literature on science and mathematics instruction and should be handled simultaneously (National Research Council, 2005). The first type is concepts about the nature of the discipline itself (what it means to

TABLE 7.1

Sample Concepts Useful in Curriculum Development

Change	Life and death	Scale
Constancy	Models	Signs and symbols
Evolution	Origins	Systems
Family	Patterns	Time
Good and evil	Patterns of change	Truth
Knowledge	Power	Wisdom

engage in doing mathematics and science, including concepts such as proof, skepticism, and control). The second type is concepts that are central to the understanding of the subject matter (such as function and gravity).

The Center for Gifted Education at The College of William and Mary has developed several series of curricular units that are organized around key concepts. Each set of units, all of which are organized around the ICM, explores one or more central concepts within the specific discipline addressed and promotes understanding of interdisciplinary connections. The language arts curriculum focuses on the concept of *change*, with the various units delving into some of the nuances of change, such as cyclical change and social versus individual change (Center for Gifted Education, 1999; also see chapter 8 in this volume). The first set of science units (Center for Gifted Education, 1997b) focuses on the concept of *systems*, and a more recent series uses both *systems* and *change* as key concepts (VanTassel-Baska, Bracken, Stambaugh, & Feng, 2007; also see Chapter 10). Some units in the center's social studies curriculum are organized around the concept of *systems*, while others focus on such concepts as *cause and effect*, *authority*, and *perspective* (see Chapter 11 in this volume).

The development of each of these concepts into foundations for a curriculum involved the development of examples and generalizations, to be discussed below, and also a review of the concepts as they applied to various disciplines. Such a review of previous theory and treatment of the concept assists the curriculum developer in ensuring that the treatment of the concept within the curriculum reflects the principles and practices of the related content disciplines. In the Center for Gifted Education's curriculum development projects, several concept papers have been written to demonstrate these connections as a support to the curriculum developers and to teachers wishing to implement the curriculum successfully (Boyce, 1992; Pence, 1999; Sher, 1991). Concept papers at this level of detail certainly are useful to the curriculum developer; however, more abbreviated concept maps can be developed to support smaller curricular efforts from the practitioner.

SUPPORTING STUDENT CONCEPT DEVELOPMENT

Concepts, as discussed above, underscore all human thought and communication, and individuals develop conceptual understandings as a part of the natural learning process (Ehrenberg, 1981). Nevertheless, a more structured process of concept development also can be guided and supported by a teacher's intervention. Teachers can provide excellent contexts in which students may undergo a process of concept development that is well organized and leads step-by-step to deeper understandings. The concept development model to be explained here is based on the work of Taba (1962), a major theorist in the area of curriculum development. The process is a constructivist one that asks students to take what they already know about a concept, organize and reflect upon it, develop generalizations, and then apply those generalizations back to previous knowledge. The role of the teacher is to help students arrive at these generalizations on their own by scaffolding a sequence of steps and providing guiding questions as needed to facilitate the process. This scaffolding strategy is embedded in most of the Center for Gifted Education's units. "The Concept of Change" lesson (Center for Gifted Education, 1998a), which follows on the next two pages, illustrates how students move through the stages of the concept development model to arrive at generalizations about change.

Change is used as the central organizer in the Center for Gifted Education's series of language arts units (Center for Gifted Education, 1999). In these units, students progress through the stages of this activity in an early lesson, at the conclusion of which they are presented with a list of the following generalizations about the concept:

- Change is everywhere.
- Change is linked to time.
- Change may be positive or negative.
- Change may happen naturally or be caused by people.
- Change may be perceived as orderly or random.

These generalizations were developed based on a review of literature in various disciplines about change, with central ideas organized into these five statements accessible to student understanding from early school years. Such a prepared list of generalizations is useful to the curriculum developer in organizing lessons to address the concept comprehensively; in an instructional context, however, students' own generalizations should be aligned with this list and validated through discussion and activities throughout a related unit. For example, if students develop the generalization "Change may happen fast or slow," teachers may wish to use this language in further discussions throughout the unit along with or in place of "Change is linked to time." Similarly, if students generalize

SAMPLE LESSON
THE CONCEPT OF CHANGE

Instructional Purpose:
- To develop understanding of the concept of change.

Activities and Questions:
1. Divide students into groups of four or five. Give each group several large sheets of paper for recording ideas. Each section of the activity that follows should incorporate small-group work followed by whole-class debriefing.

2. Have students generate examples of the concept of change that are derived from their own understanding and experiences with changes in the world. Encourage students to try to provide at least 25 examples.

Guiding questions:
- What words come to mind when you think about change?
- What kinds of things change? What are some specific examples of things that change?
- What is it about those things that changes?
- How do you know when something has changed?
- What evidence can you examine to decide whether change has occurred?

3. Once an adequate number of examples has been generated, have students group examples together into categories. This process allows students to search for interrelatedness and to organize materials. Students should be able to explain their reasoning for their categories and seek clarification from each other in a whole-class discussion. Teachers should ensure that students have accounted for all of their examples of change through the categories they established.

Guiding questions:
- How might you categorize your examples of change into groups?
- What could you call each group? Why?
- What steps do you need to take to be sure that all of your changes fall into groups?
- Might some of your changes belong in more than one group?
- What is another way you might choose to group your examples? What other categories might you use?
- What are some general characteristics of change you can now identify, based on the work you have done so far?

4. Next, ask students to think of nonexamples of the concept of change. Begin the brainstorming process with the instruction, "Now list examples of things that do not change." Encourage students to think carefully about nonexamples and discuss ideas within their groups. Each group should strive to list six to eight nonexamples.

Guiding questions:
- What are some things that do not change?
- What are some things that always seem the same or always happen the same way?
- What evidence or proof do you have that these things do not change?
- How might you group the nonexamples?
- What can you call each of these groups?
- How are the groups of things that do not change similar to or different from the groups of things that do change?
- Think about the following ideas and whether they show change: routines or habits, rules and regulations, table manners, laws, customs of cultures, seasonal cycles. Explain your answers. If these ideas show change, where would they fit in your categories of change? If they do not, where would they fit with your categories of things that do not change?

5. Have students work to determine generalizations about the concept of change. Encourage them to use their lists of examples, categories, and nonexamples to help them. Then, present a list of prepared generalizations developed from a review of literature sources related to the concept and essential for the discipline under study. Through discussion, align student generalizations with the prepared generalizations and post both sets for use throughout the unit of study.

Guiding questions:
- A generalization is a descriptive statement that explains something that is always or almost always true about a concept. What generalizations can you make about change?
- Use your examples and categories to guide your thinking and write several statements that are generalizations about change.

Note. Adapted from *Autobiographies* (pp. 37–38), by the Center for Gifted Education, 1998, Dubuque, IA: Kendall/Hunt. Copyright 1998 by the Center for Gifted Education.

that "Change may be predictable or unpredictable" from their discussion, teachers should invite students to consider the ways in which this statement relates to the generalization, "Change may be perceived as orderly or random," and the ways in which it is different. Then, throughout further work in the related unit, students' own generalizations may be applied, along with the original unit set.

Curriculum developers also may want to add essential questions within a unit as a further tool for stimulating student thinking about the concept. Some essential questions linked to the generalizations about *change* might be as follows:

- How has the idea of change evolved differently in different cultures and time periods?
- Why are some societal changes judged to be good and others bad?
- What patterns of change are all around us?

Wiggins and McTighe (1998) explained that essential questions (a) go to the heart of a discipline, (b) recur naturally throughout one's learning and in the history of a field, and (c) raise other important questions. By adding essential questions to a curriculum unit, curriculum developers help students focus their thinking on broad aspects of the generalizations and provide teachers with a basis for further lesson planning and development.

As a concluding step to the concept development model, students are asked to reexamine their examples with the generalizations in mind, demonstrating how particular examples support the generalizations. Figure 7.1 illustrates how this portion of the activity may be presented in graphic form.

This versatile model is applicable to almost any concept, although sometimes it requires additional instruction prior to the activity to orient students toward an understanding of the term used as the concept label. For example, students may need to explore a particular example of a system to understand its definitional features before they begin working to generate their list of examples and nonexamples. However, once students have an initial understanding, the overall model may be applied. The Texas Association for the Gifted and Talented (1991) identified nine important universal themes and concepts and created generalizations for each of them (see Figure 7.2). Each of these concepts is applicable across a variety of disciplines and student developmental levels, and because of their depth and abstraction, as well as their widespread applicability, they provide a strong context for differentiation through the types of questions and activities different students may work with as they develop understanding of the concepts at their own levels of readiness.

One feature to note about the process described here is the difference between the concept development or concept formation model as outlined above (Taba, 1962) and a concept attainment model (Bruner, Goodnow, & Austin, 1967). Concept attainment bears some similarity to the model described above, but the order and orientation of the procedures are quite dif-

Directions: Write 3–5 examples to illustrate each of the generalizations.

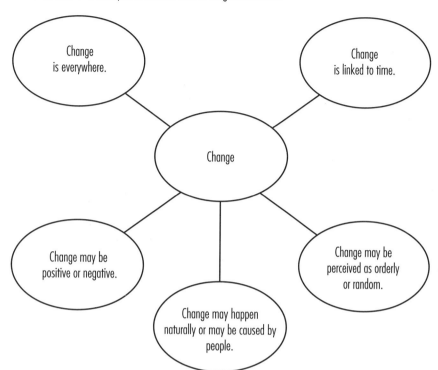

Figure 7.1. The change model. From *Autobiographies* (p. 43), by the Center for Gifted Education, 1998, Dubuque, IA: Kendall/Hunt. Copyright © 1998 by the Center for Gifted Education. Reprinted with permission.

ferent. In a concept attainment model, students are given a list of examples and nonexamples and asked to figure out to what concept these lists refer. The concept development model used above is somewhat more open-ended in its orientation and encourages divergent contributions from students' own experiences and ways of thinking.

The two student examples in Figures 7.3 and 7.4 illustrate the power of an open-ended stimulus to capture student understanding of key generalizations about concepts. The first writing sample was crafted by a fourth-grade girl who was asked to choose one of the generalizations about the concept of change and show its relevance to her life. She chose to focus on how change relates to time. The second selection was developed by a fourth-grade boy who decided to focus on the generalization that "Change is everywhere."

Each example illustrates the student's capacity to find personal relevance in studying the concept and to deepen his or her understanding of his or her own life as a result. The first student recognized the power of reading in her life as a developmental progression, while the second gained insight into how his writing had become more sophisticated.

Conflict	**Patterns**
• Is composed of opposing forces. • May be natural or made-made. • May be intentional or unintentional. • May allow for synthesis and change.	• Have segments that are repeated. • Allow for prediction. • Have internal order. • Are enablers.
Exploration	**Power**
• Requires recognizing purpose and responding to it. • Confronts the unknown. • May result in new findings or the confirmation of findings.	• Is the ability to influence. • Is connected to a source. • Is always present in some form. • May take many forms.
Force	**Structure**
• Attracts, holds, or repels. • Influences or changes. • Is interdependent with inertia. • May be countered with equal or greater force.	• Has parts that interrelate. • Is no stronger than its weakest component. • May be combined to form larger structures. • Provides support and can be supported.
Order	**Systems**
• May be natural or constructed. • May allow for prediction. • Is a form of communication. • May have repeated patterns. • Is reciprocal with chaos. • Leads to chaos and vice versa.	• Have parts that work to complete a task. • Are composed of subsystems. • Have interdependent parts that form a symbiotic relationship. • May be influenced by other systems. • Interact. • Follow rules. • Have inputs, outputs, elements, and boundaries.
Relationships	
• Everything is related in some way. • Are purposeful. • Change over time.	

Figure 7.2. Sample concepts and related generalizations.

My Reading Change

This story is all about how I developed reading skills. Before I learned to read from the time I was about 9 months old, to when I was about 4 years old, I liked books. When I was about 3, I would always want to hear the same books—Pee Wee Scouts books and Oz books, both of which, in fact, are series.

The process of learning to read started when I was about 4. I don't remember too much about starting, but I have a few scraps of memory. One memory picture about preschool and kindergarten reading is of me reading a beginner book and having trouble with some of the words. It was a rectangle-shaped book. Another vivid memory is, in kindergarten, the class was reading a book together and I was reading ahead a little because I already knew how to read. In first grade, I must have completed the beginner book stage, though I have no memories of first-grade reading. In second grade I liked to read an awful lot. One of the books I read in second grade was *Aliens Don't Wear Braces*. In third grade, I was almost as much of a reader as I am now. I even had a reputation for being a major reader! This year I can read at least one book a day. One day this year, I read 123 pages of small print in a few hours.

Each year I get a little faster at reading and the stuff I read changes. Reading has become an enormous part of my life, so this was a monumental change for me. I can't remember a time when books were not part of my life. And it's no wonder. It all started before I was even a year old!

—9-year-old girl

Figure 7.3. Student example 1.

Change Is Everywhere

I think that the generalization about change, "Change is everywhere," is most true. You don't have to agree with me, but I do think that, if you listen closely, you will understand my point. My opinion is supported by the following three reasons.

My first reason is that a large part of change is natural, and there is no place where nature is absent. Some examples of natural change are orbits, plant growth, animal evolution, and erosion. Two important examples of natural change are continental drift and seasons. Continental drift is definitely everywhere. Wherever there are continents, there is continental drift. Seasons are also everywhere, though they may differ in different places. Some examples of seasonal change are the changing of the leaves and having snow fall.

My second reason is that cultural change is a part of change and it is everywhere. Wherever there are groups of people, there is cultural change. There are lots of cultural things that occasionally change. Some change frequently. Here are some examples of cultural change: holidays (change dates and the way they are celebrated), politics, technology, human knowledge, languages, religions, industrial product crazes, customs, and styles. One cultural change that happened very recently was the Presidential election.

My third reason is that personal change is an aspect of change, and it is definitely everywhere. Wherever there are individuals, there is personal change. Some things that fit into the personal category of change are interests, ages, feelings, opinions, and so forth. An example of personal change that happened to me very recently was that I moved from third grade, to summer vacation, to fourth grade. Now I have different ideas and opinions, and I think that some of the pieces I wrote in third grade that are supposed to be funny are a little too outward. That means that my idea of subtlety is changing.

For the above three reasons, I think that the statement, "Change is everywhere" is most true. I hope that now you understand my opinion.

— 9-year-old boy

Figure 7.4. Student example 2.

Ehrenberg (1981) identified several key points that summarize the benefits of the concept development lesson for encouraging student thinking:

- Students must focus on several examples and nonexamples of the concept.
- Students must gather and verify information as to the concept-relevant characteristics of each individual example and nonexample.
- Students must note how the examples vary and yet are still examples of the concept.
- Students must note what is alike about all of the examples of the concept.
- Students must generalize that what is alike about all the examples they've examined also is true of all other examples of the concept.
- Students must note how the nonexamples resemble examples, but, particularly, how they differ from them.
- Students must generalize about the characteristics that distinguish all examples of the concept from any item that might resemble them in some way.

MOVING FROM A LESSON TO A CURRICULUM

Within the framework of a curricular unit, the concept development activities described above can serve as an explicit introduction to a concept that is then embedded throughout a content-based unit of study. The generalizations

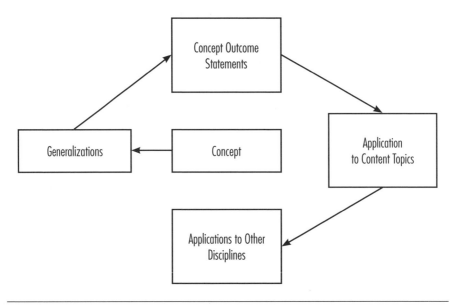

Figure 7.5. Concept Development Model. Adapted from *A Guide to Teaching a Problem-Based Science Curriculum* (p. 25), by the Center for Gifted Education, 1997, Dubuque, IA: Kendall/Hunt. Copyright © 1997 by the Center for Gifted Education. Adapted with permission.

developed in the initial lesson, along with details of the definition, examples, and categories related to the concept, provide guidelines for student outcomes and for questions and activities that reinforce student understanding and ability to apply the concept within and across disciplines for deeper understanding of content. This curricular process of developing generalizations, outcomes, and applications is illustrated graphically in Figure 7.5.

The outcomes related to the concept represent the most critical element of this process for the curriculum developer, because these outcomes and the curricular framework of which they are a part serve as the foundation for the instruction that follows. Lessons that provide applications of the concept within and across disciplines should focus on how best to guide students in their progress toward achieving these outcomes, which are designed to represent how students' understanding of the concept and its disciplinary applications has been enhanced.

Possible applications of concepts may vary considerably from one unit to another, depending on the concept, the developmental level of the students, and the discipline under study. However, one general application that relates across disciplines and across concepts is the development and implementation of core questions. Questions that encourage students to recognize and define examples and nonexamples of the concept or to apply the concept generalizations to specific instances based in the content under study support students in developing a deeper understanding of the concept. A set of such questions should be prepared in advance of teaching a given lesson to ensure that the discussion is maintained at a higher level, although the need for additional probing questions will undoubtedly arise during the course of the implementation of the discussion.

For example, in a Center for Gifted Education language arts unit focusing on the concept of *change*, students are asked to explain how a story by Edgar Allen Poe illustrates human and natural control over change or how a Nathaniel Hawthorne story uses changing times of day to symbolize larger implications of the links between change and time (Center for Gifted Education, 1998b). In a social studies unit exploring the concept of cause and effect within the context of a study of the American Revolution, students are asked to analyze the chain of related effects resulting from the taxes instituted by Parliament in the 1760s, as well as the causes of these taxes in the first place; they also are asked to consider how a generalization addressing the predictability of effects relates to the debates of the Continental Congress in early 1776 (Center for Gifted Education, 2003b). In a science unit using the concept of *systems* to explore acid-base chemistry, students are asked to analyze how organisms within an ecosystem represent interdependent systems and how this interdependency is affected by the introduction of an acidic input (Center for Gifted Education, 1997a). In a mathematics unit using the concept of *models* to explore populations, students examine existing mathematical models and create new ones to represent real-world phenomena; for example, students are asked to determine the accuracy of $y = 3^x$ as a predictor of population size for a bacteria culture (Johnson & Sher, 1997).

Another way in which a concept may be embedded into the curriculum is to encourage students to see connections across discrete reading selections or topics throughout a unit and to demonstrate how the combination of content elements contribute to their understanding of the concept. For example, throughout a social studies unit that explores the concept of authority within the context of the period of the Renaissance and Reformation in Europe, students examine examples of symbols and symbolic actions that demonstrate authority and compare the origins and effects of these symbols throughout the period (Center for Gifted Education, 2005). Figure 7.6 demonstrates an example of how students record reflections about change throughout the course of a language arts unit, leading to a closing discussion about the concept, the literature selections, and students' own personal responses.

In addition to the overall organization of the curriculum under one concept, curricula for the gifted also should encourage students to develop their awareness of multiple concepts affecting what they read, hear, discuss, and understand. Consequently, questioning strategies should encourage students to identify other ideas underscoring the content they encounter. Students should be encouraged to recognize themes and ideas that appear frequently within given reading selec-

Literature Selection	Changes in Relationships	Changes That Can Be Perceived as Positive	Changes That Can Be Perceived as Negative	Changes in You as a Result of Reading
"Autobiographia Literaria"				
"Ghost Cat"				
"Literary Lessons" from *Little Women*				
"All Summer in a Day"				
"Ode to my Library"				
"Charles"				
Your own story				

Figure 7.6. Change matrix. From *Autobiographies* (p. 61), by the Center for Gifted Education, 1998, Dubuque, IA: Kendall/Hunt. Copyright © 1998 by the Center for Gifted Education. Reprinted with permission.

tions or other sources, and also across selections, and to demonstrate their understanding of how these concepts are elaborated. For example, language arts lessons may consistently ask students to identify key ideas in a reading selection and to highlight specific evidence from the text that communicates an understanding about that idea. Activities that engage students in examining primary sources in social studies, be they government documents, letters, political cartoons, photographs, or other types of sources, may include questions that encourage students to identify the key ideas being communicated within the source, the evidence that supports their understanding of that idea, and how our understandings of the idea today are similar to and different from the way the concept was understood at the time the source was produced.

The development of concept maps also is an effective tool for encouraging students to advance their understanding of a concept. To construct a concept map, the student must identify the concept or concepts, arrange them spatially, and specify relationships among them (Jonassen, 2006). For example, the illustration in Figure 7.7 shows a fully completed concept map about the topic of plants in the Clarion unit entitled *Budding Botanists at Work* (Center for Gifted Education, 2007). This concept map is used as an instructional tool; at the beginning of the unit, students' first version of the map will show fewer elements and connections, and then students are given the opportunity to expand the elements and connections as their knowledge of the topic of plants evolves. Similarly, in the Center for Gifted Education's *Navigator* series of novel study

Sample Concept Map for Plants

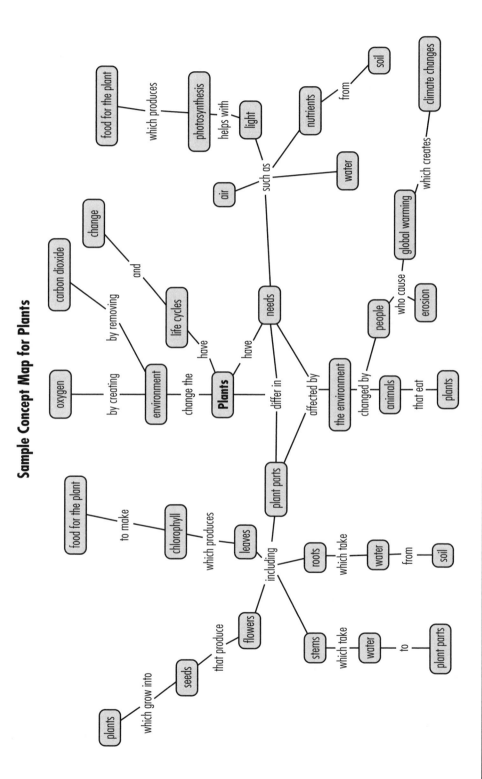

Figure 7.7. Sample concept map for plants. From *Budding Botanists at Work* (p. 136), by Center for Gifted Education, 2007, Williamsburg, VA: Author. Copyright 2007 by Center for Gifted Education. Reprinted with permission.

guides (see Chapter 8), students are encouraged to construct concept maps demonstrating how key ideas are represented within the context of the particular novel they are reading. Concept maps are also effective devices for assessing student learning (Novak, 2005), discussed more fully in the following section.

ASSESSING CONCEPT LEARNING

Because concepts are a critical dimension in the ICM, concept learning must be assessed routinely. Strategies that encourage more open-ended responses allow students to demonstrate their understanding of concepts through illustration and application. We have used several assessment approaches in our curriculum development work at the Center for Gifted Education. Some of these strategies measure how students grasp the larger, overarching concept of a unit, such as *change*, *systems*, or *cause and effect*. Another strategy assesses students' understanding of narrower, more endemic concepts using concept maps.

Concept maps are an excellent tool for assessing content learning, but teachers can find it difficult to quantify changes in learning when using these maps on a pretest-posttest basis. According to Jonassen (2006), the primary unit of analysis should be the proposition (two concepts and the labeled line connecting them). Weight also should be given to comprehensiveness, organization, and accuracy. Other criteria involve the number of levels of hierarchies, interconnectedness, and embeddedness.

A new assessment technique emerged from the Center for Gifted Education's work on Project Clarion (VanTassel-Baska et al., 2007) in using concept maps to assess content learning. Project Clarion produced new science units for the primary grades and built on earlier Center work on problem-based learning in science. A concept map technique was developed to measure content learning on a pretest-posttest basis. Preteaching is necessary before the test is administered to ensure that students understand what a concept map is. Figure 7.8 shows the prompt and the template for students to use in providing their responses in a unit called *Budding Botanists at Work*, designed for first and second graders. Figure 7.9 shows the scoring rubric used to assess student work. The rubric quantifies the properties of propositions, hierarchical levels, and examples.

Another instrument developed for Project Clarion focuses on a student's understanding of the overarching concept of *systems*. In this assessment, students are asked to list examples of systems, draw one example of a system and label its features (elements, boundaries, inputs, outputs, and interactions), and make at least three generalizations about systems. This assessment is included as an example with its accompanying rubric in Chapter 16.

In the Center for Gifted Education's language arts units, a concept question is embedded in the pretest and posttest on literary analysis and interpreta-

Pre-Assessment for Content

Today, I would like you to think about all the things you know about plants. Think about the words you would use and the pictures you could draw to make a concept map. Think about the connections you can make. On your concept map paper, draw in pictures and words that you know about plants. You will be drawing a concept map, just like the ones you did when we discussed the farm. Today's instruction is: "Tell me everything you know about plants."

Name: **Grade:**

Concept Map
Plants

Figure 7.8. Sample concept map preassessment. Adapted from *Budding Botanists at Work* (pp. 133–134), by Center for Gifted Education, 2007, Williamsburg, VA: Author. Copyright 2007 by Center for Gifted Education. Adapted with permission.

tion. This question typically asks students to infer what a passage of text (e.g., from a poem, story, or the like) tells us about the concept of change and to support what is said with details from the text. Because the question is open-ended, with more than one "right" answer, a rubric is used to score the response. The latest edition of the rubric has five levels of performance on the scale, arranged as follows:

0—Provides no response or a response inappropriate to the task demand.

2—Provides limited, vague, inaccurate response; only quotes from the story.

4—Provides literal description of change occurring in the story or a generalization about the concept made without support from the text.

Scoring Rubric for Content Assessment

Directions for Use: Score students on their completed maps.

	5	4	3	2	1	0
Hierarchical Level Each subordinate concept is more specific and less general than the concept drawn above it. Count the number of levels included in the total map.	Five or more levels are identified.	Four levels are identified.	Three levels are identified.	Two levels are identified.	One level is identified.	No hierarchical levels are identified.
Propositions The linking of two concepts indicating a clear relationship is given. Count the total number of propositions identified on the total map.	Twelve or more propositions are provided.	Ten to twelve propositions are provided.	Seven to nine propositions are provided.	Four to six propositions are provided.	One to three propositions are provided.	No propositions are provided.
Examples A valid example of a concept is provided. Count the total number of examples.	Twelve or more examples are provided.	Ten to twelve examples are provided.	Seven to nine examples are provided.	Four to six examples are provided.	One to three examples are provided.	No examples are provided.

Total points possible: 15

Figure 7.9. Scoring rubric for content assessment. From *Budding Botanists at Work* (p. 135), by Center for Gifted Education, 2007, Williamsburg, VA: Author. Copyright 2007 by Center for Gifted Education. Reprinted with permission.

6—Provides valid generalization about change that is supported with details from the text (meets expectations).

8—Provides at least one generalization about change with multiple applications from text and/or with analogies to real life (exceeds expectations).

During Project Phoenix, the research and development initiative that produced many of the Center for Gifted Education's social studies units, the research team also used a pretest and posttest instrument to assess different aspects of concept mastery (Little, Feng, VanTassel-Baska, Rogers, & Avery, 2007). A sample item on this instrument gave students a list of objects and asked them to code whether or not each object represents a system. Then, they were to select one object from the list that they indicated is a system and explain why it is a system. Later iterations of the social studies curriculum embedded concept questions in a comprehensive pretest and posttest that also addressed content learning. For example, in a middle school unit that explores the concept of *systems* through a focus on the U.S. government structure and the process of presidential elections, students are asked in one pretest and posttest question to identify changes that have occurred in the electoral system and to explain how those changes have influenced the interactions and outputs of the system, thereby demonstrating their understanding of these key system features while also embedding their knowledge of the content (Center for Gifted Education, 2003a).

Another strategy for measuring concept learning is through embedded assessment activities. An example of such a strategy is found in the Center for Gifted Education's problem-based science units, which also focus heavily on the concept of *systems*. This example involves having students complete and label the elements in a fish bowl. By comparing and contrasting student responses to this exercise, the teacher is able to illustrate that system boundaries are fluid and established by social construction and that the relationship of inputs, interactions, and outputs often is governed by where these boundaries are established. The fish bowl exercise can be included in a student's portfolio of work as an illustration of his or her understanding of the concept at a given point in time. The Clarion units use the same idea but instead of a fish bowl, the students are given a generalized template that can be adapted to multiple examples of systems.

The big ideas by which we come to know and understand our reality provide ample opportunity for depth and complexity in curricular design and implementation. Because they are such an essential part of our instructional focus, we need to have sufficient tools to measure whether student understanding of the concepts grows and deepens over time. Both pretest and posttest instruments, as well as embedded assessment strategies, afford us insights for

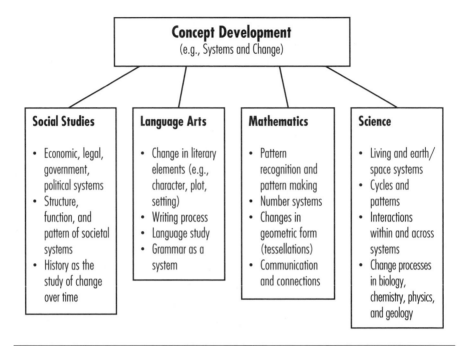

Figure 7.10. Disciplinary applications of concepts. From *Curriculum Planning and Instructional Design for Gifted Learners* (p. 48), by J. VanTassel-Baska, 2003, Denver: Love. Copyright © 2003 by Love. Reprinted with permission.

ascertaining the level of concept acquisition by students. Concept maps also are good tools to use in assessing content learning of more subject-specific concepts within a discipline area.

USING CONCEPTS TO DESIGN INTERDISCIPLINARY CURRICULA

Our discussion thus far has focused largely on discipline-specific applications of concept learning. But, in reality, concepts transcend artificial disciplinary boundaries and enable us to make important connections across bodies of knowledge. The model previously presented in Figure 7.5 shows that, once generalizations have been translated into student outcomes, these outcomes can be embedded across fields of inquiry. In fact, most of the national and state standards of learning require that higher order concepts, such as *change*, *systems*, *models*, and *scale*, be addressed within most subject matter areas. Figure 7.10 takes the concepts of *systems*, *change*, and *patterns* and shows sample applications across several major content areas.

At the elementary level, it is relatively easy for teachers to elicit applications of the same concept as the subject under study progresses from math, to

Concept	Art/Music	Psychology	Philosophy
Conflict	Conflict/Tranquility as a theme in representations of war and peace (art)	Conflict as a precondition of psychological growth (dissonance)	Conflict as an irreconcilable difference in poles of a continuum (absolutism vs. relativism)
Conflict	Conflict as a clash between tonal and atonal compositions (music)	Conflict among schools of thought, theories, and approaches	Conflict in values underlying philosophical orientations
Power	Power as an exercise of control by state or church in subject matter or treatment of arts and music	Power as psychological integration; self-control	Power in control of philosophical ideas by systems of government (democracy, communism, and totalitarianism)
Power	Power in the ability of art and music to shape emotional responses and influence behavior	Power as explanatory value in predicting individual behavior	Power as a condition of reasoning ability (logic)
Change	Change as presented in schools, theories of art and music (e.g., classical, Baroque, Rococo, Romantic)	Change as growth or regression in a sentient being	Change in philosophical perspectives across time and place

Figure 7.11. Further disciplinary applications of concepts.

language arts, to social studies, to science, to art and music. Seasonal changes addressed in science from summer, to fall, to winter, to spring may be related to symbolism in literature. Why did the protagonist have his or her crisis in winter? Why did the epiphany occur in spring? Such parallels can be extended to psychology, with questions about seasonal affective disorder (SAD), in which light deprivation appears to trigger depression in some individuals. The savvy teacher can use such interdisciplinary connections to help students appreciate the connectedness of the world.

At the middle school and high school levels, collaborative curricular planning across content areas is necessary for higher order concepts to be addressed simultaneously across subject areas within the larger curricular scope and sequence. Although multiple concepts will always be embedded within content and thus represent potential for in-depth study and exploration, collaborative decision-making around how to focus the curriculum and instruction provides students with a more targeted learning experience across disciplines. Figure 7.11 is included to show how concepts apply to an expanded array of disciplines, more akin to what is offered at the secondary level of a school system. The illustration deals with the concepts of conflict, power, and change.

It is an interesting paradox of modern life that, as progress demands increasing areas of specialization, these areas often represent the intersection of multiple disciplines. For instance, beyond training biologists generally, we train sociobiologists and psychobiologists. Such descriptors demonstrate how we have come to blend science and social science orientations in particular fields. These connections across fields often afford new professional vistas for human development.

Furthermore, the ability to integrate deep content knowledge with a larger scope of interdisciplinary concepts is key to communication and innovation in today's society. Pink (2005) argued, "We are moving from an economy and a society built on the logical, linear, computerlike capabilities of the Information Age to an economy and a society built on the inventive, empathic, big-picture capabilities of what's rising in its place, the Conceptual Age" (pp. 1–2). It is particularly important that our high-ability students come to grasp the interdependence of disciplines in understanding life and carving out a meaningful experience of it. By incorporating a focus on concept learning, we can create scaffolds for ensuring that these connections are addressed within and across classrooms.

CONCLUSION

Concept learning enables students to make connections across the disciplines and to forge a deeper understanding and appreciation of the complexity of the world we inhabit and shape to our own ends. By focusing acutely on the concept dimension of learning, the teacher elevates the level of learning from the concrete to the abstract, from the particular to the general. A theoretical model for understanding how to teach concepts both within and across the disciplines is useful for teachers and curriculum developers in supporting authentic concept learning. Taba's (1962) ideas, as operationalized in the Center for Gifted Education's curricular units, provide a template for moving from concepts, to generalizations, to outcomes, to applications in the classroom, thus supporting teachers in their guidance of student understanding of the ideas that underscore all that they learn and experience.

KEY POINTS SUMMARY

- Concept development requires student manipulation of abstract thought and higher level thinking within and across areas of learning.
- All disciplines of learning are organized by powerful ideas that help shape our understanding of these areas.
- Curricula that are organized and taught by concepts deepen and enhance student learning over time.

- Although concepts are useful for curricular organization, their real power rests in their being effective within units of study across lessons.
- Developing curricula that are concept-based requires the formation of generalizations and the transformation of those into student outcomes, followed by relevant content applications.
- Concept maps are useful tools for both instruction and assessment, and rubrics can be used to quantify the breadth and depth of understanding illustrated by these maps.
- Assessment of concept learning engages students in demonstrating deep understanding of relevant generalizations.

REFERENCES

Adler, M. J. (Ed.). (1952). *The great ideas: A synopticon of great books of the Western world.* Chicago, IL: Encyclopedia Britannica.

American Association for the Advancement of Science. (1990). *Science for all Americans.* New York, NY: Oxford University Press.

Barton, K. C., & Levstik, L. S. (2004). *Teaching history for the common good.* Mahwah, NJ: Lawrence Erlbaum.

Boyce, L. N. (1992). *The concept of change.* Williamsburg, VA: Center for Gifted Education, College of William and Mary.

Bruner, J. E., Goodnow, J. J., & Austin, G. A. (1967). *A study of thinking.* New York, NY: Science Editions.

Bryce, T., & MacMillan, K. (2005). Encouraging conceptual change: The use of bridging analogies in the teaching of action-reaction forces and the "at rest" condition in physics. *International Journal of Science Education, 27,* 737–763.

Center for Gifted Education. (1997a). *Acid, acid everywhere.* Dubuque, IA: Kendall/Hunt.

Center for Gifted Education. (1997b). *Guide to teaching a problem-based science curriculum.* Dubuque, IA: Kendall/Hunt.

Center for Gifted Education. (1998a). *Autobiographies.* Dubuque, IA: Kendall/Hunt.

Center for Gifted Education. (1998b). *Threads of change in 19th century American literature.* Dubuque, IA: Kendall/Hunt.

Center for Gifted Education. (1999). *Guide to teaching a language arts curriculum for high-ability learners.* Dubuque, IA: Kendall/Hunt.

Center for Gifted Education. (2003a). *The road to the White House: Electing the American President.* Dubuque, IA: Kendall/Hunt.

Center for Gifted Education. (2003b). *The world turned upside down: The American Revolution.* Dubuque, IA: Kendall/Hunt.

Center for Gifted Education. (2005). *The Renaissance and Reformation in Europe.* Dubuque, IA: Kendall/Hunt.

Center for Gifted Education. (2007). *Budding botanists at work.* Williamsburg, VA: Author.

Coll, R. K., France, B., & Taylor, I. (2005). The role of models and analogies in science education. *International Journal of Science Education, 27,* 183–198.

Ehrenberg, S. D. (1981). Concept learning: How to make it happen in the classroom. *Educational Leadership, 39*(1), 63–43.

Erickson, H. L. (2007). *Concept-based curriculum and instruction for the thinking classroom.* Thousand Oaks, CA: Corwin Press.

Feldhusen, J. (1988). Developing units of instruction. In J. VanTassel-Baska, J. Feldhusen, K. Seeley, G. Wheatley, L. Silverman, & W. Foster (Eds.), *Comprehensive curriculum for gifted learners* (pp. 112–150). Boston, MA: Allyn & Bacon.

Fullan, M. (1991). *The new meaning of educational change.* New York, NY: Teachers College Press.

Fullan, M. (1993). *Change forces: Probing the depths of educational reform.* Bristol, PA: Falmer Press.

Fullan, M. (2010). *Motion leadership: The skinny on becoming change savvy.* Thousand Oaks, CA: Corwin Press.

Gick, M. L., & Holyoak, K. J. (1980). Analogical problem solving. *Cognitive Psychology, 12,* 306–355.

Gick, M. L., & Holyoak, K. J. (1983). Schema induction and analogical transfer. *Cognitive Psychology, 15,* 1–38.

Goswami, U. (1991). Analogical reasoning: What develops? Review of research and theory. *Child Development, 62,* 1–22.

Johnson, D. T., & Sher, B. T. (1997). *Models: A study of animal populations.* Williamsburg, VA: Center for Gifted Education, College of William and Mary.

Jonassen, D. H. (2006). On the role of concepts in learning and instructional design. *Educational Technology Research and Development, 54,* 177–196.

Little, C. A., Feng, A. X., VanTassel-Baska, J., Rogers, K. B., & Avery, L. D. (2007). A study of curriculum effectiveness in social studies. *Gifted Child Quarterly, 51,* 272–284.

National Research Council. (2000). *How people learn: Brain, mind, experience, and school.* Washington, DC: National Academy Press.

National Research Council. (2005). *How students learn: History, mathematics, and science in the classroom.* Washington, DC: National Academies Press.

Novak, J. D. (2005). Results and implications of a 12-year longitudinal study of science concept learning. *Research in Science Education, 35*(1), 23–40.

Pence, M. (1999). *The concept of systems.* Williamsburg, VA: Center for Gifted Education, College of William and Mary.

Perkins, D. (1993). The connected curriculum. *Educational Leadership 51*(2), 90–91.

Pink, D. H. (2005). *A whole new mind: Why right-brainers will rule the future.* New York, NY: Riverhead Books.

Schack, G. (1994, November). *Designing integrated units.* Presentation at the annual meeting of the National Association for Gifted Children, Salt Lake City, UT.

Sher, B. (1991). *A guide to key science concepts.* Williamsburg, VA: Center for Gifted Education, The College of William and Mary.

Taba, H. (1962). *Curriculum development, theory, and practice.* New York, NY: Harcourt, Brace, and World.

Texas Association for the Gifted and Talented. (1991). *Curriculum guide for the education of gifted high school students.* Austin, TX: Author.

VanTassel-Baska, J. (1986). Effective curriculum and instructional models for the gifted. *Gifted Child Quarterly, 30,* 164–169.

VanTassel-Baska, J. (1995). The development of talent through curriculum. *Roeper Review, 18,* 98–102.

VanTassel-Baska, J. (Ed.). (1998). *Excellence in educating gifted and talented learners* (3rd ed.). Denver, CO: Love.

VanTassel-Baska, J., Bracken, B. A., Stambaugh, T., & Feng, A. (2007, September) *Findings from Project Clarion.* Presentation to the United States Department of Education Expert Panel, Storrs, CT.

VanTassel-Baska, J., & Wood, S. (2009). The Integrated Curriculum Model. In J. Renzulli (Ed.), *Systems and models in gifted education* (2nd ed., pp. 655–691). Mansfield Center, CT: Creative Learning Press.

Ward, V. S. (1961). *Differential education for the gifted.* Los Angeles, CA: National/State Leadership Training Institute for the Gifted and Talented.

Wiggins, G., & McTighe, J. (1998). *Understanding by design.* Alexandria, VA: Association for Supervision and Curriculum Development.

Chapter 8

Adapting Language Arts Curricula for High-Ability Learners

Catherine A. Little

*Y*ou are a fifth-grade teacher. Your school has decided to regroup students for language arts and mathematics in the next school year to serve all students' needs more effectively. You will be working with the top and above-average groups of students for language arts. Your principal has encouraged you to seek and develop curricula that will challenge these students who are already reading above grade level and excelling on their state-mandated reading comprehension tests. What will you do to work with these students effectively?

As a unified group, the language arts represent one of the four core content areas in the school curriculum. Indeed, in elementary school, this area is generally given priority over all other subjects in terms of the time and resources devoted to it, and even into the secondary years it never really loses its prominence as a centerpiece of schooling. As a result of this heavy emphasis on language arts instruction in schools, students who are gifted and talented in the verbal areas may find language arts class to be either a saving grace or a source of boredom and anguish in school. Verbally talented students often read voraciously and enjoy opportunities to interact with literature and to write. However, if classroom reading selections, the activities designed to relate to them, and the opportunities for writing and language development are not sufficiently challenging and interesting—and if there is no differentiation for advanced learners—then the extensive time spent on language arts instruction in school may be a great source of tedium to these students.

How, then, can language arts curricula and instruction be made challenging and motivating for highly able learners? How can a love for reading, writing, or language be translated into engagement in language arts activities in school? What steps can teachers and curriculum developers take to ensure that students are progressing in their learning and actively engaged in processes that will support their lifelong involvement with the language arts? A central element of achieving this level of challenge and student interest comes from the literature selections chosen for instructional purposes; another element is the type and level of questions asked for discussion and writing purposes. In addition, the language arts curriculum should encourage students to develop habits of inquiry and critical reading, and it should provide them with opportunities to delve deeply into their language and all of its complexities. These and other key elements of a challenging language arts curriculum will be discussed in the following pages.

This chapter is organized around the major elements of curricular reform discussed in Chapter 2, with emphasis on how each may be realized in strong language arts curricula and instruction for the gifted. First, the key elements of significant learner outcomes and authentic assessment are addressed, with the idea that a well-grounded curricular framework that is systematically assessed throughout the instructional process is the foundation of a strong curriculum. Following these elements, the three dimensions of the Integrated Curriculum Model (ICM; VanTassel-Baska, 1986, 1995) are discussed as they specifically relate to the language arts. The chapter then focuses in some detail on constructing meaning as the centerpiece of a language arts curriculum, followed by a discussion of strategies and resources that are especially relevant to language arts curricula and instruction, as well as the importance of interdisciplinary connections from the language arts to the other core content areas. Each section will draw upon sample lessons from the Center for Gifted Education's award-winning and research-based language arts curriculum and supplementary resources for examples of how the elements of reform may be applied to enhance curricular appropriateness for verbally talented learners. Relevant sections from sample lessons are included.

LEARNER OUTCOMES OF SIGNIFICANCE

Outcomes in the language arts content area should reflect the four primary language arts—reading, writing, listening, and speaking—as well as the structure and organization of the language itself, which underscores all of these functions. The International Reading Association (IRA) and the National Council of Teachers of English (NCTE), in their Standards for the English Language Arts (1996), emphasized three major categories of learning opportunities for students: (a) to read and interact with a wide range of literature selections, (b) to communicate effectively in writing and speaking in a variety of genres and for a variety of purposes, and (c) to develop a strong sense of language structure and to use this as a starting point for understanding various types of communication. Through appropriate activities within each of these categories, students develop skills and habits of mind to support their use of the language for a wide range of purposes and their participation as well-educated members of a literate society. These types of learning opportunities support the 12 content standards, which incorporate attention to a wide range of experiences and expectations for students in elementary and secondary education, including the range of resources students learn to use, the strategies they use for interacting with resources and communicating with others, and the dispositions they develop around communication and respect for diversity in language (NCTE & IRA, 1996).

In developing outcomes of significance in the language arts for gifted students, curriculum writers may use the standards as a starting point for developing outcomes supported by particular curricular experiences. State-level standards also are important sources, as alignment with state and local standards supports integration of advanced curriculum in the classroom. At all times, however, curriculum developers must keep in mind the necessity of holding high-ability students to levels of expectation that are well beyond minimum competency standards; therefore, curriculum developers should examine standards two or more grade levels above the intended grade level as part of the process of developing outcomes. Learning outcomes for gifted students also should embed the expectation for using advanced processing and thinking skills, such as those emphasized in Chapters 5 and 6, as well as connections with other disciplines and to the world of work. In addition, learning outcomes should reflect a focus on developing conceptual understanding, both within the language arts discipline and in ways that bridge across multiple disciplines.

The Center for Gifted Education at The College of William and Mary has developed a series of curricular units in the language arts, all organized around the ICM and incorporating six central goals common across multiple units and grade levels (Center for Gifted Education, 1999). Four of these are content goals, representing reading, writing, language study, and oral communication; one goal represents a focus on process; and one represents the conceptual organization of the curriculum. Several learner outcomes—specific enough to facilitate assessment, but general enough to apply across a range of developmental levels—also were developed for each goal. Samples of these goals and outcomes are given in Table 8.1. The third column of the table illustrates how specific goals and outcomes of the curricular units align with aspects of the Standards for the English Language Arts (NCTE & IRA, 1996). Note that both the curricular goals and the related national standards are broad in scope, while the outcomes are more specific; also note that the curricular goals and outcomes reflect attention to the advanced verbal skills and behaviors characteristic of gifted students.

Learning outcomes that are designed to target the needs of advanced students do not eliminate the expectation for performance of more fundamental skills; rather, they implicitly require that such skills be used as foundations for performance of more complex tasks. For example, skills of decoding and comprehension are presumed under the outcome of developing critical reading behaviors. By employing advanced goals that reflect the key practices and habits of mind of the language arts disciplines, curriculum developers demonstrate high overall expectations that may be applied to all students. Specific learning objectives may then be established to detail the components of these advanced goals, but also to demonstrate pathways of skill development toward goal attainment. These pathways provide the basis for scaffolding instruction to guide students toward higher levels.

For example, in the *Jacob's Ladder Reading Comprehension* series developed by the Center for Gifted Education, each goal represents advanced critical reading behaviors, while the objectives under each goal and the related questions and activities guide students through scaffolded strategies that contribute to the advanced goals. Thus, to support a goal of developing synthesis skills, the specific objectives include (a) to paraphrase important quotations from the text; (b) to summarize the main ideas presented in the text and provide support using text-based evidence; and (c) to generate new ideas based on evaluation of existing ideas (Center for Gifted Education, 2006).

HABITS OF MIND

Learner outcomes of significance in any subject area must incorporate attention to the desired habits of mind of the related disciplines. A disciplinary orientation toward curriculum and instruction represents a more challenging and complex approach, as well as one with a broader array of applications than a more skill-based, foundational approach; thus, it supports key aspects of differentiation for gifted learners. The fundamental goal of language arts education is to develop

TABLE 8.1

Learner Goals and Outcomes

Goals	Sample related outcomes	Related national standard (NCTE & IRA, 1996)
Students will be able to . . .		
Develop analytical and interpretive skills in literature.	Cite similarities and differences in meaning among selected works of literature. Make inferences based on information in given passages.	Apply a wide range of strategies to comprehend, interpret, and evaluate given texts.
Develop persuasive writing skills.	Develop a written persuasive essay, given a topic. Complete various pieces of writing using a three-phase revision process.	Employ a wide range of strategies as they write and use different writing process elements appropriately.
Develop linguistic competency.	Analyze the form and function of words in a given context. Develop vocabulary power commensurate with reading.	Apply knowledge of language structure [and] language conventions to create, critique, and discuss print and nonprint texts.
Develop listening/oral communication skills.	Evaluate an oral persuasive message according to a main idea and arguments cited to support it. Develop skills of argument formulation.	Use spoken language to accomplish their own purposes.
Develop reasoning skills in the language arts (process goal).	Apply aspects of Paul's Elements of Reasoning model through specific examples. Define a problem, given ill-structured, complex, or technical information.	Conduct research on issues and interests by generating ideas and questions and by posing problems.
Understand the concept of change in the language arts (concept goal).	Interpret change as positive or negative in selected works. Analyze social and individual change in a piece of literature.	Read a wide range of literature from many periods in many genres to build an understanding of the many dimensions of human experience.

Note. "Goals" and "Sample Related Outcomes" from *A Guide to Teaching a Language Arts Curriculum for High-Ability Learners* (pp. 63–64), by the Center for Gifted Education, 1999, Dubuque, IA: Kendall/Hunt. Copyright © 1999 by the Center for Gifted Education. Adapted with permission. "Related National Standard" from *Standards for the English Language Arts*, by the International Reading Association and the National Council for Teachers of English, 1996, Urbana, IL: Author. Copyright © 1996 by the International Reading Association and the National Council for Teachers of English. Reprinted with permission. For a complete list of standards, please visit http://www.ncte.org/standards.

literacy for the language tasks of everyday life (NCTE & IRA, 1996). Building upon and beyond this, however, language arts education also must encourage habits related to critical reading, the iterative processes of writing, and the exploration of language as the foundation for the aesthetic and intellectual experience of communication. Furthermore, the ever-expanding concept of literacy in the 21st century (e.g., Partnership for 21st Century Skills, 2009) requires that students develop skills for critical thinking, information-seeking, and communication across a variety of sources and media, all of which reflect skills that are grounded in key language arts goals, outcomes, and habits of mind.

One central focus of developing habits of mind in language arts is fostering desired behaviors in how students interact with text. Langer (1995) defined two types of experiences that characterize interactions with literature: the literary experience, in which the primary goal is "exploring horizons of possibilities" (p. 26), and the discursive experience that focuses on gaining or sharing ideas or information, in which the primary goal is maintaining a point of reference with which we develop agreements or disagreements. Key elements of developing critical reading behaviors include the ability to recognize and articulate the purpose of reading a given text and to identify how the experience of reading reflects one of the goals Langer (1995) noted. These critical reading behaviors begin with the development of proficiency in reading skills and strategies (Harvey & Goudvis, 2007), and then move into the more interpretive and evaluative skills fostered in more advanced literature study (Eckert, 2008). Each of these levels of interaction requires that students have opportunities to practice applying their skills and strategies to a variety of texts and in multiple contexts, so that they are prepared to approach new texts effectively in school settings and beyond.

Another important aspect of literate behavior, and thus a key habit of mind to promote in language arts education, is the ability to make good choices about what one will read and write (Zemelman, Daniels, & Hyde, 1993). In order to develop as lifelong readers, students need to learn strategies for finding things to read and making decisions about how they spend their time in literacy-related endeavors. Thus, in addition to critical reading behaviors, it also is important to engage students in reflecting upon their own emotional response to reading, the connections they can draw to their own lives and other learning, and the ways that reading affects the decisions and choices they make. Classroom experiences can foster these habits by providing students with broad exposure to a wide range of texts, genres, themes, authors, and topics, as well as by promoting reflective writing and conversation about reading.

In addition, it is important for teachers and curriculum developers to maintain awareness of evolving patterns of preference in student reading, as well as to recognize the many forms in which students are interacting with text. Despite concerns about the evidence of a decline in reading habits in general in young people (National Endowment for the Arts, 2004), some other evidence demonstrates that adolescents, for instance, read extensively, but much of what they read would not fit within a picture of "academic" reading because it consists of sources such as blogs, e-mails, and social network discussions (Pitcher et al., 2007). Therefore, the wise teacher or curriculum developer helps to promote connections among the varied forms of reading in which students engage, and to find in students' existing reading behaviors entry points and connections that can be made to other literature.

Fostering key habits of mind related to writing also is a central goal within language arts curriculum and instruction. Language arts classroom experiences that guide students through the steps of the writing process not only help them develop skills that will be useful throughout their education, but also give them a sense of the key habits of mind of the professional writer. However, within the structured steps of prewriting, drafting, revising, and editing fall the diverse and idiosyncratic behaviors of the individual writer. An important writing habit of mind is to define one's own writing process—elements such as favorite format for prewriting, degree of revision that occurs during drafting, and how writing time is allocated to the different steps, as well as more affective concerns regarding one's emotional state when engaging in writing. Students need to have opportunities to find themselves as writers and to discover their own most effective habits for writing, with instruction in the writing process used as a flexible foundation, not a source of rigid rules. Beyond the processes of writing, students also must work to develop their own style as writers, which involves not only practice in writing, but practice in analyzing the writing styles of others through critical reading and literature study.

The study of language also encourages the habits of mind of the critical reader and the practiced writer; the meaning we create when reading or when expressing ourselves in writing or speech is constructed on a frame of words and their combinations into grammatical structures. Thompson (1996a) emphasized the importance of formal language study focused on grammar, vocabulary, and poetics because language is both "a medium for the mind" and "a manifestation of the mind" (p. 151). Study of the structures of language, moreover, not only provides students with the tools for understanding and analyzing the texts they read, but also deepens their aesthetic appreciation for linguistic expression as an art form. Furthermore, study of English grammar and vocabulary builds students' capacity to recognize connections and patterns across languages, thereby giving them strategies helpful in learning other languages, as well as an introduction to the habits and practices of linguistics as a discipline (Haussamen et al., 2002).

AUTHENTIC ASSESSMENT

Authentic assessment in the language arts involves students in the actual processes of interacting with language through reading, writing, listening, and speaking in both classroom instruction and the real world. Reading and response activities, writing and speaking tasks, and appropriate language study experiences all can be examples of authentic assessment in this area. Assessment in the language arts should be ongoing and embedded into instruction. Tasks used for assessment purposes also should represent opportunities for student learning in themselves and should be viewed as tools for planning and organizing instruction, as well as for evaluating students for accountability purposes (Marzano, 1992; McTighe & O'Connor, 2005). Clear goals and outcomes and embedded opportunities for assessment should appear throughout a curricular document in order to promote this perspective on assessment as ongoing and deeply integrated with the overall instructional process.

An example of an authentic literary response and interpretation assessment would be to have students read a selection of literature and then respond in writing or orally to a series of targeted questions that require students to use comprehension and analysis strategies to provide a well-supported answer. Ideally, a literary response assessment task such as this engages students with a new piece of literature and requires that they demonstrate their own capacity for responding to and interpreting new literature, not their ability to remember and repeat someone else's interpretation. Again, this allows the assessment task to be an opportunity for learning, as well as for demonstration and mastery of key processes and critical reading behaviors.

In writing, assessment tasks should, simply enough, require students to write. In order for assessment tasks to be useful to teachers as diagnostic tools and manageable for scoring purposes, the expectations for student performance should be clearly stated in the instructions for the tasks. In addition, rubrics should be shared with students, along with writing models, so as to demonstrate to them what level of performance is expected. Writing tasks of varying lengths should be part of the overall assessment system, engaging students in many of the different purposes for writing and linking the format of the task with the purpose. For example, some tasks should require students to complete a written product within a designated length of time, because their opportunities in future employment and other settings may require such quick application of the writing process. In other assessment tasks, students should have opportunities to revise their writing and develop products over time. In addition, students should have opportunities for peer review activities, in which they read one another's work with a critical eye and according to a specific set of guidelines, with emphasis on the need for objective review and objective response to constructive criticism. This, too, is authentic to real-world practice in writing. Structured self-evaluation and peer evaluation should be regular components of the instruction and assessment system in the language arts classroom.

Writing tasks are more authentic in nature when they are completed for the purpose of sharing with a real audience beyond the teacher or even classmates. Students might be asked to prepare reports on a research project to be shared with other students in the school or community members. They might prepare poems, stories, or narratives about school events for publication in a class or school newsletter. Students also might be encouraged to use persuasive writing skills to write book reviews to post in online bookstores or review blogs. Across all of these types of products, a component of the instruction and assessment should be a focus on developing audience awareness—a concept that also links back to literature instruction, because students should be encouraged to seek evidence of intended audience in the texts they read as well.

Naturally, audience awareness also is a key feature of effective speaking, and emphasis on audience should infuse oral communication tasks and assessments (Chaney, 1996). Presentation of the content of written products in an oral format is one way of integrating product assignments and creating opportunities for assessment in both areas. Such presentations allow for not only assessment of the oral language skills of the presenter, but also of the listening skills of other students through peer-assessment tools and through questioning and discussion. Moreover, such economy of assessment through tasks that address multiple outcomes at once is an important consideration in planning a curriculum.

CONCEPTUALLY ORIENTED CURRICULA

The Taba (1962) concept development model discussed in Chapter 7 encourages students to delve deeply into their understanding of an abstract concept and then to apply a renewed understanding of that concept in the form of generalizations. In the language arts, there are extensive, rich options for appropriate concepts to use as curricular organizers. Literature is a common ground from which the concepts fundamental to the human experience are explored, explained, and passed down from generation to generation and culture to culture, as the list of fundamental concepts found in The Great Ideas (Adler, 1952) demonstrates. The selection of a concept for a language arts curriculum, then, is more a question of narrowing a field of appropriate options than seeking possibilities. In addition, it is important to acknowledge that in any literature study unit, students will engage with a variety of themes and concepts beyond the unit's central organizer. Therefore, curriculum developers may focus overall on one broad concept, while including opportunities to build connections to additional concepts within specific activities. Selection of an overarching concept depends primarily on ease of application across subjects and upon the types of literature to be employed. The broader the concept, the more applicable it will be to multiple units and multiple selections of literature.

In the language arts units developed at the Center for Gifted Education, *change* was selected as the central concept for discussion and development (Center for Gifted Education, 1999). Change is an extremely versatile concept because it is familiar to every individual's experience of life and of the world and because it applies to virtually every aspect of life; it also is a highly accessible concept, meaning that students of all ages and varying levels of ability can bring an initial understanding of the concept to the learning experience.

The concept of change applies specifically to language arts in a number of ways. For example, movement of a plot requires change of some kind to be occurring; character development through the course of a literature selection involves change; and the fundamental purpose of many literature selections is to change the mind of the reader in some way, as Downs (1978) demonstrated in a discussion of revolutionary literature throughout history. The evolution of a piece of writing is a process of change, and just as students might be changed in some way by the literature they read, they may seek to bring about change in others through their own writing. Study of language also provides an excellent context for examining change because of the ways that language evolves over time yet still maintains patterns. By exploring word usage and stylistic changes in writing over time, students learn about cultural values and behaviors across different periods, and they develop an increasing awareness of their own role as contributors to and users of an active, changing language.

Chapter 7 has already provided some suggestions regarding curriculum development around the concept of change and its generalizations. The sample lesson "Reflections on Change in Poetry" (Center for Gifted Education, 1998c) specifically demonstrates the embedding of the concept and its generalizations within a language arts activity. In this lesson, designed for upper elementary gifted students, an in-depth discussion of several short poems by Emily Dickinson is organized around the concept of change. The opening journal activity is meant to focus students on the occurrences of change in nature as they relate to changes in human emotion, as well as to demonstrate the cyclical nature of change and the fact that some changes are positive and some are negative. The bulk of the lesson then involves students in discussing how Dickinson's poetry demonstrates the generalizations about change (outlined in Chapter 7). Key elements of this lesson to note in considering curriculum development are the selection of literature pieces that demonstrate important features of the concept and the preparation of specific questions in advance to promote student thinking around the concept.

Beyond lessons that focus on a central organizing concept, aspects of the language arts curriculum should encourage students to identify and discuss other key concepts and themes that emerge from what they read, hear, write, and say. Questioning around themes and concepts may focus on having students identify central ideas within a text, or may ask students to explain what they infer a particular literature selection is conveying about a given concept. As explained in Chapter 5, as part of a critical thinking model, students may be asked to identify key concepts within a chain of reasoning and to explain the assumptions about those concepts held by major stakeholders. Students

SAMPLE LESSON
REFLECTIONS ON CHANGE IN POETRY

Instructional Purpose
- To develop reasoning and interpretive skills in literature by discussing poetry.
- To develop understanding of the concept of change and demonstrate its applications to literature selections.

Activities and Questions
1. Ask students to respond to the following question in their response journals: "How do the changing seasons affect your emotions?" Invite students to discuss their responses.

2. Divide the class into five groups. Assign each group a poem by Emily Dickinson, using the selections beginning with the following lines:
   - *"Presentiment is that long shadow on the lawn"*
   - *"Funny to be"*
   - *"The morns are meeker than they were"*
   - *"It sifts from leaden sieves"*
   - *"Dear March, come in!"*

   Ask each group to read the poem silently and aloud within the group and then to discuss how the poem shows that change is linked to time.

3. As a class, discuss the group of poems, using the following questions as a guide:

Literary Response and Interpretation Questions
- What is personification? How did Emily Dickinson use personification in each of these poems? Why might a poet choose to use this poetic device?
- What does the word *it* refer to at the beginning of many lines of *"It sifts from leaden sieves"*? How do you know?
- What are the secrets a century keeps?
- What is meant by the words, *"The morns are meeker than they were"*? What words might you use to describe summer mornings?
- Why is the speaker in *"Dear March"* happy to see March but not April?
- If you did not know the meaning of the word *presentiment* in *"Presentiment is that long shadow on the lawn,"* what context clues in the poem give you an idea of what it means?

Reasoning Questions
- What is the feeling the poet is trying to express in each poem? What evidence from the poem supports your response?
- What assumptions does the poet make about the century's secrets in *"Funny to be a century"*?
- How is the concept of time important in these poems?

Change Questions
- These poems demonstrate in several ways that change is linked to time. How do the other generalizations about change relate to the poem?
- What are some other signs of changing times and changing seasons that the poet did not include in these pieces?

Note. Adapted from *Literary Reflections* (pp. 169–172), by Center for Gifted Education, 1998, Dubuque, IA: Kendall/Hunt. Copyright 1998 by Center for Gifted Education. Adapted with permission.

also might be asked to identify or select a major concept from a novel and construct a concept map demonstrating how the idea is addressed throughout the text. For example, in the *Navigator* series of novel study guides developed by the Center for Gifted Education, each guide encourages students to map a central concept and to answer key questions about how the concept plays out in the novel what connections exist between the novel's treatment of the idea and how the idea is addressed in other novels students have read. Both of these questioning strategies—asking students to identify and explain key concepts, and asking them to apply their understanding of a given concept—promote students' ability to discern the key ideas in what they read and to recognize and understand the major themes that permeate world literature.

HIGHER ORDER REASONING

As discussed in Chapter 5, one of the keys to encouraging higher order thinking in students is to select a strong thinking model, teach it to students directly, and then apply aspects of that same model systematically in various contexts. In the language arts, such a thinking model makes an effective tool for teachers and for students, serving as a support structure for questioning, analyzing literature, writing and revising, and conducting research.

Paul's (1992) Elements of Reasoning, detailed in Chapter 5, represent a comprehensive model for reasoning around issues that also serves as a versatile framework for supporting critical thinking in the language arts. In literature discussions, the reasoning model provides a scaffold for the development of higher level questions around a given literature selection. For example, in the *Autobiographies* unit (Center for Gifted Education, 1998b), students are asked to read a chapter called "Literary Lessons" from Louisa May Alcott's *Little Women* and then to respond to the following reasoning questions in discussion (reasoning elements are given in italics):

- How important are a writer's powers of observation? What does the *evidence* in the chapter suggest about Jo's powers of observation?
- How is the *concept* of unselfishness played out in this chapter? In what ways did different characters display selfishness or unselfishness?
- Compare the descriptions of the writing Jo did for the contest with the writing she did for her novel. How did the *purposes* for each change the style of the writing?
- What is the difficult *issue* Jo must face with regard to her writing? What circumstances help her resolve the issue?
- What were the *implications* or *consequences* for Jo's novel when she tried to please all of her critics?

By emphasizing specific elements of reasoning in varied contexts, teachers raise students' awareness of the thinking processes they use when trying to solve a problem or draw conclusions from text. Through such practice activities, teachers help to equip students with an understanding of their own thinking that can help them when they are called upon to draw conclusions in new contexts, with new readings or questions.

Critical thinking, as discussed in Chapter 5, is not something reserved to the most highly capable or to academic contexts; critical thinking is part of daily life, from making decisions about what to wear in the morning, to evaluating options in the grocery store, to determining which candidate to vote for in a local or national election. The teaching and learning around critical thinking comes in emphasizing the awareness of it and being able to apply critical thinking elements to challenging content. Teachers can help students to build awareness of their processes of critical thinking, and the strength of the inferences and conclusions being made, by scaffolding students' work within particular critical thinking contexts. For example, in the language arts classroom, teachers can encourage students to analyze their own and one another's persuasive writing for evidence of logical reasoning. In reading, teachers can guide students toward higher level reasoning activities such as making inferences, predicting consequences, and interpreting assumptions by creating scaffolds from lower order comprehension skills to these more advanced expectations.

The *Jacob's Ladder* series from the Center for Gifted Education was designed to address such movement from lower order to higher order skills in a structured manner. These materials provide sets of questions, linked to short reading selections, that move students up a ladder of connected skills. For example, students may first be asked to sequence events from a text they have read, then interpret causal relationships among such sequenced events,

Sample 1: From *Jacob's Ladder, Level 3*		**Sample 2: From *Jacob's Ladder, Level 1***	
Creative Synthesis	The Gettysburg Address	Consequences and Implications	The Crow and the Pitcher
D3 Pretend you are an interested party from the audience (e.g., mother, father, sibling of a soldier; a soldier; a congressional leader; the secretary of war) who has just heard the Gettysburg Address. How would you react to the message of Lincoln's speech? Create a reaction to the Gettysburg Address.		**A3** What would have happened if the crow had done the following: • Kept putting his beak in the pitcher? • Flown away? • Broken the pitcher? • Waited for rain?	
Summarizing		Cause and Effect	
D2 In three sentences or less, summarize the message Lincoln is trying to convey to the American people.		**A2** What caused the water to reach the crow? What overall effect did it have on the crow?	
Paraphrasing		Sequencing	
D1 In your own words, paraphrase Lincoln's statement, "It is for us the living, rather, to be dedicated here to the unfinished work which they who fought here have thus far so nobly advanced."		**A1** What steps did the crow use to get the water? List them below in order: 1. 2. 3. 4.	

Figure 8.1. Sample *Jacob's Ladder* scaffolded questions. Adapted from *Jacob's Ladder Reading Comprehension Program, Level 3* (p. 44) and *Jacob's Ladder Reading Comprehension Program, Level 1* (p. 24), by J. VanTassel-Baska and T. Stambaugh, 2009, Waco, TX: Prufrock Press. Copyright 2009 by Prufrock Press. Adapted with permission.

and then predict consequences and implications. Thus, they are guided to link the comprehension skill of sequencing to a recognition of relationships among events, and then to apply such an understanding of relationships to be able to make logical predictions supported by evidence. Similarly, in another "ladder," students are asked to start by paraphrasing important quotations, moving then to summarizing what they have read with support, and then to synthesis of key ideas. (See Figure 8.1 for sample questions on selected ladders.) Again, students therefore move from lower order to higher order reasoning through a set of structured questions. As students review and reflect upon their work, they begin to see the steps toward higher levels of reasoning that they can use to tackle more challenging questions around more difficult texts.

In the area of writing, the reasoning model forms an effective complement to the persuasive writing emphasis in language arts curricula. Persuasive writing involves the presentation of a point of view on a given issue with evidence

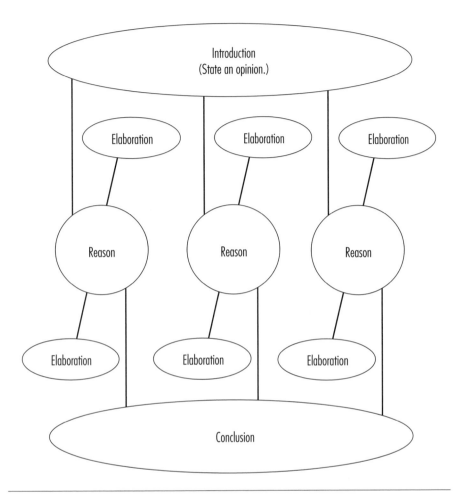

Figure 8.2. Hamburger Model for Persuasive Writing. From *A Guide to Teaching a Language Arts Curriculum for High-Ability Learners* (p. 53), by the Center for Gifted Education, 1999, Dubuque, IA: Kendall/Hunt. Copyright © 1999 by the Center for Gifted Education. Reprinted with permission.

to support it, thus reflecting key elements of reasoning. Although this type of writing is an important skill in everyday life and a foundational component of thesis development throughout education, studies of persuasive writing have demonstrated weak student performance (Gentile, 1992). Moreover, students are exposed on an increasingly frequent basis to expressions of opinion that may or may not represent well-reasoned arguments, through message boards, blogs, and comments on what they may read online. Therefore, persuasive writing and a focus on rigorous, logical argument is an important emphasis for language arts curricula, and its complexity, when coupled with intensive exploration of connections to the reasoning model, makes it particularly appropriate for gifted students. The Hamburger Model for Persuasive Writing (see Figure 8.2) demonstrates the basic format of a persuasive piece as presented to stu-

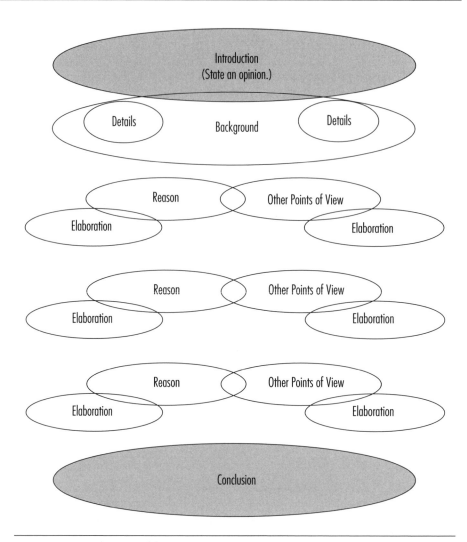

Figure 8.3. Dagwood Essay Model. From *A Guide to Teaching a Language Arts Curriculum for High-Ability Learners* (p. 54), by the Center for Gifted Education, 1999, Dubuque, IA: Kendall/Hunt. Copyright © 1999 by the Center for Gifted Education. Reprinted with permission.

dents in the Center for Gifted Education's language arts units, with a more complex version found in the Dagwood Essay Model for older students (see Figure 8.3; Center for Gifted Education, 1999).

Teaching a writing model through a deliberate strategy and targeted feedback has been found effective in previous writing research with gifted students (Schunk & Swartz, 1992); similarly, the Center for Gifted Education's units utilizing the Hamburger Model have been found effective in improving gifted students' persuasive writing skills (VanTassel-Baska, Zuo, Avery, & Little, 2002). The writing models also provide a concrete framework within which students may explore to what degree their persuasion is based on strong inferences versus weak data or inappropriate assumptions. Moreover, the standards of reasoning (Paul, 1992) and the elements together provide a framework within which students may understand and assess their own writing and that of others, including their peers' work and persuasive selections drawn from the media, literature, and historical documents. Issue-based research, also a key process skill incorporating many related language arts competencies, is closely linked to the reasoning model as well (see Chapter 6). This correspondence among persuasive writing, reasoning, and research provides a seamless set of outcomes to be addressed together within a comprehensive language arts curriculum for gifted learners.

SUBSTANTIVE CONTENT

The content of the language arts curriculum draws upon several sources for its challenge and substance; fundamentally, however, the most important foundation for the content of the language arts begins in the literature. Strong literature pieces, selected on the basis of their literary value, applicability to the lives and experiences of gifted students, degree of challenge, and relationship to the concepts central to the curriculum, are key to establishing substantive content (VanTassel-Baska, Johnson, & Boyce, 1996). The content of the curriculum then grows from the literature—through specific questions developed to encourage deep thinking about the pieces, through writing assignments that require reflection about the literature and creation of connections to other literature and to life, and through other types of projects and discussions. Moreover, the other key piece of content in the language arts—the study of language itself, its vocabulary and grammatical structures— also may be drawn from literature pieces selected for study on the basis of linguistic, as well as literary, value (Haussamen et al., 2002; also see Thompson, 1996a, 1996b).

Language arts curricula for the gifted should be deeply grounded in the study of literature and language. Thus, crucial elements of developing an appropriate language arts curriculum include the selection of rich and rigorous reading materials and the development of objectives and tasks that engage the students in high-level inquiry and interpretation experiences related to those reading materials (VanTassel-Baska, 1995; VanTassel-Baska & Stambaugh, 2005). In order to ensure that the content is both advanced and substantive, the literature selected should be at least two reading levels above the grade for which the curriculum is intended, and, at least by middle school, students should be reading world literature not necessarily aimed at young readers. In addition, the vocabulary contained in this literature should be rich, varied, and advanced to encourage students to develop their abilities in this area of language arts content, as well as to provide exposure to the wide spectrum of background knowledge that is opened through a focus on vocabulary (Baskin & Harris, 1980; Marzano, 2004).

A strong language arts curriculum for the gifted should give students opportunities to explore given literature selections in depth and then to engage in analysis and synthesis at a conceptual level across literature selections, thus involving them in advanced levels of literary criticism, rather than mere comprehension of given pieces. In writing and speaking, as well, students should learn advanced forms and styles, developing and refining their own works as they examine and practice with the works of others.

In the area of language study, rather than teaching students parts of speech, spelling, and rules of usage in isolation, teachers may instead teach grammar as a complex system of thought. Vocabulary and language study should reach beyond definitions of specific words and into stems and etymology and the fundamental structure of language at the morphological and grammatical levels. The Center for Gifted Education resources use a model called the Vocabulary Web to promote student understanding of structures within their language and to equip them with analytical tools for encountering new words. This model encourages students to begin with advanced vocabulary they encounter in their reading and to explore words at an etymological and connective level, thus increasing their own vocabulary through the in-depth study of specific words and the meaningful stems they contain. An example of a completed Vocabulary Web is found in Figure 8.4.

Throughout the language arts curriculum, gifted students should have the opportunity to engage with content in the ways that specialists in the disciplines do; they should be involved in critical analysis of literature, exploration of the history and structure of their language, and increasingly complex and refined forms of writing. They may gain access to this advanced content through classroom activities and also through extensions beyond the classroom, such as through connections with mentors who are professional writers. All of these types of approaches engage students in challenging, substantive content and encourage involvement and discussion. They also support integration of the language arts, which makes the content at once richer, more real-world applicable, and more interesting for students (Tschudi, 1991). Moreover, through the emphases described here, the language arts curriculum for gifted students can fulfill several of the aspects of differentiation discussed in Chapter 2 of this text, namely providing experiences at an advanced level through instructional strategies that promote thinking and use appropriate materials that challenge and engage students.

CONSTRUCTING MEANING

At the center of all language arts curricula and instruction is the element of constructing meaning. As we read, listen, write, or speak, we are constantly

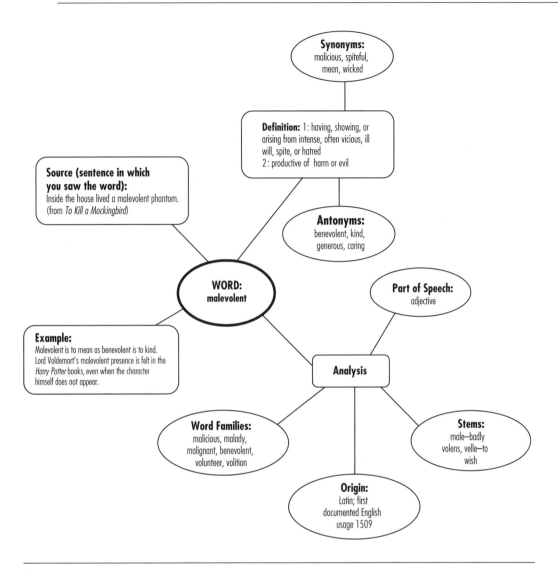

Figure 8.4. Example of a vocabulary web.

constructing our own understanding of the words, sentences, paragraphs, and pages we encounter and create; the very learning of language itself requires the construction of meaning. In language arts curricula and instruction, educators should support students in efforts to construct their own meaning and understanding of the texts they encounter, providing strategies for exploring literature both analytically and holistically. Moreover, teachers should provide ongoing and varied opportunities for students to express themselves in writing and speech, thereby helping students to refine their skills at constructing and communicating meaning.

Teachers and curriculum developers support students in constructing meaning by providing scaffolds that allow them to explore their understanding in an organized way. The Literature Web, for example, serves as an effective scaffold for exploring literature and the process of constructing meaning as one reads. Figure 8.5 demonstrates sample responses to the web based on Robert Frost's poem "The Road Not Taken." The Literature Web is based on the notion that literary understanding is found in a combination of the contributions of the text and the reader (Rosenblatt, 1991). It asks students to work with the text directly and with their own responses to delve deeper into their conceptions of the piece. Independently, students work to identify key words, feelings, ideas, images and symbols, and structural elements of a given piece; guiding questions and modeling the first few times students use the web help them to learn to focus on each of these elements and discuss their influence on the overall meaning of the piece. After completing a Literature Web independently, students work in small groups to discuss their responses, followed by a larger group debriefing. At each of these stages, students refine their understanding of the piece and their own responses to it by explaining their thoughts, pointing out supporting textual evidence, and listening to one another's perspectives. It is important to note that there are generally not specific "right" or "wrong" answers to a Literature Web, because of the focus on the reader's individual interpretation; the focus should be on drawing evidence from a text to support interpretations.

The Literature Web is a tool that may be used to support differentiation in the classroom as well. Students at a wide range of readiness levels can use the web to scaffold their analysis of and response to a piece of literature, but the literature pieces themselves might vary from one group of students to another. Students who are more advanced in their reading and reasoning levels can work with a more challenging reading that uses a complex structure or greater abstraction, while other students might use a piece in which the structure is more familiar or the ideas are more easily identified. In addition, the web itself may be introduced to students as a whole from the start, or it may be introduced an element or two at a time with different literature selections to guide students in understanding how to use it. For example, in *Beyond Words*, a primary grade unit from the Center for Gifted Education (2003), students first use just the key words and feelings elements of the web with one selection, then discuss those elements plus ideas in the next, and so forth until they have explored the web more fully.

Preplanned, higher level questions also add to the development of understanding because they facilitate guided exploration of specific and important issues by the teacher. An emphasis on higher level questions is important in fostering reading growth in students (Taylor, Pearson, Peterson, & Rodriguez, 2003), and planning questions in advance of the discussion helps to ensure that higher levels of thinking are maintained as the focus. Finally, when students are given opportunities to reflect further on their understanding through jour-

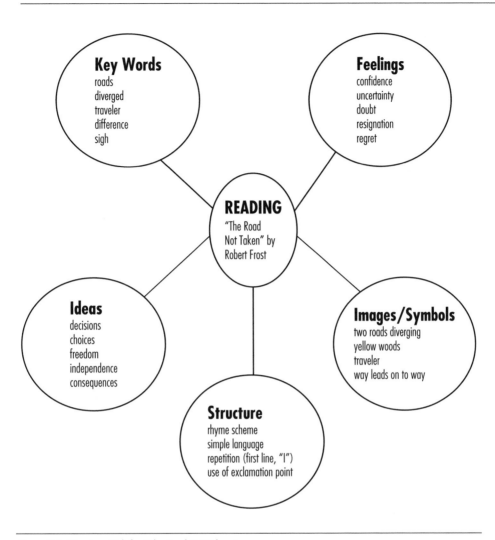

Figure 8.5. Literature Web for "The Road Not Taken."

nal responses and activities and questions that encourage comparison across multiple texts, they strengthen not only their construction of a given text's meaning, but also their ability to apply techniques of analysis to multiple contexts and new readings.

Another factor in encouraging in-depth construction of meaning is the frequent use of short literature passages in classroom discussions. When students are given opportunities to read, analyze, and discuss a text in one sitting, the holistic process is more effectively reinforced. In addition, shorter pieces allow for more in-depth discussions of a greater percentage of the literary elements in a text. Although longer pieces, such as novels, should certainly be incorporated into a language arts curriculum, teachers and curriculum developers should give careful consideration to the use of shorter pieces as the primary focus of classroom instruction in literary analysis and interpretation. When

Question category	Sample questions
While you read . . .	Why is Wilbur's escape in Chapter 3 such big news on the farm? Why do the other animals try to tell him what to do? Why do you think Mr. Zuckerman is still happy after Uncle wins the prize? Why do you think Charlotte's three children ask Wilbur to name them? Why do you think they decide to stay on the farm?
Exploring the story	How does the author change the perspective from which the story is told in Chapter 3? Why do you think he waited until Chapter 3 to start telling the reader about Wilbur's thoughts and comments? In what ways does Wilbur's life change after Charlotte starts writing about him in her web? What is good about these changes, and what might be bad about them?
Meeting the characters	Why do you think the author gave the geese their particular idiosyncrasy? What other idiosyncrasies do you see in the characters, and why do you think the author gave them those habits? How does Fern change over the course of the novel? What specific evidence shows how she is changing? In what ways does Charlotte become a leader in the barn?
Understanding the ideas	How do the human characters in the novel explain the writing in Charlotte's web? List at least four human characters and explain their responses. Why do you think their attention goes to Wilbur instead of to Charlotte? What does Charlotte teach Wilbur about the meaning of friendship?
Connecting to you	Explain what is meant by the comment that "when your stomach is empty and your mind is full, it's always hard to sleep." Have you ever had trouble falling asleep like this? Why was your mind full? What did you do to try to fall asleep? What are some of "the doubts and fears that often go with finding a new friend"? What are some of the things you think about when you first meet someone and start thinking about being friends with that person?

Figure 8.6. Sample questions from the *Navigator* for *Charlotte's Web* by E. B. White.

novel studies are employed, they also should include similar attention to having students focus on their construction of meaning. Once again, this effort is supported by tools such as the Literature Web and guiding questions. For example, in the *Navigator* novel studies from the Center for Gifted Education, guiding questions are provided for each novel within five categories that address prediction while reading, character analysis, understanding of plot, conceptual understanding, and personal connections to reading. See Figure 8.6 for sample *Navigator* questions for the novel *Charlotte's Web*.

All of the processes involved with developing written products involve students in the act of constructing meaning. Spivey (1995, 1996) noted that, throughout the process of composition, the writer is engaged in organizing and selecting content and making connections among ideas in order to create a coherent presentation of his or her own meaning and to provide a context within which readers may bring their own perspectives and thus construct meaning again. Yancey (2009) suggested that in our current era, the processes of composition are changing to become more and more interactive, and more and more people are engaged in writing for an audience on a regular basis. Therefore, fostering meaning-making within new models of composition is becoming an ever more critical element of education. The necessity of considering context, content, and audience, as well as features of format, style, and mechanics, makes the writing process a complex and challenging one and a key part of the substantive content of a language arts curriculum.

MULTICULTURAL/GLOBAL EMPHASIS

In today's society, a gradually broadening awareness of our complex human heritage and the contributions of multiple cultures and individuals to the present world has created a demand in the schools for a more representative study of many cultures in the curriculum. In addition, the growing diversity of American society has made it imperative to acknowledge and respect the diverse backgrounds of our students in both the materials presented to them and the ways in which they are presented. The Standards for the English Language Arts (NCTE & IRA, 1996) emphasize multicultural literature and study, as well as respect for diversity of language and culture, as do state and local standards for schools across the country.

One important way of establishing and maintaining a multicultural emphasis in a language arts curriculum is through the selection of literature. The literature pieces students read in the language arts classroom should reflect a wide range of cultural influences, with authors and subject matter representing varied backgrounds, experiences, and perspectives. In addition, students should be encouraged through discussions and writing activities to think about the perspectives they encounter in literature; the cultural influences on the authors, topics, and characters; and the influence of a wide range of points of view on society in general.

The diversity of authors writing high-quality literature for children and young adults continues to increase, and the content of the literature also is growing in its representation of many cultures and backgrounds. In addition, through technology, students have the opportunity to see and experience more of the world virtually from their classrooms. Nonfiction and fiction selections help to foster a more global perspective. In selecting literature for students with an eye to greater multicultural representation, teachers and curriculum developers must ensure an appropriate balance of perspectives and keep an emphasis on high quality overall. Miller-Lachman (1992) suggested several criteria to consider in making text selections to represent a broad array of cultural perspectives:

- general accuracy;
- avoidance of stereotypes;

- authentic, up-to-date, and age-appropriate language;
- attention to author's perspective;
- currency of facts and interpretations;
- concept of audience;
- integration of cultural information;
- balance and multidimensionality; and
- accurate and appropriate illustrations.

Ladson-Billings (1995) emphasized that, for curricula designed to represent and respond to diversity, the key issues for developers to consider are multiculturalism and relevance—first, that the curriculum incorporate content and materials reflecting many cultures and accurate representations of their characteristics and interactions; and, second, that the curriculum be designed in such a way that it is made relevant and comprehensible to students, with deep connections to their own diverse lives and backgrounds. These issues of multiculturalism and relevance are significant for both the curriculum development process and instructional planning, with regard to the types of grouping models, activities, and expectations used with students.

Related to the issue of a multicultural emphasis in language arts is the idea of studying additional languages. Incorporating modern languages into the curriculum, both as separate subjects and as an aspect of English study, allows students to develop a deeper understanding of the structures and history of their own language and also to expand their cultural understandings (Adler, 1984; Haussamen et al., 2002; Thompson & Thompson, 1996). Moreover, adding some degree of exploration of other languages to the study of English can raise the complexity level of the language arts curriculum for students, thus making it more challenging and engaging for verbally talented learners. Further discussion of second language study for advanced learners may be found in Chapter 12.

INTRADISCIPLINARY AND INTERDISCIPLINARY CONNECTIONS

Chapters 4–7 discussed the elements of the ICM in depth and its versatility in terms of supporting intradisciplinary and interdisciplinary connections. Curricula for gifted students should incorporate such connections in order to develop and encourage students' capacity for recognizing the complex, interdisciplinary nature of abstract concepts. Intradisciplinary connections in the language arts are natural and often allow for smoother instruction than separating the divisions of reading, writing, listening, speaking, and language study; in addition, evidence suggests valuable effects on achievement from integration of reading and writing instruction (e.g., Bottomley, Truscott, Marinak, Henk, & Melnick, 1999; Langer, 2001). These elements should be interwoven in the curriculum in such a way that students naturally come to appreciate and use the connections that exist.

Similarly, interdisciplinary connections may be made naturally from the language arts to a range of other disciplines, both in terms of content and the processes and habits of mind involved. Such integration of language arts with other disciplines promotes student learning across all subject areas and maximizes instructional time effectively (IRA, 2007). For example, literature of a period necessarily reflects the social and cultural values of that period, as well as historical events. Consequently, effective study of literature should incorporate social science connections. A lesson from a unit drawing on the literature and culture of the 1940s includes the following elements:

- discussion of a news article from *The New York Times*, December 8, 1941, about steps taken in major cities with regard to Japanese American populations following Pearl Harbor ("Entire City Put on War Footing," 1941);
- reading and discussion of the picture book *The Journey* (Hamanaka, 1990), giving background on the internment of Japanese Americans;
- reading and discussion of several poems written by an interned Japanese American woman; and
- a persuasive essay assignment regarding whether or not a similar situation could happen in the United States today (Center for Gifted Education, 1998a).

The background information provided and the critical analysis of the historical situation from multiple perspectives encourage a deeper understanding of the literature selections for students, even as the literature of a period can provide a broader and deeper understanding of historical events.

Other important interdisciplinary connections may be made with the "sister arts" of the visual arts and music. One example of how such connections may be promoted is found in an exploration of how artists of various types express their own identities in their work. In *Autobiographies* (Center for Gifted Education, 1998b), students spend much of the unit exploring themselves as writers and reading autobiographies of authors, thus developing an understanding of how life experiences affect expression in writing. In one lesson of this unit, students explore self-expression in the visual arts and in music by examining self-portraits of various artists and musical selections that reflect specific events and experiences in the lives of their composers. Students are then asked to respond to a global question: "How is every work of art in some way a reflection of the artist?"

An emphasis on nonfiction reading also helps to support active student engagement with interdisciplinary connections, promoting student learning in

Novel	Selected activities
Bud, Not Buddy by Christopher Paul Curtis	Read another historical fiction selection that takes place during the Depression and create a Venn diagram or chart to compare and contrast the way the period is described in the book you chose to the way it is described in *Bud, Not Buddy*. Then choose one aspect of life that was included in both books and read about that aspect of life in at least two nonfiction sources. (For example, you might read about Hoovervilles or bread lines or jazz bands.) Evaluate how accurate the descriptions in your novel were, based on what you find in your other sources. Write a paragraph or essay to explain what you found out.
Everything on a Waffle by Polly Horvath	*Everything on a Waffle* has characters who have traveled extensively and others who have never traveled far from home. The novel also explores the idea of tourism and what makes a place attractive to tourists. Find out about tourist attractions in your area or state. What is it about them that attracts tourists? How do "locals" feel about the tourism? What role does tourism play in your state's economy? Prepare an essay discussing the pros and cons of tourism in your area or state. Reread what Primrose "discovered that year" on pages 147–148. Although Primrose did not travel far in the novel, in what ways did she take a metaphorical "journey"? Explore some examples of stories in which a character goes off into the world to try to find something, and ends up finding it at home or inside him- or herself. Examples might include *The Wonderful Wizard of Oz* (or the movie *The Wizard of Oz*), *The Phantom Tollbooth*, or *The Neverending Story*. Then create an artistic representation that shows how *Everything on a Waffle* was in some ways a journey of discovery like the other stories you explored.
Charlotte's Web by E. B. White	In Chapter 5, Charlotte explains to Wilbur how spiders help to control the bug population in the world. Find out more about different kinds of spiders and how they interact with other living things in the ecosystem. Write a persuasive essay sharing what you discovered to help people who say they hate spiders to understand these creatures better.

Figure 8.7. Sample interdisciplinary connections and research activities from selected *Navigators.*

language arts, as well as in the content area that is the subject of the reading selection. Students should be encouraged to explore the structure of what they read and the author's style in nonfiction as well as fiction reading, and to try to explore varied forms of nonfiction in their own writing. Whatever the genre of their reading—fiction or nonfiction—students also may be encouraged to pursue interdisciplinary connections through extension assignments in which they seek further understanding of a topic or issue related to their reading. For example, in the *Navigator* series, students are given suggestions of interdisciplinary extension projects that link to each novel studied, in connection with some topic or issue within the novel or other related texts. See Figure 8.7 for samples of interdisciplinary projects related to selected novels.

In addition to these specific examples of potential intradisciplinary and interdisciplinary connections, the other most viable foundation for such connections is the abstract concept underscoring the curriculum. In the case of change, the concept is central to understanding the major strands of the language arts because change is a universal theme in all great literature, is central to understanding the writing process, and defines key approaches to teaching language study. Beyond the language arts, change also is a central concept in almost every other discipline; thus, it provides a bridge for making connections across subject areas in school and to the larger world. For example, students may explore how changes in the plot of a short story or novel are symbolic of historical events; how changes in the writing styles of novelists across their lifespans reflect changes in their societies; or how the style of one's writing changes depending on whether the writing is narrative, technical, or descriptive and what such changes reveal about the intended audience. Thus, the concept serves as an effective basis for thought-provoking connections across the disciplines.

MATERIALS AND RESOURCES

The materials and resources with which students engage as they learn are a key part of developing and implementing strong curricula. In the language arts, the focus on materials and resources must include careful consideration of what students will read, as well as an emphasis on support materials that promote understanding and growth.

Literature to support a language arts curriculum for gifted students must be carefully selected to challenge students appropriately. As mentioned previously, one strong criterion for literature selection is to select works at least two grade levels above the target group of students. Along with challenge and complexity, teachers and curriculum developers also should emphasize variety in their choices of literature in terms of author, topic, culture, time period, length, and genre. Classic literature—reflecting the best of literary accomplishment across time and cultures—should be incorporated in the curriculum throughout the school years to encourage deep and aesthetic literary experiences. At the same time, literature selections that represent the best of current writing also should be included, again representing a broad range of genres, authors, and topics.

Several texts recommending literature for gifted students have been published in the last several decades (e.g., Baskin & Harris, 1980; Halsted, 2009; Hauser & Nelson, 1988); although some of these books are many years old, the lists of criteria they provide are still viable and useful for the curriculum developer and teacher, and many of the texts they recommend still have strong appeal for readers. One set of criteria found particularly useful in the development of the Center for Gifted Education's language arts curriculum came from the work of Baskin and Harris (1980), who recommended that books for the gifted be selected according to the following criteria:

- The language used in books for the gifted should be rich, varied, precise, complex, and exciting, for language is the instrument for the reception and expression of thought.

- Books should be chosen with an eye to their open-endedness and their capacity to inspire contemplative behavior, such as through techniques of judging time sequences, shifting narrators, and unusual speech patterns of characters.
- Books for the gifted should be complex enough to allow interpretive and evaluative behaviors from readers.
- Books for the gifted should help them to build problem-solving skills and develop methods of productive thinking.
- Books should provide role models for emulation.
- Books should be broad-based in form, from picture books, to folk tales and myths, to nonfiction, to biography, to poetry, to fiction.

In addition to texts such as those cited above, several websites also make up-to-date recommendations of books from teachers, parents, and gifted students easily accessible (e.g., http://www.hoagiesgifted.org/reading_lists.htm). In addition, resources such as lists of award winners, book reviews in publications such as the *Horn Book* and on websites for booksellers, and online sources for previewing books are useful in making selections of literature for classroom use.

The emphasis on high-quality, carefully selected literature pieces does not mean there is no room in the language arts curriculum for student choice and interest to be considered in what they are expected to read. Particularly at the adolescent level, given increasing evidence of students' disconnected feelings from what they read in school (Ivey & Broaddus, 2001; Pitcher et al., 2007), attention to student engagement with literature and opportunities for choice are critical. Therefore, curriculum developers and teachers should seek to strike a balance, ensuring that students have opportunities for exposure to a broad range of literature selections; for deep engagement with challenging, complex selections chosen for a particular purpose; and for time to read some selections of their own choosing, both for pleasure and to extend upon their more structured literature study.

Beyond selection of literature for classroom lessons, discussions, and independent reading activities, curriculum developers also should have a strong sense of support materials available to supplement the curriculum. Additional discussion of criteria for evaluating materials, along with a list of some suggested titles, may be found in Chapter 14.

TECHNOLOGY CONNECTIONS

Every area of the curriculum and, seemingly, every area of life today is inextricably tied in with the technology explosion. People rely more and more each day on their technological tools to accomplish daily goals, to communicate, and to be entertained, and students in schools are increasingly connected to the world outside the classroom with a variety of electronic devices and services. Given the prevalence of technology in so many aspects of students' lives, it is increasingly important to ensure that the curriculum across content areas uses technology extensively and appropriately and also provides opportunities for students to learn appropriate use of the tools available to them.

Technology provides several major areas of support for the language arts curriculum for gifted students. One relates to the changing ways of accomplishing writing today. Yancey (2009) pointed out the frequency with which composition is done in an online and interactive format, as well as the increasing community of people who engage in writing online. Students use e-mail, texting, instant messaging, and social networking to connect with one another; therefore, they are engaged in forms of writing for communication purposes on a highly frequent basis. It is important for language arts curriculum to allow students to explore the many ways of using writing for communication, even as it emphasizes certain fundamental features of formal writing for academic purposes and, ultimately, for many career purposes. Integration of technology tools in the language arts curriculum should promote writing development by allowing students to compose, revise, edit, and share their writing using technology; by inviting students to explore varied writing styles and formats, as well as tools; and by encouraging students to critique writing that they see online. In addition, by giving attention to the varied forms of communication through technology that students use, teachers can encourage students to think carefully about purpose and audience for their writing in the decisions they make about format and formality of what they write.

Technology also provides support for student research in a variety of ways. The Internet provides unimaginable volumes of research and resources at students' fingertips, giving access to far-off places and authentic materials and texts that otherwise might be difficult or even impossible to bring to the classroom. Online sources also allow students to have easy access to authors' websites, some literary criticism on what they read, and other direct and interdisciplinary connections to their books. Many authors of children's and young adult literature maintain websites with questions and answers about their books, biographical information, and other resources. Museums and research centers about major authors throughout history also provide valuable websites. Such access to a broad range of related sources provides opportunities for promoting careful, critical thinking about the sources students use to support their research.

For language study, a number of websites draw upon several different dictionaries at once to provide definitions of words from multiple sources. There are many websites that highlight common questions and answers, as well as common errors in grammar, spelling, and usage. Several sites provide "word of the day" options—often in more than one language—for vocabulary development, in addition to etymological information, word games, and question-and-answer sections.

One excellent place for teachers to begin looking at online resources related to language arts is http://www.readwritethink.org, a site maintained through the IRA and NCTE as a support for teachers, parents, and students. Not only does the site contain extensive teacher resources, it has links and interactive activities for students, and any external website link is carefully screened to avoid sites with extensive advertisements or content that is not supportive of the goals of the two organizations. See Chapter 15 of this text for further discussion of technology resources and applications in the classroom.

INQUIRY-BASED LEARNING AND OTHER MODELS

An inquiry-based orientation to learning in the language arts involves active participation from students in both developing questions and finding answers to them, as well as skilled guidance from the teacher and the use of thinking strategies that promote exploration, analysis, and further questioning. Questioning strategies important in analyzing and interpreting literature involve encouraging students to ask questions, as well as answer them, using Socratic techniques. In language arts, inquiry-based learning can range from small-scale activities to larger scale research investigations that engage students in pursuing their own questions while they learn research processes.

The Literature Web model, as previously discussed, provides a strong example of a foundational structure that takes students deeply into their understanding of a literature selection and then lends itself to further discussion and inquiry. Carefully prepared interpretive questions that guide students deeply into an understanding of a work of literature are a hallmark of both the Center for Gifted Education's language arts units and the shared inquiry model that is the basis for the Junior Great Books program (Great Books Foundation, 1990). In both cases, the goal of the literature discussion is to encourage students to develop the habits of mind of the critical reader, including the ability to focus on central ideas and fundamental messages and to connect texts to their own lives and to their understanding of the larger world. The teacher's ability to facilitate such discussions and to follow up on student responses through probing questions and use of Socratic techniques is a key element of supporting inquiry-based learning for students in the language arts (Cawley & Corbett, 1996). See Chapter 5 for additional discussion of questioning strategies.

A research model encourages students in developing habits of inquiry by its very nature; authentic research requires that the researcher ask questions, not only find out answers to the questions posed by others. The William and

Mary Research Model (Boyce, 1997), outlined in Chapter 6, provides opportunities for such development of habits of inquiry. Research is central to all the disciplines; but, in schools, the language arts curriculum generally bears particular responsibility for teaching the skills of questioning, data collecting, and writing. Thus, appropriately challenging research should be a part of curriculum development in this area.

METACOGNITION

The final curricular reform element that is key to developing an effective language arts curriculum for gifted students is a concentration on metacognition. At a foundational level in language arts, monitoring comprehension is one of the critical reading strategies emphasized in recent literature on reading instruction (e.g., Harvey & Goudvis, 2007); similarly, planning and goal setting, as well as self-evaluation, are important parts of the writing process. Emphasizing students' overall consciousness of their processes of constructing meaning strengthens them as learners overall, and equips them with habits that will continue to guide their work as learners and thinkers. All of the emphases described in this chapter can become even richer and more meaningful for students if specific efforts are made to have students reflect upon their work systematically, including acknowledgement of their learning goals, monitoring of progress, and evaluating accomplishments. As students reflect upon themselves as readers, writers, speakers, listeners, and thinkers, they become aware of their own strengths and areas for improvement, thus encouraging growth and progress.

One natural vehicle for such reflection in the language arts is the use of journals. Student journals provide a forum for reflecting on connections between the literature they read and their own lives, both in terms of how they respond to the pieces and how reading and reflecting on the pieces changed them in various ways. Students also might use their journals as a place to note their emotional responses and preferences around what they read, to help them in making choices about the literature they read independently. Again, as has been illustrated with so many of the sections above, careful planning for attention to metacognition should be incorporated into the curricular documentation, including specific questions for journal writing, self-evaluation around given products, and other types of reflection. Moreover, the teacher should model metacognition for students. Teachers can share reflections on their own thinking processes, discussions of the way their thoughts or actions were changed by given events or encounters with literature, and the ways in which monitoring and evaluating progress has contributed to their personal development as a reader, writer, speaker, and thinker.

In using journals as a metacognitive tool, teachers can design specific questions that require students to reflect on their own thinking and how it connects to their experiences in the language arts classroom. For example, the following question appears as a follow-up to the discussion of the selection from *Little Women* mentioned earlier in this chapter:

> This chapter describes Jo's preferred conditions for writing—where she liked to be, what she wore, etc. Beverly Cleary wrote in "The Platoon System" that she liked to write when it was raining. What conditions do you prefer for writing? Describe your best writing environment and explain why you think this environment works for you. (Center for Gifted Education, 1998b, p. 113)

On a larger scale, students should be encouraged to maintain records of their progress and to reflect on their learning throughout a unit. This should be developed within a context, however, and a conceptually based curricular unit provides such a context. For example, in each language arts unit, students may reflect on how the generalizations regarding change are exemplified in each literature selection they read. However, from another vantage point, they are asked to examine how each selection changed them and, at the end of the unit, to review their portfolio of accomplishments and to discuss how they changed as writers during the course of the unit. Students also should maintain logs of their progress across long-term assignments, such as extended research activities.

CONCLUSION

Teaching language arts to high-ability learners represents a worthy challenge to teachers who must find ways to differentiate effectively for the needs of those learners. The ICM and the elements of curricular reform addressed here provide teachers and curriculum developers with a foundation upon which to build goals and units of study that are appropriately challenging for their gifted students. Across all of the elements, the differentiation features of advanced-level materials and tasks that add depth and challenge to the curriculum, as well as the use of instructional strategies and project work that promote higher order processes and complex thinking, ensure that the curriculum will support gifted students in their growth as readers, writers, and overall learners.

KEY POINTS SUMMARY

* Teaching the language arts to high-ability learners requires differentia-

tion in all of the major strands: literature, writing, language study, and oral communication.

- Selecting readings that are intellectually challenging is a cornerstone of an effective language arts curriculum for high-ability learners.
- Using short and complex reading selections for analysis and interpretation assesses student capability to handle difficult texts and allows in-depth classroom discussion of texts holistically.
- Questioning strategies may be applied to promote comprehension and to give students scaffolds to move from comprehension to more advanced levels of literary analysis and interpretation.
- Using models to teach writing allows for greater student growth.
- Writing instruction should incorporate attention to developing individual preferences and styles, through reflective activities that promote students' careful consideration of their own processes.
- Diversity in types of activity, as well as depth and complexity, characterizes a well-differentiated language arts curriculum.
- Performance-based assessment models are essential in gauging students' deep understanding of the language arts.
- Open and structured journal activities are important for promoting meta-cognition and personal reflection related to literature and writing.

REFERENCES

Adler, M. J. (1952). *Great ideas: A syntopicon of great books of the Western world.* Chicago, IL: Encyclopedia Britannica.

Adler, M. J. (1984). *The Paideia program.* New York, NY: Collier.

Baskin, B. H., & Harris, K. H. (1980). *Books for the gifted child.* New York, NY: Bowker.

Bottomley, D. M., Truscott, D. M., Marinak, B. A., Henk, W. A., & Melnick, S. A. (1999). An affective comparison of whole language, literature-based and basal reader literacy instruction. *Reading Research and Instruction, 29,* 115–129.

Boyce, L. N. (1997). *A guide to teaching research skills and strategies for grades 4–12.* Williamsburg, VA: Center for Gifted Education, The College of William and Mary.

Cawley, C., & Corbett, J. (1996). Constructing meaning through shared inquiry. In J. VanTassel-Baska, D. T. Johnson, & L. N. Boyce (Eds.), *Developing verbal talent: Ideas and strategies for teachers of elementary and middle school students* (pp. 333–356). Boston, MA: Allyn & Bacon.

Center for Gifted Education. (1998a). *The 1940s: A decade of change.* Dubuque, IA: Kendall/Hunt.

Center for Gifted Education. (1998b). *Autobiographies.* Dubuque, IA: Kendall/Hunt.

Center for Gifted Education. (1998c). *Literary reflections.* Dubuque, IA: Kendall/Hunt.

Center for Gifted Education. (1999). *Guide to teaching a language arts curriculum for high-ability learners.* Dubuque, IA: Kendall/Hunt.

Center for Gifted Education. (2003). *Beyond words.* Dubuque, IA: Kendall/Hunt.

Center for Gifted Education. (2006). *The Jacob's ladder reading comprehension program.* Williamsburg, VA: Author.

Chaney, A. (1996). Oral communication: Thinking in action. In J. VanTassel-Baska, D. T. Johnson, & L. N. Boyce (Eds.), *Developing verbal talent: Ideas and strategies for teachers of elementary and middle school students* (pp. 115–132). Boston, MA: Allyn & Bacon.

Downs, R. B. (1978). *Books that changed the world* (2nd ed.). Chicago, IL: American Library Association.

Eckert, L. S. (2008). Bridging the pedagogical gap: Intersections between literary and reading theories in secondary and postsecondary literacy instruction. *Journal of Adolescent and Adult Literacy, 52,* 110–118.

Entire city put on war footing. (1941, December 8). *The New York Times,* pp. 1, 3.

Gentile, C. (1992). *Exploring new methods for collecting students' school based writing: NAEP's 1990 portfolio study.* Washington, DC: National Center for Education Statistics.

Great Books Foundation. (1990). *Junior Great Books teacher's edition.* Chicago, IL: Author.

Halsted, J. W. (2009). *Some of my best friends are books* (3rd ed.). Scottsdale, AZ: Great Potential Press.

Hamanaka, S. (1990). *The journey.* New York, NY: Orchard Books.

Harvey, S., & Goudvis, A. (2007). *Strategies that work: Teaching comprehension for understanding and engagement* (2nd ed.). Portland, ME: Stenhouse.

Hauser, P., & Nelson, G. A. (1988). *Books for the gifted child* (Vol. 2). New York, NY: Bowker.

Haussamen, B., Doniger, P., Dykstra, P., Kolln, M., Rogers, K., & Wheeler, R. (2002). *NCTE guideline on some questions and answers about grammar.* Urbana, IL: National Council of Teachers of English. Retrieved from http://www.ncte.org/positions/statements/qandaaboutgrammar

Ivey, G., & Broaddus, K. (2001). "Just plain reading": A survey of what makes students want to read in middle school classrooms. *Reading Research Quarterly, 36,* 350–377.

International Reading Association. (2007). *Making every moment count: Maximizing quality instructional time.* Retrieved from http://www.reading.org/Libraries/Reports_and_Standards/MEMC_070620.sflb.ashx

International Reading Association, & National Council of Teachers of English. (1996). *Standards for the English language arts.* Urbana, IL: Author.

Ladson-Billings, G. (1995). Challenging customs, canons, and content: Developing relevant curriculum for diversity. In C. A. Grant (Ed.), *Educating for diversity: An anthology of multicultural voices* (pp. 327–340). Boston, MA: Allyn & Bacon.

Langer, J. A. (1995). *Envisioning literature: Literary understanding and literature instruction.* New York, NY: Teachers College Press.

Langer, J. A. (2001). Beating the odds: Teaching middle and high school students to read and write well. *American Educational Research Journal, 38,* 837–880.

Marzano, R. (1992). *Cultivating thinking in English.* Urbana, IL: National Council of Teachers of English.

Marzano, R. (2004). *Building background knowledge for academic achievement: Research on what works in schools.* Alexandria, VA: Association for Supervision and Curriculum Development.

McTighe, J., & O'Connor, K. (2005). Seven practices for effective learning. *Educational Leadership, 63*(3), 10–17.

Miller-Lachman, L. (1992). *Our family, our friends, our world: An annotated guide to significant multicultural books for children and teenagers.* New Providence, NJ: Bowker.

National Endowment for the Arts. (2004). *Reading at risk: A survey of literary reading in America* (Research Division Report #46). Washington, DC: Author.

Partnership for 21st Century Skills. (2009). *Framework for 21st century learning.* Tucson, AZ: Author. Retrieved from http://www.21stcenturyskills.org

Paul, R. (1992). *Critical thinking: What every thinking person needs to survive in a rapidly changing world.* Rohnert Park, CA: Foundation for Critical Thinking.

Pitcher, S. M., Albright, L. K., DeLaney, C. J., Walker, N. T., Seunarinesingh, K., Mogge, S., . . . Dunston, P. J. (2007). Assessing adolescents' motivation to read. *Journal of Adolescent and Adult Literacy, 50,* 378–396.

Rosenblatt, L. M. (1991). Literary theory. In J. Flood, J. M. Jensen, D. Lapp, & J. R. Squire (Eds.), *Handbook of research on teaching the English language arts* (pp. 57–62). New York, NY: Macmillan.

Schunk, D., & Swartz, C. (1992, April). *Goal and feedback during writing strategy instruction with gifted students.* Presentation at the annual meeting of the American Educational Research Association, San Francisco, CA.

Spivey, N. N. (1995). Written discourse: A constructivist perspective. In L. P. Steffe & J. Gale (Eds.), *Constructivism in education* (pp. 313–329). Hillsdale, NJ: Lawrence Erlbaum.

Spivey, N. N. (1996). Reading, writing, and the construction of meaning. In J. VanTassel-Baska, D. T. Johnson, & L. N. Boyce (Eds.), *Developing verbal talent: Ideas and strategies for teachers of elementary and middle school students* (pp. 34–55). Boston, MA: Allyn & Bacon.

Taba, H. (1962). *Curriculum development, theory, and practice.* New York, NY: Harcourt, Brace, & World.

Taylor, B. M., Pearson, P. D., Peterson, D. S., & Rodriguez, M. C. (2003). Reading growth in high-poverty classrooms: The influence of teacher practices that encourage cognitive engagement in literacy learning. *The Elementary School Journal, 104,* 3–30.

Thompson, M. C. (1996a). Formal language study for gifted students. In J. VanTassel-Baska, D. T. Johnson, & L. N. Boyce (Eds.), *Developing verbal talent: Ideas and strategies for teachers of elementary and middle school students* (pp. 149–173). Boston, MA: Allyn & Bacon.

Thompson, M. C. (1996b). Mentors on paper: How classics develop verbal ability. In J. VanTassel-Baska, D. T. Johnson, & L. N. Boyce (Eds.), *Developing verbal talent: Ideas and strategies for teachers of elementary and middle school students* (pp. 56–74). Boston, MA: Allyn & Bacon.

Thompson, M. C., & Thompson, M. B. (1996). Reflections on foreign language study for highly able learners. In J. VanTassel-Baska, D. T. Johnson, & L. N. Boyce

(Eds.), *Developing verbal talent: Ideas and strategies for teachers of elementary and middle school students* (pp. 174–188). Boston, MA: Allyn & Bacon.

Tschudi, S. (1991). *Planning and assessing the curriculum in English language arts.* Alexandria, VA: Association for Supervision and Curriculum Development

VanTassel-Baska, J. (1986). Effective curriculum and instructional models for talented students. *Gifted Child Quarterly, 30,* 164–169.

VanTassel-Baska, J. (1995). Talent development through curriculum: The Integrated Curriculum Model (ICM). *Roeper Review, 18,* 98–103.

VanTassel-Baska, J., Johnson, D. T., & Boyce, L. N. (Eds.). (1996). *Developing verbal talent: Ideas and strategies for teachers of elementary and middle school students.* Boston, MA: Allyn & Bacon.

VanTassel-Baska, J., & Stambaugh, T. (2005). *Comprehensive curriculum for gifted learners* (3rd ed.). Boston, MA: Allyn & Bacon.

VanTassel-Baska, J., & Stambaugh, T. (2009). *Jacob's ladder reading comprehension program: Level 1.* Waco, TX: Prufrock Press.

VanTassel-Baska, J., & Stambaugh, T. (2009). *Jacob's ladder reading comprehension program: Level 3.* Waco, TX: Prufrock Press.

VanTassel-Baska, J., Zuo, L., Avery, L. D., & Little, C. A. (2002). A curriculum study of gifted student learning in the language arts. *Gifted Child Quarterly, 46,* 30–44.

Yancey, K. B. (2009). *Writing in the 21st century: A report from the National Council of Teachers of English.* Urbana, IL: National Council of Teachers of English. Retrieved from http://www.ncte.org/library/NCTEFiles/Press/Yancey_final.pdf

Zemelman, S., Daniels, H., & Hyde, A. (1993). *Best practice: New standards for teaching and learning in America's schools.* Portsmouth, NH: Heinemann.

Chapter 9

Adapting Mathematics Curricula for High-Ability Learners

Dana T. Johnson

Y*ou are a middle school mathematics teacher who is responsible for a class of sixth graders. In your class you have students of average ability and a cluster group of students who are mathematically gifted. The school district is pressuring you to make sure that all of your students pass the state performance tests in May, so you have been pushing hard on skills listed in the state standards for sixth grade. It is October. One of your students comes to you and complains that she already knows the material because most of the topics were covered in previous years, and even the new material is covered painfully slowly. What can you do to meet her instructional needs while covering the bases with the rest of the class?*

Many changes in instructional delivery have occurred with the publication of national standards documents in the content areas. *Principles and Standards for School Mathematics* (National Council of Teachers of Mathematics [NCTM], 2000) does not mention gifted students explicitly, but it clearly acknowledges that students are not all the same. For all students, the standards place a greater emphasis on areas that traditionally have been emphasized for the gifted. All students are now expected to complete a core curriculum that has shifted its emphasis away from computation and routine problem practice toward real-world problem solving, communication, and connections to other disciplines and the real world. Reasoning is now a major emphasis for all students. "Mathematical thinking and reasoning skills, including making conjectures and developing sound deductive arguments, are important because they serve as a basis for developing new insights and promoting further study" (NCTM, 2000, p. 15). This emphasis continues to be explicitly noted in recent studies and reports on teaching mathematics to gifted learners (see National Mathematics Advisory Panel, 2008; Sheffield, 2006).

Research supports the practices advocated in the NCTM (2000) *Principles and Standards for School Mathematics*. Grouws and Cebulla (1999) included the following among research-based best practices in mathematics curricula and instruction:

- *Opportunity to learn.* When students are exposed to new material, achievement increases. Teachers must ensure that students are given the opportunity to learn important content that is new to them.
- *Focus on meaning.* Student learning increases when instruction is focused on meaningful development of important mathematical ideas. Instruction should build on student intuition and make connections to other subjects, student interests, and students' past knowledge and experience.
- *Learning new concepts and skills in the context of solving problems.* Students can develop understanding of important mathematical ideas when given nonroutine problems to solve. It is not necessary to begin with skill development; in fact, if students are drilled too much initially on isolated skills, they may have a harder time making sense of them later.
- *Opportunities for discovery.* Research suggests that students benefit from a balance of practice and invention. Frequent use of nonroutine problems can help students build new knowledge.
- *Openness of student solution methods.* When students develop their own solution methods, they are better able to apply mathematical knowledge to new problems.
- *Use of small groups.* Working with others can enhance achievement. The tasks chosen should be appropriate for group work and should involve important concepts and ideas, not just skill work. By "putting their heads together," students can learn more than they might have learned on their own.
- *Whole-class discussion following individual and group work.* Students should present solutions to problems and discuss each other's methods and reasoning. In this context, teachers may identify misconceptions and seize opportunities for guiding understanding.
- *Teaching mathematics with a focus on number sense.* This involves being able to compute mentally, to estimate, to move between various representations of numbers, to judge the relative magnitude of numbers, and to judge the

reasonableness of numerical results. An integrated approach seems preferable to focusing on a single skill.

- *Long-term use of concrete materials by students.* The "hands-on" approach can improve student concept development and improve attitudes toward mathematics.
- *Student use of calculators.* Studies show calculator use enhances understanding of arithmetical concepts and problem-solving skills, as well as improving student attitudes toward mathematics (Hembree & Dessart, 1986). Calculators can be used as a tool for mathematical discovery.

These approaches are integrally linked and supportive of each other. Many of these practices are exemplified in the excellent eighth-grade Japanese geometry class shown on the videotape, Eighth-Grade Mathematics Lessons, produced as part of the Third International Mathematics and Science Study (Office of Educational Research and Improvement, 1999). They also have been supported by the National Research Council recommendations on how to teach mathematics in the classroom, based on contemporary learning research (Donovan & Bransford, 2005).

The current trend in mathematics curricula and instruction for all students is moving toward what has traditionally been advocated for gifted learners (VanTassel-Baska & Stambaugh, 2006). In light of this trend in which all students should engage in higher level processes, how should mathematics curricula look different for mathematically gifted students?

This chapter will explore the Integrated Curriculum Model (ICM) and the elements of curriculum reform as they apply to strong curricula for mathematically gifted students. It will emphasize several specific content-related issues, including attention to acceleration and pacing, along with depth and complexity, as well as the need for independent work and conceptual organization. Sample lessons will be used to illustrate key ideas, and specific suggestions for adaptation of existing lessons will be offered at the end of the chapter.

LEARNER OUTCOMES OF SIGNIFICANCE

The three dimensions of the ICM—content, process, and concept—provide a context for exploring ways to differentiate the standards and adapt curriculum and instruction for gifted students' learning needs. Table 9.1 provides some examples for grade 7 goals and outcomes linked to the three dimensions of the ICM and to the national mathematics standards.

The sequential nature of the mathematics curriculum and the tendency of mathematics textbooks to incorporate a considerable amount of review (Flanders, 1987), particularly at the elementary level, underscore the importance of devel-

TABLE 9.1

Outcomes of Significance

Dimension	Goal	Outcome	Link to principles and standards
Concept	Develop an understanding of what constitutes proof and how to show that proof.	Prove that the diagonals of a rectangle divide the rectangle into four triangles of equal area.	• Recognize reasoning and proof as fundamental aspects of mathematics; • make and investigate mathematical conjectures; • develop and evaluate mathematical arguments and proofs; and • select and use various types of reasoning and methods of proof.
Process	Improve problem-solving skills.	Solve problems presented on the Math Forum "Problem of the Week" and submit a clear and accurate solution to the forum by e-mail.	• Build new mathematical knowledge through problem solving; • solve mathematical problems that arise in other contexts; • apply and adapt a variety of appropriate strategies to solve problems; and • monitor and reflect on the process of mathematical problem solving.
Content	Analyze the behavior of numerical sequences.	Write the next three terms of a given sequence; write a symbolic expression for the nth term; and determine whether the sequence converges—if it does, show what the limit is.	• Use symbolic forms, including iterative and recursive forms, to represent relationships arising from various contexts.

Note. "Link to Principles and Standards" from *Principles and Standards for School Mathematics* (pp. 52–58, 296), by the National Council of Teachers of Mathematics (NCTM), 2000, Reston, VA: Author. Copyright © 2000 by NCTM. All rights reserved. Reprinted with permission.

oping appropriate learner outcomes in mathematics for gifted students across a range of years and courses instead of within only one school year or unit of study. Within and across courses, developing curricular goals and activities for gifted learners requires careful attention to the process by which a student is placed into a particular mathematics course, the degree of review, and pacing. These issues will be discussed further in the sections that follow.

PLACEMENT AND ASSESSMENT

Acceleration has a long tradition as a method for successfully serving the needs of gifted students in mathematics (Stanley, Keating, & Fox, 1974; Swiatek, 1993, 2007). However, effective use of acceleration practice in mathematics requires careful assessment of student achievement and determination of areas of need. Thus, diagnostic testing for placement is a key consideration in developing and implementing mathematics programs for gifted students. Beyond such diagnostic testing for placement, authentic assessment of student learning, including both formative and summative assessment techniques, also is a central feature to incorporate into curriculum development and implementation. Most gifted programs require multilevel screening approaches to ensure that the process of identification for programs will be predictive of program success (Colen, 2007).

Placement

Educators should determine the best curriculum placement for students in mathematics using a diagnostic-prescriptive approach. The learners in any given grade level or content area are diverse in their needs, but the diversity can be more extreme in the area of mathematics because of the sequential nature of the skills required. Precocious students who are required to proceed at the average pace for their grade level can become negative toward the subject due to boredom. It is imperative that a diagnostic-prescriptive mechanism be in place to identify the level and appropriate placement for students who already have achieved mastery of math skills. In elementary and middle grades, this can be accomplished by giving a version of an end-of-year test to see how much students already know. Those who have mastered 80% or more of the desired objectives should be placed in a more advanced class, along with a plan to address any apparent knowledge gaps that were uncovered on the pretest. If more than a small group of such students exists in a given school at a given grade level, the school might offer a course that is based on the next year's math content. If the numbers do not warrant a special class, a few students may be included with the next grade's math class, especially if there is a cluster group or a whole class of gifted math students in that grade. For students who are accelerated in mathematics classes, advanced performance in later coursework is supported by research (Sowell, 1993; Swiatek, 2007). For the top 1% of students, the appropriate level of challenge (depending on interest and learning style) may be an independent study approach such as Stanford University's Education Program for Gifted Youth (EPGY), in which students work independently and are in e-mail contact with a tutor (Ravaglia, Suppes, Stillinger, & Alper, 1995) or a distance learning course offered by talent search programs (Lee & Olszewski-Kubilius, 2006).

Two cautions are in order with regard to special arrangements for advanced mathematics learning. Whenever possible, students should work at least some of the time in a setting in which they are able to interact with others of their ability level and readiness for advanced content, rather than only working independently. An extracurricular activity, such as participation in the mathematics coaching and competition opportunities provided by a MathCounts team (MathCounts Foundation, 2000), might be the way to accomplish this for the student who is not in a class with his or her peers. Also, long-term planning needs to take place to make sure that students do not discontinue taking mathematics just because they have exhausted the available courses in high school. Additional courses such as Advanced Placement (AP) statistics may be added to the high school curriculum, or students may be scheduled to attend courses at a local college or university for dual enrollment credit, where there are likely to be other gifted students also participating in coursework.

Authentic Assessment

One thing gifted students can do well (even without instruction) is solve routine math problems. In order to document real growth and understanding, multiple means of assessment are important for gifted students. If the teacher asks, "How can I give these students the opportunity to show what they know and can do?," this should generate assessment ideas that go beyond the typical test situation. Authentic performance-based tasks in the mathematics classroom might include a math journal that asks students to explain their problem-solving methodologies and choices and their understanding of concepts; presentations of problem solutions to the class; or independent and small-group project work. Performance-based tasks should be embedded within units of study to allow for ongoing assessment; for example, in a unit on volumes and surface areas of geometric solids, a student might be given a cone, cylinder, rectangular prism, and sphere and asked to find the volumes and surface areas, correct to within a given margin of error. The following example is a more open-ended and challenging task that might appear as a summative assessment of a unit on surface area and volume:

> Use the next 50 minutes to write an organized explanation of the big ideas that you have learned during this unit on surface area and volume of three-dimensional figures. This should include not only formulas for all solids we encountered in class, but also explanations of where the formulas came from and examples of applications of these formulas in solving problems.

Or, another example on the same content might be a take-home assessment that challenges the student to do the following:

> You are a city planner who is tasked with making a recommendation for building a water storage tank for 100,000 gallons of water. Analyze all of the three-dimensional solids we have studied by showing (a) the dimensions of each that would be needed to contain the 100,000 gallons and (b) how much surface area each has (as the tower needs to be painted every 10 years). Make your recommendation based on which

structure would require the least amount of paint. Your work will be evaluated based on completeness, clarity, accuracy, and organization.

Each of these examples gives students a chance to show what they know. Unlike a multiple-choice test, they require students to demonstrate real understanding, not just good guesses.

HABITS OF MIND

Learner outcomes of significance in any content area and the assessments used to measure achievement of these outcomes should reflect an emphasis on encouraging students to develop the habits of mind of the related disciplines. The standard mathematics curriculum gives students problems that are usually solvable by the methods that are taught by example. This is fine for building a repertoire of mathematical skills, but it is not enough to build the mathematical habits of mind that mathematicians typically employ. These include creativity, tenacity, skepticism, and collaboration.

Mathematically gifted students need to experience the open-ended exploration that is the essence of what mathematicians do. They should be encouraged to both create problems and solve them, to think of questions that have not been asked of them, and to wonder if things are always true and then attempt to find out. If their only assignments are drill problems on one section of the textbook that are due the next day, students are not experiencing and developing the tenacity required for a problem that takes weeks or months to solve. Collaboration with others is important in the real problem-solving world, as reflected in the joint authorship by several mathematicians of many articles appearing in mathematical journals. Skepticism is an important quality of mathematical reasoning, as one should not be too accepting of any result until one can see the reason that it is true or disprove it with a counterexample.

Consider this question that I heard discussed by a math professor and an honors thesis student at The College of William and Mary: If two positive integers are selected at random, what is the probability that they will be relatively prime (that the largest common factor is one)? A person needs to have some content background in probability and a small amount of number theory to think about this, but it is a question that should be accessible to middle school students. The process of posing questions like this one, studying the patterns, and providing solutions (often collaboratively and over an extended period of time) is what mathematicians do. It is higher order thinking at its best and should be experienced by gifted students as much as possible in their school life. Typical textbook problems expect students to be able to solve them within a class period or overnight. Mathematicians often spend years working on a proof. To get a sense of real mathematics, high-ability students need to work on problems that are not easily solved in a short period of time.

SUBSTANTIVE CONTENT

A curriculum based on substantive content in mathematics that supports the development of mathematical habits of mind should reflect consideration of both depth and breadth, as well as careful attention to pacing. Again, pretests and ongoing formative assessments support the integration of these considerations in working to challenge mathematically gifted students. At the beginning of each unit, a pretest should be administered so that the content can be differentiated for those who have already mastered it.

Pacing

Because of the sequential nature of a mathematics curriculum, the pace of instruction is especially important. Once a student is placed at the appropriate level, the instruction should proceed at a faster pace than that of an average class. Therefore, moving a student to a higher grade level is not sufficient differentiation if the new class is not paced with gifted math students in mind. A high-ability fourth grader who is moved into a fifth-grade math class that covers the basics of fifth-grade math still needs differentiated curriculum. The most precocious students may be able to handle a compressed course, such as summer classes offered by talent search programs, in which students can master as much as a year's worth of material in 3 weeks. Various studies report the success of these programs in preparing students for more advanced courses (Lee & Olszewski-Kubilius, 2006; Mills, Ablard, & Lynch, 1992; Miller, Mills, & Tangherlini, 1995). In the time gained by faster pacing, more depth and breadth of content can be addressed. At the beginning of each unit, a pretest should be administered so that the content can be differentiated for those who have already mastered some or all of it.

Depth Considerations

The abilities of the mathematically gifted require that the treatment of topics be at a deeper level than would be provided for average students. For example, in the primary grades, students spend a large amount of time learning addition facts. The gifted should, instead, be engaged with questions that go beyond the skill level, such as looking for patterns in addition. They should grapple with open-ended situations, such as the nature of various sums of odd and even integers, addressing questions such as the following:

- Why is the sum of two odds always even?
- What can you say about the sum of three odd integers?
- What is true about the sum of any number of odd integers?
- Why is that result always true?

In an algebra course, students learn the quadratic formula for solving quadratic equations. High-ability students should be asked to prove the formula using a general quadratic form of $ax^2 + bx + c = 0$.

An example from geometry might look like the one below.

Make two cylinders from the same size paper. Which has greater volume?

a. Begin with piece of paper that is 8.5" by 11". Roll and tape it into a cylinder so that it is 11" tall.
b. Begin with another piece of paper the same size as the first. Cut it in half by cutting parallel to the shorter side. Tape the two pieces together along the 5.5" sides to make a rectangle that is 5.5" by 22". Roll and tape it into a cylinder so that it is 5.5" tall. For all students, this is a problem that will explore deeper thinking about volume. Below are three levels of depth that can be used to solve the problem. The teacher can set expectations for different student groups whose needs for depth are greater.
- *Concrete*: Pour beans into the two cylinders to see that the shorter one holds more.
- *Numerical*: Apply the formula for volume of a cylinder to show that the short one holds more.
- *Abstract*: Extend the question. What is the ratio of the volumes? Will that ratio be the same if the dimensions of the paper change?

Allowing student choices of tasks can encourage self-selection of depth. One example would be to assign point values to problems and tell students to choose any combination of problems that would give a total of 100 points.
- *5 points each*: Given two numbers, find the least common multiple (LCM) and greatest common divisor (GCD).
- *10 points each*: Given three numbers, find the LCM and GCD.
- *50 points*: Given two numbers m and n, show a general method for finding the LCM and GCD. Extend the method for any collection of numbers no matter how large.

In the sample lesson entitled "Patterning" (pp. 197–198), fourth-grade students engage in an investigation of a pattern made of regular polygons. All fourth graders should be expected to fill out the table through the 10th term in both activities. Others may be able to determine the answer for 100 terms. In addition, gifted students should be asked to write a formula for the general term, n. The third activity on the page is an extension that asks for a generalization of finding the perimeter of a figure made of any number of polygons with any given number of sides (i.e., using two variables). The spectrum of task demands in the lesson can be adapted from first grade through algebra. First graders may not be able to write notation for their ideas, but they can describe the relationships they see in words.

Using pattern blocks as a manipulative in the "Patterning" lesson can be a useful tool for all students. Gifted students may abandon the manipulative early, but it is productive and inspirational to thinking as they begin the process. This is a more abstract task demand, taking the activity to a higher level of complexity and abstraction that is appropriate for these students. This activity can be followed by more examples in which numerical data are given in function tables so that students have practice in determining general patterns from abstract data.

At the secondary level, the choice of textbooks for gifted students makes a big difference in terms of availability of challenging problems and applications. Within these texts, teachers should not merely require correct answers, but also should emphasize detailed and careful explication of thought processes used. Alternative and creative solutions to problems should be shared and discussed. Textbooks should be supplemented with interesting problems such as the following geometry example: Draw any 5-pointed star. What do you think the sum of the angles of the five points is? Can you prove it?

Breadth Considerations

With the time gained by moving more quickly through the core curricular material, it is possible to include some extra content that will benefit and interest strong math students. This might be thought of as analogous to the difference between (a) getting on the interstate and driving from point A to point B as fast as possible and (b) taking a few exits along the way to explore museums, historical sights, natural phenomena, and so forth. The enrichment may be either within a topic already under study, or it may be topics that are not usually included.

An example of enrichment within a topical unit of study is extending the study of square numbers to other "figurate" numbers. These would include triangular numbers or pentagonal numbers, which can be explored with drawings as well as numbers.

The study of number bases other than base 10 is another example of

SAMPLE LESSON: PATTERNING

Directions:

1. Place square pattern blocks end to end as shown.

a. One unit is the length of the side of the square. Study the patterns and determine the perimeters for figures that are made of 10 squares and 100 squares. Enter your answer in the table.

Number of Squares	Perimeter
1	4
2	6
3	8
4	
10	
100	
n	

b. Write a formula for the perimeter of a figure made this way with any number, n, squares. Show or tell why it works.

2. Repeat the activity with hexagonal pattern blocks as shown.

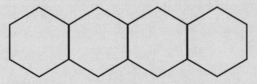

Number of Hexagons	Perimeter
1	6
2	10
3	14
4	18

Number of Hexagons	Perimeter
10	
100	
n	

a. Fill in the table for 10 hexagons and for 100 hexagons.
b. Write a formula for the perimeter of a figure made of *n* hexagons. Explain why it works.

3. Suppose you constructed figures in a similar way using regular polygons such as pentagons, octagons, or any number of sides that we will call *s*. Can you write a formula that tells you the perimeter of the figure made of *n* polygons, each of which has *s* sides?

enrichment that can be used in elementary school to enrich the study of place value. This would include counting in the new base, representation of numbers in various bases, addition and subtraction within a new base, and the study of place value in early civilizations, such as base 20 in Mayan culture and base 60 in Babylonian culture.

Another idea is to study Roman numerals. Roman numerals represent a topic that is not required to be taught, as there is no mention of it in the NCTM standards. So, a serious treatment of this number system as an example of a system that does not use place value would be an enriching experience for students.

As a cautionary note, however, both types of breadth considerations must be tailored to the gifted population. If the activity is one that would benefit all students, it is not sufficiently differentiated for the gifted. For example, if students are shown "number guessing tricks," many will only learn the trick. The purpose for high-ability students should be to discover and explain why the trick works. In other words, there must be depth within the breadth.

Math games and puzzles also are a good source of enrichment. Rather than just playing the game or solving the puzzles, students should analyze their own strategies to maximize the benefit of the activities. Questions that can model thinking for students are listed in Table 9.2.

Games or puzzles may be a type of enrichment that focuses on breadth, while the level of questions asked or the expectation of a product can increase the depth. An example using a game called Nim is shown on the following page.

Competitions

Academic competitions can provide strong enrichment, especially for middle and high school students. In addition to exposure to challenging con-

TABLE 9.2

Questions to Stimulate Thinking in Games and Puzzles

Example question	Content, process, and concepts supported
What strategies can I use to win or solve the puzzle?	Analysis
What happens if . . .?	Making inferences
Does it always work to do this?	Proof
Can I account for all possibilities?	Use of symbols and notation

A GAME OF NIM

Place sticks or other objects in 3 rows as shown here.

Procedure:
Two players take turns removing sticks according to these rules:
- Each person takes 1, 2, or 3 sticks each time.
- The sticks you take must come from within the same row. (Do not take some from one row and some from another row on the same turn.)
- The person who takes the last stick loses.

Questions to Think About:
1. What patterns of sticks are winning patterns? In other words, how should you leave the sticks after your move so that the other person loses?
2. Is it better to go first or second? Does it matter? Why or why not?
3. What if the rules are changed so that the person who takes the last stick wins instead of loses? How does this change your strategies?

Extensions:
- Add a row of seven sticks to the set up for the game. Do your strategies need any adjusting?
- Suppose you extended the pattern for 10 rows. How many sticks would you need? How many would you need for 100 rows? How many for any number, n, rows?
- Design a tournament for your class.

tent, contests provide an expectation of higher order thinking and a chance to interact with students of similar interests and abilities. They also are an excellent way for students to understand how they are faring with their talent development process in mathematics and establish a culture of excellence in doing mathematics (Assouline & Lupkowski-Shoplik, 2005). Karp (2003) studied the lives of former winners of mathematical Olympiads, finding them to be highly accomplished and productive in adulthood as a group, similar to Lubinski and Benbow's (2006) finding of creative and productive lives in adulthood, based on successful participation in the talent search competition at the middle school level.

Teachers who support such competitions should use some of the contest problems as classroom activities so that students who participated in the contest can share their strategies and get some feedback. Among popular contests are Math Counts, Math Olympiads for Elementary and Middle Schools, Continental Math, and American Mathematics Competitions.

CONCEPTUALLY ORIENTED CURRICULA

Concepts such as *proof*, *logic*, *systems*, *cycles*, or *models* can provide a more abstract way of organizing curricula. The lens of such a concept forces students to look beyond skills and discrete facts, reflecting the complexity and practices of the discipline of mathematics. A teacher might organize learning around a theme such as problem solving, as is done in *The Challenge of the Unknown* (Maddux, 1986). In these supplementary materials, students examine applications of real-world problem solving via nontraditional lenses. The concept of models is used as the theme of a middle school unit from the Center for Gifted Education: *Models: A Study of Animal Populations* (Johnson & Sher, 1997). This is a problem-based learning unit inspired by the problem of the overpopulation of deer in a suburban community. Mathematics and science are integrated in the unit so that the mathematics arises naturally as needed to support solutions to the problem. The unit concept of models includes physical, conceptual, and mathematical examples. It uses models to study population growth through activities such as examining deer data, growing bacteria, and studying a hypothetical set of data regarding plant growth that assumes doubling every day.

Another example of conceptual organization of content is the following sample lesson, "Properties and Operations," from a prealgebra unit developed by the South Carolina Consortium for Gifted Education (Peeples, 1994). In this lesson, mathematical concepts such as inverses and identities are studied as properties of an abstract number system, instead of in terms of how they apply to multiplication and addition in the set of whole numbers.

SAMPLE LESSON:
PROPERTIES AND OPERATIONS

Operation * (call it "star") is defined in the table below. It gives the result of combining two elements from the set A where A = {R, S, T, U} by using operation *. To read the table, locate the first element in the left column and the second element in the top row. The result is found where the row of the first element intersects the column of the second element. For example, T * U = T as shown.

*	R	S	T	U
R	S	R	T	U
S	U	T	R	S
T	R	S	U	T
U	T	U	S	R

1. Find S * T
2. Find U * U
3. Find T * S
4. Find R * T
5. Is operation * commutative? How do you know?
6. Is there an identity element for operation *? Explain.

A sample lesson on "Patterns of Rational Numbers" is included below. It could be part of a unit on patterns or a unit on the broad mathematical concepts of rational numbers and number systems. This also represents a comprehensive example of "deeper treatment" of content that most classrooms treat at the topical level of computation with fractions. The lesson requires students to investigate patterns of the decimal forms of rational numbers and ask them to discover the reasons why some terminate while others repeat.

SAMPLE LESSON:
PATTERNS OF RATIONAL NUMBERS

Background:
This lesson would be embedded in a unit on the real number system. The set of real numbers can be thought of as the union of two sets of numbers, the rational numbers (numbers that can be written as the ratio of two integers, such as $\frac{3}{4}$, $\sqrt{25}$, or 1.4) and the irrational numbers (numbers that cannot be written as the ratio of two integers, such as π or $\sqrt{2}$). What we call "frac-

tions" are a representation of rational numbers in fraction form. A decimal representation of a rational number is obtained by dividing the numerator of a fraction by the denominator. This lesson would be preceded by a lesson that teaches the concept of rational numbers that uses examples and nonexamples to determine what is meant by a rational number. This lesson will span more than one class period.

Prerequisites:

Knowledge of prime numbers, how to determine the prime factorization of a composite number, and ability to change fractions to decimals (with and without a calculator).

Objective:

Students will determine (without dividing) whether a given proper fraction will yield a repeating or terminating decimal form and will explain how the underlying principles determine the structure of the decimal form.

Activities and Questions:

1. Review the concept of rational numbers. Ask students what is meant by a rational number. Be sure they see the link between the word "ratio" and rational. Then ask them to distinguish between fractions and rational numbers. (All rational numbers can be written in fraction form. For example, 0.3 is a rational number. It has several possible representations, among which is $\frac{3}{10}$, the fractional form.) Have students find the decimal form of $\frac{1}{43}$ on a calculator. Ask: Is this the exact value or a rounded value? How can you tell? Allow discussion. Possibly use a Need to Know Board to record ideas as follows.

What do we know?	What do we need to know?	How can we find out?

2. As part of the "finding out" phase, use the following list of fractions for gathering data. Have students write the decimal form for each fraction. They may use a calculator.

$$\frac{1}{2} \qquad \frac{1}{3} \qquad \frac{3}{4} \qquad \frac{8}{9} \qquad \frac{5}{8} \qquad \frac{1}{11}$$

3. Make a two-column table on the board and separate the fractions from step 2 into two lists.

Fractions that convert to repeating decimals	Fractions that convert to terminating decimals

4. Use the following question as the basis of a discussion about the nature of fractions: If we choose any fraction and divide the numerator by the denominator to generate a decimal form, will the resulting decimal form always fall into one of the two categories above? Or could the decimal form be a nonrepeating, nonterminating decimal? Why? (The answer is that all fractions will convert to either a repeating or terminating form. If students are having trouble, have them examine the process of long division used in changing from fraction form to decimal form. They should see that eventually they will run out of different possibilities for remainders so either the remainder will be zero or they will re-encounter the original dividend, thus revisiting the previous cycle of divisors.)

5. Ask students to go back to the table and study the entries. In small groups they should see if they can form a conjecture that will predict which category a given fraction belongs to. Have them write up their findings but don't have the students share them yet.

6. Call the attention of all groups to the list of fractions below. Ask them to use their conjectures to assign these fractions to the table. (No actual division should be allowed until after they have made a decision. Then they can check on the calculator.)

$$\frac{6}{7} \qquad \frac{17}{125} \qquad \frac{199}{200} \qquad \frac{5}{13} \qquad \frac{9}{80} \qquad \frac{15}{24} \qquad \frac{11}{24}$$

If they were not right, they can revise the conjecture and choose some more fractions to guess and check. (Note: You may suspect that a group has discovered the rule if they are consistently placing fractions in the right group. Do not let them give away the rule to other students if they have discovered it.)

7. If the students are having trouble, prompt their thinking with questions such as these:

•   Does the outcome depend on the numerator? How can you find out? (Gently nudge them, but do not tell them directly. Write out the list of simplified fractions with the same denominator but different numerators and study their placement in the two groups. Do another list using another common denominator. This incorporates elements

of good experimental design—holding one variable constant [the denominator] and repeated trials.)
- Does it depend on the denominator? How can you find out? (You can use a similar method as described above.)

Teacher Background:
A fraction (in simplest form/lowest terms) terminates in its decimal form if the prime factors of the denominator are only 2's and 5's or a combination of 2's and 5's. Otherwise it repeats. In the examples listed below, factor the denominators into prime factors and see what you get.

$\frac{1}{2} = 0.5$

$\frac{4}{5} = 0.8$

$\frac{3}{10} = 0.3$

$\frac{4}{25} = 0.16$

$\frac{3}{16} = 0.1875$

$\frac{7}{20} = 0.35$

$\frac{1}{3} = 0.\overline{3}$

$\frac{1}{15} = 0.0\overline{6}$

$\frac{7}{30} = 0.2\overline{3}$

$\frac{3}{7} = 0.\overline{428571}$

$\frac{9}{22} = 0.4\overline{09}$

$\frac{5}{13} = 0.\overline{384615}$

8. Have each group report on its findings and through discussion make sure all have discovered the rule. Then ask about $\frac{3}{12}$. It is a terminating decimal—but the prime factorization of the denominator is $2 \times 2 \times 3$, so shouldn't it repeat? Encourage discussion.
   (Answer: $\frac{3}{12}$ is not in lowest terms. The rule only applies to fractions that are completely simplified.)

9. Have students write in their math journals using a prompt such as this: Explain why the decimal form of $\frac{3}{11}$ is repeating and the decimal form of $\frac{3}{40}$ terminates.

10. Lead a whole-class discussion using questions such as the following:
    - Is our reasoning in this problem an example of inductive or deductive reasoning? Why?
    - How do we know this "rule" that we have conjectured is always true?
    - Is it sufficient to show it works for 10 examples? 100? 1,000? (inductive reasoning)
    - What can you see about the structure of our number system that makes this work? (Answer: Ours is a decimal system. This means

that each digit represents a group of some power of 10. Because $10 = 2 \times 5$, you can convert each fraction whose denominator contains only factors of 2's and 5's into an equivalent fraction whose denominator is some power of 10. When the denominator is a power of 10, the decimal form terminates. For example, $\frac{4}{25} = \frac{16}{100} = 0.16$. This is deductive reasoning, as we are reasoning from known facts and relationships and applying them to this particular situation.)

Assessment:

Ask students to write the following in their math journals:

1. Which of the following fractions terminate in their decimal form?

$$\frac{3}{8} \qquad \frac{4}{15} \qquad \frac{7}{9} \qquad \frac{7}{50} \qquad \frac{1}{40} \qquad \frac{9}{36} \qquad \frac{7}{99} \qquad \frac{55}{56} \qquad \frac{3}{20} \qquad \frac{1}{14}$$

Write a short paragraph telling how you made those decisions.

2. Explain the underlying principles of our number system that make these "fraction to decimal patterns" work.

Homework:

Design a pretest that consists of 10 fractions on a page. Ask an adult (e.g., family member, neighbor, your English teacher) to circle the fractions that he or she thinks will terminate in their decimal form. (Do not let them actually divide.) If that person does not get them right, teach him or her how to do it using what you have learned about the patterns of rational numbers. Then give the adult a posttest to see if your teaching was effective. Be prepared to report about your experience to the class. (The debriefing of this assignment may include discussion about how well known this pattern is among adults.)

Application:

Why do we care about this characteristic of fractions?

- We use calculators so much that we are used to the decimal display of most numbers we use. Try dividing 1 by 23 on the calculator. The display probably reads 0.0434782. You are a smart person—now you know more than the calculator is telling you. Is the displayed value exact?
- Until recently, stock prices on the New York Stock Exchange (NYSE) were given in rational form, rounding prices to the nearest eighth of a dollar. Now, the prices are given in decimal form. What are the advantages and disadvantages of each system of reporting and bookkeeping?
- Fabric is measured to the nearest ⅛ of a yard in fabric store. Why do you think eighths are the fraction of choice?

Extension:

Think about the following question: What is the maximum number of decimal places necessary before the decimal representation of a fraction will either repeat or terminate?

- Make a plan for finding out.
- Carry out the plan.
- Use your hypothesis to predict the number of places required in the cycle of repeating digits in the decimal expansion of ¼₇.
- Write a description of what you decided and how you found out.
- Discuss with the whole class and see if all of the students reached the same conclusion. If you did not, argue for your point of view or acknowledge that your result was flawed.

Assessment for This Extension:

1. Assume that you are Dr. Math at the Math Forum (http://mathforum.org) and a student sends you the question below. Write a response to the student in your math journal.

> Dear Dr. Math,
>
> A section about rational and irrational numbers in our algebra textbook has the following question: A student who used long division to find the repeating decimal form for $\frac{1}{17}$ claimed that there were 20 digits in the repeating block of digits. Is this correct? Please explain.
>
> The textbook answer says that there can be no more than 16 digits in the repeating block. Do you have to divide it out to figure this out, or can you predict the number of digits without dividing?
>
> Thanks,
> A Lost Student

2. Let R represent a rational number that has a repeating decimal expansion. Let T represent a rational number that has a terminating decimal expansion.

- What can you say about the nature of $R + T$? Can you prove it?
- What can you say about the nature of R/T? Can you prove it?
- What can you say about the nature of T/R? Can you prove it?

The concept of *closure* means that when two elements of a set interact under a given operation, the result is a member of the original set. For example, the set of even integers is closed under the operation of addition because when you add two even integers, the result is an even integer. But the set of positive integers is not closed under subtraction because sometimes when you

subtract two positive integers, you get a result that is not a positive integer (3 – 5 = -2).
Is the set of {R} closed under addition? How do you know?
Is the set of {T} closed under addition? How do you know?

3. Pythagoras was an ancient Greek mathematician who was born in 572 BC. His followers thought that any magnitude could be expressed as a rational number. When they discovered this was not true, they were deeply upset. Read more about this discovery and report to the class.

HIGHER ORDER REASONING

Higher order questions can bring about the type of reasoning required to explore the depth and breadth of mathematical content and concepts indicated in the sections above. A study by Friedman and Lee (1996) showed that higher cognitive levels of teacher questions elicited higher cognitive levels of student responses. Gavin et al. (2006) reported a similar finding with their M^3 curriculum, used with students from Title 1 schools.

By emphasizing induction, deduction, analysis, and synthesis, teachers can guarantee higher level reasoning opportunities in the classroom. Both inductive and deductive reasoning are used in mathematics. Inductive reasoning is used when one makes a generalization about what usually happens based on particular examples (e.g., examining a set of ordered pairs and then writing a function based on them). Reasoning from known principles to particular situations uses deductive reasoning (e.g., concluding that a square is a rectangle by reasoning from the definition of a rectangle: A rectangle is a parallelogram with four right angles, therefore, the square is a particular instance of a rectangle). Both types of reasoning should be understood and discussed as underlying processes in mathematical thought, as illustrated in the sample lesson, "Patterns of Rational Numbers." Moreover, analysis and synthesis should be emphasized in mathematical learning as part of the effort to move away from discrete facts and skills.

Reasoning Through Communication

If reasoning is required to solve a problem, students should be asked to explain their reasoning in writing or orally. This process can help develop, reinforce and assess substantive concepts. Words, symbols, diagrams, pictures, or manipulatives can be used to show why concepts work as they do. Students who become used to explaining will develop the habit of asking themselves, "Why does this work?"

Using a problem-solving journal is a wonderful tool for individual com-

The vertices of a square lie on the midpoints of a larger square. If the area of the larger square is 8 square units, find the area of the smaller shaded square. Explain your reasoning.

Figure 9.1. Area of an inscribed square.

munication. We have all heard students ask, "If I can do it in my head, do I have to show my work?" By requiring an explanation, not just calculations on the page, teachers increase the task demand. Students will need modeling of what is meant by an explanation. The tendency is to merely write down calculations, but the real goal is for someone who has no idea how to solve the problem to understand it from what is written. An example is given in Figure 9.1. Some students may say that they see the answer is 4 because it looks about right, but by pressing them for a solution rather than an answer the problem is more challenging, and ultimately more learning will occur. Emphasis on process rather than merely correct answers is important.

By requiring writing, teachers also are able to assess student understanding of concepts and processes. For example, a prompt such as, "Write a story that illustrates $1\frac{3}{4} \div \frac{1}{2}$" would tell which students understand the concept of division rather than just their rote skill in solving the problem.

Group problem solving can produce solutions to problems that would not be solved by students working alone. When heterogeneous partners or larger groups work on problems, they can build on each other's ideas, challenge misconceptions, and refine their thinking through discussion. Whole-class discussions contribute to students seeing other ways of thinking about solutions and can serve as a vehicle to summarize the major ideas that students have worked on individually or in groups.

In college-level courses, communication about mathematical ideas is required. Students who have never been held to serious explanations are at a disadvantage. In the world of professional mathematicians, communication is key. There is much collaborative work, followed by written papers that are subject to peer review and opportunities for talks that explain the work of the individual. We should be cultivating skills that will support later opportunities. Often bright students who breezed through K–12 math courses are stumped when required to explain concepts in college courses. They may interpret their clumsiness as lack of talent, while it may simply be a case of lack of experience.

INQUIRY-BASED LEARNING

A discovery approach to seeking and finding patterns works well in mathematics, but it takes more careful planning of activities. Such an approach requires "nudging" students toward results, rather than telling them. For example, rather than being told, elementary students should be expected to develop the rules for addition of fractions. High school geometry students should figure out the conditions under which two triangles are congruent and then prove why. By posing questions, teachers can push students toward the habits of mind of mathematicians instead of merely training them in algorithmic skills and problem-solving strategies. Teachers can make routine questions more open-ended in order to set the stage for inquiry-based learning. Manipulative materials should be part of this approach; just because students are gifted does not mean that they do not need, or cannot benefit from, concrete representations of ideas. However, they may move more quickly than other students from the concrete to the abstract. For instance, students might use cubes to model volume and surface-area problems when the ideas are being introduced, but they would not continue to use them every time they work a problem.

Encouraging habits of mathematical inquiry also requires that students engage in individual and small-group problem solving and projects. Gifted students are capable of working on substantive math tasks independently. Self-pacing activities, such as Techniques of Problem Solving (TOPS, 1980) cards or Visual Thinking cards (Seymour, 1983), can provide such an experience. However, rather than working toward answers only, students should document their solutions in a math journal so that the process of solving problems is emphasized, rather than the answers themselves. The solutions become products, rather than accumulated points. These kinds of tasks can be a good basis for group problem solving and discussion.

Gifted students also should be engaged in some longer term student-directed projects in which they can work independently or in groups. One such project might be the planning and building of 3-D fractal structures, such as a Sierpinski pyramid (a self-replicating structure made of tetrahedra) or Menger's Sponge (similar to the pyramid, but cubic in nature). This should entail a presentation that explains the fractal principles that are used in the design of the structure. Other project ideas might be "Learn the game of Sprouts. Write an analysis of the game" or "Write a guide to doing the operations (addition, subtraction, multiplication, and division) in base six (or any other base)."

Principles of depth and breadth that were discussed earlier also apply to the implementation of projects. An example from arithmetic that seems deceptively trivial on the surface is the following problem: Arrange the digits 1–9 so that they form a correct sum in the form XXX + XXX = XXX (where each X represents a different number). The typical expectation in a regular classroom would be to have students find one solution. However, there are somewhere in the neighborhood of 300 solutions. Finding and cataloging solutions and making generalizations about patterns would make a wonderful, long-term, group project. In a unit on place value, this would be a depth extension of the topic.

MATERIALS AND RESOURCES

Relying on standard math textbooks is not adequate for providing the necessary depth and breadth of content. However, a number of new curriculum projects have been funded under research grants, especially from the National Science Foundation and the Javits Act, since the 1990s. They include various elements of best practice, but are not intended to meet all of the needs of high-ability learners. Multiple resources, including the Internet, print sources, and communication with experts, need to be used for both teacher planning and student investigations.

Examples of new areas of study are fractals, topology, and logic. An inspirational source for problems in these areas and others that could be independently carried out is *Mathematics: A Human Endeavor* (Jacobs, 1994). Websites such as MegaMath (http://www.c3.lanl.gov/mega-math/index.html) and The Math Forum (http://mathforum.org) are filled with ideas for extensions in the classrooms or use as independent projects. Both depth and breadth can be incorporated in high-level applications of mathematical ideas.

Mathematics units also have recently been developed by the Center for Gifted Education. *Beyond Base Ten* (Johnson, 2008a), intended for students in grades 3–6, focuses on the representation of numbers by using place value and non-place-value systems. Bases other than base 10 are featured through the context of early civilization number systems and then compared to current number systems. *Spatial Reasoning* (Johnson, 2008b), a unit for students in grades 2–4, approaches spatial reasoning through one-, two-, and three-dimensional tasks and includes transitions and representations from three- to two-dimensional objects. Another new unit called *Moving Through Dimensions* (Center for Gifted Education, 2010) exposes students in grades 6–8 to interesting real-world problems in multiple dimensions.

INTERDISCIPLINARY AND INTRADISCIPLINARY CONNECTIONS

According to Galileo, mathematics is the language of the universe. There are unlimited ways of applying it to other content areas and real-world problems. These applications should be important and well integrated, not just word problems that disguise skills in sentences. One such example is given in *Models: A Study of Animal Population* (Johnson & Sher, 1997), in which mathematical models are studied in the context of animal populations. Mathematical analyses can lend support to the research work in other content areas. They can be the glue for the data and evidence part of a persuasive argument in other disciplines. Moreover, real-world connections to the concepts and principles of mathematics may be explored as part of, or extensions to, lessons in the mathematics classroom. For example, the following two questions were used to extend the sample lesson, "Patterns of Rational Numbers":

*   Until recently, stock prices on the New York Stock Exchange (NYSE) were given in rational form, rounding prices to the nearest eighth of a dollar. Now, the prices are given in decimal form. What are the advantages and disadvantages of each system of reporting and bookkeeping?
*   Fabric is measured to the nearest ⅛ of a yard in fabric stores. Why do you think eighths are the fraction of choice?

CONSTRUCTING MEANING
AND METACOGNITION

The inquiry-based and higher order reasoning elements that are discussed above are the main tools used to guide students toward building meaning about the relationships and significance of mathematical ideas. Students should be asked to share the process they used in solving problems. If the teacher models thinking and questions students for deep understanding and processes, students will be better prepared for further study at the university level. A math journal is a good tool for encouraging and documenting thinking. The following example demonstrates an opportunity for students to develop their understanding of the key concepts further and to reflect upon their thinking process. The goal is not to get answers, but to investigate numerical relationships, share strategies of problem solving, form conjectures, and reflect on how old results and new information support or erode the conjectures. After students work alone on the first question, a discussion can be held so that students share and support their conclusions and strategies aloud. Various strategies for solving the problem may give students insights into alternate strategies for the second and third questions.

Suppose the post office only has stamps of the denominations 5 cents and 7 cents.
1. What amounts of postage can you buy? Explain your conclusion in your journal.

2. What if the denominations are 3 cents and 5 cents? Explain. Did you use the same strategy as you did in Question 1? How did the discussion of Question 1 affect your thinking about Question 2?
3. What if the denominations are 15 cents and 18 cents? Explain.
4. Based on what you figured out from these test cases, can you make a prediction about what amounts of postage you can buy if the only stamp denominations are 3 cents and 7 cents?

TECHNOLOGY RESOURCES

Technological resources, such as spreadsheets, graphing calculators, specialized software, and the Internet, are wonderful tools for student exploration and discovery in mathematics. If self-paced acceleration is desired, the mathematics portion of the EPGY program at Stanford is worth considering. It covers content from kindergarten to college. Students must be able to work independently, but they have access to an online tutor (see http://epgy.stanford.edu).

By middle school, gifted students should be exposed to a graphing calculator as a powerful tool for making mathematical discoveries. The function tables and statistical lists allow data to be examined for numerical patterns, while the graphing capabilities expose the geometry of the patterns. Any scientific calculator is a treasure trove of examples of inverse functions—from addition and subtraction, to the exponential and logarithmic functions—so students can carry out multitudes of calculations to see how inverse functions "undo" each other. They can then make generalizations based on the patterns observed. The calculator makes problem solving the focus rather than computation. For example, the purpose of a question such as, "How long is one billion seconds?" is to determine and implement a strategy rather than just divide large numbers.

Programming is an important skill for students who are interested in mathematics and science. Elementary students can learn a lot about programming by using a Logo program. Logo is a user-friendly programming language that incorporates spatial reasoning along with programming; students give commands to the Logo turtle, telling it how far to go and in what direction. The graphing calculator is a good tool for teaching programming to middle and high school students. Middle school students should be able to write simple programs such as one that will prompt the user to enter numbers and then calculate the average and the median of those numbers. High school students should be able to write a program for solving quadratic equations. Setting up a spreadsheet for a project is another kind of programming task. One example is to create a grade-keeping program in which grades carry various weights and need to be averaged.

The Internet is a rich source of enrichment, as many powerful mathematical ideas that are not included or barely mentioned in textbooks are presented here. For example, at Mega Mathematics (http://www.c3.lanl.gov/mega-math/index.html), a project of the Computer Research and Applications Group of Los Alamos National Laboratory, students can explore the concept of infinity at the Infinity Hotel, learn about knot theory, or find out about graph theory. Students also can interact with Sierpinski triangles while discovering the patterns that unfold within them at http://math.rice.edu/~lanius/fractals/sierjava.html.

There are many challenging problems presented on the Internet for students to solve. For example, they might go to the Math Forum (http://mathforum.org) and choose "Problems of the Week," where they will find problem categories of math foundations, geometry, prealgebra, algebra, discrete math, and trigonometry and calculus. They can submit their solutions (not merely answers, but detailed descriptions of the steps they took and why) and perhaps have them published on the website. Students with advanced skills and abilities will not feel so different or isolated when they see the interesting solutions to hard problems that other students have submitted to sites such as this.

CONCLUSION

Once gifted students are placed in a grade level or course that is appropriate for their level of mathematical maturity and content knowledge, teachers are faced with the question of whether or not the curriculum of the operative classroom is challenging and rewarding. How can teachers of mathematics make their lessons more in line with some of the elements that have been addressed in this chapter?

1. Begin with the best curricular materials possible that reflect multiple characteristics of appropriate resources for gifted learners as discussed in this chapter and in Chapter 14. Draw from specialized resources, not just the basal textbook.
2. Reorganize the mathematical content under larger concepts such as *patterns*, *systems*, or *proof*.
3. Pretest students before each chapter or unit so that the needs of the students are clear and time is not wasted on material they already know.
4. Redesign some of the lessons you already teach by telling less and giving students more opportunities to explore ideas and make discoveries.
5. Craft higher level questions that probe student thinking so that facts and algorithms are not the only end product of learning.
6. Make assessment opportunities more open-ended, not just traditional skill-based tests. Presentations of solutions to challenging problems, projects, group problem solving, and math journals can be included.

7. Give opportunities for independent exploration with clear guidelines about process and product expectations.
8. Include some topics that go beyond the required content of your course. The Internet can be a good resource for this. See Chapter 14 for some resources that will help you.
9. Require all students in your gifted program to learn some computer programming or learn to program a graphing calculator. Both are excellent environments for higher level thinking.
10. Have students keep a math journal in which they document problem-solving processes and results.
11. Focus on challenging problem solving, not just skill-building, concepts.
12. Seek help from experts in mathematics if the interests and needs of your students go beyond your level of expertise.

The key question teachers should ask themselves in a planning mathematics curriculum is: Where is the thinking? If it is not there, it is not an appropriate curriculum for the gifted.

KEY POINTS SUMMARY

- A mathematics curriculum has to be accelerated before it can be effectively enriched.
- Treating mathematics as conceptual, rather than topical, raises the level of thinking for high-ability learners.
- Emphasis on problems that are nonalgorithmic enhances mathematical challenge.
- The use of computer programming and graphing calculators provides powerful learning enhancements for the gifted.
- Students should be asked to explore problems rather than be told answers and should explain their reasoning in the solutions.
- Use of math manipulatives deepens the understanding of mathematics concepts for all learners, including the gifted.
- Mathematics curricula can be diversified through effective use of puzzles, games, competitions, challenging problems, and selected websites.

REFERENCES

Assouline, S., & Lupkowski-Shoplik, A. (2005). *Developing math talent: A guide for educating gifted and advanced learners in math.* Waco, TX: Prufrock Press.
Center for Gifted Education. (2010). *Moving through dimensions: A mathematics unit for high-ability learners in grades 6–8.* Waco, TX: Prufrock Press.

Colen, Y. S. (2007) In my opinion: a call for early intervention for mathematically gifted elementary students: A Russian model. *Teaching Children Mathematics, 13,* 280–284.

Donovan, M. S., & Bransford, J. D. (Eds.). (2005) *How students learn: Mathematics in the classroom.* Washington DC: National Academies Press.

Flanders, J. R. (1987). How much of the content in mathematics textbooks is new? *Arithmetic Teacher, 35,* 18–23.

Friedman, R. C., & Lee, S. W. (1996). Differentiating instruction for high-achieving/gifted children in regular classrooms: A field test of three gifted-education models. *Journal for the Education of the Gifted, 19,* 405–436.

Gavin, M. K., Casa, T. M., Adelson, J. L., Carroll, S. R., Sheffield, L. J., & Spinelli, A. M. (2007). Project M3: Mentoring mathematical minds—A research-based curriculum for talented elementary students. *Journal of Advanced Academics, 18,* 566–585.

Grouws, D. A., & Cebulla, K. (1999). Fostering effective mathematics instruction: Implications from research. In G. Cawelti (Ed.), *Handbook of research on student achievement* (pp. 117–134). Arlington, VA: Educational Research Service.

Hembree, R., & Dessart, D. J. (1986). Effects of hand-held calculators in precollege mathematics education: A meta-analysis. *Journal for Research in Mathematics Education, 17,* 83–99.

Jacobs, H. R. (1994). *Mathematics: A human endeavor.* New York, NY: Freeman.

Johnson, D. T. (2008a). *Beyond base ten: A mathematics unit for high-ability learners in grades 3–6.* Waco, TX: Prufrock Press.

Johnson, D. T. (2008b). *Spatial reasoning: A mathematics unit for high-ability learners in grades 2–4.* Waco, TX: Prufrock Press.

Johnson, D. T., & Sher, B. T. (1997). *Models: A problem-based study of animal populations.* Williamsburg, VA: Center for Gifted Education, The College of William and Mary.

Karp, A. (2003). Thirty years after: The lives of former winners of mathematical Olympiads. *Roeper Review, 25,* 83–87.

Lee, S. L., & Olszewski-Kubilius, P. (2006). A study of instructional methods used in fast-paced classes. *Gifted Child Quarterly, 50,* 216–237.

Lubinski, D., & Benbow, C. (2006). Study of mathematically precocious youth after 35 years: Uncovering antecedents for the development of math-science expertise. *Perspectives on Psychological Science, 1,* 316–345.

Maddux, H. C. (Ed.). (1986). *The challenge of the unknown: Teaching guide.* New York, NY: Norton.

MathCounts Foundation. (2000). *How MathCounts works.* Retrieved from https://mathcounts.org/Page.aspx?pid=207

Mills, C. J., Ablard, K. E., & Lynch, S. J. (1992). Academically talented students' preparation for advanced-level coursework after individually paced precalculus class. *Journal for the Education of the Gifted, 16,* 3–17.

Miller, R., Mills, C., & Tangherlini, A. (1995). The Appalachia model mathematics program for gifted students. *Roeper Review, 18,* 138–141.

National Council of Teachers of Mathematics. (2000). *Principles and standards for school mathematics.* Reston, VA: Author.

National Mathematics Advisory Panel. (2008). *Foundations for success: The final report of the National Mathematics Advisory Panel.* Washington, DC: U.S. Department of Education.

Office of Educational Research and Improvement. (1999). *Attaining excellence: A TIMSS resource kit: Third International Mathematics and Science Study* [Multimedia kit]. (Available from the National Center for Education Statistics, U.S. Department of Education, 555 New Jersey Ave. NW, Washington, DC 20208-5574)

Peeples, S. (1994). *Ideas from algebra: Operations, variables, properties.* Columbia, SC: South Carolina Council for Gifted Education.

Ravaglia, R., Suppes, P., Stillinger, C., & Alper, T. (1995). Computer-based mathematics and physics for gifted students. *Gifted Child Quarterly, 39,* 7–13.

Seymour, D. (1983). *Visual thinking.* Palo Alto, CA: Seymour.

Sheffield, L. J. (2006) Mathematically promising students from the space age to the information age. *Teaching Methods in Mathematics Education, 3,* 104–109.

Sowell, E. J. (1993). Programs for mathematically gifted students: A review of empirical research. *Gifted Child Quarterly, 37,* 124–132.

Stanley, J., Keating, D., & Fox, L. (1974). *Mathematical talent.* Baltimore, MD: Johns Hopkins University Press.

Swiatek, M. A. (1993). A decade of longitudinal research of academic acceleration through the Study of Mathematically Precocious Youth. *Roeper Review, 15,* 120–123.

Swiatek, M. (2007). The talent search model: Past, present and future. *Gifted Child Quarterly, 51,* 320–329.

TOPS: Techniques of problem solving. (1980). Palo Alto, CA: Seymour. (Available from Pearson Learning)

VanTassel-Baska, J., & Stambaugh, T. (2006). Mathematics curriculum for the gifted learner. In J. VanTassel-Baska & T. Stambaugh (Eds.), *Comprehensive curriculum for gifted learners* (3rd ed., pp. 122–139). Boston, MA: Allyn & Bacon.

Chapter 10

Adapting Science Curricula for High-Ability Learners

Janice I. Robbins

Your school has recently redefined the gifted program and now the faculty is preparing to provide services in each core content area rather than in a general "thinking skills" resource class. Your principal has asked you as lead science teacher to work with a small committee to propose adaptations to accommodate the needs of gifted learners within the science curriculum. During your first committee meeting, you encourage members to share their ideas. One teacher asks, "What should differentiation in science look like in my classroom? I am comfortable with language arts differentiation, but science is more challenging. Should I use a different textbook with my advanced students?" You know that the classroom teachers will be looking to your committee for guidance in determining what makes an effective curriculum for highly able students. What will you do to support the teachers and their students?

The goal of a differentiated curriculum for high-ability students in science is to promote learning experiences that enable those students to grow in conceptual understanding and procedural competence. The differentiated curriculum guides instruction that engages students in the ways of knowing and doing science. An effective approach to differentiation begins with a clear understanding of the nature of science as practiced professionally and how that translates to K–12 instruction, as well as a definitive view of the high-ability learners themselves.

THE NATURE OF SCIENCE AND CURRENT RESEARCH

Science by its very nature is a process that seeks to explain the natural world. It is more than a collection of facts, more than a body of knowledge, and more than an investigative process. Scientists, guided by their innate curiosity and past experiences, seek new information about the world around them in order to deepen their understanding of scientific phenomena. They develop hypotheses, test their ideas, and propose new theories supported by their findings. They recognize that their ideas are subject to challenge and change; solutions in science are never final. Scientists engage in work that is both about the discovery of new ideas and the refinement of old ones.

HIGH-ABILITY STUDENTS IN SCIENCE

A strong parallel exists between the characteristics of gifted students and those of eminent scientists. Researchers (Proctor & Capaldi, 2006; Simonton, 1988, 1992; Thagard, 2004) found that scientists exhibited high intellectual ability, curiosity, personal drive and persistence, analytical skills, and creativity. Studies of students with a proclivity for science (Brandwein, 1995; Consuegra, 1982; Subotnik, 1993) reveal similar traits. Both groups enjoy challenges and problem solving; both are self-motivated and generally show intense interest in one particular area of science. When provided with classroom resources and activities that replicate scientists' ways of knowing, high-ability learners become more definitive and focused on work in specific areas of science. Brandwein (1995) suggested that:

> Science proneness begins in a base of a general giftedness and develops its component skills in verbal, mathematical, and in time, the non-entrenched tasks of problem seeking, finding, and solving in specialized science fields. Eventually, given favorable ecologies, science proneness can shift to an expression in work showing science talent. (p. 104)

Differentiation in science requires that, just like scientists who engage in

TABLE 10.1

Relationship of Advanced Science Curriculum to the ICM

Integrated Curriculum Model	Focus in advanced science curriculum
ICM advanced content dimension	
Conceptually oriented	Clearly articulate extended conceptual frameworks for science topics.
Substantive content	Explore fewer science topics in depth.
ICM process/product dimension	
Constructing meaning	Incorporate real-world investigations.
Higher order reasoning	Teach reasoning skills directly and apply reasoning skills to investigations.
Metacognition	Include expectations for reflection, self-analysis, and critiquing of investigative work.
Habits of mind/dispositions	Emphasize curiosity, objectivity, skepticism, and persistence.
ICM issues/themes dimension	
Interdisciplinary and intradisciplinary connections Deep understanding of ideas	Focus on unified and connected ideas via overarching concepts such as *systems*, *change*, and *evolution*.
Models of teaching and learning	
Inquiry-based learning	Use specific models and strategies such as problem-based learning and the Wheel of Scientific Investigation and Reasoning. Use real-world problems and theoretical modeling.

investigations drawn from their own curiosity, experiences, and interests, high-ability students participate in active explorations that increase their motivation and self-efficacy in science.

The ICM Related to Reform Elements in Science

VanTassel-Baska (1992, 1998a; VanTassel-Baska & Stambaugh, 2006) provided a clarifying focus on the curriculum needs of high-ability learners. Her Integrated Curriculum Model (ICM) incorporates three interrelated dimensions responsive to aspects of gifted learners: advanced content, advanced process/product, and complex issues/themes. The ICM has been used as the framework for science units developed by the Center for Gifted Education at The College of William and Mary for use with high-ability students for the past 20 years. The units serve as effective and beneficial examples of curriculum for the gifted (Feng, VanTassel-Baska, Quek, O'Neil, & Bai, 2005) that, over time, result in significant growth in scientific research design skills. Table 10.1 shows the ICM's elements as applied to a focus in the advanced science curriculum.

Learner Outcomes of Significance

Current research efforts in science and science education provide a better understanding of how scientists complete their work and how students learn science. In a recent report, the National Research Council's Committee on Science Learning (2007) summarized research from cognitive and developmental psychology, science education, and the history and philosophy of science to provide a new view of the developing science student, one who is capable of significantly more than previously believed. The report, based on a synthesis of the research, describes specific proficiencies in science in terms of student outcomes, including abilities to do each of the following:

- know, use, and interpret scientific explanations of the natural world;
- generate and evaluate scientific evidence and explanations;
- understand the nature and development of scientific knowledge; and
- participate productively in scientific practices and discourse.

Table 10.2 presents examples of high-ability learner outcomes aligned with the dimensions of the ICM and related to the National Research Council's work (2007), as well as the National Science Education Standards (National Research Council, 1996).

CONCEPTUALLY ORIENTED CURRICULUM

Common themes cross multiple disciplines and are frequently used by professionals as ways of thinking and generalizing. The *Atlas of Science Literacy* (Project 2061, 2007), a useful curriculum tool that maps science concepts and skills across grades K–12, highlights the importance of introducing students to the themes or overarching concepts that cross multiple disciplines, as well as multiple fields in science. Central to the introduction of these overarching concepts is the importance of guiding students to understanding how science is centered in universal ideas.

The use of an overarching concept within a unit of study exposes students to key ideas, themes, and principles within and across domains of knowledge. Aesthetic appreciation of powerful ideas in various representational forms also is viewed as an important outcome. As students apply their understanding of an overarching concept to their current and developing knowledge, they begin to articulate and internalize generalizations that are associated with the concept, connecting them to future work across multiple disciplines. Overarching concepts incorporated into William and Mary science units include *change*, *systems*, *patterns*, and *cause and effect*. Students are guided to apply these overarching concepts to their work in science, especially in articulating broad

TABLE 10.2

Learner Outcomes for High-Ability Students

ICM dimension	Goal	Examples of related outcomes for high-ability students	Related national science standards
Advanced content	Know, use, and interpret scientific explanations of the natural world. Understand the nature and development of scientific knowledge.	Develop a concept map in response to a key question about the content.	Unifying content and processes standard (i.e., systems, order, and organization; evidence, models, and explanation; change, constancy, and measurement; evolution and equilibrium; form and function).
Process/product	Use creative thinking to support conceptual growth.	Develop analogies and metaphors to describe a natural object or phenomenon.	Not specifically addressed in national standards.
Issues/themes	Expand problem-solving abilities.	As a group, determine criteria for a resolution to a real-world problem scenario (PBL).	Science as a human endeavor.
	Conduct scientific inquiry. Generate and evaluate scientific evidence and explanations.	Plan the steps in a scientific experiment based on a specific scientific question.	Abilities necessary to do scientific inquiry. Understanding about scientific inquiry.
	Apply data collection skills.	Conduct an experiment with repeated measures and compare data tables to results from another student.	Using multiple process skills—manipulation, cognitive, and procedural.
	Conduct data analysis.	Use data to formulate conclusions from an experiment.	Science as argument and explanation.
	Communicate scientific findings. Participate productively in scientific practices and discourse.	Record specific findings from a given experiment.	Communicating science explanations.
	Use technology to enhance and expand inquiry.	Complete electronic records; use software to organize data sets.	Understanding about science and technology.

generalizations. In this way, they work like scientists who must justify their conceptualizations and findings as they elaborate on their generalizations.

CONSTRUCTIVE MEANING AND SUBSTANTIVE CONTENT

Students with high potential in science need to be exposed to advanced content in ways that promote learning with understanding. This can be accomplished through emphases on strong and focused concept development, using models such as concept mapping (Novak, 1998) and Taba's (1962) teaching strategies for concept development. In addition, conceptual understanding is strengthened through wide reading, student discourse, and writing focused on the essence and interconnection of ideas. Recognizing the work of science educators who have published more than 3,500 studies on students' understanding of science concepts (Pfundt & Duit, 1994), Mintzes and Wandersee (2005) proposed several knowledge claims endorsed by cognitive scientists, including two that are especially pertinent to gifted students' development of advanced content:

1. The differential ability to solve problems in novel, real-world settings is attributable primarily to the advantage conferred on individuals possessing a highly integrated, well-differentiated framework of domain-specific knowledge which is activated through concentrated attention to and sustained reflection on related objects and events.
2. Successful learners in science make meanings by restructuring their existing knowledge frameworks through an orderly set of cognitive events (i.e., subsumption, superordination, integration, and differentiation). (p. 76)

Students use their conceptual frameworks and apply their knowledge when presented with additional information, weaving the new ideas into their existing knowledge structures. Thus, the effective curriculum for high-ability students provides significant exposure to new information, including the current work of experts in scientific fields as well as data from multiple sources, so that students' knowledge structures continue to expand.

INQUIRY-BASED LEARNING

All scientists work to improve our knowledge and understanding of the world. In the process of scientific inquiry, scientists connect evidence with logical reasoning. Scientists also apply their imagination and creativity as they

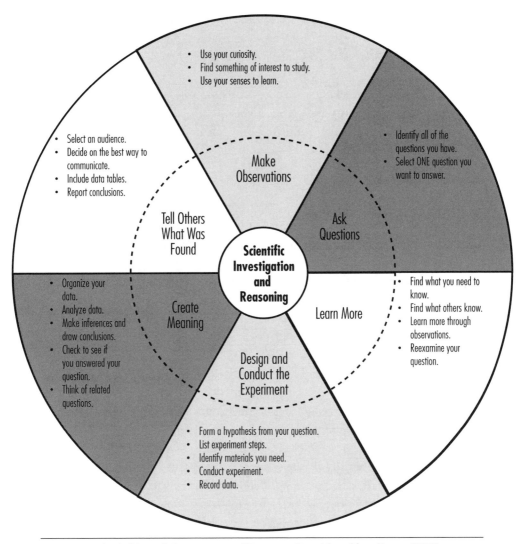

Figure 10.1. Wheel of Scientific Investigation and Reasoning. From Adapted from Kramer (1987).

devise hypotheses and explanations that make sense of the evidence. Students can strengthen their understanding of particular science topics through investigations that cause them to employ evidence gathering, logical reasoning, and creativity. The National Science Education Standards (National Research Council, 1996) specifically address inquiry as a critical component of all students' science learning.

The Wheel of Scientific Investigation and Reasoning (Center for Gifted Education, 2006; see Figure 10.1) is a model that contains the specific processes involved in scientific inquiry. The wheel was developed to highlight the important actions scientists use when engaging in an investigation. Although the wheel presents six different components of the investigation process, it is neither prescriptively sequential nor static. When scientists work, they engage in these processes, but certainly not in a step-by-step way.

Bridgman (1949) made this point decades ago when he wrote,

> The scientist, in attacking a specific problem, suffers no inhibitions or precedent on authority but is free to adopt any course that his ingenuity is capable of suggesting to him . . . In short, science is what scientists do, and there are as many scientific methods, as there are individual scientists. (p. 12)

A scientist may be engaged in an experiment that results in additional questions. Because the scientist is ready to test out new hypotheses related to these questions, she may move directly to an additional experiment prior to completing an overall analysis that may incorporate evidence from several experiments. In addition, great scientists often experience "aha" moments that move their thinking beyond the obvious and generate new and groundbreaking ideas.

Make Observations

De Duve (2002), a Nobel-Prize-winning biologist, stated that science is "based on observation and experiment, guided by reason" (p. 285). As scientists observe, their focus is on getting accurate data and using observation and measurements taken in all kinds of situations. They use instruments to enhance their own natural abilities. Effective observations help students to use the information they gather to form questions about specific phenomena. Careful observations, coupled with reasoning, enable students to construct models and explanations of natural phenomena.

An effective curriculum incorporates the scientific skills of observation to ensure that students work with precision and accuracy as they record their observations of important phenomena. The use of appropriate instruments that are sensitive measures is critical to the work of gifted students who may experience extreme frustration with poor instruments. Students need to learn what evidence is relevant and offer their interpretations of the meaning of the evidence. Successful learners receive teacher guidance, encouragement, and practice in collecting, sorting, and analyzing evidence and in building arguments based on it.

Ask Questions

Scientific investigations are usually initiated through a problem to be solved or a question to be asked. Selecting just the right question or clearly defining the problem to be addressed is critical to the investigation process. High-ability learners have intense curiosity and are easily overwhelmed by the actual number of questions they can generate. These students need guidance in developing and maintaining a focus narrow enough for investigation, with additional questions preserved for future investigations. This act of focusing, narrowing, and determining a goal and objective is important for gifted students. As students develop questioning skills, they deepen their understanding of various factors and how to isolate particular variables related to their questions.

Learn More

To clarify their questions, scientists learn more by reviewing bodies of scientific knowledge documented in texts and previously conducted investigations. When scientists get conflicting information, they continue their observations, looking for deeper insights that may result in the revision of their previously formed questions. Gifted students in science should be guided to deeper, focused, and more detailed readings related to their questions. Learning about prior works of scientists is highly motivating to high-ability learners, not only providing new information, but also motivating them to emulate the work of professional scientists.

Design and Conduct an Experiment

Scientists use their collection of relevant evidence, their reasoning, and their imagination to develop a hypothesis. Sometimes scientists have more than one possible explanation for the same set of observations and evidence. Often when additional observations and testing are completed, scientists modify current scientific knowledge. In simulating the work of real scientists, it is important for students to have direct experiences with establishing hypotheses, identifying and isolating variables, determining methods and materials, collecting and recording data, and repeating experiments.

To test out hypotheses, scientists design experiments that will enable them to control conditions so that their results will be reliable. Scientists repeat their experiments, doing it the same way it was done before and expecting to get very similar although not exact results. It is important to control conditions in order to make comparisons. High-ability learners benefit from diligently pursuing repeated measures, as well as alternative hypotheses. An effective curriculum helps advanced students to grow in numeracy and in the understanding of important quantitative concepts like magnitude, scale, and models.

Create Meaning From the Experiment

Scientists analyze the data that are collected from the experiment to add to the existing body of scientific knowledge. They organize their data using data tables and graphs and then make inferences from the data to draw conclusions about whether their question was answered and about how effective their experiments were. Scientists also create meaning by comparing what they found to existing knowledge. The analysis of experimental data and processes often leads to identification of related questions and future experiments.

Tell Others What Was Found

In the investigative process, scientists often work as a team, sharing findings with each other so that they may benefit from the results. Students need experiences that direct them to draw conclusions and then compare their thinking to that of others, analyzing and justifying their own thinking while also being open to other ideas.

HIGHER ORDER REASONING

The most critical component in science curriculum for high-ability students in science is the development of scientific reasoning. Students engaged in scientific activity must learn how to apply analytical skills to all aspects of the scientific process. Science requires a focus on explanation, prediction, control, and interpretation based on logical thinking. By applying scientific reasoning, gifted students approach learning with a more critical mind, often questioning things that otherwise might have gone unchallenged. They exhibit a desire to test things and critically review outcomes. This disposition is the mark of a scientific mind: seeing the questions and seeking the answers through empirical results.

Paul and Elder (2003) suggested that an accomplished scientific thinker possesses habits of scientific thought that become second nature. They delineated scientific thought as incorporating essential intellectual standards such as clarity, precision, and logic applied to fundamental elements of scientific thought contained in the their Reasoning Model. When students use this model they engage in reasoning that addresses matters of scientific purpose, questions, information, inferences, concepts, assumptions, implications, and points of view.

Curriculum for high-ability science students integrates advanced content with higher order reasoning. Too often student misconceptions in science are reinforced rather than modified, lost in years of science education that limits student thinking. Rather than the accumulation of facts and the practice of completing predefined labs, advanced science students should be engaged in developing sound conceptual foundations and applying their deepening and evolving conceptions of the world to new issues and problems.

METACOGNITION

Young scientists, just like their professional counterparts, must reflect upon their own thinking and determine how thorough, how precise, and how logical they have been. The metacognitive process trains young scientists to expand their capacities for logic, accuracy, breadth, completeness, and precision. Findings by Schraw and Graham (1997) supported the value of including direct instruction, interaction with peers, and self-reflection as strategies for improving the metacognition of gifted students. As students practice metacognition, the development of their conceptual frameworks in science is enhanced. Students more readily note inconsistencies and look for resolution to perceived incongruities. Effective metacognition may move learners to begin to question their previous conception, their evidence, hypothesis, or some misinformation used in their cognitive processing. Many opportunities for the expansion of metacognitive processing exist within the science curriculum. Any activity that incorporates multiple ways of thinking and multiple responses is an appropriate medium for metacognition. Students may be asked to explain their thinking in the development of a particular hypothesis. They may be required to articulate their predictions with reasons. They may be asked to support their findings with specific evidence from multiple experiments. In science, questions and discrepancies are many, posing opportunities for students to think about their thinking.

MODELS OF TEACHING AND LEARNING

One teaching model that is particularly applicable to the world of science is problem-based learning (PBL). Problem-based learning is a curriculum framework and instructional model that provides a sophisticated content and high-level process situated in a community-based problem. The model helps students to enhance their self-efficacy, confidence, and autonomous learner behaviors. This teaching and learning model has its origins in the field of medicine, where it is used to help medical students learn to work with real medical problems in a simulated setting prior to actual responsibility for patient diagnosis and treatment.

PBL begins with an ill-structured problem. Students work in groups to analyze the problem and conduct research and experimentation, all the while working toward a resolution of the problem. The teacher serves as a coach and resource rather than as a director. Throughout the problem-solving sessions, students engage in activities that will help them to gain more knowledge about the situation and a deeper understanding of the factors that affect the problem and its possible solutions or resolutions.

PBL is a form of curriculum as experience. Rather than beginning with knowledge and information provided by the teacher, followed by a problem to solve, PBL begins with a problem through which students move to generate knowledge and information they deem necessary in the resolution of the problem. The teacher works as a facilitator and supportive guide rather than as a direct provider of information.

The College of William and Mary's Center for Gifted Education has developed a series of PBL units situated in the sciences, allowing students to engage in experimental research as part of their learning experience. Each unit incorporates an overarching concept developed throughout unit lessons, advanced content through the use of expanded resources, in-depth topics, advanced reading, primary sources, and a focus on scientific processes including scientific investigation and reasoning. Research evidence supports the use of problem-based learning and the effectiveness of the William and Mary science units when used with high-ability learners (see Chapter 19 for specific details of the studies).

AUTHENTIC ASSESSMENT

Tools for the assessment of advanced learning in science should match identified student outcomes and flow from instructional activities. Units of study developed at the Center for Gifted Education provide good examples of performance-based pre- and postassessments that seek to measure student progress in advanced content, process, and overarching concepts. Use of these performance-based assessments has allowed for the documentation of student growth (VanTassel-Baska, Bracken, Stambaugh, & Feng, 2007) in higher order concepts, scientific investigation, and content mastery. Preassessments enable teachers to determine students' prior knowledge and process skills. Preassessments also establish a baseline against which to measure and document progress. The results of the preassessment can be used to guide modifications in instruction and to help students see their areas of strength and need. In the process of modifying instruction, new challenges can stimulate thinking. For example, students might be provided with a question such as, "Does music affect plant growth?" and then be asked to design an experiment that responds to the question. A simple rubric designed to measure the important components of experimental design would be used for pre- and postassessments. Assessments that require open-ended responses are the most effective in enabling advanced learners to show what they know.

MULTIMEDIA AND TECHNOLOGY

Recent studies (Hegarty, 2005; Kozma & Russell, 2005; Lowe, 2005) on the practices of professional scientists show that they use computer programs, videos, models, pictures, diagrams, graphs, and electronic collaboration on a regular basis. Highly effective uses of multimedia and technology for advanced learners include precision instruments, databases to retrieve and/or contribute to, virtual labs that allow the use of materials and specimens that are not available in the classroom, and electronic connections to real scientists. Such multimedia tools help students engage in real science activities where the investigation is not about finding the correct answer to a prescribed "lab" but rather exploring multiple possibilities and using observation and analytical skills to promote expanded questioning and thinking.

One promising way of exposing students to the work of real scientists is through reading the lab notes of current scientists. A recent breakthrough in the area of communication and collaboration is the use of electronic laboratory notebooks, which offer a partial solution to the need for scientists to be able to reconstruct what happened during an experiment and for students to follow along with the scientists' thinking.

MATERIALS AND RESOURCES

An effective curriculum for high-ability learners extends beyond the standard textbook and resource adoptions and uses specific materials that promote advanced content and higher order thinking (VanTassel-Baska, 1998b). Materials should include specialized tools and instruments, lab and field study access, and exposure to the work of real-world scientists. Visual depictions such as photos and video clips and access to electronic records and databases should be included. A search for such materials involves significant time and expertise, requiring careful reviews to ensure that the materials are suitable for the age and grade level of the students, as well as their readiness for advanced work. The following Internet resources are offered as starting places for such a search.

Interactive Projects and Resources

- *JASON Science* (http://www.jason.org/public/whatis/start.aspx) is a nonprofit subsidiary of the National Geographic Society. JASON Science connects young students with great explorers and events to inspire and motivate them to learn science. Its core curriculum units are designed for fifth- through eighth-grade classrooms but are flexible enough to be adapted for higher or lower grades.

- *FOSSweb* (Full Option Science System; http://www.fossweb.com) has evolved into a curriculum for students and their teachers in grades K–8 over the past 20 years, with the support of the National Science Foundation (NSF) and the University of California at Berkeley.
- *The GLOBE Program* (Global Learning and Observations to Benefit the Environment; http://www.globe.gov/r), working in partnership with NASA and National Science Foundation (NSF) Earth System Science Projects, is a worldwide hands-on, primary and secondary school-based science and education program that promotes inquiry-based investigations of the environment and the Earth system.
- *WISE* (Web-based Inquiry Science Environment; http://wise.berkeley.edu) is a simple yet powerful learning environment on the Internet where students examine real-world evidence and analyze current scientific controversies. Curriculum projects for grades 5–12 are included.
- *The Illinois Mathematics and Science Academy (IMSA) PBL Network* (http://pbln.imsa.edu/students/index.html) is a leader in problem-based learning, providing training at the K–12 levels and beyond. IMSA provides a practical, research-based framework to enable classroom teachers to implement the model.
- *NASA Quest Challenges* (http://quest.nasa.gov/challenges) are web-based, interactive explorations designed to engage students in authentic scientific and engineering processes. The solutions relate to issues encountered daily by NASA personnel. The content of NASA Quest Challenges follows real NASA tasks. As students work in teams to mirror NASA career roles, agency experts are available to answer questions and to encourage a proper design process. The interaction with scientists occurs via Q&A, chats, interactive webcasts, and posted feedback on the website.
- *Science Olympiad* (http://soinc.org) is a national nonprofit organization dedicated to improving the quality of K-12 science education, increasing male, female, and minority interest in science; creating a technologically-literate workforce; and providing recognition for outstanding achievement by both students and teachers. These goals are achieved by participating in Science Olympiad tournaments and noncompetitive events, incorporating Science Olympiad into classroom curriculum, and attending teacher training institutes.

Units of Study

The Center for Gifted Education has developed a series of science units for use in classrooms nationally that span K–8 levels of inquiry. The most recent units have been developed under the auspices of a Javits-funded project (Project Clarion). These units contain lesson plans that illustrate well the principles just described that align with the science standards, illustrate the ICM at work, and also demonstrate the opportunity for students to practice real science in the classroom.

The following lesson plan exploits the use of The Wheel of Scientific Investigation and Reasoning to guide students in conducting their own experiments on the effects of the sun. It is taken from *Weather Reporter*, a unit designed for second- and third-grade students.

SAMPLE LESSON: THE SUN'S EFFECT ON THE TEMPERATURE OF SUBSTANCES (GRADES 2–3)

In prior lessons in this unit on weather, students learned that weather data are collected and recorded using instruments. The overarching concept of change is integrated into unit lessons. Students are also involved in lessons about how scientists work and explore the Wheel of Scientific Investigation and Reasoning in the process.

Instructional Purpose:
- To initiate an investigation of the temperature of sand in the sun vs. black dirt in the sun.
- To apply investigative processes including making observations, asking questions, and learning more.

Materials:
- 1 small bag of black dirt per group
- 1 small bag of sand per group
- 2 identical plastic cups per group
- 2 thermometers per group
- 1 ruler per group
- Heat lamps to share
- Student science logs

Lesson Activities:
1. Ask students to describe how scientists get answers to their questions. Emphasize the importance of observations and questioning. Remind students that scientists have different instruments for use in their work. For example, weather reporters often use thermometers to measure temperature.

2. Create groups of 3–4. Provide each group with thermometers and remind students of the way to handle these instruments properly. Ask a student to explain how a thermometer is read.

3. Provide each group with one copy of Our Observations Comparing Black Dirt and Sand, two cups, one bag of sand, and one bag of soil.

4. Explain that students are going to design and conduct a scientific investigation. Remind them of the importance of careful observations and data collection.

5. Ask each group to use a ruler to measure 1 ½ inches below the top of their cups and to mark a line at the 1 ½-inch mark. Then ask students to fill one cup with dirt to the mark and one with sand. Ask students to record their observations of the two cups. Tell students that in addition to the materials they already have, they will have access to heat lamps that will simulate the heat from the sun.

6. Tell students that you have a question for them: How does heat (sunlight) affect the temperature of black dirt and sand? Ask students to tell you other questions they have, recording them on chart paper.

7. Next, ask students to talk with their group members to consider one of the questions that they feel could be tested and then to design an experiment that would help them find an answer. Tell students to record their question and the steps they will take to conduct their experiment.

8. After all groups have designed their experiment, allow students to conduct their test and record results. Remind students to record their results carefully and talk about something they can say about heat and their soil and sand materials.

9. Invite groups to share their questions and experiments and record statements of their findings on a class chart. Tell students that scientists often have new questions as a result of their experiments. Ask students if they have new questions and record these on a chart. Let students know that their findings will be used in the next few lessons. Ask them if there are a few things they feel they know for sure about heat and soil/sand. Record these on the class "Findings" chart.

10. Ask students in what ways today's experiments relate to the concept of "change." Ask how they think time might impact results.

11. Assessment through observation of student work: Look for students' ability to develop related questions, use materials appropriately, design meaningful experiments, record results, and draw conclusions from results.

Extension: Provide materials and additional time for students to conduct similar experiments outdoors and at different times of the day. Allow students to explore additional common materials to compare temperature readings under different heating conditions. Introduce students to different kinds of thermometers and include different scales (Fahrenheit, Celsius, and Kelvin).

Our Observations
Comparing Black Dirt and Sand

	Black Dirt	Sand
Observations without heat		
Observations when soil and sand are heated		

Note. Adapted from Center for Gifted Education. (2007). *The weather reporter.* Williamsburg, VA: Author.

The next lesson is taken from the unit *Animal Populations* (Center for Gifted Education, 2001), used in middle school gifted programs. Students study physical, conceptual, and mathematical models as they participate in a problem-based science unit on animal population and biology. The unit exploits the connections between science and mathematics, allowing students ample opportunity to use quantitative skills in the data collection, analysis, and interpretation of their results from experiments.

SAMPLE LESSON:
INTRODUCTION TO EXPERIMENTAL
DESIGN: DEER REPELLENTS (GRADES 7–8)

Prior to this lesson, students were presented with a scenario related to a bug bite (Lyme disease) and attempts to control the spread of the disease in a local community. Students reasoned that deer in the area spread the disease and that control of the population might be considered. This lesson introduces the experimental design process.

Instructional Purpose:
* To introduce the principles of experimental design.
* To allow students to design an experiment to test the efficacy of deer repellents.

Materials:
- Bar of bath soap
- Cheesecloth or nylon net
- Copies of school district policy on use of animals in student research
- Letter from Uncle Lou
- Experimental Design Diagram

Assessment:
- Evaluate the whole-group discussion and small-group discussions for student understanding of experimental design.
- Review the Experimental Design Diagram for student understanding of experimental design.

Activities:
1. Read the letter from Uncle Lou in which he shares a trick his neighbors used to keep deer out of their apple orchard. They hung soap in cheesecloth bags from their trees when the apples were getting ripe and said the deer would not go near the trees. Ask them how they could find out if Uncle Lou is correct.

2. Ask students how a scientist might approach this question.

3. Ask students to work in small groups to respond to the questions: What do we need to find out? What materials do we have? How can we use the materials to help us? What do we think will happen (hypothesis)? What will we need to observe or measure to answer our scientific question? Ask students to explain and justify their answers.

4. Ask each small group to describe its approach to the class. Remind the students that the experiment they are proposing involves live deer.

5. Once groups have finished the brainstorming process, give students copies of the Experimental Design Diagram. Tell them that this guide will help them design their plan for an experiment.

6. Direct each group to record an experimental protocol.
   - List the materials you will need.
   - Write a description of what you will do.
   - What data will you collect?
   - Design a data table to collect and analyze your information.

7. When they have finished, check their work to be sure that each experi-

ment they have designed has appropriate controls, constants, and one independent variable; also be sure that each experiment meets the requirements for ethical treatment of animals.

Extensions:
1. Invite a guest speaker who is an expert on the ethical treatment of animals in research settings to speak to the students.
2. An alternative to the experiment would be to assess the efficacy of other deer deterrents such as noise makers, fencing, lights, and the like.
3. Another alternative design for the experiment would be to have students test various types of soap.
4. Remind students that experiments can be done on animal models, as well as with deer. For example, mice or mealworms could be used when testing whether soap repels hungry animals.

Experimental Design Diagram

Title of Experiment:
Hypothesis (Educated guess):
Independent Variable (The variable you change):
Dependent Variable (The variable that responds to changes):
Observations/Measurement to Make:
Constants (All things that remain the same):
Control (The standard for comparing experimental effects):

Note. Adapted from Center for Gifted Education. (2001). *Animal populations: A study of physical, conceptual, and mathematical models.* Dubuque, IA: Kendall/Hunt.

CONCLUSION

Science curriculum for high-ability learners should focus on both short- and long-term student outcomes. Teachers who embrace the potential of these students for advanced postsecondary and professional work in the sciences offer continuing challenges that promote new learning every day. An effective science curriculum for high-ability learners incorporates the Integrated Curriculum Model and the strands of scientific proficiency outlined by the National Research Council (2007) of the National Academy of Sciences. Such a curriculum promotes the expansion of conceptual knowledge combined with skills necessary for effective scientific investigations. It includes higher level thinking and scientific reasoning that mimics that of professional scientists. It provides advanced learners with the time necessary for extended investigations, experiences involving real solutions to real problems, opportunities for discourse, and access to models of scientific thought that motivate and challenge. As a result of exposure to an advanced science curriculum, students come to know what questions science can and cannot answer, understand the methods scientists use to answer questions, and have experience with making reasoned judgments about scientific findings.

KEY POINTS SUMMARY

- An effective curriculum for advanced learners in science supports their growth in applying scientific reasoning to the quest for understanding the world.
- Effective science curriculum for high-ability learners is an active blend of content and process skills that strengthen student growth in conceptual understanding.
- Scientific investigations for advanced learners require reflective analysis (metacognition), as well as critical reviews by others, thus promoting scientific collaboration.
- A challenging science curriculum engages high-ability learners in an advanced quantitative focus with emphasis on the development of precision, numeracy, scale, magnitude, and modeling.
- Selected use of multimedia resources provides advanced learners with alternative ways of viewing data, as well as access to scientific phenomena not otherwise possible in a classroom setting.
- Exposure to and involvement in the real work of scientists is highly desirable and possible through electronic interactive projects and connections.
- The ICM, connected to specific proficiencies in science, is an effective framework for developing curriculum for high-ability learners that demonstrates positive effects for both students and teachers.

REFERENCES

Brandwein, P. F. (1995). *Science talent in the young expressed within ecologies of achievement* (RBDM 9510). Storrs, CT: National Research Center on the Gifted and Talented.

Bridgman, P. W. (1949, December). Scientific method. *The Teaching Scientists, 342.*

Center for Gifted Education. (2001). *Animal populations: A study of physical, conceptual, and mathematical models.* Dubuque, IA: Kendall/Hunt.

Center for Gifted Education. (2006). *Wheel of scientific investigation and reasoning.* Williamsburg, VA: Author.

Center for Gifted Education. (2007). *The weather reporter.* Williamsburg, VA: Author.

Consuegra, G. F. (1982). Identifying the gifted in science and mathematics. *School Science & Mathematics, 82,* 183–188.

De Duve, C. (2002). *Life evolving: Molecules, mind, and meaning.* Oxford, England: Oxford University Press.

Feng, A., VanTassel-Baska, J., Quek, C., O'Neil, B., & Bai, W. (2005). A longitudinal assessment of gifted students' learning using the Integrated Curriculum Model: Impacts and perceptions of the William and Mary language arts and science curriculum. *Roeper Review, 27,* 78–83.

Hegarty, M. (2005). Multimedia learning about physical systems. In R. E. Mayer (Ed.), *The Cambridge handbook of multimedia learning* (pp. 447–466). New York, NY: Cambridge University Press.

Kozma, R., & Russell, J. (2005). Multimedia learning of chemistry. In R. E. Mayer (Ed.), *The Cambridge handbook of multimedia learning* (pp. 409–428). New York, NY: Cambridge University Press.

Lowe, R. K. (2005). Multimedia learning of meteorology. In R. E. Mayer (Ed.), *The Cambridge handbook of multimedia learning* (pp. 429–446). New York, NY: Cambridge University Press.

Mintzes, J. J., & Wandersee, J. H. (2005). Research in science teaching and learning: A human constructivist view. In J. Mintzes, J. Wandersee, & J. Novak (Eds.), *Teaching science for understanding* (pp. 59–92). Burlington, MA: Elsevier Academic Press.

National Research Council. (1996). *National science education standards.* Washington, DC: National Academy Press.

National Research Council, Committee on Science Learning, Kindergarten Through Eighth Grade. (2007). *Taking science to school: Learning and teaching science in grades K–8.* Washington, DC: The National Academies Press.

Novak, J. (1998). *Learning, creating, and using knowledge.* Mahwah, NJ: Lawrence Erlbaum.

Paul, R., & Elder, L. (2003). *A miniature guide for students and faculty to scientific thinking.* Dillon Beach, CA: Foundation for Critical Thinking.

Pfundt, H., & Duit, R. (1994). *Bibliography: Students' alternative frameworks and science education* (4th ed.). Kiel, Germany: Institute of Science Education.

Proctor, R., & Capaldi, E. (2006). *Why science matters: Understanding the methods of psychological research.* Maldon, MA: Blackwell.

Project 2061. (2007). *Atlas of science literacy*. Washington, DC: American Association for the Advancement of Science.

Schraw, G., & Graham, T. (1997). Helping gifted students develop metacognitive awareness. *Roeper Review, 20,* 4–8.

Simonton, D. K. (1988). *Scientific games: A psychology of science.* New York, NY: Cambridge University Press.

Simonton, D. K. (1992). The social context of career success and course for 2,026 scientists and inventors. *Personality and Social Psychology Bulletin, 18,* 452–463.

Subotnik, R. F. (1993). Adult manifestations of adolescent talent in science. *Roeper Review, 15,* 164–169.

Taba, H. (1962). *Curriculum: Theory and practice.* New York, NY: Harcourt, Brace.

Thagard, P. (2004). How to be a successful scientist. In M. E. Gorman, R. D. Tweney, D. C. Gooding, & A. P. Kincannon (Eds.), *Scientific and technological thinking* (pp. 159–171). Mahwah, NJ: Lawrence Erlbaum.

VanTassel-Baska, J. (1992). *Effective curriculum planning for gifted learners.* Denver, CO: Love.

VanTassel-Baska, J. (1998a). *Excellence in educating gifted and talented learners* (3rd ed.). Denver, CO: Love.

VanTassel-Baska, J. (1998b). *Planning science programs for high-ability learners* (ERIC Digest E546). Reston, VA: ERIC Clearinghouse on Disabilities and Gifted Education.

VanTassel-Baska, J., Bracken, B. A., Stambaugh, T., & Feng, A. (2007, September). *Findings from Project Clarion.* Presentation to the United States Department of Education Expert Panel, Storrs, CT.

VanTassel-Baska, J., & Stambaugh, T. (2006). *Comprehensive curriculum for gifted learners* (3rd ed.). Needham Heights, MA: Allyn & Bacon.

Chapter 11

Adapting Social Studies Curricula for High-Ability Learners

Molly M. Sandling

As a high school social studies teacher, you teach 90-minute blocks of sophomore geography. You have a textbook, researched and written several years ago, that provides a limited overview of the major concepts and world regions you cover in your course. The abstract nature of the concepts and the changing events and boundaries in the world require you, the classroom teacher, to locate additional resources around which to construct classroom activities and assignments. The tasks of identifying resources and planning goals and activities are further complicated by the heterogeneous grouping of your classes. Although many, if not most, of your students have little or no prior knowledge of the material, some of the gifted students have such extensive knowledge of given topics and interest in the related issues that they seek a level of complexity and detail that would overwhelm those encountering the information for the first time. Given the time-consuming and complex task of finding and organizing materials and activities to meet your goals, how do you adapt your curriculum and instruction to challenge the gifted learner effectively?

The task of teaching social studies is complicated by the great number of disciplines included in the term—history, geography, economics, and political science, to name just a few—and the vast body of content details, as well as procedural and conceptual knowledge. World events and issues are constantly changing in ways that affect our understanding of the social studies disciplines, and textbooks cannot keep current with the state of the world. Complicating the teacher's task still further, particularly in the elementary grades, is the relatively limited amount of time allocated to social studies during the school day—time that, always short, has eroded further in the era of No Child Left Behind (National Council for the Social Studies, 2007).

Moreover, limitations on curricular materials may make it difficult for a teacher to provide sufficient resources for a diverse group of students to explore topics adequately at levels appropriate to their needs. The nearly unlimited resources available on the Internet provide access to a great wealth of information in a variety of useful forms, yet also present the teacher with the almost overwhelming challenge of finding appropriate materials to supplement, or substitute for, a textbook's presentation of information. Once materials are located, the teacher must then construct meaningful activities in which to use them. In addition, lessons must introduce the ideas and processes of the social sciences to an increasingly uninformed majority of students while challenging gifted students with greater depth and advanced content.

This chapter provides teachers with examples and suggestions for differentiating social studies curricula and instruction to respond to advanced learners. The chapter explores the elements of curricular reform from Chapter 2 as they apply in this domain. Within the context of two grant-funded initiatives in the late 1990s and early 2000s, the Center for Gifted Education at The College of William and Mary developed social studies units addressing a wide range of content topics and grade levels. As in previous chapters, examples from these existing materials are used throughout the chapter to demonstrate the reform elements at work.

LEARNER OUTCOMES OF SIGNIFICANCE AND HABITS OF MIND

An overarching goal of social studies curricula and instruction in general is to "help young people develop the ability to make informed and reasoned decisions for the public good as citizens of a culturally diverse, democratic society in an interdependent world" (Bragaw, 1996, p. 12). Despite the diversity of disciplines covered by "social studies" in schools, the habits of mind required to achieve this goal are similar. Students become good citizens in part by understanding the problems of the world, and these problems are more deeply understood when approached from the multiple perspectives of the various disciplines. By studying the world's various cultures in anthropology, the interaction of places and peoples in geography, the sequence of events in history, or the social causes and consequences of human behavior in sociology, a student gains a deeper understanding of what is happening in the world, allowing him or her to make reasoned decisions more effectively. Furthermore, such reasoning ability is achieved not by memorizing a series of facts from a textbook, but by developing key habits of mind used by practitioners of the social science disciplines:

- analyzing documents and other sources of all sorts to detect bias, weigh evidence, and evaluate arguments;
- distinguishing between fact and conjecture and between the trivial and the consequential;
- viewing human subjects nonjudgmentally and with empathy instead of present-mindedness and ethnocentrism;
- recognizing and analyzing the interplay of change and continuity;
- recognizing the complexity of causality and avoiding easy generalizations and stereotypes while analyzing how change occurs;
- recognizing that not all problems have solutions;
- understanding how people and cultures differ and what they share; and
- analyzing how the actions of others, past and present, influence our own lives and society.

Developing these habits of mind in our students requires teachers to teach inclusiveness and complexity through active learning and critical inquiry. Students must study the many people whose actions and interactions with others have shaped world events. Students also must be repeatedly confronted with the reality that what they are studying was not inevitable—different choices made by many different people could have led to dramatically different outcomes. Learner outcomes reflecting this level of complexity are important for all students; for high-ability learners, whose learning needs require more complex challenges, such challenging outcomes are necessary. An example of a key goal and related learner outcomes is demonstrated in Table 11.1 with alignment to national standards for history (National Center for History in the Schools, 1996).

Beyond the goal and outcome level, every lesson should incorporate behaviors requiring the use of significant social science habits of mind and also should encourage critical inquiry. A basic geography lesson on maps, for example, can have students question why a map is drawn a certain way, rather than merely reading the map: Why is the world map centered on the U.S. or on the Atlantic? How else could it be drawn? How does the choice of colors or symbols for the data shown on the map reveal the point of view of the cartog-

TABLE 11.1

Key Goal and Related Learner Outcomes

Goal	Sample Student Outcomes	Related National Standards
Develop skills in historical analysis and primary source interpretation.	Define the context in which a primary source document was produced and the implications of context for understanding the document.	*Historical Research Capabilities* • Marshall contextual knowledge and perspectives of the time and place and construct a sound historical interpretation.
	Analyze a document to define a problem, argument, assumptions, and expected outcomes.	*Historical Issue—Analysis and Decision Making* • Marshall evidence of antecedent circumstances and contemporary factors contributing to problems and alternative courses of action.
	Evaluate the influence of author and audience bias in a given document.	*Historical Comprehension* • Reconstruct the literal meaning of a historical passage. • Identify the central questions the historical narrative addresses.
	Describe an author's intent in producing a given document based on understanding of text and context.	*Historical Analysis and Interpretation* • Identify the author or source of the historical document or narrative. • Compare and contrast differing sets of ideas, values, personalities, behaviors, and institutions.
	Validate a source as to its authenticity, authority, and representativeness.	*Historical Research Capabilities* • Interrogate historical data.
	Research short- and long-term consequences of a given document.	*Historical Analysis and Interpretation* • Challenge arguments of historical inevitability. • Hypothesize the influence of the past.
	Analyze effects of given sources on interpretation of historical events.	*Historical Analysis and Interpretation* • Analyze cause-and-effect relationships and multiple causation, including the importance of the individual, the influence of ideas, and the role of chance.

Note. "Goal" and "Sample Student Outcomes" from *Defining Nations: Cultural Identity and Political Tensions* (p. 5), by M. M. Sandling, 2000, Williamsburg, VA: Center for Gifted Education, College of William and Mary. Copyright © 2000 by the Center for Gifted Education. Reprinted with permission. "Related National Standards" from *National Standards for History* (pp. 18–19), by the National Center for History in Schools, 1996, Los Angeles: Author. Copyright © 1996 by the National Center for History in Schools. Reprinted with permission.

rapher? What responses do these colors or symbols elicit from the observer? How does the scale of the map affect the specificity of the data for a given location? How would a different scale change the types of interpretations possible from this map?

Social science habits of mind can be developed through the use of specific strategies that students may employ in a variety of contexts. For example, Reasoning About a Situation or Event (see Figure 11.1) is an application of Paul's (1992) Elements of Reasoning. The activity guides students to identify the key stakeholders involved in a given circumstance, to determine their points of view and explore the assumptions and beliefs that underlie these points of view, and then to evaluate the implications of the coexistence of these diverse positions. This approach may be used across social studies courses to help students focus on the complexity of world events and to develop an awareness of the possibilities for alternative outcomes.

This graphic organizer also may be used to structure student research in preparation for demonstrating their understanding of an issue and the different perspectives in a role-play. Working from a given situation, students or groups of students take on the position of one of the stakeholders they have listed in the chart. Using historical documents or primary sources related to current issues, they establish the perspective and assumptions of their stakeholder and use that information to formulate a presentation of their wants and desires related to the specific event. For instance, students may take on the roles of worker or management and each formulate a position on a key issue being disputed during the early years of the Industrial Revolution; they may take part in a UN-style debate over an international issue; or they may take on the perspectives of the representatives of different states at the Constitutional Convention. Following time for background research, each stakeholder presents his or her agenda to the group. After hearing the perspectives of each stakeholder, the group members can negotiate and attempt to reach a resolution that is agreeable to all parties involved.

This process not only requires students to engage in the research and analytical strategies of social science practitioners, but it adds complexity to their understanding of the event, and engages the student more personally in the material. All of the social science disciplines incorporate analysis of documents and other sources and rely upon this analysis to promote understanding of the perspectives involved. By emphasizing strategies for primary source analysis in the curriculum, teachers provide challenging reading materials, as well as complex interpretive tasks, that support students in developing the habits of critical inquiry that they can then use every day in confronting the enormous amount of information they receive from the newspaper, television, Internet, and other sources.

Beyond general strategies, certain content lends itself better to teaching specific habits of mind. In the sample lesson "Tensions in the Former Yugoslavia"

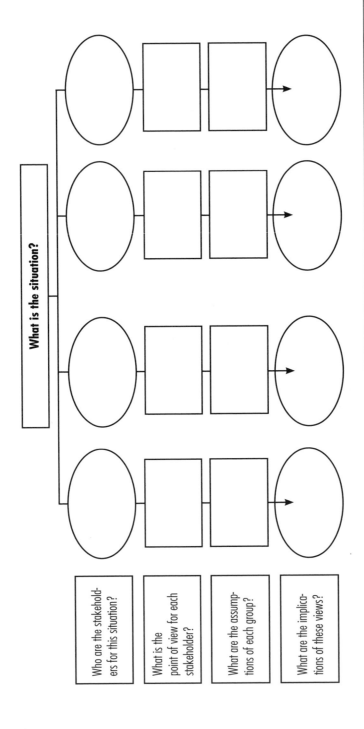

Figure 11.1. Reasoning about a situation or event. From *Defining Nations: Cultural Identity and Political Tension* (p. 67), by M. M. Sandling, 2000, Williamsburg, VA: Center for Gifted Education, College of William and Mary. Copyright © 2000 by the Center for Gifted Education. Reprinted with permission.

(Sandling, 2000), the situation in the Balkans following the break-up of the former Yugoslavia and the continued repercussions of it provides an opportunity for students to grapple with the idea that people and cultures differ, but share a common humanity; to explore the complexity of cause; and to consider the possibility that not all problems have workable solutions. Court cases, such as the Sacco and Vanzetti case in the 1920s (see the sample lesson "Sacco and Vanzetti" [Center for Gifted Education, 2001a]), can be presented to students first without their outcomes, thus allowing students to weigh evidence and evaluate arguments while stressing historical empathy as they attempt to understand the values and views of the historical actors. Engagement in real-world issues, with emphasis on the complexity of circumstances, encourages critical reasoning even as it helps students develop a knowledge base of social science content, thus representing several significant areas of learner outcomes in this subject.

HIGHER ORDER REASONING

In order to develop the habits of mind of the social sciences and to achieve significant outcomes, students must move beyond memorization and repetition of facts to active analysis and higher order thinking. In the social sciences, each discipline addresses various questions that students should attempt to answer as they begin developing disciplinary skills and habits of mind. Anthropologists attempt to understand human and societal development while recognizing the value of all cultures. Economists analyze how the choices people make about resources then affect public policy and international interactions. Geographers examine where things are located and why and how the interactions among these locations shape the world. Historians study human activity and thinking in past societies and try to construct an understanding of the effects of past actions on the contemporary world. Political scientists focus on how public choices are made, by whom, for what purposes, and with what consequences, both locally and globally. Sociologists study the patterns and organization of human behavior and the causes and consequences of that behavior. Questions of these types have no answer that students can look up in a book and memorize; instead, students must have opportunities to learn how to find and examine sources of information and draw conclusions.

Students need a structure to guide their reasoning and to help them identify the questions to be asked. Once such a method has been taught to students and they have developed some proficiency with using it, they can use it in any discipline and in their daily lives. Paul's (1992) Elements of Reasoning model, outlined in Chapter 5, serves as a useful and versatile tool in social studies courses. As they use and reflect upon the Elements of Reasoning, students

SAMPLE LESSON:
TENSIONS IN THE FORMER YUGOSLAVIA

Instructional Purpose:
- To identify cross-cutting and overlapping cleavages in populations.
- To use maps to examine the ethnic divisions in the former Yugoslavia.
- To write a persuasive paragraph using evidence.

Activities and Questions:
1. Simulate the process of group formation. Tell students to form groups with other students in the classroom based on shared elements of their identity (e.g., aspects of family, race, ethnicity, beliefs, values, nationality, social aspects, class, time, and place). Give them no further directions.

2. Have each group report on what elements of identity unite the group. Then, ask questions that will require students to question the way they grouped themselves:
   - All of you are students in this school and in this class, so why didn't you all group together?
   - In what ways are you different from others in your group? In what ways are you like students in the other groups? Why did you choose the particular elements you did for grouping purposes?
   - In what other ways could you form yourselves into groups? On which elements of identity might you base those decisions? How would the makeup of the groups change?
   - What can we learn about how people identify and group themselves based on this activity?

3. Point out to students that, depending on what elements of identity they stressed, they may find themselves in different groups with different people; that, in some way or another, they share an element of their identity with every other student. Explain that they have divided themselves based on *cross-cutting cleavages.* Draw a circle on the board and demonstrate that, if the students divide on religion, it may divide them according to this line (draw a line through the circle), but if they divide based on something else, it will divide them differently (draw a different line). Explain that some societies are like this. Ask what the benefits would be of having a society that is divided by cross-cutting cleavages. What would be the drawbacks? What other ways can a society be divided besides cross-cutting cleavages?

4. Explain that the other division discussed by geographers is *overlapping*

cleavages. What do you think this means? Draw another circle with one line through it and say that, in some groups, the people are divided by religion, by nationality, and by economic status and that all of the lines fall in the same place, so the group is always divided into the same subgroups no matter what element of identity you look at. What are the benefits of a society's being divided by overlapping cleavages? The drawbacks? Can you think of a place in the world where this is the case?

5. Tell students that they are going to look more closely at the effect of the collapse of communism by studying the area of the former Yugoslavia. With the end of a common political identity, people in former communist areas sought to identify themselves as countries and political boundaries shifted. Today, students will look at cleavages in those areas and discuss why there has been such tension in a region that has existed for many, many years, and how it is necessary to examine the history of the area in order to understand the present.

6. Break students into small groups and have each group represent the Serbians, Bosnians, or Croatians of the former Yugoslavia. Provide each group with relevant documents to read and encourage them to identify the groups in conflict in their region and the issues that divide these groups. Give the students the form for Reasoning About a Situation or Event (see Figure 11.1) and have them identify the central issue and major stakeholders. Then, have each group complete the point of view, assumptions, and implications for one stakeholder, followed by a large-group sharing and discussion for the overall chart based on the following questions:
   - What are the implications of the interactions of these various assumptions?
   - What has caused these very different points of view to develop?
   - Are the cleavages in this society overlapping or cross-cutting?
   - What are the potential areas of conflict in this situation?
   - What are the potential areas of compromise in this situation?
   - What are the possible resolutions for this situation?
   - What would have to happen for those resolutions to be possible?
   - What might be obstacles to achieving a resolution in this situation?
   - What elements of identity are being stressed in this situation?
   - How is identity influencing the tensions and the possibilities of resolution?
   - Is it possible for these people to continue living together in one country? What would have to happen for that to work?

7. Share with students accounts of experiences in Kosovo from Mertus' (1999) *Kosovo: How Myths and Truths Started a War.* Ask students to consider the following questions: Who is stirring up the divisions? How is identity being used to make people act?

8. Give students a map depicting the ethnic groups of Serbia. Ask students how they would draw political boundaries in this region to best resolve the situation. Have them present their solution to the class along with a justification for it. (To facilitate this process, you could give groups of students a map on an overhead transparency that they could then put up for the class to see, or use the overhead and erase the lines between groups.) Ask:
   - How small of a group should an individual country be?
   - In general, where should political boundaries be drawn in the world and according to which elements of identity?
   - What other issues are at stake when drawing political boundaries?
   - Have students read articles about the declaration of Kosovo independence. Ask: Why do some countries recognize the independence of Kosovo and others don't? Does this mark the end of the issues of identity and cleavage in the Balkans? Why or why not? How might this affect other groups?

9. Ask students to individually write an answer to the following scenario:

   You are a Department of State official. Write a memo to the President about what the United States' role should be in the former Yugoslavia and in regards to Kosovo independence. What potential conflicts might you encounter and what possible compromises can be reached?

Note. From *Defining Nations: Cultural Identity and Political Tension* (pp. 50–64), by M. M. Sandling, 2000, Williamsburg, VA: Center for Gifted Education. Copyright 2000 by the Center for Gifted Education. Adapted with permission. Suggested resources: Serbia: excerpts from speeches given by Radovan Karadzic to key Serb Democratic Party [SDS] activities in the fall of 1991; Bosnia: excerpts from a 1994 speech by Alija Izetbegovic; Croatia: excerpts from the letter from the Deputy Prime Minister and Minister for Foreign Affairs of Croatia (January 29, 1994), letter from the Permanent Representative of Croatia to the UN (September 15, 1994), and letter from the President of the Republic of Croatia (Franjo Tudjman) to the UN Secretary-General (January 12, 1995). All reprinted in Trifunovska (1999).

SAMPLE LESSON:
SACCO AND VANZETTI

Instructional Purpose:
- Describe both sides taken in the Sacco and Vanzetti trial.
- Examine primary sources (e.g., speeches, court records) and construct the positions of the prosecution and the defense.

Activities and Questions:
1. [Lesson to be taught in the context of studying the period of the 1920s in the United States and the Red Scare of that time.] Give students a brief overview of the events surrounding the arrest of Sacco and Vanzetti from background information. Then, divide students into small groups and share documents on the case, including details of the arrest and evidence and the defendants' final statements to the court (from Monk [1994], *Ordinary Americans*). Assign half of the group to be the prosecution and the other half of the group to be the defense. Briefly establish the position of each side: The prosecution believes the men are guilty and wants them convicted, while the defense feels they are innocent and unjustly accused.

2. Give students the "Assessing an Issue" handout and have them complete their side's influences on point of view and evidence based on their role. Then, bring students together in a large group and discuss the two sides. Once the evidence is established, discuss and further develop the position statements for each side.

3. Ask:
   - Why did the two groups have different reactions to Sacco and Vanzetti when they were examining the same incident and the same evidence?
   - Do some factors influence the decision more than others do? Which ones and why? Give examples and explain (e.g., *bias* or *point of view, beliefs*). Have students discuss the influences on the prosecution's and defense's viewpoints and add them to their sheets. If all that was different was your point of view, what does that tell you? What does this mean for us when we look at documents, listen to someone speak, or encounter information? (*We need to be careful—they could be twisting the truth or seeing it differently because of their point of view. The information may be wrong because of how someone saw it.*)
   - What are some ways we can prevent our point of view from making us misinterpret information we receive? (*Be aware of our point of view, try to take other points of view.*)

4. Ask students to weigh both sides and hypothesize or guess what they think the jury decided. Encourage healthy mini-debate. Explain the jury's actual decision, reiterating the Red Scare social and political context.
   • What does this case reflect about the workings of the political system during this time?
   • How did the inputs of the Red Scare affect the processes of the political system?

5. Close with the 1977 court decision to reopen the case and reverse the 1921 decision as described in the background information.

Handout
Assessing an Issue

Issue:

Prosecution's Position:

Defense's Position:

What are the possible influences on their particular viewpoints?
   Influences on Prosecution's Viewpoint:

   Influences on Defense's Viewpoint:

	Supporting Argument	
	Prosecution	Defense
Evidence:	1.	1.
(Key points of support)	2.	2.
	3.	3.
	4.	4.
	5.	5.

should draw on other material being studied to attempt to identify and examine the various perspectives and assumptions held by the author, theorist, or speaker being analyzed. The students also should identify the evidence being used by the thinker, whether it is the author of the document or themselves, and consider how the assumptions one holds affects his or her interpretation of the evidence and shapes the inferences being drawn. Students then can recognize the possibilities for varied interpretations and conclusions about issues and gain a more complex understanding of past and present events. The graphic organizer, Reasoning About a Situation or Event (see Figure 11.1), provides a framework within which students may identify different points of view in a situation and then examine the reasons for each and the possible outcomes related to each perspective. Thus, it helps students avoid thinking of historical events as inevitable. Moreover, the Elements of Reasoning also provide foundations for developing strong questions for discussion and writing about historical events and documents. Their alignment to key elements of persuasive writing (discussed in Chapter 8) is relevant for writing in social studies as well.

CONCEPTUALLY ORIENTED CURRICULA

As discussed in Chapter 7, an emphasis on abstract concepts in the curriculum promotes higher order thinking and interdisciplinary connections. Identifying and organizing information under an "umbrella" concept helps to generate questions for investigation and discussion and aids in analyzing new experiences or evidence (Beyer, 1971). In addition, concept development is a tool that enables students to evaluate evidence and construct chains of causality. Students' ability to do advanced reasoning and real-world problem solving around challenging content is enhanced by their knowledge of important concepts and how they function within and across disciplines.

A conceptual framework for organizing and understanding information is critical in all of the disciplines, including the social sciences. Social science content, whether government, history, economics, or geography, consists of large amounts of factual knowledge, much of which is rather abstract in nature (e.g., the concepts of supply and demand in economics). Also, many aspects of the social sciences are comparative in nature, and students are repeatedly called upon to compare familiar events and processes with other places, circumstances, and historical periods (Schecter & Weil, 1996). For example, students may be asked to analyze the similarities and differences between aspects of the Revolutionary War and the Civil War in the United States, or between the two World Wars in Europe. Concept-based instruction in social studies is crucial in making the volume of information meaningful; without the concepts, students get lost in the isolated facts and cannot perceive the whole or make use-

History Concepts	General Social Science Concepts	Political Science Concepts
Community Society Revolution Progress Authority	Systems Causality Change Time Patterns Justice Law Liberty Conflict Culture Ethnicity Nationalism Authority	The State Tyranny Leadership Aristocracy Democracy
Economic Concepts		Geographic Concepts
Scarcity Productions Interdependence Specialization Market		Place Movement Region Location Diffusion

Figure 11.2. Concepts in the social sciences.

ful comparisons (Kneip, 1989; Wesley & Wronski, 1973). Thus, incorporation of concept development activities represents one of the central best practices in social studies instruction (Shaver, 1991).

Because the social sciences are concerned with aspects of the human condition, many of the universal concepts discussed in Chapter 7 apply well to this subject area. Moreover, each of the social science disciplines is built upon a foundation of specific concepts that are critical to understanding that discipline. Figure 11.2 lists some of the major concepts that are relevant across all of the social sciences, along with some of the discipline-specific concepts that can be used to inform instruction in each of these areas.

When concepts are to be used as a focus for instruction, it is important for students to be introduced to the concept directly and then be given many opportunities to practice using that concept within the content area. As described in Chapter 7, students should build a basic understanding of the chosen concept through a process of identifying and categorizing examples, then generating nonexamples of the concept. The process concludes with students' development of several generalizations or statements about the concept that are always or almost always true (Taba, 1962). Curriculum developers and teachers preparing to guide students through this process should have a guiding set of generalizations representing key understandings for students to learn and apply. These key understandings should be fundamental to the concept itself but also points that will most effectively illuminate the content and support students in making connections within and across content areas. For example, in a unit using the concept of *authority* to examine the changes that occur from the Renaissance through the age of Absolute Monarchs, the Enlightenment, and into Imperialism, the following generalizations may help to engage students with the important content of the historical period (Sandling & Sandling, 2005).

- *Authority may be derived from a person or a position.* This generalization alerts students to the different natures of authority, whether it be based on knowledge one has, the position one holds, or a person's natural charisma, which may help students to understand why a particular person has authority despite lack of knowledge, a strong personality, or any legitimate claim to it.

- *The legitimacy of authority is grounded in the culture and values of that place and time.* This challenges students to gain a deeper understanding of the values of a given place and time and then have a better awareness of why people would have followed a particular leader.

- *Enduring authority rests with institutions, not individuals.* This generalization is key to understanding the particular historical period in question, because it was a time noted for the growth of institutions of government, constitutional monarchies, and republics not based on birth.

- *Authority is demonstrated through symbols, symbolic actions, and procedures.* This generalization helps to guide students in noticing the variety of ways that authority is expressed, so they can be alert to watching how these change over time and why. It also provides opportunities to focus on how outsiders, such as European explorers and colonizers, responded to the symbols of authority when confronting a new society. This prompts careful consideration of the interactions between the groups.

- *Authority changes in response to other expressions of power.* In the time period being studied, the nature of political authority changed significantly and the power of other institutions, notably the church, declined. This generalization was designed to help students see the chains of causality that contributed to the changes that occurred.

Although the examples and explanations demonstrate key connections between the generalizations and the particular period under study, the overall concept (authority) and generalizations certainly apply across human history. Therefore a unit organized around these generalizations provides opportunities for students not only to understand the Renaissance and Reformation period, but also to build connections to a much broader range of history as well as their own time.

Throughout a unit grounded in a concept such as *authority*, students may be guided to use the unit generalizations and their own developing key understandings in their consideration of primary and secondary source readings and other class materials. By varying the approach to the concept throughout a unit of instruction, a teacher also can differentiate the degree of complexity to help students develop in-depth understanding. The sample lesson "Sacco and Vanzetti" (Center for Gifted Education, 2001a), which linked to the concept of *systems,* did not ask students to analyze a specific system fully; instead, students focus only on the influence of one major event on a political system, with acknowledgement of other influences within the larger context. The sample lesson "Tensions in the Former Yugoslavia" (Sandling, 2000) addressed the concept of *nationalism* with an added level of complexity that asks students to look at how nationalism shapes and is shaped by the concept of *identity.* In conjunction with developing generalizations about authority as described above, groups of students read different documents that illustrate views of authority in the period under study. The documents may be assigned to groups based on level of student readiness for varying degrees of complexity in the sources, providing differentiated challenge levels while engaging all students in a higher level exploration of the concept. With such variation and yet consistency in the treatment of central concepts, the curriculum supports students in deep reflection upon the place of those concepts within their understanding of the world.

SUBSTANTIVE CONTENT

Inextricably linked with conceptual learning is substantive content—drawing upon the complex knowledge, principles, and questions that represent the essence of the social sciences disciplines. High-ability students can quickly grasp the vocabulary and basic facts presented in class or in a textbook. To be challenged, these students need to go deeper into content, engaging in the habits of mind of the discipline. In order to move beyond simplistic, rote memorization, gifted students need rich sources of information from which to draw conclusions, as well as strong guiding questions to support their exploration and understanding of these information sources.

One key element to help achieve this goal is to use primary source documents in social studies education. Using primary sources as central reading materials, with textbooks only as supplements, can greatly increase the complexity of the learning process for students. Primary sources engage students in the historian's task of trying to construct an understanding of past people and events instead of reading and digesting someone else's summary; such sources offer students in history, geography, and other courses a more direct exploration of the perspectives, biases, and emotions of the stakeholders, and they are not influenced by the degree of hindsight that affects secondary source accounts. For example, when studying the Imperialist expansion of European countries during the 19th century, students can read documents and discern the reasons Europeans desired and justified taking control of most of the African and Asian continents. These documents also provide insight into the values and perspectives Europeans held about themselves and the indigenous peoples of the lands they were taking over. Students can compare these perspectives with documents from Chinese, African, and Indian leaders regarding the European Imperialists to gain a more multicultural and complex view of this time period, as well as a greater understanding of later conflicts and interactions between the various groups.

The difficulty with this approach is that primary sources can be dense and challenging for students. At least initially, students will need scaffolding to help them make sense of the documents. Figure 11.3 is a model for analyzing primary sources that helps students make meaning out of a historical source. First, students explore key aspects of a source's context, the time and place from which the document arose. This section assists students in making connections between the document and the larger scope of what they are studying, and in identifying the cultural values and assumptions that shaped the tone and message of the text. The second section guides students through an analysis of the text. This section helps students to analyze the point and perspective of the text and evaluate the influence of the author's intent or conditions on the message conveyed. Finally, students engage in critical analysis of elements of reliability, authenticity, and potential and actual consequences; such questions help students identify the importance and effects of the document. Although in some circumstances students may not be able to find answers to all of the questions in this last section, consideration of these issues engages them in the ways of thinking used by professional historians. This model enables students to gain a deeper insight into the meaning of the text while making connections between various information and drawing conclusions of their own. In addition to the general model for analyzing primary sources, learners also may benefit from specific, structured questions that guide their understanding as they read a particular source, especially if that source is dense or lengthy. Guiding questions may be used to check comprehension and encourage reading strategies such as making inferences and predicting outcomes, in addition to using reasoning strategies to strengthen their understanding of the source.

Secondary sources are, of course, useful and important for students to review for background knowledge and wider perspectives; indeed, many of the questions on the analysis chart in Figure 11.3 are generally best answered from a review of related secondary sources. Secondary sources also are useful for teacher reference and for content coverage across the span of a course because of the great volume of information generally included. Nevertheless, teachers of high-ability learners should consider how much of the secondary material students can cover on their own, leaving class time for in-depth analysis of primary sources, maps, and the writings of theorists in the social sciences. For example, instead of memorizing a list of causes of World War I, students can read documents and study events of the time to develop their own tentative

---

Document Title:

Establishing a context and intent for the source:

> Author:
> Time/When was it written?
> Briefly describe the culture of the time and list related events of the time:
> Purpose (Why was the document created?)
> Audience (For whom was the document created?)

Understanding the Source:

> What problems/issues/events does the source address?
> What are the main points/ideas/arguments?
> What assumptions/values/feelings does the author reflect?
> What actions/outcomes does the author expect? From whom?

Evaluating/Interpreting the Source:

> *Authenticity/Reliability.* (Could the source be invented, edited, or mistranslated? What corroborating evidence do you have about the source? Does the author know enough about the topic to discuss it?)
>
> *Representative.* (How typical is the source of others of the same period? What other information might you need to find this out?)
>
> What could the consequences of this document be? (What would happen if the author's plans were carried out? What could happen to the author when people read this? How might this document affect or change public opinions?)
>
> What were the actual consequences? What really happened as a result of this document? Short-term? Long-term?
>
> What new or different interpretation does this source provide about the historical period?

Figure 11.3. Analyzing primary sources. From *The Road to the White House* (pp. 192–193), by the Center for Gifted Education, 2000, Williamsburg, VA: Author. Copyright © 2000 by the Center for Gifted Education. Reprinted with permission.

understandings of key issues, followed by a guided debriefing with the teacher. Rather than just reading that Thomas Paine's *Common Sense* or the writings of John Locke influenced the patriots in the Revolutionary period, students can read from *Common Sense* or *Two Treatises on Government* and compare the concepts and rhetoric in those documents to those found in the Declaration of Independence. Even in the elementary grades, students can begin to work with primary sources in full or excerpted form, particularly when the study of these sources is guided with questions that highlight points of key understanding for students, such as points of similarity around the laws of nature and the rights of man in excerpts from the documents just noted. Similarly, students studying government or economics should explore the actual writings of political theorists and economists and work with teacher guidance to understand the theories of these thinkers.

In addition to the use of primary source documents, students also should engage in exploration of the tools and concepts of the discipline as a component of substantive content, thus connecting the three dimensions of the ICM and encouraging development of disciplinary habits of mind. History students can analyze artifacts (or images of them), as well as the archaeological record, to draw conclusions about groups who may have not been powerful or notable enough to have documentary evidence; or they may read diaries and journals of individuals from different walks of life to add to their understanding of the culture and values of a given time or place. Geography students, instead of merely learning how to use scale to measure distance on a map, can develop an understanding of what scale is and how the scale of the map affects the detail and perspective of the data it presents. Students can analyze how the information they derive from a map at a national scale compares to the information taken from a county scale map and extrapolate about the effect of scale for a map viewer. Sociology students can conduct interviews or observations of human behavior to test and evaluate the theories and concepts covered in class. Students can then identify the strengths and usefulness of these theories as well as the limitations of them. These students, along with students of economics, should learn about the descriptive and predictive models used in their disciplines and practice their use. Simulations of political situations, such as Model Congress, Model UN, or model Supreme Courts, can allow students to use authentic tools and concepts within content study.

Content also can be made more substantial through activities that broaden the scope of information covered, making it more multicultural or global in focus, and through activities that provide students with materials that allow them to explore and draw conclusions. The sample lesson "Chinese Thought and Education" (Center for Gifted Education, 2001b) is an example of substantive content for primary students. This lesson not only teaches students who Confucius was, but has them analyze and interpret some of his sayings. The sample lesson "Tensions in the Former Yugoslavia" (Sandling, 2000) does not *tell* students the causes of the conflict; rather, the students explore documents to build an understanding of the tensions. Students analyze multiple perspectives in the conflict, thereby coming to appreciate the difficulty in resolving the issues and the continuing repercussions of the initial breakup of the country.

As students wrestle with greater complexity in the content they encounter, their learning can be supported and centered through the integration of the other key dimensions of the ICM. A structured model for reasoning and a focus on a central concept allow students to bring disparate pieces of content together and to analyze the patterns they see and the anomalies in those patterns. Thus, while advanced processes and abstract concepts increase the level of challenge, they also provide a common ground for students to work from as they deepen their content knowledge.

MULTICULTURAL/GLOBAL EMPHASIS

One way rich content and a realistic paradigm of the world can be achieved in social studies education is by expanding one's view to incorporate a greater number of human actors. In addition, given the growing interdependence and interconnectedness of our increasingly globalized world, it is imperative for students to examine and recognize the role of different peoples in different parts of the world in global economic and political systems. A broader understanding emerges when students examine the multiple perspectives and experiences of a given event or situation, whether that is a historical event, a current economic trend, or the distribution of resources. Students should be exposed to the perspectives of diverse ethnic and economic groups, and should attempt to view issues, events, and concepts from the viewpoints of these groups. Incorporating these multicultural perspectives especially benefits high-ability students by enabling them to confront and make sense of the complexity of society.

Textbooks and instruction have long focused on the powerful and the successful, as well as the perspective of the present, examining the viewpoints and actions of the individuals and groups who have most obviously created the world we live in today. Little time has traditionally been spent on people, ideas, and cultures that failed or were overwhelmed by others. The problem with this approach is that the less powerful still shaped the world in which we live; in their interactions with the "winners," ideas were exchanged and the winners were affected by the act of overwhelming or replacing the less successful. Expanding one's view beyond the winners also can mean looking at the voices of ethnic, racial, religious, and ideological minorities. Their ideas were not the ones the majority followed, but society was influenced by their existence and had to respond to them. For example, "Sacco and Vanzetti" (Center for Gifted Education, 2001a) looks at two Italian immigrant anarchists who were part of a radical fringe group in the United States in the early 20th century. Although these two men and those who shared their ideas were not successful in achieving their goals, U.S. citizens at the time responded strongly to them, which resulted in an overall effect on U.S. behavior and views. Today, American memory and thought have been shaped by the treatment and deaths of these two men. By expanding social studies instruction to include the perspectives of multiple cul-

SAMPLE LESSON:
CHINESE THOUGHT AND EDUCATION

Instructional Purposes:

- To explore the ancient Chinese system of education and civil service examinations.
- To introduce the Chinese philosopher Confucius and his teachings.
- To recognize the importance of following rules for behavior.

Activities and Questions:

1. [Lesson presented in the context of a study of ancient China.] Tell students that, in ancient Chinese societal structure, most people were peasants; generally, they were poor farmers. There were some merchants who sold and traded goods; the merchants were higher in the societal structure than the peasants and usually were wealthier. Above these were the group known as the scholar-gentry, who held important positions in the government. Have students think about how people who work for the government get to their positions. Ask them to imagine being locked into a small, closet-size room for several days to take a very hard test. Explain that this is how the Chinese tested people who wanted to work for the government or in the "civil service." The exams tested people's knowledge of books of history, poetry, and philosophy, including the teachings of an influential Chinese philosopher called Confucius.

2. Distribute a handout of the following text and read with students.

    Confucius was a great philosopher, or thinker, of ancient China. He was born about 2,500 years ago, in about 551 B.C. The dynasty ruling in China at that time was called the Chou or Zhou dynasty, but many other powerful families had control over different areas of the country, and these families and their armies fought many battles with one another.

    Confucius was very interested in learning when he was young, but not everyone in his time was allowed to have a formal education, only the children of the royalty and nobility. Confucius' father had a job in the government, so Confucius was able to study with tutors. He loved to learn and tried to learn everything he could. He hoped someday he could be a government official who advised the rulers on wise decisions, but he had trouble finding such a position and getting rulers to listen to him. Many other students listened to Confucius, though, and soon he started teaching others what he had learned and was learning. He traveled around the country and taught anyone who wanted to learn from him. He had many ideas about how peo-

ple could get along with each other by following certain rules and customs. He also thought the government should always be trying to make life better and safer for the people. Even though Confucius never found the kind of job helping rulers that he wanted, he had many followers throughout his life who learned from him and tried to follow his teachings.

We do not have any of Confucius' own writings, but his students wrote down many of his important ideas after he died. These teachings were collected in a book called the Analects. *An example of Confucius' teaching is in the statement, "Do not do unto others, what you would not want others to do to you."*

Write this statement on the board and ask students to explain what they think the statement means and if they have heard similar statements before.

3. Divide students into small groups. Give each group one of the quotes listed below. Ask each group to read the quote, discuss the meaning of the quote and then choose a way to share the teaching with the class. They may choose to draw a picture of an event the quote might apply to, act out a situation, or write a group story relating to the quote. Invite students to share what their groups have done.
   - I hear and I forget. I see and I remember. I do and I understand
   - Our greatest glory is not in never falling, but in rising every time we fall.
   - If you make a mistake and do not correct it, this is called a mistake.
   - Learn as if you were following someone with whom you could not catch up, as though it were someone you were frightened of losing.
   - Put me in the company of any two people at random—they will invariably have something to teach me.

Wrap up the discussion by explaining to students that the influence of Confucius was strong and long-lasting in Chinese society and the value he placed on learning was a value that has been shared by many in Chinese society throughout history. Remind students of the comment earlier in the lesson that those who took the civil service exams had to know of Confucius' teachings. Also discuss with students the idea of working hard to learn and how that relates to the idea of working hard in general; remind them of the readings on Chinese farming they studied previously and the value placed on hard work by the Chinese people. Do you think Confucius valued hard work? Why or why not?

Note. Adapted from *Ancient China: The Middle Kingdom* (pp. 96–103), by the Center for Gifted Education, 2001, Williamsburg, VA: Author. Copyright 2001 by the Center of Gifted Education. Adapted with permission.

tures, educators help students to see the contingency of events and how the decisions, actions, and interactions of many individuals, rather than an inevitable sequence of events, shaped our world. This awareness of the possibilities for change can then lead students to take social action now and in the future. With solid instruction in the habits of mind of the social sciences, students can develop informed opinions on important issues and work to address those issues, thus achieving key goals of civic education (Banks, 1995; Bragaw, 1996).

Beyond a focus on individuals and specific events, a balanced multicultural emphasis in the social studies curriculum also requires examining situations in their larger global context over extended periods of time to explore the world's complexity and its interconnectedness. For example, the Great Depression—or any economic trend, including the recent economic downturn—was not solely dependent on conditions in the United States, but was a result of decisions and conditions around the world. In a study of the Great Depression, students should examine related historic events, including World War I reparations and the rise of consumer spending and credit, as well as global patterns of loans and trade tariffs, to be able to understand more fully how the economy could become so fragile. "Tensions in the Former Yugoslavia" (Sandling, 2000) looks at multiple perspectives within a context and has students look at the event in its larger global setting. Students first analyze the multiple ethnic groups at odds in the former Yugoslavia and then analyze the larger repercussions of this ethnic division by examining how the tension shaped U.S. actions and how the status of Kosovo can affect the foreign relations of the U.S. and Russia, neither of whom are in the Balkans.

Awareness of the global context and global connections is critical in helping students understand past and current world events. In geography or economics class, students can analyze the system of global food production and how demand in developed countries for luxury crops, such as coffee, cocoa, and tropical foods, has altered the agricultural patterns and products in less developed countries and contributed to our increasing interdependence. This awareness of the global setting can help students to realize that the current emphasis on biofuels and higher gas prices globally can combine with unrest and drought to create both a massive food shortage in less-developed countries and higher prices in U.S. grocery stores at the same time. Such study of complex interactions can challenge and stimulate students while also promoting the habits of mind required in the social sciences.

Teachers and students can use current event articles and other publications to illustrate and help define various perspectives on key issues. Another way students can gain multiple cultural perspectives is through a global learning experience. Teachers can partner their class with students in other countries. Students can then send letters, pictures, or class products back and forth or use technologies such as webcasts, e-mail, and videoconferencing or electronic transfer of pictures or products to communicate and learn about one another (Gibson, Rimmington, & Landwehr-Brown, 2008). The ability to ask questions and view personal stories will further deepen students' understanding of cultural differences and similarities and demonstrate tangible ways in which people in other countries are connected to their own lives. Politics, economics, history, and geography do not happen in a vacuum; they are all shaped by national and international forces. By confronting events in their larger global setting, students gain a deeper understanding of why things happen as they do, which enables them to address today's important issues more knowledgeably and effectively.

INTERDISCIPLINARY AND INTRADISCIPLINARY CONNECTIONS

People are not only influenced by the actions of other individuals and political and social organizations, they also are affected by things such as religion, music, art, and literature. In turn, the cultural products of a people are influenced by political, economic, and military events. Therefore, curriculum that draws connections across a broad array of disciplines can shed light on what motivates and influences human actions. Gifted learners can make connections at abstract levels and benefit from a more holistic approach, rather than compartmentalizing history, government, literature, and music. The resulting instruction does not just involve reading a piece of literature and identifying how the time period is reflected in it; instead, students examine the interplay between literature and reality and increase their understanding of both.

The social studies reflect important connections, as they combine multiple social science disciplines into one school subject. Within social studies, various fields of study can enrich one another. For example, the geography of the Balkans helps explain the historic and current events in that region; an understanding of politics sheds greater light on the significance of the Sacco and Vanzetti case; and geographic regions and boundaries in the U.S. influence the process of electing a President. Map analysis in history lessons helps students understand the effect of the physical geography on human action. A study of the physical landscape traversed by the Silk Road combined with an understanding of the transportation technology of the time helps students understand European perspectives about China during the Renaissance, and an analysis of the geography of the Indian subcontinent enables students to explain the limits of the spread of Islam into the region and the resulting religious divisions that continue to create tension.

Not only do such connections enrich students' experience of learning, they also build stronger fundamental skills and habits of mind. Geography teachers need to build students' knowledge of history in order to analyze population pyramids and resulting population structures around the world, as well as to explain the distribution of languages and culture groups on Earth and the resulting disputes over control of territory that currently exist. The geographic distribution of economic activities can be more thoroughly understood with an understanding of the different political systems and agendas, past and present, and the role of governments in the economy. Likewise, economics teachers can have students analyze maps of physical geography, geographic distance, resource distribution, and climates to better understand the various factors that shape economic decisions. Using the skills, resources, and knowledge of the various disciplines helps students to make connections, deepen their understanding of the material, and develop greater complexity in their conceptions of the individual disciplines.

Connections to areas across a broader array of content also can enrich and inform the social studies. Literature lends itself easily to enhancing history and geography instruction. The study of literature written in a given place or time can capture and demonstrate key aspects of a culture, and the study of high-quality historical fiction can provide insights into the past. Music may be used to demonstrate the values of the creators and the people who listened to it. Lyrics and music from a particular folk society or even popular rock and roll of various eras can be analyzed for the priorities, views, and values of peoples or times. From the songs that were passed down for generations or given considerable radio and MTV play time, students can extrapolate the sentiments and perspectives of the larger population. Music can be used to view changes in values over time or between societies. Students can compare the sound of Gregorian chant to the music of Mozart or Bach and discuss the cultural and technological changes that occurred to result in the changes in musical taste during this period.

Art and architecture can be analyzed in similar ways. Students can evaluate the form and purpose of structures such as the Chateau de Versailles, the pyramids of Egypt, or modern skyscrapers to identify the values or ways of life of different ages. Students can compare structures from the same culture at different points in time, such as medieval castles and the Chateau de Versailles, to identify changing conditions. In addition, they can view two different locations during the same period, such as a European medieval castle and a Japanese feudal castle, to add to a multicultural awareness and comparison of cultural differences, despite political similarities. The study of folk housing structures can provide a record for groups who may not have left other written documents. From an analysis of Native American or African folk housing students can analyze something about the environment they lived in based on the materials available and structural features of the home, their ways of life, and their values based on the size, layout, and orientation of the buildings. Understanding physical science concepts makes geographic features and environmental issues such as the Dust Bowl crisis of the 1930s or present global warming more meaningful, and mathematics can be used to increase an understanding of the Electoral College system, the effect of immigration quotas, or the effects of population growth. Because the social studies are concerned with so many aspects of human life across time and place, the interdisciplinary connections that may be made to this content area are endless. Building such connections around key outcomes and applications of concepts and higher level thinking processes in curriculum ensures that students' learning experience will be enriched and advances their overall growth as learners and citizens.

TECHNOLOGY CONNECTIONS

The use of technology in the classroom can help provide advanced content and also assist in developing social science habits of mind in students. Technology resources open a broad range of sources that students can access to learn more about their social science topics, as well as provide tools that students can use in engaging with the content and sharing it beyond their specific classroom setting.

Various technology tools allow students to apply their different learning preferences to different product forms. Students who are verbal learners can use word processing and desktop publishing to type papers, make newspapers or advertisements, or generate surveys. They also can use programs such as ePublishing to create books with pictures that illustrate their ideas and text. Auditory and visual students can use presentation software to share their research or persuasive arguments, or they can express their creativity by integrating music, images, and narration in a Photo Story production. Students can use spreadsheets to analyze the data gained by surveys like geographers, political pollsters, and sociologists do. GoogleEarth allows students access to satellite imagery of the Earth that they can use to examine changing conditions, contrast land use patterns, and analyze the extent of deforestation and desertification, much like practicing geographers. Increasing availability of GIS (geographic information system) programs allows students to manipulate layers of data about a site and analyze the effects of proposed or current land uses. The computer provides an ever-increasing range of possibilities that can be adapted to meet the technological abilities of the students.

Computers also enable students to use a wider array of resources than were traditionally available in libraries prior to the recent Information Age. The Internet allows students to do research, explore their interests, and extend what they have learned in the lesson. Hypermedia learning environments provide students with the ability to click on various links and nodes based on their own interests and knowledge levels. These environments allow gifted students to bypass information they already know and pursue areas of interest to them (Greene, Moos, Azevedo, & Winters, 2008). The Internet provides access to images and text of a wide range of primary source materials. For example, students can view items such as World War II propaganda from various countries or posters from Mao Zedong's China, and many of these sites also provide historical commentary and contextual information about the documents. Students can use the Internet to take virtual tours of historic sites such as ancient Roman villas, Auschwitz, a tenement in New York City, or a cathedral; political sites such as the White House and U.S. Supreme Court; or countries such as Bangladesh for a geographic perspective. Computer technology can integrate the geographic conditions with history and allow students to explore the 1906 San Francisco earthquake on GoogleEarth and see how the physical event affected human systems. Art collections or artifact collections can be viewed online to add complexity to topics being studied or as a means of examining cultures that lack a written tradition. Also, the immediate access to news sources enables students to connect past events with current developments. Students can use major world news sources to find out what is currently going on with groups, issues, or disputes covered in class, thereby gaining much more up-to-date information than a textbook could provide.

Television and video can be used to provide students with visual images of the people, conditions, or events being studied, adding complexity to basic facts and statistics found in print material. For example, geography students can discuss population growth around the world, but watching the Zero Population Growth video (Population Connection, 2000) and seeing dots appear and start to fill the continents to demonstrate population growth makes the statistics more powerful. Newer technologies in schools such as SAFARI Montage and Discovery Education Streaming provide teachers with a wide array of visual media to choose from that support learning objectives. When used effectively, documentary footage of the past or of other cultures can make material more meaningful and help students to construct a more complete understanding of it. In order for such understanding to emerge, however, visual media should not be used for presentation only; students need to be asked to engage with it. They may be asked to complete responses or reflections on what the video added to their understandings, discuss comparisons of events or groups, or participate in other analytical exercises that engage them with the material presented. Video also can be used creatively by students; video products may be a tool for authentic assessment. Students can create TV advertisements, talk shows, or newscasts; recreate historic events; develop film documentaries; or create other projects to demonstrate their learning in a real-world task. Many schools have the small, handheld Flip Video cameras that will record up to 90 minutes of footage, allowing students to film projects during class time. Students may share their work with broader audiences through online media options.

Internet communication technologies can allow students to interact with students in other states or countries to learn about other areas of the world. Teachers can initiate partnerships with other schools, and students can e-mail or instant message their peers to share information about each group's respective home and lifestyle. These exchanges may allow students to see another country's perspective on historic events or present-day issues. Products made electronically, such as Photo Stories and e-books, can be sent back and forth to allow students to share images and information with one another (Gentry, 2008; Gibson et al., 2008). Students can plan, create, and transmit webcasts to students in other locations. The exchange of information can enhance students' multicultural understandings and make students more aware of their own cultural assumptions (Gibson et al., 2008). Thus, technology allows students to explore topics with more depth, viewing images and obtaining information that helps them build a more complex understanding of the material being studied. (See Chapter 15 for further discussion of technology resources and applications.)

Students' use of technology resources in social studies education should be part of careful planning for the most effective learning experiences. Technology used instructionally or for assessment needs to be incorporated as a tool to support the learning endeavor, not as a substitute for teaching or a time-filler. In addition, planning should include attention to issues of safety and appropriate use for students. Such concerns also promote modeling and fostering of critical thinking; students should be encouraged to seek information on the perspective and background of the publishers of Internet sites, learn ways of assessing the reliability of online sources, and be cautious in their interactions through online communication. Indeed, beyond the critical thinking skills they learn to use in these contexts, social studies students also can be encouraged to explore how changing technologies affect educational needs and access, communication systems, and societies overall; thus, technology represents not only tools and resources for students in social science, but also a key topic for content study.

INQUIRY-BASED LEARNING

Inquiry teaching was introduced formally to social studies education in the early 1970s. The main goal of this approach was not to provide students with a particular amount of predetermined content; rather, the focus was on teaching children how to learn, acquire information, make meaning from experiences, and find solutions on their own, as well as to formulate their own attitudes and values based on these experiences (Beyer, 1971; Brown, 1996). To achieve these goals, inquiry teaching stressed the development of concepts, generalizations, and intellectual skills instead of presentation of information and memorization.

By stressing the skills for gaining knowledge and examining assumptions and conclusions, the core of inquiry teaching is useful and valid no matter how students' and society's perspectives change. In inquiry teaching, students follow a series of steps. The process begins as teachers allow students to generate and define problems to be solved without limiting the questions to a specific syllabus. In order for students to define a problem, they must become aware of the problem and its immediacy and relevance to their own experience (Beyer, 1971). An examination of current events could provide teachers with a variety of issues that relate to course content. Teachers in a history or geography class may draw upon conflicts or tensions in the news to stimulate student curiosity about what the issues are and how they echo similar conflicts in the past or in other places, thus engaging students in research that will connect events in the students' lives with course content. Government or sociology teachers may draw upon current cases in the courts or legislation being debated or proposed to engage students in the issues and processes of those disciplines. Once a topic has been chosen, teachers can present an argument with which the teacher knows students will strongly disagree or that contradicts student biases. Teachers also may introduce conflicting opinions on a topic that may raise questions for students concerning both sides' viewpoints. These approaches will evoke student concerns and responses and, therefore, a desire to pursue the problem. Whatever the initial approach, inquiry teaching encourages questions that grow out of students' own experiences and beliefs (Beyer, 1971; Brown, 1996).

Once the students have chosen and defined a problem to be studied, they must examine their existing knowledge and data, draw logical inferences, and develop a hypothesis, or tentative response to the problem. The hypothesis is crucial, as it guides the investigation of the data and establishes a goal for the inquiry process. Student hypotheses might address a way to resolve a dispute that is on the news, an economic plan for a struggling country, a bill that would meet the needs of the population, a UN resolution, or a justification for a particular court decision. The students then need to gather relevant evidence that supports and possibly contradicts the hypothesis, evaluate the evidence for credibility, and analyze the data for trends, similarities, and differences. Students then look for relationships between the evidence and their hypothesis, testing their assumptions against the facts. The process ends as students draw a conclusion based on the experience and generalize the conclusion to new data or experiences. Throughout the process, the teacher piques student curiosity, guides students through the process, and models the use of skills, but does not directly supply information concerning the content (Brown, 1996). In order to facilitate inquiry, teachers need a considerable knowledge of whatever content the students choose to pursue, and the open-endedness of the process may make it difficult for teachers and media center staff to assemble resources and plan ahead of time. These methods emphasize the authenticity of tasks and the real-life contexts of students instead of topics and units designed by scholars (Beyer, 1994). In its emphasis on analytical and evaluative skills, inquiry instruction also provides scaffolding for students as they develop the abilities required for critical evaluation of data sources. Considering the many information sources inundating contemporary society, these skills are crucial for student development (Beyer, 1994; Wheeler, 1996).

Similar to inquiry instruction in its open-ended aspects and focus on real-world problems, problem-based learning (PBL) also is an effective model for supporting complex learning in social studies (Stepien, Gallagher, & Workman, 1993). PBL, discussed in more detail elsewhere in this book as it relates to science instruction, engages students in the exploration of a real-world, ill-structured problem. Often, the challenge for social studies teachers, particularly in history, is identifying real-world problems that are open-ended, given that the events already have happened and have had a resolution. One strategy is for history teachers to focus on historical events as a mystery to be solved (Scheuerell, 2008). Teachers can create questions out of events to which even historians lack definitive answers, such as what happened to the Roanoke Colony or Amelia Earhart, and during the steps of the problem-solving process introduce information that adds to students' understanding of the world at that time and the values and cultures of the people. Students can try to figure out why people would want to leave their farms to work in the harsh conditions of the first factories or why large numbers of people chose to leave their homes for a dangerous and uncertain trip across an ocean or the Great Plains (Scheuerell, 2008). Government and economics teachers can have students investigate why governments or other high-level decision makers would want to change policies or practices, and sociology teachers can have students explore the reasons for social changes we see around us (Savoie & Hughes, 1994). The challenge for teachers and curriculum developers of this approach is how to turn the unit content into a mystery to be solved, giving students only the outcomes and making them research the causes. The preplanned lessons that the students experience as they work through the problem can build the content knowledge of the period or concepts that meet the objectives of the unit of study. Problem-based learning, like the inquiry approach described above, encourages not only the habits of inquiry in the disciplines, but also the habit of recognizing the complexity of problems in the real world and the need for a balanced and multifaceted approach to solving them.

The Elements of Reasoning model (Paul, 1992) outlined in Chapter 5 and discussed earlier in this chapter also reflects an inquiry-oriented notion that students need to be taught how to think, not just what to think (Paul, Binker, Martin, Vetrano, & Kreklau, 1995). Under this perspective on education, teachers are questioners, not transmitters of knowledge, and they encourage students' metacognitive awareness. In addition, social studies teachers must encourage another dimension of inquiry: the "traits of the reasoning mind," such as intellectual empathy, courage, and humility (Paul, 1992; Paul & Elder 2001). Social studies education that seeks to develop responsible citizens must not foster the development of thinking skills while "ignoring the ultimate use to which the learner puts them" (Paul et al., 1995, p. 5). Through emphasis on responsibility within inquiry, teachers can underscore the importance of empathy for the perspectives of others, the need to clarify issues and justify judgments based on evidence, and the habit of considering the implications and possible contradictions of one's own thinking (Paul et al., 1995).

CONSTRUCTING MEANING

The integration of substantive content, the reasoning taught in inquiry methods, and the concepts that guide organization of connections all enable students to construct meaning from the information they encounter. This is the task of social scientists: to take discrete facts, details, and sources; analyze them; and use the pieces of information to draw conclusions about the people, times, and places they are studying. For example, historians use photographs, letters, court records, title records, and artifacts to create a narrative of what happened in the past, how it happened, and why. Therefore, if we are to develop the social science habits of mind and obtain significant outcomes from students, they must be able to construct meaning from the information they encounter in the classroom and beyond, guided by structures that planned curriculum and targeted instruction help to establish. To allow students to construct meaning, teachers must not ask questions just to receive specific student answers or provide sources just to give students specific facts to be learned. Rather, the teacher must provide contexts within which students can build understanding through their interactions with particular tasks and resources. In the sample lesson "The Emergence of the Renaissance: Humanism," the teacher does not simply define humanism for students. Instead, students are given primary documents and asked to extrapolate the characteristics of ideal citizens to a humanist and what humanism is. From this information they are then asked to analyze how these ideas might bring about change and what the nature of that change might be in Europe at the time, thereby combining new information with previously learned understandings about the place and period. Thus, students are not merely receiving information; they are analyzing, synthesizing and evaluating data.

As with inquiry, teaching the process of constructing meaning requires scaffolding with strategies and tools students may use while they work to

SAMPLE LESSON:
THE EMERGENCE OF THE
RENAISSANCE: HUMANISM

Instructional Purposes:
- To analyze the reasoning behind humanism and the emergence of the Renaissance.
- To hypothesize how the new ideas of the Renaissance could affect authority in Europe.

Activities and Questions:
1. [To be used in a unit covering the transition from the Middle Ages to the Renaissance and Reformation]. Review with students the results of the Black Death. Explain to students that the collapse of the existing social order and assumptions about the structure of authority led to the rise of new ideas about humankind. Today the students will study a school of thought called humanism.

2. Explain to students that to understand the new ideas of this time, they will analyze documents describing the ideas of some of the Renaissance thinkers. Divide students into four groups. Give each group one document and a copy of the Reasoning of the Humanists chart. Have each group read and analyze its document together using its column of the chart. (You may wish to use large chart paper for each group as well as the individual paper copies to create a large class chart for posting in the classroom.)

3. When students are finished, have them switch groups so that they are in groups of four students, with one student from each of the earlier groups. Have the new groups share their findings from their readings. Have each student fill in the information on their charts.

4. Then, have students work in their new groups to discuss the questions found under the chart. Have groups share their ideas and discuss as a class.

5. Share a formal definition and summary of the ideas of humanism with students and ask:
   - How is this a major shift in thinking from the Middle Ages?
   - What events we have studied may help to explain why this change is happening?
   - What assumptions about authority does humanism make?
   - Where does authority get its legitimacy, in the eyes of humanists?

- What would these thinkers list as characteristics of an ideal citizen during the Renaissance? Brainstorm a list.
- What are the implications of humanism for European society?
- How might this affect the authority of kings and of the church? Why?
- How might this cause the kings and the church to change?
- What might you expect to see happen in Europe as a result of the spread of these ideas?

6. To assess student understanding, have students write from the perspective of a person living at the time humanism emerged. Have them write in their journals their thoughts, responses, and reflections on those new ideas and what they think should happen in Europe as a result.

Reasoning of the Humanists

	Vasari	Mirandola	Bruni	Erasmus
Point of view: According to this writer, what is wrong with society at the time? What criticisms is the writer making about society or the situation of the world?				
Assumptions: What assumptions does the writer make about the Roman Empire? What other assumptions does the writer make about the past?				

	Vasari	**Mirandola**	**Bruni**	**Erasmus**
Inferences: What are the conclusions the writer is drawing? Where does the writer see the solutions to the problems in society? What does the writer think should be done?				
Implications: What are the implications of this person's writing? For whom?				

1. How are the ideas in the chart above a challenge to existing authority systems in Europe? How might these ideas affect the current authority systems in Europe?
2. How do we see values in society changing from reading these documents? How are values different? How might these changes affect the legitimacy of the current authority figures/systems?

Note. Adapted from *The Renaissance and Reformation in Europe* (pp. 123–126, 139), by M. Sandling and G. Sandling, 2005, Dubuque, IA: Kendall/Hunt. Suggested documents include excerpts from Giorgio Vasari, *The Lives of the Painters, Sculptors, and Architects*; Pico della Mirandola, *Oration on the Dignity of Man*; Leonardo Bruni, *The Painting of Leon Battista Alberti*; Erasmus, *An Exhortation to the Diligent Study of Scripture.*

understand the content. In the humanism lesson example, students are given guiding questions with which to analyze the documents and their perspectives and to evaluate the effects of these writings on ideas of authority at the time. The framework for analyzing primary sources, illustrated in Figure 11.3, is another example of an organizer that helps students construct meaning from a document. Answering these questions takes the student beyond reading comprehension and memorization of facts to constructing a more complex understanding of the text and the time period. The same goal can be accomplished in a class discussion through a well-constructed questioning sequence.

All of these approaches to guiding students in constructing meaning require that curriculum developers and teachers have access to and understanding of the content at appropriate levels of depth, and that they use questioning and activities such as the analysis organizer noted above to draw out students' thinking. Several studies of students' historical thinking have demonstrated that throughout elementary and secondary school, students may be developing significant misconceptions about the history they are learning—misconceptions that are fostered by certain approaches to teaching and that are not discovered through fact-based assessment (Barton & Levstik, 2004; Wineburg, 2001). Rather, students must have opportunities to express their understandings of historical content and key ideas, so that teachers may recognize and address major misconceptions before they become too deeply seated in students' understanding. Thus, again, questioning that really requires students to explain the way they are making meaning of the content is critical in the social studies classroom.

MATERIALS AND RESOURCES

A teacher's ability to provide students with substantive content that reflects multiple perspectives and allows them to construct meaning depends largely upon the materials and resources made available in the classroom. Moreover, given that research in many of the social science disciplines relies extensively on interpretation of documents, artifacts, maps, and other resources, supporting student learning through the use of strong sources encourages essential social science habits of mind. Consequently, the selection of appropriate resources is an important element of good social studies teaching and curriculum development. With gifted students in particular, issues of providing challenge and complexity arise in both materials selection and the development of activities around them.

Students should have access to a variety of resources that reflect diverse points of view and provide insight into the topic or issues under study. They should represent a wide enough range to enable students to examine both the "big picture" and the complex details. Secondary accounts or summaries often can help provide the big picture and allow students to analyze subsequent interpretations of a given event, while primary sources can highlight the perspectives and viewpoints of the historical actors and help students to evaluate why events transpired as they did. For example, while studying the meeting of world leaders at Versailles to decide the terms of peace following World War I, students might be presented with a textbook summary of the actors and conditions in conjunction with the German Septemberprogramm outlining German goals in the war, President Wilson's Fourteen Points, and a document from a British government agency outlining British goals for the peace. With such a collection of sources, students do not simply record the outcome of the treaty, but can compare and contrast the goals and values of the various participants, analyze the possibilities for other outcomes, and apply their knowledge of the war and European history to evaluate both how the meeting resulted in the Treaty of Versailles and its possible consequences for Europe.

Both teacher and students should have access to general and specific resources that not only achieve the purpose of the lesson or unit, but also support extensions. Sufficient resources will provide the means for students to pursue their interests and go beyond the classroom activities. However, a potential danger arises with the tendency to amass too large a selection of materials. Today, technology provides us with easy access to a greater wealth of information than ever before. This can make it tempting to provide students with large numbers of resources, which has the potential to overwhelm students and make a lesson too difficult. Moreover, many of the resources available on the Internet are not of high quality, as discussed previously. Careful selection and parsimony are as important as breadth when choosing materials for classroom use.

Variety is a central issue in considering materials selection, with several dimensions to address. A variety of resources will be necessary to obtain a multicultural perspective, but some groups whose perspectives are critical to a given topic may not have written sources, or their writings and views have not been preserved or are not available. Teachers and curriculum developers therefore need to try to find other materials that might provide insights into the experiences of these people in order to have a more authentic multiple perspective emphasis. Teachers can use images of architecture, art, and other artifacts to have students extrapolate information about groups who have left a limited written record. Such variety in form as well as content also can help to promote student interest and engagement in the content. Visual sources and varied perspectives may draw in students who would not be initially attracted by written documents or the majority viewpoints but will find an interest in the overall topic that will eventually lead them to more in-depth study. Primary artifacts will provide insights into individual feelings and experiences, helping illuminate the perspectives that shaped events. Secondary sources will be useful in providing more general knowledge on a topic and will provide a summary of multiple people's experiences, helping students to make sense of the details they encounter. Again, while amassing a variety of sources, teachers and curriculum developers should be primarily concerned with the purpose and specific contribution each source will make to students' overall understanding of the major concepts and content under study.

The *length* of a selection also is important to consider when planning for use of given sources. Even for students who are advanced readers, use of short selections is advisable. Short, yet substantive reading selections enable teachers to provide lessons in which students can quickly read and comprehend the material, thus allowing more time for in-depth discussion of the issues and concepts contained in the document. If a desired document is fairly lengthy, it may be more beneficial to provide the excerpts that relate most directly to the lesson, with a note to remind students that they are seeing only an excerpt. In addition, even when excerpted, primary sources may still be quite lengthy and complex, so guiding questions to support students' understanding as they read can be helpful. This issue of length is significant across grade levels, but is perhaps most important in planning learning experiences for younger students who may be ready to begin to grapple with the concepts in a document but not in its full length or original form.

When choosing any source, curriculum developers must first consider the *reliability* and *representativeness* of that source. Primary sources reflect the ideas of individuals. If students are going to be drawing conclusions and making generalizations from the documents, then the sources must be reflective of the ideas of a large percentage of the population or group being studied, or must be highlighted as unusual within that group through corroboration with other sources. If students use documents that reflect the views of one person or a small minority, then the conclusions the students make will be inaccurate. Documents reflecting a minority position are still useful and can provide students with important information about alternative ideas at the time and add to the complexity of history, but their limited nature needs to be kept in mind. In addition, the purpose of the document is an important consideration. The author's purpose can shape the way information is conveyed, what details are shared or omitted, and how events are portrayed, possibly affecting the accuracy of student conclusions.

Secondary sources also are susceptible to bias. When choosing secondary sources beyond the textbook, consider the sources and perspective of the author. No secondary source is purely objective, but some are more agenda-driven than others. Also consider the reliability of a secondary source: Is the author speaking knowledgeably on the topic, or is it ill-informed opinion? Questions of reliability are of even greater significance with Internet-based sources; it is important for curriculum developers and teachers to know who has supplied the information, because many websites do not have clearly identifiable editors or publishers. Students should be encouraged to develop a habit of examining the reliability and bias of a source, because this is a skill that will be useful to them. However, although students benefit from critiquing their sources, the classroom teacher has to choose sources responsibly in the first place for use in classroom activities and to meet educational objectives.

AUTHENTIC ASSESSMENT AND PRODUCTS

If teachers are striving to have their students engage in the habits of mind of practitioners of particular disciplines, thereby constructing meaning of the content they encounter, then assessment of students must go beyond reading and answering comprehension and recall questions, and tests must not be limited to multiple-choice tasks. Students should be assessed on their performance of the tasks required of historians, geographers, economists, or political scientists. Activities that can be used in any of the disciplines include debates on key issues, designing museum exhibits on a particular event or group, or developing policy statements for a given country or group about what actions it should take locally and globally. Such activities require not only content learning, but also an emphasis on strong reasoning skills and deep understanding of values, assumptions, and concepts, as well as facts.

Assessment in social studies, as in any of the content areas, should be an ongoing process, occurring not only as the culmination of a unit of study, but within each lesson. Again, such assessment should be based at least partially on tasks that engage students in the practices of the discipline they are studying. Geography students can construct maps, create and justify regions in a country, or decide how to draw political boundaries to resolve conflicts or best represent voters. History students can evaluate primary sources for authenticity and corroborate information across multiple sources, put historic figures on trial, and discuss events and issues from the perspectives of different people. Such tasks require students to demonstrate their understanding of sources and the context in which events occurred; consequently, they also provide opportunities to assess students on multiple goals beyond knowledge of the facts, particularly specific process goals related to the practices of the discipline and conceptual understanding that supports conclusions students draw across sources and contexts.

Small- or large-scale products that represent student understanding of the content are useful assessment sources. Product development tasks should require students to consider and apply their understanding of major ideas, as well as demonstrate their own creative input to the process; they should be engaging and promote creativity while still emphasizing rigor in the content demands. For example, students may create original artwork that incorporates the themes and values of the Harlem Renaissance of the 1920s or the Italian Renaissance of the 15th and 16th centuries, or a piece of wartime propaganda that incorporates the ideas and agendas of a war. In political science classes, students can draft legislation and have mock Congresses or simulate an election campaign by writing campaign speeches, developing platforms, and lobbying for changes. Sociology students can create questionnaires around research issues of interest, poll students or community members, and analyze their data to draw conclusions about human behavior. All of these methods require students to use the skills and information they have gained in the classroom to construct an original expression of what they have learned. Some of the products students develop should be short-term in nature, completed in a single class period or as a homework assignment, so that they can be used as formative assessments and allow teachers to measure the level of mastery of content being achieved and reteach or supplement instruction as needed. Other assignments could be longer term, not only to deepen students' understanding of issues in depth, but also to encourage their metacognition and project-management skills.

One other key issue related to assessment in social studies is the consideration of prerequisite knowledge. Many social studies teachers face the challenge of helping students to learn volumes of facts in order to achieve established standards. However, when considering gifted students in particular, pretesting prior knowledge is essential to ensuring that students' class time will not be wasted. By assessing students early in a year or a unit of study on the prerequisite content, or by allowing them to read some background information and then to complete an assessment on that information, teachers free up time from content presentation for these students and expand the time available for engaging in more in-depth, issue-based research and product development. Thus, challenging independent or small-group product assignments may be used as a differentiation strategy to provide engaging learning opportunities for students who may move more quickly through certain content than their classmates.

In order to accomplish all of the assessment goals discussed here, assessment in social studies should incorporate pretesting and posttesting, performance-based tasks in addition to more traditional tests, and ongoing formative assessment through lesson activities. Furthermore, students should be involved in the assessment process through an emphasis on self-evaluation in the classroom, a key component of the next topic, metacognition.

METACOGNITION

The goal of social studies curricula and instruction is not just to teach students the material, but also develop in them the skills they need to be responsible citizens, including behaviors of making decisions based on careful planning and review of available information. In addition, professionals in the disciplines recognize that a key element of the research process is to support the validity of findings and conclusions. Therefore, not only should students learn how to construct meaning from information they encounter, but they also should be able to articulate how they accomplished this task. Often, students arrive at conclusions but cannot explain their inferential process; similarly, students may be able to recognize bias in what they read, but are often unable to trace their own interpretations to track the evidence supporting that inference about bias (Barton & Levstik, 2004). Students need to have opportunities to learn and practice reasoning skills that will allow them to analyze their own thinking. Applying the reasoning model to their own writing or arguments can help them identify their point of view and assumptions, demonstrate the evidence they have that supports or contradicts these views, and evaluate their conclusions. Students can be asked to outline or brainstorm a paper or verbal argument using Paul's (1992) Elements of Reasoning model in order to help them analyze their own reasoning more directly.

Students also need to develop the skills necessary to explicate and carry out the research processes of the disciplines and for civic engagement. Long-term assignments are useful for helping students learn to plan, monitor, and evaluate their own work, the essential components of metacognition. Students should be given long-term assignments in which they must set a goal, plan how to fulfill the requirements, monitor their progress, and then evaluate their products as well as what they learned from the experience. These assignments can be individual projects such as research papers, mini-museums, or travel journals that allow students to focus on goal-setting and completion. These assignments can be tied to classroom activities such as Model Congress or simulated campaigns that allow students to extend their experience to learning how to take action in group settings and adjust to the needs of others (National Council for the Social Studies [NCSS], 2008). To help students develop these skills, teachers should provide structure to guide students through long-term projects and actively model metacognition in the classroom and encourage students to be more conscious of their thinking and overall progress. Students should then be assessed not only by the teacher, but also by their own self-evaluation of their performance. Self-evaluation promotes personal responsibility for projects as well as a sense of independence in goal-setting and self-regulation that students will ultimately need to succeed as practitioners of their chosen disciplines in further academic and career settings.

CONCLUSION

Adapting social studies curricula for high-ability learners centers around students' use of the analytical skills of practitioners and access to primary sources that provide depth in understanding. In order to use the resources in ways that promote their learning, students must have a sufficient background in the content, aided by the use of concepts, and be given instruction and scaffolding in the process of critical thinking. Through the selection of materials at various levels for different students and varying degrees of scaffolding and flexible grouping, teachers can appropriately challenge gifted students within a heterogeneously grouped classroom. Being successful in this endeavor requires a teacher not only to have a good knowledge of the content, but also to be willing to ferret out a variety of engaging and appropriate resources and develop contacts with fellow teachers and practitioners of social science disciplines. Classroom teaching does not, and should not, happen in a vacuum. Constant collaboration with other teachers and social science practitioners will allow a teacher to gain new insights and ideas for the benefit of students.

KEY POINTS SUMMARY

- Active learning and critical inquiry are central tenets in teaching gifted students the social science habits of mind.
- The use of specific thinking models and tools over time can enhance student understanding of important aspects of social studies learning.
- Teaching universal concepts in the social sciences serves to bind together disparate strands of the curriculum while encouraging high-level inquiry.
- Concepts in the social sciences may be general, such as systems or causality, or specific to the subdisciplines, such as leadership and tyranny in a study of political science.
- Use of extensive primary source material that the students must analyze, synthesize, and evaluate emphasizes higher order thinking and problem solving more than the use of survey-like secondary sources.
- Incorporating multicultural points of view on history is essential to a broader understanding of significant events and eras.
- Use of technology can expose students to multiple perspectives on current issues and lead to a stronger emphasis on assessing credibility of sources.

REFERENCES

Banks, J. (1995). Multicultural education: Historical developments, dimensions, and practice. In J. A. Banks & C. A. M. Banks (Eds.), *Handbook of research on multicultural education* (pp. 3–24). New York, NY: Macmillan.

Barton, K. C., & Levstik, L. S. (2004). *Teaching history for the common good.* Mahwah, NJ: Lawrence Erlbaum.

Beyer, B. K. (1971). *Inquiry in the social studies classroom: A strategy for teaching.* Columbus, OH: Merrill.

Beyer, B. K. (1994). Gone but not forgotten—Reflections on the new social studies movement. *The Social Studies, 85,* 251–255.

Bragaw, D. (1996). The social studies: The civic process. In Social Science Education Consortium (Ed.), *Teaching the social sciences and history in secondary schools: A methods book* (pp. 10–36). Belmont, CA: Wadsworth.

Brown, R. H. (1996). Learning how to learn: The Amherst project and history education in the schools. *The Social Studies, 87,* 267–273.

Center for Gifted Education. (2000). *The road to the White House.* Williamsburg, VA: Author.

Center for Gifted Education. (2001a). *The 1920s: A system of tensions.* Williamsburg, VA: Author.

Center for Gifted Education. (2001b). *Ancient China: The middle kingdom.* Williamsburg, VA: Author.

Gentry, J. (2008). E-publishing's impact on learning in an inclusive sixth grade social studies classroom. *Journal of Interactive Learning Research, 19,* 455–467.

Gibson, K. L., Rimmington, G. M., & Landwehr-Brown, M. (2008). Developing global awareness and responsible world citizenship with global learning. *Roeper Review, 30,* 11–23.

Greene, J. A., Moos, D.C., Azevedo, R., & Winters, F. I. (2008). Exploring differences between gifted and grade-level students' use of self-regulatory learning processes with hypermedia. *Computers and Education, 50,* 1069–1083.

Kneip, W. (1989). Social studies within a global education. *Social Education, 53,* 399–403.

Mertus, J. A. (1999). *Kosovo: How myths and truths started a war.* Berkeley: University of California Press.

Monk, L. R. (Ed.). (1994). *Ordinary Americans: U.S. history through the eyes of everyday people.* Alexandria, VA: Close Up.

National Center for History in the Schools. (1996). *National standards for history.* Los Angeles, CA: Author.

National Council for the Social Studies. (2007). *Social studies in the era of No Child Left Behind: A position statement of the National Council for the Social Studies.* Retrieved from http://www.socialstudies.org/positions/nclbera

National Council for the Social Studies. (2008). *A vision of powerful teaching and learning in the social studies: Building social understanding and civic efficacy.* Author. Retrieved from http://www.socialstudies.org/positions/powerful

Paul, R. (1992). *Critical thinking: What every person needs to survive in a rapidly changing world.* Rohnert Park, CA: Foundation for Critical Thinking.

Paul, R., Binker, A. J. A., Martin, D., Vetrano, C., & Kreklau, H. (1995). *Critical thinking handbook: 6th–9th grades: A guide for remodeling lesson plans in language arts, social studies, and science.* Santa Rosa, CA: Foundation for Critical Thinking.

Paul, R., & Elder, L. (2001). Critical thinking: Nine strategies for everyday life: Part 1. *Journal of Developmental Education, 24,* 40–41.

Population Connection. (Producer). (2000). *World population* [DVD]. Available from http://www.populationeducation.org

Sandling, M. M. (2000). *Defining nations: Cultural identity and political tension.* Williamsburg, VA: Center for Gifted Education, The College of William and Mary.

Sandling, M., & Sandling, G. (2005). *The Renaissance and Reformation in Europe.* Dubuque, IA: Kendall/Hunt.

Savoie, J. M., & Hughes, A. S. (1994). Problem-based learning as classroom solution. *Educational Leadership, 52*(3), 54–57.

Schecter, S. L., & Weil, J. (1996). Studying and teaching political science. In Social Science Education Consortium (Eds.), *Teaching the social sciences and history in secondary schools: A methods book* (pp. 137–170). Belmont, CA: Wadsworth.

Scheuerell, S. (2008). The great migration: Using a problem-based learning approach and the Internet. *Social Studies Research and Practice, 3*, 68–79.

Shaver, J. P. (Ed). (1991). *Handbook of research on social studies teaching and learning.* New York, NY: Macmillan.

Stepien, W. J., Gallagher, S. A., & Workman, D. (1993). Problem-based learning for traditional and interdisciplinary classrooms. *Journal for the Education of the Gifted, 16*, 5–17.

Taba, H. (1962). *Curriculum development, theory, and practice.* New York, NY: Harcourt, Brace, and World.

Trifunovska, S. (1999). *Former Yugoslavia through documents: From its dissolution to the peace settlement.* The Hague, Amsterdam: Martinus Nijhoff.

Wesley, E. B., & Wronski, S. P. (1973). *Teaching secondary social studies in a world society* (6th ed.) Lexington, MA: Heath.

Wheeler, R. (1996). Rx for social studies. *Social Education, 60*, 313–314.

Wineburg, S. (Ed.). (2001). *Historical thinking and other unnatural acts.* Philadelphia, PA: Temple University Press.

Chapter 12

Adapting World Languages for High-Ability Learners

Bronwyn MacFarlane

Y*ou are a high school teacher of world languages who is responsible for teaching several levels of your target language. In your class, you have a significant number of high-functioning students along with students of average and below-average abilities. It is October and one of your students in the beginning level comes to you and expresses that she mastered the material covered in Level 1 (which you are now teaching) in her previous district's middle school language program. As a result of the small class enrollment in the upper level classes of the world language program, the principal and counselor plan to consolidate the upper levels into one class and have asked for your input to present to the school board. There also is discussion and interest in moving some of the world language classes into an online service delivery model. Finally, the district is preparing for the upcoming state review of the instructional program, and a planning meeting to prepare for that review is set 2 weeks from now. You have been charged with the responsibility of submitting the world language curriculum report. What can and should you do?*

During the course of teaching world languages in public school settings, many students enrolled in my advanced French class revealed that they participated in the elementary gifted program as younger students. During that preliminary year in the classroom, I predicted that the pattern of performance of advanced foreign language students who also were identified as gifted in elementary school would be advanced in the secondary classroom, and indeed it was. Making that connection and merging the areas of world language instruction and gifted education became an area of focus in developing a highly dynamic and creative classroom to serve high-ability students in the French program. A recent study of world language teacher practices in advanced classrooms revealed a lack of differentiated instruction for gifted world language learners (MacFarlane, 2008). This chapter will explore appropriate curriculum and instructional planning for teaching world languages to talented language students, using the Integrated Curriculum Model (ICM) as a framework for differentiation.

THE PAST AND PRESENT OF WORLD LANGUAGE EDUCATION

The language teaching profession has been in search of a single, ideal method, generalizable across diverse learner groups and one that would successfully teach all students a foreign language in the classroom (Brown, 2002). Subsequently a succession of methods has been described in the historical literature, each one more or less discarded in due course as a new method took its place. The "method obsession" can be traced to Francois Gouin's 1880 publication of *The Art of Teaching and Learning Foreign Languages*, followed by Charles Berlitz at the turn of the century with the Direct Method. This approach in turn was supplanted by the Audiolingual Method of the late 1940s, followed by the burst of innovation in the "spirited seventies" with "designer" methods (Nunan, 1989) such as Community Language Learning, Total Physical Response, the Silent Way, Suggestopedia, and others (Brown, 2002).

At least eight language teaching methods are in practice today including (1) the Grammar-Translation Method, (2) the Direct Method, (3) the Audio-Lingual Method, (4) the Silent Way, (5) Suggestopedia, (6) Community Language Learning, (7) the Total Physical Response Method With Storytelling, and (8) the Communicative Approach. No comparative study has consistently demonstrated the superiority of one method over another for all teachers, all students, and all settings (College Board, 1986; Snow, 1994). How a particular method is manifested in a world language classroom depends heavily on the individual teacher's interpretation of the method's principles. Some teachers may prefer to practice one method to the exclusion of others while other teachers may prefer to pick and choose in a principled way among the methodological options that exist, creating their own unique blend (Snow, 1994).

The method obsession may have brought about its own demise with the realization of one size does not fit all, especially beyond the early, beginning stages of language development. David Nunan (1991) explained that

> It has been realized that there never was and probably never will be a method for all, and the focus in recent years has been on the development of classroom tasks and activities which are consonant with what we know about second language acquisition, and which are also in keeping with the dynamics of the classroom itself. (p. 228)

From a paradigm that once focused almost exclusively on grammar, translation, and the memorization of dialogues, the profession has largely embraced teaching for communicative competence (Rifkin, 2006).

As a field of research, World Language Education inquires into cognitive, social, and institutional dimensions of language instruction in institutional settings and draws insights from social and educational psychology (Kramsch, 2000), with many world language education scholars focusing their attention on the common set of issues in the schooling process, including diversity, scope and sequence with articulation to college, teacher preparation, and curriculum design. At a philosophical and pedagogical level, language learning is about making meaning, and world language teachers share many beliefs about learning and instruction with teachers in other content areas. Constructivist and social constructivist learning theories are consistent with the communicative approach to world language teaching and learning (Met, 1999); thus, their viewpoints have prevailed in recent years and affected the way that teachers perceive student learning and the way that they teach.

World language teaching methods are applied in a "local knowledge" context dependent upon particular institutions, classrooms, and learners. Teacher cognition has been "situated" in practice, and it is important to consider the effects of context upon teacher decision-making and teaching and learning (Crandall, 2000; Lave, 1988). Research in second language acquisition and pedagogy almost always yields findings that are subject to interpretation rather than providing conclusive evidence (Brown, 2002), leading to teachers using an eclectic approach to language pedagogy. It is the dynamic application of a compendium of instructional techniques, selected by the teacher in a principled approach and based on perceived student needs, that characterizes and reshapes situational practice in the language classroom.

RESEARCH ON BEST PRACTICE INSTRUCTION IN WORLD LANGUAGE EDUCATION

The prevailing view among world language educators today is that the goal of world language instruction is to prepare students to function effectively in the real-life situations they are likely to encounter (American Council on the Teaching of Foreign Languages [ACTFL], 2006; Franklin, Shaw, & Grbic, 2004; Met, 1999). This has garnered the prevailing terminology of "proficiency-orientated instruction" and "communicative language teaching." The National Standards for Foreign Language Learning represent the movement toward communication as a primary goal of foreign language education (Met, 1999).

The research base for communicative language instructional practices is both direct and indirect. Some evidence directly supports practices associated with the communicative approach; however, other practices may be inferred from research on cognition, information, processing, and sociocultural theory. Although the research on emerging practices may be limited or indirect, it is necessary to note that there is a scant body of research to support past approaches to world language teaching, such as the grammar-based approach (Met, 1999). It is ironic that world language education has been late to join the realm of interdisciplinary unit development with the other content areas, because, by its very nature, world language education is concerned with bridging disciplines (Reagan & Osborn, 2002).

PLANNING WORLD LANGUAGE CURRICULUM AND INSTRUCTION FOR HIGH-ABILITY LANGUAGE LEARNERS

A "principled approach" to language teaching incorporates a specific and systematic process of using diagnosis, treatment, and assessment to account for communicative and situational needs anticipated among designated learners and to diagnose for appropriate curriculum in harmony with distinctive learning goals (Brown, 2002). This process enables teachers to systematically evaluate the accomplishment of curricular objectives and assists them in revising activities, lessons, materials, and curricula.

Understanding the Role of Standards in Developing Curriculum for the Gifted

To understand the syntax of the foreign language standards, it is necessary to consider the history of foreign language education. World language classes at the secondary level morphed from an almost exclusive focus on language

TABLE 12.1

Sample Tiered Activity for a Middle School World Language Curriculum

Middle School World Language
Standard: Students should be able to achieve a level of written expression that would be comprehensible to the nonsympathetic (i.e., not the teacher) native reader.

Basic:	**Advanced:**
Write a letter to a pen pal. Describe something that is important to you and why. Use correct verb conjugations and at least three different tense forms.	Write a letter to the editor of the local bilingual newspaper to support K–12 world language education programs in the schools. Clearly state your case and argue your point with at least three reliable sources.

building blocks such as grammar, vocabulary, and pronunciation, to a focus on communicative proficiency and cultural competency. The standards incorporate understandings about the nature of second language acquisition; language processing skills in the classroom in the areas of listening, speaking, reading, and writing; and an interdisciplinary approach drawing from academic disciplines of study. The "5 C's" of the national foreign language standards focus on (1) *communicating* in languages other than English, (2) gaining knowledge and understanding of other *cultures*, (3) *connecting* with other disciplines and acquiring information, (4) making *comparisons* to gain insight into the nature of language and culture, and (5) participation in multilingual *communities* at home and around the world.

Differentiating by instructional objective and cognitive level is where the standards can be used in developing a curricular blueprint for the world language program sequence at a more rigorous level appropriate for the gifted student. In keeping with the dimensions of the ICM, strong curricula for world languages must engage students in advanced and accelerated content, higher level processes, and the world of themes, concepts, and ideas. World language teachers and curriculum writers should emphasize content-related issues while attending to appropriate challenge, depth, complexity, and pacing. The curriculum should provide for both independent learning and interactive dynamic communications. The development of appropriate learner outcomes for gifted language students requires attention to specific language standards and best practices for designing curriculum for the gifted. Table 12.1 illustrates a tiered activity for a world language lesson at the middle school level.

A teacher of gifted students must know and understand the specific subject content of the language taught at a deeper level while also possessing strong facility of pedagogical skills. She must be attuned to her environment. The school functions around a set of customs and traditions (Cattani, 2002). Through careful observation and listening, it is possible to understand how to replicate accepted ways of doing things at the school and also consider new ways to promote the study of language by scanning the environment, making adjustments, and asking the right questions.

Understanding the resources available and cultivating collaboration across the language department and schoolwide team will assist in planning the K–12 world language learning sequence that defines what and when gifted learners will be ready for certain curricular experiences in their language development. A comprehensive language program vision, philosophy, and the use of a curriculum blueprint will assist in the sequence planning of a vertically aligned K–12 language program. In concert with VanTassel-Baska's (2003) philosophy of curriculum for the gifted, the gifted language learner needs a curricular program that is grounded in the recognition of individual differences and unique learning needs. The gifted world language student needs a curriculum that is responsive to his or her individual learning rate, style, and complexity and set in an instructional environment that encourages and nurtures inquiry, flexibility, and divergent thinking. The world language education profession offers a large number of options categorized as second language "treatments" or learning experiences. This is evidenced by the 38 language teaching techniques outlined by Crookes and Chaudron (1991, pp. 52–54), ranging from controlled (e.g., drills, dialogues, reading aloud, display questions/answers), to semicontrolled (e.g., referential questions/answers, cued narratives, information gap activities), to free (e.g., role-plays, problem solving, interviews, discussion).

The curriculum writer also must consider an abundance of whole-class, group-work, and pair-work activities (Brown, 2002). Strategies that allow for more open-ended, interactive, and generative learning behavior are most beneficial to gifted learners (VanTassel-Baska, 2003). Although teachers in world language departments may be left to formulate a sequence of using these techniques, the use of a curriculum blueprint will assist in the "principled approach" to planning a vertical and horizontal sequence of developing gifted language learners.

DESIGNING AN ARTICULATED WORLD LANGUAGE PROGRAM AND CURRICULUM FOR THE GIFTED

Foreign languages are most often offered and taught as separate subjects from the core content areas (Schulz, 1999). How a school district chooses to schedule the course offering may impact the instructional options that would lead to increased proficiency. World language program options include (a) traditional scheduling in a daily 50-minute class period, (b) block scheduling in a longer classroom period every other day, (c) intensive programs that meet for extended periods of time daily, (d) immersion programs that provide more than 4 hours daily of subject matter instruction in the targeted language, (e) study abroad programs that provide guided travel and opportunities for academic and emotional growth, and (f) multilevel classes in which students at different instructional levels are combined in a single classroom (Schulz, 1999). The decision to create multilevel classes may be driven more by administrative reasoning such as low enrollments at advanced levels, teacher shortages, or scheduling conflicts rather than by what is the most effective teaching format for language acquisition.

Technological interfaces are available and in use in schools for world language programs as either support materials or stand-alone programs. Articulation and sequencing of world language study across the K–12 spectrum must be clearly aligned to take learners from the early novice stages to advanced levels. The sequencing of world language learning must be articulated with a planned calendar through the units of study, quarter, semester, academic year, and summer months. An academic year calendar plan of language development, with an auxiliary summer calendar, may be useful in guiding the ongoing development of linguistic skills and practice in the K–12 pipeline.

CREATING A COMMUNITY OF TALENTED LINGUISTS

Research studies have defined specific instructional strategies found to be effective in second language learning including (a) extensive exposure to the target language at an early age with continuing instruction; (b) opportunities to hear and use the language comprehensibly with others; (c) frequent opportunities to apply the language in purposeful, real-life tasks; (d) integration of cultural instruction in making meaning for socioculturally appropriate functioning; (e) explicit instruction in learning strategies for developing skills in the target language and learner autonomy; (f) explicit instruction in listening, reading, and writing for meaning with grammatical competence; (g) opportunities to use technological resources to enhance language learning and practice; and (h) appropriate assessment to measure student progress in producing a second language and identifying instructional needs for continued growth (Fares & Zinke, 2008; Met, 1999; Mulhair, 2008).

Determining which type of foreign language instruction is best depends on a number of variables: the learner's age, aptitude, and motivation; the amount of time available for instruction; and the difference between the native and the foreign language (American Educational Research Association [AERA], 2006). Language skills for development are classified as listening, speaking, reading, and writing. The great variety of programs for teaching students who do not know a specific target language can be divided into four general categories, although what happens in classrooms is sometimes a mix of strategies: (a) direct instruction of the target language; (b) specially designed target language instruction with primary language support; (c) "sheltered immersion," or special instruction in the target language; or (d) no special services (Amselle, 1997). These four modes of teaching world languages may produce variability across language classrooms, impacting student acquisition.

Positive effects from instruction have been verified through regression analyses that isolated the differential strength of several variables in predicting phonological performance (Elliot, 1997; Moyer, 1999) including pronunciation (Elliot, 1995). Findings on instructional practices suggest that learners reported feedback inconsistency as one problem among many in their quest for phonological attainment, and learners also would appreciate more attention to phonological accuracy in the classroom. Successful second language teachers emphasize interpersonal communication in using the language competently with others rather than an overemphasis on verb conjugations (Franklin et al., 2004). For example, Chela-Flores (2001) suggested activities for sustained dialogue and paragraph utterances that could be incorporated naturally throughout the instructional sequence from beginning through advanced levels.

Brown (1994) suggested fostering "good language learner" characteristics among students in second language classrooms through targeted instructional activities. Table 12.2 has been modified with the gifted student in mind.

MATERIALS AND RESOURCES

Selecting materials appropriate to gifted language students is another important component of curriculum planning. Technology provides many different types of language learning opportunities, but it is important to consider who should study online or with distance-delivered courses as such options may not be appropriate for all students. The Internet's strength in teaching second languages lies in its use as a repository and channel for reading and hearing authentic language (Allen et al., 2004). World language program coordinators and teachers also collect materials and resources that cultivate language skills through the visual aspects of the classroom environment. Such a rich educational environment positively impacts student learning. Figure 12.1 suggests purposeful materials for extending the curriculum through world language bulletin board displays.

TABLE 12.2

Curriculum Principles and Instructional Activities to Develop
Characteristics of the Good Language Learner

Curriculum principles related to developing characteristics of the good language learner	Instructional activities related to developing characteristics of the good language learner
Lower inhibitions.	• Develop hypotheses and communication opportunities. • Model role-plays and skits. • Sing cultural songs that impact correct pronunciation. • Use group work. • Use humor. • Discuss language production fears in small groups.
Encourage risk taking.	• Praise students for sincere effort in using the target language. • Use fluency exercises for language production. • Set up learning centers. • Encourage outside-of-class assignments to speak, write, or otherwise try out the language.
Build students' self-confidence.	• Tell students explicitly of your belief in their production abilities. • Ask students to conduct self-evaluations of their strengths and what they know or have accomplished in the target language.
Help students develop intrinsic motivation.	• Develop vision by keeping goals in front of students regarding explicit rewards (beyond the final exam) for learning the target language.
Promote cooperative linguistic communication.	• Direct students to communicate in small groups. • Use learning centers. • Set up opportunities for audio communications between students and classes.
Encourage students to use right-brain processing.	• Use oral-fluency exercises in which students must produce (oral or written) a high amount of productivity. • Do rapid "free writes." • Use audio, film, and rapid passage reading in class.
Promote ambiguity tolerance.	• Keep theoretical explanations brief. • Occasionally translate into English to clarify a word or meaning. • Encourage students to ask the teacher and their classmates questions.
Help students use their intuition.	• Correct selected errors, preferably those that interfere with learning. • Allow students to deduce an explanation of errors from the correction.
Get students to make their mistakes work for them.	• Audio record students' oral production and ask them to identify errors as well as have other students identify and correct errors. • Do not always give them the correct form and encourage them to catch it. • Have students make lists of their common errors and work on correcting errors on their own.
Get students to set their own goals.	• Explicitly encourage or direct students to go beyond the classroom goals. • Have them make lists of what they will accomplish on their own in a particular week. • Have students make specific time commitments at home to study the language. • Provide extension ideas to lessons.

- Visual aids (to build knowledge and understanding)
- Objectives and rubrics (to inform students of learning goals and criteria for submitted work)
- Charts and tables with grammatical content (to represent advanced content in graphic organizers for student comprehension)
- World-language-related humor, including posters with jokes and cartoons (to illustrate multiple perspectives)
- Current event articles from journals, newspapers, and magazines (to connect the study of world languages to everyday living)
- Political spectra (to illustrate multiple perspectives)
- Timelines (to graphically illustrate the relation of time and events)
- Examples of professionals in careers using world language skills (to enhance career development)
- "What would you do?" prompts (to stimulate student reflection and discussion)
- Displays of student work products (to recognize student growth and accomplishment)
- Quotes by historical or contemporary individuals (to inspire students into action)

Figure 12.1. Extension materials with cognitive purpose for world language classroom displays and bulletin board visuals.

THE INTEGRATED CURRICULUM MODEL AND ADVANCED PLACEMENT FOREIGN LANGUAGE CLASSES

The Integrated Curriculum Model (ICM) was developed for high-ability learners to guide the process of differentiation. The model has three dimensions: (a) an advanced content focus in core areas; (b) high-level process and product work in critical thinking, problem-solving, and research; and (c) intra- and interdisciplinary concept development and understanding (see Chapter 2 for a fuller explanation). The ICM has been used as a basis to develop specific curriculum units in language arts, mathematics, science, and social studies that are aligned with state standards and differentiated for high-ability students, and it also may be applied as a differentiation tool for remodeling world language curriculum in schools for high-ability students.

The current trend in gifted education is the decision by schools to serve gifted students in alternative learning formats such as Advanced Placement, International Baccalaureate, dual-credit classes, online learning, and off-campus options including mentorships and internships (VanTassel-Baska & Johnsen, 2007). The Advanced Placement (AP) program has provided millions of students a chance for early exposure to rigorous and challenging content in individual course packages from the College Board (Ewing, 2006; Gallagher, 2004). However, alternative services provided to high-ability students are dependent upon the contextual setting as urban and rural schools have different and unique issues in managing gifted services (Lewis, 2000).

In a study of Advanced Placement world language teacher perceptions and instructional differentiation practices, AP teachers reported that they did not differentiate classroom instruction for gifted learners (MacFarlane, 2008).

However, the alignment of world language curriculum and programs that meet the needs of gifted students can be purposefully designed to match the theoretical dimensions of the ICM, as shown below using AP French as an example.

The AP French language syllabus aligns with the issues/themes dimension of the ICM through designing the curriculum around major ideas to encompass a broad conceptual understanding of the advanced content under a thematic umbrella such as "Relationships" or "Revolution." This conceptual umbrella provides the basis to develop the four language skills in a variety of settings, types of discourse, and topics. The AP French language exam also aligns with the issues/themes dimension of the ICM as the exam requires students to form a well-developed spoken discourse on a particular topic.

The advanced content dimension is a critical element for a world language course to be accelerated to a level equal to that of a college freshman-level course. Both the AP French syllabus and the exam require instructional materials to be used that include authentic written texts such as newspaper and magazine articles, literary texts, and other nontechnical writings that develop students' advanced reading abilities. Both the syllabus and the exam require instructional materials, activities, assignments, and assessment items to be appropriate to an advanced level of study and include a variety of authentic audio and/or video recordings that develop students' listening abilities as well.

The process/product dimension of the ICM conceptually aligns with the AP French syllabus and exam as the course provides frequent opportunities for students to use higher order thinking processes such as analysis, reasoning, evaluation, and synthesis across the areas of reading comprehension, listening comprehension, compositional writing, problem solving, and creating dialogue in the language. The syllabus and exam also require students to produce advanced products in writing a variety of compositions, reciting poetry, and performing/conversing in French.

French exam items (College Board Advanced Placement Program, 2010) align with each dimension of the ICM and require students to work with advanced content in reading and listening passages in the target language; to practice and apply advanced higher order thinking processes such as analysis, evaluation, and synthesis; and to create products in writing and oral discourse.

In addition to applying the theoretical underpinnings of the ICM to world language curriculum development, the application of the William and Mary teaching models such as the Literature Web and Paul's (1992) reasoning model also may be applied and field-tested in world language teaching. Table 12.3 illustrates how the ICM aligns with both the AP French syllabus and exam.

TABLE 12.3

Alignment of the ICM With the AP French Syllabus and Exam

Integrated Curriculum Model dimensions	Advanced Placement (concepts from the French course syllabi and examination) The course provides students with a learning experience equivalent to that of a third-year college course in French language.
Issues/themes dimension	Syllabus: The courses provide students with regular opportunities, in class or in a language laboratory, to develop the four language skills in a variety of settings, types of discourse, and topics.
	Exam: Students form a well-developed spoken discourse.
Advanced content dimension	Syllabus: The teacher uses French almost exclusively in class and encourages students to do likewise.
	Syllabus and exam: Instructional materials include authentic written texts such as newspaper and magazine articles, literary texts, and other nontechnical writings that develop students' reading abilities.
	Syllabus and exam: Instructional materials, activities, assignments, and assessments are appropriate to this level and include a variety of authentic audio and/or video recordings that develop students' listening abilities.
Process/product dimension	Syllabus: The course provides instruction and frequent opportunities to write a variety of compositions, recite poetry, and perform/converse in French.
	Exam: Forty minutes each of reading comprehension, listening comprehension, and compositional writing; 20 minutes of fill-in word and verb functions and a speaking portion.

DELIVERY DILEMMAS

World language learning is faced with several dilemmas. There is a lack of instructional time that is necessary for acquiring a second language that impacts student performance and self-efficacy. The typical student who begins studying a world language in Grade 7 or 9 is exposed only to a fraction of the contact hours required to achieve a high level of proficiency in a second language (Goranson & Howland, 1999). In Teaching English to Speakers of Other Languages (TESOL) research, students usually receive only a few hundred hours of instruction, spread over several years, and only students who are exceptionally gifted or motivated or who have out-of-school exposure acquire the ability to use the language effectively (Lightbrown, 2001). This situation should lead teachers to do more differentiation based on skill attainment, not less, and to group gifted language learners together to heighten their learning potential.

Delivery of world language instruction occurs in several different program models, many of which are part-time, intermittent, and limited in contact hours. The Saturday School model, for example, is delivered only one day a week with 6 days in between that lack reinforcement of language learning. To combat this reality, the Saturday School model must carefully plan integration into the week's educational system by including instruction on 3 days during the school week and use technology with language learning software programs to extend listening exposure during the week.

The benefits of language proficiency are known to extend well beyond linguistics. The skills students develop while learning a language can directly affect their performance in other subjects as well. Children who study world languages statistically outperform non-language-learning students in English, math, science, and social studies (Franklin et al., 2004).

Research also has been conducted in specific language areas. VanTassel-Baska (1987) found that one year of Latin benefited students significantly in enhancing English vocabulary learning and linguistic competency, even in comparison to students taking a Greek and Latin roots course in English. These benefits could drive the expectation that second language programming would be involved as an essential part of a gifted student's curriculum; however, the opposite appears to be more the practice. Although No Child Left Behind (NCLB, 2001) legislation purports that all content areas are core subjects, school administrators may perceive content areas that are not assessed to be not as essential as those that are assessed. Such conclusions have an impact on student opportunities to learn second languages as schools have cut or eliminated language programs (Franklin et al., 2004). As language programs are cut and expectations of language proficiency suffer from lack of instructional time, negative attitudes toward language programs may develop, even as reports encourage the integration of world languages into core curriculum (National Association of State Boards of Education, 2003).

ALIGNING RESEARCH-BASED INSTRUCTIONAL STRATEGIES TO WORLD LANGUAGE CURRICULUM AND INSTRUCTION

Instructional strategies such as higher level thinking and problem solving, metacognition, and teaching for conceptual understanding that have been found to be effective for core subject areas (Marzano, Pickering, & Pollack, 2001) may enhance world language learning even though the application of these pedagogical skills has not been studied extensively in world language learning. There are few specific world language instructional strategies that have been crowned with the moniker "best practice." Indeed, in accordance to the expectations for scientific research studies set forth by the Institute of Education Sciences to be worthy of becoming part of the What Works

Clearinghouse, only *one* strategy tied to world language instruction was designated with a plus (+) sign of approval. This one instructional strategy focused on the intervention of peer tutoring and response groups.

LANGUAGE APTITUDE: ASSESSMENT AND DIAGNOSIS

As with any type of learning, a student's individual characteristics have an impact on how well she grasps a subject. In world language learning, an individual's aptitude and motivation can be key components in her individual trajectory of language acquisition (AERA, 2006). Foreign language aptitude tests consist of several components including sensitivity to sound, which is important for pronunciation. Sensitivity to structure impacts the student's grasp of grammar, and level of memory determines how well a student learns and retains foreign vocabulary (AERA, 2006). An optimal aptitude test should measure and predict development of competence and performance, implicit acquisition and explicit learning, and knowledge of language and ability for use (Robinson, 2005). Whether an aptitude test predicts these elements is a question of great consequence to the decisions made by learners, teachers, and program administrators. Aptitude tests inform the decision-making process in determining the likelihood of a student's success and the costs involved in second language acquisition learning. Such costs can be considerable, especially for the high end of real-world L2 use where it is most starkly and validly defined in accomplishing high-level goals (Robinson, 2005).

Assessment is an important component in education and in understanding language learning and the variables that are related to it. Unfortunately, this area has received even less attention in world language education than curriculum and instruction. Norris (2005) discussed the limitations associated with this lack of attention and recommended developing appropriate assessments that would satisfy current needs for data. Measures are needed that inform educators about vocabulary size and depth, native-like fluency, phonology, sociopragmatic sensitivity, discourse competency, syntactic complexity, and any number of other outcomes of advanced foreign language learning (Norris, 2005). Furthermore, assessment of the impact of the curriculum program on gifted learners is one of the most important aspects in curriculum design work (VanTassel-Baska, 2003), and related assessment is needed for judging the efficacy of world language programs with the gifted language learner population. Nontraditional assessments such as portfolios and performance-based assessment may authentically assess high-level language performance and provide language teachers with credible evidence of student growth, while program evaluation can provide district personnel with information about program impact over time.

TEACHER PREPARATION AND PROFESSIONAL DEVELOPMENT IN WORLD LANGUAGE EDUCATION

Quality professional development serves a vital function in helping educators improve their classroom practice. In a study examining how world language teachers are trained, Wilbur (2007) found that the methods of teaching used in world language methods courses vary extensively from the instructors' training background, to inconsistencies in syllabi, to the ways instructors evaluate the preservice teachers. However, the most salient research outcome was that the methods employed range vastly across teacher training institutions. Furthermore, the majority of AP teachers have received little, if any, explicit training on working with gifted students (Hertberg-Davis, Callahan, & Kyburg, 2006; Westberg, 1994). Moreover, gifted teacher preparation development and regulations vary from state to state and even from district to district (VanTassel-Baska & Brown, 2007). Thus, the effectiveness of world language teachers with gifted students is in question.

In a study examining Advanced Placement world language teacher perceptions of high-ability world language students and their use of differentiated instructional approaches, findings indicated teachers held somewhat positive attitudes toward providing needs and support for gifted students and the social value of gifted persons in society (MacFarlane, 2008). Teachers held ambivalent attitudes about the instructional practice of ability grouping, the rejection of gifted students by others, and the practice of actively advocating for gifted learners. Teachers reported somewhat negative attitudes toward the instructional practice of acceleration. Findings further revealed limited teacher use of differentiated strategies in the AP classroom and limited teacher training in gifted education pedagogy, yet a positive relationship between high and low student achievement and teachers' training background in gifted education (MacFarlane, 2008).

The implications for practice from this study point to the need for gifted education training for Advanced Placement world language teachers on the characteristics of high-ability students and differentiated instructional practices that are found to be effective for increased student achievement. Specifically, professional development is needed for teachers that addresses (a) differentiated curriculum for the gifted with an emphasis on remodeling AP curriculum to meet high-ability student needs, and (b) the use of advanced instructional practices with specific information regarding effective delivery and classroom management techniques. Implications for research include the need for more studies on AP teachers' attitudes and practices in relation to gifted learners and a set of studies focusing on effective instructional practices for teaching world languages (MacFarlane, 2008).

Although the case has been made for the value of a world language education component in a school curriculum and the value of second language study for gifted students, trends show specific areas where curriculum, instruction, assessment, and professional development can be improved among world language education programs by strategically incorporating what is known in the gifted education literature to improve educational learning experiences for talented language students.

CONCLUSION

World language education offers a learning environment for natural interdisciplinary connections across content domains and a diverse array of instructional approaches for teaching the language content. World language curriculum must incorporate the elements of curricular reform and explore the dimensions of the Integrated Curriculum Model if it is to respond effectively to the needs of gifted learners. World language teachers need more training on best practices in teaching their subject area (ACTFL, 2008) and in using pedagogy that constitutes best practice for working with the gifted language learner. By building the connection between world language learning and gifted education, it is possible to map a comprehensive approach to teaching world languages well to high-ability learners.

KEY POINTS SUMMARY

- World language curriculum development for the gifted may employ the ICM as an effective way to differentiate course syllabi in the dimensions of acceleration of content, higher level skills and processes, generative products, and use of themes and concepts that provide interdisciplinarity of thought.
- Use of research-based best practices in instruction, found to be effective in other subjects, should be used in the teaching of world languages to elevate gifted student learning.
- World language instructional delivery systems must be based on the realities of second language learning in respect to time and resources.
- The development of a comprehensive articulated vertical curriculum sequence for the world language K–12 program for gifted learners needs to occur.
- Consistent use of assessment and evaluation techniques deemed appropriate for gifted learners need to be employed within the world language program.

- There is a need for ongoing professional development for teachers in world language content, pedagogy, and assessment skills related to working with gifted learners.

REFERENCES

Allen, M., Mabry, E., Mattrey, M., Bourhis, J., Titsworth, S., & Burrell, N. (2004). Evaluating the effectiveness of distance learning: A comparison using meta-analysis. *The Journal of Communication, 54*, 402–420.

American Council on the Teaching of Foreign Languages. (2006). *Standards for foreign language learning: Preparing for the 21st century* (2nd ed.). Yonkers, NY: Author.

American Council on the Teaching of Foreign Languages. (2008). *Standards for foreign language learning: Preparing for the 21st century* (3rd ed.). Yonkers, NY: Author.

American Educational Research Association. (2006). Foreign language instruction: Implementing the best teaching methods. *Research Points: Essential Information for Education Policy, 4*(1), 1–4.

Amselle, J. (1997). Adios, bilingual ed. *Policy Review, 86*, 52–55. Retrieved from http://www.hoover.org/publications/policyreview/3572952.html

Brown, H. D. (1994). *Teaching by principles: An interactive approach to language pedagogy*. Englewood Cliffs, NJ: Prentice Hall Regents.

Brown, H. D. (2002). English language teaching in the "post-method" era: Toward better diagnosis, treatment, and assessment. In J. Richards & W. Renandya (Eds.), *Methodology in language teaching: An anthology of current practice* (pp. 9–18). New York, NY: Cambridge University Press.

Cattani, D. H. (2002). *A classroom of her own: How new teachers develop instructional, professional, and cultural competence*. Thousand Oaks, CA: Corwin Press.

Chela-Flores, B. (2001). Pronunciation and language learning: An integrative approach. *International Review of Applied Linguistics, 39*, 85–101.

College Board. (1986, October). Speech delivered by Hanford, G. The SAT and Statewide Assessment. *Vital Speeches of the Day, 52*(24), 765. Retrieved February 2, 2008, from Academic Search Complete database.

College Board Advanced Placement Program. (2010). *French language course description*. New York, NY: College Board. Retrieved from http://apcentral.collegeboard.com/apc/public/repository/ap-french-course-description.pdf

Crandall, J. (2000). Language teacher education. *Annual Review of Applied Linguistics, 20*, 34–55.

Crookes, G., & Chaudron, C. (1991). Guidelines for classroom language teaching. In M. Celce-Murcia (Ed.), *Teaching English as a second or foreign language* (2nd ed., pp. 46–66). Boston, MA: Heinle & Heinle.

Elliot, A. (1995). Foreign language phonology: Field independence, attitude, and the success of formal instruction in Spanish pronunciation. *Modern Language Journal, 79*, 530–542.

Elliot, A. (1997). On the teaching and acquisition of pronunciation within a communicative approach. *Hispania, 80*, 95–108.

Ewing, M. (2006). *The AP program and student outcomes: A summary of research.* Retrieved from http://professionals.collegeboard.com/data-reports-research/cb/ap-student-outcomes-summary-research

Fares, G., & Zinke, L. (2008). *AP Spanish language teacher's guide.* New York, NY: College Board. Retrieved from http://apcentral.collegeboard.com/apc/public/repository/spanish_lang_teachers_guide.pdf

Franklin, K., Shaw S., & Grbic, N. (2004). Applying language skills to interpretation: Student perspectives from signed and spoken language programs. *Interpreting, 6,* 69–100.

Gallagher, J. J. (2004). Public policy and acceleration of gifted students. In N. Colangelo, S. G. Assouline, & M. U. M. Gross (Eds.), *A nation deceived: How schools hold back America's brightest students* (Vol. II, pp. 39–45). Iowa City, IA: The Connie Belin & Jacqueline N. Blank International Center for Gifted Education and Talent Development.

Goranson, D., & Howland, M. (1999). *A guide to K–12 program development in world languages.* (ERIC Document Reproduction Service No. ED462005)

Gouin, F. (1880). *L'art d'enseigner et d'etudier les languages* [The art of teaching and learning foreign languages]. Paris, France: Librairie Fischbacher.

Hertberg-Davis, H., Callahan, C. M., & Kyburg, R. M. (2006). *Advanced Placement and International Baccalaureate programs: a "fit" for gifted learners?* (RM06222). Storrs: University of Connecticut, The National Research Center on the Gifted and Talented.

Kramsch, C. (2000). Second language acquisition, applied linguistics, and the teaching of foreign languages. *The Modern Language Journal, 84,* 311–326.

Lave, J. (1988). *Cognition in practice.* New York, NY: Cambridge University Press.

Lewis, T. (2000). Adopting standards for technology education. *Journal of Industrial Teacher Education, 38,* 71–90.

Lightbrown, P. (2001). L2 instruction: Time to teach. *TESOL Quarterly, 35,* 598–599.

MacFarlane, B. (2008). *Advanced Placement world language teacher perceptions of high ability students and differentiated instruction* (Unpublished doctoral dissertation). The College of William and Mary, Williamsburg, VA.

Marzano, R. J., Pickering, D., & Pollack, J. (2001). *Classroom instruction that works: Research-based strategies for increasing student achievement.* Alexandria, VA: Association for Supervision and Curriculum Development.

Met, M. (1999). Research in foreign language curriculum. In G. Cawelti (Ed.), *Handbook of research on improving student achievement* (2nd ed., pp. 86–111). Arlington, VA: Educational Research Service.

Moyer, A. (1999). Ultimate attainment in L2 phonology: The critical factors of age, motivation, and instruction. *Studies in Second Language Acquisition, 21,* 81–108.

Mulhair, M. (2008). *AP French language teacher's guide.* New York, NY: College Board. Retrieved from http://apcentral.collegeboard.com/apc/public/repository/AP_French_Language_Teacher_Guide.pdf

National Association of State Boards of Education. (2003). *The complete curriculum: Ensuring a place for the arts and foreign languages in America's schools. The report of the NASBE study group on the lost curriculum.* Alexandria, VA: Author.

No Child Left Behind Act, 20 U.S.C. §6301 (2001).

Norris, J. (2005). Assessing advanced foreign language learning and learners: From measurement constructs to educational uses. In H. Byrnes, H. Weger-Guntharp, & K. Sprang (Eds.), *Educating for advanced foreign language capacity: Constructs, curriculum, instruction, assessment* (pp. 167–187). Washington, DC: Georgetown University Press.

Nunan, D. (1989). *Understanding language classrooms: A guide for teacher-initiated action.* Englewood Cliffs, NJ: Prentice-Hall.

Nunan, D. (1991). *Language teaching methodology: A textbook for teachers.* New York, NY: Prentice-Hall.

Paul, R. (1992). *Critical thinking: What every person needs to survive in a rapidly changing world.* Sonoma, CA: Foundation for Critical Thinking.

Reagan, T. G., & Osborn, T. A. (2002). *The foreign language educator in society: Toward a critical pedagogy.* Mahwah, NJ: Lawrence Erlbaum.

Rifkin, B. (2006). Studying a foreign language at the postsecondary level. *The Language Educator, 2,* 48–51.

Robinson, P. (2005). Aptitude and second language acquisition. *Annual Review of Applied Linguistics, 25,* 46–73.

Schulz, R. A. (1999). Foreign language instruction and curriculum. *Education Digest, 64*(7), 29–37.

Snow, R. (1994). Abilities in academic tasks. In R. Sternberg & R. Wagner (Eds.), *Mind in context: Interactionist perspectives on human intelligence* (pp. 3–37). New York, NY: Cambridge University Press.

VanTassel-Baska, J. (1987). A case for the teaching of Latin to the verbally talented. *Roeper Review, 9,* 159–161.

VanTassel-Baska, J. (2003). *Curriculum planning and instructional design for gifted learners.* Denver, CO: Love.

VanTassel-Baska, J., & Johnsen, S. K. (2007). Teacher education standards for the field of gifted education: A vision of coherence for personnel preparation in the 21st century. *Gifted Child Quarterly, 51,* 182–205.

VanTassel-Baska, J., & Brown, E. (2007). Toward best practice: An analysis of the efficacy of curriculum models in gifted education. *Gifted Child Quarterly, 51,* 342–358.

Westberg, K. L. (1994). Teachers who are good with the gifted. *Instructor, 104*(2), 65.

Wilbur, M. (2007). How foreign language teachers get taught: Methods of teaching the methods course. *Foreign Language Annals, 40,* 79–101.

Chapter 13

Adapting Arts Curricula for High-Ability Learners

Hope E. Wilson

The school board has recently requested that all departments develop programs to meet the needs of advanced learners. As a fine arts teacher, how will you address the needs of the talented artists, performers, or composers in your classes, as well as the needs of the intellectually gifted students? What components of your curriculum are most effective in developing the talents of these students? What does curriculum for talented learners in the fine arts look like?

Despite the emphasis of recent legislation (No Child Left Behind Act [NCLB], 2001) on reading, mathematics, and science skills, many researchers have noted the importance of the fine arts in the education of students (e.g., Fuller, 1994; President's Committee on the Arts and Humanities & Arts Education Partnership, 1999). Fine arts experiences for students can provide opportunities for the development of talent in diverse artistic areas (Clark & Zimmerman, 1998), as well as support for other domains of the curriculum, such as social studies and reading (Americans for the Arts, 2006;

Arts Education Partnership & President's Committee on the Arts and the Humanities, 1999; Eisner, 1998; Ruppert, 2006). Thus, fine arts in education can be seen as more than enrichment activities, but as a central component of a comprehensive curriculum (Rasmussen, 1998).

This chapter will include information about both the visual and performing arts, although greater emphasis and examples will be drawn from the visual arts. Both domains, however, include similar characteristics regarding creative expression and enrichment opportunities. However, they also represent distinct areas of the curriculum with different objectives, critical thinking skills, and technical skills required. Aspects of a curriculum for high-ability students, both artistically gifted and intellectually gifted, are addressed individually, with attention to both types of arts needs.

VISUAL AND PERFORMING ARTS

The visual arts include domains such as drawing, painting, sculpture, print-making, textile and fabric arts, and computer graphic design. The visual arts include both two- and three-dimensional products, requiring different technical skills. The performing arts include music, dance, and theater, all performed in three-dimensional space.

Talent in all domains of the visual and performing arts includes not only the domain-specific technical skills, but also includes nonintellectual aspects such as motivation and creativity (Winner, 2000). Curriculum in the arts needs to include an emphasis on the production and performance of art, as well as aesthetics, history, and criticism (Asmus, Lee, Lindsey, Patchen, & Wheetley, 1997; Clark, Day, & Greer, 1987).

Integrated Curriculum Model Connections

Just as in the academic areas of learning, the arts require the same types of differentiation in order to make them appropriate for gifted learners. They require that learning be pitched at a challenge level above functional skill; they require that students develop content-relevant higher order skills and processes, and that they focus on a conceptual understanding of what they are learning. Moreover, both the visual and performing arts are driven by generative products and performances that attest to high-level skills and interpretative capacities at work (VanTassel-Baska, Evans, & Baska, 2008). Thus, the discussion that follows focuses on how the Integrated Curriculum Model (ICM) may be interpreted in arts areas for purposes of curriculum development. It also incorporates the core elements of curriculum design that have been used in the William and Mary work over the past two decades.

TABLE 13.1

Concepts for the Visual Arts Curriculum

Theme	Content areas
Influence	Andy Warhol, Frida Kahlo, Vincent Van Gogh
Identity	Self-portraits (e.g., Frida Kahlo, Rembrandt van Rijn, Vincent Van Gogh)
Abstraction	Wassily Kandinsky, Pablo Picasso, Jackson Pollock
Representation	Leonardo da Vinci, Claude Monet, Georgia O'Keeffe
Aesthetics	Multicultural aesthetic values (e.g., Western Renaissance, Islamic Art, Asian Calligraphy)

CONCEPTUALLY ORIENTED CURRICULUM

The arts are inherently conceptually based and deal with the abstract. They deal with the representation of an object, story, idea, or concept in a new medium. For example, even in the most realistic of portraits, the artist is capturing a three-dimensional object (in this case, a person) in two-dimensional space, with oil paint on canvas. A ballet captures the story of a young girl and the magic of Christmas toys in *The Nutcracker* through dance and movement. More abstract concepts can similarly be portrayed through purely musical forms.

Conceptually Oriented Curriculum in the Visual Arts

Many concepts and themes may be appropriate for focus in curriculum in the visual arts. A unit on art history may center on the theme of "influence." Influence encompasses the essence of the history of art, in that artists are influenced by their culture and exert influence onto their culture in a reciprocal relationship. Students studying this aspect of art history might investigate the influences on various artists, such as Japanese prints on the works of Post-Impressionist painters. They also could look at the personal experiences of artists, such as the tragic bus accident injury of Frida Kahlo and its influence on her later self-portraits. The theme could be investigated through the artwork of artists who deliberately incorporated the influence of their culture into their work, such as pop artist Andy Warhol. In addition, students could investigate how art has influenced the larger culture, such as in Pablo Picasso's *Guernica*.

Other themes for the visual arts could include the themes or concepts of abstraction, representation, or identity. See Table 13.1 for a list of concepts and possible artists, techniques, or activities to support each concept.

Learner Outcomes of Significance

The focus of curriculum in the fine arts includes not only instruction in technique and production of art, but also addresses critical thinking about visual representations, historical context, and aesthetic values. There is research to suggest that many students talented in the visual arts also are intellectually gifted (e.g., Clark & Zimmerman, 2001). Thus, programs should provide for both of these needs.

Curriculum for talented students in the fine arts must have two foci. First, the curriculum must address the needs of students who are intellectually gifted, students who are ready for greater academic challenges and more complex questioning and reasoning. Secondly, the curriculum must provide opportunities and instruction for students with gifts in the visual arts to further develop their talents. The curriculum must provide for the general intellectual and academic capabilities of gifted learners and the more specific talents and potentials in fine arts areas. Students in fine arts classes may need differentiation in either, both, or neither of these areas. Teachers of the gifted in the arts need to incorporate objectives designed for the various areas of giftedness represented within their classes.

Learner Outcomes of Significance in the Visual Arts

Winner (1997) has indicated that talent in the visual arts is demonstrated by precocity, marching to one's own drummer, and a rage to master. Talented artists can be thought of as possessing creativity, aesthetic sensitivity, high levels of motivation, and conviction of purpose (Michael, 1983). They often are identified by their portfolios or individual pieces of artwork. In a survey of more than 350 professional artists, 85% cited experiences in childhood, including experiences in school, as important to their artistic development (Michael, 1970). Curriculum for talented visual artists should include outcomes that deal specifically with the development of skills and artistic expression, as well as the development of creativity and motivation. Curriculum in the visual arts for intellectually gifted students, on the other hand, should focus on the development of thinking skills surrounding the visual arts.

As far back as 1966, Eisner wrote about the importance of education in the arts, for both the general population of students and for those with talent in the arts. He identified three areas of concentration for the art curriculum, including productive, critical, and historical objectives (Eisner, 1966). More recent developments in the arts have included Discipline-Based Art Education (DBAE) and developmental theories. No similar model exists for the other performing arts areas, although adherence to the arts standards would accomplish similar ends in curriculum.

SUBSTANTIVE CONTENT

Too often in the fine arts, curriculum has comprised various teacher-led activities, representing little cohesion and connection to deeper art objectives. In other words, art lessons have typically focused on the product (performance, recital, drawing, painting, or sculpture) rather than student learning. These lessons fail to show substantive content that is a key component of curricula for gifted learners. Teachers of the fine arts need to focus on substantive content emphasizing student learning and growth of talent, rather than perfected final products. Curricula in the fine arts should favor the processes that students learn rather than the products that they produce.

Substantive Content in the Visual Arts

The national standards for the visual arts produced by the Kennedy Foundation for the Arts (Consortium of National Arts Education Associations, 1994) can provide a starting point for educators in the development of curriculum. In addition to the national standards, most states have developed standards that provide a guide for instruction (e.g., Texas, New York, Wisconsin, and California). The national standards are organized by six content standards with specific objectives varying on grade levels. These incorporate art production, evaluation, history, aesthetic structures, and connections to other disciplines. Thus, substantive content, even as outlined by the visual arts standards, moves beyond the creation of artwork to deeper understandings about the fundamental, theoretical, and historical basis for the discipline. Discipline-based art education (DBAE) also emphasizes the various components of the substance of art: art production, art history, art criticism, and aesthetics.

Art Production

Substantive content in the visual arts begins with art production. The foundation of any visual arts program is the creation of artwork. The presentation and instruction in this area, however, must go beyond step-by-step drawing exercises and teacher-directed products. Clark and Zimmerman (1987, 1992, 1994, 1995, 1998) over the years have recommended authentic materials and studio spaces for advanced students in the visual arts, which also would entail greater student autonomy in the art production process. Studio models of art instruction also emphasize the importance of student-directed art production (Wilson, 2007). In particular, important problem-solving processes are involved when students make decisions about subject, style, media, and/or technique in the creation of art. Teachers may need to scaffold this independence for students, depending on developmental level, by offering narrower choices (that can become broadened as learner competencies grow) or assisting with the development of ideas.

Substantive content in art production also should include meaningful exposure to a variety of techniques and media. Thus, students should have opportunities to explore media and gain familiarity with expression in two- and three-dimensional techniques, including painting, drawing, printmaking, fiber, and sculpture. Although attention to developmentally appropriate choices in materials is important for art instructors, it also is necessary for instructors to be aware that talented students may be ready for more advanced materials at earlier ages. Whereas intaglio printmaking techniques may not typically be introduced until high school, middle school or even elementary school-aged artists who are talented may benefit from exposure to this technique. In addition, students should be encouraged to explore a variety of techniques and styles when working with various media. For example, students should explore both wet- and dry-brush techniques when introduced to watercolor painting. Students also should be encouraged to use expressive, realistic, abstract, and other styles in the production of art.

Art History

The historical context and legacy of art is an important element of instruction in the visual arts. By situating art projects and assignments within an historical framework, teachers help students gain a deeper understanding of their own artistic endeavors. In addition, historical styles can provide a source of inspiration for a student's independent work. Substantive content in art history requires attention not only to the visual aspects of historical art styles, but also political, cultural, and societal influences. For example, a discussion of Pablo Picasso's Cubist painting *Guernica* should include not only a formal analysis of Cubism's abstraction of forms in geometric planes and the departure of Cubism from earlier stages of Picasso's career, but also information about the cultural influences of greater exposure to African Art and the overwhelming devastation of the Spanish Civil War. For intellectually gifted learners in particular, the deeper analysis of art history can provide greater levels of rigor to the curriculum that is most appropriate for their development.

Art Criticism and Aesthetics

The ability to discuss artwork is the core of the art criticism and aesthetics disciplines. The discussion should go beyond evaluation, to theorizing and interpreting works of art. This discourse about art should include students' own work, the work of peers, and the work of professional artists (both historical and contemporary). Substantive content in this area must incorporate an understanding

TABLE 13.2

Substantive Content in the Visual Arts

Discipline	Activity
Art production	Painting, drawing, printmaking, sculpture
Art history	Research into art movements, cultural contexts, and development of artistic expression
Art criticism	Discussion of formal aspects (i.e., line, color, balance, contrast, unity) and composition in historical, contemporary, and student-created pieces of art
Aesthetics	Evaluation of the value of art, the creation of art, and comparison of the various aesthetic values across cultures

of the formal aspects of the visual arts (such as color, line, form, balance, harmony, or contrast). It also must include meaningful judgment about works of art, going beyond initial subjective assessments, and encouraging analysis and justifications of opinions and conclusions. These assessments made by students must include information about the cultural contexts and impacts on society. Substantive content, interpreted as using great art pieces across time and cultures, should encourage students to engage in discourse, analyzing the many dimensions of these great works of art, music, theater, or dance.

Substantive content in the visual arts must lead students to greater understanding of the nature and the creation of art. Instruction in art production should encourage students to explore a variety of media, techniques, and styles, and give opportunities to develop skills independently. Art history, art criticism, and aesthetics encourage students to analyze the relationship between the formal aspects of design, the culture of the artists, and the role of today's society in works of art. Sample classroom activities for each of these disciplines are given in Table 13.2.

INTRADISCIPLINARY AND INTERDISCIPLINARY CONNECTIONS

The ubiquitous nature of the arts in our society makes these disciplines particularly suited for the development of connections within the curriculum. Many programs have been developed to emphasize the integration of arts into other disciplines (e.g., Adams & Russ, 1992; Consortium of National Arts Education Associations, 2002; Murfee, 1995; Strand, 2006), despite some objections that art should be taught as a discipline in and of itself and valued for its own strengths, rather than its ability to contribute to other content areas (Catterall, 1998; Hetland & Winner, 2001; Winner & Hetland, 2003). When incorporating art into other disciplines (and vice versa) curriculum developers must maintain the integrity of both areas. In other words, meaningful and

TABLE 13.3

Integrating the Visual Arts

Content area	Sample activities
Language arts	Book illustrators (Eric Carle and Maurice Sendak) Paintings that tell a story (Norman Rockwell) Writing about art (descriptive, journaling, how-to)
Mathematics	Geometric planes (Henri Matisse) Tessellations (M. C. Escher)
Science	Scientific observation (James John Audubon) Color and light (color field painters) Chemistry (ceramics, printmaking)
Social studies	Art history Cultural influence of the arts Geography (spread of the Renaissance) Studies of diverse cultures
Music/Performing arts	Harlem Renaissance Illustrate musical piece

substantive art objectives must be used along with objectives in other disciplines. The arts provide the basis for visual thinking skills, as well as an outlet for and place for the development of, creativity and artistic expression. When used in authentic ways, they can increase motivation and student learning in other content areas, as well as provide connections between diverse areas of curriculum.

Interdisciplinary Connections in the Visual Arts

Many content areas can be integrated in visual arts curricula. Table 13.3 provides a description of activities demonstrating integration between art and content areas.

Language arts. Sample art lessons that meaningfully integrate the language arts include discussions of visual storytelling and the role of illustration in book publishing. For elementary-aged students, artist/illustrators such as Eric Carle or Maurice Sendak can provide the foundation for exploring collage techniques or creative expression. Conceptually, the link between parts of a story (such as character, setting, and climax) can be compared to components of figurative works of art such as background, figures, and focal point. Artwork that tells a story, such as many of the paintings and illustrations by Norman Rockwell, also can be used to connect to reading comprehension strategies such as making inferences and finding details and main ideas. Finally, the visual arts support writing skills when students are asked to richly describe their own or others' art pieces. These writing activities can work to reinforce students' understandings of vocabulary terms and formal aspects of design, as well as develop skills of descriptive writing. Other writing tasks may include reflective writing and how-to papers describing art techniques and procedures.

Mathematics. Mathematics might seem like an unlikely area to integrate with art. However, many mathematical concepts, especially in geometry, are quite similar to the visual art concepts. For example, when working with shapes in a geometric plane, a discussion of transformations (rotations, translations, and reflections) and congruency of shapes fits perfectly with a discussion of Henri Matisse's collages and his concept of "painting with scissors." Other ways that art and math combine is in the tessellations of M. C. Escher, the golden ratio of Classical Greek architecture, and the abstract symbols and iconography in the artwork of many cultures.

Science. For centuries there was much less of a distinction made between the arts and the sciences. Artists such as Leonardo da Vinci dabbled in the physical and natural sciences as much as they created masterpieces of fine art. James John Audubon used his scientific skills of observation to document the various species of North American birds in his classic book of illustrations. The keen observation skills of scientists also are vital for students of the visual arts. Thus, lessons discussing the scientific method can easily be integrated with life drawing lessons about observing and representing the information presented.

In addition to the similar skill sets necessary for both disciplines, many of the techniques and processes creating artwork rely on knowledge of the chemical changes and scientific properties of matter. For example, the Color Field painters of the modern period were deeply concerned with the properties of light and the color spectrum. The chemical changes involved in firing ceramics and the properties of various glazes have been vital for artists throughout the centuries. Finally, complex chemical reactions occur in printmaking processes, such as etching. Thus, lessons on art techniques and new media can be firmly integrated with a deeper understanding of the scientific processes.

Social studies. Most easily conceptualized is the deep connection between social studies and art. In fact, many of the core strands of the national art standards incorporate the idea of the link between the creation of art and the context of society. A rich, deep understanding of a piece of art necessarily involves a rich and deep understanding of the culture and society of the arts. Similarly, a complete understanding of culture must include an understanding of art. Geography skills can be reinforced by studying the spread of art movements, such as the Renaissance throughout Europe, beginning in Italy and moving through Northern Europe. Finally, diverse cultures can be compared and contrasted through their artwork even today, from Balinese craftsmen and painters to those in China and South America.

Intradisciplinary Connections in the Fine Arts

The integration of the various disciplines that integrate the fine arts is another area of potentially rich learning for students. Many visual artists have been inspired by music and the performing arts and vice versa. The work during the Harlem Renaissance in the United States is a prime example of multiple areas of the arts building from one another's creative endeavors. Many schools work to create a sense of this atmosphere by providing celebrations that incorporate performances by students alongside exhibit of student artwork. Many art programs for the gifted encourage collaboration across art forms to enhance understanding of the contribution of each to the overall effect of performance. For example, students collaborate on an opera production that fuses the visual arts, theater, and music in a seamless way. Teachers can enrich these experiences for students by taking a more proactive role in directing and encouraging students to learn from each other and other artists working in different media or expression styles. As another example, for a warm-up activity, students could be asked to illustrate a piece of music using abstract lines and colors.

AUTHENTIC ASSESSMENT

Assessment in the fine arts can prove to be a source of uncertainty for many educators. It is difficult to test a student's knowledge with traditional assessments in a field dominated by subjective judgments. For the purposes of identification of talented students and documenting effectiveness of programs, some researchers have developed formalized assessment tasks for the fine arts (e.g., Clark, & Zimmerman, 1991, 2001; Oreck, Owen, & Baum, 2003). However, assessing the arts still remains subjective and highly personal (Willis, 2002).

One of the most common ways to formally assess a student's progress in the fine arts is through the use of rubrics, checklists, or product descriptors. Rubrics may be used holistically, with one set of descriptors describing overall product or performance quality, or they may be used analytically, separating the product or performance into components and assessing each separately. Another common approach to assessing student performance in the arts is through live performance via auditions in music, dance, and theater, and the use of portfolios for the visual arts of painting, sculpture, and architecture. The rubric approach often can be used by expert panels of judges from each arts area to determine the quality of a performance or product.

Art inherently lends itself to authentic assessment in that students are most often actively engaged in the work of professionals (i.e., creating art) and thus assessed on their progress in these endeavors. The assessment of the fine arts should, therefore, focus on objectives that are meaningful for practitioners of the discipline. For example, in the visual arts a focus on craftsmanship would be especially important for a student completing a graphic design project, but may be less important for a student inspired by the abstract expressionist Jackson Pollack. These assessments may be more authentic and capture student investment in the process by creating opportunities for students to have input into their creation of the rubric. Thus, the assessment can be more closely tied to the objectives of the student artists in the creation of their work. In addition, students can be asked to self-assess their own work, adding additional layers of authenticity.

Another aspect of authentic assessment common to fine arts classrooms is group or individual critique. Professional artists and performers often work together to evaluate, encourage, and analyze one another's artwork or performance. Educators can work to cultivate an environment of encouragement and constructive criticism in their classrooms. Some common ways of conducting a critique include "sandwich critiques," where the identification of areas for improvement are surrounded (or sandwiched) by more positive comments; sticky note critiques, where suggestions are written on notes and attached to works of art; or the use of oral or written prompts to guide discussion or written papers about specific aspects of the student work or performance. These techniques for art critiques can provide valuable and authentic formative assessments for students and guide the direction of their art.

HIGHER ORDER REASONING

The arts have long been exalted for their emphasis on higher order reasoning skills (e.g., Gardner, Winner, & Kircher, 1975; Koroscik, 1984; Ring, 2000; Winner, 1986, 2007). In the production of, for example, a painting, students are asked to solve complex visual problems, such as how to represent a three-dimensional object, concept, idea, or image in a two-dimensional plane. The work of analyzing, interpreting, and evaluating pieces of art develop higher order reasoning skills. These skills can be enhanced through the use of questions to elicit these behaviors, with teachers' attending to the development of such skills in discourse with students. When eliciting subjective opinions from students about artwork, it is important for teachers to continue questioning to encourage students to provide details and specific justification for their opinions. Table 13.4 indicates questions (based on Anderson & Krathwohl's [2000] revision of Bloom's taxonomy) teachers may ask to elicit higher order thinking and reasoning from students.

Both critical and creative thinking processes are essential in the fine arts for the development of higher order reasoning in talented students. By creatively finding novel ideas and modes of expression in the fine arts and then critically analyzing the results, advanced students can develop their talents.

TABLE 13.4

Higher Order Thinking Questions by Levels of Bloom's Revised Taxonomy

Thinking level	Example questions
Remember	What is the subject of this painting? What instruments are used in this performance?
Understand	What style of dance is seen in this performance? Would you classify this play as classical, modern, or absurdist?
Apply	What message do you think the artist/composer/choreographer is trying to convey in this piece?
Analyze	What piece of artwork is similar to this piece? How is this play similar or different from others by the same playwright?
Evaluate	Would you hang this artwork in your bedroom? Why or why not? How would you assess this piece of music in respect to mood, theme, and style? Is it the best example from this composer, do you think?
Create	How would you change this piece of art? How could you use this piece of art as an inspiration for your own creation?

CONSTRUCTING MEANING

The fine arts provide unique opportunities for students to construct meaning in their learning. The act of creative expression itself is a version of meaning construction in that artists are exploring their own thoughts, feelings, and ideas through personal and/or creative endeavors. Studies of aesthetics, art history, or design properties can similarly be developed through constructivist approaches emphasizing the creation of meaning.

Constructing Meaning in the Arts

One approach to teaching in the visual arts is particularly oriented toward constructing meaning. The studio model extends talent development in the visual arts beyond sets of assignments and projects toward an ability to construct a solution to visual problems (Perry, 1987). Studio models encourage students to develop talents in more authentic environments and situations, and they allow students to develop independent ideas and make choices about media, subject, and/or style. Teachers in this type of approach act as guides and facilitate artistic endeavors rather than direct artistic projects. In the other arts areas, the studio model also prevails, especially in music, where students engage in original composition and perform independently in small ensembles, with the guidance of a teacher.

Metacognition

Metacognition is an important piece of the artistic process, especially for advanced and talented students. The process of reflection on the act of producing creative products allows students to grow and develop as artists. This process, when completed as a written reflection, internal thought process, or oral discussion with peers or an instructor, gives students the opportunity to evaluate the effectiveness of their own strategy used in the creative processes, find areas of strength and areas of continued growth, and investigate new ways to explore the act of creating art. Curricula for talented artists should incorporate activities and time for students to reflect on their final products as well as the processes that contributed to their creation. These processes include both the physical techniques used (whether the body movements involved in dance, the vocal chords in a solo, or the techniques used in watercolor painting), but also the internal processes of the development of ideas and decision-making strategies that led to the final product or performance. Art or performance journals to record thoughts and evaluations are one way to encourage this metacognitive piece in the curriculum. Other teachers ask students to write reflections about their work as they complete the pieces or performances. As an alternative to written reflections, time might be set aside for small-group discussions about the process or teacher conferences with students. Finally, artists' statements about a collection of work or a portfolio might serve as a guide for students to think reflectively about the process of creative expression through the fine arts.

Multicultural/Global Emphasis

Teachers of the fine arts must be aware of the differences in the arts across the globe and appreciate the various artistic endeavors of diverse cultures. This multicultural and global perspective is especially important for talented students to introduce new sources of inspiration and new styles in the creation of art. Although art instruction in the United States tends to have a Western emphasis, educators should intentionally include a variety of perspectives.

Throughout the history of Western art, artists have drawn inspiration from non-Western cultures. Pablo Picasso was fascinated by African masks, the Impressionists and Post-Impressionists were influenced by Japanese prints, and Frida Kahlo incorporated indigenous Mexican colors, patterns, and traditional symbols in her paintings. However, non-Western art should not be studied only through the lens of its influence on Western art, but explored through the aesthetic values of each individual culture. Students benefit from learning and experiencing the various aesthetic values around the globe, as well as the diverse roles that art has played in culture. The intricate and abstract designs of Islamic art, the simplicity and elegance of Japanese Sumi-e paintings and calligraphy, the bold colors of Latin American traditions, and the geometric abstractions of African art all add richness and complexity to students' understandings of the arts.

MATERIALS AND RESOURCES

The materials and resources for advanced students in the arts must provide appropriate opportunities for the continued development of talent. Clark and Zimmerman (1994, 1995, 1998) recommend advanced materials and resources such as individual studio spaces for students. Although such resources may not always be possible for schools to provide, attention to providing advanced materials and resources for talented artists is warranted. In elementary school, while typical tempera paint may serve most students, advanced students may be ready to work with acrylic paints and canvas, rather than paper. However, care also should be taken to ensure the safety of students when working with materials. Oil paints and solvents contain hazardous chemicals, tools for sculpting and printmaking may have sharp edges, and teachers must judge the developmental appropriateness of materials and the precautions for student safety.

In the area of music, access to quality instruments is a concern, especially at the elementary level where students may not be able to afford home lessons. In all of the performance areas, access to the appropriate venues to practice and perform are the major considerations beyond the core tools needed such as scripts, choreography, and arrangements. Libraries may be tapped for access to recordings needed for musical performance and dance and for copies of plays to be performed.

SELECTED RESOURCES

A Community Audit for Arts Education: Better Schools, Better Skills, Better Communities (Kennedy Center Alliance for Arts Education Network, 2007)
Provides a checklist/survey for schools and communities to evaluate the state of arts education.

Americans for the Arts (http://www.americansforthearts.org)
This website includes an advocacy toolkit for communities, resources and literature pertaining to the educational benefits for the arts, and ideas for community involvement.

ArtsEdge: The Kennedy Center (http://artsedge.kennedy-center.org)
This website provides links to art standards, advocacy toolkits, and current research pertaining to art education.

"Ten Lessons the Arts Teach: The Arts and the Creation of Mind" (Eisner, 2002)

This short article provides a list of the value of arts education and its importance to student learning and development.

Resources About Artists

The Metropolitan Museum of Art, New York (http://www.metmuseum.org)

The official website for The Metropolitan Museum of Art provides images of much of the museum's collection, as well as accompanying information. It also includes a timeline of art history, and teachers can set up a personal gallery from the museum's collection to access later.

The Modern Museum of Art, New York (http://www.moma.org)

The official website for The Modern Museum of Art (MoMA) includes interactive museum tours for both the MoMA galleries and the PS1 contemporary gallery that is appropriate for even the youngest of art students. Much of the collection is available online.

WebMuseum Paris (http://www.ibiblio.org/wm)

This website provides background information and links to examples of artwork for a comprehensive list of visual artists.

CONCLUSION

This chapter has presented important ideas for designing and developing a curriculum in the visual and performing arts for gifted learners, whether they are talented in one area or intellectually gifted in academic areas as well. It has assumed that the arts are both a vehicle for production and aesthetic appreciation. Linkages to both the Integrated Curriculum Model and key elements of contemporary curriculum design have been made through addressing the importance of concepts, substantive content, and higher level skills and processes to be used. Examples, drawn primarily from the visual arts, have illuminated the ideas shared.

KEY POINTS SUMMARY

- The arts require differentiation for gifted learners to the same degree as do academic subjects.
- Both the visual and performing arts require an emphasis on aesthetic

appreciation and production, addressed through a common set of standards in each area.

- The arts provide an important bridge and interdisciplinary connections to academic subjects to enhance learning.
- The arts may be taught through various approaches, but gifted learners benefit from a constructivist model in which they take charge of their own learning at key stages in the development of expertise.
- Collaboration across arts areas provides deepened appreciation and understanding of intradisciplinary work.

REFERENCES

Adams, H. M., & Russ, J. C. (1992). Chaos in the classroom: Exposing gifted elementary school children to chaos and fractals. *Journal of Science Education and Technology, 1,* 191–209.

Americans for the Arts. (2006). *Highlights from key national research on arts education.* Retrieved from http://www.artsusa.org/public_awareness/artsed_facts/002.asp

Anderson, L. W., & Krathwohl, D. R. (Eds.). (2000). *A taxonomy for learning, teaching, and assessing: A revision of Bloom's taxonomy of educational objectives.* Boston, MA: Allyn & Bacon.

Arts Education Partnership, & President's Committee on the Arts and the Humanities. (1999). *Champions of change: The impact of the arts on learning.* Retrieved from http://www.aep-arts.org/files/publications/ChampsReport.pdf

Asmus, E., Lee, K., Lindsey, A., Patchen, J. H., & Wheetley, K. (1997). Discipline-based arts education: A conceptual framework for learning and teaching the arts. *Visual Arts Research, 23,* 114–123.

Catterall, J. S. (1998). Does experience in the arts boost academic achievement? A response to Eisner. *Art Education, 51*(4), 6–11.

Clark, G. A., & Zimmerman, E. (1987). Tending the special spark: Acceleration and enriched curricula for highly talented art students. *Roeper Review, 10,* 10–17.

Clark, G. A., & Zimmerman, E. (1991). Screening and identifying gifted/talented students in the visual arts with Clark's drawing abilities test. *Roeper Review, 13,* 92–97.

Clark, G. A., & Zimmerman, E. (1992). *Issues and practices related to identification of gifted and talented students in the visual arts.* Storrs: University of Connecticut, The National Research Center on the Gifted and Talented.

Clark, G. A., & Zimmerman, E. (1994). *Programming opportunities for students gifted and talented in the visual arts.* Storrs: University of Connecticut, The National Research Center on the Gifted and Talented.

Clark, G. A., & Zimmerman, E. (1995). You can't just scribble: Art talent development. *Educational Forum, 59,* 400–423.

Clark, G. A., & Zimmerman, E. (1998). Nurturing the arts in programs for gifted and talented students. *Phi Delta Kappan, 79,* 747–753.

Clark, G. A., & Zimmerman, E. (2001). Identifying artistically talented students in four rural communities in the United States. *Gifted Child Quarterly, 45*, 104–114.

Clark, G. A., Day, M. D., & Greer, W. D. (1987). Discipline-based art education: Becoming students of art. *Journal of Aesthetic Education, 21*, 129–193.

Consortium of National Arts Education Associations. (1994). *National standards for arts education: What every young American should know and be able to do in the arts.* Retrieved from http://artsedge.kennedy-center.org/teach/standards.cfm

Consortium of National Arts Education Associations. (2002). *Authentic connections: Interdisciplinary work in the arts.* Retrieved http://www.naea-reston.org/pdf/INTERart.pdf

Eisner, E. (2002). Ten lessons the arts teach: The arts and the creation of mind. In National Art Education Association (Ed.), *What the arts teach and how it shows* (pp. 70–92). New Haven, CT: Yale University Press. Retrieved from http://www.naea-reston.org/tenlessons.html

Eisner, E. W. (1966). Arts curricula for the gifted. *Teachers College Record, 67*, 492–501.

Eisner, E. W. (1998). A response to Catterall. *Art Education, 51*(4), 12–13.

Fuller, F. (1994, April). The arts for whose children? A challenge to educators. *NASSP Bulletin, 78*, 1–6.

Gardner, H., Winner, E., & Kircher, M. (1975). Children's conceptions of the arts. *Journal of Aesthetic Education, 9*(3), 60–77.

Hetland, L., & Winner, E. (2001). The arts and academic achievement: What the evidence shows. *Arts Education Policy Review, 102*(5), 3–11.

Kennedy Center Alliance for Arts Education Network. (2007). *A community audit for arts education: Better schools better skills better communities.* Retrieved from http://www.kennedy-center.org/education/kcaaen/resources/CAudit6-9.pdf

Koroscik, J. S. (1984). Cognition in viewing and talking about art. *Theory Into Practice, 23*, 330–345.

Michael, J. A. (1970). *A handbook for art instructors and students based upon concepts and behaviors.* New York, NY: Vintage Press.

Michael, J. A. (1983). *Art and adolescence: Teaching art at the secondary level.* New York, NY: Teachers College Press.

Murfee, E. (1995). *Eloquent evidence: Arts at the core of learning.* Washington, DC: President's Committee on the Arts and Humanities. Retrieved from http://www.nasaa-arts.org/publications/eloquent.pdf

No Child Left Behind Act, 20 U.S.C. §6301 (2001).

Oreck, B. A., Owen, S. V., & Baum, S. M. (2003). Validity, reliability, and equity issues in an observational talent assessment process in the performing arts. *Journal for the Education of the Gifted, 27*, 62–94.

Perry, P. J. (1987). Arts and new horizons. *Gifted Child Today, 10*(5), 36–37.

President's Committee on the Arts and Humanities, & Arts Education Partnership. (1999). *Gaining the arts advantage: Lessons from school districts that value arts education.* Retrieved from http://www.aep-arts.org/files/publications/GAAReport.pdf

Rasmussen, K. (1998). Arts education: A cornerstone of basic education. *Curriculum Update, 6*, 1–3.

Ring, L. M. (2000). The t in art is for thinking. *Gifted Child Today, 23*(3), 36–43.

Ruppert, S. S. (2006). *Critical evidence: How the arts benefit student achievement.* Retrieved from http://www.nasaa-arts.org/publications/critical-evidence.shtml

Strand, K. (2006). The heart and the journey: Case studies of collaboration for arts integrated curricula. *Art Education, 108,* 29–34.

VanTassel-Baska, J., Evans, B., & Baska, A. (2008). The role of the arts in the socio-emotional development of the gifted. In J. VanTassel-Baska, T. L. Cross, & R. Olenchak (Eds.), *Social-emotional curriculum for gifted students* (pp. 227–258). Waco, TX: Prufrock Press.

Willis, S. (2002). What art educators value in artwork. *Visual Arts Research, 28*(1), 61–67.

Wilson, H. E. (2007, July). *Differentiation for the elementary art room: Artist's workshop.* Paper presented at the Biennial World Council of Giftedness.

Winner, E. (1986). Children's perception of "aesthetic" properties of the arts: Domain-specific or pan-artistic? *British Journal of Developmental Psychology, 4,* 149–160.

Winner, E. (1997). Giftedness vs. creativity in the visual arts. *Poetics, 24,* 349–377.

Winner, E. (2000). The origins and ends of giftedness. *American Psychologist, 55,* 159–169.

Winner, E. (2007). Visual thinking in arts education: Homage to Rudolf Arnheim. *Psychology of Aesthetics, Creativity, and the Arts, 1,* 25–31.

Winner, E., & Hetland, L. (2003). Beyond the evidence given: A critical commentary on critical links. *Arts Education Policy Review, 104,* 13–21.

Chapter 14

Selecting Resources and Materials for High-Ability Learners

Linda D. Avery and Kimberley Chandler

Y*ou are a newly hired teacher, assigned to work as a gifted resource teacher. Your new boss is sending you to a conference on gifted education and has given you a purchase order for selecting and purchasing new curricular materials for use in the gifted program. You arrive at the conference exhibit hall and see dozens of booths with materials for teaching gifted students. You want to take advantage of your time browsing to make the best decisions possible about what to buy. However, there are so many materials with different features that you feel a little overwhelmed.*

Much of this book has addressed the issue of how to design curricula for the gifted and how to adapt curricula already in place. However, it is not always necessary or practical to reinvent the wheel when it comes to finding appropriate curricula to use in teaching gifted students. For many years there was a dearth of gifted education curricula built around content-based standards, scope and sequence, and appropriate differentiation in substance and process, but major inroads in recognizing and addressing this gap have occurred in recent years. One of the benefits of the introduction of national and state standards for the core content areas has been to develop consensus on what is important to teach. This has made curriculum development efforts more uniform and cohesive and led to the creation of materials that already address the stated standards, yet go beyond them in a way that is appropriate for gifted students; this is especially true of materials developed under the auspices of the Jacob K. Javits Act.

The ability to select good curriculum materials for gifted students is, in itself, an important proficiency for gifted education professionals. In fact, the Teacher Knowledge and Skill Standards for Gifted and Talented Education developed by the National Association for Gifted Children (NAGC) and the Council for Exceptional Children (CEC) articulated two specific standards relevant to this skill set (VanTassel-Baska & Johnsen, 2007). These standards state that competent teachers of the gifted will be able to (a) select curriculum resources, strategies, and product options that respond to cultural, linguistic, and intellectual differences; and (b) select and adapt a variety of differentiated curricula that incorporates advanced, conceptually challenging, in-depth, distinctive, and complex content. Defensible curriculum selections must be made at both the classroom and the program level. This chapter provides a framework for executing these decisions that can help teachers as well as program coordinators approach the selection process in a thoughtful and systematic way.

A good core curriculum is an essential foundation for creating an exemplary gifted program. In some ways, it is the glue that holds the program together as students move from one grade level to another. A well-documented and clearly articulated curriculum is a valuable tool for new teachers and can significantly reduce the amount of time that is spent in instructional preparation. Appropriate curricula for gifted learners address multiple learning goals simultaneously. The goals that are embedded in the curriculum developed by the Center for Gifted Education at The College of William and Mary include the following overarching dimensions:

- to deliver content knowledge that is substantive, up-to-date, and essential to an understanding and ability to use major concepts;
- to develop inquiry and reasoning skills that encourage high levels of student engagement in the process of constructing meaning;
- to demonstrate practices and "habits of mind" that give students experience in the behavior and thinking of experts in the field; and
- to provide opportunities for students to make inter- and intradisciplinary connections.

The selection of the print and media resources that support the implementation of program curricula (curriculum units, teacher guides, student texts, reference materials, and other supplemental resources to extend or enrich the core content) requires careful planning and attention. Educators often are bombarded by resource exhibits and fairs, promotional mailings, publishing catalogs, and even Internet advertisements, but without a template to assess the quality and utility of these materials, it is difficult to make informed decisions. This chapter provides advice in making materials acquisition decisions that are research based.

The purpose of this chapter is twofold. The first goal is to provide specific guidelines for selecting curricular resources for classroom use with gifted students and to describe the elements of a curriculum assessment checklist that was developed and utilized by the Center for Gifted Education. This checklist addresses three important dimensions of curriculum appropriateness: general design, specific content emphases, and accommodations or aspects appropriate for the advanced learner. The second goal of the chapter is to identify both core and supplemental curriculum units and resources that are suitable for gifted learners in each of the four content areas. These lists include curriculum materials developed by the Center for Gifted Education, curriculum materials from other publishers that were reviewed using the procedure and criteria described in this chapter, and resources that have been found to be useful additions to classroom libraries to reinforce and complement learning.

CURRICULAR SELECTION PROCESS

Curricular selection decisions cannot be made lightly as they impact the expenditure of limited resources and are expected to last multiple academic years. As a result, it is important to utilize a review and decision-making process that is efficient, defensible, and wise. A collaborative process that capitalizes on the knowledge and expertise of a number of professionals (teachers, media specialists, consultants, and administrators) helps to bring a balanced perspective to the choices that are made. The process also should be dynamic in that it is revisited annually to incorporate research advances and evolving technology. Like all systemic processes, curricular review is never complete, but is always in a stage of recycling.

The model used by the Center for Gifted Education to conduct a review of core curricula is presented in Figure 14.1. This review process was done in the late 1990s and revealed that there was a significant void in coherent and challenging curricula for gifted learners in many of the core areas. The review effort itself became a catalyst for the Center for Gifted Education's intensive curriculum work.

The model identifies four steps in the curriculum review process. The first step is to identify or develop the criteria that will be used. The criteria that were employed by the Center for Gifted Education were organized around three critical elements: (a) principles of sound curricula in general, (b) important

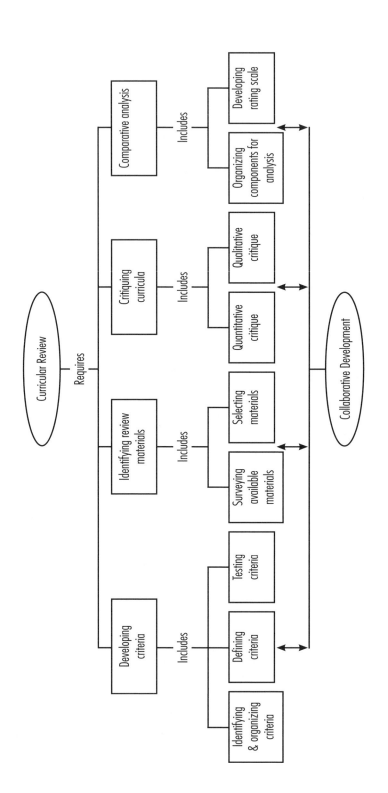

Figure 14.1. Model of the curricular review process. From *A Guide to Teaching a Problem-Based Science Curriculum for High-Ability Learners* (p. 79), by the Center for Gifted Education, 1997, Dubuque, IA: Kendall/Hunt. Copyright © 1997 by the Center for Gifted Education. Reprinted with permission.

features of the specific content area (language arts, mathematics, social studies, science) drawn from the literature and research base on effective teaching of that subject, and (c) relevant characteristics of the gifted student. Any checklist or rating scale that is developed for this process should attend to all three dimensions. The application of these criteria should be phased in sequentially. If materials do not meet the criteria identified in the first category (sound curricula in general), there is little need to continue with further examination. If the materials do meet the first set of criteria, but not the second set (content-area features), the review of these materials can be truncated at this point. By implementing the application of the materials review in this way, time is maximized.

The next three steps are fairly obvious. Step 2 requires one to identify and acquire the materials to be reviewed. Step 3 is the actual implementation of the review by the individual or group of people involved (examining the materials and completing the rating forms). Step 4 focuses on conducting a comparative analysis across all of the material reviewed, whether units, texts, or supplemental resources, in order to make informed decisions. In Step 3, provisions should be made to attend to both quantitative and qualitative factors. In Step 4, provisions should be made to determine how the results of Step 3 will be compiled across reviewers (e.g., narrative summaries, score totals, ranking by reviewer) to facilitate the discussion and selection process. If multiple people are involved in the review, Step 4 may require that time be set aside for them to meet as a group to share their perceptions and concerns.

It is our belief that, in order for educators to make informed decisions about instruction, they must first become informed consumers (Center for Gifted Education, 1997). Because textbooks are the primary curriculum in more than 95% of U.S. public schools (Lockwood, 1992), the selection of materials and resources has powerful instructional consequences. Based on the Center for Gifted Education's findings in conducting curricular reviews across the four content areas, no single program will meet the needs of all students at a given grade level. Basal texts, in particular, have been found to be particularly lacking in their capacity to meet the needs of the high-ability learner. "Supplementary materials should not automatically be equated with 'enrichment,'" but should instead be examined with an eye toward alignment with curricular standards and instructional objectives (Johnson, Boyce, & VanTassel-Baska, 1995, p. 41).

The next section of this chapter presents the criteria that were developed by the Center for Gifted Education for use in reviewing materials for high-ability learners. These criteria are presented to educators to help expedite the first step in the curricular review and selection process.

Phase 1: General Curricular Design Features

The first phase of curricular review, incorporating the first set of criteria for consumers to consider in selecting materials, concerns features of general curricular design. This phase acknowledges that a strong curriculum has certain key elements no matter who its intended student audience may be. Although these features may seem at first glance to reflect the foundations of introductory education coursework in curriculum development and methods, they nevertheless do not always appear in useful or fully developed form in many curricular resources.

Phase 1 includes eight categories of criteria to review, including aspects that appear in broad curricular frameworks, as well as within specific lesson plans (Center for Gifted Education, 1997, 1999; Gregory, 2000; Johnson & Sher, 1997). The eight categories, with their specific criteria and brief descriptions, are as follows:

1. Rationale and Purpose
   a. Overtly stated, clear, and understandable
   b. Presented logically and delineate how material fits into larger scope and sequence of program
   c. Identify learning goals and learning outcomes that are consonant with one another
   d. Learning goals are deemed substantive and worthy of time allocation
   e. Where relevant, learning goals are aligned with state and local standards and testing

2. Lesson Objectives
   a. Clear and understandable
   b. Measurable
   c. Related to overall rationale and purpose

3. Activities
   a. Used to explore, reinforce, clarify, and extend content
   b. Use of concrete experiences/manipulatives
   c. Balance of teacher facilitation and student direction
   d. Possibilities for flexible grouping to allow independent, cooperative, or collaborative learning

4. Instructional Strategies
   a. Varied to include lecture, inquiry activities, group and independent work, and engagement with core teaching/learning models
   b. Opportunities for students to discover ideas and concepts
   c. Opportunities for open inquiry through problem finding, problem solving, and decision making

    d. Use of various types of questions, such as convergent, divergent, and evaluative

    e. Opportunities for students to reflect upon and evaluate their own thinking

5. Assessment Procedures

    a. Use of well-designed pretests and posttests linked to core goals and outcomes

    b. Use of performance-based modes of assessment, such as portfolios

    c. Use of multiple means of assessment, including observation and self-assessment

    d. Opportunities for extending learning embedded throughout the lessons

    e. Use of rubrics or clearly stated criteria for assessment

6. Materials and Resources

    a. Engaging style of presenting information

    b. Well-aligned with national and state standards of learning

    c. Evidence of attention to multiculturalism or cultural diversity

    d. Evidence of attention to multiple perspectives

    e. Background material for teachers incorporated

    f. Bibliography for teacher support and student extensions

    g. Supportive handouts to enhance learning

    h. Use of print and nonprint resources

    i. Opportunities for students to learn how to use multiple resources

7. Technology

    a. Reasonably up-to-date

    b. Appropriate for age and task

    c. Enhances and complements instruction and learning

    d. Opportunities to assess student technology competence and to teach necessary skills

8. Extensions

    a. Worthwhile and related activities and resources for students to pursue beyond the classroom

    b. Quality homework assignments

    c. Orientation to parents on how to help students' extended learning

Phase 2: Content-Area Emphases

Although the features outlined above can be generalized across content areas to represent essential curricular features no matter what the subject, each discipline has its own important principles, practices, and habits of mind that are key to support in student learning. Moreover, the treatment of content varies significantly from one subject area to another, with major differences in processes and conceptual elements. Consequently, a curricular review should take into account specific criteria related to the content area under study, and an interdisciplinary curriculum should be reviewed according to as many of the criteria as are relevant.

A first step in the review of a curriculum in relation to the content dimension is to consider the alignment of the materials with national, state, and local content standards. Standards-based reform has had a profound effect on curricular, instructional, and assessment practices and serves as the linchpin of educational accountability initiatives. In our experience, the convergence between national and state standards in the major disciplines is currently quite strong. Nevertheless, this issue of alignment of content with discipline-specific standards should be a first step in the review of all of the content areas. The following pages outline additional key criteria in each of the four major content areas.

Language arts. The language arts standards at both the national and state levels are largely focused on the development and mastery of communication skills (International Reading Association & National Council of Teachers of English, 1996). In a sense, the "process" skills associated with reading, writing, listening, and speaking form the basis of the "content" standards in the discipline of language arts. The standards have become more challenging as a result of an increased emphasis on literary analysis and interpretation, higher order thinking skills, interdisciplinary study, and sensitivity to cultural diversity. The eight criteria (VanTassel-Baska, 1998) detailed below focus on the key features of educational reform that have influenced this discipline:

- integration of the language arts of reading, writing, listening, speaking, and language study;
- emphasis on developing critical reading behaviors;
- incorporation of high-quality multicultural literature and cultural study opportunities;
- choice of literature reflecting cognitive and affective considerations;
- evidence of balanced perspectives presented;
- employment of interdisciplinary approaches to connect language arts to other disciplines;
- incorporation of techniques for enhancing thinking skills; and
- use of questions for discussion that emphasize high-level thinking.

The William and Mary language arts units employ advanced-reading-level literature as the catalyst for learning. Based on the Integrated Curriculum Model (ICM), the units teach advanced content through the selection of challenging reading material to strengthen literary analysis and interpretation, vocabulary building, and grammar. The units also focus on teaching reasoning and persuasive writing. The concept addressed across most of the units is change. There are currently 10 units in print that address student needs in grades 1–12. Significant student learning gains from the implementation of four of these units (covering grades 2–8) have been documented and reported in the professional literature (VanTassel-Baska, Zuo, Avery, & Little, 2002).

The Center for Gifted Education also has produced supplemental materials in the language arts called the *Navigator Novel Study Guides* (*Navigators*). These are collections of task demands intended to support group or independent study of classic novels. The *Navigators* encourage advanced readers to develop their skills in analyzing and interpreting literature through structured questions and activities that highlight themes and concepts, literary elements, and real-world connections contained within the books. They also promote vocabulary building and writing skills by exploring and emulating the language and style of authors.

The *Jacob's Ladder Reading Comprehension Program* is a learning journey for students that begins with targeted readings from short stories, poetry, and nonfiction sources and moves through an inquiry process from basic understanding to critical analyses. There are three levels of this program, one for lower elementary, one for upper elementary, and one for middle school, but they may be used at different grades depending on the students' abilities. This program was created based on student needs and teacher requests for additional scaffolding within the language arts curriculum. Each ladder in the program focuses on a different set of skills, from lower to higher order; students "climb" each ladder by answering lower level questions and then moving to higher level questions or rungs at the top.

Mathematics. In the discipline of mathematics, the introduction of content standards (National Council of Teachers of Mathematics, 2000) has dramatically impacted the threshold expectations for all students, with many states requiring competency in Algebra I in eighth grade as a condition for graduation. The impact of No Child Left Behind (NCLB, 2001) also has forced schools to examine the alignment between the math standards that are taught and mandated tests at the state and national levels (Cavanagh, 2007; Weaver, 2004). The National Center for Education Statistics (NCES) has now conducted four rounds of international comparisons of student performance across countries, and the results of these comparative analyses have brought additional attention to the domains of math and science. The 2003 results were mixed (NCES, 2004). Previous reports at the 4th- (NCES, 1997), 8th- (NCES, 1996), and 12th-grade (NCES, 1998) levels had demonstrated the relatively poor performance of U.S. students in world comparisons. The 2003 results showed no measurable changes overall for fourth graders in math, but an increase in the performance of Black students showed that the gap between Black and White students was narrowing. At the eighth-grade level, scores in both math and science improved in addition to the narrowing of the gap between Black and White students (NCES, 2004). Recent research in both math and science has demonstrated that the mere presence of content standards is not sufficient to guarantee curricula that lead to high-quality instruction and achievement (Schmidt, Wang, & McKnight, 2005).

The impetus to keep our nation economically competitive in a global marketplace has led to mathematics standards that emphasize concept learning and reasoning skills in addition to mastery of challenging math content. The nine criteria (Johnson & Sher, 1997) set forth below will help educators evaluate curriculum materials and resources in mathematics in the wake of these tougher standards:

- organization of content around major mathematical ideas;
- depth in coverage of important mathematical concepts;
- progression from the concrete to the abstract presented in an understandable manner;
- inclusion of the history of mathematical ideas, concepts, and mathematicians;
- opportunities for both inductive and deductive reasoning;
- encouragement of divergent thinking and multiple solutions;
- emphasis on communicating ideas using various modes, including oral, written, and visual forms;
- connection of mathematics to real-world and other disciplines; and
- opportunities for students to develop habits of mind of mathematicians, such as curiosity, tenacity, skepticism, and respect for evidence.

The Center for Gifted Education has developed units in the area of mathematics. One unit, *Beyond Base Ten*, is targeted to grades 3–6 and focuses on the representation of numbers by using place value and non-place-value systems. Bases other than base 10 are featured through the context of early civilization number systems. *Spatial Reasoning*, a unit developed for students in grades 2–4, and *Moving Through Dimensions*, for students in grades 6–8, approach spatial reasoning through one-, two-, and three-dimensional tasks and include transitions and representations from three- to two-dimensional objects.

Science. The proliferation of advances in science and technology has become so commonplace in the last century that we often fail to appreciate the scope and magnitude of the changes that have taken place. Many of the fascinating questions with which we wrestle in modern society are grounded in scientific developments. Dilemmas such as balancing ecological protections with energy demands; deciding to what extent stem cell research, cloning, and genetic engineering should be regulated; finding an optimal match between military might and world peace; and deciding what constitutes the initiation and cessation of life are endlessly recast in the wake of scientific and technological progress. Responses to such issues are increasingly complex and sophisticated and require a citizenry that values accuracy, precision, and parsimony in assessing information and has the capacity to identify and reason through alternative choices and consequences.

Recent commentary on the science standards praises the standards for changing the way science is addressed, particularly at the elementary level (Bybee & Van Scotter, 2007; Yager & Enger, 2006). Concerns continue to be voiced, however, about the scope and the focus of the standards, at least in how they are translated into curriculum at the district level. Wheeler (2007) proposed the identification of anchors, common points of reference across grade levels and districts, that will ensure some uniformity in content coverage. Other critics want to see the inquiry process that is central to the conduct of science expanded to address areas such as theory and model-building, data collection and analysis, constructing arguments, and using specialized ways of talking, writing, and representing phenomenon (Duschl, Shouse, & Schweingruber, 2008).

The Trends in International Math and Science Study (TIMSS) data (NCES, 2004) cited the same pattern for student performance on science as on math. At the fourth-grade level, there was no evidence of change from prior years' scores; at the eighth-grade level there was some improvement. Again, differences between Black and White student scores at both levels were narrowed. There also is evidence in the literature that for states that did not conduct statewide testing on science standards until the provisions of NCLB went into effect there was a scramble to refocus on science content in the elementary schools (Boyle & Bragg, 2005; Cavanagh, 2005).

The impact of educational reform in science has been to emphasize the "big picture" through concept development and higher order thinking skills. The standards encourage inquiry-driven models; typically organize content across specific categories such as physical science, life science, and Earth and space science; and try to foster scientific habits of mind that lead students to career paths in this area. The following 12 criteria focus on such aspects of science curriculum reform (Center for Gifted Education, 1997; Johnson et al., 1995):

- coverage of important science concepts in depth;
- accurate and understandable presentation of science;
- linking of topics to broad scientific concepts (intradisciplinary connections);
- linking of topics to ideas outside of science (interdisciplinary connections);
- balance of qualitative and quantitative information;
- balance of theoretical and practical science;
- presence of moral, ethical, and historical dimensions of science and technology;
- opportunities for open-ended scientific investigation (not simply verification exercises);
- laboratory and field work integral to, and integrated with, the curriculum;
- opportunities for students to work together to investigate real-world scientific technological problems;

- inclusion of instruction on building and testing hypotheses; and
- allowance for questioning of assumptions and presentation/exploration of diverse opinions on scientific issues.

The William and Mary science curriculum units use problem-based learning (PBL) as the catalyst to engage students in scientific inquiry. After being confronted with a real-world problem, the students become scientists themselves to collect data and propose solutions. The science units are built around the concepts of *systems* and *change* as a way to link components together, add depth to the content, and make interdisciplinary connections. The first eight units that were developed cover grades 2–8. Research data collected from the implementation of six of these units showed significant student learning gains in science process skills (VanTassel-Baska, Bass, Ries, Poland, & Avery, 1998). These data helped convince an expert panel appointed by the U.S. Department of Education to identify the units among the nine most promising efforts in the country in this subject matter.

More recently, the Center for Gifted Education has developed eight new units for use with students in grades K–3. These units incorporate the Wheel of Scientific Investigation and Reasoning, a graphic organizer that scaffolds the scientific research process; students make observations, ask questions about the world around them, read and learn about their new topic, design and conduct experiments, and discuss and present their findings. An evaluation of the impact of these units on student learning showed significant gains on a standardized achievement test in science and on a measure of critical thinking over a comparison group (VanTassel-Baska, Bracken, Stambaugh, & Feng, 2007).

Social studies. Although the original development of national standards in the various subjects of the social studies (e.g., Center for Civic Education, 1994; National Council for the Social Studies, 1994) engendered a level of controversy and debate, many of the issues have appeared to have been resolved over the years as states have increasingly adopted their own sets of standards (Bettis, 2004; Kenney, 2004). Initial criticisms suggested that the standards covered too much material and were burdensome to teachers (Saunders, 1996), overly praised native cultures while sanctioning European achievements (Saxe, 1995), and undermined the importance of plurality (Whelan, 1995). Evans and Pang (1995) defended the standards as an excellent and inclusive guide to the broad topics and themes appropriate to the study of history, and Mirel and Angus (1994) indicated that the standards helped to equalize quality and access to challenging programs and courses (as cited in Gregory, 2000). Perhaps more than in any other discipline, the articulation of standards for the social studies energized discussions about the substance, scope, and nature of social studies education, and resulted in the inclusion of economics and politics in a curriculum that had focused almost exclusively on history and geography at the elementary level.

Even recently, proponents of the social studies standards have reiterated that the standards do not call for knowledge of an extensive list of facts, nor do they set out an expectation for rote memorization; what they do call for is the ability to analyze and apply information in the decision-making process (Adler, Dougan, & Garcia, 2006). Unfortunately, this content is often marginalized because of the current emphasis on reading and math precipitated by NCLB (Risinger, 2006; VanFossen, 2005). A proposed solution to this dilemma has been to integrate social studies content into the core domains of language arts, math, and science (Hinde, 2005; Olwell & Raphael, 2006). One element of this solution is to use biography and autobiography in the language arts to teach history and civic leadership (Sandmann, 2002).

Aspects of educational reform reflected in the social studies standards echo many of the same concerns and themes as the other discipline areas: the importance of critical inquiry and conceptual learning, an emphasis on problem solving and reasoning, recognition of cultural diversity, and connectedness to current events and real-world issues. The following 12 criteria (Gregory, 2000) can be used to structure a review instrument for this subject area:

- use of critical inquiry as an analytical tool by students;
- emphasis on the meaning and the process of history;
- use of simulations or scenarios that involve students directly in problem solving;
- use of multiple perspectives in viewing issues or events;
- strong focus on the well-organized essay as a grading tool;
- engagement of students with primary source material;
- provisions for direct field experience;
- balance of knowledge skills and values;
- evidence of attention to multiculturalism or cultural diversity in the selection of reading material;
- instruction in problem finding, problem solving, and addressing real-world issues and current events;
- provision of opportunities for linking content to current events so that relevance is established; and
- emphasis on depth, rather than breadth.

The Center for Gifted Education has developed 12 social studies units with attention to the criteria listed. These units use historical periods and events as the catalyst for student learning. Students actively engage in document analysis, issue-based research on current events, and reasoning through situations to master historical content. Students then connect this new learning to an overarching concept such as *systems* or *cause and effect* to gain a deeper understanding of history and its relationship to other areas of study within and beyond social studies. When five of these units were implemented with 1,200 students in heterogeneous classrooms, results showed significant student growth on measures of conceptual thinking, content learning, and critical thinking (Little, Feng, VanTassel-Baska, Rogers, & Avery, 2007). In addition, treatment effects were evident for the whole sample and consistent across gender.

Phase 3: Essential Features for Gifted Learners

The third phase in the curricular review and selection process focuses on the specific needs of high-ability students. These students' abilities are accelerated in relation to the general population, and their academic or intellectual precocity often manifests itself in rate, degree, and depth of learning behavior. Such learning needs require that the curriculum be sufficiently differentiated to optimize cognitive and affective development. The 12 criteria that we have found useful in reviewing materials for high-ability students are listed below (Center for Gifted Education, 1997, 1999; Gregory, 2000; Johnson & Sher, 1997):

- selected activities, resources, and materials are sufficiently challenging for advanced learners;
- organizing concept is treated in sufficient depth;
- opportunities are provided for creative production;
- opportunities are provided for integrating higher order thought processes;
- issues, problems, and themes are sufficiently complex;
- ample opportunities are provided through unit activities for students to construct meaning for themselves;
- both content and instruction provide for a sufficiently high level of abstraction;
- reading material is sufficiently advanced;
- different levels of ability are provided for by the unit;
- open-ended questions that encourage multiple or divergent responses are identified for the teacher;
- opportunities are provided for independent learning; and
- opportunities are provided for meaningful project work.

The five essential differentiation features that one should keep in mind in assessing the appropriateness of curricula for gifted learners deal with complexity, depth, challenge, creativity, and acceleration (VanTassel-Baska, 2003). Materials that successfully incorporate these differentiation features are able to address multiple instructional goals simultaneously. In addition, they provide sufficient opportunities for student work that promotes integration and synthesis of learning. In some cases, this requires the selection of alternative texts and resources; in other cases, the issue is one of supplementation. It is important to keep in mind how the different pieces of a curriculum work together to ensure that instruction is both at a high level and on target. This holistic orientation is achieved by looking at the frequency and distribution of the criteria that are met by each resource reviewed.

CURRICULAR RESOURCES FOR HIGH-ABILITY LEARNERS

As a component of the curriculum development work at the Center for Gifted Education at The College of William and Mary, the center has both developed a variety of curricular materials and reviewed a wide variety of materials within each major subject area. On the basis of the criteria outlined in this chapter, a number of resources have been identified as appropriate for use with high-ability learners, as well as teacher resources that are particularly helpful in framing curricula for these students. Teachers will need to make selections from these lists based on their instructional objectives and the level of student development.

Language Arts

American Federation of Teachers. (1998). *Building on the best, learning from what works: Seven promising reading and English and language arts programs.* Washington, DC: Author.

Anders, G., & Beech, L. W. (1990). *Reading: Mapping for meaning.* Kent, CT: Sniffen Court Books.

Anderson, P. S., & Lapp, D. (1988). *Language skills in elementary education.* New York, NY: Macmillan.

Baskin, B. H., & Harris, K. H. (1980). *Books for the gifted child.* New York, NY: Bowker.

Boyce, L. N. (1997). *A guide to teaching research skills and strategies in grades 4–12.* Williamsburg, VA: Center for Gifted Education.

Center for Gifted Education. (n.d.). *Libraries link learning: Resource manual for use with at-risk gifted children (K–2).* Williamsburg, VA: Author.

Center for Gifted Education. (2002). *Navigator series.* Williamsburg, VA: Author.

Center for Gifted Education. (2009). *Notes from a writer: Resources and activities for gifted children.* Williamsburg, VA: Author.

Center for Gifted Education. (2010). *Autobiographies* (2nd ed.). Dubuque, IA: Kendall/Hunt.

Center for Gifted Education. (2010). *Beyond words* (2nd ed.). Dubuque, IA: Kendall/Hunt.

Center for Gifted Education. (2010). *Change through choices* (2nd ed.). Dubuque, IA: Kendall/Hunt.

Center for Gifted Education. (2010). *Guide to teaching a language arts curriculum for high-ability learners* (2nd ed.). Dubuque, IA: Kendall/Hunt.

Center for Gifted Education. (2010). *Journeys and destinations* (2nd ed.). Dubuque, IA: Kendall/Hunt.

Center for Gifted Education. (2010). *Literary reflections* (2nd ed.). Dubuque, IA: Kendall/Hunt.

Center for Gifted Education. (2010). *The 1940s: A decade of change* (2nd ed.). Dubuque, IA: Kendall/Hunt.

Center for Gifted Education. (2010). *Patterns of change* (2nd ed.). Dubuque, IA: Kendall/Hunt.

Center for Gifted Education. (2010). *Persuasion* (2nd ed.). Dubuque, IA: Kendall/Hunt.

Center for Gifted Education. (2010). *Threads of change in 19th century American literature* (2nd ed.). Dubuque, IA: Kendall/Hunt.

Center for Gifted Education. (2010). *Utopia* (2nd ed.). Dubuque, IA: Kendall/Hunt.

Chinn, C. A., Anderson, R. C., & Waggoner, M. A. (2001). Patterns of discourse in two kinds of literature discussion. *Reading Research Quarterly, 36*, 378–411.

Costa, A. L. (Ed.). (1991). *Developing minds: A resource book for teaching thinking* (Rev. ed., Vols. 1–2). Alexandria, VA: Association for Supervision and Curriculum Development.

Guthrie, J. T., Schafer, W. D., & Huang, C.-W. (2001). Benefits of opportunity to read and balanced instruction on the NAEP. *Journal of Educational Research, 94*, 145–162.

Halsted, J. W. (2002). *Some of my best friends are books: Guiding gifted readers from preschool to high school* (2nd ed.). Scottsdale, AZ: Great Potential Press.

Kaufer, D. S., Geisler, C. D., & Neuwirth, C. M. (1989). *Arguing from sources: Exploring issues from reading and writing.* New York, NY: Harcourt Brace Jovanovich.

Kaye, S. M., & Thomson, P. (2007). *Philosophy for teens: Questioning life's big ideas.* Waco, TX: Prufrock Press.

Lucas, S. E. (1986). *The art of public speaking* (2nd ed.). New York, NY: Random House.

Marzano, R. J. (1991). *Cultivating thinking in English and the language arts.* Urbana, IL: National Council of Teachers of English.

McKeague, P. (2005). *Writing about literature: Step by step* (8th ed.). Dubuque, IA: Kendall/Hunt.

Miller, R. K. (1992). *The informed argument: A multidisciplinary reader and guide* (3rd ed.). Fort Worth, TX: Harcourt Brace Jovanovich.

Norton, D. E. (1982). Using a webbing process to develop children's literature units. *Language Arts, 59*, 348–356.

Parnes, S. J. (1975). *Aha! Insights into creative behavior.* Buffalo, NY: DOK Publishers.

Paul, R. (1992). *Critical thinking: What every person needs to survive in a rapidly changing world.* Sonoma, CA: Foundation for Critical Thinking.

Paul, R., Binker, A. J. A., Jensen, K., & Kreklau, H. (1990). *Critical thinking handbook: 4th–6th grades. A guide for remodeling lesson plans in language arts, social studies, and science.* Rohnert Park, CA: Sonoma State University, Center for Critical Thinking.

Polette, N. (2001). *The research book for gifted programs K–8* (Rev. ed.). Marion, IL: Pieces of Learning.

Reading Manipulatives. (n.d.). *Latin roots match-ups.* Phoenix, AZ: Author.

Rottenberg, A. T., & Winchell, D. H. (2008). *Elements of argument: A text and reader* (9th ed.). Boston, MA: Bedford Books.

Swicord, B. (1984). Debating with gifted fifth and sixth graders—Telling it like it was, is, and could be. *Gifted Child Quarterly, 28,* 127–129.

Taylor, B. M., Peterson, D. S., Pearson, P. D., & Rodriguez, M. C. (2002). Looking inside classrooms: Reflecting on the "how" as well as the "what" in effective reading instruction. *The Reading Teacher, 56,* 270–279.

Thompson, M. C. (1995). *Classics in the classroom.* Unionville, NY: Royal Fireworks Press.

Thompson, M. C. (1995). *Word within the word III.* Unionville, NY: Royal Fireworks Press.

Thompson, M. C. (2001). *Magic lens I.* Unionville, NY: Royal Fireworks Press.

Thompson, M. C. (2002). *Grammar island.* Unionville, NY: Royal Fireworks Press.

Thompson, M. C. (2002). *Magic lens II.* Unionville, NY: Royal Fireworks Press.

Thompson, M. C. (2003). *Caesar's English II.* Unionville, NY: Royal Fireworks Press.

Thompson, M. C. (2003). *Grammar town.* Unionville, NY: Royal Fireworks Press.

Thompson, M. C. (2003). *Grammar voyage.* Unionville, NY: Royal Fireworks Press.

Thompson, M. C. (2003). *Magic lens III.* Unionville, NY: Royal Fireworks Press.

Thompson, M. C. (2003). *Word within the word I.* Unionville, NY: Royal Fireworks Press.

Thompson, M. C. (2003). *Word within the word II.* Unionville, NY: Royal Fireworks Press.

Thompson, M. C., & Thompson, M. B. (2001). *Caesar's English I.* Unionville, NY: Royal Fireworks Press.

Thomson, P. (2009). *The Old Testament for teens: A guide to critical issues and perspectives.* Waco, TX: Prufrock Press.

Toulmin, S., Rieke, R., & Janik, A. (1979). *An introduction to reasoning.* New York, NY: Macmillan.

VanTassel-Baska, J., Johnson, D. T., & Boyce, L. N. (Eds.). (1996). *Developing verbal talent: Ideas and strategies for teachers of elementary and middle school students.* Boston, MA: Allyn & Bacon.

VanTassel-Baska, J., Zuo, L., Avery, L.D., & Little, C.A. (2002). A curriculum study of gifted-student learning in the language arts. *Gifted Child Quarterly, 46,* 30–44.

VanTassel-Baska, J., & Stambaugh, T. (2008). *Jacob's ladder reading comprehension program, Level 1.* Waco, TX: Prufrock Press.

VanTassel-Baska, J., & Stambaugh, T. (2008). *Jacob's ladder reading comprehension program, Level 2.* Waco, TX: Prufrock Press.

VanTassel-Baska, J., & Stambaugh, T. (2008). *Jacob's ladder reading comprehension program, Level 3.* Waco, TX: Prufrock Press.

Villaume, S. K., & Brabham, E. G. (2002). Comprehension instruction: Beyond strategies. *The Reading Teacher, 55,* 672–676.

White, D. A. (2005). *The examined life: Advanced philosophy for kids.* Waco, TX: Prufrock Press.

Mathematics

Assouline, S., & Lupkowski-Shoplik, A. (2005). *Developing math talent: A guide for educating gifted and advanced learners in math.* Waco, TX: Prufrock Press.

Bank Street College Project in Science and Mathematics. (1995). *Maya math* [Computer software]. Pleasantville, NY: Sunburst/WINGS for Learning.

Barbeau, E. J., & Taylor, P. J. (2009). *Challenging mathematics in and beyond the classroom: The 16th ICMI Study.* New York, NY: Springer.

Burger, E., & Starbird, M. (2009). *The heart of mathematics: An invitation to effective thinking* (3rd ed.). New York, NY: Wiley.

Gavin, M. K., Chapin, S. H., Dailey, J., & Sheffield, L. J. (2006). *Project M3: Level 3: Awesome algebra: Looking for patterns and generalizations.* Dubuque, IA: Kendall/Hunt.

Gavin, M. K., Chapin, S. H., Dailey, J., & Sheffield, L. J. (2006). *Project M3: Level 3: Digging for data: The search within research.* Dubuque, IA: Kendall/Hunt.

Gavin, M. K., Chapin, S. H., Dailey, J., & Sheffield, L. J. (2006). *Project M3: Level 3: Unraveling the mystery of the MoLi Stone: Place value and numeration.* Dubuque, IA: Kendall/Hunt.

Gavin, M. K., Chapin, S. H., Dailey, J., & Sheffield, L. J. (2006). *Project M3: Level 3: What's the me in measurement all about?* Dubuque, IA: Kendall/Hunt.

Gavin, M. K., Chapin, S. H., Dailey, J., & Sheffield, L. J. (2007). *Project M3: Level 4: Analyze this! Representing and interpreting data.* Dubuque, IA: Kendall/Hunt.

Gavin, M. K., Chapin, S. H., Dailey, J., & Sheffield, L. J. (2007). *Project M3: Level 4: At the mall with algebra: Working with equations and variables.* Dubuque, IA: Kendall/Hunt.

Gavin, M. K., Chapin, S. H., Dailey, J., & Sheffield, L. J. (2008). *Project M3: Level 5: Record makers and breakers: Using algebra to analyze change.* Dubuque, IA: Kendall/Hunt.

Gavin, M. K., Chapin, S. H., Dailey, J., & Sheffield, L. J. (2008). *Project M3: Level 5: Treasures from the attic: Exploring fractions.* Dubuque, IA: Kendall/Hunt.

Jacobs, H. (1994). *Mathematics: A human endeavor* (3rd ed.). New York, NY: W. H. Freeman.

Johnson, D. T. (2008). *Beyond base ten: A mathematics unit for high-ability learners in grades 3–6.* Waco, TX: Prufrock Press.

Johnson, D. T. (2008). *Spatial reasoning: A mathematics unit for high-ability learners in grades 2-4.* Waco, TX: Prufrock Press.

Johnson, D. T. (2010). *Moving through dimensions: A mathematics unit for high-ability learners in grades 6-8.* Waco, TX: Prufrock Press.

Katzoff, S. (1992). *Twists and turns and tangles in math and physics: Instructional material for developing scientific & logical thinking.* Baltimore, MD: Johns Hopkins University Center for Talented Youth.

SET Enterprises. (n.d.). *SET* [Card game]. Fountain Hills, AZ: SET Enterprises. Available at http://www.setgame.com

Sheffield, L. J. (2003). *Extending the challenge in mathematics: Developing mathematical promise in K–8 students.* Thousand Oaks, CA: Corwin Press.

Serra, M. (2007). *Discovering geometry: An investigative approach* (4th ed.). Emeryville, CA: Key Curriculum Press.

Sobel, M. A., & Maletsky, E. M. (1998). *Teaching mathematics: A sourcebook of aids, activities, and strategies* (3rd ed.). New York, NY: Allyn & Bacon.

The University of Chicago School Mathematics Project. (1995). *Transition mathematics* (2nd ed.). Glenview, IL: Scott, Foresman.

Science

Center for Gifted Education. (1997). *Guide to teaching a problem-based science curriculum.* Dubuque, IA: Kendall/Hunt.

Center for Gifted Education. (2007). *Acid, acid everywhere: Exploring chemical, ecological, and transportation systems* (2nd ed.). Dubuque, IA: Kendall/Hunt.

Center for Gifted Education. (2007). *Animal populations: A study of physical, conceptual, and mathematical models* (2nd ed.). Dubuque, IA: Kendall/Hunt.

Center for Gifted Education. (2007). *Electricity city: Designing an electrical system* (2nd ed.). Dubuque, IA: Kendall/Hunt.

Center for Gifted Education. (2007). *No quick fix: Exploring human body systems* (2nd ed.). Dubuque, IA: Kendall/Hunt.

Center for Gifted Education. (2007). *Nuclear energy: Friend or foe? Examining nuclear power from a systems perspective* (2nd ed.). Dubuque, IA: Kendall/Hunt.

Center for Gifted Education. (2007). *Something fishy: Exploring an aquatic ecosystem* (2nd ed.). Dubuque, IA: Kendall/Hunt.

Center for Gifted Education. (2007). *What a find! Analyzing natural and cultural systems* (2nd ed.). Dubuque, IA: Kendall/Hunt.

Center for Gifted Education. (2007). *Where's the beach? Examining coastal erosion* (2nd ed.). Dubuque, IA: Kendall/Hunt.

Center for Gifted Education. (2008). *Water works: A physical science unit for high-ability learners in grades K–1.* Waco, TX: Prufrock Press.

Center for Gifted Education. (2008). *What's the matter? A physical science unit for high-ability learners in grades 2–3.* Waco, TX: Prufrock Press.

Center for Gifted Education. (2010). *Budding botanists: A life science unit for high-ability learners in grades 1–2.* Waco, TX: Prufrock Press.

Center for Gifted Education. (2010). *Dig it! A life science unit for high-ability learners in grades 1–2.* Waco, TX: Prufrock Press.

Center for Gifted Education. (2010). *How the sun makes our day: An earth and space science unit for high-ability learners in grades K–1* Waco, TX: Prufrock Press.

Center for Gifted Education. (2010). *Invitation to invent: A physical science unit for high-ability learners in grade 3.* Waco, TX: Prufrock Press.

Center for Gifted Education. (2010). *Survive and thrive: A life science unit for high-ability learners in grades K–1.* Waco, TX: Prufrock Press.

Center for Gifted Education. (2010). *Weather reporter: An earth and space science unit for high-ability learners in grade 2.* Waco, TX: Prufrock Press.

Center for Gifted Education. (n.d.). *The curriculum assessment guide to science materials.* Williamsburg, VA: Author.

Cothron, J. H., Giese, R. N., & Rezba, R. J. (2000). *Students and research: Practical strategies for science classrooms and competitions* (3rd ed.). Dubuque, IA: Kendall/Hunt.

Cothron, J. H., Giese, R. N., & Rezba, R. J. (2000). *Science experiments and projects for students* (3rd ed.). Dubuque, IA: Kendall/Hunt.

Lawrence Hall of Science. (1990–present). *Full option science system* (FOSS). Berkeley, CA: The Regents of the University of California. Available at http://www.delta-education.com/fossgallery.aspx?subID=&menuID=2

Lawrence Hall of Science. (1990–present). *Great explorations in math and science (GEMS).* Berkeley, CA: The Regents of the University of California. Available at http://lawrencehallofscience.org/gems/gemsguides.html

National Science Resources Center. (1991–present). *Science and technology for children* (STC). Burlington, NC: Author. Available at http://www.nap.edu/catalog/nsrc/index.html

Sher, B. T. (2003). *Notes from a scientist: Resources and activities for gifted children* (2nd ed.). Williamsburg, VA: Center for Gifted Education.

Sher, B. T. (2004). *A guide to key science concepts* (2nd ed.). Williamsburg, VA: Center for Gifted Education.

Social Studies

Bronowski, J. (1973). *The ascent of man.* Boston, MA: Little, Brown.

Bruner, J. S. (1968). *Man: A course of study (MACOS).* Washington, DC: Education Development Center.

Center for Gifted Education. (2003). *A house divided? The Civil War: Its causes and effects.* Dubuque, IA: Kendall/Hunt.

Center for Gifted Education. (2003). *Ancient China: The middle kingdom.* Dubuque, IA: Kendall/Hunt.

Center for Gifted Education. (2003). *Ancient Egypt: Gift of the Nile.* Dubuque, IA: Kendall/Hunt.

Center for Gifted Education. (2003). *Building a new system: Colonial America 1607–1763.* Dubuque, IA: Kendall/Hunt.

Center for Gifted Education. (2003). *The 1920s in America: A decade of tensions.* Dubuque, IA: Kendall/Hunt.

Center for Gifted Education. (2003). *The 1930s in America: Facing depression.* Dubuque, IA: Kendall/Hunt.

Center for Gifted Education. (2003). *The road to the White House: Electing the American President.* Dubuque, IA: Kendall/Hunt.

Center for Gifted Education. (2003). *The world turned upside down: The American Revolution.* Dubuque, IA: Kendall/Hunt.

Center for Gifted Education. (2005). *The Renaissance and Reformation in Europe.* Dubuque, IA: Kendall/Hunt.

Center for Gifted Education. (2006). *Defining nations: Cultural identity and political tensions.* Dubuque, IA: Kendall/Hunt.

Center for Gifted Education. (2006). *Primary sources and historical analysis.* Dubuque, IA: Kendall/Hunt.

Center for Gifted Education. (2007). *Guide to teaching social studies curriculum*. Dubuque, IA: Kendall/Hunt.

Clark, K. (1969). *Civilization*. New York, NY: Harper & Row.

Nisbet, R. (1980). *History of the idea of progress*. New York, NY: Basic Books.

Ravitch, D. (Ed.). (1990). *The American reader: Words that moved a nation*. New York, NY: Harper Perennial.

Ravitch, D., & Themstrom, A. (Eds.). (1992). *The democracy reader: Classic and modern speeches, essays, poems, declarations, and documents on freedom and human rights worldwide*. New York, NY: Harper Perennial.

Roleff, T. L. (Ed.). (2003). *Immigration: Opposing viewpoints*. San Diego, CA: Greenhaven Press.

CONCLUSION

Sound curriculum development requires incredible investments of time, energy, and expertise. Furthermore, curricular units that are created by individual teachers often are underdeveloped and idiosyncratic to the extent that other teachers cannot use them effectively. It is our firm belief that it should not be necessary to reinvent the curriculum wheel, particularly for every academic bandwagon that rolls down the road. In fact, it often is a more efficient use of resources to select and integrate materials that have been successfully reviewed by district staff.

Having a prescribed set of criteria to use in curricular review facilitates the implementation of the process. Furthermore, the phasing in of the use of these criteria through three stages allows staff members to discard materials that fail to meet the criteria in the early stages of the process. Even as an aid to individual teachers charged with purchasing materials while attending conferences and exhibits, these criteria can help focus one's thinking about important elements of appropriate resources and materials for high-ability learners.

The use of criteria also serves other purposes for teachers. Because several new curriculum units were designed to embrace the content standards, it is easier for teachers to see the match between the objectives of their instruction and the product that is under consideration.

The good news is that the resources available to address the needs of advanced learners have become more relevant and sophisticated as the tenets of educational reform have begun to impact the whole educational system. Major initiatives to recognize and address the needs of gifted students have occurred in the last decade. The Center for Gifted Education's curriculum work has led the way in developing and improving the materials available for use with gifted students. Curriculum units developed by the Center for Gifted Education are designed around the criteria discussed in this chapter, and many of these units have demonstrated empirical learning gains with high-ability students.

Also worthy of mention is an initiative launched in 1996 by NAGC's Curriculum Studies Network. This initiative created a competition process to select exemplary gifted curriculum units based on a rubric that is employed by a panel of professionals. This rubric is based on 12 key features (Purcell, Burns, Tomlinson, Imbeau, & Martin, 2002). Each year at its annual conference, NAGC announces the winners of this competition and provides an opportunity for attendees to meet the authors and review the curricula. All of the William and Mary units that have been submitted for this competition have been selected as winners, but other curriculum units also have received this accolade. One of the strong features of this NAGC initiative is that it has called attention to the importance of the link between a theoretical model and its translation into a clearly articulated and structured classroom game plan. Although the curriculum work of the Center for Gifted Education emanated from the Integrated Curriculum Model (VanTassel-Baska, 1986), other award-winning units are derived from different models including the Kaplan Grid (Kaplan, 1986), the Renzulli Multiple Menu Model (Renzulli, Leppien, & Hays, 2000), and the Parallel Curriculum Model (Tomlinson et al., 2002).

In selecting any curriculum product, particularly those that are the cornerstones of the classroom experience, decisions should be made on the basis of a close examination of the product itself, not a stamp of approval or endorsement from an external source. By selecting products that are coherent, challenging, and educationally defensible, one builds a strong foundation for the instructional process. The integrity of these decisions can impact the quality of the program, the investment students are willing to make in their own learning, the instructional expertise of the teachers involved, and the support of parents for the programs. These judgments should not be taken lightly.

KEY POINTS SUMMARY

- The introduction of content standards in the core curriculum areas has been a catalyst for educational reform that has impacted classroom instruction. Because of federally mandated testing requirements in the No Child Left Behind legislation, reading and mathematics instruction have become the central focus of most school district programs, resulting in diminished time for science and social studies.
- In the last decade, many new educational materials, particularly the William and Mary curriculum units, have been produced to address these content standards and to incorporate student assessment techniques to measure learning.
- It often makes more sense to select materials that have already been devel-

oped and tested with gifted learners than to create curricular materials from scratch.

- The use of a structured checklist can aid both in examining materials and in making decisions about materials and resources.
- Three phases have been suggested for conducting such a review. Phase 1 focuses on general curricular design features, Phase 2 on exemplary content area emphases, and Phase 3 on essential elements for high-ability learners.
- Although the review process is sequenced so that time is allocated to the most promising materials, a holistic perspective should be taken when choosing among potential texts or resources.
- We must continue to press publishers to supply data on curriculum effectiveness in order to stay focused on the right questions in making resource decisions.

REFERENCES

Adler, S., Dougan, A., & Garcia, J. (2006). NCATE has a lot to say to future social studies teachers: A response to Sam Wineburg. *Phi Delta Kappan, 87,* 396–400.

Bettis, N. C. (2004). Illinois school reform and the social sciences: 1985 to the present. *Social Studies, 95,* 239–242.

Boyle, B, & Bragg, J. (2005). No science today—The demise of primary science. *Curriculum Journal, 16,* 423–437.

Bybee, R. W., & Van Scotter, P. (2007). Reinventing the science curriculum. *Educational Leadership, 64*(4), 43–47.

Cavanagh, S. (2005). As test date looms, educators renewing emphasis on science. *Education Week, 24*(29), 1–2.

Cavanagh, S. (2007). State tests, NAEP often a mismatch: Bars defining "proficient" unaligned, study shows. *Education Week, 26*(4), 1–2.

Center for Civic Education. (1994). *National standards for civics and government.* Calabasas, CA: Author.

Center for Gifted Education. (1997). *Guide to teaching a problem-based science curriculum.* Dubuque, IA: Kendall/Hunt.

Center for Gifted Education. (1999). *Guide to teaching a language arts curriculum for high-ability learners.* Dubuque, IA: Kendall/Hunt.

Duschl, R. A., Shouse, A. W., & Schweingruber, H. A. (2008). What research says about K–8 science learning and teaching. *Educational Digest, 73*(8), 46–50.

Evans, R. W., & Pang, V. (1995). National standards for United States history: The storm of controversy continues. *Social Studies, 86,* 270–274.

Gregory, T. (2000). *Social studies curricula for gifted learners in elementary and middle school* (Unpublished master's thesis). The College of William and Mary, Williamsburg, VA.

Hinde, E. R. (2005). Revisiting curriculum integration: A fresh look at an old idea. *Social Studies, 96,* 105–111.

International Reading Association, & National Council of Teachers of English. (1996). *Standards for the English language arts*. Urbana, IL: Authors.

Johnson, D., Boyce, L. N., & VanTassel-Baska, J. (1995). Science curriculum review: Evaluating materials for high-ability learners. *Gifted Child Quarterly, 39,* 36–43.

Johnson, D. T., & Sher, B. T. (1997). *Resource guide to mathematics curriculum materials for high-ability learners in grades K–8*. Williamsburg, VA: Center for Gifted Education, The College of William and Mary.

Kaplan, S. N. (1986). The grid: A model to construct differentiated curriculum for the gifted. In J. S. Renzulli (Ed.), *Systems and models for developing programs for the gifted and talented* (pp. 180–193). Mansfield Center, CT: Creative Learning Press.

Kenney, M. (2004). The implementation of the national geography standards in Colorado: To everything there is a season. *Social Studies, 95,* 247–249.

Little, C. A., Feng, A. X., VanTassel-Baska, J., Rogers, K. B., & Avery, L. D. (2007). A study of curriculum effectiveness in social studies. *Gifted Child Quarterly, 51,* 272–284.

Lockwood, A. (1992). Whose knowledge do we teach? *Focus on Change, 6,* 3–7.

National Center for Education Statistics. (1996). *Pursuing excellence: A study of U.S. eighth-grade mathematics and science teaching, learning, curriculum, and achievement in international context* (NCES 97–198). Washington, DC: U.S. Government Printing Office.

National Center for Education Statistics. (1997). *Pursuing excellence: A study of U.S. fourth-grade mathematics and science achievement in international context* (NCES 97–255). Washington, DC: U.S. Government Printing Office.

National Center for Education Statistics. (1998). *Pursuing excellence: A study of U. S. twelfth-grade mathematics and science achievement in international context* (NCES 98–049). Washington, DC: U.S. Government Printing Office.

National Center for Education Statistics. (2004). *Trends in international mathematics and science study* (TIMSS) 2003. (NCES 2005005). Washington, DC: U.S. Government Printing Office.

National Council for the Social Studies. (1994). *Expectations of excellence: Curriculum standards for social studies*. Silver Springs, MD: Author.

National Council of Teachers of Mathematics. (2000). *Principles and standards for school mathematics*. Reston, VA: Author.

No Child Left Behind Act, 20 U.S.C. §6301 (2001).

Olwell, R., & Raphael, N. (2006). The problems of elementary social studies: Are curricular and assessment sprawl to blame? *Social Studies, 95,* 222–224.

Purcell, J. H., Burns, D. E., Tomlinson, C. A., Imbeau, M. B., & Martin, J. L. (2002). Bridging the gap: A tool and technique to analyze and evaluate gifted education curricular units. *Gifted Child Quarterly, 46,* 306–321.

Renzulli, J. S., Leppien, J. L., & Hays, T. S. (2000). *The Multiple Menu Model: A practical guide for developing differentiated curriculum.* Mansfield Center, CT: Creative Learning Press.

Risinger, C. F. (2006). Teaching what we should be teaching using the Internet. *Social Education, 70,* 197–198.

Sandmann, A. L. (2002). *Linking literature with life: The NCSS standards and children's literature for the middle grades.* Silver Springs, MD: National Council for the Social Studies.

Saunders, R. M. (1996). National standards for United States history. *Social Studies, 87*, 63–67.

Saxe, D. W. (1995). The national history standards: Time for common sense. *Social Education, 60*, 44–48.

Schmidt, W. H., Wang, H. C., & McKnight, C. C. (2005). Curriculum convergence: An examination of US mathematics and science content standards from an international perspective. *Journal of Curriculum Studies, 37*, 525–559.

Tomlinson, C. A., Kaplan, S. N., Renzulli, J. S., Purcell, J., Leppien, J., & Burns, D. (2002). *The parallel curriculum: A design to develop high potential to challenge high-ability learners.* Thousand Oaks, CA: Corwin Press.

VanFossen, P. J. (2005). Reading and math take so much of the time: An overview of social studies instruction in elementary classrooms in Indiana. *Theory and Research in Social Education, 33*, 376–403.

VanTassel-Baska, J. (1986). Effective curriculum and instructional models for the gifted. *Gifted Child Quarterly, 30*, 164–169.

VanTassel-Baska, J. (Ed.). (1998). *Excellence in educating gifted and talented learners* (3rd ed.). Denver, CO: Love.

VanTassel-Baska, J. (2003). *Curriculum planning and instructional design for gifted learners.* Denver, CO: Love.

VanTassel-Baska, J., Bass, G., Ries, R., Poland, D., & Avery, L. (1998). A national pilot study of science curriculum effectiveness for high ability students. *Gifted Child Quarterly, 42*, 200–211.

VanTassel-Baska, J., Bracken, B. A., Stambaugh, T., & Feng, A. (2007, September). *Findings from Project Clarion.* Presentation to the United States Department of Education Expert Panel, Storrs, CT.

VanTassel-Baska, J., & Johnsen, S. K. (2007). Teacher education standards for the field of gifted education: A vision of coherence for personnel preparation in the 21st century. *Gifted Child Quarterly, 51*, 182–205.

VanTassel-Baska, J., Zuo, L., Avery, L. D., & Little, C. A. (2002). A curriculum study of gifted-student learning in the language arts. *Gifted Child Quarterly, 46*, 30–44.

Weaver, P. E. (2004). The culture of teaching and mentoring for compliance *Childhood Education, 80*, 258–261.

Wheeler, G. F. (2007). Strategies for science education reform. *Educational Leadership, 64*(4), 30–34.

Whelan, M. (1995). Right for the wrong reasons: National history standards. *Social Education, 60*, 55–57.

Yager, R. E., & Enger, S. (2006). *Exemplary science preK–4: Standards-based success stories.* Arlington, VA: National Science Teachers Association.

Chapter 15

Learning From and Learning With Technology

Del Siegle and Melissa S. Mitchell

Y*ou are a gifted resource teacher in your middle school, which has received some extensive technology upgrades through grant funding and district-wide technology initiatives. You have experimented with some of these resources with your gifted students, and you have been asked to provide some support to your fellow teachers in learning about the available resources and how to integrate them into instruction and how to use them to support differentiation. Where will you begin?*

Although curriculum development and differentiation in general are of paramount interest and importance to educators of the gifted, the place of technology within that overall endeavor is undoubtedly an issue that ranks high in interest and concern. Technological innovations touch all aspects of our lives. Not only are new technologies emerging every day, older technologies are being combined in new ways (Siegle, 2005b). Technology is changing the way we work, how we communicate with each other, and how we learn. Within a context of developing, selecting, and implementing content-based curriculum for high-ability learners, such as curriculum developed under the Integrated Curriculum Model (ICM), technology presents (a) extensive sources for access to more advanced content, as well as communication with experts in the disciplines; (b) contexts for developing and applying critical and creative thinking skills; and (c) tools for constructing and sharing sophisticated products. Moreover, technology supports exploration of abstract concepts and their interdisciplinary applications, providing students a wider vista in which to recognize those concepts and a broader canvas on which to convey their understandings.

The purpose of this chapter is to share how educators of the gifted and talented can use technology to enhance their students' gifts and talents, both by building their knowledge of and skill with technological tools and by using such tools to promote learning and creative productivity across all content areas. We begin by describing how students today differ from their predecessors in terms of their attitudes toward and use of technology. We review a brief history of technology use in education and describe the importance of professional development in integrating technology into the classroom. We then provide a rationale for using technology with gifted and talented students, and we share some ways to enhance student learning through technology.

LEARNERS TODAY AND TECHNOLOGY

Call them "Generation M" (Kaiser Family Foundation, 2005), "Generation Me" (Twenge & Campbell, 2009), or "Gen Mobile" (Breck, 2007). Call them "digital natives" (Prensky, 2001). Whatever we call them, today's students live in a world in which being plugged into technology is a way of life. Almost every part of their lives has some root in the technological revolution. They watch digital TV, they talk and text on digital mobile phones, they surf the digital Internet, they listen to digital music and watch digital movies on their iPods, and they document their experiences with digital photos and videos. They communicate through technology; they are plugged into their iPhones, their mp3 players, their Xboxes, their social networking sites, and their virtual reality.

Not only are today's students surrounded by technology, they are using it more often, more skillfully, and in different ways than their predecessors. Unlike many of their teachers, today's students do not see technology as a complex addition but rather an integral part of their lives and learning environment (Besnoy, Housand, & Clarke, 2009). They spend more than 6 hours each day accessing a variety of media (Kaiser Family Foundation, 2005). This amounts to almost as much time as would be spent at a full-time job (Owston, 2009). However, most of the time students spend using technology is spent at home—outside of school (Lenhart, Arafeh, Smith, & Macgill, 2008; Macgill, 2007)—in part because many schools have not embraced the digital revolution nor incorporated it extensively into their classrooms. Project Tomorrow (2009) noted:

> [S]urveys collected for the past six years as well as student and educator focus groups conducted across the nation have consistently shown that students, for the most part, more readily embrace the use of technology than their parents, teachers or principals. Students openly acknowledge that they have to "power down" when they enter the schoolhouse, and then "power back up" to resume their technoinfused lives outside of school. (p. 1)

In order to promote connections between today's "digital native" learners and the classroom instruction they experience, schools must consider ways of incorporating technology more extensively. Not to do so is to ask students to flourish in an environment of outdated information and unfriendly learning spaces that are comfortable and familiar to one generation, but awkward and foreign to another. Moreover, providing greater technology integration helps to ensure a learning experience for students that is more authentic to their own ways of approaching knowledge acquisition, interpersonal interactions, and problem solving through the use of technological tools.

TECHNOLOGY EVOLUTION IN EDUCATION

Over the past three decades, educators have progressed through three distinct stages of computer use in the classroom (Valdez et al., 2000). Initially, educators saw computers as an opportunity to automate print, most frequently as self-correcting worksheets. Drill and practice and tutorial programs abounded. Although these innovations in the early 1980s lessened a teacher's burden of correcting papers and provided students with immediate feedback, they did little to promote student innovation and creativity or to advance integration with the curriculum.

In the 1990s, a shift occurred in technology use in education. Driven by the development of productivity tools for business, educators shifted computer use in the classroom from a delivery instrument to a productivity tool. Word processing was the first of these tools to become a staple of educational computing. Spreadsheets and presentation tools followed, and the emergence of the Internet began to change processes of information-gathering and communication. Tools for developing more professional-looking and innovative products, including sound and video as well as posters, documents, and web pages, opened opportunities for student creativity in developing and sharing their ideas. Students were able to collect data from a variety of online sources, analyze and organize their information, and create impressive multimedia projects that communicated their understanding of the material.

The third phase, which features data-driven virtual learning, is now in its infancy. With this phase, students combine a number of technology skills for a set purpose. The key feature is data collection and analysis for a strategic purpose in a particular contextual setting and content area. Digital data are expected to surge fivefold in the next 3 years, which opens new worlds of discovery for data sleuths (Lohr, 2009). Knowing how to find and use data to address problems will be the paramount 21st-century skill.

The first phase of technology use that we described above represents "learning *from* technology" (Reeves, 1999). Learning from technology implies that the students are passive players in a learning process in which technology is used to teach or remediate basic skills. Typically, technology in this arena consists mainly of computer tutors or learning/CD-ROM software; technology that falls into this category most often includes older equipment, pre-Internet software, and very basic software packages. These types of technologies often are referred to as "Web 1.0," meaning that they were the first generation of technological tools.

The second and third phases described above fall under the "learning *with* technology" umbrella (Reeves, 1999). Learning with technology implies that students are active participants in the learning process. The learning with technology category employs computers as a medium through which students can access a wealth of other knowledge. Learning with technology describes the usage of all forms of technology, not just computers, in ways that ensure that the student is an active participant in the learning process. These types of technologies often are referred to as "Web 2.0," the second and current generation of technology. In this chapter, we will concentrate on learning with technology.

TEACHERS' USE OF TECHNOLOGY AFFECTS HOW STUDENTS USE TECHNOLOGY

For technology tools to be most effective in the classroom, teachers must be willing and able to incorporate those tools purposefully into the curriculum. In order for that to happen, beyond the clear need for availability of the tools in the first place, teachers must feel comfortable not only with the technology itself, but with their own ability to use and share it.

Professional development is an integral component of successful technology integration in the classroom (Penuel, Korbak, Yarnall, & Pacpaco, 2001; Wenglinsky, 1998). Staples, Pugach, and Himes (2005) reported that before teachers can fully integrate technology, three essential factors need to be in place: (a) administrative and technical support, (b) adequate resources to support technology, and (c) teacher leadership to advocate for, demonstrate, and evaluate technology.

Some studies have shown that a blended approach to professional development for technology integration is most successful. This approach includes professional development workshops, curricular examples, and a peer-support system (Penuel et al., 2001; Voogt, Almekinders, van den Akker, & Moonen, 2005). Peer-support systems are effective and should not be overlooked (Parr, 1999; Zhao & Frank, 2003). Providing teachers with opportunities to explore applications and to work with peers on the integration of those applications will increase technology use in the classroom (Voogt at al., 2005; Zhao & Frank, 2003). As do most people, teachers need time to experiment with a new technology to develop a comfort level with its operation. Providing laptops for teachers to take home is one example of a way to improve teachers' comfort level with a technology (Parr, 1999; Somekh, Mavers, & Lewin, 2002), and an improved comfort level increases the likelihood that technology will be integrated into the classroom environment (Wenglinsky, 1998).

The number of tools and initiatives introduced within a given span of time also affects level of integration. Zhao and Frank (2003) recommended that administrators limit the number of innovations they introduce at any given time. Limiting the number of new technologies that come onto the scene will allow those innovations to be given more resources and receive more use. Teachers will gain experience and thereby be more able to use them in the classroom.

Schools increase technology use when they (a) provide adequate professional development (both group and individual time), including time for teachers to apply the technology in their own setting; (b) allow teachers personal access to computers that they can take home and explore on their own in order to develop their confidence and skill levels; and (c) establish a peer and administrative support network through which teachers can solicit information and assistance as well as be assured that technology efforts will be supported administratively and financially.

Another support for professional learning about technology tools may come from teachers' own students. Some teachers may find that classroom roles will be reversed when they are exploring new technology tools (Rossman, 1984; Siegle, 2005b); many students relish the opportunity to assist a teacher with technology. Teachers may want to consider the implementation of a SWAT team (Students Working to Advance Technology; SWAT, 2002) of students who serve as technology assistants, as it will prove beneficial to both students (by allowing them to showcase their talents) and to teachers (by providing them with willing and able tech support).

WHAT TECHNOLOGY SKILLS DO STUDENTS NEED?

Many of today's students have learned to search for, evaluate, and analyze information online outside of the school context; others learn very quickly once presented with new technology tools. Through social networking they are expanding their view of the world and are learning to socialize, communicate, and exchange ideas with people from around the globe. Through their use of the Internet and other open-source media, they are learning not only programming but also the principles of economic supply and demand. Many can record, edit, and produce impressive multimedia productions. Students learn through trial and error how to navigate the information pathways they explore to find what they need and how to use the tools available to them; as in any learning context, some students develop these skills more quickly and ably than others. In fact, some researchers (O'Brien & Friedman-Nimz, 2006; O'Brien, Friedman-Nimz, Lacey, & Denson, 2005; Siegle, 2007a) have proposed a type of giftedness focusing on technology. Technological giftedness appears to manifest itself in three distinct ways: those who excel at writing computer code (programmers), those who excel at using software (interfacers), and those who excel at working with the actual technology equipment (fixers; Friedman-Nimz, personal communication, April 23, 2006).

So, what technology skills should gifted students have, whether technologically gifted or not, and what role should schools play in developing those skills? Moreover, how can technology emphases be integrated with other premises of good curriculum for advanced learners?

As in each of the specific content areas addressed earlier in this text, attention to technology in the curriculum for advanced learners should echo the important elements of good curriculum overall as well as the specific strengths and needs of advanced learners. Several professional organizations have provided guidance in the development of significant learner outcomes in the area of technology.

Partnership for 21st Century Skills

A popular set of standards related to technology learning are the 21st century learning skills, which were compiled by the Partnership for 21st Century Skills (2007). Not only do students need to have a basic competency in core subjects, they also need to be able to integrate these with 21st-century interdisciplinary themes (awareness of global issues and literacy in economics, business, entrepreneurship, civics, and health). Such themes represent outgrowths of major overarching concepts as outlined in Chapter 7 and in the specific content chapters of this text. As technology grows, the world shrinks; knowledge of how that world works then becomes increasingly more important. The use of technology also is said to develop "soft skills" such as flexibility, initiative, adaptability, and self-direction. These skills are necessary for successfully navigating the increasingly complex global environment (Partnership for 21st Century Skills, 2007), with its rapid changes and abundance of information.

Not only must students know how to employ the information technology at their fingertips effectively, they need to know how to be savvy consumers of that information. They must be literate in the information they are using, the media they utilize to find that information, and the means by which they are communicating with one another.

International Society for Technology in Education

The International Society for Technology in Education (ISTE, 2007) also has recommended a set of standards and performance indicators for students. In a technology-driven society, ISTE has suggested that all curricula reinforce the ideas of creativity, communication, and high-level thinking skills, as well as digital citizenship and technological capabilities. ISTE (2008) has encouraged teachers to "facilitate and inspire student learning and creativity . . .; design and develop digital age learning experiences and assessments . . .; model digital age work and learning . . .; promote and model digital citizenship and responsibility . . .; and engage in professional growth and leadership" (p. 1).

The above standards provide some key components of technology use and skills that students should possess. They also address several common components that Davis, Rimm, and Siegle (2011) noted are evident in many curricular models for the gifted and talented; in addition to promoting critical and creative skills and problem solving, technology tools may be integrated to support advancing content and differentiation overall. Educators can use technology to enhance each of the following components of appropriate curriculum for the gifted:

- tasks often are differentiated to accommodate different skill levels and learning styles;
- content often is presented above grade level;
- a variety of creative and critical thinking skills are explicitly taught;
- the emotional needs of gifted students are addressed through group and individual options;
- curriculum often is built around general themes or "big ideas," which assists with differentiation;
- interdisciplinary curriculum provides for depth and complexity of thought; and
- authentic methodologies and products enhance student learning and motivation.

USING TECHNOLOGY TOOLS
TO ENHANCE LEARNING

Reflecting their identity as digital natives, many gifted and talented learners possess a large skill set pertaining directly to the new technologies and literacies (Prensky, 2006), as well as the capacity to learn how to use new technologies quickly. Gifted students' combination of advanced learning abilities in specific content areas, comfort with existing technology tools, and readiness to learn new tools easily suggests that many opportunities are possible for providing differentiated learning experiences through technology integration. In the remainder of this chapter, we will describe different tools and resources that can help educators purposefully incorporate technology into the classroom to enhance student learning and encourage talent development. The technologies are presented in five categories based on purpose for use: (a) as an information resource, (b) as an interactive learning tool, (c) as a communication tool, (d) as a production tool, and (e) as a tool for instruction and interaction in the classroom. Although some of the examples appear in more than one category, they will be discussed in each section according to the relevant ways of using them to support learning.

Technology as an Information Resource

New literacies. Technology is changing exponentially, and the information that is readily available online grows by the second. As the technology grows, so too does the need for students to develop skills to understand, synthesize, and employ the information that technology makes available to them (Leu, Kinzer, Coiro, & Cammack, 2004). These skills and the related strategies and dispositions related to reading, comprehending, and learning from the Internet are referred to as the "new literacies" and represent a growing field of study and research (Coiro, Knobel, Lankshear, & Leu, 2008).

The Internet removes many of the common information resource barriers that in the past have frequently created learning ceilings for gifted and talented students:

> The Internet . . . [has] the most extensive and accessible collection of information available to students. Since gifted and talented students require greater depth and breadth of information than other students, the Internet is an important resource for them. Many gifted students are passionate about esoteric topics, and they require advanced information that cannot be found in most school and local libraries. The Internet meets their quest for content related to their passion areas

above and beyond what is available in textbooks and local libraries. (Siegle, 2005a, p. 30)

The new literacies include facility with accessing, understanding, evaluating, and applying information from the Internet; in other words, students need to know how to find information, how to determine whether that information is accurate or reliable, and how to use and synthesize that information (Leu et al., 2004). This requires the use of both their technical skills and their critical and creative thinking skills as they navigate the information they encounter. Literacy in this form is paramount in today's society; before students can learn from the Internet and all of the related technological resources, they must develop the fundamental literacy skills necessary for that learning to occur.

Skills in evaluating content resources are especially relevant for gifted students who may be seeking levels of knowledge and understanding about a topic well beyond what their peers and even their teacher will explore; although teachers can exercise some control over the web resources students access in the classroom, students must develop skills in assessing the material they find on their own. McCoach (2002) suggested that students be taught to evaluate web content according to three criteria: reliability, authorship, and purpose. She proposed that students consider some of the following when evaluating web content:

- Has the web content been through any sort of review process?
- Does the site provide citations or references for print material that supports the information contained on the site?
- Does the site provide links to other reputable websites? Is the site listed within other reputable websites?
- Does the site provide contact information?
- Are the author's credentials provided on the site?
- Is the content on a personal web page, or is it on one that is associated with a reputable organization?

Students' capacity to determine answers to these types of questions is an important learning outcome that cuts across all content areas and bears implications for their lives beyond school.

Creating conceptual space. In addition to providing more information at a greater level of depth and complexity, technology also makes the information available quickly and fairly easily, provided that the students and their teachers are skilled in searching and selecting content. Having information readily available at the student's fingertips frees conceptual space, an individual's available mental data for solving a problem or task (Amabile, 1983, 1996). In other words, if a student is freed from the logistical and basic skill details of answering simple questions and finding foundational information, the student has more time and conceptual resources to think about the larger picture of a problem to be solved. With more and more information at their fingertips, students' need to retain mountains of facts through rote memorization is minimized. This allows for more time and space to be devoted to higher levels of thinking and problem solving.

Technology as an Interactive Learning Tool

Virtual learning environments. Students are increasingly flocking to the virtual world for entertainment, communication, and now for education. Virtual environments, such as Second Life (http://secondlife.com), Active Worlds (http://www.activeworlds.com), or SIMS (http://www.thesims3.com), can provide students with access to a wealth of content resources and simulated problem-solving activities, as well as many opportunities for creative exploration. For example, the widely popular Second Life provides students with opportunities to participate in health assessment simulations, fly into the depths of the solar system, become one with a cell, and even join National Oceanic and Atmospheric Administration (NOAA) experiments. Students also can observe classes or visit lectures from colleges and universities such as Harvard University, Ohio University, Bowling Green State University, Vassar College, and the University of Edinburgh.

Second Life was designed for users over the age of 18, and there are many more noneducational sites on the Second Life grid. Although the creators of Second Life monitor the grid for unwanted material, educators will want to proceed cautiously in this virtual world, and may wish to consider the alternative, Teen Second Life. Teen Second Life (http://teen.secondlife.com) was designed specifically for students under 18, and educators need to have special permission to take part in Teen Second Life. Second Life and Teen Second Life encourage students to learn programming and design basics. Libraries, universities, art galleries, and interactive field trips abound on the grid, and students can take part in simulations geared around history, medicine, language, and science. See Second Life's Spotlight on Education (http://education.secondlife.com) or Top 20 Educational Locations in Second Life (http://simteach.com/wiki/index. php?title=Top_20_Educational_Locations_in_Second_Life) for specific ideas about educational applications of this resource.

Some virtual learning environments do not require the user to be immersed in the environment to the extent described above. The term *virtual learning environment* also can be used to describe interfaces such as Blackboard (http://www.blackboard.com), Udutu (http://www.udutu.com), and Moodle (http://moodle.org), which facilitate synchronous and asynchronous distance learning; and programs such as Renzulli Learning (http://www.renzullilearning.com), which provide teachers with enrichment activities for gifted students. Across all of these types of virtual environments, classroom use provides opportunities for students to access information and learning tasks beyond their physical setting. Through purposeful integration of guiding questions, challenging problems, and opportunities for students to share and discuss their experiences, teachers can help to ensure that student interaction in these environments helps them to grow as learners and creative thinkers.

Digital game-based learning (DGBL). Game-based learning using technology tools has been occurring in classrooms for many years, with advances in the demands of the games growing along with the capacities of the technology. *Lemonade Stand* (updated and available online at http://www.coolmath-games.com/lemonade) and *The Oregon Trail* (now in its fifth edition) were among the first learning-focused digital games. The Oregon Trail, set during the 19th-century period of Westward expansion, involved planning a family trip from the East Coast across the Oregon Trail to the West Coast. Players had to develop a survival plan, battle the wilderness and the trials and tribulations that came with driving a covered wagon across the continent, and be prepared to establish a new life in the Oregon Territory. Although the technology has vastly improved and the skills students learn while playing are far more advanced than they were in the past, the focus of the game on having students learn through an interactive, life-like experience has not changed since its initial release.

Today's digital games have players communicating and collaborating with other players from around the globe, using critical thinking skills to develop means of solving complex problems and making complicated decisions. Some games, like *Rollercoaster Tycoon* (http://www.atari.com/rollercoastertycoon) and *My Sims* (http://www.ea.com/games/mysims), require players to develop, manage, maintain, and grow complex environments. Games such as *Civilization III* (http://www.2kgames.com/index.php?p=games&platform=PC&title=civ3c) not only have players developing complex environments, but also learning how key concepts in history and civics play into the development of civilizations. Collaborative games such as *Rune Scape* (http://www.runescape.com/title.ws) have players learning to work together, often across great distances, to solve complex problems and make group decisions.

As they play a game, students learn to solve problems using a method quite similar to that of scientists. Players formulate a hypothesis about how to solve a problem, they test that hypothesis, and they revise it until they reach success (Van Eck, 2006). After three decades of development, video games are ubiquitous and sophisticated. Students respond positively to them and often are more motivated within a gaming environment. Digital game-based learning often presents problems that appear "real" and interesting to the gamer.

In order to be effective as an instructional tool, DGBL must be aligned with the curriculum, with identification of intended learning outcomes and opportunities to assess thinking and transfer of skills. Effective DGBL includes at least one (and preferably all) of the following components: (a) pre-instruction, during which the curriculum is introduced as a starting point for game play; (b) co-instruction, during which the curricular material is taught simultaneously with the game play; and (c) post-instruction, during which the game play is aligned with the curricular material after play is completed (Van Eck, 2006). There are a number of websites that will help teachers align the game with their curriculum (e.g., http://www.gamesparentsteachers.com; http://brainmeld.org), and teachers should look for "mod programs," games that can be modified to meet instructional needs, rather than tailoring the curriculum to off-the-shelf games (Halverson, 2009). Gifted students also may be able to have their curriculum compacted with the aid of DGBL (Van Eck, 2006).

Online gifted programs. Many gifted and talented students have advanced learning needs beyond what their local schools can provide, particularly when students are highly advanced in one or more areas, when they attend school in small districts and rural areas, or when their particular combination of interests and needs demands a complicated schedule (e.g., taking more classes than might be offered in a regular school day). Online classes are an excellent solution for each of these situations (Siegle, 2004), and a recent meta-analysis by the U.S. Department of Education found that "students in online learning conditions performed better than those receiving face-to-face instruction" (Means, Toyama, Murphy, Bakia, & Jones, 2009, p. ix).

Online learning may provide gifted students with a learning community filled with students of similar interests and abilities (Ng & Nicholas, 2007), thereby providing them with some of the social benefits that have been documented in special out-of-school courses for gifted learners through talent searches and similar programs. Moreover, in many online courses, students can work independently, be provided with greater challenge, and have their pace and level of learning matched by the curriculum. Differentiation may occur in ways that are less obvious to other students, and the gifted student can develop close relationships with online instructors as mentors in the area of interest.

In a recent study, almost half of middle and high school students surveyed expressed interest in taking an online course, and 40% indicated that they believe online classes should be part of an ideal school; yet only 10% have been given a chance to take an online course through their school (Project Tomorrow, 2009). Nevertheless, some (Christensen, Horn, & Johnson, 2008) have predicted that up to half of all high school classes will be delivered online by 2019.

Schools that wish to develop online classes can conduct them on a variety of online learning platforms. In addition to the commercial platforms (such as Blackboard), Moodle (http://moodle.org) and Sakai (http://sakaiproject.org/portal) are two free, open-source course management systems that schools may wish to consider using. Educators who have taught online report that the experience improved their effectiveness as a teacher by helping them:

- encourage students to be more self-directed,
- facilitate student-centered learning,
- facilitate collaboration between students,
- take time to differentiate instruction,
- better understand how students were doing, and
- give more personal attention. (Project Tomorrow, 2009, p. 6)

Many universities offer online courses that are appropriate for gifted and talented students, particularly advanced secondary students. Most of these courses are at the college/university level, which allows for acceleration and possible curriculum compacting; some are self-paced, while others are more directed and may involve synchronous or asynchronous interaction with other students. Several programs, including the Education Program for Gifted Youth (EPGY) at Stanford University (http://epgy.stanford.edu), offer accelerated online classes that high-achieving students can take on their own or as part of a high school diploma program. The Center for Talented Youth (CTY) at Johns Hopkins University (http://cty.jhu.edu/ctyonline) has been offering distance courses since 1983. Ten thousand students each year enroll in their distance academic courses for gifted students. Wallace (2005) reported that the gifted students who participated in CTY were satisfied with the program.

Project ASPIRE (http://www.bsu.edu/academy/aspire/index.htm; Cross & Burney, 2005) works with middle and high school students in the Midwest in the areas of mathematics and science. The program's key goals are to assist teachers in increasing the rigor level of math and science courses, as well as help increase the number of Advanced Placement (AP) offerings through the use of distance education. There also are a number of schools that provide advanced curricula with distance access (Rice, 2006), such as A. Linwood Holton Governor's School (http://www.hgs.k12.va.us/index.htm) and Clark County Virtual High School (http://www.ccsdde.net).

Prior to enrolling in an online course outside a student's school, a student should be guided in finding the answers to the following questions:

- What are the dropout and completion rates for the course?
- How transferable are the course credits?
- Does the course instructor hold certification or a degree in the course topic?
- Is the pace of the course negotiable?
- How much interaction is built into the course?
- Is the course self-contained or are additional materials needed?
- Are any special hardware, software, or technology skills needed for the course? (Siegle, 2005b, p. 45)

Technology as a Communication Tool

The Internet's simple capacity to connect people is as important today as its role as the primary repository of knowledge (Siegle, 2008a). Technologies today have made a vast world incredibly small. A letter sent from a computer in Maine can reach India in a matter of seconds. Instant communication is a way of life; send a message, and within an instant a message is received in return. Beyond the world of text communication, those same people in Maine and India can talk face to face through a wide variety of free video software programs. Today's young people are enmeshed in a world of technology-based communication and evolve quickly with new tools; for example, texting is overtaking e-mail as a primary mode of communication for young people. Technology tools for communication provide opportunities for interaction that break down classroom walls and give students access to a much wider community of learners and teachers.

Video conferencing. Two-way video conferencing is now a viable teaching and learning option, especially given that it utilizes existing equipment: a computer with either a built-in or external webcam, a microphone, and an Internet connection. Windows Live Messenger (http://messenger.live.com) and AOL Instant Messenger (http://www.aim.com) are popular text messaging options that also include a free videoconferencing feature. Skype (http://www.skype.com) is a popular alternative Internet phone service that also features a free videoconferencing function. Each of these options is free but requires users to download software and to register with a unique login and password. An alternative for videoconferencing is MeBeam (http://www.mebeam.com), which does not require a registration login or software installation.

Using videoconferencing, teachers can have students talk with experts, collaborate on projects with other students, hold debates, conduct book talks, share their expertise, and visually experience cultures anywhere on the planet (Siegle, 2008a). With minimal equipment and setup time, videoconferencing opens new worlds for students. For gifted students in particular, such connections with other students or with experts in different fields may provide the kind of mentorship they need to advance their learning in a content area of strength and interest.

Social networking. Social networking sites are an increasingly integrated part of the digital landscape. Two thirds of all global Internet users now regularly visit a social network or blog site (Nielsen Company, 2009). According to Nielsen (2009), sites such as Facebook (http://www.facebook.com) and MySpace (http://www.myspace.com) are surpassing e-mail for the purpose of communication, and LinkedIn (http://www.linkedin.com) is a major source for professional networking. Given the prevalence of this form of communication, it is important for students to have opportunities to learn how to use such sites to their advantage.

As in the virtual learning environments such as Teen Second Life, social networking sites allow students to interact with others who possess similar abilities and interests. These sites may support students in maintaining some of the friendships developed in special programs for gifted students outside of school time, and potentially in working on projects with some of these friends. Social networking broadens a student's peer group and may help to respond to the challenges some gifted students face in finding friends with shared interests and values in their school environment. From more of an academic perspective, social networking sites also provide opportunities for students to access information or join "groups" around particular areas of interest. For example, students might find it interesting to "friend" their local senator or house representative and thereby to learn more about the political process and the work these individuals conduct.

Several cautions are warranted about use of social networking sites and other digital communication tools. Teachers and parents need to be aware of the level of openness of social networking sites and conscious of student activities online in general, particularly in contexts that engage students in interactions with people unknown to them. Cyber bullying is becoming an area of concern to educators and parents (Hinduja & Patchin, 2008).

In addition, students should learn that despite privacy functions, online information is rarely completely secure. Also, they must be guided to understand that their online activities, including social networking and involvement in virtual environments, give impressions of them to others just as their interpersonal activities in their physical environments do. This issue has raised several different kinds of concerns. Some are concerned that as students grow and become more aware of social physical standards, they are conforming their virtual selves to meet these standards rather than portraying an accurate representation of their own selves (Boss, 2009). Other concerns emerge around whether students' online personae present aspects of themselves that could negatively affect activities such as job-hunting and applying for special programs and for college. Thus, students must be guided in learning about how to present themselves authentically but also in ways fully appropriate for a public context.

Online publishing. There is an increasing number of ways in which students and teachers can use the Internet to develop and share ideas and products. Many schools and districts provide space for teachers to publish their own class web pages; students and teachers also can use specific software or online resources to develop web pages. For example, Google provides a tool called Google Sites with which individuals can create sites and control access to them. Web design, whatever tool is used to approach it, provides a range of learning challenges for students, from selecting content to share, to managing visual design and organization, to updating information.

Blog sites such as LiveJournal (http://www.livejournal.com), Blogger (http://www.blogger.com) from Google, or even the blog opportunities through social networking sites allow students the opportunity to express their thoughts to a much wider audience than their own classroom. Most of these sites are free, and access to them usually can be controlled by the blogger. Students can not only write their own blogs but also interact with bloggers who have similar interests. A quick search of the Internet will easily produce a blog to fit the most esoteric interest. Caution should be taken, however, to alert students that anything written in a blog, no matter how high the security level, may still be seen by unwanted eyes.

A wiki is another publishing opportunity. A wiki is simply a website that can easily be edited by more than one person. One advantage of creating a site as a wiki is that it can be edited from anywhere that Internet access is available and by anyone who is given permission to edit it. Student access to a wiki site can range from simple viewing rights for a few students to full editing rights for all. Wiki sites are created with an easy-to-use interface that is no more difficult to use than a word processing program. Two commonly available wiki sites are PBworks (http://pbworks.com/academic.wiki) and Google Sites (http://sites.google.com). Almost everything that can be created on a website can be created with a wiki with the advantage of allowing multiple people access for editing and controlled viewing and editing (Siegle, 2008b). Building upon the concept of collaborative knowledge, teachers can employ wikis in the classroom, allowing students the opportunity to research, write, review, edit, and publish information collaboratively. In this way, wikis foster interactions among students and between students and teachers.

Blogs and wikis can be employed in the classroom in a number of creative ways. Students can share knowledge about topics that interest them. They can collaboratively plan a class project or field trip (Siegle, 2008b). Students engaged in a problem-based learning (PBL) unit can work collaboratively on updating an online Need to Know Board (see Chapter 10). Teachers can post homework questions to a blog or wiki and have students work collaboratively; students can post questions they have about homework or readings and have the chance for either the teacher or a fellow student to provide assistance. In a simpler format, teachers can post worksheets for their students to easily locate and complete (Bernard, 2009).

YouTube (http://www.youtube.com) allows users to upload their creative videos to the Internet for the world to see. Some students use YouTube, and other such publishing sites or social networking sites, to express their feelings, to demonstrate technical knowledge, to collaborate with others, or simply to show off their talents. Students upload everything from video game shots, to videos of their "Rock Band" debuts, to compilations of their own animation. Publishing work on the Internet provides the student with a wider audience that is more in tune with that student's particular interests.

Telementoring. Mentoring itself is a useful tool to provide gifted students with assistance that the regular classroom teacher, enrichment teacher, or parents may not be able to provide. The nature and diversity of gifted students' interests and specific talents often demand resources beyond the confines of the school. Mentors provide content sophistication that would normally not be accessible from traditional sources (Siegle, McCoach, & Wilson, 2009). Telementoring (also known as virtual mentoring, e-mentoring, or iMentoring) opens the door to a great number of possibilities; not only do more and varied mentors have the opportunity to assist students, but students in areas where mentors are scarce will be able to find someone with whom to work.

Telementoring usually is divided into three types of programs: (a) mentor experts who agree to respond to questions, (b) mentors who are paired with a single learner, and (c) mentors who work in partnerships (Riel, n.d.). Mentor experts usually have short e-mail interactions with students, although there are sites such as MadSci network (http://www.madsci.org) that list answers to students' questions. The most successful telementoring experiences are three-component partnerships that involve students, their teachers, and mentors (Siegle et al., 2009). The International Telementor Program (ITP; http://www. telementor.org) is one example. It provides academic mentoring support from professionals of ITP sponsor companies. All student/mentor communication is project focused and facilitated by a teacher or parent.

Telementoring has some unique advantages over traditional mentoring. It:

- provides a means of connecting thousands of professionals with students on a scale that is impractical in traditional face-to-face mentoring;
- matches students with appropriate mentors without geographic limitation;
- allows convenient, consistent, weekly communication between students and mentors and creates an archive of all communication;
- eliminates scheduling problems between mentors and students because an e-mail communication can be sent any time; and
- provides the opportunity for students to work on long-term projects with their mentors and allows mentors to see the influence they are having on students. (International Telementor Program, n.d.).

Production Tools

Technology tools have come a long way from early word processing applications and opportunities for students to engage in simple programming. Many tools now exist for students to develop and share products in a variety of formats and for a wide range of audiences. These tools also represent a range in the technical challenges they present to students; therefore, just learning to use some of the more difficult tools may provide students with a stimulating challenge.

Office Suite to cloud computing. Most educators are familiar with Microsoft Office Suite, the software package that allows students to do word processing, program spreadsheets, build databases, design publications, and organize presentations. These types of programs are critical for students to learn as more and more universities and employers expect that their applicants will be proficient in them. Students who are highly proficient in the basic applications also can be challenged to explore more advanced features of each program and to apply them to enhanced products.

For schools with limited resources, several alternatives to the full Microsoft Office Suite exist. First, Sun Microsystems offers a free and open productivity suite (download from http://www.openoffice.org) that is similar to the Microsoft Office Suite. In addition, counterparts to the Microsoft Office software are quickly becoming part of a phenomenon known as *cloud computing*. As computers are becoming smaller, and other programs are requiring more memory space, people are turning to cloud computing as a way to access programs such as those available in Microsoft Office. Cloud computing allows access to both the programs and the documents via the Internet. The program runs through the Internet, rather than being installed and running on the user's computer. The user can be on any computer with Internet access and can access and modify his or her documents, spreadsheets, or presentations. Google Docs (http://docs.google.com) currently offers free word processing, spreadsheets, forms, and presentation options this way.

Not only does the production software mentioned here allow students the means to express themselves, their studies, their research, and their creativity, but with cloud computing, they can do it from anywhere there is a computer and Internet, without the prohibitive cost (monetary and memory) of software. Moreover, sharing features of these Internet-based tools will allow multiple students to work on and edit files at the same time, supporting development of collaborative skills.

Video editing. Young people today are surrounded by visual images and drawn to viewing and creating videos. Given the increasing access to tools for creating, editing, and sharing videos, educators can take advantage of the opportunities provided by such tools for students to develop and share their work in video format. Video projects, like writing projects and other formats for sharing ideas, promote problem solving and critical and creative thinking as students consider their content and audience and the best way of communicating what they have to share. Most traditional school writing projects can easily be modified for a video project. For example, instead of writing a persuasive essay, students might design the structure of their argument and present it in the format of a documentary intended to influence public opinion. Other possible options for video presentations include creating commercials, developing newscasts, writing and producing plays, creating a video yearbook, demonstrating a skill for others to learn, creating music videos, interviewing local leaders, collecting oral histories, and conducting book talks (Siegle, 2009b, pp. 14–15).

Apple Inc. made video editing commonplace with iMovie more than a decade ago. The software is currently packaged with Apple's iLife suite. Microsoft's response to iMovie is Windows Movie Maker, which is distributed free (http://www.microsoft.com/windowsxp/downloads/updates/moviemaker2.mspx) and was included with the XP installation. Movie Maker is currently part of the free Live Essentials bundle that Microsoft offers for Windows 7 (http://windows.microsoft.com/en-us/windows7/products/features/windows-live-essentials). Using these easy-to-learn resources, students equipped with a digital video camera can begin to produce impressive video productions that can be shared with classmates or with an external audience via YouTube or a social networking site of choice.

Sound editing. Audacity (free download from http://audacity.sourceforge.net for Windows, Mac, or Linux) is the PC answer to GarageBand, which is developed by Apple Inc. Both programs allow students to edit existing music files and to create their own sound. Students can use GarageBand or Audacity in conjunction with the video editing tools to create impressive soundtracks to accompany the video that reflect some aspect of their interests or research.

Students also can use these sound editing tools to create audio projects, rather than written ones. Performing a song, reading poetry, acting out a scene from a play, or narrating their report through GarageBand or Audacity will make the project more authentic, entertaining, and meaningful. Such performances can be captured for use with video editing software or simply kept as a keepsake on a CD (Bernard, 2009). Students also can create and edit audio for podcasts (described later in this chapter).

Programming. Although computer programming has always interested a core set of students, it is once again regaining some of the popularity it held when computers such as the Commodore PET 2001, Tandy's Radio Shack TRS-80, and the Apple II were first introduced (Siegle, 2009a). Writing computer code is an excellent exercise in problem solving. A plethora of free options exist for educators who wish to introduce students to computer programming. The requirements range from simple programs that need minimal skills to rather complex code-writing exercises.

Seymour Papert (1980) at MIT believed that students at a very young age should be solving problems and programming computers—and that computers should not be programming students. He developed the LOGO language to introduce very young children to programming. LOGO provides premathematical children with problem-solving and reasoning experiences as they create shapes with the now familiar "turtle." A variety of free versions of this early programming language can be downloaded from the Internet (http://www.softronix.com/logo.html), although students may find some of the later generations of programming software that are featured in the next few paragraphs more motivational.

Also developed at MIT, Scratch (http://scratch.mit.edu) is intuitive programming software tailored for a video game generation. It allows students (ages 8 and up) to use building blocks and play to develop the programming language. Once students have mastered the language, they can create games, animations, and with the right add-on, robots and other mechanical gadgets. In the process students learn important mathematical and computational ideas as they think creatively, reason systematically, and work collaboratively.

Alice (http://www.alice.org) is a 3D programming environment developed at Carnegie Mellon University. Similar to Scratch, in Alice students create their own interactive stories, animations, games, music, and art and can share their creations on the Internet. One version of Alice is geared for middle school students, and a second version is geared for high school and college students. How programs such as Alice are used, however, does matter for some groups of students. For example, women are currently underrepresented in computer science; Alice may be one option to erase this gap. One study compared programming time of a group of middle school girls using the storytelling function of the Alice program versus a group using Generic Alice; the study found that those girls who also employed the storytelling function with Alice spent 42% more time programming and were more than three times as likely to sneak extra time to continue working on their programs than the nonstorytelling group (51% of Storytelling Alice users vs. 16% of Generic Alice users sneaked extra time; Kelleher, 2006).

DreamSpark (https://www.dreamspark.com) is a Microsoft initiative to encourage future programmers that provides students with free software design and development tools, such as Visual Basic (Prabhu, 2009). Writing computer code is not for everyone, but those who enjoy it often find it addictive. Computer programming can be a valuable tool in gifted and talented educators' arsenal of learning activities. The skills necessary for writing computer code closely match many common characteristics associated with gifted students (Siegle, 2009a).

Tools for Classroom Instruction and Interaction

Chalk alternatives. There are several alternatives to the traditional blackboard and even to the static white board that has become more customary in classrooms. SMART Technologies (http://smarttech.com) offers a wide range of innovative classroom tools. The interactive SMART Board allows the user to manipulate images using not only the standard stylus, but also by touch. The

SMART technology also includes student pads with which students write on the board from their desks, hand-held "clickers" that allow a whole classroom of students to answer a question (with results tabulated and graphed on the board), and a table at which students can interact, by touch, with images and words displayed on the screen.

A less expensive alternative to the SMART technology is the Mimio Interactive (http://www.mimio-boards.com). This device hooks on the edge of a standard white board and captures every stroke written on the board with a specially designed stylus. Teachers need only capture the image before erasing the board and starting over again. In this way, teachers can provide students with notes taken straight from the board.

Assistive technology. Assistive technology has a wide range of uses for all students. Although designed for use with students who have impairments, these technologies can provide new levels of differentiation to respond to various learning style needs and preferences. Programs such as ReadPlease (http://www.readplease.com) and Kurzweil 3000 (http://www.kurzweiledu.com), which can turn texts into audio files, provide support for students who have difficulty reading and for those who may prefer a combination of listening and seeing what they are to read. Such programs, along with books available on CD or for mp3 download, provide another dimension to reading and also the opportunity for students to discuss the different experiences of reading and listening to text.

Other technology resources support students in translating their thoughts into text or graphic form. Dragon NaturallySpeaking (http://www.nuance.com/talk) is a speech-to-text program that allows the user to speak the words he or she would like to have typed. Several sources offer free mind mapping software to help guide students in diagramming connections among concepts. A wide range of choices may be found with a quick Internet search; some sources include FreeMind (http://freemind.sourceforge.net/wiki/index.php/Download) and View Your Mind (http://www.insilmaril.de/vym).

Podcasting. Podcasts are on-demand audio recordings that students can play on their computers or mp3 players. Their initial popularity has waned, but they are still an excellent tool. Podcasting allows teachers to record a lecture, a lesson, or a lab and then post it online for students to hear. Some students may take poor notes during class because they are paying attention to the lecture, and other students may not pay very good attention to the lecture because they are trying to take good notes. Through the use of a podcast, students can revisit the lecture and be able to fill in the gaps in their notes, take notes, or just resolidify their understanding of the material.

Students also can create podcasts on material they are learning. Students may wish to create a weekly news broadcast about events in their school or community. They may present results of a research project through this format, making it available for listeners beyond the time and audience of an in-class presentation. The extent of possible podcast topics is limited only by the creativity of the teacher and students. Talented students will undoubtedly generate myriad ideas for possible podcasts (Siegle, 2007b). Students can edit the audio for their podcasts with a program like Audacity or GarageBand.

Online videos. TeacherTube (http://www.teachertube.com), similar to YouTube, is a site where teachers, parents, and other educators can post and watch instructional videos. Teachers will find creative ideas on how to present material, as well as new and exciting ways to get students intrigued and involved with the curriculum. YouTube itself also is a resource for videos that may provide different perspectives on a problem or innovative ideas, as well as being a location for students to post their own videos, as noted earlier. However, as with any of the general-access websites described here, YouTube should be used only with careful monitoring in the classroom.

E-books. Some believe that textbooks will soon go the way of the scroll, as many schools move away from textbooks and into e-books and other digitally based resources (Lewin, 2009). Electronic books come in a variety of formats. Some e-books can be read online with a standard web browser or downloaded for viewing on personal computers or handheld devices. Others require special software or a special device to read them. A free Microsoft Reader can be downloaded from Microsoft's website (http://www.microsoft.com/reader) for one type of e-book format. E-Books Directory (http://www.e-booksdirectory.com), Project Gutenberg (http://www.gutenberg.org), and The Online Book Page (http://onlinebooks.library.upenn.edu) are among the many websites that offer free online books (for a list of the top 25 sites, visit http://educhoices.org/articles/Online_Libraries_-_25_Places_to_Read_Free_Books_Online.html). Books in the public domain often are available for free, and the range of titles will open new opportunities for language arts lessons. In addition to books in the public domain that are free, many online bookstores offer electronic versions of popular titles with a price that is similar to that of a book in print. These books often are designed for handheld e-book readers such as COOL-ER (http://www.coolreaders.com), Kindle (http://www.amazon.com/Kindle), and Sony Reader (http://www.sonystyle.com). Google Books (http://books.google.com) offers previews of selected pages from a wide range of books. Such previews may provide the "hook" to draw students into a particular book that they may go on to read in its entirety.

Shelfari (http://www.shelfari.com), a social networking site for book lovers, provides teachers with the opportunity to create a virtual library that their students can access. Teachers can stock the shelves of their library with required or recommended readings and collaborate with other teachers on suggested reading material. Using Shelfari, teachers can have students post reviews and reports on books and make suggestions for other students. Shelfari also provides teachers with a unique social networking opportunity to discover and discuss what other teachers are reading.

CONCLUSION

There is a wide range of technology that teachers can use to enhance the curriculum and learning for gifted students. Technology tools can provide access to advanced content; opportunities for students to solve challenging, ill-structured problems and to develop critical thinking skills; varied creative product options; and ways for students to integrate their thinking about concepts to new contexts. The examples of technology tools provided here are by no means exhaustive. In addition, what we present today may be outdated tomorrow. The only constant with technology is that it will change. Educators who fail to embrace technology and its changing nature will fall behind. Worse, their students' motivation and learning will suffer. We have merely scratched the surface of possible technology that can be used to enhance curriculum for the gifted. Successful implementation of technology is only limited by the teachers' creativity and understanding of their curriculum. With creative thought, any curriculum can be enhanced with technology to be more relevant and motivating for students and to provide challenging and stimulating tasks that will advance students' skills and learning experiences.

KEY POINTS SUMMARY

- Today's students use technology extensively and rely on a wide variety of technological tools, yet often their classroom experiences do not integrate technological tools with learning activities.
- Technology tools can promote learning goals related to all dimensions of the Integrated Curriculum Model through an emphasis on access to higher level content; a focus on the problem solving and critical thinking skills needed to use tools to achieve a particular purpose; opportunities to develop sophisticated products that can be shared with an extensive, authentic audience; and a broad array of contexts in which to explore concepts and their interdisciplinary connections.
- Effective integration of technology with the curriculum requires careful consideration of the learning goals in the content area, the technology skills needed to use particular tools to achieve those goals, and the differentiated guidance students will require based on their technology and content-area readiness.
- Early technology use in classrooms focused on drill-and-practice activi-

ties; the 1990s saw greater classroom use of word processing and other product development tools, as well as the wider emergence of the Internet; more recent years have seen ongoing growth of opportunities to learn with technology and to use technological tools to access and analyze information for particular purposes.

- Professional development is critical for supporting teacher implementation of technology in the classroom. Such professional development should include time for teachers to learn about and practice with technology tools, as well as ongoing classroom support.

- Student needs for technology skills include the technical understanding of how to use tools as well as how to be wise consumers of information. They must develop problem-solving and communication skills to support their use of a variety of tools and programs.

- Technology tools for classroom integration include those that are used (a) as an information resource, (b) as an interactive learning tool, (c) as a communication tool, (d) as a production tool, and (e) as a tool for instruction and interaction in the classroom.

REFERENCES

Amabile, T. M. (1983). *The social psychology of creativity.* New York, NY: Springer-Verlag.

Amabile, T. M. (1996). *Creativity in context: Update to "The social psychology of creativity."* Boulder, CO: Westview.

Bernard, S. (2009, June/July). Kids talk tech. *Edutopia, 22.*

Besnoy, K. D., Housand, B. C., & Clarke, L. W. (2009). Changing nature of technology and the promise of educational technology for gifted education. In F. A. Karnes & S. M. Bean (Eds.), *Methods and materials for teaching the gifted* (3rd ed., pp. 783–802). Waco, TX: Prufrock Press.

Boss, S. (2009, June/July). Beauty and the avatar. *Edutopia,* 34–38.

Breck, J. (2007). Gen mobile: Kids of the commons. *Educational Technology, 47*(2), 30–34.

Christensen, C. M., Horn, B., & Johnson, C. W. (2008). *Disrupting class: How disruptive innovation will change the way the world learns.* New York, NY: McGraw-Hill.

Coiro, J., Knobel, M., Lankshear, C., & Leu, D. J. (Eds.). (2008). *Handbook of research on new literacies.* Mahwah, NJ: Lawrence Erlbaum.

Cross, T. L., & Burney, V. H. (2005). High ability, rural, and poor: Lessons from Project Aspire and implications for school counselors. *Journal of Secondary Gifted Education, 16,* 148–156.

Davis, G., Rimm, S. B., & Siegle, D. (2011). *Education of the gifted and talented* (6th ed.). Boston, MA: Pearson/Allyn & Bacon.

Halverson, R. R. (2009, April). *Game design as educational research.* Paper presented at the annual meeting for the American Educational Research Association, San Diego, CA.

Hinduja, S., & Patchin, J. W. (2008). *Bullying beyond the schoolyard: Preventing and responding to cyberbullying.* Thousand Oaks, CA: Corwin Press.

International Society for Technology in Education. (2007). *National educational technology standards (NETS*S) and performance indicators for students.* Retrieved from http://www.iste.org/Content/NavigationMenu/NETS/ForStudents/2007Standards/NETS_for_Students_2007_Standards.pdf

International Society for Technology in Education. (2008). *National educational technology standards (NETS*T) and performance indicators for teachers.* Retrieved from http://www.iste.org/Content/NavigationMenu/NETS/ForTeachers/2008Standards/NETS_T_Standards_Final.pdf

International Telementor Program. (n.d.). Retrieved from http://www.telementor.org

Kaiser Family Foundation. (2005). *Executive summary: Generation M: Media in the lives of 8–18 year-olds.* Retrieved from http://www.kff.org/entmedia/upload/Executive-Summary-Generation-M-Media-in-the-Lives-of-8-18-Year-olds.pdf

Kelleher, C. (2006). *Motivating programming: Using storytelling to make computer programming attractive to middle school girls* (Unpublished doctoral dissertation). Carnegie Mellon University, Pittsburgh, PA.

Lenhart A., Arafeh S., Smith A., & Macgill A. R. (2008). *Writing, technology and teens.* Retrieved from http://www.pewinternet.org/PPF/r/247/report_display.asp

Leu, D. J., Jr., Kinzer, C. K., Coiro, J., & Cammack, D. (2004). Toward a theory of new literacies emerging from the Internet and other information and communication technologies. In R. B. Ruddell & N. Unrau (Eds.), *Theoretical models and processes of reading* (5th ed., pp. 1568–1611). Newark, DE: International Reading Association.

Lewin, T. (2009, August 8). In a digital future, textbooks are history. *The New York Times.* Retrieved from http://www.nytimes.com/2009/08/09/education/09textbook.html?scp=1&sq=in%20a%20digital%20future,%20textbooks%20are%20history&st=cse

Lohr, S. (2009, August 5). For today's graduate, just one word: Statistics. *The New York Times.* Retrieved from http://www.nytimes.com/2009/08/06/technology/06stats.html

Macgill, A. R. (2007). *Parent and teen Internet use.* Retrieved from http://www.pewinternet.org/Reports/2007/Parent-and-Teen-Internet-Use.aspx

McCoach, D. B. (2002). Using the Web for social studies enrichment. *Gifted Child Today, 25*(3), 48–52.

Means, B., Toyama, Y., Murphy, R., Bakia, M., & Jones, K. (2009). *Evaluation of evidence-based practices in online learning: A meta-analysis and review of online learning studies.* Washington, DC: U. S. Department of Education Office of Planning, Evaluation, and Policy Development Policy and Program Studies Service. Retrieved from http://www.ed.gov/rschstat/eval/tech/evidence-based-practices/finalreport.pdf

Ng, W., & Nicholas, H. (2007). Technology and independent learning: Conceptualizing the use of online technologies for gifted secondary students. *Roeper Review, 29,* 190–196.

Nielsen Company. (2009). *Global faces and networked places: A Nielson report on social networking's new global footprint.* Retrieved from http://server-uk.imrworldwide.

com/pdcimages/Global_Faces_and_Networked_Places-A_Nielsen_Report_on_
Social_Networkings_New_Global_Footprint.pdf

O'Brien, B., & Friedman-Nimz, R. (2006, November). *Timing is everything: The emergence of technology talent.* Paper presented at the 53rd annual convention of the National Association for Gifted Children, Charlotte, NC.

O'Brien, B., Friedman-Nimz, R., Lacey, J., & Denson, D. (2005). From bits and bytes to C++ and Web sites: What is computer talent made of? *Gifted Child Today, 28*(3), 56–63.

Owston, R. D. (2009). Digital immersion, teacher learning, and games. *Educational Researcher, 38,* 270–273.

Papert, S. (1980). *Mindstorms: Children, computers, and powerful ideas.* New York, NY: Basic Books.

Parr, J. M. (1999). Extending educational computing: A case of extensive teacher development and support. *Journal of Research on Computing in Education, 31,* 280–291.

Partnership for 21st Century Skills. (2007). *21st century skills standards: A Partnership for 21st Century Skills epaper.* Retrieved from http://www.21stcenturyskills.org/documents/21st_century_skills_standards.pdf

Penuel, B., Korbak, C., Yarnall, L., & Pacpaco, R. (2001, March). *Silicon Valley challenge 2000: Year 5 multimedia project report.* Report prepared for Joint Venture: Silicon Valley Network.

Prabhu, M. T. (2009). Microsoft offers free software for high schoolers. *eSchool News, 12*(5), 8.

Prensky, M. (2001). Digital natives, digital immigrants. *On the Horizon, 9*(5), 1–2.

Prensky, M. (2006). Listen to the natives. *Educational Leadership, 63*(4), 8–13.

Project Tomorrow. (2009). *Learning in the 21st Century: 2009 trends updated.* Retrieved from http://www.blackboard.com/resources/k12/Bb_K12_09_TrendsUpdate.pdf

Reeves, T. C. (1999). *A research agenda for interactive learning in the new millennium* (ED-MEDIA 99 Keynote Address Paper). Retrieved from http://itech1.coe.uga.edu/~treeves/EM99Key.html

Rice, K. L. (2006). A comprehensive look at distance education in the K–12 context. *Journal of Research on Technology in Education, 38,* 425–448.

Riel, M. (n.d.). *Tele-mentoring over the Net.* Retrieved from http://edc.techleaders.org/LNT99/notes_slides/presentations/riel-tues/telement.htm

Rossman, M. (1984). How to use the computer in science class (and how not to). *Classroom Computer Learning, 4*(7), 12–18.

Siegle, D. (2004). Learning online: A viable alternative for gifted and talented students. *Duke Gifted Letter, 4*(4), 7.

Siegle, D. (2005a). Six uses of the Internet to develop students' talents and gifts. *Gifted Child Today, 28*(2), 30–36.

Siegle, D. (2005b). *Using media & technology with gifted learners.* Waco, TX: Prufrock Press.

Siegle, D. (2007a). Identifying and developing technological giftedness: Exploring another way to be gifted in the 21st century. *Gifted Education Communicator, 38*(1), 18–21.

Siegle, D. (2007b). Podcasts and blogs: Learning opportunities on the information highway. *Gifted Child Today, 30*(3), 14–19.

Siegle, D. (2008a). Free options for Internet videoconferencing: Moving beyond e-mail and chat. *Gifted Child Today, 31*(4), 14–18.

Siegle, D. (2008b). Working with wikis. *Gifted Child Today, 31*(1), 14–17.

Siegle, D. (2009a). Developing student programming and problem-solving skills with Visual Basic. *Gifted Child Today, 32*(4), 24–29.

Siegle, D. (2009b). Literacy in the 21st century: The fourth R—Video recording. *Gifted Child Today, 32*(2), 14–19.

Siegle, D., McCoach, D. B., & Wilson, H. E. (2009). Extending learning through mentorships. In F. A. Karnes & S. M. Bean (Eds.), *Methods and materials for teaching the gifted* (3rd ed., pp. 519–563). Waco, TX: Prufrock Press.

Somekh, B., Mavers, D., & Lewin, C. (2002, April). *Broadening access to the curriculum through using technology to link home and school: A critical analysis of reforms to improve educational attainment for all K–12 students.* Paper presented at the annual meeting of the American Educational Research Association, New Orleans, LA.

Staples, A., Pugach, M. C., & Himes, D. J. (2005). Rethinking the technology integration challenge: Cases from three urban elementary schools. *Journal of Research on Technology in Education, 37*, 285–311.

SWAT. (2002). *Students working to advance technology.* Retrieved from http://www.swatweb.net

Twenge, J. M., & Campbell, W. K. (2009). *The narcissism epidemic: Living in the age of entitlement.* New York, NY: Free Press.

Valdez, G., McNabb, M., Foertsch, M., Anderson, M., Hawkes, M., & Raack, L. (2000). *Computer-based technology and learning: Evolving uses and expectations.* Oak Brook, IL: North Central Regional Educational Laboratory.

Van Eck, R. (2006). Digital game based learning: It's not just the digital natives who are restless. *EDUCAUSE Review, 41*(2), 16–30.

Voogt, J., Almekinders, M., van den Akker, J., & Moonen, B. (2005). A "blended" in-service arrangement for classroom technology integration: Impacts on teachers and students. *Computers in Human Behavior, 21*, 523–539.

Wallace, P. (2005). Distance education for gifted students: Leveraging technology to expand academic options. *High Ability Studies, 26*, 77–86.

Wenglinsky, H. (1998) *Does it compute? The relationship between educational technology and student achievement in mathematics* (Educational Testing Service Policy Information Report). Retrieved from http://ftp.ets.org/pub/res/technolog.pdf

Zhao, Y., & Frank, K. A. (2003). Factors affecting technology uses in schools: An ecological perspective. *American Educational Research Journal, 40*, 807–840.

Chapter 16

Assessing Student Learning

Joyce VanTassel-Baska and Li Zuo

Y*ou are a middle school teacher who would like to obtain a more complete profile of how your gifted students are progressing. You surmise that the annual state test does not begin to tap into their abilities, and tests you have created also are limited to factual content, using short-answer formats. If you knew more about appropriate measures to assess the learning of your gifted students in your subject area, you would use them and adapt the curriculum accordingly. How can you appropriately assess learning in gifted students?*

The purposes of student assessment are to examine the effectiveness of classroom teaching and learning, as well as to plan for future instruction based on student learning needs. Constructing an effective assessment tool is not an easy task in the sense that it must not only cover the objectives of a curriculum, but cover them in a way that is technically adequate. In the case of assessing gifted students' learning, it also is necessary to increase the task difficulty level so as to provide opportunities for those students to demonstrate the advanced thinking of which they are capable.

This chapter discusses some of the guidelines in curriculum-based assessment construction, with particular focus on high-ability learners. Examples of assessments from Advanced Placement (AP), the International Baccalaureate (IB), and the Center for Gifted Education's science units are provided to illustrate the concepts under discussion and their application.

TECHNICAL CONSIDERATIONS IN ASSESSMENT

Depending on the use of a test, different levels of technical adequacy are required. A test that is used for the determination of eligibility for a special service (e.g., a gifted program) must be highly valid and reliable. For a teacher-made classroom assessment, however, the demand on its technical adequacy is less stringent.

Two major properties of technical adequacy are reliability and validity. Other important considerations are test fairness and, particularly in the case of high-ability learners, test ceiling. The following explanation of these constructs may be supplemented by test manual descriptions, if needed.

Reliability

Reliability refers to the consistency of examinees' test scores over repeated administrations of the same test or alternate test forms. Such consistency gives the assurance that the test is measuring an individual's true ability. There are several ways to estimate an instrument's reliability using test data. Administering the instrument twice to the same group of examinees with an interval in between, the test-retest method, yields the reliability coefficient of stability. Administering two forms of the same instrument one after another to the same group of examinees, the alternate form method, yields the coefficient of equivalency. Combining the two methods by testing and retesting with alternate forms yields the coefficient of both stability and equivalence. That reliability is usually lower because it combines both types of errors due to test construction and examinees' performance over time.

A reliability coefficient of .85 means that 85% of the observed score variance is attributable to true score variance (Crocker & Algina, 1986). A high reliability, typically above .85, is generally found in well-established intelligence tests and achievement tests. Teacher-made classroom tests generally are not subjected to reliability studies because of their relatively low-stakes nature, nor are they expected to meet a high reliability standard. Yet,

TABLE 16.1

Table of Specifications

	Content Goal Emphases					
Test Item	Geography	Weather	Civilization	Political System	Economy	Religion
1	√					
2		√				
3			√			
4			√			
5				√		
6					√	
7						√
8				√		
9	√					
10					√	

it may be important to conduct a test-retest reliability check to ascertain stability of the measure.

Validity

Although the reliability coefficient indicates the consistency of examinees' scores, it does not ensure defensible inferences drawn about examinees' knowledge or behavior. The basis for such inferences needs to be established through studies in which test developers or test users collect evidence to demonstrate an instrument's *validity*, which is the degree to which the test measures what it purports to measure and thus justifies the inferences made.

Content validity refers to the inference that can be made about an examinee's knowledge of a domain or construct of specific interest from his or her performance on the test (Crocker & Algina, 1986). It is the most relevant type of validity for classroom assessment. Content validity can be established by having content experts check the test items to determine whether or not they assess what they are supposed to assess. The test maker, of course, should make sure before seeking expert review that the test covers the instructional objectives and curricular contents for assessment. A helpful method of checking the coverage is to map out the test items against content or skills to be assessed in a table of specifications. The layout should present a balanced coverage if all of the objectives or content areas are of equal importance. Table 16.1 gives an example of a table of specification. Matching the assessment with curricular goals or objectives also means selecting the right assessment approach for a particular goal or set of objectives. When the goal specifies that students should be able to conduct a scientific experiment, a paper-and-pencil approach will not adequately assess its attainment. For that particular goal, performance assessment is a superior tool.

Fairness

A good test should not be biased in favor of or against any individual because of his or her gender, culture, language, or experience. Bias occurs when a test contains vocabulary or tacit knowledge that is specific to a subculture, but is irrelevant to the test purpose; when a test is given to students who have different degrees of familiarity with the employed test format; and when the test calls for the use of a lab device to which students have had varied exposure. Students from another culture, students who speak another language, and students with learning disabilities are some of those for whom accommodations may need to be made in order to ensure a fair assessment of their ability.

Test Ceiling

Test ceiling refers to the maximum score allowed on a test. An easy test that allows too many students to achieve the highest score possible is said to have a low ceiling, which means it fails to discriminate for high-end students. Tests that are designed for use with gifted learners should pay special attention to this problem, providing sufficiently difficult tasks and scoring protocols with room for varied levels of performance near the top. Often criterion-referenced tests are too easy for gifted learners, as are traditional standardized measures, which are calibrated to do a good job of discriminating performance in the middle but not at the extreme ends of the test. State tests suffer from ceiling effect in that the advanced level of the test in most states is too broad a category to use for discriminating how able students may be in a given subject area.

AUTHENTIC ASSESSMENT

In recognition of the limitations of standardized tests and the need to assess students' high-level skills, performance-based and authentic assessment has been seen as an appropriate and viable alternative to assess gifted students' knowledge and skills in content domains. Products, portfolios, and other performance-based approaches have long been advocated for gifted learners to demonstrate their ability to apply and synthesize knowledge (Moon, Brighton, Callahan, & Robinson, 2005; VanTassel-Baska, 1992, 2008). Yet, the trend in the new millennium for all students has been to move away from any assessment that is not based on multiple-choice questions, as state tests have become more and more high stakes (Marion, 2009). Now, as we face problems with the overuse of tests, as well as the use of lower level and narrowed tests, there is a renewal of interest in tests that aid instruction, motivate learners, and provide a better picture of high-level learning (Goertz, 2009).

Several considerations important in developing and implementing more authentic and performance-based assessment systems with high-ability learners are addressed below. They focus on technical adequacy issues, the need to use assessments for improving learning, and the range of assessment types that may be appropriate for use with the gifted learner.

Target High-Level Skills

Given the depth and complexity of gifted learners' cognitive abilities, tests for this population should emphasize high-level thinking and processing skills. That is, the test should go beyond simple recollection of knowledge or facts and require students to operate at higher levels of application, analysis, synthesis, and evaluation. Task demands for gifted learners can make use of the following thinking processes often identified as central to differentiation (Marzano, Pickering, & McTighe, 1993):

- comparing,
- classifying,
- induction,
- deduction,
- error analysis,
- constructing support,
- abstracting,
- analyzing perspectives,
- decision making,
- investigation,
- experimental inquiry,
- problem solving, and
- invention.

By the same token, expectations for students' performance conveyed, for instance, through scoring rubrics should reflect the same high standards for complexity and sophistication to bring out the best products that gifted learners are capable of generating.

Use Multiple Approaches

To monitor student performance and inform instruction, a teacher needs

TABLE 16.2

Assessment Tools for Writing

	Writing Projects	Research Products	Metacognitive and Organizational Products
Formative tools • Portfolio of work in progress	Three graded essays in second draft form with peer and teacher commentary	Outline for research paper	Annotated bibliography of research paper references
Summative tools • Portfolio of completed work	Final draft essays (three or more)	Research paper	Self-assessment of completed portfolio

to collect student performance data all the way through a learning module or unit, using formative and summative assessments. Formative assessments are used to monitor student progress during instruction, while summative assessments are given at the end of instruction for the purpose of certifying mastery or assigning grades (Gronlund, 1998). A sample set of formative and summative assessment tools in the area of writing is illustrated in Table 16.2. Although some approaches are more suitable for one type of assessment (e.g., portfolios may be used for formative, rather than summative, assessment), some approaches can be used for both. In order to examine a student's performance from various perspectives and under different conditions, it is desirable for teachers to employ multiple assessment approaches in both oral and written form. A combination of approaches generally works to both the teacher's and the student's advantage because different approaches can supplement one another to provide a more comprehensive picture of a student's performance.

Identify Purpose

An emphasis on performance-based tasks does not need to entirely replace standardized tests when the latter may function effectively. For instance, although a performance task can allow students to demonstrate their actual writing ability, students also may construct their own sentences in such a way as to bypass their weak areas in grammar and sentence structure. If language mechanics are the focus of an assessment, then a standardized test can better cover a large number of grammar and language points in a relatively short time. It is, therefore, a more efficient tool for examining students' mastery in that area. The key is to select an appropriate approach based on the purpose of the assessment. In a pull-out enrichment program, for example, embedded assessment tasks have proven to be the most useful in fulfilling the purpose of continuity in interrupted instructional time (Tal & Medijensky, 2005). Generally, if content mastery is being assessed, a paper-and-pencil test with close-ended items may be preferable. If higher order thinking and problem solving are being assessed, a more performance-based approach would be appropriate.

ISSUES IN ASSESSING GIFTED STUDENTS' LEARNING

Differentiation for gifted learners typically calls for the use of advanced content, deep processing, and quality products. When differentiation is occurring, gifted students tend to get harder books to read and more challenging projects to complete than their regular classmates. How do teachers assess their learning outcomes in such a way that these students feel properly rewarded for their extra labor? How can we encourage gifted students to strive for a higher level when they always compare favorably with their peers in the classroom? And, in attempting a challenging project, how should teachers appropriately weigh the emphasis on students' efforts and final results? A finding that has consistently emerged from district-wide evaluations of gifted programs is that gifted students are not evaluated regularly for their learning in the programs (VanTassel-Baska, 2008). That, in part, speaks to the complexity of the problem.

Another technical issue with performance assessment is its typically low-scoring interrater reliability (Stiggins, 1991). Therefore, quality control in scoring and repeated use of such an assessment over time to collect multiple samples of student performance can help ensure a reliable assessment of a student's ability. Use of assessments in science, the language arts, and social studies at the Center for Gifted Education have demonstrated strong interrater reliability (.8 and higher) when teams of educators have been trained in using the assessments, when they are monitored for scoring problems, and when discussions are held about problem student work and how it should be scored, resulting in tighter guidelines for scoring.

Even given the power of this approach to assessment, it is important to stress the downside of employing such a model (Lazer, 2009). Concerns from the psychometric community continue to be troublesome in respect to the level of technical adequacy that can be acquired with this approach to assessment, the resources and cost of designing such assessments well, and the limits on generalizability that can be claimed.

MODELS FOR ASSESSMENT

The examples that follow provide a concrete representation of performance-based assessment tools that have been and continue to be employed effectively with gifted learners. Both examples meet the technical adequacy requirements discussed in this chapter.

International Baccalaureate and Advanced Placement Assessments

At the high school level, the academic provisions for gifted and high-ability learners often primarily consist of International Baccalaureate (IB) and Advanced Placement (AP) courses. These courses are calibrated to be "advanced" to a typical college-level course at a selective school in various subject areas. Because of their emphasis on advanced-level work, the assessment approaches employed in IB and AP programs are illustrative of assessments commonly used with academically oriented gifted learners.

The IB assessment model measures the performance of students against the main objectives of the program by using a combination of external and internal assessment methods in both written and oral modes. External assessments are provided and scored by the International Baccalaureate Organization (IBO). Internal assessments, which are also provided by the IBO, are scored by classroom teachers who are required to send representative scores of high, low, and average levels to the IBO for verification of their having correctly used the scoring rubric. The purpose of this is to ensure that students are assessed fairly according to international standards. On example is the IB Language A1 assessment model. Its externally assessed components are commentary and essay papers on seen and unseen texts and two written assignments of comparative and imaginative/creative nature. The external assessments account for 70% of the overall Language A1 assessment. The internally assessed component consists of two compulsory oral activities, one commentary on a teacher-selected extract, and one oral presentation on a student-selected topic. The oral component accounts for 30% of the total assessment (International Baccalaureate Organization, 1999). Scoring rubrics for the written work typically contain six levels to differentiate the degrees of none, little, some, adequate, good, and excellent demonstrations of required ability, skills, or presentation. These assessments demand abilities such as appreciation, interpretation, comparison, critique, analysis, evaluation, and creativity.

The AP exam in each course provides another example of carefully constructed and scored responses that require depth of knowledge and thought. The exams generally contain two question types: multiple choice and free response. The multiple-choice section emphasizes the breadth of the student's knowledge and understanding of the content. The free-response section emphasizes the application of these core principles in greater depth in solving more extended problems or analyzing complex issues and texts (e.g., College Board Advanced Placement Program, 1999a, 1999b, 1999c, 1999d). For example, a student taking an exam in English Language and Composition might be asked to analyze the rhetoric of a given passage; a student taking English Literature and Composition might be asked to use examples from literature selections he or she has read to support a generalization about character or plot in literature. Students taking a science or statistics exam may be given a situation and asked to design an experiment to answer a question of interest. In general, the free-response questions are designed so that different students are able to draw upon the different experiences and texts they have encountered in their courses in order to respond to the question, thus allowing choice for both teacher and student while still maintaining a common course framework.

The free-response section is scored against carefully developed guidelines that are drafted by individual item developers, reviewed and revised collectively by a task committee, and modified based on student responses. Scorers of the free-response section are trained to apply the guidelines using exemplary student responses. Sample free-response questions for all exams, demonstrating the emphasis on higher level thinking required of students, are available through the College Board at http://www.collegeboard.com.

Along with demonstrating emphasis on higher level skills, the AP and IB exams also illustrate the proper use of different test formats to serve different purposes of assessment. Moreover, these exams are exemplary for high-stakes testing in terms of their careful construction with consideration of the technical concepts discussed earlier in this chapter. For example, the free-response questions in the AP Physics exam (College Board Advanced Placement Program, 1999a) were first developed by members of the AP Physics Development Committee, then reviewed and revised by the committee collectively in a meeting, and finally combined with multiple-choice items written by physics content experts at the Educational Testing Service (ETS). Such a detailed and collaborative development procedure helps to ensure the quality of questions. Free-response questions are assembled with multiple-choice items in such a way that the two parts complement each other to cover the content and skills called for by the test specifications.

Although the resources available to the College Board and the IBO for developing their assessments far exceed the resources available to the average classroom teacher or district curriculum developer, the procedures used by these organizations are instructive in terms of developing even small-scale classroom assessments. The emphases on determining key principles, concepts, and content for assessment; using multiple formats for question development; encouraging review by a group of educators and content experts; and developing and revising careful scoring guidelines based on the test framework and student response are important considerations that teachers and curriculum developers may use as foundations for creating strong assessments.

Center for Gifted Education Science Unit Assessments

Another example of the use of performance-based assessment tools may be found in the science units developed for high-ability learners by the Center for Gifted Education at The College of William and Mary (Center for Gifted Education, 1997), which assess learning in multiple ways. Student learning outcomes are an ultimate indicator of the effectiveness of curricular intervention. These outcomes include oral and written forms of assessment of product, process, and concept in accordance with the Integrated Curriculum Model (ICM). Ideally, curricular intervention that starts with a curriculum developer's theoretical conceptions should result in tangible student gain to complete the cycle of curriculum development. That successful translation from theory to reality depends on both the soundness of the theory and sensitive measurements well aligned with the theory.

This section will analyze an example of one assessment instrument used in the Center for Gifted Education's science curriculum, with exploration of key features that influenced the selection of the instrument and its incorporation into the curriculum. Specifically, the following pages will explore the two forms of the instrument, scoring, content validity and reliability, student examples, and instructional needs indicated by the assessments. This exploration also will serve to illustrate the importance of a reliable and valid instrument in the study of curriculum effectiveness.

Description of the instruments and scoring. The Diet Cola Test was developed by Marilyn Fowler Cain (1990) to assess students' understanding of experiments. It is an open-ended test that requires students to design an experiment to determine whether or not bumble bees are attracted to diet cola. A parallel form to the Diet Cola Test, the Earthworm Test, asks students to design an experiment to find out whether or not earthworms are attracted to light (Adams & Callahan, 1995). Both instruments were adopted in the Center for Gifted Education's science units to be used on a pre- and posttest basis for their adequate reflection of the unit objectives to develop student experimental research skills, the similar age range targeted, and their sufficiently high ceilings (VanTassel-Baska, Bass, Ries, Poland, & Avery, 1998).

Students' responses are scored according to a checklist of science process skills, with points assigned for addressing each skill and additional points for skills addressed in greater detail:
- plans for *safety*,
- stating the *problem* or *question*,
- giving a *hypothesis*,
- describing three *steps* or more,
- arranging steps in a *sequential order*,
- listing *materials* needed,

- plans to *repeat testing*,
- defining *terms*,
- plans for *observation*,
- plans for *measurement*,
- plans for *data collection*,
- plans for *interpreting data*,
- plans to make *conclusions based on data*, and
- plans to *control variables*.

Reliability of the instrument. The National Research Center on the Gifted and Talented at the University of Virginia conducted reliability and validity studies on the Diet Cola Test. The study included 180 students in grades 4–8 who were nominated by their teachers as being good in science and employed the method of test-retesting (10-week interval) with alternate forms. Researchers established the reliability of stability and equivalency of the instrument as .76 (Adams & Callahan, 1995).

Validity of the instrument. The same study at the National Research Center on the Gifted and Talented at the University of Virginia investigated the instrument's content validity and construct validity. The purpose of content validation is to assess whether or not the items adequately represent a performance domain of specific interest (Crocker & Algina, 1986). In this respect, the instrument was said to "exhibit content validity with a clear match between the task and its indicators of success and the criteria of science aptitude suggested by the literature" (Adams & Callahan, 1995, p. 16). The purpose of construct validity is to examine whether or not the instrument correlates highly with other instruments that measure similar constructs of interest. Three instruments were selected to correlate with the Diet Cola Test: the science portion of the Iowa Tests of Basic Skills, the Group Embedded Figures Test, and the Test of Basic Process Skills. The results showed low correlations with varied degrees of statistical significance between the Diet Cola Test and other instruments. Therefore, the test was cautioned as not being a suitable identification instrument for making decisions about the aptitude of specific individuals.

Given the use of the Diet Cola Test in the Center for Gifted Education's science units, it is more relevant to establish its content validity by examining its match with the objectives of the units and its coverage of the targeted high-level skills in unit instruction.

Match between the instrument and unit objectives. In light of the findings from the analysis of the National Education Longitudinal Study (NELS) data (Hamilton, Nussbaum, Kumpermintz, Kerhoven, & Snow, 1995) that the instructional variables of working on experiments in class, problem solving, and promoting scientific understanding were the best predictors of achievement in quantitative science by 10th grade, the William and Mary science units put emphasis on the scientific process, in which students conduct scientific inquiry through the use of experimental design. The units focus on the objectives of developing student abilities to explore a new scientific area, identify meaningful questions within that area, demonstrate good data as appropriate, evaluate results in light of the original problem, make predictions about similar problems, and communicate understanding to others (VanTassel-Baska et al., 1998). The Diet Cola Test, being a performance test that requires students to design an experiment in order to study a given problem, can evaluate fairly well student learning with respect to most of the objectives in the units.

Match between the instrument and the instructional approach. The specific approach used for instruction in the science units from the Center for Gifted Education is problem-based learning (PBL). Each unit presents students with a problem scenario and proceeds to have them define the problem and ways to solve it. The related science and scientific experiments are introduced in the process of students' exploring and investigating the problem. This problem-based approach is reflected well in the Diet Cola Test, a desirable feature that adds to the authenticity of the instrument.

Match between the instrument and targeted high-level thinking. As a science curriculum developed for high-ability learners, the units provide materials and instruction that are sufficiently challenging, in-depth, and varied to meet their learning needs. Through an integrated approach of teaching scientific topics and processes within an overarching concept of *systems*, the units aim to train students in their ability to perform systems thinking and apply what they have learned in an intra- or interdisciplinary way. Accordingly, the assessment for this kind of learning should give due emphasis to higher level thinking skills, as called for by the tasks in the instrument.

Students' pretest and posttest performance. Most units (four out of six on which data were collected) showed a statistically significant effectiveness when treatment students were compared with their own prior performance or with their peers who received no curricular intervention. To illustrate students' increased understanding in experimental design and data collection after their exposure to the units, three sample responses from fifth graders were presented as follows (grammar and spelling are not corrected).

Treatment effect and revealed instructional needs. The implementation results of the science unit showed that, compared with students who did not use the unit, those who participated in unit instruction performed significantly better on the posttest after taking into consideration the pretest difference between the treatment and comparison groups. Content analysis of student performance showed that students were weak in (a) stating a plan for interpreting data, (b) stating a plan for making conclusions based on data, (c) planning to control variables, (d) planning to repeat testing, and (e) planning to

EARTHWORM/DIET COLA
TEST RESPONSES

Student A
Pretest Response:

First, I would put some earthworms in a container. There would be lights and some dirt. I would put several different earthworms in it. If more earthworms liked the light than that would be right. If more didn't like the light then that would be right. I would try this with about seven groups and decide if they liked light. (Score = 5)

Posttest Response:

Materials: Diet Cola, 3 large containers, 3 small containers, 6 bees

Hypothesis: If you give bees diet cola then they will be attracted to it.

1. Gather 6 bees, diet cola, 3 large containers, 3 small containers.
2. Put 2 bees in each large container.
3. Pour 5 ml of diet cola in each small container.
4. Set the small container of diet cola in each large container that has bees in it.
5. Watch and observe to see if the bees are attracted to the diet cola.
6. You should record if the bees like the diet cola on a chart like below.

Bees   *If they are attracted to Diet Cola*

1
2
3

(Score = 11)

Student B
Pretest Response:

No, earthworms don't like light. How I know that is because I took an earthworm and put it on some dert and if it liked sun light it would stay on top of the dert but it didn't it went into the dert where it's dark. (Score = 4)

Posttest Response:

Title of experiment is — Are bees attracted to diet cola?

Materials: a room with nothing in it, 4 bees in a jar, a cup of diet cola, and a Pepsi

Step by step on how to do the experiment: First you take the diet cola & put it in the room when you take the Pepsi and put it in the room by the diet cola. Then you take the jar of 4 bees and release them in the room & then in about 5 mins. see which one they like better & if they don't like neither of them.

How will you know: Look in each cup & see how much they drink out of each cup. The data I will be collecting is: how much diet cola & Pepsi they drink.

Data Table

Diet Cola   Pepsi

(record information here)

(Score = 12)

Student C
Pretest Response:

I don't think earthworms like light, because most of them live underground unless it rains or something and they get washed out of the dirt. I could always do an experiment to make sure, thow. For an experiment, I might take an earthworm with some kind of light, and dirt, and see if it stays out in the light, or trys to get away from the light by going under the dirt.

(Score = 5)

Posttest Response:

Title: "Are bees attracted to diet cola?"

Hypothesis: I don't think bees are attracted to diets, just to regular. For example: Coke, Sprite, Dr. Pepper.

Materials: Bee, diet cola, container

Description of what I would do: Take one can of diet cola and pour about 1 cup of it into a dish, bowl, etc. Then release a bee about a foot away and see if it moves toward the diet cola. If it does—you know bees like diet cola, but if it moves away from the diet cola, or doesn't respond to it you know bees don't like diet cola. When you are done with your experiment carefully release your bee, pour out your soda, and put back the way you found them.

What will you record: If the bees are attracted to the diet cola or if they are attracted to the non diet liquids.

Data Table:

Tries	1	2	3	4	5	6

Reactions:

(Score = 12)

practice safety (VanTassel-Baska et al., 1998). More instructional attention is needed in implementing the corresponding component of the curriculum.

Project Clarion Assessments

The use of performance-based assessments with K–3 populations using ICM-designed units of study have yielded strong learning gains at each level of implementation and for each unit of study (see Kim et al., 2010). The use of the Diet Cola Test prototype was employed for all units to assess gains in scientific process design, using a modified rubric. Content mastery was assessed through pre- and post-concept maps that engaged students in demonstrating their understanding of key science topics taught in the units such as plants,

1. Give *five* examples of things that are "systems."
   -
   -
   -
   -
   -

2. Draw *one* example of a system that you know.

3. Label at least *five* features of your system.

4. What are *three* things you can say about *all* systems?
   - All systems _____.
   - All systems _____.
   - All systems _____.

Figure 16.1. Preassessment for the concept of *systems.*

magnetism, and force. The mastery of the macro-concept used in each unit was assessed by students' responding to a set of questions about the concepts of *systems* and *change* (see Figure 16.1). Rubrics also were developed for each of these assessments (see Figure 16.2), and exemplars were provided after the first year of data collection.

Primary age students were able to handle the task demands on this performance-based assessment fairly well after they had experienced a unit of study, especially the first three parts of the assessment. Sample responses demonstrated students' capacity to be more fluent in providing examples of systems and providing more detailed drawings. Generalizations remained challenging for all learners. Ability differences prevailed, however, favoring gifted learners (Bland, VanTassel-Baska, Bracken, Feng, & Stambaugh, 2010). However, the assessment met the technical adequacy standards of validity, reliability, fairness, and ceiling.

Other Assessment Approaches in Science

As mentioned before, teachers need to use formative and summative assessments in a variety of modes to monitor and evaluate student progress over time and to avoid putting undue weight on a single high-stakes test. The assessment opportunities for formative assessment in the William and Mary science units include the following:

	5	4	3	2	1
Examples of the concept	At least five appropriate examples are given.	Four appropriate examples are given.	Three appropriate examples are given.	Two appropriate examples are given.	One appropriate example is given.
Systems representation	The drawing contains a recognizable system, with functioning parts.	The drawing contains most of the major elements of a system.	The drawing contains some elements of a system.	The drawing contains a few elements of a system.	The drawing contains only one object.
Features of a system	The drawing contains at least five elements or other features of a system.	The drawing contains four elements or other features of a system.	The drawing contains three elements or other features of a system.	The drawing contains two elements or other features of a system.	The drawing contains one element or other feature of a system.
Generalizations	Three appropriate generalizations are made about systems.	Three somewhat appropriate generalizations are made about systems.	Two appropriate generalizations are made about systems.	One appropriate generalization is made about systems.	Only a statement about systems is made.

Figure 16.2. Rubric for scoring the concept assessment of *systems*.

- the student's problem log, which is a written compilation of the student's thoughts about the problem (each lesson contains suggested questions for students to answer in their problem logs, which also can be used by the student to record data and new information that he or she has obtained during the course of the unit);
- experimental design worksheets, which can be used to assess a student's understanding of experimental design and the scientific process, as well as to record information about what was done and what was found during student-directed experimentation; and
- teacher observation of student participation in large- and small-group activities.

Opportunities for summative assessment include the following:
- the final resolution activity, which involves a small-group presentation of a solution to the unit's ill-structured problem, the quality of which will reflect the group's understanding of the science involved, as well as the societal and ethical considerations needed to form an acceptable solution; and
- final unit assessments, which allow the teacher to determine whether or not

individual students have met the science process, science content, and systems objectives listed in the goals and objectives at the beginning of the unit.

Assessments in Other Subject Areas

Just as the Center for Gifted Education at The College of William and Mary has refined existing performance-based approaches in science, staff also have developed and refined assessment approaches for the language arts (VanTassel-Baska et al., 2002) and social studies (Little, Feng, VanTassel-Baska, Rogers, & Avery, 2007). All of them adhere to the principles outlined above for the science assessments in respect to establishing technical adequacy, tailoring existing assessments to meet the demands of the curriculum, and developing rubrics and exempla for easier teacher implementation and use. Because these verbal areas of the curriculum are interdisciplinary by their very nature, the performance-based assessments used to assess student learning are more diversified than in science, exploiting content mastery, writing proficiency, literary analysis and interpretation, higher level thinking, and concept attainment. Results in student learning from the use of these assessments have been reported elsewhere (see VanTassel-Baska & Stambaugh, 2008).

ADVANTAGES AND DISADVANTAGES OF ALTERNATIVE ASSESSMENTS IN JUDGING GIFTED STUDENT LEARNING OUTCOMES

Much has been written in this chapter and elsewhere (see VanTassel-Baska, 2008) about the positive aspects of using alternative assessment for the gifted to gauge so-called "real learning." It is certainly true that products, open-ended elaborated task demands, and portfolios all afford the advantages of having sufficient ceiling, representing a creative response mode, being focused on the curriculum taught (curriculum-based), providing a mode of assessing higher level thinking and problem solving, and, perhaps most importantly, offering diagnostic information for improving instruction. Yet, these advantages must be seen in the perspective of the limitations of these approaches to assessment as well. Such limitations may be seen as the difficulties with generalizability beyond a particular class of learners, the problems inherent in obtaining interrater reliability among teachers using a given performance-based assessment (PBA) rubric, and the narrow scope of skills that can be tapped through such an assessment. In the final analysis, however, these approaches used in tandem with more standardized measures offer an important portrait of gifted students—one that provides social comparison data to their age group as well as

TABLE 16.3

Advantages and Disadvantages of Alternative Assessments

Advantages	Disadvantages
• Are domain-specific	• Lack generalizability
• Have sufficient ceiling	• Challenge to develop rubrics, score, and establish
• Offer an opportunity to assess higher level skills	interrater reliability
• Can be designed around content standards	• Do not assess full range of skills
• Provide creative and elaborated response mode	• Difficult to demonstrate technical adequacy
• Offer diagnostic information for instruction	

unique data on individual growth and development. Table 16.3 delineates the advantages and disadvantages just described.

THE LANDSCAPE OF ASSESSMENT FOR THE GIFTED

Educators need to think about appropriate assessment approaches for use in gifted programs by asking themselves what the assessment is capable of providing, what outcomes of learning need to be assessed, and the purpose for which the assessment will be used. Table 16.4 shows the relationship among different types of assessments, both traditional and alternative, that may be useful in assessing gifted students' learning. Both on- and off-level achievement measures are useful to document mastery learning in specific subjects. State assessment tests illustrate the level of proficiency attained, with gifted learners expected to reach proficiency in all areas and achieve at the advanced level in their areas of giftedness. Off-level national tests such as the SAT and ACT, used routinely with middle-school-age gifted learners, assess advanced levels of learning in specific academic areas. The AP and IB tests described in this chapter also are highly useful to calibrate advanced learning for gifted students in high school that translates into college placement and/or credit. Performance-based models at all levels provide important diagnostic data to teachers and other educators on the acquisition of content-based higher level skills and concepts within an academic semester or year. Product assessments may be useful tools to assess longer term learning of higher order skills and processes across years in a gifted program. Finally, portfolios have the capacity to demonstrate the nature as well as the extent of gifted student learning over a designated period of time, usually at least a year.

The use of these assessment approaches should be carefully considered and used in combination for different audiences to illustrate different aspects of gifted student learning. Because the high-stakes state assessments must be a

TABLE 16.4

Assessment Type by Purpose and Use in Gifted Programs

Type of assessment	Application/purpose	Use in gifted programs
State achievement tests (on-level)	Mastery oriented on a narrow set of skills and content	To assess current levels of mastery and ensure reasonable growth
Standardized achievement tests (off-level at elementary level)	Mastery oriented for the gifted	To assess "real" gifted student achievement in an area
Advanced Placement/International Baccalaureate (secondary)	Advanced mastery in subject areas	To assess levels of gifted students' advanced learning
Performance-based (all levels)	Pre/post or time series	To assess short-term growth in advanced skills and processes
Product-based (all levels)	Pre/post over multiple years	To assess enhancement of research and problem-solving skills
Portfolios (all levels)	Evolving competencies based	To assess the process of learning as it unfolds in key dimensions

part of the picture, it may be wise to combine these results with performance-based models to gauge instructional level and off-level assessments that do not suffer from ceiling effect. In such a combination, we emerge with a more authentic picture of gifted learners' current functioning in subject area learning.

CONCLUSION

Effective and reliable assessment is not an easy task, and for gifted students it is even harder, given the nature of the learner and the nature of the learning in the program. Just as evaluation of gifted programs is a weak area in gifted education, so too is assessment for gifted students. Although we can learn from the general assessment literature, we have a great need to build practice and experience in this area, creating performance and portfolio approaches that clearly demonstrate enhanced learning for this population of learners.

KEY POINTS SUMMARY

- Effective practice in assessment requires attention to technical details of reliability, validity, test fairness, and test ceiling. Test ceiling is a particularly important consideration in the development of assessments for high-ability learners.
- Expectations for student performance on assessments for high-ability learners should be at a high level, requiring the employment of analysis,

synthesis, and evaluation skills; these expectations should be conveyed to students through both the questions asked and the rubrics employed for scoring.

- A combination of formative and summative, standardized and performance-based assessments should be employed to develop a clear understanding of student progress and learning needs in each area of the curriculum.
- The Advanced Placement and International Baccalaureate programs employ assessments that illustrate effective measurement practice for gifted learners by incorporating accelerated content, requirements for higher level thinking, and varied response tasks relevant to the subject areas.
- The Center for Gifted Education science, social studies, and language arts curricula provide another example of performance-based learning assessments for high-ability learners, incorporating emphasis on higher level task demands relevant to the subject area and scoring rubrics that have a sufficiently high ceiling.

REFERENCES

Adams, C. M., & Callahan, C. M. (1995). The reliability and validity of a performance task for evaluating science process skills. *Gifted Child Quarterly, 39,* 14–20.

Bland, L. C., VanTassel-Baska, J., Bracken, B. A., Feng, A. X., Stambaugh, T., & Kim, K. H. (2010). *Assessing science reasoning and conceptual understanding in the primary grades using multiple measures of performance: Project Clarion.* Manuscript submitted for publication.

Cain, M. F. (1990). The diet cola test. *Science Scope, 13*(4), 32–34.

Center for Gifted Education. (1997). *Guide to teaching a problem-based science curriculum.* Dubuque, IA: Kendall/Hunt.

College Board Advanced Placement Program. (1999a). *Released exams: 1998 AP Physics B and Physics C.* New York, NY: College Entrance Examination Board and Educational Testing Service.

College Board Advanced Placement Program. (1999b). *5-year set of free-response questions 1995–1999: English.* New York, NY: College Entrance Examination Board and Educational Testing Service.

College Board Advanced Placement Program. (1999c). *Released exam 1997: AP statistics.* New York, NY: College Entrance Examination Board and Educational Testing Service.

College Board Advanced Placement Program. (1999d). *Released exam 1998: AP environmental science.* New York, NY: College Entrance Examination Board and Educational Testing Service.

Crocker, L., & Algina, J. (1986). *Introduction to classical and modern test theory.* New York, NY: Holt, Rinehart, & Winston.

Goertz, M. (2009, December) *Overview of current assessment practices*. Presentation to the National Academies of Science, Washington, DC.

Gronlund, N. E. (1998). *Assessment of student achievement* (6th ed.). Boston, MA: Allyn & Bacon.

Hamilton, L. S., Nussbaum, E. M., Kumpermintz, H., Kerhoven, J. I. M., & Snow, R. E. (1995). Enhancing the validity and usefulness of large-scale educational assessments: II. NELS: 88 science achievement. *American Educational Research Journal, 32*, 555–581.

International Baccalaureate Organization. (1999). *International Baccalaureate Language A1 guide*. Geneva, Switzerland: Author.

Kim, K. H., VanTassel-Baska, J., Bracken, B. A., Feng, A., Stambaugh, T., & Bland, L. (2010). *Project Clarion: Three years of science instruction in Title I schools among K-third grade students*. Manuscript submitted for publication.

Lazer, S. (2009, December). *Technical challenges with innovative item types*. Presentation to the National Academies of the Sciences, Washington, DC.

Little, C., Feng, A. X., VanTassel-Baska, J. Rogers, K. B., & Avery, L. D. (2007). A study of curriculum effectiveness in social studies. *Gifted Child Quarterly, 51*, 272–284.

Marion, S. (2009, December). *Changes in assessments and assessment systems since 2002*. Presentation to the National Academies of the Sciences, Washington, DC.

Marzano, R. S., Pickering, D., & McTighe, S. (1993). *Assessing student outcomes: Performance assessment using the dimensions of learning model*. Alexandria, VA: Association for Supervision and Curriculum Development.

Moon, T., Brighton, C. M., Callahan, C. M., & Robinson, A. (2005). Development of authentic assessments for the middle school classroom. *Journal of Secondary Gifted Education, 16*, 119–133.

Stiggins, R. J. (1991). Facing the challenges of a new era of educational assessment. *Applied Measurement in Education, 4*, 263–273.

Tal, R. T., & Medijensky, S. (2005). A model of alternative embedded assessment in a pull-out enrichment program for the gifted. *Gifted Education International, 20*, 166–186.

VanTassel-Baska, J. (1992). *Planning effective curriculum for gifted learners*. Denver, CO: Love.

VanTassel-Baska, J. (2002). Assessment of gifted student learning in the language arts. *Journal of Secondary Gifted Education, 13*, 67–72.

VanTassel-Baska, J. (Ed.). (2008). *Alternative assessments with gifted and talented students*. Waco, TX: Prufrock Press.

VanTassel-Baska, J., Bass, G., Ries, R., Poland, D., & Avery, L. D. (1998). A national study of science curriculum effectiveness with high-ability students. *Gifted Child Quarterly, 42*, 200–211.

VanTassel-Baska, J., & Stambaugh, T. (Eds.). (2008). *What works: 20 years of curriculum development and research for advanced learners*. Waco, TX: Prufrock Press.

Chapter 17

Aligning Curriculum for the Gifted With Content Standards and State Assessments

Tamra Stambaugh

In this age of educational accountability and an increased focus on international competitiveness to succeed in a global economy (Friedman, 2005), those who teach gifted students cannot ignore the impact of subject-specific content standards as a springboard for modifying and implementing appropriate curriculum and instruction for gifted learners. Educators of the gifted can no longer approach the curriculum as a set of activities that are unrelated to the content standards or general classroom instruction. Instead, leaders in gifted education must be deliberate in their selection and planning of content-based instruction and find ways to infuse standards in a systemic way across all grade levels.

Educators of the gifted must be concerned with how to develop expertise and provide advanced instructional opportunities for gifted learners as part of a talent development process, catering to the unique advanced abilities of the gifted child. Can this be accomplished within a standards-based system? Of course. Content-specific standards play a significant role in the development of expertise and talent in gifted students. Research focused on the development of expertise aligns with the philosophical underpinnings of the standards movement when implemented appropriately.

First, the development of expertise is content-specific (Amabile, 1996; Bransford, Brown, & Cocking, 1999; Bransford & Donovan, 2003; Simonton, 2004). Gifted students must be introduced to the habits of mind and tools of the discipline at earlier ages. There is little evidence to suggest that the teaching of isolated thinking skills transfers to content-specific domains without the explicit incorporation of the advanced processes within a given discipline (French & Rhodes, 1992; Perkins & Salomon, 1989). Therefore, teachers who plan instruction for gifted learners should ensure that the advanced processes they teach (e.g., higher level thinking skills, creative problem solving) are embedded within the core standards.

Second, metacognitive approaches are critical to the development of expertise and learning (Bransford et al., 1999; Bransford & Donovan, 2003; Palincsar & Brown, 1989). Students need time to reflect on their own learning and thinking. Teachers can facilitate this process through the incorporation of reflective activities within a content area. Expertise can be developed through metacognitive approaches such as (a) discussion groups about the processes of a given activity and how students viewed their processes of approaching a difficult task, (b) reflection journals, (c) deliberate questioning strategies that help students analyze assumptions or errors in their thinking, and (d) constructive feedback about the process of thinking like a professional in a given field.

Moreover, the development of expertise within a content-specific domain occurs over time with continued practice of challenging content (Bloom, 1985; Csikszentmihalyi, Rathunde, & Whalen, 1993; Simonton, 2004). Studies of gifted adolescents and eminent persons who have contributed significantly to a field did so with a lot of practice and hard work within a content-specific domain. Students need exposure to challenging opportunities that increase in complexity as their knowledge and skills increase, if they are to continue to achieve at high levels.

WHY STANDARDS?

When I first started my career in gifted education, I was advised to create lessons that focused on processes, generally void of content, and to ignore what was being taught in the general education classroom. I was cautioned against overlapping my instruction with favored general education classroom activities or lessons, especially the reading of certain novels that were reserved for a specific grade. As the standards movement gained a stronghold, many teachers of the gifted were overheard saying that the standards movement did not apply to their teaching because they taught processes that were transferable across all domains. Likewise, teachers felt the standards were unnecessary and too easy for gifted students and therefore of no value. Both of these beliefs are erroneous.

The National Research Council, informed by cognitive scientists, sponsored the publication of a series of books entitled *How People/Students Learn* (Bransford et al., 1999; Bransford & Donovan, 2003). The authors suggested that the transfer of learning occurs when (a) new knowledge is linked to pre-existing ideas or schema within a content-specific discipline; (b) knowledge is connected and organized around important concepts within and across disciplines; and (c) deliberate strategies within a content area are taught, providing a framework for understanding.

Although standards are not fail-proof, there are stated benefits for all students. VanTassel-Baska (2003) explained that standards (a) provide a framework to prepare students for work in the 21st century, (b) ensure quality and consistency across districts, (c) encourage a stronger focus on content-discipline and the habits of mind of professionals within the field, and (d) provide a template in which to plan instruction. When teachers embrace the intent of standards, they then can use them as a springboard for modifying and adjusting content to provide accelerated curriculum for the most precocious learners. Tomlinson (1999) also outlined the importance of using standards as a springboard for differentiating instruction for gifted learners. She explained that teachers must know where they are going with a lesson in order to arrive at a goal. Standards provide this roadmap and allow students to develop expertise in their areas of talent.

Barriers to standards also exist when they are used to confine and hold students back instead of allowing them the opportunity for continual progress. Standards can impede learning if they are not differentiated or adjusted based on student readiness. Moreover, simply teaching to the test hinders gifted student progress. When standards are appropriately aligned and adapted to meet the needs of gifted students, these students are more likely to show positive growth. Wright, Horn, and Sanders (1997) found that students in the top 20% are less likely to show positive academic gains when compared to their previous year's test scores unless student learning is linked to content standards and differentiated. They postulated that when students of high ability are unsuccessful it is because of a "lack of opportunity to proceed at their own pace, lack of challenging materials, lack of accelerated course offerings, and concentration of instruction on average or below-average students" (Wright et al., 1997, p. 66). They continued by saying, "This finding indicates that it cannot be assumed that higher-achieving students will make it on their own" (p. 66).

CONSIDERATIONS FOR ALIGNING STANDARDS

There are six main principles to consider when aligning the curriculum to content standards. Educators of the gifted must (a) know their students and how to provide accommodations for them, (b) understand the intent of the standards and plan activities and products accordingly, (c) select appropriate curriculum and materials that match and enhance the standards, (d) differentiate the standards by applying features of the Integrated Curriculum Model (ICM), (e) ensure that assessment and instruction are commensurate, and (f) develop a scope and sequence as a guide for teachers of gifted students.

Know Your Students

Students arrive in classrooms with unique abilities and varying degrees of readiness. When aligning curriculum to standards, teachers of the gifted must continually keep their students in mind so they know to what extent the standards may need to be modified or accelerated. This may include preassessing students' skills and appropriately adjusting the standards, if necessary, to meet the needs of these advanced students. Preassessment options, whether formal or informal, provide data to assist teachers with providing appropriate curriculum and instructional activities to better meet student needs.

Know the Intent of the Standards and Plan Activities and Task Demands Accordingly

Too many times teachers plan lessons around preferred activities as opposed to the standards. This is quite tempting to do. As educators we want students to enjoy learning and are always looking for new activities to incorporate into our lessons. Although many activities may be appropriately linked to existing standards, teachers must deliberately discipline themselves to *look at the standard first* and then determine the learning demands, based on their acquired knowledge of varying students' readiness levels. Consider this illustration:

> Mrs. Jones' class is studying plants. She cites the following standard and representative check for understanding as a guide for class activities:
>
> Guiding question: How are plant and animals cells organized to carry on the processes of life?
>
> Grade level expectations: (GLE 0207.1.1) Recognize that plants and animals are made up of smaller parts and use food, water, and air to survive.

Check for understanding: (GLE 0207.1.1) Design a new living thing and explain how it would acquire food, water, and air. (Tennessee Department of Education, 2009, p. 3)

Upon the conclusion of her plant unit, Mrs. Jones asks her students to create a brand-new plant using a variety of art materials. Students showcase their new plant during a plant show that is open to the entire school. During the event students explain the name of their plant and outline what inspired them to make it.

This plant-creating tradition has been in existence for several years and fondly remembered by matriculating students. This activity is engaging and provides an interesting culminating activity to conclude the unit. However, the teacher failed to closely examine the intent of the standard and ignored the overarching conceptual understanding of how living cells are organized to survive. Instead she focused on the product of plant creation and commensurate event, ignoring the substantive part of the standard—how different parts of the plant have specific uses for survival. Teachers must understand the intent of the regular standard before they can adapt it or modify for gifted learners.

Select Appropriate Materials That Match and Enhance the Standards

Similar to the previous point, standards are to be considered first, not curriculum or activities. Teachers must resist the temptation to select a favorite unit or activity without considering how that curriculum matches the standards. Teachers do not need to develop a new curriculum but rather match research-based curriculum, already piloted and found to be effective with gifted learners, to standards to be addressed. Standards are identified first and then such materials and curricula are selected that will enable students to learn and practice the content embedded within the listed standard. To accomplish this, leaders and teachers should (a) examine the standards to be taught and modified for gifted learners as necessary; (b) align the standards with the sections and task demands presented within the curriculum to on- and above-grade-level standards; (c) determine the gaps between the standards and the curriculum based on the alignment; and (d) select appropriately advanced supplemental materials to fill gaps.

It is rare to find one textbook that meets all of the state standards, especially given the differences in standards and subsequent assessments across states. Instead, a curriculum team that includes teachers of the gifted, content experts, and curriculum specialists should be convened to examine textbooks and determine which chapters or lessons align with each cluster of higher level standards. This is even more critical for gifted students as much of the curriculum, especially

Standard (Ohio Content Standards, grades 11–12, p. 61)	Textbook chapter	Teacher response to meet the standard
d.11.10 *Analyze* issues related to the *use* of different types of taxes to fund public goods and services including (a) proportional tax, (b) progressive tax, and c) regressive tax.	The textbook provides definitions of proportional, progressive, and regressive tax and outlines examples each.	After reading the textbook, the students will debate which tax is best given a set of community circumstances.

Figure 17.1. Example of standard, text, and supplemental activity.

that used in Title I schools for language arts, emphasizes lower level basic skills and factual recall, rather than higher level processes (Tivnan & Hemphill, 2005).

Sometimes teachers must create new task demands to meet the intent of the standard, using the textbook as a resource for background knowledge. The facts are included in the textbook but it is up to the teacher to guide students to use the book as a student resource and create high-level task demands that embed the content with the advanced processes required by the intent of the standards. Figure 17.1 provides an example of how teachers can supplement the text to meet the standard. Note that the textbook provides basic definitions and examples, both lower levels of Bloom's taxonomy. The standard asks that students analyze the use of the types, not simply "define." The teacher needs to supplement the text to meet the standard by including a higher level activity.

Differentiate the Standards by Applying the Integrated Curriculum Model Features

The ICM can be used as a framework to guide the alignment of curriculum content standards and state assessments. Figure 17.2 outlines the relationship between the research on the development of expertise, the ICM framework, and differentiation, all of which have been previously discussed in this book. These models can be used to guide instruction and can be adjusted to meet the needs of gifted learners. Teachers may use one or all of the components of the ICM (e.g., issues/themes, process/product, advanced content) and commensurate models (e.g., Literature Web, primary document analysis, Paul's [1992] Elements of Reasoning model) as a means for aligning and differentiating standards. Examples and further discussion are provided in the next section.

Ensure That the Assessment Matches the Instruction and Standards

This concept sounds simple, but it is one of the most common mistakes teachers make when administering assessments. For sake of illustration, imagine that a teacher of the gifted pulled students out of the classroom for language

The Integrated Curriculum Model dimensions	Development of expertise	Framework for aligning and differentiating content standards	How differentiated
Issues/themes	Linkage of content to overarching ideas and essential understandings within and across disciplines	Taba Concept Development (e.g., systems, change, cause and effect)	Abstractness
Process/product	Provision of frameworks that enhance the understanding of a discipline and allow students to practice the craft of an acting professional	Paul's (1992) Reasoning Model, inquiry-based investigations, research	Depth, complexity, challenge
Advanced content	Linkage to content standards and subject-specific disciplines for the transfer or learning	Integration of higher level standards across grade levels; content-based models that support habits of the discipline (e.g., literature web, problem-based learning)	Acceleration

Figure 17.2. How the Integrated Curriculum Model links to the development of expertise.

arts instruction. Students read advanced classical literature and discussed their interpretations of varying ideas about the text, focusing on how the literary elements impact the main ideas of the text. Upon conclusion of the novel, a test was administered to all students. The test required that students write a persuasive essay outlining their thoughts about the theme of the book. Although the students had great ideas, the rubric for assessing their writing focused mostly on the development of a thought and the mechanics of writing. Consequently students did not perform as well on the assessment because the instruction was about literary analysis and the assessment focused on writing mechanics.

Another example of this frequently occurs in science. Consider a common standard to be taught in an elementary science classroom: Students will plan and conduct experiments by creating questions, formulating hypotheses, designing accurate data tables, and making inferences about findings. The teacher implements this standard by allowing students to conduct experiments. The teacher introduces a scientific concept, writes the question for experimentation on the board, provides a detailed outline of the experiment, demonstrates it in front of the class, and then, if time permits, allows students to follow similar directions to conduct the experiment. Upon conclusion of the unit, students are asked to determine how they would design a question and create an experiment to test it. Few students pass. Why? The instruction did not match the assessment or the standard. The standard specifically states that "students will *plan* and *conduct* experiments by *creating questions* ..." Even though the assessment matched the standard, the lessons did not align because students conducted preplanned experiments and did not have the opportunity to plan and conduct their own experiments by creating their own testable questions, given specific phenomena.

Develop a Scope and Sequence for the Gifted

School district leaders and teachers must work together to create a comprehensive plan that outlines which standards will be taught at which grade levels, and to what level these standards are taught or differentiated. A scope and sequence should be designed for each content area and embed advanced processes such as critical thinking and problem solving within each discipline, linked to and adapted from the standards. VanTassel-Baska and Stambaugh (2006) suggested that districts select a small group of key personnel that includes those familiar with curriculum and standards across grade levels as well as those familiar with gifted learners and their instructional needs and development. The team should use the current standards as a springboard for the scope and sequence development and include advanced requirements and differentiated opportunities for gifted learners. The document should be piloted and revised as necessary based on user feedback, changes in regular standards, and student assessment results (VanTassel-Baska & Stambaugh, 2006).

THE ICM: A GUIDE TO DIFFERENTIATING STANDARDS

The Advanced Content Dimension

The advanced content dimension of the Integrated Curriculum Model outlines the need for accelerated curriculum and the selection and teaching of the most rigorous standards. Acceleration for the gifted has been well researched and found to be effective, regardless of whether acceleration occurs within a subject area or through grade skipping (Colangelo, Assouline, & Gross, 2004). When planning instruction for the gifted, one must consider how to infuse advanced or accelerated content within the standards framework. To accomplish this, teachers must first know the sequence of standards, including what was taught in previous grades and what will be taught in following grades. Acceleration may involve more than adopting the next grade level standards. VanTassel-Baska and Stambaugh (2006) described acceleration as (a) fewer tasks assigned to master standards, (b) preassessment of skills and deliberate selection of instruction and content, and (c) the clustering of standards by higher order thinking skills.

The inclusion of advanced or accelerated content may not be accomplished simply by incorporating the next grade level curriculum standards to the previous grade. This is most aptly illustrated in mathematics. A typical third-grade standard requires students to multiply one-digit numbers whereas a typical fourth-grade standard requires students to multiply two-digit numbers. Although this may be the progression from one grade level to the next, both grade-level standards include basic calculation principles instead of advanced processes that add depth. In this instance, acceleration might include a problem-solving component such as combining addition, subtraction, multiplication, and division to arrive at a target number, instead of progressing to more basic calculation.

Another example comes from language arts. Note the progression of the standard requirement from one grade level to the next:

Fourth Grade, 4.2: *Identify* the influences of setting on a selection . . .
Fifth Grade, 5.2: *Explain* the influence of setting . . .
Sixth Grade, 6.2: *Identify* the features of setting and <u>explain</u> its importance in literary text . . . (Ohio Department of Education, 2009)

The verbs are italicized to emphasize what is intended by the standard. The fourth- and fifth-grade standards require students to identify or explain the setting, respectively, whereas the sixth-grade standard combines identifying and explaining. The standard also links the setting to the plot. To effectively accelerate the curriculum for gifted learners, a teacher may cluster the standards by using the most difficult standard first, ensuring that students identify and explain the relationship between setting and plot, using a more advanced or accelerated reading selection as well. Then the teacher may use the Literature Web to help the students not only identify and explain but analyze the impact of setting on the main idea or theme, also providing more advanced content.

The Advanced Process/Products Dimension

The current standards also may be adapted by applying advanced processes and products, such as those used by experts in the field, to add depth, complexity, and challenge. Specific advanced processing models such as Paul's (1992) Elements of Reasoning model and the William and Mary Research Model provide a framework to guide teachers in adjusting the standards to meet the needs of gifted learners.

Paul's (1992) Elements of Reasoning model may be used holistically or may be separated as a question-asking tool for the differentiation of standards. Figure 17.3 provides examples of typical standards and adjustments to that standard using the reasoning model as a template. The more facets of Paul's Elements of Reasoning model incorporated, the more challenging the standard.

Subject	Typical standard	Adjusted for gifted by applying Paul's (1992) model
Math	The student will describe when one might use percentages versus actual numbers and use real-world examples.	The student, when given specific *evidence* or data, will determine whether percentages or actual numbers should be used to portray the data. The student will describe the *assumptions* made when reporting numbers versus percentages and vice versa.
Language arts	The student will interpret, analyze, and evaluate a variety of texts by determining author bias and point of view.	The student will interpret, analyze, and evaluate a variety of texts by determining how author *assumptions* and *point of view* impact the *theme/concept* of the text, providing *evidence* for each.
Social studies	The student will identify how climate and landforms influence where people settle in a state.	The student will identify the *implications and consequences* of geography and climate on settlement trends and current state demographics given state data (*evidence*).
Science	The student will identify different pollutants in the environment and its contributors.	The student will explain the *long- and short-term consequences* of pollution in the environment and provide evidence to persuade its contributors to stop polluting.

Figure 17.3. Using Paul's (1992) reasoning model to differentiate standards in content areas.

The William and Mary Research Model, closely linked to Paul's (1992) Elements of Reasoning model, also may be used to add depth and complexity to the standards for gifted learners. Independent research is commonly used as a preferred way for teachers of the gifted to differentiate for their students, allowing time for these students to pursue an area of interest. Many times, however, the research conducted is low-level and students are instructed to examine a topic of interest superficially, simply repeating learned facts. To illustrate, consider that a student wants to learn more about spiders. In most classrooms the student would read a few books on spiders and retell what he learned by creating a poster or PowerPoint presentation that outlines newly discovered facts and shares interesting photos. Instead, to add more depth and complexity to the assignment, teachers should help students advance from a topic to an issue. A topic is a broad area of study whereas an issue has two sides for debate so that students must evaluate various points of view and make an informed decision based on the evidence provided. Continuing with the spider illustration and switching from a topic to an issue, students may choose to research the implications and consequences on the ecosystem if everyone killed spiders in their homes. Figure 17.4 shows examples of how topics can become issues and add more depth to the assignment. Then students should follow the prescribed William and Mary Research Model, outlined in Chapter 6. Once

Typical topic	Issues: Adjusted for the gifted
Bugs	Which bug is most important to the environment? Why?
Thomas Jefferson	What are the implications and consequences of Jefferson's policies on current government operations?
Influence of progress in the sciences	Is scientific progress positive or negative? Why or why not?

Figure 17.4. Examples of topics versus issues.

an issue is determined, it is easily linked to the research process standards in a typical language arts classroom and also may be aligned with advanced content standards in a specific discipline.

The Issues/Themes Dimension

The issues/themes dimension of ICM also is used to adjust standards for gifted learners. Linking learned content from all disciplines to overarching themes that apply to all content areas provides abstractness to the learning process. Because gifted students are more whole-to-part in their thinking and learning preferences (Rogers, 2001), adjusting standards by incorporating an overarching theme not only addresses their unique characteristics but provides abstract learning opportunities for each student to link seemingly unrelated content together. Consider the generalizations of *systems* (Center for Gifted Education, 1999):

- The interactions and outputs of a system change when its inputs, elements, or boundaries change.
- Systems can be productive or dysfunctional.
- Many systems are made up of smaller systems.
- Systems are interdependent.
- Over time, human systems adapt, change priority, or are replaced.

These generalizations may be applied to add depth to various content areas. Figure 17.5 provides examples of sample systems discussions linked to standards in a variety of content areas. Of course, other concepts such as *cause and effect*, *change*, *order and chaos*, or *power*, for example, may be used instead.

STATE ASSESSMENTS AND ALIGNMENT

There is much controversy about the use and benefit of state assessments. Due to an emphasis on all students passing the test, gifted students, who may be able to pass the assessment prior to any teaching, are not a primary focus for instruction in a regular classroom (Ramirez, 2007). When misused, high-

Sample standard	Adjusted using generalizations of systems
Define symbiotic relationships in plants and animals. Provide real-world examples of each.	Explain how symbiotic relationships impact the food chain. Identify all systems affected.
Identify character traits and relationships among different characters given a fictional text.	Systems can be functional or dysfunctional. Explain the family system of the main character. Is that system functional or dysfunctional? Justify your answer.
Compare the American political system with that of other democracies.	Compare the American political system with that of other democracies. Explain your comparisons in terms of inputs, outputs, elements, and boundaries.
Explain how acid rain impacts the environment.	What is the impact of acid rain on the weather system, the ecosystem?
Classify various plants and animals according to their characteristics. Describe differences between plant and animal structures.	Identify the inputs, outputs, boundaries, and elements of plant and animal systems. Describe what happens if one part of a system fails to work in a predictable manner.

Figure 17.5. Examples of standards differentiated by issues/themes by subject area.

stakes assessment drives instructional practices in negative ways, and its results for our best learners is catastrophic. Gentry (2006) outlined impediments to high-stakes tests for gifted students. She explained that schools focus on the test instead of learning, a situation that has led to a deficit-based mindset focused on students who need remediation so that they can pass the test. She reported that gifted students' needs are ignored and, in many instances, gifted programs are no longer in existence because teachers are afraid to excuse students from test preparation. Moreover, Popham (2001) argued that high-performing schools enroll significantly wealthier students than low-performing schools, deeming state assessments as inequitable in their sanctions.

Because each state selects its own content standards and accountability measures, there are vast differences between the levels of assessments across states. Some states have very rigorous assessments while other state assessments are less advanced. In this age of accountability, the adage "what gets measured gets done" is especially true. There are three major assumptions that must be met before assessments should drive decisions about teaching and learning.

- Assumption 1: The test matches the standards;
- Assumption 2: The test measures worthwhile and higher level skills and concepts; and
- Assumption 3: The test is reliable and supports valid inferences.

Educators and parents need to be intelligent consumers of assessments and advocate for high-level, valid and reliable measures of progress. District and state leaders should publicize standards alignment charts matched to assessment items, provide an analysis of higher and lower level skills tested based on item analyses from prior state assessments, and make reliability and validity data readily available. How does the state assessment correlate with standardized achievement tests and ability assessments? Does the test actually measure what it intends to measure? Is the test reliable over time? What is the internal consistency in results between test and retest situations? If a test does not measure what is intended or if a test is not reliable, even the best instruction will not seem to be effective.

The following list of considerations will help teachers who work with gifted students align assessments and instruction in a way that is best suited to gifted students' needs:

1. *Incorporate ongoing diagnostic assessments to guide instructional planning and placement.* Chapter 5 provided strategies to assist teachers with ways to incorporate advanced content standards and higher level thinking processes to better meet the needs of the gifted. Because assessment guides instruction, and instruction is guided by standards, all three are intertwined. Consequently, if one follows the presented strategies for aligning and adapting instruction with standards, then there is no need to worry about the final assessment if it is linked to the standards. Teachers should create higher level task demands and assessments to determine what students know and what learning should happen next.

   Preassessments, matched to standards and administered before each unit, can be used as a guide to help teachers determine to what extent the standards must be adapted to provide ongoing learning and the development of content-expertise.

2. *Teach for learning, not to the test.* If a test measures higher level skills, it is more difficult to actually teach to a test because the measure assesses more than basic, isolated facts. Teachers who teach only to the test waste valuable learning time and guarantee failure. It is virtually impossible to guess every test item that will be covered. If teachers focus specifically on learning, they are more likely to prepare students not only for the test but also for critical skills that will be necessary to compete successfully in the 21st century.

3. *Help students analyze their test-taking skills.* Although mundane practice tests should not be a focus of instructional time, students need to know how to prepare for a test-taking situation. Many gifted students learn whole-to-part and are skilled at dealing with ambiguity and multiple ways of thinking about a situation. These characteristics are positive but could be a hindrance in certain test-taking situations because some gifted students may overthink an answer. Throughout the school year, teachers can begin to pose questions that help students analyze which answer is best, allowing time for metacognitive discussions. Many school districts conduct item analyses that show which questions were commonly missed by various

subgroups of students. My experience has been that gifted students tend to miss the easiest questions and master the most difficult. If teachers can model throughout the school year ways to analyze questions linked to the content studied, students will be able to learn from their mistakes.

4. *Use testing as a learning tool.* We learn from our mistakes, and we also learn by discussing our thinking processes. If diagnostic assessments, matched to standards, are a focus of instruction, teachers can provide feedback regarding errors students make so that students are able to discern and analyze their own strengths and weaknesses and set goals for future learning. Whether we agree with assessments or not, gifted students in particular must become used to and proficient at taking assessments because, at least in our current system, assessments serve as a gatekeeper for the next level of education and attainment. Although students may be quite proficient at learning content and higher level skills, they may not be as proficient in a structured test setting. It is better for them to learn these skills earlier as the stakes in elementary and middle school are not as great as high school when students begin taking Advanced Placement and college entrance exams.

CONCLUSION

Standards do not have to be a barrier to gifted student learning. Research suggests that coupling advanced content with the higher level processes practiced by professionals and the conceptual focus of intra- and interdisciplinary learning is critical to the development of expertise (VanTassel-Baska & Stambaugh, 2008). By aligning and adapting content standards to the Integrated Curriculum Model features and using research-based materials already aligned, teachers are able to successfully merge standards and gifted education. Ongoing assessment of these standards should guide instruction and will positively impact student learning in this age of accountability.

KEY POINTS SUMMARY

- Standards and gifted education are not dichotomous; they can and should be complementary.
- Standards must be differentiated for gifted learners if academic achievement gains are expected.
- When differentiating standards for the gifted, educators must recognize their students' needs, know the intent of the standards, and understand the content being differentiated.

- The Integrated Curriculum Model can be used as a framework to differentiate standards for gifted learners.
- The purpose of standards is to be focused on student content acquisition and learning, not passing a test.

REFERENCES

Amabile, T. (1996). *Creativity in context*. Boulder, CO: Westview Press.

Bloom, B. (Ed.). (1985). *Developing talent in young people*. New York, NY: Ballantine.

Bransford, J. D., Brown, A. L., & Cocking, R. (Eds.). (1999). *How people learn: Brain, mind, experience and school*. Washington, DC: National Academy Press.

Bransford, J. D., & Donovan, S. (Eds.). (2003). *How students learn: History, math and science in the classroom*. Washington, DC: National Academy Press

Center for Gifted Education. (1999). *No quick fix*. Dubuque, IA: Kendall/Hunt.

Colangelo, N., Assouline, S. G., & Gross, M. U. M. (2004). *A nation deceived: How schools hold back America's brightest students* (Vol. 1). Iowa City: The University of Iowa, The Connie Belin & Jacqueline N. Blank International Center for Gifted Education and Talent Development.

Csikszentmihalyi, M., Rathunde, K., & Whalen, S. (1993). *Talented teenagers: The roots of success and failure*. New York, NY: Cambridge University Press.

French, J. N., & Rhodes, C. (1992). *Teaching thinking skills: Theories and practice*. New York, NY: Taylor & Francis.

Friedman, T. (2005). *The world is flat*. New York, NY: Farrar, Straus and Giroux.

Gentry, M. (2006). No child left behind: Gifted children and school counselors. *Professional School Counseling*. Retrieved from http://www.thefreelibrary.com/No+Child+Left+Behind:+gifted+children+and+school+counselors-a0153359894

Ohio Department of Education. (2009). *Academic content standards*. Retrieved from http://www.ode.state.oh.us/GD/Templates/Pages/ODE/ODEPrimary.aspx?Page=2&TopicID=1695&TopicRelationID=1696

Palincsar, A. S., & Brown, A. L. (1989). Classroom dialogues to promote self-regulated comprehension. In J. Brophy (Ed.), Advances in research on teaching (pp. 35–72). Greenwich, CT: JAI Press.

Paul, R. (1992). *Critical thinking: What everyone needs to survive in a rapidly changing world*. Sonoma, CA: Foundation for Critical Thinking.

Perkins, D., & Salomon, G. (1989). Are cognitive skills context-bound? *Educational Researcher, 18*(1), 16–25.

Popham, W. (2001). *The truth about testing: An educator's call to action*. Alexandria, VA: Association for Supervision and Curriculum Development.

Ramirez, E. (2007, November 2). For talented students, challenges to grow. *US News and World Report*. Retrieved from http://www.usnews.com/articles/education/2007/11/02/gifted-students.html

Rogers, K. (2001). *Re-forming gifted education: How parents and teachers can match the program to the child*. Scottsdale, AZ: Great Potential Press.

Simonton, D. K. (2004). *Creativity in science: Chance, logic, genius, and zeitgeist.* Cambridge, England: Cambridge University Press.

Tennessee Department of Education. (2009). *Grade 2—Life science.* Retrieved from http://tennessee.gov/education/ci/sci/doc/SCI_Grade_2.pdf

Tivnan, T., & Hemphill, L. (2005). Comparing literacy reform models in high poverty schools: Patterns of first grade achievement. *The Elementary School Journal, 105,* 419–442.

Tomlinson, C. A. (1999). *The differentiated classroom: Responding to the needs of all learners.* Alexandria, VA: Association for Supervision and Curriculum.

VanTassel-Baska, J. (2003). *Curriculum planning and instructional design for gifted learners.* Denver, CO: Love.

VanTassel-Baska, J., & Stambaugh, T. (2006). *Comprehensive curriculum for gifted learners* (3rd ed.). Needham Heights, MA: Allyn & Bacon.

VanTassel-Baska, J., & Stambaugh, T. (Eds.). (2008). *What works: 20 years of curriculum development and research.* Waco, TX: Prufrock Press.

Wright, S. P., Horn, S. P., & Sanders, W. L. (1997). Teacher and classroom context effects on student achievement: Implications for teacher evaluation. *Journal of Personnel Evaluation in Education, 11,* 57–67.

Chapter 18

Professional Development to Support Successful Curriculum Implementation

Catherine A. Little and Kristina Ayers Paul

When adopting new curricula and considering related professional development for teachers, school leaders are faced with the challenge of planning and implementing professional learning experiences that are of sufficiently high quality to support teachers' needs and that demonstrate the alignment between the curriculum and the goals of the school and district. Professional development around advanced curriculum as described in this text also must include an emphasis on the particular learning needs of high-ability students and how the curriculum responds to those needs, as well as demonstrating, in many cases, how teachers may differentiate the curriculum for a wider range of learners in their classrooms. Furthermore, professional development planning must include attention to sustained support for teachers as they implement new curriculum, as well as how to evaluate both the formal professional learning experience and the classroom changes that are the intended result.

Throughout all of the curriculum development and implementation projects alluded to in this book, the related professional learning of teachers has always been a key concern. Each of the curriculum initiatives from the Center for Gifted Education at The College of William and Mary has included attention to professional development for teachers, and several of the research initiatives have specifically addressed teacher learning and change in practice over time (e.g., VanTassel-Baska et al., 2008). This chapter reviews key considerations for implementing professional learning initiatives related to the implementation of content-based curriculum for high-ability learners. The discussion includes important findings from the literature on what makes professional development effective in changing teacher practice, as well as specific examples drawn from our own experiences working with teachers and schools to implement curriculum for advanced students in the major content areas.

THE PROFESSIONAL DEVELOPMENT DEMANDS OF CONTENT-BASED CURRICULUM FOR HIGH-ABILITY LEARNERS

The central goal of most professional development in education is to support desired student outcomes, such as learning and achievement gains, by promoting teacher learning and changes in classroom practice. Professional development encompasses not only the specific, structured activities in which educators participate, but also the overall process of learning, reflection, and growth that they experience. As highlighted by a recent report on the status of teachers' professional learning nationally, "Effective professional development is intensive, ongoing, and connected to practice; focuses on the teaching and learning of specific academic content; is connected to other school initiatives; and builds strong working relationships among teachers" (Darling-Hammond, Wei, Andree, Richardson, & Orphanos, 2009, p. 5).

The challenges of developing and implementing professional development experiences that reflect the principles of effective professional development are many, including the issue of allocating sufficient time to build and implement meaningful learning experiences for educators. This challenge is especially salient with regard to professional development on curriculum for advanced learners, because the depth and breadth of teacher understanding must go far beyond simply knowing the format and structure of the curriculum. As described throughout this book, curriculum targeting the needs of advanced learners should focus on advanced content and should represent high levels of rigor in the processes students use to engage with the content. To facilitate gifted student learning effectively, teachers implementing such curriculum need to have concomitantly higher knowledge and pedagogical skills in the content area. In addition, curriculum organized around abstract, interdisciplinary concepts requires that teachers have time and opportunity to discuss and reflect upon the ideas themselves to prepare to guide students through applications of the concepts to diverse areas of knowledge.

Moreover, professional development experiences in this area should include opportunities for teachers to learn about and discuss the common characteristics and behaviors of gifted learners and their likely responses to advanced curricular experiences. Within a context of many competing priorities, rarely do the needs of gifted learners and the curriculum intended to respond to their needs top the list. Nevertheless, several key studies have demonstrated the importance of providing professional development experiences focusing on the characteristics and learning needs of gifted learners, as well as the relatively limited knowledge among general education teachers about this population of students (Brown et al., 2005; Hansen & Feldhusen, 1994; Siegle & Powell, 2004; Westberg & Daoust, 2003). Therefore, professional development experiences providing guidance on the curriculum itself, the strategies and content it entails, and the characteristics and needs of advanced learners are critical for effective curricular adoption. Furthermore, these experiences must be sustained over time to support teachers' learning and promote growth in their professional practice.

KEY FEATURES OF EFFECTIVE PROFESSIONAL DEVELOPMENT

Research on the effectiveness of professional development has been somewhat limited by the difficulty of measuring direct connections between teachers' professional learning and outcomes such as increased student engagement or achievement. Traditionally, much of the research on "effective" professional development has primarily relied upon teacher satisfaction measures as a data source (Guskey, 2000; Lawless & Pellegrino, 2007; Richardson, 2003). Increasingly, however, research has begun to demonstrate linkages of professional development to outcomes such as changes in teacher knowledge and classroom practice, and in some cases has begun drawing connections to student outcomes as well (e.g., Garet, Porter, Desimone, Birman, & Yoon, 2001; Kennedy, 1999; Richardson, 2003). Among the key features of effective professional development emerging from the literature are the following:

- worthwhile, meaningful content as a focus;
- strong coherence of professional learning initiatives with teachers' work assignments and with content standards;
- acknowledgement of teachers' existing beliefs and practices, along with efforts to encourage and develop participant buy-in to new initiatives.

- active engagement of teachers during professional development activities, including opportunities to engage with specific instructional approaches and student data;
- opportunities for teachers to work together collaboratively;
- sustained attention to professional development, including follow-up at the school and classroom level beyond initial learning experiences; and
- support from school administration.

Content, Coherence, and Teacher Attitudes

Just as this text has highlighted the necessity of including substantive content and significant learner outcomes in curriculum for students, professional development planners should emphasize a similar attitude toward quality content in learning experiences for teachers. The content of professional development should engage teachers, like students, in content learning that is central to the disciplines to be taught and that reflects disciplinary habits of mind; moreover, professional learning should focus on the pedagogical content knowledge teachers need to work with students in the content areas. The focus on quality content and coherence go hand in hand; a professional learning activity with interesting, challenging content will not ultimately have much effect on students if it is not connected to what teachers are expected and able to teach in their classrooms.

The issue of coherence is a particularly important consideration in light of evidence about factors influencing change in teacher attitudes and beliefs, which are integrally related to changes in learning and practice. Guskey (1986) has argued that professional development activities alone are unlikely to change teacher attitudes and beliefs; rather, such changes result after teachers try out something they have learned through a professional development activity and see the effects on their own students. As Richardson (2003) also pointed out, teachers' adoption of new instructional strategies hinges in large part on the experience of actually trying out the new strategies with their own students and seeing positive results:

> When these new activities engage the students, do not violate the teacher's particular need for control, match the teacher's beliefs about teaching and learning, and help the teacher respond to system-determined demands for such outcomes as high test scores, they are deemed to work. If they do, they are internalized and absorbed into the teacher's repertoire. (p. 403)

Clarke and Hollingsworth (2002) theorized that teacher attitudes change as a result of a complex collection of factors, including results with students among other salient outcomes. They also highlighted the interaction of new information with teachers' understanding of their own context, as well as their opportunities to reflect upon new learning and its application in that context. These perspectives support the importance of sustained, ongoing opportunities for teachers to reflect upon their implementation of new methods, how those methods align with their established practices and perspectives, and how the results they see with students affect their attitudes and understanding.

The acknowledgement of the complex nature of teachers' professional learning requires that we move beyond thinking of professional development as a "training paradigm built on knowledge consumption" to an "inquiry and problem-solving paradigm built around knowledge production" (Little, 1993, p. 139). As Tomlinson (1995) stated, "people are more likely to act their way into belief than to believe their way into acting" (pp. 85–86).

Active Engagement and Collaboration

The National Staff Development Council's (NSDC, 2001) *Standards for Staff Development* emphasized the importance of considering what we know about learning when designing professional development activities. This includes attention to the ways in which teachers engage with content during professional learning activities; specifically, NSDC encouraged that whenever possible, teachers should experience what their students will experience by participating, as learners, in the instructional approaches they will subsequently use in their own classrooms. Through such experiences, teachers are able to see instructional approaches modeled, consider their own questions about the content and the pedagogical methods, and reflect on the connections to their work.

Teachers also should have opportunities to work together with colleagues in learning the content of the professional development activity, considering its applications in their own settings, and developing supplementary materials relevant to their own implementation. The community aspect of professional learning is important in promoting school goals and collegial support for implementing new initiatives.

Active engagement and collaboration are important not only in the introduction of new content in professional development, but also in ongoing initiatives that encourage teachers to discuss, reflect upon, and plan for continued classroom implementation of curriculum. Working with student assessment data is a particularly important aspect of this ongoing engagement; teachers need to have opportunities to come together with results from their own students and to share and discuss the implications of those results for further instruction.

Sustained Attention and Administrative Support

The importance of sustained attention to professional learning, as opposed to a focus on "one-shot" workshops with no follow-up, has been strongly emphasized throughout the professional development literature over the last several decades. The NSDC (2001) standards included a consistent thread of emphasis on continuous learning, ongoing engagement, and the recognition that brief, one-shot sessions are unlikely to spur the achievement of goals for professional learning. Sustained attention, such as through workshop follow-ups, job-embedded strategies, and in-classroom supports, helps to maintain a focus on specific goals and to facilitate responses to emerging teacher questions and concerns.

Planners of professional development initiatives must assemble a repertoire of approaches to support teachers' sustained professional learning over time. Not only must the planned professional development experiences align with the goals of the school and district, but they also must be meaningful for teachers, relevant to their classroom assignments, and sufficiently sustained to support teacher learning as it develops over time. A single workshop that introduces content-based curriculum is an important introductory approach, but is insufficient to support learning and changes in practice over time. As teachers engage with new methods and materials, their questions and areas of concern change; the challenges they face upon first trying something new in their classrooms may be quite different from the challenges they face after they and their students have begun to get used to the new approaches (Little & Fogarty, 2009). Therefore, scheduled follow-up activities, as well as supports in the classroom through peer and mentor coaching or peer support structures, are critical to providing teachers with the support they need to implement new methods and materials successfully.

Such ongoing support efforts, in addition to initial professional development experiences, require administrative support in both concrete and abstract forms. Supportive administrators demonstrate their investment in professional learning initiatives through allocation of time and resources, as well as through their own participation, demonstration of interest in learning and growth, and moral support for teachers. For example, Vavasseur and MacGregor (2008) noted the importance of direct principal involvement in online discussions among teachers; principals provided both pressure and support that teachers found to be influential in their own engagement in emerging online communities and integration of technology in the classroom. School leaders play an important role in articulating and reinforcing the links between student learning and teacher professional learning, as well as building the structures needed to promote ongoing professional growth (NSDC, 2001).

PLANNING PROFESSIONAL DEVELOPMENT FOR CURRICULUM IMPLEMENTATION

The complexity of the key features addressed above demonstrates that there is not one silver bullet that will guarantee change in teacher practice connected to professional development. Careful consideration of these features in professional development planning is important in promoting successful implementation of curriculum through supportive opportunities for teacher learning, clear alignment with other local goals and initiatives, and intensive focus on responding to student needs within the context of the habits of mind of the disciplines.

Within the context of supporting the successful implementation of content-based curriculum for high-ability learners, professional development planning must reflect the key features above while giving attention to several important considerations specific to a curriculum implementation initiative. These considerations include developing learning experiences that allow teachers to understand the structure of the curriculum and its instructional and assessment approaches; resources for teachers to support their understanding of the curriculum, its content, and the student characteristics to which it responds; and opportunities for teachers to try out the curriculum and share their experiences, questions, and insights. All of these experiences must be planned within a conscious consideration of the particular context in which teachers are working, as well as clear evidence of teacher and student needs regarding the area of the curriculum under study. The sections that follow will address important contextual considerations in planning professional development around content-based curriculum and then describe initial and follow-up learning experiences for teachers to support implementation.

Situating Professional Learning in Context

An important aspect of planning professional development on curriculum is assessing the unique context within which the curriculum will be implemented and the needs of the stakeholders within that context. Considerations include the match between the new curricular initiative and the existing school initiatives; the individual teachers' experiences, attitudes, and knowledge that determine their readiness to learn and implement the new curriculum; and the dynamic organizational factors that are unique to each school and district. The match with existing school initiatives must be assessed through careful review of the features of particular curricular materials and local standards and practices. Frequently, curriculum developers include some discussion of alignment with national standards, often in their supporting materials (e.g., Center for Gifted Education, 1999). In addition, local student assessment data may provide information regarding the needs of a school or district. Disaggregated data demonstrating growth patterns among the highest achieving students may provide important evidence regarding the need for more advanced curriculum for this population, particularly if these data show little growth for gifted learners or demonstrate a ceiling effect. These indicators may demonstrate that the assessments themselves are too low-level for this population to be able to show growth, but they also may provide indicators regarding low levels of curricular expectations for advanced learners.

Birman, Desimone, Porter, and Garet (2000) identified coherence as a critical component of professional development that promotes changes in teacher knowledge and classroom practice. In their definition, coherence refers to how professional development connects to teachers' classroom practice and their professional goals, as well as the standards and goals that guide the overall curriculum and instruction in schools. Ensuring coherence with teachers' job expectations requires careful analysis of existing needs within the larger picture of school and district goals. Professional development needs within a district may be assessed using a range of data sources, including teachers' reported perceptions of need (gathered through surveys, focus groups, and the like); classroom observation results; and student data (including results from authentic, performance-based classroom assessments as well as state tests and other standardized instruments).

Decision-makers also must consider the differences among teachers in assessing needs and determining directions for professional development. One key difference among teachers to consider is the various levels of experience that teachers bring to any professional development initiative. Teachers function at different developmental levels based on their experience just as students do, and newer and more experienced teachers vary in their attitudes as well as their learning needs (Anderson & Olsen, 2006). Several researchers have explored questions of differential teacher choices and responses with regard to professional development, finding significant differences among teachers based on personal factors (e.g., age, interests) and environmental factors (e.g., characteristics of specific schools and teaching-learning contexts; Higgins, 2006; Joyce & Showers, 2002; Kwakman, 2003; Paul, Little, & McCoach, 2009; Torff & Sessions, 2008).

Clearly, teachers' specific grade level and subject assignment are critical; professional development is unlikely to achieve coherence with teachers' daily work if it is not relevant to their domain of practice. Moreover, teachers' perception of *meaningfulness*—a term closely related to *coherence* as one considers professional practice—also has been demonstrated to be a major factor in influencing levels of participation, along with perceptions of feasibility of the practice for implementation in their own contexts (Kwakman, 2003).

Another contextual factor that plays a key role in teachers' attitudes and, therefore, the likelihood that professional development will promote changes in practice is the school climate around the expectations that administrators have for teachers. As previously noted, administrative support is critical for effective professional development and implementation of curriculum; in a context in which administrators insist that all classrooms be working on the same page of the same textbook at the same time each day, a curriculum designed around differentiation is unlikely to be implemented effectively.

All of these contextual considerations are important in professional development planning, both to guide organization of the content and to develop structures that can be used to support implementation of new curriculum. Facilitators of professional development around content-based curriculum need to understand the individual learning needs of teachers, including teacher background and experience in understanding the characteristics and needs of gifted learners. Facilitators also need to understand the context within which the curriculum for advanced learners will be implemented—whether it be heterogeneous classrooms, pull-out programs, self-contained programs, or some other context—in order to provide appropriate recommendations for implementation and differentiation. Planners should make use of student data to provide evidence of learning needs and related standards to emphasize. Recognition of key contextual details also helps in planning for resource support. Professional development planning around curriculum implementation should include identification of individuals within the school or district who may have prior experience with the curriculum and can serve as mentors to teachers who are trying it for the first time.

Guided by an understanding of contextual needs and resources, professional development planners may then turn to the "nuts and bolts" of the learning activities for teachers, including both initial learning experiences and the follow-up supports that will promote fidelity of implementation.

Initial Professional Development Activities: Frameworks, Content, and Instructional Approaches

Perhaps the most fundamental objective in professional development around content-based curriculum is for teachers to become familiar with the curriculum itself. The framework and intended outcomes, organization, instructional and assessment approaches, and resources within the curriculum should be among the key features initially addressed in the professional development context. In addition, initial workshops may need to provide teachers with opportunities to learn the specific content addressed by the curriculum, particularly if it is focused on content that is unfamiliar, presented differently, or more advanced than material they have previously taught. Curriculum developers frequently provide guidance and resources for organizing professional learning about the materials or for contacting experts who will help to plan and facilitate professional learning experiences (e.g., see http://cfge.wm.edu/professional.htm; http://www.projectm3.org). Often, the programs outlined by these developers are grounded in the experience of piloting professional development sessions along with piloting the curricular materials themselves.

Within each of the Center for Gifted Education's major curriculum development initiatives, a professional development module has been prepared, piloted, and revised based on experiences in schools and feedback from teachers and administrators. These modules have included initial overview workshops on the center's curriculum, as well as guidelines for follow-up support and advanced sessions for professional learning. Although workshops alone are insufficient for providing the full support for professional learning that teachers generally need for curriculum implementation, the workshop format, *when paired with follow-up activities*, may be among the more effective ways of introducing information to teachers and providing them with a common overview of new curriculum or of particular instructional or assessment approaches. The experience should introduce the curriculum and allow teachers structured time to consider the relationship between the new material and their existing standards and expectations, as well as to begin making plans collaboratively with colleagues for how to solidify this relationship in practical terms. The experience should engage teachers actively in the kinds of learning activities their students will engage in upon use of the curricular materials. Ideally, the experience should include real examples of student work that resulted from use of the curriculum.

Initial workshops on the center's curriculum generally begin with an overview of the Integrated Curriculum Model (ICM) and the curriculum framework of the specific set of materials. Then, the majority of the workshop is focused on introducing and practicing each of the major teaching models, as outlined in the content chapters of this text. See Figures 18.1 and 18.2 for sample outlines of workshops on language arts and social studies curricula.

Structured engagement with the instructional approaches of the curriculum reflects the NSDC (2001) standard on quality teaching as a key component of professional development, as well as literature cited above regarding active engagement and transfer to classroom practice (e.g., Garet et al., 2001). The teaching models are used not only to demonstrate the pedagogy to teachers, but also in many cases to introduce or reinforce the content of the curriculum for teachers. In the workshop introducing the curriculum's instructional approaches, teachers have the opportunity to play the student role as they participate in each model, but then replace their teacher "hat" as they consider applying the models in their own classrooms; after each model is piloted, discussion follows about the experience of each model, its applications in the curriculum, and considerations for particular groups of learners and classroom

Outline of Topics

Each topic includes facilitator guidance and opportunities for small-group practice and discussion.

A. Introduction and Curriculum Framework
    a. Integrated Curriculum Model
    b. Linkages to High-Ability Learner Characteristics and Needs
    c. Language Arts Goals and Outcomes
    d. Overview of Assessment Approaches
    e. Research Findings to Support Curriculum Effectiveness
B. Concept Development: The Concept of Change
    a. Concept Model Practice and Debriefing
    b. Applications of Concept in Language Arts Units
C. Constructing Meaning Through Literature
    a. Guidelines for Selecting Literature
    b. Literature Web Practice and Debriefing
    c. Additional Questioning Within Lessons
    d. Overview of Supplementary Reading Resources
D. Persuasive Writing
    a. Hamburger Model Practice and Debriefing
    b. Overview of Writing Assessments
    c. Writing Applications
E. Reasoning
    a. Overview of Reasoning Model
    b. Reasoning Model Practice and Debriefing
    c. Applications of Reasoning Model
F. Research
    a. Overview of Research Model
    b. Research Model Practice and Debriefing
G. Vocabulary and Language Study
    a. Vocabulary Web Practice and Debriefing
    b. Overview of Language Study Activities
    c. Development of Language Study Task Cards
H. Unit Review and Implementation Guidelines
    a. Discussion of Unit Organization
    b. Sample Interdisciplinary Connections From Various Units
    c. Sample Resources to Support Implementation
    d. Questions and Answers Regarding Implementation

Figure 18.1. Workshop on language arts curriculum for high-ability learners.

settings. This follow-up debriefing is an opportunity for facilitators to provide teachers with additional resources that they may need to build their content knowledge further or to guide extensions to learning for students.

For example, during a language arts overview workshop for teachers, one section of the workshop is devoted to examining the Literature Web (see Chapter 8). A short reading, such as a poem, is introduced, and teachers engage with the Literature Web as their students eventually will—they complete it

Outline of Topics

Each topic includes facilitator guidance and opportunities for small-group practice and discussion.

A. Introduction and Curriculum Framework
      a.   Integrated Curriculum Model
      b.   Linkages to High-Ability Learner Characteristics and Needs
      c.   Social Studies Goals and Outcomes
      d.   Overview of Assessment Approaches
      e.   Research Findings to Support Curriculum Effectiveness
B. Reasoning About a Situation or Event
      a.   Situation Activity Practice and Debriefing
      b.   Overview of Applications of Activity
C. Primary Source Analysis
      a.   Overview of Key Considerations With Primary Sources
      b.   Primary Source Analysis Practice and Debriefing
      c.   Applications of Primary Source Model Across Units
D. Concept Development: The Concepts of Systems and Cause and Effect
      a.   Concept Model Practice and Debriefing
      b.   Applications of Concept in Social Studies Units
E. Persuasive Writing
      a.   Hamburger Model Practice and Debriefing
      b.   Overview of Writing Assessments
      c.   Writing Applications
F. Reasoning
      a.   Overview of Reasoning Model
      b.   Reasoning Model Practice and Debriefing
      c.   Applications of Reasoning Model
G. Projects and Connections
      a.   Overview of Research and Additional Projects in Units
H. Unit Review and Implementation Guidelines
      a.   Discussion of Unit Organization
      b.   Sample Interdisciplinary Connections From Various Units
      c.   Sample Resources to Support Implementation
      d.   Questions and Answers Regarding Implementation

Figure 18.2. Workshop on social studies curriculum for high-ability learners.

independently, then discuss it in a small group, and then engage in a large group debriefing led by the workshop facilitator. Following this, the facilitator reviews some of the questioning and facilitation strategies that were used, explains how differentiation might occur with the Literature Web by using different readings with different groups of students, discusses additional questions that would follow a Literature Web discussion in the classroom, and answers questions. During this portion of the discussion, teachers return to their professional roles and are encouraged to discuss and ask questions about the process of implementing the web, now that they have experienced completing one. Likewise, in workshops in science, social studies, or mathematics, teachers are encouraged first to engage in the kinds of problem solving, experimentation, or document analysis their students will experience, followed by a debriefing that includes discussion of how the experience of facilitating the lesson would be different with fourth graders or seventh graders or whoever the target population might be.

Beyond the focus on the teaching models, introductory workshops on the center's curricular materials include an overview of research results demonstrating the effectiveness of the curriculum, along with specific samples of student work from implementation in classrooms. This combination of larger scale group data as well as individual student samples provides different types of evidence to support the quality of the curriculum and its influence on students. Larger scale research results tend to be important for demonstrating the quality of curriculum to decision-makers such as administrators and school boards. Specific student data may be more meaningful to classroom teachers who are considering what the curriculum may look like for their specific students. In addition, the student samples allow teachers to engage in discussion of assessment and differentiation issues. A session on student work and large-scale data also should include discussion of the assessment approaches used in the curriculum, with opportunities for teachers to consider and discuss among themselves how the assessment approaches may fit within and extend their own assessment and grading frameworks.

Finally, introductory workshops on the center's materials generally include opportunities for teachers to examine the curriculum units themselves, along with supplementary materials such as books, websites, artwork, and other resources that appear within lessons or extension activities. Question-and-answer sessions, along with written responses to frequently asked questions, provide opportunities for teachers to explore details of implementation.

All of the above components of an initial workshop on content-based curriculum may be provided with varying levels of detail and intensity, depending on the amount of time allocated for an introductory session. Ideally, introductory curriculum workshops should occur over multiple days—2 at a minimum, 3–4 for optimal exposure. This allows facilitators to guide teachers to sufficient levels of depth with the instructional approaches and the content, as well as to allow teachers to digest the materials and bring questions. Workshops that occur over several days provide greater room for facilitators to blend instruction in the content with focus on the instructional approaches, as well as to differentiate the experience as teacher needs and strengths emerge in the learning context. Often, such workshops may be provided during the summer, to allow teachers to learn the material and have preparation time before they begin to implement curriculum with their students in the fall.

Follow-Up Activities to Sustain Professional Learning and Implementation

Beyond initial learning opportunities for teachers, additional professional development components are necessary to support the implementation of new curriculum. Follow-up support should include organized sessions for further professional development, as well as providing resources and guidance that teachers may use on an ongoing basis within the classroom.

Organized follow-up sessions on curriculum implementation can address a variety of important topics. Professional development facilitators might organize workshops to occur several weeks or months after curriculum implementation has begun, in order to review teaching models and to encourage teachers to share their experiences of the models and the questions, successes, and challenges they encountered during instruction. Rigorous curriculum as described in this text is not easy to implement in classrooms, and teachers who show great enthusiasm in an introductory workshop may feel less eager as they experience some of the challenges that emerge in the classroom. Also, given that content addressed in initial workshops is likely to be quite extensive, follow-up support is needed to provide refreshers and additional information, as well as to promote fidelity to the curriculum as it is intended.

Another important area of focus in follow-up sessions is review of student products; teachers bring evidence of their students' work in response to the curriculum, and then they review the products collaboratively and discuss the evidence of learning and plans for ongoing instruction. Such a focus on student products facilitates a deeper understanding for teachers of the connections between the new curriculum, instructional strategies, and student learning, as well as makes the experience much more personal than even the student samples provided from other classrooms could. When teachers see their own students' evidence of learning as a result of the implemented strategies, the impetus is no longer on the professional development designer to convince the teachers that the new curriculum is a worthwhile endeavor.

In some cases, follow-up sessions may be opportunities for teachers to work collaboratively to develop supplementary materials to accompany the curriculum. For example, teachers might work to develop learning centers that extend the curriculum. Kwakman (2003) emphasized the value teachers place on professional learning that engages them in developing products for classroom use; such experiences combine the use of research-based curriculum with context-specific supplementary resources that enhance each individual teacher's instruction.

Schools and districts also may choose to use online resources to maintain a repository of locally developed materials. For example, several districts that have implemented the Center for Gifted Education curriculum widely across their schools have built extensive collections of online resources for teachers implementing the curriculum, combining resources originally assembled by the curriculum developers with specific, locally relevant materials. These might include alignments with local standards and pacing guides; guidelines for implementing the units in a range of settings specific to the context; and contact information for local teachers with experience in using the materials (e.g., see http://www.montgomeryschoolsmd.org/curriculum/enriched).

Another direction for follow-up professional development sessions might be further exploration of the advanced content addressed in the curriculum, again to ensure that teachers have sufficient background knowledge in this content area to facilitate student learning. Planning for advanced content learning may require a different facilitator who can provide the depth necessary for teachers to grow in the dimension of content knowledge.

Perhaps even more than in introductory sessions, follow-up sessions should be differentiated to respond to teachers' needs. School leaders and professional development facilitators should use evidence from observations in classrooms, from student learning data, and from teachers' expressed questions to determine the focus of follow-up sessions, and may provide multiple sessions to address different needs among the group of teachers. Teachers may form small groups to work together in planning and implementing the curriculum, supporting one another around shared goals and concerns that emerge over time. There often is a significant discrepancy between teachers' verbal enthusiasm about new strategies and what the actual use of those strategies looks like in the classroom, related to the emergence of new questions as well as teachers' deeply held beliefs, attitudes, and concerns (Brighton, 2003; Little & Fogarty, 2009). Therefore, building specific plans for follow-up support in organized sessions and more informal communications is critical in supporting implementation.

Follow-up support for professional learning is not limited to scheduled meetings. Many other forms of support may be provided for teachers as they implement curricular change in the classroom. For example, a peer support system or mentoring system may be established whereby teachers spend time in one another's classrooms observing implementation of curriculum, then follow up with discussions to review the experience. Such a system may include opportunities for teachers to watch one another to see a lesson or approach modeled by a teacher well-practiced in its use, or the system may focus on having teachers with more experience in the curriculum observe teachers who are novices and provide feedback. In such a case, the more advanced teacher may play the role of a coach supporting fellow teachers' implementation.

Professional development planners may decide to encourage teachers to interact online in professional learning communities focused on implementation of the curriculum; in such a context, teachers who may have limited opportunities to interact in person during the school day can engage in longer, reflective conversations about their practice and collaborate on the development of supplementary resources to support and extend implementation (e.g., Vavasseur & MacGregor, 2008).

An instructional specialist, administrator, or outside consultant also may provide coaching to support curriculum implementation. Several of the major curriculum development initiatives supported by the Jacob K. Javits funding have included ongoing follow-up support in classrooms by project teams as part of the research and development effort (e.g., Gavin, Casa, Adelson, Carroll, & Sheffield, 2009; VanTassel-Baska et al., 2008). Evidence from a recent study of the implementation of Center for Gifted Education language arts units over several years demonstrated that initial professional development followed by at least 2 years of classroom support was related to the best evidence of changes in practice and implementation of key differentiation features related to the curriculum (VanTassel-Baska et al., 2008).

Whether online or in person, through scheduled meetings or classroom interactions, follow-up learning experiences for teachers promote curriculum implementation in several different ways. They provide opportunities for teachers to ask and discuss the questions that emerge as they implement new curriculum, they encourage collegial support among teachers in the process of trying new curriculum, and they promote differentiation by encouraging a focus on assessing student learning as it emerges from implementation.

EVALUATING PROFESSIONAL DEVELOPMENT ON CONTENT-BASED CURRICULUM

Planning, implementing, and evaluating professional development around content-based curriculum requires thorough attention to setting goals, gathering data, and assessing outcomes to determine the degree to which goals have been met. The success of curriculum implementation may not be evaluated merely by asking teachers whether they liked a workshop; rather, evaluation should focus on evidence of teacher learning of knowledge and skills, changes in classroom practices, and organizational supports for implementation. Student learning must be considered as a key data source for making formative and summative judgments around the overall success of curriculum implementation, including the professional learning activities that were part of the implementation process.

Time, money, and resources are precious when it comes to prioritizing systems and services for professional development. Therefore, it is important that school leaders evaluate the effectiveness of these efforts to ensure that resources are being leveraged effectively. Evaluation of professional learning initiatives should include examination of all of the data sources noted above, as well as the evidence of key features of professional development discussed throughout this chapter. Little and Paul (2009) provided a framework for planning and evaluating workshop experiences as a component of an overall professional development initiative. That framework has been adapted here to provide key guidelines for professional development planners to consider in planning and evaluating programs designed to support teacher implementation of content-based curriculum for high-ability learners. See Table 18.1 for a format useful in applying these elements in a planning or evaluation context.

The guidelines provided can help educators responsible for professional development on content-based curriculum to calibrate a plan that is coherent and meaningful to teachers and appropriate for the context within which they practice. It also can help to foster a climate that is conducive to powerful learning for teachers, and to ensure that specific professional learning experiences include the elements that are known to be effective in supporting growth in teachers' professional practice. Evaluators also might use the framework as a list of benchmarks they would expect to see in a high-quality system of professional development to support the implementation of content-based curriculum.

CONCLUSION

Curriculum effectiveness relies upon the skills of the classroom teacher in implementing the curriculum as it was intended and in providing the differentiated support needed by specific groups of students in specific classrooms. Carefully planned, responsive, and sustained professional learning opportunities are critical in providing teachers with the foundation they need to begin using curricular materials and in supporting them as they become proficient in implementation. Teachers, like their students, need learning experiences that are substantive, rigorous, and engaging to achieve significant outcomes; it is the responsibility of professional development planners to organize, facilitate, and evaluate these experiences to promote the highest levels of learning for the educators who will implement curriculum, ultimately leading to higher quality learning experiences for students.

KEY POINTS SUMMARY

- Professional development on content-based curriculum should provide guidance on the curriculum itself, the strategies and content it entails, and the relevant characteristics and needs of advanced learners.
- Professional development must include not only introductory workshops,

TABLE 18.1

Planning and Evaluation Tool: Key Components of Strong Professional Development for Content-Based Curriculum

Key components	Criteria	Guiding questions	How does your professional learning experience meet each criterion?
Coherence and meaningfulness	**Requisite knowledge:** Designers build a collection of professional learning experiences, including initial and follow-up activities, that provide the subject-matter knowledge, instructional skills, and understanding of the curriculum that are expected of teacher participants, with consideration of the varying backgrounds teachers may bring to the endeavor.	Have teachers of various readiness levels been provided with the proper scaffolding to implement the curriculum thoughtfully and with appropriate rigor and fidelity?	
	Connections to the standards: The learning experiences offer specific and explicit connections to standards. Not only do facilitators ensure that connections exist as they *plan* a high-quality learning experience, they also devote specific attention *during* the learning experience to having teachers identify, explore, or review those connections.	Are teachers able to recognize and articulate the connections between the curriculum and local/state standards for student learning?	
	Connections to evidence of effectiveness: Professional development experiences include opportunities for teachers to see evidence demonstrating the effectiveness of the curriculum, including attention to features most critical for replicating positive outcomes for students.	Is convincing evidence of the effectiveness of the curriculum provided in a way that demonstrates relevance to teachers' own context?	
	Connections to present practices: Teachers are given guided opportunities to make connections between their existing classroom practices and the new strategies that are *expected* of them within the curriculum.	Are teachers encouraged to explore connections to present practice and to analyze ways the new curriculum connects with, builds upon, and differs from existing instruction?	
	Student-centered: The professional development experiences maintain a focus on K–12 students, centering on intended student outcomes of the curriculum, specific learning implications for high-ability students, and consideration of strategies for differentiation for varied learning needs.	Are teachers guided in predicting, observing, responding to, and assessing a range of student responses to the curriculum?	
	Assessment of student learning: The professional development program provides experiences with assessment of student learning as detailed in the curriculum resources and with student data to inform instructional decision making.	Do teachers have the opportunity to practice and reflect upon using assessment data to make instructional decisions within the context of the curriculum?	

Key components	Criteria	Guiding questions	How does your professional learning experience meet each criterion?
Learning climate	**Professionalism:** Professional development experiences promote a climate of professionalism and respect.	Do teachers feel they are respected as professionals engaged in meaningful learning?	
	Contextual relevance: Professional development planning includes careful assessment of contextual needs and uses teacher input as well as classroom-based data to guide goal setting and organization of the learning experience.	Have teachers been consulted regarding needs and goals for professional learning? Have local data been used in determining needs?	
	Interactive, responsive climate of inquiry: Teachers involved in implementation of the curriculum are given extensive opportunities for active engagement with colleagues and professional development leaders, with emphasis on expressing their ideas, asking questions, and sharing their experiences related to implementation of the curriculum.	Is there a free and timely exchange of questions, comments, and sharing of experiences in implementing the curriculum?	
	Facilitation of a reflective dialogue: Facilitators of the professional development experiences use prompts and questions effectively to encourage teachers to reflect collaboratively upon experiences and to strive for higher levels of expertise in their implementation.	Do facilitators use questions that encourage teacher response and provide feedback that promotes teacher learning and changes in practice?	
Professional development process	**Format of professional development experiences:** Appropriately varied delivery formats are used that respond to the professional development objectives at different stages of curricular implementation. A balance of scheduled professional development events and job-embedded strategies are used to support the teachers' implementation of the curriculum.	Are varied and targeted formats used to promote professional learning and attention to learning objectives of each stage of the curriculum implementation?	
	Modeling of instructional strategies: Teachers have the opportunity to experience, as learners, the instructional strategies that they are expected to incorporate in their implementation of the curriculum, including questioning strategies, teaching models, and other specific pedagogical techniques.	Have teachers observed other teachers or professional development facilitators using the strategies they are expected to implement?	
	Specific opportunities for discussion: Purposefully planned opportunities to discuss teachers' experiences with the curriculum are provided. Discussions may be guided by specific questions related to the curriculum or left open to allow issues to emerge that are most relevant to the teachers.	Is adequate time set aside for discussion that focuses solely on the implementation of the curriculum?	
	Effective use of time: Professional development experiences make effective use of time to support the expectations for teacher participation and provide sustained attention over the duration of implementation.	Is sufficient time provided prior to and during implementation to ensure efficient, effective professional learning?	

Key components	Criteria	Guiding questions	How does your professional learning experience meet each criterion?
Professional development process	**Provision of resources:** Teachers implementing content-based curriculum have access to and knowledge of the resources and supplies needed for successful implementation of the curriculum.	Do teachers understand and have access to everything that they need to implement the curriculum? Are they aware of all of the resources available to them if they should choose to seek additional materials or support beyond what is already provided?	
	Formative assessment of teacher learning needs: The professional development program includes methods of assessing the learning needs of the teachers throughout all stages of curricular implementation, including measures of teacher content learning, classroom practice indicators, and self-assessment and reflection data.	Have data been collected and analyzed throughout the professional development program to support effective modifications and adjustments to respond to the changing needs of teachers throughout each stage of curriculum implementation?	
	Differentiation: The professional development program provides formats and learning options that respond to varying participant readiness and experience levels. Flexible activities with multiple entry points, respectful discussion, and responsive grouping patterns are among the strategies that are used to provide a differentiated response to the range of participant needs, and ongoing assessment provides support for differentiated guidance.	Are the individual learning needs of teachers considered in the delivery and facilitation of the professional development experiences?	

but sustained opportunities over time for teachers to learn, apply, and reflect on their understanding and use of content-based curriculum.

- Research-based features of effective professional development include meaningful content, coherence with standards and teacher expectations, responsiveness to individual differences in teacher knowledge and attitudes, opportunities for active engagement and collaboration, sustained learning opportunities over time, and administrative support.

- Differences in teacher experience, attitudes, and school climate play an influential and complex role in teachers' reception of professional development initiatives, and must be considered in the planning process.

- Classroom data from students and teachers should be used to inform professional development, including initial experiences and ongoing activities and support.

- Initial professional learning experiences on content-based curriculum should present a thorough overview of materials, engage teachers as learners in the instructional strategies, and provide time for collaboration and reflection.

- Sustained support for curriculum implementation should combine scheduled sessions with in-classroom support and should include attention to review of student products emerging from instruction.

REFERENCES

Anderson, L., & Olsen, B. (2006). Investigating early career urban teachers' perspectives on and experiences in professional development. *Journal of Teacher Education, 57*, 359–377.

Birman, B. F., Desimone, L., Porter, A. C., & Garet, M. S. (2000). Designing professional development that works. *Educational Leadership, 57*(8), 28–33.

Brighton, C. (2003). The effects of middle school teachers' beliefs on classroom practices. *Journal for the Education of the Gifted, 27*, 177–206.

Brown, S. W., Renzulli, J. S., Gubbins, E. J., Siegle, D., Zhang, W., & Chen, C. (2005). Assumptions underlying the identification of gifted and talented students. *Gifted Child Quarterly, 49*, 68–79.

Center for Gifted Education. (1999). *Guide to teaching a language arts curriculum for high-ability learners.* Dubuque, IA: Kendall/Hunt.

Clarke, D., & Hollingsworth, H. (2002). Elaborating a model of teacher professional growth. *Teaching and Teacher Education, 18*, 947–967.

Darling-Hammond, L., Wei, R. C., Andree, A., Richardson, N., & Orphanos, S. (2009). *Professional learning in the learning profession: A status report on teacher development in the United States and abroad.* Dallas, TX: National Staff Development Council.

Garet, M. S., Porter, A. C., Desimone, L., Birman, B. F., & Yoon, K. S. (2001). What makes professional development effective? Results from a national sample of teachers. *American Educational Research Journal, 38*, 915–945.

Gavin, M. K., Casa, T. M., Adelson, J. L., Carroll, S. R., & Sheffield, L. J. (2009). The impact of advanced curriculum on the achievement of mathematically promising elementary students. *Gifted Child Quarterly, 53*, 188–202. doi:10.1177/0016986209334964

Guskey, T. R. (1986). Staff development and the process of teacher change. *Educational Researcher, 15*(5), 5–12.

Guskey, T. R. (2000). *Evaluating staff development.* Thousand Oaks, CA: Corwin Press.

Hansen, J. B., & Feldhusen, J. F. (2004). Comparison of trained and untrained teachers of gifted students. *Gifted Child Quarterly, 38*, 115–123.

Higgins, T. E. (2006, April). *Pressures of participation: Factors influencing teachers' involvement in ongoing professional development programs.* Paper presented at the annual meeting of the American Educational Research Association, San Francisco, CA.

Joyce, B. R., & Showers, B. (2002). *Student achievement through staff development* (3rd ed.). Alexandria, VA: Association for Supervision and Curriculum Development.

Kennedy, M. (1999). Form and substance in mathematics and science professional development. *NISE Brief, 3*(2), 1–7.

Kwakman, K., (2003). Factors affecting teachers' participation in professional learning activities. *Teaching and Teacher Education, 19*, 149–170.

Lawless, K. A., & Pellegrino, J. W. (2007). Professional development in integrating technology into teaching and learning: Knowns, unknowns, and ways to pursue better questions and answers. *Review of Educational Research, 77*, 575–614. doi:10.3102/0034654307309921

Little, C. A., & Fogarty, E. A. (2009, November). *Reflecting on change: Concerns of teachers implementing differentiated reading instruction.* Presentation at the annual convention of the National Association for Gifted Children, St. Louis, MO.

Little, C. A., & Paul, K. A. (2009). Weighing the workshop: Assess the merits with six criteria for planning and evaluation. *Journal of Staff Development, 30*(5), 26–30.

Little, J. W. (1993). Teachers' professional development in a climate of educational reform. *Educational Evaluation and Policy Analysis, 15*, 129–151. doi:10.3102/01623737015002129

National Staff Development Council. (2001). *NSDC's standards for staff development.* Oxford, OH: Author.

Paul, K. A., Little, C. A., & McCoach, D. B. (2009, April). *Development of the pathways to professional development scale.* Paper presented at the annual meeting of the American Educational Research Association, San Diego, CA.

Richardson, V. (2003). The dilemmas of professional development. *Phi Delta Kappan, 84*, 401–406.

Siegle, D., & Powell, T. (2004). Exploring teacher biases when nominating students for gifted programs. *Gifted Child Quarterly, 48*, 21–29.

Tomlinson, C. A. (1995). Deciding to differentiate instruction in middle school: One school's journey. *Gifted Child Quarterly, 29*, 77–87.

Torff, B., & Sessions, D. (2008). Factors associated with teachers' attitudes about professional development. *Teacher Education Quarterly, 35*, 123–134.

VanTassel-Baska, J., Feng, A. X., Brown, E., Bracken, B., Stambaugh, T., French, H., . . . Bai, W. (2008). A study of differentiated instructional change over three years. *Gifted Child Quarterly, 52*, 297–312.

Vavasseur, C. B., & MacGregor, S. K. (2008). Extending content-focused professional development through online communities of practice. *Journal of Research on Technology in Education, 40*, 517–536.

Westberg, K. L., & Daoust, M. E. (2003, Fall). The results of the replication of the classroom practices survey replication in two states. *The National Research Center on the Gifted and Talented Newsletter*, 3–8.

Chapter 19

Implementing Innovative Curriculum and Instructional Practices in Classrooms and Schools: Using Research-Based Models of Effectiveness

Joyce VanTassel-Baska

This final chapter focuses on the implementation considerations necessary to make curricular innovation work on a larger scale than that of individual classrooms. It explores the importance of assessment as a part of the mosaic that charts student progress across years within and across learning areas and showcases the effectiveness data available to guide teacher practice. The chapter also explores research-based best practices in professional development that must be emphasized within and across schools in order to sustain innovative practice, and it addresses the leadership dimension so essential to institutionalizing meaningful school reforms. Finally, it lays out 10 lessons of curriculum development found essential to the work of the Center for Gifted Education over 20 years, concluding with commentary on innovation and how to sustain it over time.

CURRICULUM EFFECTIVENESS RESEARCH

Creating effective curricular and instructional models requires that a significant amount of attention goes to the development of an effective accountability system. The use of assessment tools that facilitate student learning at the same time that they provide useful data for future instructional planning is the hallmark of performance- and portfolio-based assessment techniques, which have been discussed in the content and assessment chapters of this text (Chapters 8–11 and 16). Yet, it is systematic data collection on high-ability students over time that best demonstrates the effectiveness of any curricular model as a tool for enhancing significant and important learning. The Integrated Curriculum Model (ICM) has been tested substantially in the areas of science and language arts in particular, using quasi-experimental research designs that compared pre-test-posttest performance of students participating in The College of William and Mary's Center for Gifted Education units in these areas with the performance of similar students who were not taught using the units. The presentation of claims for student learning in each area follows, demonstrating specifically the results related to the specific curriculum, as well as supporting the notion of ongoing data-collection efforts to maintain high-quality curriculum development and implementation. In each content area, details and results of earlier studies are presented first, followed by discussion of more recent studies that have occurred since the first edition of this text.

Science Curriculum Effectiveness Data

The Center for Gifted Education's problem-based science units for high-ability learners in grades 2–8 have been rigorously evaluated to ensure both effectiveness in promoting student learning gains and acceptance by teachers. Not only have the units and accompanying training materials undergone four major revisions in the course of their development, the next-to-last edition of the units was field-tested across multiple school districts.

The goals of the program across all of the units have consistently been threefold: (a) to develop student understanding of the concepts of *systems* and *change*, (b) to develop specific content learning that is unit dependent, and (c) to develop scientific research processes. More specific learning outcomes have been delineated under each of these broad overarching goals, in keeping with the intent of the National Science Standards and the Benchmarks for Science Literacy that call for substantive content linked to high-level scientific processes and the understanding of meaningful scientific concepts (American Association for the Advancement of Science, 1990; National Research Council, 1996).

Although the units are designed to have assessments addressing all three of the major science learning goals given above, the research design investigating the curriculum's effectiveness focused explicitly on student application of the scientific method. Findings related to two of the units, *Acid, Acid Everywhere* and *What a Find!* (Center for Gifted Education, 1997a, 1997b), are presented here for illustrative purposes. Further discussion of the design of the units themselves may be found in Chapter 10.

Design. The sample for the evaluation of effectiveness of each unit was composed of volunteer teachers and their classrooms from our national network of schools, including districts from the states of Illinois, Florida, Connecticut, South Carolina, Ohio, Indiana, and Virginia. These districts also agreed to collect comparison data from classes of students of comparable ability in the same schools. The actual numbers of participating teachers varied by curricular unit being evaluated. Data were collected from 42 teachers covering 45 experimental classrooms for *Acid, Acid Everywhere*, with 10 comparison teachers covering 17 classrooms. For *What a Find!*, data were collected from 20 teachers covering 27 experimental classrooms, with 3 comparison teachers and classrooms. All teachers who participated in the field-testing of units received implementation training lasting 2–5 days.

Students included in the sample were all average, above-average, or high-ability learners and were drawn from urban, suburban, and rural districts. All pull-out and self-contained classrooms contained only high-ability learners, but other organizational models also were represented in the sample.

Experimental and comparison classrooms were assessed on a pretest and posttest basis. Posttests were administered at the conclusion of the implementation process, after approximately 20–36 hours of instruction.

Instruments and procedures. Claims regarding the evidence of effectiveness of the science curriculum in promoting student learning are based on the use of the Diet Cola Test (Cain, 1990). The Diet Cola Test measures a student's ability to apply the scientific method and to demonstrate scientific reasoning skills.

The instrument has alternate forms, which made it very useful for the pretest-posttest design employed in the evaluation. Its reliability was documented by the National Research Center on the Gifted and Talented at the University of Virginia (Adams & Callahan, 1995), and its psychometric properties are reasonably high. It is an open-ended, performance-based assessment using a rubric with a ceiling of 21 points to rate student responses. It was the only instrument found in the literature to be appropriate for gifted students in science across the elementary and middle school age ranges due to its sufficiently high ceiling. It also is fairly quick to administer, taking only 30–40 minutes.

Data analysis and results. The analysis of the data for the two science units yielded statistically significant results, showing that students in the experimental or treatment classrooms outperformed students in the comparison classrooms on the posttest, with statistical controls in place for between-group differences in pretest scores. Effect sizes also were calculated to give a measure of how educationally important the significant differences are.

For *Acid, Acid Everywhere,* the experimental classrooms had an adjusted mean posttest score of 6.81 (statistical adjustment based on pretest scores in the two groups). The adjusted mean score for the comparison group was 5.41. For *What a Find!,* the adjusted mean on the Diet Cola Test for the experimental group was 5.95, and for the comparison group, it was 4.07. Both of these sets of results demonstrated statistically significant differences between treatment and comparison classes, indicating that the higher scores in the treatment group could be attributed to the use of the curriculum and not just to chance. The effect sizes also demonstrated that the differences were educationally important. More detailed descriptions of the study and the results may be found in other publications (see Feng, VanTassel-Baska, Quek, O'Neil, & Bai, 2005; VanTassel-Baska, Bass, Ries, Poland, & Avery, 1998).

Teacher questionnaire results. In addition to student test data, the effectiveness of the science units was assessed by asking teachers to respond to a curricular unit evaluation questionnaire. Forty-two teachers from 15 school districts completed the questionnaire for *Acid, Acid Everywhere.* Demographic data from this form demonstrated that the range of classes participating in the study included various grouping patterns, from self-contained gifted classes to heterogeneous classrooms, and that the teachers were generally experienced, with several years of working with gifted and talented students and of teaching science.

The questionnaire then asked teachers to indicate their perceptions of the unit, based on their experience teaching it. Most teachers reported positive perceptions of the unit. Teachers found the unit to be highly appropriate for high-ability students in terms of goals and outcomes, as well as exercises and activities. They also felt that it promoted active student involvement and that it was motivating for students. The overall judgment of the units by pilot teachers seemed to center on four main points:

- the units had applicability across a broad range of learners,
- the units were well designed and documented important curricular elements for teachers,
- the units were enjoyable and motivating for both students and teachers, and
- teachers would use the units again.

Evidence of Effectiveness for Project Clarion

Although the problem-based learning (PBL) units discussed above address all three major goals in the science curriculum framework (i.e., the concepts of *systems,* specific content learning, and scientific reasoning), the PBL curriculum studies focused explicitly on student application of scientific research and integrating students' understanding of science content and inquiry, reasoning, and problem-based reasoning skills. In the more recent units developed under Project Clarion, we addressed the development of curiosity in science and critical and creative thinking, as well as emphasizing concept development in *systems* and *change* and the scientific research process. The PBL was part of the units, not the lead feature as in the earlier curriculum development work. Goals and student outcomes are aligned to the National Science Education Standards. Each lesson includes instructions that detail the purpose, time needed, suggestions on how to implement the lesson, and ways to conclude and extend the exercise. Three sample units are described below to illustrate different grade levels and science domains.

Budding Botanists (grades 1–2, 13 lessons) is a life science unit that engages students in a scenario-based approach to observe and investigate plant life. The macroconcept of *systems* guides students as they assume the role of botanists. Team members seek to understand the structure, nature, and life cycle of plants, and to answer questions such as, "How can plants be used to fuel cars?" *Budding Botanists* received a 2008 NAGC Curriculum Studies division award for outstanding curriculum and has been recommended by the National Science Teachers Association (NSTA) as a strong curriculum in science for young children.

Dig It! (grade 2, 15 lessons) is an Earth and space science unit that involves students in a problem-based approach to investigate humanity's effects on the environment, the importance of natural resources, and sound conservation practices. The macroconcept of *change* guides students as they assume the role of a preservation park planner. Team members examine examples of environmental pollution and conservation with hands-on scientific experiments and demonstrations.

Invitation to Invent (grade 3, 16 lessons) is a physical science unit that connects the scientific investigation process with creative problem solving. The macroconcept of *systems* guides students as they assume the role of inventor to solve an everyday problem using simple and complex machines. Students conduct investigations that support their learning about force, motion, and friction. Students also learn about the six simple machines and how they are put together to form more complex machines. This unit also received an endorsement from NSTA as a strong science curriculum for young students.

Research design. In the recent 5-year, multidistrict Clarion studies, we used a quasi-experimental design to test the efficacy of the units in K–3 classrooms, using the Metropolitan Achievement Test, the Test of Critical Thinking, and three performance-based measures to assess content, concept, and scientific research process skills. Comparison data were collected within other Title I schools in the same district. After 24 hours of instruction, posttests were administered to both groups. Analyses included MANOVA.

Sample. The Clarion sample involved three school districts with 48 classrooms, of which 43 were controls. All experimental teachers received 3 days of training on implementing the units of study, 2 days before implementation began and one during the project implementation period. Additionally, each received an end of implementation debriefing opportunity in person with project staff.

Instruments. Project effectiveness in the Clarion study also was assessed on a revised form of the Cain (1990) Diet Cola Test, which assesses students' application of scientific method and scientific reasoning skills. Additional instruments used in Project Clarion included two other project-developed performance-based assessments, one standardized achievement measure (Metropolitan Achievement Test), and one critical thinking measure (Test of Critical Thinking).

Data collection procedures. Data for Project Clarion were collected by project staff at each school site between 2006–2008. These data included the pre-post measures described previously, as well as fidelity of implementation data from teachers in the experimental group.

Data analysis and results. Posttest analyses were conducted using an ANCOVA that covaried pretest between-group differences. MANOVAs were conducted and effect sizes calculated. The Project Clarion results showed significant and important gains for all groups of Title I learners in respect to ability (gifted, average, low ability) and minority status (African American, Asian American, Hispanic American, Caucasian) across 2 years of data collection on all measures employed. Effect sizes were in the moderate range (i.e., $d = .32$ to .56; Kim et al., 2010). The second and third year of data collection revealed growth on performance-based measures in content, scientific process, and concept development, with moderate effect sizes (i.e., $d = .32$ to .62). The scientific process assessment was administered to experimental and control students in the third year of data collection and showed significant differences for second graders but not third graders in science process skills (Bland et al., 2010).

Interpretation and discussion of results. Project Clarion results suggested a trajectory of learning gains on different dimensions of science learning as a result of exposure to the 24 hours of classroom instruction in science concepts, content, and process for students in Title I classrooms receiving the intervention. However, learning on the science achievement scale was less impressive in the third-year results, suggesting the need for an instrument with a stronger curricular-content match to the concept-based units.

Teacher and student feedback. Although enhanced student learning is the primary indicator of curriculum effectiveness, teachers' favorable subjective impressions about their experiences with materials and related instructional strategies also are important. Such experiences support teacher acceptance of the materials and contribute to sustained use over time. Teacher acceptance was evaluated using a questionnaire administered at the conclusion of the implementation process. Teacher evaluation outcomes supported the quality of the units in respect to benefits to learners, applicability to science standards, and ease of implementation. In Project Clarion, teachers also rated the units of study individually, with project staff using the results to guide final revisions of the units. Focus groups were employed to evaluate training and unit implementation; results suggested that the experience was helpful and illuminated what Title I students could do if given the opportunity to be actively engaged in high-quality science curriculum.

Language Arts Curriculum Effectiveness Data

The Center for Gifted Education's language arts curriculum units have been evaluated for effectiveness in terms of teaching literary analysis and interpretation and persuasive writing as language arts manifestations of higher level thinking (VanTassel-Baska, Zuo, Avery, & Little, 2002). As such, the study discussed in the following sections contributes to our understanding of the importance of embedding higher order skills into content and builds on prior understanding of effective research-based strategies for teaching writing (e.g., Burkhalter, 1995).

Design and purpose of the study. By using a quasi-experimental design, the researchers sought to demonstrate the effects of particular units of study on gifted learners at primary, intermediate, and middle school levels. Each unit was organized around the ICM and, therefore, sought to enhance learning through an integrated approach of using advanced literature, embedding a reasoning model into the teaching of the language arts, requiring a high-quality student product, and teaching the major concept of *change* as it applies to literature, writing, language study, and oral communication.

Sample. Seventeen public school districts and one private school furnished student data for this study. The districts and schools were quite diverse, drawn from rural, urban, suburban, or exurban settings across 10 states: Colorado, Connecticut, Illinois, Indiana, Maryland, Ohio, South Carolina, Utah, Virginia, and West Virginia. The private school was located in an urban area. In all, 46 schools across these districts participated in the study.

Students participating in the study (N = 2,189) were all identified gifted learners in grades 2–8 in their local school district. Given the relative standard of giftedness applied to identification procedures at the local level coupled with the variety of state definitions of giftedness (Karnes & Stephens, 2000), the range of general ability and verbal aptitude varied in the sample to some extent. Identification criteria employed in the 10 participating states included ability and aptitude measures coupled with teacher recommendations. Threshold scores ranged from 94%–99% for both identification on group ability measures and on-group, on-grade verbal aptitude measures.

Curriculum treatment. The curriculum materials used in the study were four of a series of six units, organized around the ICM curricular framework developed under a federal Jacob K. Javits grant in the mid-1990s. The goals of the units are outlined in Chapter 8 on language arts. The units included pretests and posttests for literary analysis and interpretation and for persuasive writing. Other assessments, including both formative and summative measures, also were included. The four units included one written for grades 2–3, two for grades 4–6, and one for grades 7–9. This study focused on the pretest-posttest results of the literature and writing tests. Each of the teachers involved in the study received 1–4 days of training on the curricular materials. The training workshops were conducted by project staff, local teachers, or administrators who had themselves been trained for workshop leadership. Workshops introduced teachers to the curricular framework and to the specific teaching models used in the units, with discussion of how those models promoted accomplishment of the goals.

Instrumentation. The two assessments used in the study measured literary analysis and persuasive writing skills. The same task demands were consistent across the units, although different stimuli were used to evoke student responses in each unit. At the beginning and end of each unit, students were asked to read a selection and complete the two assessments based on that selection. Both assessments were piloted with relevant populations and formed the basis of an earlier curriculum effectiveness study (VanTassel-Baska, Johnson, Hughes, & Boyce, 1996). The first assessment was a performance-based test of literary analysis and interpretation. This test, modeled on the reading portion of the National Assessment of Educational Progress (National Assessment Governing Board, 1992), included four questions that addressed the following topics: (a) main idea, (b) analysis of a quote, (c) relationship of the concept of *change* to the selection, and (d) creating a title with a rationale to support it. The second assessment was a performance-based persuasive writing assessment that asked students to develop an argument to support whether or not they would require all the students in their grade to read the given selection (Center for Gifted Education, 1999b). In each unit, students read and responded to a different selection in the pretest than in the posttest, although the two selections in each unit represented the same genre.

Scoring. The rubric for the literature test gave a range of 0–3 points for each of the four questions, for a total score range of 0–12. The rubric for the writing test was based on Toulmin's (1958) criteria for judging quality of claim, data, and warrant as adapted by Burkhalter (1995). This rubric gave a range of 0–20 total points, with a 0–6 range for each of the elements of claim, data, and warrant, and a 0–2 range for the conclusion (see Table 19.1 for a sample rubric).

Method. As in the science study discussed earlier in this chapter (VanTassel-Baska et al., 1998), the statistical test used to compare treatment and comparison classes in the language arts study was ANCOVA, which controls for between-group differences. The results of these analyses indicated statistically

TABLE 19.1

Persuasive Writing Scoring Rubric

Claim or Opinion	
0	No clear position exists on the writer's assertion, preference, or view, and context does not help to clarify it.
2	Yes/no alone or writer's position is poorly formulated, but reader is reasonably sure what the paper is about based on context.
4	*meets expectations:* A clear topic sentence exists, and the reader is reasonably sure what the paper is about based on the strength of the topic sentence alone.
6	*exceeds expectations:* A very clear, concise position is given and position is elaborated with reference to reasons; multiple sentences are used to form the claim. Must include details that explain the context.
Data or Supporting Points	
0	No reasons are offered that are relevant to the claim.
2	One or two weak reasons are offered; the reasons are relevant to the claim.
4	At least two strong reasons are offered that are relevant to the claim.
6	*meets expectations:* At least three reasons are offered that are relevant to the claim.
8	*exceeds expectations:* At least three reasons are offered that are also accurate, convincing, and distinct.
Elaboration	
0	No elaboration is provided.
2	An attempt is made to elaborate at least one reason.
4	More than one reason is supported with relevant details.
6	*meets expectations:* Each reason (3) is supported with relevant information that is clearly connected to the claim.
8	*exceeds expectations:* The writer explains all reasons in a very effective, convincing, multi-paragraph structure.
Conclusion	
0	No conclusion/closing sentence is provided.
2	A conclusion/closing sentence is provided.
4	*meets expectations:* A conclusion is provided that revisits the main ideas.
6	*exceeds expectations:* A strong concluding paragraph is provided that revisits and summarizes main ideas.

Note. From *Patterns of Change* (p. 31), by the Center for Gifted Education, 2003, Dubuque, IA: Kendall/Hunt. Copyright © 2003 by the Center for Gifted Education. Reprinted with permission.

significant differences on the posttests for literary analysis and interpretation and for persuasive writing favoring the treatment group, which again means that higher mean scores on the posttests could be attributed to the use of the curricular units. For the literary analysis test, the adjusted mean score on the posttest for the treatment group was 6.86, while the comparison group had an adjusted mean score of 5.88. On the persuasive writing test, differences were even more dramatic, with the treatment group achieving an adjusted mean posttest score of 11.34, while the comparison group had an adjusted mean score of 7.59. The effect sizes were medium to large, again indicating both educational importance of the results and statistical significance.

These analyses were conducted across four language arts units; the results of separate analyses, conducted at the unit level, are consistent with the results combined across units. In other words, virtually any language arts unit within the Center for Gifted Education's curriculum can be implemented and expected to generate significant treatment effect.

Additional tests were run to compare performance by gender and by socio-economic status (SES) within the treatment group. In the gender comparison, results showed that there were no differences by gender for literature, but found a statistically significant difference for persuasive writing ($p < .01$). However, that difference was found to be of little practical importance when effect size was computed. This suggests that boys and girls benefitted relatively equally from their exposure to the literature curriculum. The SES comparison was conducted using schoolwide data on percentage of students on free or reduced lunch programs to categorize schools as high or low SES. This comparison yielded no statistically significant differences between the groups and demonstrated clearly, especially in writing, that students from high- and low-SES groups can benefit from using the curriculum. Additional details on the results of the language arts study may be found elsewhere (see VanTassel-Baska et al., 2002).

Discussion. The data suggested that the use of the Center for Gifted Education's language arts units produces significant and important gains for gifted learners in key aspects of the language arts, as assessed by demonstration of high-level thinking on performance-based measures. Because of the integration of goals within the units, these findings contribute to our understanding of teaching literature and writing in an integrated way, teaching for deeper understanding, and teaching for thinking within a subject area. All of these are important aspects in enhancing learning when teaching to the new standards and to reflect research on teaching both literature and writing (e.g., Applebee & Langer, 2009). The deliberate use of instructional models, such as the Literature Web, Hamburger Model, and Paul's (1992) Element of Reasoning model within the curriculum to promote student automaticity in thinking and writing about ideas appears to have impacted student learning positively (see Chapters 5 and 8 for explication of the relevant instructional models).

The treatment was effective with both economically disadvantaged and economically advantaged students. It also was equally effective with males and females when educational importance was used as the criterion to examine small differences. The grouping model used showed minimal evidence of impact on student performance, with all grouping models showing strong evidence of learning gains. Clearly, students benefitted from their exposure to the Center for Gifted Education's curriculum units in language arts, and these benefits were documented in terms of learning outcomes of statistical and educational significance on performance-based assessment measures. Furthermore, this study showed how a curriculum derived from standards-based reform can be assessed using instruments that require demonstration of higher order reasoning in the language arts domain. Such assessments then provide data to support professional development and continuous improvement of curricular implementation.

Evidence of Effectiveness From Project Athena

Based on the growing research evidence on the use of the Center for Gifted Education's language arts units with gifted learners, the team at William and Mary began a 3-year longitudinal study that used the curriculum in Title 1 schools and inclusive classrooms with all learners (VanTassel-Baska, Bracken, Feng, & Brown, 2009).

Using an experimental design, 28 experimental classrooms implemented a William and Mary language arts unit in grades 3, 4, or 5. More rigorous assessment was included in this study: an investigator-developed Test of Critical Thinking (TCT) and the use of the reading comprehension section of the Iowa Tests of Basic Skills (ITBS) in addition to the performance-based measures used in the earlier language arts studies.

The longitudinal sample for this 3-year study was 1,346 students, with 735 in the experimental group and 611 in the control group. Formal training for teachers in the implementation of the units was conducted for 4 days across each year. Data analysis featured the use of MANOVA to assess pretest-posttest results for between-group differences. Effect sizes were calculated for all groups. Results suggested that students in experimental classes showed significant and important educational gains in critical thinking across 3 years ($p < .05$) with effect sizes at the moderate level. Although students in the control group also showed significant gains in critical thinking, significant differences favored the experimental group with small effect sizes of $\eta^2 = .037$. All groups within the experiment showed gains, including gifted, high readers/promising learners, and typical learners. On the ITBS reading comprehension subtest, both the experimental and control students showed significant growth. Performance-based measures also yielded significant and educationally important results for the experimental students in all ability groups, suggesting that the curriculum is effective with a broad range of learners.

Data also were collected on teacher change as a result of both training and use of a differentiated curriculum. Pretest-posttest data using a classroom observation instrument (the Classroom Observation Scale–Revised [COS-R]) suggest that teachers in the experimental group showed significant growth patterns in the use of key elements of differentiation (i.e., critical thinking, creative thinking, accommodation to individual differences) across 2 years of implementation of the William and Mary units of study in comparison to control group teachers not trained in the curriculum. Third-year results did not show added growth.

The results of this 5-year Javits project demonstrated the power of using more high-level materials with all learners, not just the gifted, as well as illustrating the importance of using multiple approaches to assess learning and multiple pathways for learning. The project team also developed a reading comprehension program, entitled *Jacob's Ladder*, to enable students to move to higher level thinking, once comprehension has been attained.

Evidence of Effectiveness From Social Studies Curriculum

One comprehensive study has been conducted to date to examine the efficacy of the social studies units of study developed by the Center for Gifted Education under the Javits-supported Project Phoenix (Little, Feng, VanTassel-Baska, Rogers, & Avery, 2007). In a quasi-experimental study of using social studies units modeled on the ICM, conducted with Title I students in grades 3–8, results suggested that significant and important learning gains were accrued for students in selected classrooms on the dimensions of content mastery, concept development, and higher level thinking. Teacher results confirmed the unevenness of student learning as connected to implementation fidelity, although group analyses suggested that teachers enhanced their ability to use selected differentiation strategies as a result of the training and curriculum differentiation use designed into the units. Subanalyses showed growth for both gifted and nongifted students in the study and for low socioeconomic learners, as well as minority students.

This study of the efficacy of the social studies units suggested the need for further work, using standardized instruments, as well as performance-based ones to assess student learning. Teacher development findings are consonant with other later studies, suggesting that randomly selected, untrained teachers can grow in important ways in their differentiation practices if they have sufficient training coupled with a curriculum already differentiated for their use.

Other Assessment Approaches

In addition to core assessments of accountability for student learning, a content-based system of assessment must include formative approaches that allow teachers to understand how students are progressing, as well as end-of-unit cumulative product assessments. The Center for Gifted Education's units contain several different assessment components so that teachers have maximum opportunities for gathering student assessment information (see Figures 19.1 and 19.2).

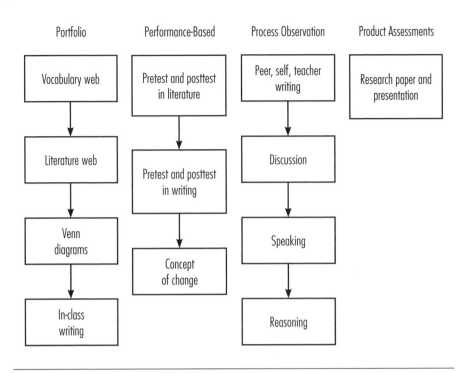

Figure 19.1. Assessment tools for language arts units.

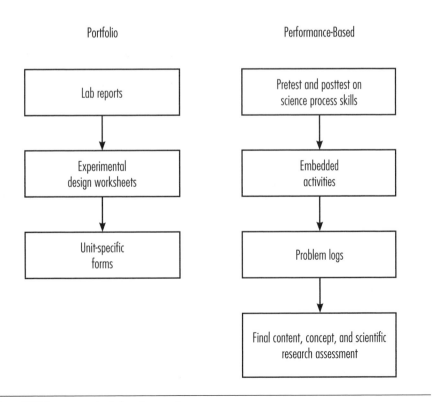

Figure 19.2. Assessment tools for science units.

PROFESSIONAL DEVELOPMENT

An age of meaningful accountability calls out for school contexts in which teacher learning is as paramount a concern as student learning. Therefore, a key need area within a system of curriculum and instruction is an effective plan and a follow-up evaluation mechanism for professional development. Guskey (2000) has argued that our accountability system for judging the efficacy of professional development is weak and has suggested that we need to consider several areas for assessing effectiveness. These include the following:

- participants' reactions,
- participants' learning,
- organizational support for change,
- use of knowledge and skills, and
- student learning outcomes (results).

When planning professional development programs for teachers of the gifted, administrators and professional development coordinators need to focus on the elements that research suggests have been the most critical. These include selecting content topics that respond to real, as opposed to perceived, need. Thus, in implementing reform-based principles, it is necessary to ascertain those principles teachers routinely employ and those they need to develop. A recent analysis of classrooms (VanTassel-Baska et al., 2008) demonstrated that teachers of the gifted need more emphasis on the use of individualization techniques, critical thinking, problem solving, and metacognition, because the pattern of data suggests greatest discrepancy between observed and desired teacher behavior in these dimensions. Thus, workshops on the implementation of appropriate curricular units should stress these skills.

A second research-based best practice in professional development involves emphasizing student learning in key areas as the goal and using student-learning data as the best evidence of effective professional development work. The Center for Gifted Education's professional development model (see Figure 19.3) encourages teachers to collect student data on the models taught through professional development and to use these data to make adjustments in their teaching. Only then can the claim of effective professional development be made.

A third area of research-based professional development practice involves the follow-up mechanisms that are in place in schools to encourage active experimentation with new teaching strategies and models (e.g., Guskey, 2002). It is clear that many schools are not positioned to engage in meaningful professional development practices, given the limited organizational support for such activities. Principals and teacher teams must be actively engaged in ensuring that practices learned are tried out and supported in everyday practice. Evidence suggests

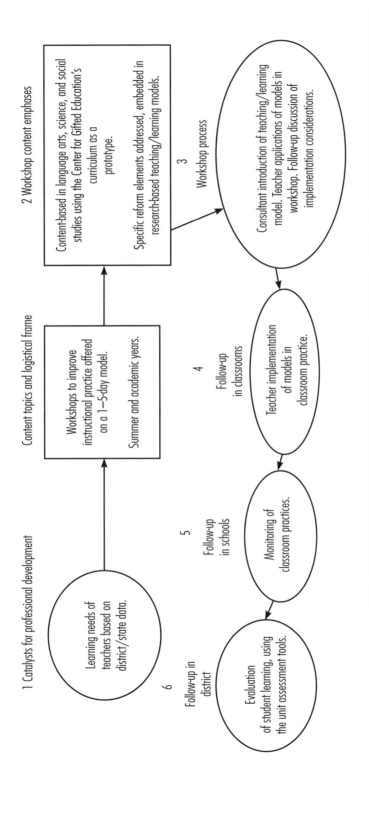

Figure 19.3. The Center for Gifted Education's professional development model.

that teachers practice a strategy or model before they make judgments about it based on how students react. If students respond favorably, then teachers are more apt to adopt positive attitudes and beliefs about using a new model for learning (Guskey, 2000). Our experience with the Center for Gifted Education's professional development model suggests similar findings. Results from teacher implementation data in science, for example, consistently showed that teacher enthusiasm for problem-based learning increased as they saw their students' motivation increase with use of the pedagogy (VanTassel-Baska et al., 1998).

Another key finding from the professional development literature suggests that training on practices embedded in content and materials to be used in classrooms aids student learning, and, thus, it enhances the likelihood that teachers will continue employing the practice (Kennedy, 1999). This strategy has been extensively employed in National Science Foundation (NSF) projects over the past two decades, as well as in the curricular implementation workshops through the Center for Gifted Education at The College of William and Mary. A major emphasis in such training involves the teaching of a core model, practice, feedback, and then a demonstration of how and where it may be found in a unit of study or constructed into one. Closely linked to this demonstration is showing how the model is aligned to the teaching of the content area under discussion based on the demands of state standards. Thus, teachers leave a workshop with a contextual base for the use of the technique.

Moreover, recent studies on professional development support the use of research-based learning strategies, such as those employed in the William and Mary curriculum, to promote student achievement and positively affect teacher behaviors (Johnson, Kahle, & Fargo, 2006; VanTassel-Baska et al., 2008). In specific studies using gifted samples, Gentry and Keilty (2004) and Gubbins et al. (2002) found that cluster teachers needed support in compacting the curriculum and systematically employing higher level skills and strategies in their teaching. Matthews and Foster (2005) found that the resource teacher model of professional development was efficacious as long as it was dynamic and ongoing. More generic research-based elements known to influence classroom practice, such as emphasizing content knowledge, providing opportunities for active learning, maintaining coherence with other learning activities, addressing teachers' attitudes, sustaining intensity, and ensuring collective participation (Garet, Porter, Desimone, Birman, & Yoon, 2001) also are critical to the success of professional development practices.

Finally, research-based best practice in professional development supports the need for a match between the sophistication of the learning and the duration of training opportunities. In-depth summer training options appear to work well as a first-stage effort when the learning to be accrued is complex, because they offer more intensive time away from the classroom. However, more follow-up training opportunities are required onsite to ensure faithful implementation of such practices, coupled with further in-depth and advanced training opportunities during actual implementation of the curriculum innovation.

The Role of Leadership in Reform-Based Practice

There has never been a time when instructional leadership has been in greater demand than it is now as we prepare to implement a substantial curricular learning reform agenda. The needs for such leaders must first evolve from a sound theoretical sense of what educational leadership is all about. Minimally, they must be schooled in the following principles, which are derived from theory:

- Leadership is about accepting the multiple realities of working in an organization (Bolman & Deal, 1991).
- School leaders have to accept their role in the change process as involving human relations skills and task commitment skills, using the organizational structure to advance innovation, and helping the school create meaning for its members.
- Leadership is about integrity, using power to help people grow (Burns, 1978). A school leader also has to attend to the overall growth and development of teachers, making them stronger tomorrow than they are today and providing them the tools to continue the challenge of growth in a politically charged environment.
- Leadership is about building learning communities and managing them in contemporary educational environments (Gardner, 1990). School leaders also must attend to overall management of learning-centered environments that demand dynamic principles of leadership to be enacted and flexible approaches and styles to be used.
- Leadership is about accepting and creating challenge through reflection, intention, and action (Kouzes & Posner, 1995). School leaders need to be proactive and clear about their goals and the strategies to enact them. Thus, both action and accompanying communication habits have to be effectively enacted in order for change to be successfully implemented.

In addition, school leaders must deliberately monitor classrooms on a regular basis to ensure that a given model is being implemented and done well. If the desired practice is critical thinking, for example, then the principal could use a simple checklist like the one in Table 19.2 to discern the use of these behaviors.

However, in order to implement such a checklist, the school leader must be able to recognize these behaviors when they are in use. Because most of the reform strategies focus on higher level skill and concept development approaches, some training for administrators is warranted to ensure that reform

TABLE 19.2

Classroom Observation Form: Critical Thinking Strategies

The teacher used activities or questions that enabled students . . .	Yes	No	Comments
1. to make judgments or evaluate situations, problems, or issues	❏	❏	
2. to compare and contrast	❏	❏	
3. to generalize from specific data to the abstract	❏	❏	
4. to synthesize and summarize information within or across the disciplines	❏	❏	
5. to debate points of view or develop arguments to support ideas	❏	❏	

Note. From *Classroom Observation Form* (p. 2), by the Center for Gifted Education, 1999, Williamsburg, VA: Author. Copyright © 1999 by the Center for Gifted Education. Reprinted with permission.

practices are understood well enough to be effectively monitored. Thus, training for administrators in the models that teachers have learned, to the extent necessary for recognizing their use and judging the efficacy of their delivery, is crucial. For example, a principal observed in an elementary school spent time in the classrooms every day, assessing the behaviors associated with the successful implementation of the Center for Gifted Education's language arts curriculum, and, based on his observations, he discerned the need for follow-up in-service in key areas for specified teachers only, thus successfully differentiating the professional development plan based on real data from the classroom.

Leadership must be sensitive to the need for policy change and monitoring (Swanson, 2007). In any innovation, there will be continued need for support from a community that values the innovation; forward progress on converting the innovation to school, district, and even state policy; and the mechanisms and will to collect research data on its effectiveness at all levels of the schooling enterprise. This process also implies that there is a leader in place over time who can shepherd these changes through a system designed to continue the status quo rather than innovation.

Leadership also must be motivational and even inspirational in schools in order to lift the spirits of teachers and students who are engaged in the difficult work of enhancing learning. Thus, principals must be aware of the need for honoring the culture and symbolically rewarding the efforts that go on within it (Peterson, 2001). A high priority must be placed on accolades for enhanced learning. One school district, for example, rotates board meetings to each school in the district and asks the principal of each school to stage a performance demonstrating student learning. In addition, at each board meeting, students who received awards during the past month are individually recognized, along with their parents, for their accomplishments. The event is handled in such a way that the experience is one of celebration. This is an example of a learner-centered school district, in which learners are the focus of adult activities and evidence of learning is rewarded. Talent development must be recognized in order to demonstrate that it is valued sufficiently in a school context.

FINAL LESSONS

As schools and districts consider implementation of the ideas presented in this book, it may be helpful to consider the lessons we have learned over the past 20 years of curriculum design, development, field-testing, and efficacy research at The College of William and Mary, in our quest to upgrade curriculum and instructional quality for the gifted learners in our schools.

Lesson #1: Curriculum Design Matters

All William and Mary curricula feature the Integrated Curriculum Model (ICM) as the guiding theoretical framework for curriculum design. The Center for Gifted Education units have been piloted in schools nationwide and found to improve student achievement, not only in the specific content areas, but also in critical thinking and understanding overarching concepts. Each unit, regardless of the content focus, features the following blueprint specifications:
- a curriculum framework that identifies learning goals and anticipated outcomes;
- authentic assessments for content, concept, and process as a guide for diagnostic and prescriptive instruction, as well as formal assessment;
- emphasis on higher level thinking and reasoning through questioning and activities;
- inquiry-based, meaningful, hands-on, and minds-on experiences;
- use of graphic organizers;
- inclusion of accelerated reading and advanced resources;
- use of a broad-based concept (e.g., *systems*, *cause-effect*, *change*) to elevate understanding of the subject under study;
- metacognition and reflection components;
- incorporation of interdisciplinary, real-world research;
- use of teaching models to scaffold instruction and to promote higher level thinking skills;
- strong content emphasis that focuses on discipline-specific skills and concepts; and
- use of technology.

These features have stood the test of time and varied use to represent core design variables for inclusion in any curriculum designed for use with gifted learners.

Lesson # 2: The Curriculum Development Process Matters

All of the curriculum developed by the Center for Gifted Education over the past 20 years has followed not only a set of design specifications consistent with curriculum reform, but also a consistent approach to development.

We have begun to develop each unit with a review of relevant research on the topic, age level of the student, and the best practices for teaching in the discipline under study. This research phase also takes into account alignment with state standards and curriculum reform research in each subject matter. These findings then are used as the basis for creating a draft set of lessons. These lessons are tried out in relevant classrooms and revised, based on student receptivity and teacher feedback. Next, an entire unit of study is prepared for piloting in one teacher's classroom. Multiple data sources are used to judge the effectiveness of the unit after implementation, including teacher log notes, student learning results, and outside expert review. Revisions then are made to each unit, based on triangulation of the feedback. The units are field-tested at multiple sites with different teachers and data collected on treatment fidelity, student growth, and teacher perceptions of effectiveness. Based on these data, the units are revised a second time before they are disseminated nationally. This multiple stage process allows us to refine the product, based on sources of evidence, to enhance its use as an agent of positive learning.

Lesson #3: Curriculum Development Work for High-End Learning Requires Collaboration With Content Experts and Teachers

Discipline-specific expertise is needed to design, develop, and refine curricula to be used with our best learners. Essential content understandings that are core to understanding the discipline need be developed and articulated. Content experts must be an integral part of unit design and review at the beginning stages of development, as well as provide critiques of later drafts of work.

Similarly, a curriculum that will significantly enhance student achievement must be created with strong teacher involvement. Collaboration among grade-level teachers, content specialists, and educators of the gifted at all phases of curriculum development produces a higher quality product. Collaboration time should be apportioned to the critical tasks of curriculum development and piloting, discussing student assessments, grouping mechanisms, and alignment to relevant standards.

Lesson #4: Student Exposure to Repeated Models Over Time Enhances Student Achievement and Learning Transfer

Curriculum delivery requires the use of carefully selected teaching and learning models over time. Research-based, packaged curriculum that has been extensively piloted is more likely to be sustained over time and lead to statistically and educationally important gains in student achievement when compared to idiosyncratic teacher-created materials (VanTassel-Baska, 2003) or strategies devoid of content emphases (Westberg & Daoust, 2003). When students are consistently introduced to the same models (e.g., Paul's [1992] Elements of Reasoning model, the Persuasive Writing Model, problem-based learning) over time, learning is continually enhanced (Feng et al., 2005). Moreover, students are more likely to internalize the processes inherent to each model so that their thinking becomes more automatic and thus transfers to new learning situations with ease.

Lesson #5: High-Level Curriculum May Be Used Successfully With All Learners

Recent Center for Gifted Education studies of science and language arts curriculum effectiveness in heterogeneous Title I classrooms have shown that a curriculum written for gifted learners also is effective with nongifted learners, given the use of proper differentiation, scaffolding, and flexible grouping techniques (VanTassel-Baska et al., 2009; VanTassel-Baska et al., 2008). Scaffolding may be in the form of a supplemental curriculum or specific differentiated strategies and pacing. In language arts, *Jacob's Ladder* was developed to provide additional scaffolding in reading to expose less-experienced students with models that bridge lower level to higher level thinking. *Navigator* novel studies were written so that students could have more choice in novel selections and differentiated activities at a given reading level. In science, specific models were developed to scaffold students' thinking in planning scientific investigations. Pacing of units also was modified within the regular classroom, and instructional grouping encouraged effective discussions.

Lesson #6: Promising Learners From Low-Income Backgrounds and Students of Color Benefit From High-Powered Curriculum

The research evidence we have collected over multiple projects, as well as evidence collected by our colleagues (e.g., Swanson, 2006), has suggested that the William and Mary units are effective with these special populations of promising learners. In fact, the data suggest that, given enough time, these students perform at comparable levels to more advantaged learners in selected areas like persuasive writing (VanTassel-Baska et al., 2002). In Title I schools, all groups showed significant and important growth in key areas of language arts, social studies, and science learning after using the units, including groups of diverse learners. The use of such curriculum, however, must be accompanied by faithful use of the teaching-learning models that scaffold instruction at higher levels of discourse and thought, particularly for less-experienced learners in a subject area.

Lesson #7: Use of Curriculum-Based Assessment Documents Authentic Learning

Assessment should be aligned to the curriculum and standards taught within any given discipline. Many standardized assessments, while important, are broad-based and may not be sensitive enough to show specific student learning associated with a curriculum intervention. Therefore, pre- and post-curriculum-based assessments are an essential component for measuring the effectiveness of a curriculum on student achievement. In each William and Mary curriculum unit, the first lesson or set of lessons provides a curriculum-based assessment, matched to content, thinking and problem-solving processes, and overarching concepts so that teachers may use the assessment as a diagnostic tool for instruction. The last lesson of each unit contains a postassessment to assess gains in student achievement over the course of the unit.

Assessments have been developed specifically for our curriculum projects to measure aspects of content, concept, and process learning in students and aspects of teacher behaviors and attitudes. Not only is it important to match assessment to judging the efficacy of curriculum, but also to study teacher variables of interest.

Lesson #8: Professional Development on Curriculum Materials Enhances Faithful Implementation

When teaching gifted students, not only does curriculum matter, but the teacher is key. When students in the top 20th percentile grow in achievement, their success may be attributed to placement with highly effective teachers (Sanders & Rivers, 1996). When advanced students do not make noted gains, it may be caused by a lack of opportunity to proceed at their own pace or to be accelerated in their learning, lack of challenging materials, or the concentration of instruction on average or below-average students (Wright, Sanders, & Horn, 1997). Instead, teachers need to use critical thinking and metacognition routinely to enhance student learning (Wenglinsky, 2000).

Likewise, advanced instructional practices are more likely to be sustained when a curriculum, embedded with differentiation strategies, is provided as the basis for professional development (VanTassel-Baska et al., 2008). Direct training, along with ongoing, on-the-job professional development concerning use and implementation of new curricula, greatly increases overall effectiveness because teachers do not have to make inferences on their own about how to use new strategies they have learned.

Lesson #9: Fidelity of Implementation of Innovative Curriculum Efforts Requires Monitoring

Our work suggests that in order for curriculum to be implemented well, it must be monitored to ensure that teachers are using strategies both frequently and effectively (VanTassel-Baska & Brown, 2007). Such monitoring is a significant part of a curriculum effectiveness research protocol, but also should be an ongoing part of ensuring that professional development results in improved student learning (Guskey, 2000). Whether such monitoring is done by the principal or his designee, the instructional coach, the leaders of a grade level team, or a mentor is not what matters, as each school has its own system for instructional management. What does matter is that there is documentation to demonstrate how teachers are using higher level thinking and problem solving in their classrooms in a way that enhances student engagement and achievement over time.

Lesson #10: Institutionalization of Innovative Curriculum and Instruction Requires Ongoing Attention

One of the critical issues in conducting curriculum intervention studies is the long-term sustainability of the innovation after the project is completed. There are several factors that are likely to encourage or discourage innovation and change. For example, we have learned that innovation is difficult to maintain after project funding subsides due to competing resources, competing priorities with the overarching school reform agenda, and a lack of monitoring and attention of administrators (Brown, 2007). Schools that have been able to sustain curriculum interventions, particularly for advanced students, have emphasized ongoing assessment and monitoring of high-end student achievement and instituted policies that require the use of research-based curriculum (VanTassel-Baska, Avery, Hughes, & Little, 2000). Schools also have recognized that results in student achievement and changes in teacher behaviors happen over time with guided and intensive professional development and monitoring (Borko, Mayfield, Marion, Flexer, & Cumbo, 1997; VanTassel-Baska et al., 2008).

THE IMPORTANCE OF INNOVATION IN SCHOOLS

Ongoing innovative work serves many important functions in a school district. It serves to catalyze teachers and principals around authentic learning issues and to energize all school staff in proactive ways (Brown, Avery, VanTassel-Baska, Worley, & Stambaugh, 2006). Yet, the newness of innovative work also sparks self-doubt and forces teachers to use problem-solving skills in the best sense of Polya's (1957) notion that we are never problem solving until we hit situations that we cannot handle.

Innovative work also underscores the importance of effort, persistence, and practice of new ideas until they are owned by the individual and institutionalized by the system. One of the realities of innovative work in schools is that it takes concentrated energy over time to make it work. Sufficient time must be allocated to working through implementation problems in order for teacher automaticity to set in and routine learning for students to be attained. Research on innovation (see Shavinina, 2003, 2009) also suggests the need for collaborative work among the key human players in the process. Strong central-office leadership, the principal's involvement and support for key aspects of the given project, and teacher interest, enthusiasm, and deep understanding of the innovation are all essential to its success.

Some of the real values of establishing a climate for innovation in schools are the lessons on lifelong learning that it provides. Teachers and principals become more attuned to their own learning states and the new insights that emanate from them. They become more aware of educational practices, more reflective about them, and more intellectually engaged with the world of schools beyond a single entity.

Finally, innovative work challenges us to examine the adequacy of current practices in ways that are healthy. We should question the fruits of reform, consistently asking what anyone is *learning* as a result of our efforts. Whether we are parents, teachers, or administrators, our focus has to be on the results of learning. This tenet also should guide educators engaged in the throes of innovation, to help them to stay focused on the goal, rather than just the means.

CREATING A SYSTEM OF LEARNING

In order for curriculum and instruction to result in authentic student learning, a systemic model for implementation has to be in place. This model must take into account ongoing assessment results in multiple areas and modalities, professional development that is both data-driven and needs-based, and leadership that is knowledgeable and proactive about the relationship between teacher behaviors and student learning. It also must support recognition of the climate of innovation as a backdrop to the process. Such a systemic model would provide the annealing substance necessary to make quality content-based curricula for high-ability learners a reality in all classrooms (see Figure 19.4).

Connectivity among these elements is central to successful implementation of any instructional innovation. In the case of the ICM, such coherence is

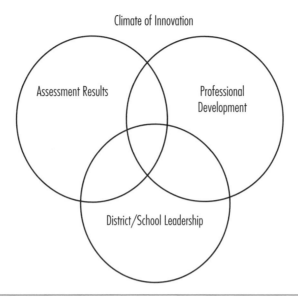

Figure 19.4. Systemic model for implementation.

critical to success, as the sophistication level required by teachers to implement the curriculum is requisitely high.

CONCLUSION

In the final analysis, this book is about learning. It is focused on content-based learning, to be sure, but its real message lies in the recognition of the importance of serious and sustained efforts to enhance the learning of our best learners in schools. This group will not take care of itself. Research on talent development (Bloom, 1985; Csikszentmihalyi, Rathunde, & Whalen, 1993) suggests that these students need as much attention as, if not more than, other students in order to help them to optimize their learning potential in life.

Although successful practices in school are not life, they bear a strong resemblance, especially in relationship to habits of mind. If our best learners are not challenged by school, then these habits will not be instilled in such a way as to guarantee transfer and automaticity of response in meeting life's challenges. Do we not owe the gifted and high-ability students under our care the support necessary to have them thrive in the world as citizens ready to solve problems and expend effort in achieving goals, as well as professionals in their chosen areas?

This book has sought to provide the positive response to that question in the format of research-based approaches to achieving such a worthy goal. Future research will continue an emphasis on curriculum effectiveness studies in subject areas as well as the use of the curriculum with special populations of gifted learners, including at-risk and learning-disabled students. As we learn more about what gifted and high-ability learners can do at different stages of development, we are forced to tackle more advanced learning models that will challenge them even more in classroom settings, and we must have the courage to provide the level of differentiation to which they are entitled.

KEY POINTS SUMMARY

- Successful implementation of research-based curriculum and instructional approaches requires a supportive system of ongoing assessment, professional development, and leadership.
- The Center for Gifted Education's science curriculum has demonstrated significant and important learning gains in the area of experimental design. Moreover, teachers found it to be motivating and challenging for students. Recent studies have shown the efficacy of the ICM approach to curriculum organization for Title I students at all ability levels in K–3 settings.
- The Center for Gifted Education's language arts units enhanced student learning significantly and importantly in the areas of literary analysis and interpretation and persuasive writing. Recent studies have shown the efficacy of this curriculum with all learners in Title I settings at grades 3–5.
- The Center for Gifted Education's social studies curriculum enhanced student learning in concept development, content mastery, and higher level thinking skills in selected classrooms at grades 3–8.
- Research-based best practices in professional development include training on the materials developed for use in classrooms, expecting to provide professional development for at least 4 days per year across 2 years, the inclusion of follow-up onsite support strategies for implementation, and a plan for assessing student learning.
- Leadership in curricular innovation requires vision, integrity, a sense of community, and a proactive stance.
- Lessons of importance in curriculum innovation focus on the need for attention to design and process in developing curriculum, the use of content experts, the need for regular use of scaffolds of learning that reach all learners, the need for varied and appropriate assessments, the critical role of professional development wedded to the curriculum framework, and the necessity of curriculum monitoring and ongoing vigilance to ensure institutionalization.
- A climate of experimentation can facilitate the institutionalization of curriculum innovation.

REFERENCES

Adams, C. M., & Callahan, C. M. (1995). The reliability and validity of a performance task for evaluating science process skills. *Gifted Child Quarterly, 39,* 14–20.

Applebee, A. N., & Langer, J. A. (2009). What is happening in the teaching of writing? *English Journal, 98,* 18–28.

American Association for the Advancement of Science. (1990). *Science for all Americans: Project 2061.* New York, NY: Oxford University Press.

Bland, L. C., VanTassel-Baska, J., Bracken, B. A., Feng, A. X., Stambaugh, T., & Kim, K. H. (2010). *Assessing science reasoning and conceptual understanding in the primary grades using multiple measures of performance: Project Clarion.* Manuscript submitted for publication.

Bloom, B. S. (Ed.). (1985). *Developing talent in young people.* New York, NY: Ballantine.

Bolman, L. G., & Deal, T. E. (1991). *Reframing organizations: Artistry, choice, and leadership.* San Francisco, CA: Jossey-Bass.

Borko, H., Mayfield, V., Marion, S. F., Flexer, R. J., & Cumbo, K. (1997). *Teachers developing ideas and practices about mathematics performance assessment: Successes, stumbling blocks, and implications for professional development.* Los Angeles: University of California, National Center for Research on Evaluation, Standards, and Student Testing (CRESST).

Brown, E. (2007, April). *Project Athena: Scaling up reform through implementing innovation: A cross-analysis of school district case studies.* Paper presented at the annual meeting of the American Educational Research Association, Chicago, IL.

Brown, E., Avery, L, VanTassel-Baska, J., Worley, B., & Stambaugh, T. (2006). A five-state analysis of gifted education policies: Ohio policy study results. *Roeper Review, 29,* 11–23.

Burkhalter, N. (1995). A Vygotsky-based curriculum for teaching persuasive writing in the elementary grades. *Language Arts, 72,* 192–196.

Burns, J. M. (1978). *Leadership.* New York, NY: Harper & Row.

Cain, M. F. (1990). The diet cola test. *Science Scope, 13*(4), 32–34.

Center for Gifted Education. (1997a). *Acid, acid everywhere: A problem-based unit.* Dubuque, IA: Kendall/Hunt.

Center for Gifted Education. (1997b). *What a find!* Dubuque, IA: Kendall/Hunt.

Center for Gifted Education. (1998). *Autobiographies.* Dubuque, IA: Kendall/Hunt.

Center for Gifted Education. (1999a). *Classroom observation form.* Williamsburg, VA: Center for Gifted Education, College of William and Mary.

Center for Gifted Education. (1999b). *Guide to teaching a language arts curriculum for high-ability learners.* Dubuque, IA: Kendall/Hunt.

Center for Gifted Education. (2001). *Patterns of change.* Dubuque, IA: Kendall/Hunt.

Csikszentmihalyi, M., Rathunde, K. R., & Whalen, S. (1993). *Talented teenagers: The roots of success and failure.* New York, NY: Cambridge University Press.

Feng, A., VanTassel-Baska, J., Quek, C., O'Neil, B., & Bai, W. (2005). A longitudinal assessment of gifted students' learning using the Integrated Curriculum Model: Impacts and perceptions of the William and Mary language arts and science curriculum. *Roeper Review, 27,* 78–83.

Gardner, J. W. (1990). *On leadership*. New York, NY: The Free Press.

Garet, M. S., Porter, A. C., Desimone, L., Birman, B. F., & Yoon, K. S. (2001). What makes professional development effective? Results from a national sample of teachers. *American Educational Research Journal, 38,* 915–945.

Gentry, M., & Keilty, B. (2004). Rural and suburban cluster grouping: Reflections on staff development as a component of program success. *Roeper Review, 26,* 147–155.

Gubbins, E. J., Westberg, K. L., Reis, S. M., Dinnocenti, S. T., Tieso, C. L., Muller, L. M., . . . Burns, D. E. (2002). *Implementing a professional development model using gifted education strategies with all students* (Report RM02172). Storrs: University of Connecticut, National Research Center on the Gifted and Talented.

Guskey, T. (2000). *Evaluating professional development*. Thousand Oaks, CA: Corwin Press.

Guskey, T. R. (2002). Does it make a difference? Evaluating professional development. *Educational Leadership, 59*(6), 45–51.

Johnson, C. C., Kahle, J. B., & Fargo, J. D. (2007). Effective teaching results in increased science achievement for all students. *Science Education, 91,* 371–383.

Karnes, F. A., & Stephens, K. R. (2000). State definitions for the gifted and talented revisited. *Exceptional Children, 66,* 219–238.

Kennedy, M. (1999). Form and substance in mathematics and science professional development. *NISE Brief, 3*(2), 1–7.

Kim, K. H., VanTassel-Baska, J., Bracken, B. A., Feng, A., Stambaugh, T., & Bland, L. (2010). *Project Clarion: Three years of science instruction in Title I schools among K–third grade students*. Manuscript submitted for publication.

Kouzes, J. M., & Posner, B. Z. (1995). *The leadership challenge*. San Francisco, CA: Jossey-Bass.

Little, C. A., Feng, A. X., VanTassel-Baska, J., Rogers, K. B., & Avery, L. D. (2007) A study of curriculum effectiveness in social studies. *Gifted Child Quarterly, 51,* 272–284.

Matthews, D., & Foster, J. (2005). A dynamic scaffolding model of teacher development: The gifted education consultant as catalyst for change. *Gifted Child Quarterly, 49,* 222–230.

National Assessment Governing Board. (1992). *Reading framework for the 1992 national assessment of education progress*. Washington, DC: U.S. Department of Education.

National Research Council. (1996). *National science education standards*. Washington, DC: National Academy Press.

Paul, R. (1992). *Critical thinking: What every person needs to survive in a rapidly changing world*. Rohnert Park, CA: Foundation for Critical Thinking.

Peterson, K. (2001, June). *Shaping school culture for quality teaching and learning*. Presentation to the National Leadership Institute, College of William and Mary, Williamsburg, VA.

Polya, G. (1957). *How to solve it: A new aspect of mathematical method* (2nd ed.). Princeton, NJ: Princeton University Press.

Sanders, W., & Rivers, J. (1996). *Cumulative and residual effects of teachers on future student academic achievement* (Research Progress Report). Retrieved from http://downloads.heartland.org/21803a.pdf

Shavinina, L. V. (2003). *The international handbook on innovation.* Oxford, UK: Elsevier Science.

Shavinina, L. V. (2009). Innovation education for the gifted: A new direction in gifted education. In L. V. Shavinina (Ed.), *International handbook on giftedness* (pp. 1257–1267). London, England: Springer.

Swanson, J. (2006). Breaking through assumptions about low-income, minority gifted students. *Gifted Child Quarterly, 50,* 11–24.

Swanson, J. (2007). Policy and practice: A case study of gifted education policy implementation. *Journal for the Education of the Gifted, 31,* 131–164.

Toulmin, S. E. (1958). *The uses of argument.* Cambridge, England: Cambridge University Press.

VanTassel-Baska, J. (2003). *Curriculum planning and instructional design for gifted learners.* Denver, CO: Love.

VanTassel-Baska, J., Avery, L. D., Hughes, C. E., & Little, C. A. (2000). An evaluation of the implementation of curriculum innovation: The impact of William and Mary units on schools. *Journal for the Education of the Gifted, 23,* 244–272.

VanTassel-Baska, J., Bass, G., Ries, R., Poland, D., & Avery, L. D. (1998). A national study of science curriculum effectiveness with high-ability students. *Gifted Child Quarterly, 42,* 200–211.

VanTassel-Baska, J., Bracken, B., Feng, A., & Brown, E. (2009). A longitudinal study of reading comprehension and reasoning ability of students in elementary Title I schools. *Journal for the Education of the Gifted, 33,* 7–37.

VanTassel-Baska, J., & Brown, E. (2007). Towards best practice: An analysis of the efficacy of curriculum models in gifted education. *Gifted Child Quarterly, 51,* 342–358.

VanTassel-Baska, J., Feng., A., Brown, E., Bracken, B., Stambaugh, T., French, H., . . . Bai, W. (2008). A study of differentiated instructional change over three years. *Gifted Child Quarterly, 52,* 297–312.

VanTassel-Baska, J., Johnson, D. T., Hughes, C. E., & Boyce, L. N. (1996). A study of language arts curriculum effectiveness with gifted learners. *Journal for the Education of the Gifted, 19,* 461–480.

VanTassel-Baska, J., Zuo, L., Avery, L. D., & Little, C. A. (2002). A curriculum study of gifted student learning in the language arts. *Gifted Child Quarterly, 46,* 30–44.

Wenglinsky, H. (2000). *How teaching matters: Bringing the classroom back into discussions of teacher quality.* Princeton, NJ: The Milken Family Foundation and Educational Testing Service.

Westberg, K. L., & Daoust, M. E. (2003, Fall). The results of the replication of the classroom practices survey replication in two states. *The National Research Center on the Gifted and Talented Newsletter,* 3–8.

Wright, S. P., Sanders, W. L., & Horn, S. P. (1997). Teacher and classroom context effects on student achievement: Implications for teacher evaluation. *Journal of Personnel Evaluation in Education, 11,* 57–67.

NAGC-CEC Teacher Knowledge & Skill Standards for Gifted and Talented Education

NAGC – CEC Teacher Knowledge & Skill Standards for Gifted and Talented Education

Standard 1: Foundations

Educators of the gifted understand the field as an evolving and changing discipline based on philosophies, evidence-based principles and theories, relevant laws and policies, diverse and historical points of view, and human issues. These perspectives continue to influence the field of gifted education and the education and treatment of individuals with gifts and talents both in school and society. They recognize how foundational influences affect professional practice, including assessment, instructional planning, delivery, and program evaluation. They further understand how issues of human diversity impact families, cultures, and schools, and how these complex human issues can interact in the delivery of gifted and talented education services.

K1	Historical foundations of gifted and talented education including points of view and contributions of individuals from diverse backgrounds.
K2	Key philosophies, theories, models, and research that supports gifted and talented education.
K3	Local, state/provincial and federal laws and policies related to gifted and talented education.
K4	Issues in conceptions, definitions, and identification of individuals with gifts and talents, including those of individuals from diverse backgrounds.
K5	Impact of the dominant culture's role in shaping schools and the differences in values, languages, and customs between school and home.
K6	Societal, cultural, and economic factors, including anti-intellectualism and equity vs. excellence, enhancing or inhibiting the development of gifts and talents.
K7	Key issues and trends, including diversity and inclusion, that connect general, special, and gifted and talented education.

Standard 2: Development and Characteristics of Learners

Educators of the gifted know and demonstrate respect for their students as unique human beings. They understand variations in characteristics and development between and among individuals with and without exceptional learning needs and capacities. Educators of the gifted can express how different characteristics interact with the domains of human development and use this knowledge to describe the varying abilities and behaviors of individuals with gifts and talents. Educators of the gifted also understand how families and communities contribute to the development of individuals with gifts and talents.

K1	Cognitive and affective characteristics of individuals with gifts and talents, including those from diverse backgrounds, in intellectual, academic, creative, leadership, and artistic domains.
K2	Characteristics and effects of culture and environment on the development of individuals with gifts and talents.
K3	Role of families and communities in supporting the development of individuals with gifts and talents.
K4	Advanced developmental milestones of individuals with gifts and talents from early childhood through adolescence.
K5	Similarities and differences within the group of individuals with gifts and talents as compared to the general population.

Standard 3: Individual Learning Differences

Educators of the gifted understand the effects that gifts and talents can have on an individual's learning in school and throughout life. Moreover, educators of the gifted are active and resourceful in seeking to understand how language, culture, and family background interact with an individual's predispositions to impact academic and social behavior, attitudes, values, and interests. The understanding of these learning differences and their interactions provides the foundation upon which educators of the gifted plan instruction to provide meaningful and challenging learning.

K1	Influences of diversity factors on individuals with gifts and talents.
K2	Academic and affective characteristics and learning needs of individuals with gifts, talents, and disabilities.
K3	Idiosyncratic learning patterns of individuals with gifts and talents, including those from diverse backgrounds.
K4	Influences of different beliefs, traditions, and values across and within diverse groups on relationships among individuals with gifts and talents, their families, schools, and communities.
S1	Integrate perspectives of diverse groups into planning instruction for individuals with gifts and talents.

Standard 4: Instructional Strategies

Educators of the gifted possess a repertoire of evidence-based curriculum and instructional strategies to differentiate for individuals with gifts and talents. They select, adapt, and use these strategies to promote challenging learning opportunities in general and special curricula and to modify learning environments to enhance self-awareness and self-efficacy for individuals with gifts and talents. They enhance the learning of critical and creative thinking, problem solving, and performance skills in specific domains. Moreover, educators of the gifted emphasize the development, practice, and transfer of advanced knowledge and skills across environments throughout the lifespan leading to creative, productive careers in society for individuals with gifts and talents.

K1	School and community resources, including content specialists, that support differentiation.
K2	Curricular, instructional, and management strategies effective for individuals with exceptional learning needs.
S1	Apply pedagogical content knowledge to instructing learners with gifts and talents.
S2	Apply higher-level thinking and metacognitive models to content areas to meet the needs of individuals with gifts and talents.
S3	Provide opportunities for individuals with gifts and talents to explore, develop, or research their areas of interest or talent.
S4	Preassess the learning needs of individuals with gifts and talents in various domains and adjust instruction based on continual assessment.
S5	Pace delivery of curriculum and instruction consistent with needs of individuals with gifts and talents.
S6	Engage individuals with gifts and talents from all backgrounds in challenging, multicultural curricula.
S7	Use information and/or assistive technologies to meet the needs of individuals with exceptional learning needs.

Standard 5: Learning Environments and Social Interactions

Educators of the gifted actively create learning environments for individuals with gifts and talents that foster cultural understanding, safety and emotional well being, positive social interactions, and active engagement. In addition, educators of the gifted foster environments in which diversity is valued and individuals are taught to live harmoniously and productively in a culturally diverse world. Educators of the gifted shape environments to encourage independence, motivation, and self-advocacy of individuals with gifts and talents.

K1	Ways in which groups are stereotyped and experience historical and current discrimination and implications for gifted and talented education.
K2	Influence of social and emotional development on interpersonal relationships and learning of individuals with gifts and talents.
S1	Design learning opportunities for individuals with gifts and talents that promote self-awareness, positive peer relationships, intercultural experiences, and leadership.
S2	Create learning environments for individuals with gifted and talents that promote self-awareness, self-efficacy, leadership, and lifelong learning.
S3	Create safe learning environments for individuals with gifts and talents that encourage active participation in individual and group activities to enhance independence, interdependence, and positive peer relationships.
S4	Create learning environments and intercultural experiences that allow individuals with gifts and talents to appreciate their own and others' language and cultural heritage.
S5	Develop social interaction and coping skills in individuals with gifts and talents to address personal and social issues, including discrimination and stereotyping.

Standard 6: Language and Communication

Educators of the gifted understand the role of language and communication in talent development and the ways in which exceptional conditions can hinder or facilitate such development. They use relevant strategies to teach oral and written communication skills to individuals with gifts and talents. Educators of the gifted are familiar with assistive technologies to support and enhance communication of individuals with exceptional needs. They match their communication methods to an individual's language proficiency and cultural and linguistic differences. Educators of the gifted use communication strategies and resources to facilitate understanding of subject matter for individuals with gifts and talents who are English language learners.

K1	Forms and methods of communication essential to the education of individuals with gifts and talents, including those from diverse backgrounds.
K2	Impact of diversity on communication.
K3	Implications of culture, behavior, and language on the development of individuals with gifts and talents.
S1	Access resources and develop strategies to enhance communication skills for individuals with gifts and talents including those with advanced communication and/or English language learners.
S2	Use advanced oral and written communication tools, including assistive technologies, to enhance the learning experiences of individuals with exceptional learning needs.

Standard 7: Instructional Planning

Curriculum and instructional planning is at the center of gifted and talented education. Educators of the gifted develop long-range plans anchored in both general and special curricula. They systematically translate shorter-range goals and objectives that take into consideration an individual's abilities and needs, the learning environment, and cultural and linguistic factors. Understanding of these factors, as well as the implications of being gifted and talented, guides the educator's selection, adaptation, and creation of materials, and use of differentiated instructional strategies. Learning plans are modified based on ongoing assessment of the individual's progress. Moreover, educators of the gifted facilitate these actions in a collaborative context that includes individuals with gifts and talents, families, professional colleagues, and personnel from other agencies as appropriate. Educators of the gifted are comfortable using technologies to support instructional planning and individualized instruction.

K1	Theories and research models that form the basis of curriculum development and instructional practice for individuals with gifts and talents.
K2	Features that distinguish differentiated curriculum from general curricula for individuals with exceptional learning needs.
K3	Curriculum emphases for individuals with gifts and talents within cognitive, affective, aesthetic, social, and linguistic domains.
S1	Align differentiated instructional plans with local, state/provincial, and national curricular standards.
S2	Design differentiated learning plans for individuals with gifts and talents, including individuals from diverse backgrounds.
S3	Develop scope and sequence plans for individuals with gifts and talents.
S4	Select curriculum resources, strategies, and product options that respond to cultural, linguistic, and intellectual differences among individuals with gifts and talents.
S5	Select and adapt a variety of differentiated curricula that incorporate advanced, conceptually challenging, in-depth, distinctive, and complex content.
S6	Integrate academic and career guidance experiences into the learning plan for individuals with gifts and talents.

Standard 8: Assessment

Assessment is integral to the decision-making and teaching of educators of the gifted as multiple types of assessment information are required for both identification and learning progress decisions. Educators of the gifted use the results of such assessments to adjust instruction and to enhance ongoing learning progress. Educators of the gifted understand the process of identification, legal policies, and ethical principles of measurement and assessment related to referral, eligibility, program planning, instruction, and placement for individuals with gifts and talents, including those from culturally and linguistically diverse backgrounds. They understand measurement theory and practices for addressing the interpretation of assessment results. In addition, educators of the gifted understand the appropriate use and limitations of various types of assessments. To ensure the use of nonbiased and equitable identification and learning progress models, educators of the gifted employ alternative assessments such as performance-based assessment, portfolios, and computer simulations.

K1	Processes and procedures for the identification of individuals with gifts and talents.
K2	Uses, limitations, and interpretation of multiple assessments in different domains for identifying individuals with exceptional learning needs, including those from diverse backgrounds.
K3	Uses and limitations of assessments documenting academic growth of individuals with gifts and talents.
S1	Use non-biased and equitable approaches for identifying individuals with gifts and talents, including those from diverse backgrounds.
S2	Use technically adequate qualitative and quantitative assessments for identifying and placing individuals with gifts and talents.
S3	Develop differentiated curriculum-based assessments for use in instructional planning and delivery for individuals with gifts and talents.
S4	Use alternative assessments and technologies to evaluate learning of individuals with gifts and talents.

Standard 9: Professional and Ethical Practice

Educators of the gifted are guided by the profession's ethical and professional practice standards. They practice in multiple roles and complex situations across wide age and developmental ranges. Their practice requires ongoing attention to professional and ethical considerations. They engage in professional activities that promote growth in individuals with gifts and talents and update themselves on evidence-based best practices. Educators of the gifted view themselves as lifelong learners and regularly reflect on and adjust their practice. They are aware of how attitudes, behaviors, and ways of communicating can influence their practice. Educators of the gifted understand that culture and language interact with gifts and talents and are sensitive to the many aspects of the diversity of individuals with gifts and talents and their families.

K1	Personal and cultural frames of reference that affect one's teaching of individuals with gifts and talents, including biases about individuals from diverse backgrounds.
K2	Organizations and publications relevant to the field of gifted and talented education.
S1	Assess personal skills and limitations in teaching individuals with exceptional learning needs.
S2	Maintain confidential communication about individuals with gifts and talents.
S3	Encourage and model respect for the full range of diversity among individuals with gifts and talents.
S4	Conduct activities in gifted and talented education in compliance with laws, policies, and standards of ethical practice.
S5	Improve practice through continuous research-supported professional development in gifted education and related fields.
S6	Participate in the activities of professional organizations related to gifted and talented education.
S7	Reflect on personal practice to improve teaching and guide professional growth in gifted and talented education.

Standard 10: Collaboration

Educators of the gifted effectively collaborate with families, other educators, and related service providers. This collaboration enhances comprehensive articulated program options across educational levels and engagement of individuals with gifts and talents in meaningful learning activities and interactions. Moreover, educators of the gifted embrace their special role as advocate for individuals with gifts and talents. They promote and advocate for the learning and well-being of individuals with gifts and talents across settings and diverse learning experiences.

K1	Culturally responsive behaviors that promote effective communication and collaboration with individuals with gifts and talents, their families, school personnel, and community members.
S1	Respond to concerns of families of individuals with gifts and talents.
S2	Collaborate with stakeholders outside the school setting who serve individuals with exceptional learning needs and their families.
S3	Advocate for the benefit of individuals with gifts and talents and their families.
S4	Collaborate with individuals with gifts and talents, their families, general, and special educators, and other school staff to articulate a comprehensive preschool through secondary educational program.
S5	Collaborate with families, community members, and professionals in assessment of individuals with gifts and talents.
S6	Communicate and consult with school personnel about the characteristics and needs of individuals with gifts and talents, including individuals from diverse backgrounds.

About the Editors

Joyce VanTassel-Baska is the Jody and Layton Smith Professor Emerita at The College of William and Mary in Virginia, where she developed a graduate program and a research and development center in gifted education. Formerly, she initiated and directed the Center for Talent Development at Northwestern University. She also has served as the state director of gifted programs for Illinois, as a regional director of a gifted service center in the Chicago area, as coordinator of gifted programs for the Toledo, OH, public school system, and as a teacher of gifted high school students in English and Latin. Dr. VanTassel-Baska has published widely, including 27 books and more than 500 refereed journal articles, book chapters, and scholarly reports. Her major research interests are on the talent development process and effective curricular interventions with the gifted.

Catherine A. Little is an assistant professor in educational psychology at the University of Connecticut. She teaches courses in gifted and talented education and in the undergraduate honors program in education. She previously served as visiting assistant professor in gifted education at The College of William and Mary, and as curriculum coordinator at the Center for Gifted Education there. Catherine received her Ph.D. in educational policy, planning, and leadership from William and Mary. Her research interests include professional development, teacher talent development, and curriculum differentiation. She has written or cowritten several curriculum units as well as book chapters and journal articles related to curriculum implementation and other issues in gifted education.

About the Authors

Linda D. Avery is currently retired but undertakes occasional contractual work in program evaluation, curriculum development, and grant writing, working from her home in Seville, OH. She was previously the manager of the Center for Gifted Education at The College of William and Mary. She received her Ph.D. in educational policy, planning, and leadership from that institution in 1999. She was integrally involved in Project STAR (identification of low-income and minority gifted students) and Project Phoenix (social studies curriculum development). Her earlier work was in state government programs, first in Michigan and then in Illinois. Over the course of her career, she conducted several state and many local gifted program evaluations, did extensive grant-writing, and published book chapters, journal articles, and research and evaluation reports. She also has conducted training on curriculum implementation in many states across the country.

Elissa F. Brown is the Statewide Director of Secondary Projects for the North Carolina Department of Public Instruction. In that role, she facilitates coordination of large-scale state initiatives for middle and high schools. Additionally, she serves as Regional Lead for Region 5 in the Statewide System of Support model. She recently served as state consultant for academically/intellectually gifted with the North Carolina Department of Public Instruction. Prior to her appointment in North Carolina, she was the director of the Center for Gifted Education at The College of William and Mary in Williamsburg, VA. She has taught undergraduate and graduate courses in education for many universities. Elissa received her bachelor's degree in education from the University of Georgia and a master's in educational administration from Western Carolina University. She received her Ph.D. in educational policy, planning, and leadership from The College of William and Mary. She serves on the board of directors of the North Carolina Association for Research in Education. She has been a high school principal, U.S. ED grant manager, central office administrator, and teacher.

Kimberley Chandler is the curriculum director at the Center for Gifted Education at The College of William and Mary. Kimberley completed her Ph.D. in educational policy, planning, and leadership with an emphasis in gifted education administration at The College of William and Mary. Her professional background includes teaching gifted students in a variety of settings, serving as an administrator of a school district gifted program, and providing professional development training for teachers and administrators. She also has served as an adjunct instructor for gifted education endorsement courses for the University of Virginia, Casenex, Inc., and The College of William and Mary. Currently, Kimberley is the chair of the NAGC Early Childhood Network, co-chair of the NAGC Education Committee, and member-at-large representative for the AERA Special Interest Group for Research on Giftedness, Creativity, and Talent. Her research interests include curriculum policy and implementation issues in gifted programs and the design and evaluation of professional development programs for teachers of the gifted.

Dana T. Johnson is an instructor in the mathematics department and the School of Education at The College of William and Mary. In her early teaching career, she taught middle and high school mathematics. Dana has worked on many projects with the Center for Gifted Education since its beginning in 1988, including developing curriculum and teaching enrichment classes. She has been involved in most of the center's major curriculum development initiatives, and she has written several mathematics curriculum units for high-ability learners. Dana coedited the 1996 book *Developing Verbal Talent* with Joyce VanTassel-Baska and Linda Neal Boyce and authored

"Mathematics Curriculum for Gifted Learners" in *Comprehensive Curriculum for Gifted Learners.*

Bronwyn MacFarlane is assistant professor of gifted education in the Department of Educational Leadership at the University of Arkansas at Little Rock (UALR). She teaches graduate-level courses and works with the UALR Center for Gifted Education. Bronwyn holds school leadership qualifications for district superintendency, the principalship, counseling, and teaching social studies, French, and gifted education. She received the NAGC Outstanding Doctoral Student Award; The College of William and Mary School of Education Dean's Award for Excellence; The College of William and Mary Excellence in Gifted Education Doctoral Award; and the International P.E.O. Scholar Award. She is coeditor of *Leading Change in Gifted Education: The Festschrift of Dr. Joyce VanTassel-Baska* (2009, with Dr. Tamra Stambaugh). With diverse experiences as a classroom teacher, Academic Dean administrator, professional development facilitator, and university graduate school faculty member, Bronwyn is actively involved with new research initiatives, reviewing and assisting school programs, and developing curriculum.

Melissa S. Mitchell is a doctoral student studying gifted education at the University of Connecticut. She currently serves as the editorial assistant for the *Journal of Advanced Academics.* Prior to entering the doctoral program, Melissa worked as an academic counselor and adjunct faculty member at a postsecondary institution in Maine. Her research interests include educational technology, rural education, and underachievement.

Kristina Ayers Paul is a doctoral candidate in educational psychology at the University of Connecticut, where she also is an online instructor of graduate courses in gifted education and a graduate assistant at the Neag Center for Gifted Education and Talent Development. During her time with the Neag Center, she has served as the coordinator for the external evaluation of the Connecticut Teacher Quality Partnership Grant Program, as well as the onsite coordinator for Confratute, the University of Connecticut's summer institute for enrichment learning and teaching. Kristina was a teacher and coordinator of early elementary gifted services before coming to the University of Connecticut to focus on research and evaluation of gifted education programs and services. She is an avid presenter at regional and national conferences, focusing on educational technology, evaluation, and professional development.

Janice I. Robbins is director of Project Civis at The College of William and Mary, where she also serves as adjunct assistant professor of education. She was formerly interim director of the Center for Gifted Education at The College of William and Mary. She served as chief of curriculum for the Department of Defense Education Activity, directing curriculum, instruction, and assessment at stateside and overseas schools. She is a former elementary and middle school principal and coordinator of gifted programs in Fairfax County Public Schools in Virginia. Janice earned her Ph.D. in educational research and evaluation from Virginia Tech.

Molly M. Sandling is a social studies teacher at Jamestown High School in Williamsburg, VA, responsible for 10th- and 11th-grade courses in AP Human Geography and AP U.S. History. Molly received a bachelor's degree in history from The College of William and Mary and a master's in history from Yale University. She worked at the Center for Gifted Education while pursuing a master's degree in secondary social studies education and continues to work with the center on curriculum development. Molly has authored or coauthored seven of the center's social studies units and has presented on social studies curricula for the gifted at several conferences and institutes.

Beverly T. Sher earned a BA in molecular, cellular, and developmental biology and in Russian from the University of Colorado in 1979 and a Ph.D. in biology from California Institute of Technology in 1985. She was a science consultant for the Center for Gifted Education in the early 1990s, and is currently a visiting assistant professor of biology at The College of William and Mary as well as the college's health professions advisor. She is the mother of three highly gifted children.

Del Siegle is an associate professor of educational psychology in the Neag School of Education at the University of Connecticut, where he was honored as a Teaching Fellow. Prior to earning his Ph.D., Del worked as a gifted and talented coordinator in Montana. He is past president of the National Association of Gifted Children and serves on the board of directors of The Association for the Gifted (CEC-TAG). He is co-editor of the *Journal of Advanced Academics* and authors a technology column for *Gifted Child Today*. Del's research interests include web-based instruction, motivation of gifted students, and teacher bias in the identification of students for gifted programs.

Tamra Stambaugh is a research assistant professor of special education and director of Programs for Talented Youth at Vanderbilt University. She is the coauthor of the most recent edition of *Comprehensive Curriculum for Gifted Learners* and coeditor of *Overlooked Gems: A National Perspective on Low-Income Promising Students*, the *Jacob's Ladder Reading Comprehension Program* (both with Dr. Joyce VanTassel-Baska), and *Leading Change in Gifted Education* (with Dr. Bronwyn MacFarlane). Tamra also has authored or coauthored journal articles and book chapters on a variety of topics focusing on curriculum, policy, instruction, and leadership. Her current research interests include the impact of accelerated curriculum on student achievement, teacher effectiveness, and talent development factors, especially for students of poverty.

Jeanne M. Struck serves as the supervisor of gifted and fine arts for the Williamsburg-James City County School division in Virginia. She also is the author of one of the elementary social studies units from the Center for Gifted Education and has coordinated social studies implementation efforts as an intern with Norfolk Public Schools. She has taught 24 years in public schools, working with culturally and economically diverse gifted students. In 1999, she received the A. Harry Passow Teacher Scholarship from the National Association for Gifted Children. In 2001, Jeanne received both the Doctoral Student Award and the Research Division Dissertation Award from NAGC. Jeanne completed her Ph.D. from The College of William and Mary in May 2002.

Hope E. Wilson completed her Ph.D. in educational psychology with an emphasis on gifted education at the University of Connecticut. She is an assistant professor of elementary education at Stephen F. Austin State University in Nacogdoches, TX. Hope is a coauthor of *Letting Go Of Perfect: Overcoming Perfectionism in Kids*, a guide for parents and educators. She was the assistant editor at the *Journal of Advanced Academics* for 3 years, and has been published in *Journal for the Education of the Gifted*, *Gifted Child Today*, and the *Journal of Advanced Academics*. Her cartoons are a regular feature in *Teaching for High Potential*. Hope's research interests have included gifted identification, acceleration, academic self-concept, and arts integration for gifted students.

Index